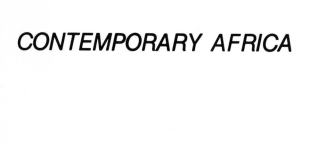

CONTEMPORARY AFRICA

AFRICA

- Bissau Capitals of Countries

250   500 miles
500   1000 kms

kl

MEDITERRANEAN SEA

Rabat
Algiers
MOROCCO
TUNISIA
Tripoli
El Aiún
WESTERN
SAHARA
ALGERIA
LIBYA
ARAB
REPUBLIC
OF EGYPT
Cairo
RED SEA

MAURITANIA
Nouakchott
MALI
NIGER
CHAD
SUDAN
Khartoum
FRENCH
TERRITORY
OF THE AFARS
AND ISSAS
Djibouti

SENEGAL
THE GAMBIA
Banjul
Bissau
GUINÉ–BISSAU
Dakar
Bamako
Niamey
Ouagadougou
Fort-Lamy
Addis
Ababa

Conakry
Freetown
SIERRA LEONE
Monrovia
LIBERIA
REPUBLIC OF
GUINEA
UPPER
VOLTA
IVORY
COAST
Abidjan
GHANA
TOGO
BENIN
Accra
Lagos
Porto-Novo
NIGERIA
CENTRAL
AFRICAN
REPUBLIC
Bangui
ETHIOPIA
SOMALI REPUBLIC
Mogadishu

CAMEROUN
Yaoundé
Bata
EQUATORIAL GUINEA
Libreville
GABON
REPUBLIC OF THE CONGO
REPUBLIC
OF ZAIRE
Brazzaville
Kinshasa
Cabinda
Luanda
UGANDA
Kampala
Kigali
RWANDA
Bujumbura
BURUNDI
KENYA
Nairobi
Zanzibar
Dar es Salaam
TANZANIA
INDIAN
OCEAN

ATLANTIC OCEAN

ANGOLA
ZAMBIA
Lusaka
Lilongwe
MOZAMBIQUE
Salisbury
ZIMBABWE
(RHODESIA)
NAMIBIA
(S.W. AFRICA)
Windhoek
BOTSWANA
Gaborone
Pretoria
Mbabane
SWAZILAND
Maputo
Maseru
LESOTHO
REPUBLIC OF
SOUTH AFRICA

CONTEMPORARY AFRICA
Geography and Change

Edited by

C. GREGORY KNIGHT
Associate Professor of Geography
The Pennsylvania State University

JAMES L. NEWMAN
Associate Professor of Geography
Syracuse University

Prentice-Hall, Inc. Englewood Cliffs, New Jersey

Library of Congress Cataloging in Publication Data
Main entry under title:

Contemporary Africa.

   Bibliography: p. 505
   Includes index.
   1. Africa, Sub-Saharan—Description and travel—
Addresses, essays, lectures. 2. Africa, Sub-Saharan—
Economic conditions—Addresses, essays, lectures.
3. Africa, Sub-Saharan—Rural conditions—Addresses,
essays, lectures. 4. Urbanization—Africa, Sub-
Saharan—Addresses, essays, lectures. I. Knight,
C. Gregory. (date) II. Newman, James L. (date)
DT352.C595   916.7   76-4902
ISBN 0-13-170035-9

© 1976 by Prentice-Hall, Inc., Englewood Cliffs, New Jersey

Printed in the United States of America

10 9 8 7 6 5 4 3 2 1

PRENTICE-HALL INTERNATIONAL, INC., London
PRENTICE-HALL OF AUSTRALIA PTY. LIMITED, Sydney
PRENTICE-HALL OF CANADA, LTD., Toronto
PRENTICE-HALL OF INDIA PRIVATE LIMITED, New Delhi
PRENTICE-HALL OF JAPAN, INC., Tokyo
PRENTICE-HALL OF SOUTHEAST ASIA PTE. LTD., Singapore

Contents

II   PARAMETERS OF CHANGE   *49*

III   RURAL CHANGE   *189*

28   Africa in the World Economy   *443*
      Douglas W. Lister

29   Tourism   *457*
      Anthony V. Williams

30   European Economic Presence in Francophone Africa:
      The Ivory Coast   *466*
      Douglas W. Lister

31   Persistent Colonialism in Southern Africa
      Harm J. de Blij   *478*

32   Liberation Movements:
      Guine Bissau and Mozambique   *495*
      Robert W. McColl

      Bibliography   *507*

      Author Index   *531*

      Subject Index   *536*

Preface

The last different place. Africa.
Explore Africa.
Discover Ethiopia.
A Personal Safari in East Africa.
Spend your next vacation on a safari in the jungles
    and plains of Africa.

These phrases from tourist advertisements may encapsulate the viewpoints of many Americans and Western Europeans toward Africa. In spite of an increasing number of popular films, television specials, art exhibits, and returning Peace Corps volunteers, Africa remains largely unknown, characterized by images of tribal life, jungles and plains, wildlife, and exotic forms of art, music, and dance. That these images of Africa persist into the late 20th century cannot be attributed to what we *do* know about Africa, but more to whether we really *care* to learn about Africa.

The purpose of this volume is to build a different set of images of Africa: of African society characterized less by exotic cultures than by motivations and dynamics of change parallel to our own; of African landscapes not populated by herds of wild animals but as complex resources for sustaining societies; of African history in interaction with the world; of African development creating economic systems, social institutions, and spatial organizations increasingly like those found elsewhere; of perils and potentials for African change in the future. Here, Africa is portrayed through the eyes of scholars immersed in Africa and African studies. Most contributors are geographers, with their particular blend of social *and* environmental orientation; history and economics are professed by others. Together, our portrait of Africa may evoke in you an interest beyond the level of curiosity. The future of Africa, though largely in African hands, is also in your attitudes, contributions, teaching, and votes. By sharing our knowledge of (and affection for) Africa with you, we think you will join us in a strong commitment to Africa's welfare.

PLACE NAMES

As this book goes to press, many place names in contemporary Africa are changing. The capital of independent Mozambique is now Maputo (former Lourenço Marques) as noted on the frontispiece; other names in that country are likely to change as well. Dahomey is officially Benin, and Malawi's new capital at Lilongwe will be followed by capital city changes in Nigeria and Tanzania in the coming decade. The frontispiece has official place names as we go to press, but in the text you will find some traditional names remaining.

ACKNOWLEDGEMENTS

This volume could not have been produced without the enthusiastic support of the contributors, both in responding to our initial queries and in producing manuscripts with a dispatch remarkable in academia. To them we can only express our thanks and hope that what we have assembled aids their continuing pursuit of African studies. We are very grateful to Pam and Gerry Zeck for graphical design and to Ken Laurie for his cartographic skills. The Syracuse University Cartographic Laboratory provided additional cartographic contributions. We also wish to thank Diane Knight for preparation of indices and our typists, Sue McMahon, Nina McNeal, and Colleen Kristula.

C. Gregory Knight
James L. Newman

Contemporary Africanists

THE EDITORS

C. Gregory Knight is associate professor of geography at The Pennsylvania State University. His research experience in Tanzania and Nigeria has focused on interactions among resource management, folk science, and rural development.

James L. Newman is associate professor of geography at Syracuse University. His interests in population, environment, and food supply have focused on East Africa and the Sahelian region.

THE CONTRIBUTORS

J. Oladipo Adejuwon is professor of geography at the University of Ife, Nigeria. His research on African ecology and resource management has concentrated on West Africa with particular attention to Nigeria.

Eileen Hadley Berry is a doctoral student at Clark University. She has lived in North Africa, Sudan, and East Africa, and completed research there with a principal focus on employment and development.

Len Berry is professor of geography and dean of the graduate school at Clark University. His African research interests on environment, natural resources and rural development with emphasis on arid lands, have concentrated on Sudan and East Africa.

Jacquelyn L. Beyer is professor of geography and environmental studies at the University of Colorado, Colorado Springs. Her interests include land and water utilization problems in western United States and Africa, including four years teaching and research at the University of Cape Town.

Harm J. de Blij is professor of geography at the University of Miami in Coral Gables, Florida. His field experience includes work in Swaziland, Mozambique, Tanzania and Kenya.

Richard R. Brand is associate professor of geography at Edinboro State College in Pennsylvania. His research on urban geography and urban planning has been focused on West Africa, particularly on Accra, Ghana.

Michael Olanrewaju Filani is lecturer in geography at the University of Ibadan, Nigeria. He has studied transportation systems in both the industrialized and developing areas.

Charles M. Good is associate professor and head of geography at Virginia Polytechnic Institute and State University. He has held administrative and research positions in Ghana and Uganda.

Peter R. Gould is professor of geography at The Pennsylvania State University. His primary research interests are on human geography and methodology; he has worked in Ghana and Tanzania.

Milton E. Harvey is professor of geography at Kent State Unversity. His research on African urban development is primarily in West Africa.

Robert Heussler is professor of history at the State University of New York, College at Geneseo. His research has extended widely across Africa and the developing world. His chapter (4) was prepared during a national fellowship at the Hoover Institution on War, Revolution and Peace at Stanford University.

Douglas W. Lister is an economist who has undertaken research in the Ivory Coast. He is now Loan Officer/Economist with the World Bank in Kinshasa, Zaire. His views, expressed in chapters prepared before joining the World Bank, should not be ascribed to the Bank or its affiliated organizations.

Gavin Maasdorp is principal research fellow in the Department of Economics at the University of Natal in Durban, South Africa. He has worked extensively in Swaziland and Lesotho, and is the Natal Region chairman of the South African Institute of Race Relations.

Robert W. McColl is associate professor of geography at the University of Kansas. His principal research on the political geography of conflict has been applied to the study of insurgency in Asia, urban America and Africa.

G. J. Afolabi Ojo is professor of geography at the University of Ife, Nigeria. His research on cultural and behavioral geography and environmental resource management have been primarily focused on Nigeria.

Oyediran Ojo is senior lecturer in geography at the University of Lagos, Nigeria. His research and teaching on tropical climatology have taken him to Uganda and the United States in addition to work in Nigeria.

Philip W. Porter is professor of geography at the University of Minnesota. He has undertaken research on population, agricultural development, and agroclimatology in Liberia, Tanzania, Kenya and Uganda.

R. Mansell Prothero is reader in geography and director of the African Mobility Project at the University of Liverpool, U.K. He has conducted research widely in Africa on population and as consultant to the World Health Organization.

J. Barry Riddell is associate professor of geography at Queens University, Canada. His research interests in transportation, migration, and modernization have focused on Sierra Leone.

Marilyn Silberfein is assistant professor of geography at Temple University. She is temporarily with the Manpower Development Division of the U.S. Agency for International Development, and has field research experience in Kenya and Tanzania.

John W. Sommer is associate professor of geography and acting dean of Social Sciences at the University of Texas at Dallas. He has lived in the Middle East and Africa, and has carried out research on African urbanization in Senegal and Gambia.

Ian D. Thomas is senior lecturer in population studies in the School of Development Studies, University of East Anglia, U.K. He lived in Tanzania for many years, where his research and teaching focused on African population geography and related development planning. He has been a census advisor to Tanzania and Ethiopia.

Reuben K. Udo is professor and head of geography at the University of Ibadan, Nigeria, where he also serves as dean of social sciences. His work has primarily focused on population geography and Nigeria.

Anthony V. Williams is associate professor of geography at The Pennsylvania State University and Visiting Rockefeller Professor at the University of Ibadan. His research interests include population and development.

Ben Wisner is a visiting fellow at the Institute of Development Studies at the University of Sussex, U.K. The founding editor of *Antipode*, his interests in social wholeness and human liberation have taken him to teaching and research positions in Kenya and Tanzania.

Burton O. Witthuhn is professor and chairman of geography at Edinboro State College in Pennsylvania. His field research experience on modernization includes Ethiopia and Uganda.

THE CARTOGRAPHER

Ken W. Laurie prepared the cartography for *Contemporary Africa* at the Syracuse University Cartographic Labs. He is currently a graduate student at Western Illinois University.

ILLUSTRATIONS

1

Introduction

C. GREGORY KNIGHT
JAMES L. NEWMAN

The continent of Africa consists of two distinct, but intertwining cultural realms. Africa north of the Sahara is part of the wider Arab world; to the south of the Sahara lies Black Africa. The Sahara appears to pose a formidable barrier separating these realms, but this is more of an illusion created by Western images of deserts than a reality. For centuries, indeed millenia, it has served more as a bridge than a barrier between north and south. Goods, peoples, and ideas have freely moved across it, and these contacts continue today in such forms as Pan-Africanism, the Organization of African Unity, and the collaboration in addressing Third World concerns in the United Nations.

Nevertheless, there are enough major differences between Arab and Black Africa so that each realm deserves treatment in its own right. The focus in this book is on Black Africa, or, as it usually is called, Africa south of the Sahara.[1] Frequent reference will be made to the continent as a whole, but the overall intent is to keep discussion geographically restricted. Indeed, some chapters deal only with tropical Africa, excluding both northern and southern Africa.

[1] The phrase sub-Saharan Africa frequently is encountered but as James (1967) has noted, this is a misnomer because "sub" refers to beneath or under.

COMMONALITIES OF BLACK AFRICA

There are a number of attributes that make treatment of Black Africa as a unit both important and meaningful. For one thing, it is just now entering the "rapid growth" phase of the demographic transition. Death rates have begun to plummet, while at the same time birth rates have remained high. Within coming decades, Black Africa will experience the highest rate of population growth of any major world region, equalling, perhaps even exceeding, the present Latin American experience. In consequence, the various nations will have to resolve many common population-resource-environment issues. What formal population growth policies should be instituted? What are the trade-offs between the need for rapid economic development and the maintenance of environmental quality? How can the surge of people to the large cities be accommodated? These and many similar questions will be discussed throughout this volume.

Black Africa seems to have suffered more severely from alien impact than any other part of the world, with the possible exception of island areas that were decimated by disease and bloodshed caused by such contact. First came the slave trade, which took away millions and degraded both the people and the land. In the wake of the slave trade came European colonialism, with its suppression of the indigenous evolution of society and polity. Fostered by both was the imposition of the myth of the "Dark Continent," awaiting the arrival of European culture, technology, and religion to lift the people from their "state of savagery." Today, all the nations of Black Africa share a common goal of doing away with these legacies and of searching for legitimate self-identities.

One means of establishing self-identity is to turn to the past, and to reinterpret history through African rather than European eyes. Brought to the present, historical identity may take the form of campaigns for "authenticity," such as the practice of abandoning Christian names in favor of African ones advocated in Zaire in the early 1970's. Recognizing the value of traditional art, music, and dance similarly establishes identity—whether they are displayed at festivals or encouraged by specially-financed institutes. There is a paradox in the identity search—the past connotes identification with local ethnic groups, sometimes called "tribes." The present requires nationalism for continuing political unity and development; the future may call for even greater international cooperation. Most African countries became independent *states* in the period around 1960, but few have yet developed as unified *nations*. Regional and sometimes ethnic diversity may influence political processes to the disadvantage of development; it occasionally explodes into secessionism and warfare, as in Nigeria, Chad, Sudan, and Ethiopia. Nevertheless, increasing economic and educational opportunities, accompanied by a felt spirit of *harambee* ("let us pull together"— Swahili) suggest at least as promising a future for the African nation as such conditions promised for European and American nations at a similar stage of their evolution.

As part of the Third World, Black Africa is caught up in the related processes of change, growth, development, and modernization. These terms are sometimes used interchangeably, but this book attempts to incorporate some meaningful distinctions between them. *Change* refers to any alteration in society, in its structure, institutions, or behavior. Such change may result from internal innovation, or it may evolve from cross-cultural contacts and either voluntary diffusion or imposition. *Growth* is simply an increase in magnitude, such as population growth or economic growth. Economic growth may involve a greater mobilization of existing resources or increased productivity, neither necessarily requiring an accompanying *change*. A linkage between economic growth and change may be termed *development*. Conceptually, development also connotes nonproductive results of increased productivity such as schools and health facilities. Development has come to mean a transformation of both rural and urban areas, with greater economic flows and increased human welfare. As does development, *modernization* incorporates both growth and change, but here these processes are seen as moving in a specific direction. Modernization is a pervasive commitment of resources and society to a particular form of development, that characterized by the Western world. Spatially, modernization means an economy and society focused on the city and on secondary (resource-processing) and tertiary (service-providing) rather than primary (resource-extracting) activities. Some writers have viewed modernization from the individual viewpoint, emphasizing an orientation toward achievement underlain by aspirations, values, and attitudes all focused on increased economic welfare and its concomitants. Others have viewed modernization as a political, social, and economic as well as psychological process, and still others have viewed it as incorporating new innovations in organization among components of society and in their spatial configuration (Lerner, 1958; McClelland, 1961; Hagen, 1962; Soja, 1968; Riddell, 1970; Gould, Chapter 27, this book). Thus transportation and communication are important elements in the spatial channeling of modernization. There is certainly a circularity of cause-and-effect in the modernization process, and for this reason we will embrace all of its major connotations—individuals, economic activities, and spatial organization.

There are several important dimensions of modernization in Africa. In terms of basic development, Africa has virtually untapped human and natural resource potentials. The prevailing relatively high disease rates and limited educational opportunities mean that human abilities are largely unexploited. The mineral and energy resources of the continent are being used as raw material exports, but their full role as resources for local modernization has yet to be developed. There is increasing concern with maintaining environmental quality during the development process, as suggested by commitments in Nigeria's recent development plans and the location of the United Nations Environmental Programme in Nairobi, Kenya.

In planning for development, Africa illustrates a wide range of economic and social experiments. On a national level commitments range from *laissez faire* capitalism in Ivory Coast and Nigeria to socialist-oriented planning in Guinea, Tanzania, and Zambia. Internally, virtually every country is experimenting with a variety of development plans—from those designed to augment rural production, develop new rural settlements, and improve transportation, to industrial investments. Also, African universities and research institutes are playing crucial roles in development planning. Regardless of specific strategies, African countries still remain tied to the developed world. These ties are strongest with the former metropolitan colonial powers.

Economic dependency holds the threat of neo-colonial control of development, and specialization on a few major export commodities imposes the uncertainty of the vagaries in world prices. Within and between countries there are vast differences in economic and physical well-being. We have come to recognize similar disparities within developed areas, but in Africa the difference between urban elites and country peasants is severe, creating problems of unfulfilled expectations in achieving the "good life" which seems increasingly focused on Western-oriented consumption patterns. Pastoral societies are the major exception, and they demonstrate that all aspects of modernity are not universally attractive.

Black Africa shares a kind of dynamism rooted in the past and extending to the present. The great migrations that carried Bantu-speaking peoples widely throughout central and southern Africa, the emergence of the major states of precolonial Africa, and the rapid spread of New-World crops once they were introduced all indicate a propensity to change. In contemporary Africa this can be seen in a rapidity of change unusual in world experience. Africa has accomplished in two or three generations deeds that took two or three centuries in the Western world. Where can this dynamism be detected? It can be seen in the crowds moving along roads to rural

A rural market in Ankole District of Uganda suggests a linkage that ties together African economies and brings products from world markets to African consumers. This 28-day market is one of many cyclical or periodic markets that occur widely in Africa. (Photograph by C. M. Good)

Downtown Nairobi, Kenya, the commercial center for Kenya and eastern Africa, is a node for communications and trade, representing the focal role of cities in the modernization of Africa. (Photograph provided by Kenya Information Services)

markets; it can be seen in the eagerness of students who recognize education as still a rare privilege; it can be seen in the great cities of Africa; it can be seen in rural experiment stations.

The dynamics of change have not meant an erasing of things African, but rather a syncretism of African and other cultural features. Sometimes cultural traits crossing ethnic boundaries become reinterpreted, as R.S.V.P. on engraved wedding invitations was thought to mean "Rice and Stew Very Plenty" by some Nigerians in Chinua Achebe's *No Longer at Ease*. More frequently, non-African features have been blended with African. New-World music has syncretised with African music to form the widely popular "High Life." Christian church services may include hymns set to African rhythms and accompanied by drums: the Zairois *Missa Luba* celebrates the Latin Roman Catholic Mass in traditional African modes—antiphonal (leader and chorus) singing and music emphasizing percussion. Western dress has been accepted in many areas; but in others, traditional styles now use machine-woven cloth. New clothing styles have emerged offering alternatives to traditional local or formal "coat-and-tie" Western dress. Especially prominent is the "African suit" made popular by Tanzania's Julius Nyerere. Indigenous markets and towns now incorporate modern sectors—from bus depots and automobile repair facilities to the skyscraper additions to cities like Ibadan.

Finally, Black Africa has shared recently a kind of "benign neglect" by the Western world following a flurry of interest in the early 1960's. This can be seen, for example, in abysmally low levels of foreign aid offered by the United States compared to its own national wealth or its military aid elsewhere in the world. Only three and one-half percent of America's total foreign aid from 1945 to 1974 was directed to Africa (U.S. AID 1975). Initial response to the Sahelian drought of the early 1970's was far slower than would have resulted from a military insurgency threatening an equal number of lives elsewhere. Scholarship aid to African students, loans and outright grants for development, and continuing active concern for Africa's progress have fallen more to international agencies (such as the World Bank and United Nations Development Fund), religious organizations extending efforts to health and agricultural programs, and philanthropic foundations (Rockefeller, Ford) than to bilateral arrangements between countries. The petroleum resources of Nigeria will do far more to attract American interest and dollars than a commitment aroused by conscience toward bettering the lot of Africa!

THE STUDY OF AFRICA

Who studies Africa? How is the study of Africa organized?

Africa has been important in both basic and applied areas of the natural and social sciences. For historical geologists, Africa was the locus of initial evidence that pointed to the past migrations of the continental masses on the earth's surface (continental drift). Africa was the core of ancient Gondwanaland (as indicated by even a cursory examination of the possible matching of the African and South American coastlines, and as confirmed by geophysical, geological, and botanical analysis), the consequences of which include her plateau-like nature with the familiar problems of upriver navigation hampered by rapids and falls; her wealth of potential water power and mineral resources associated with the crystalline Gondwana shield; and a critical lack of fossil fuels in most of the area south of the Sahara. Africa has been important for our understanding of world vegetation and animal distributions. It has served as a natural laboratory for ecologists, zoologists, entomologists, and other biological scientists.

Africa constitutes a particularly significant locale for the pursuit of archeological investigations. Egypt, of course, has long been of interest, but increasing attention is being focused south of the Sahara as evidence mounts from such sites as Olduvai Gorge in Tanzania and the Omo Basin in Ethiopia that hominids took their first tentative steps as man on the savanna lands of eastern and southern Africa.

Among the social sciences, anthropology owes much of its development as a discipline to researchers working in Africa. The numerous and varied cultures of the continent, many relatively untouched by direct Western contact until well into the twentieth century, have provided a fertile ground for probing the inner workings of individual societies and for studying processes in a cross-cultural perspective. Initially concerned with traditional ways of life, more recently anthropologists have turned their attention to the dynamics of culture change and modernization. In this endeavor they have been joined by sociologists, who have concentrated largely on urban phenomena.

The era of independence centering around 1960 for contemporary African states sparked the interest of political scientists in such topics as nation building, one-party democracies, and international relations. Indeed, from the point of view of inquiry the decade of the 1960's in Africa can be said to have belonged to political science. Unfortunately, economists have done much less research in Africa, compared to the other social sciences. This is particularly disappointing in light of the pressing needs for economic development.

In the realm of applied sciences, Africa has called for contributions by the technologically oriented engineering and agronomic professions, as well as by applied social scientists working in planning, education, social services, and similar areas. The American Peace Corps, Canadian External Aid programs, and similar European organizations have provided opportunity for face-to-face interaction between Africans and non-Africans in applied science areas, while formal aid and exchange programs have carried similar import at a governmental level. African expertise, developed in African training colleges and universities as well as abroad, has brought fundamental knowledge and applied technologies to Africa from the technologically advanced world. Indeed, in Africa there is great promise that technological and scientific "know-how" will be more than advanced; it will be incorporated into new social institutions with goals and motivations different from our own, perhaps providing new perspectives on human well-being and new models of long-run harmony of human beings in their natural and social environment.

African literature, art, and music play an increasing role in world studies in the humanities. In addition to the rich traditional literature of Africa (much of it oral), contemporary African writing reflects the historical experience, values, attitudes, aspirations, and social and environmental milieus in ways simply impossible to capture in formal scientific study. In fact, a literary excursion into the works of such modern African writers as Achebe, Aluko, Abrahams, Ngugi, and Paton is richly rewarding. In North America and Europe we are fortunate to have permanent and traveling collections of African art which are increasingly accessible. Words are insufficient in doing justice to an Ife bronze or Makonde carving in ebony. They must be seen first hand! Illustrative and interpretive volumes on African art and architecture are appearing more frequently and are one avenue toward understanding the Africans' place in the larger world of these fields. Similarly, the study of African musicology has added in strong measure to a rich appreciation of traditional, non-Western musical form. Visiting cultural troups of music and dance—or even phonograph records—make these aspects of African humanities so accessible to us that unavailability is no longer an excuse for ignorance.

Cross-cutting the sciences and humanities in the study of Africa are three additional perspectives—African studies, history, and geography. These three areas are viewed as cross-cutting because each is essentially a structure in which data are viewed rather than a specific set of data to be addressed. African studies, for example, places individual expertise (in anthropology, economics, or other fields) in a wider African context with strong interdisciplinary connections. On university campuses and in government agencies, for example, groups of African scholars offer courses and undertake research, mutually enhancing their efforts by continued interdisciplinary dialogue. In a related way, African historians build from the universal human experience of living in time to focus upon selected special aspects of historical processes: economic history, social change, political evolution.

Just as human societies live in time, so too they live in geographical space. Geographers focus on spatial dimensions and interconnections in various aspects of natural and social environment. The work of geographers in Africa may be differentiated by the *kinds* of phenomena they address (the range is well illustrated by the chapters in this book) and the *scale* at which they work, from microscale studies of small communities to macroscale studies of regional or continental processes. Overriding the apparent disparity in geographical studies in Africa is a firm commitment to a viewpoint focused on the spatial organization of phenomena and on explanations that synthesize time and space as critical stages upon which the play of natural and human events is performed. Since, for the interim, we are going to be geographers looking at Africa, let us ask how geographers organize their study and synthesis of information dealing with this area.

THE GEOGRAPHY OF AFRICA

In communicating African information, geographers have adopted several alternative strategies. These may be seen as an interweaving of topical (or systematic) and spatial (or regional) approaches. A topical approach discusses the specific spatial patterns of environmental (climates, vegetation, soils, minerals) and human (agriculture, transportation, settlements) processes, their causes and their consequences. A regional approach uses a strategy of breaking larger spatial units into smaller components. Typically, the smaller components then are addressed topically. Thus a single chapter on Africa south of the Sahara in a world geography may be wholly topical. Many African geography texts have been a combination, with topical introductory chapters on the whole continent, followed by regional (often country-by-country) discussion, again focused topically. Books by Hance (1975), Harrison Church *et al.* (1971), Hodder and Harris (1967), Mountjoy and Embleton (1967), Stamp and Morgan (1972), and Grove (1970) are indispensable for specific analyses on African regions and countries.

An important alternative to the traditional formula has been the recent emergence of topically or regionally focused studies and collections. For example, series of texts and atlases for specific countries have initiated what we hope might become continental-wide coverage of similar materials in the future. Examples include work on Nigeria (Udo 1970a), Rhodesia (Kay 1970), Zambia (Davies 1971), Tanzania (Berry, 1970), and East Africa (Morgan 1972). Collaborative materials on specific topics have been particularly exciting, including Thomas and Whittington's *Environment and Land Use in Africa* (1969) and a forthcoming volume on *Environmental Resource Management in Nigeria* edited by Adejuwon and Ojo. Monographs, too, make the geographical literature large and varied (Soja, 1968; Riddell, 1970; Newman, 1970; Hance, 1970; Ojo, 1966; Knight, 1974; Prothero, 1965). Citations here only begin to indicate the vast and rapidly growing geographical literature on Africa. What, then, is the function of this volume?

This book is designed to provide a *framework* for learning that is not (indeed, cannot be) a beginning and an end in itself. Our plan (and we will come back to it below in more detail) is to provide information on various geographical *processes* with selected substantive information. We hope that one major result of this excursion is your interest and search for additional and supplementary materials, now and in the future. We trust that building by extension and by analogy (with data from sources suggested throughout the volume), you will find these perspectives to be productive; that is, letting you continue learning and focusing on topics you believe to be most critical and interesting. We also hope that this kind of strategy will allow comparison of Africa with other world areas undergoing similar forms of economic and social transition [for example, Melanesia (see Brookfield and Hart, 1971)]. Finally, we believe that frameworks are more intellectually enduring than data. Indeed, as you are reading this book, the data are changing, and if our plan is successful, your experience will enable you to understand how and why this is so, and to carry this understanding beyond the here and now.

What, then, is our framework for understanding Africa? Fundamental to this book are processes of spatial change, of changes in the nature and distribution of phenomena and in their complex interrelationships. We are interested in the traditional questions we all remember from primary school: what? where? why? and how?

What? The measure of significance here is man. The kinds of topics we address are related to the human experience in nature and society, and represent a combination of the basic requisites of social survival and elements of modernization as a pervasive process and direction of change.

Where? Each of the topics is illustrated by specific geographical examples at a variety of scales. Important here is our ability to see the implications and consequences of processes operating at one scale on events at other scales. Equally important is linking processes to patterns in real space: as we read about them, as we see them on maps, and hopefully, as we see them in Africa.

Why? Why have various directions and motivations for change occurred in traditional societies, in colonial powers, in impinging Western economic systems, and in contemporary African aspirations? What processes link human beings to environment and people to people, and what consequences do these processes have in time and across space?

How? What are the trajectories of these processes? And, most critically, how can we create models or conceptualizations of change that explain the past, predict the future, and perhaps prescribe policy to implement desirable states (Abler, Adams and Gould, 1971:573)? The chapters in this book are as much an assessment of whether these tasks are possible as they are answers. Honest, but by no means discouraging, answers to the most pointed questions are:

Can we (geographers and related social scientists studying Africa) explain? *Partially.*
Can we predict? *Tentatively.*
Can we prescribe? *We must. There is no alternative.*

Our explanations are only partial because (1) social science is simply not theoretically well developed, and (2) it is frequently difficult to apply the most advanced social scientific techniques in the absence of requisite data. The economist Stolper (1966) refers to this problem as "Planning Without Facts." Our predictions are tentative because we simply cannot control, if indeed specify, all contingencies. Nevertheless, it is possible to extrapolate informally or to predict formally as a guide to alternative futures. Planning or prescription must take place. Day-to-day decisions on locating extension offices, building hospitals, upgrading roads, plus more embracing decisions of allocation of government funds for development among sectors of the economy and regions of geographical space *will be made.* We simply hope that these decisions are arrived at with as complete a knowledge of past processes as possible, and with a means of incorporating new understanding as it evolves.

But this is not a "state-of-the-art" manual for planners in Africa. Rather, it is an introduction to a complex and evolving set of patterns and processes from a geographical perspective. We hope that it evokes both a feeling for Africa and an understanding of the basic issues discussed. We hope, too, that you come to share some of our commitment to Africa and to development of our research and teaching topics. Learning is discovery, and this book shares some of the ways geographers discover Africa and simultaneously advance their disciplinary queries.

Because there is no single, correct way to organize our discussion, we must relate some of the rationale behind the structure we have chosen. This structure hinges on processes of change with specific emphasis on modernization. We will summarize some of the basic notions of modernization in a spatial context, and then we will briefly describe the sequence of material that lies ahead.

MODERNIZATION AS A SPATIAL PROCESS

Earlier we suggested that modernization was a pervasive commitment of society and its resources to a spatial form of development centered on the city, with accompanying economic, social, psychological, and political implications for all areas. Modernization has been approached spatially in two directions, one stressing geographical patterns of indicator phenomena and the other examining processes of spatial development focused on growth poles.

Modernization as a geographical pattern can be described as essentially a spatial coincidence or correlation of phenomena as an indication of a dynamic process of change. The work of Soja (1968, Kenya), Witthuhn (1968, Uganda), Riddell (1970, Sierra Leone; see Chapter 25, this book), Gould (1970, Tanzania; see Chapter 27, this book), and, on a microscale, Knight (1974, rural Tanzania) all use selected indicators of modernization to derive patterns at specific times which are apparently related to various dynamics of change such as evolution of transportation networks, diffusion of cash cropping, and the like. These studies, in general, do not tell us *how* the pattern developed, and they are only suggestive of *why* strong spatial correlations should be found. In a word, they point to a process in space and time, and suggest a framework for subsequent detailed examination of the process.

If the geographers have shown us that patterns of change are not random in space, but clustered—on a national scale largely focused on cities—what processes are suggested by the patterns? One is the important role of transportation networks, tying rural areas to urban centers providing markets, information, and economic inducements for development (Taaffe, Morrill, and Gould, 1963). Eventually, the focal role of transportation can be incorporated into a larger conceptual framework akin to modernization termed the "space economy" (Board, Davies and Fair, 1970), where urban nodes and the links between them suggest a spatial structure of an economy. An additional, yet related process, is the diffusion of change in space. This simply refers to processes by which innovations are communicated and eventually instituted in new areas. Such processes may be based on contiguity (as Knight, 1974, found in coffee cultivation in rural Tanzania) or may move downward through the urban hierarchy (as Riddell, 1970, found for hospitals, post offices, banks and other facilities in Sierra Leone). The diffusion process has been examined by many researchers (Hagerstrand, 1952; Rogers, 1962, 1969), but it has received surprisingly little attention in Africa. Clearly, understanding diffusion dynamics is important in hastening implemented change.

Parallel to the findings of geographers is the emergence in the last decade of the economic concept of growth poles (Darwent, 1969). Actually the term, which has come to mean development focused on urban areas, is a misnomer with respect to its original usage. The French economist Perroux (1950) designated growth poles as those firms or industries whose position and role *in the economy* made them dominant, propulsive elements for growth. A spatial connotation that links a number of related concepts was added later. Among these concepts are the basic geographical notion of the *nodal* or *functional region* (Whittlesey, 1954); Boudeville's (1968) conception of the *polarized region*: Friedmann's (1966) *center-periphery model* of "polarized development"; Myrdal's (1957) notion of *cumulative causation* focusing development on urban areas; and Hirschman's (1958) *growth pole* argument.

Descriptively, all of these models suggest a dominant role of urban areas in the economy and development of a region from which the city draws resources and people and to which it spreads some benefits. A dualistic economy develops in which the growth pole or center advances, while the periphery declines comparatively. In other words, benefits flowing from the city ("trickling down"—Hirschmann, 1958; "spread"—Myrdal (1957) are far less than the demands placed by the city on its region ("polarization"—Hirschmann; "backwash"—Myrdal). Why are growth poles focal in the development process? Friedmann (1968) suggests six effects concentrated at the center. The dominance effect connotes the ability of the center to draw upon regional resources. The information effect results from the increased spatial interaction focusing on the center. As a focus for change, the center has a psychological effect favoring innovation. Similarly, as a center in which values, behaviors, and institutions are being altered, a modernizing effect induces greater acceptance of and conformity to rapid change. Linkage effects mean that the center is itself a creator of new demands resulting in compounding change. Finally, location of industry at the center creates conditions of greater efficiency and lower development costs, the production effect (Berry, 1969). The latter is essentially Myrdal's (1957) cumulative causation model, which suggests that a combination of external economies (linkages between industries which are located near each other), attraction of the center, and available labor compound to focus development on the center (Keeble, 1967).

If these models stress an inherent inequality in the process of development, why should this occur? According to Nichols (1969), trickle down or spread from poles *should* occur because:

1. Diminishing returns in the center make investment outside more attractive.
2. Ideas generated and demonstrated in the center may be applied elsewhere.
3. The center draws excess labor from rural areas and allows modernization there.
4. Increased center income raises demand in peripheral areas.

On the other hand, many benefits may not spread:

1. Diminishing returns to investment in centers may be offset by external economies or psychological attractions.
2. Knowledge of investment opportunities in the periphery may be obscured.
3. Central location may be critical for command of the market.
4. The demand for primary products from agricultural regions is not very elastic (that is, does not benefit strongly by economic growth in the center).
5. Rural to urban migration removes the most able and educated segments of the rural population (Nichols, 1969:195).

These observations suggest that whereas growth poles have had an important, if not crucial role in development to date, as a prescriptive element for future planning they may have undesirable consequences. Alternative strategies building from growth pole theory might include conscious and carefully designed spatial redistribution of some pole benefits; improved linkages of transportation, communication and organization between centers and peripheral regions (Logan, 1972); and designation of new, lower level growth poles in rural areas (Logan, 1972; Mascarenhas and Claeson, 1972).

Modernization, then, is the creation of a unified viewpoint tying together environment, people, and their social and economic institutions in an interrelated spatial network. Certainly modernization is not the only framework for viewing contemporary Africa. Apparent economic and social benefits of the modernization process exact economic and social prices—loss of local socio-economic independence; commitment to a larger and increasingly alien community structure; vulnerability to the vagaries of the national and world economy; increasing pressure upon man-land relationships; and potential loss of traditional values and notions of the good life. Nevertheless, modernization is crucial to Africa because it encapsulates many of the hopes and designs for, and effects of, change in the late twentieth century. Modernization is unquestionably geographical and indeed historical. As a process impinging upon Africa and Africans, it is to be hoped that African people and planners acting on their behalf will intervene in the process of improving human welfare. Examining this process in space and time, the geographer's holistic viewpoint is critical for integrative understanding and planning. And, finally, modernization provides that critical need for our continued learning—a framework upon which to build, giving meaning and relevance to data that intrigue our minds.[2]

THE SAFARI AHEAD

Writing (and reading) is a linear process. Yet the very material about which we write is circular, intertwined, and without beginning or end. Nevertheless, in response to linearity constraints we have created seven major sections for this book.

The first section, *The Persistence of the Past*, suggests dimensions of historical experience in Africa that remain as legacies (positive and negative). Here we say this is the way it has been, for better or for worse, and attempt to isolate critical elements as we look toward the future. The cultural milieu of Africa and the impact of the colonial period are chosen for particular discussion.

Section II, *Parameters of Change*, focuses upon a number of related elements in African geography that are crucial in planning for future change. Among these are population dynamics, natural resources and their human significance, and questions of human

---

[2] For an excellent review of the modernization concept and a critique of its use in geographic research, see de Souza and Porter (1974).

physiological well-being. While recognizing the close relationship between rural change and dynamics of modernization focused in urban areas, we attempt to isolate the rural impact of modernization, the principal features of urban areas, and the processes that tie these areas together. Thus Section III, *Rural Change*, examines the way in which rural societies have responded to pressures for change, from the exigencies of population growth and meeting national development goals, to the opportunities provided by cash cropping and wage labor employment.

Traditional, pre-European cities of Africa were foci of culture and industry, a role that continues in African cities today. In *Urban Change*, Section IV, the opportunities and problems associated with urbanization are addressed, from industrial development to urban planning to coping with problems of massive, uncontrolled urban growth.

Linkages tying urban and rural areas into a single system include transportation networks, migration patterns, and marketing systems. These topics are explored in Section V, *Rural-Urban Systems*.

Emergent spatial patterns of modernization suggest the interrelated nature (in space and time) of rural and urban change in the context of historical legacy and parameters of change (Section VI, *Modernization*). This section reflects the spatial structure of responses to both internal and external dynamics of African nations.

The final section (VII), *Africa in the World*, explores a variety of problems that place Africa within the larger world milieu. Viewed geographically, these include Africa's place in the world economic system, the continued role of external linkages in trade and tourism, and the difficult problems posed by continued white minority domination in some parts of Africa.

As you read you undoubtedly will find relationships among chapters and topics that do not follow the sequence of the book. We hope you will free yourself of the shackles of our organization and follow a sequence of your own design. Although the authors of the chapters were aware of the sequence to be published, each designed his or her contribution to link to a number of related concepts, the appropriate chapters being cited in the text. We also hope you will test the ideas and concepts presented here on other African areas. And, finally, we hope that Africa ceases to be an abstraction for you and becomes populated by real people, real problems, and real potentials.

I

THE PERSISTENCE OF THE PAST

The past persists, shaping the present and the future. So far, even if it wished to do so, no human society has been able to cut itself off from its own history. The most far-reaching social and political revolutions inevitably wind up carrying over prior attitudes and institutions into their "new" orders. Perhaps some day an anti-past technology will be developed, but this seems to be a highly unlikely eventuality, as even imaginative science fiction writers realize. In their future worlds the past somehow asserts itself just as in today's world.

Africa's long and varigated history means that a large array of factors and their impacts on contemporary society could be discussed. The great medieval kingdoms of the savanna belt of western Africa—Ghana, Mali, Gao, Bornu-Kanem—left their legacy on political patterns and processes. The slave trade stamped its mark indelibly on population distributions and the location of economic activities. Colonialism drew territorial boundaries that continue to influence communication systems. Traditional kinship obligations remain in force and often conflict with the demands of modern entrepreneurship. Influences such as these will be discussed repeatedly in the coming chapters.

A portion of the structure at Zimbabwe in Rhodesia, one of many architectural and artistic monuments to African creativity. (Photograph by H. J. de Blij)

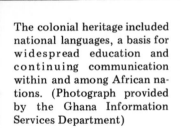

The colonial heritage included national languages, a basis for widespread education and continuing communication within and among African nations. (Photograph provided by the Ghana Information Services Department)

Universities established during the colonial period now provide higher education for African students as well as research oriented to the needs of developing nations. (Photograph at the University of Nairobi provided by Kenya Information Services)

More specifically, the present section of the book focuses on some of the legacies of the past that have particularly wide ranging consequences. Chapter 2 presents the diversity of peoples and cultures that most of the countries have inherited. A case is made for "ethnicity" as one of the most critical factors in shaping political life on the continent. It also shows how an old intellectual legacy—race—still plagues references to Africa. Chapter 3 deals with the compartmentalization of political space that resulted from European conceptions of territorial order. It documents how many of the boundaries that were drawn were incongruent with African realities. Yet, almost without exception, these same boundaries remain in force today. Finally, Chapter 4 is concerned with the heritage left by local officials in former British-ruled Africa. It demonstrates their importance in shaping patterns of rural economic change and also in influencing African attitudes toward administration. It also demonstrates how perspectives can change when the individual is looked at rather than a large-scale political system.

2

The Mosaic
of Peoples

JAMES L. NEWMAN

No matter how they are viewed, the peoples of Africa are arranged in patterns of great diversity. The shortest-statured people in the world (Pygmoids) live in close proximity to the tallest (Tutsi). Skin colors vary widely. Over 800 distinct African languages have been identified and the actual figure probably is closer to 1000. Subsistence modes cover a spectrum from paleolithic-like hunting and gathering, to nomadic pastoralism, to shifting cultivation, to paddy-rice cultivation, to livestock ranching, to dairy farming, to all the occupations associated with urban-industrial society. Islam in its several traditions and all conceivable branches of Christianity are intermixed with traditional forms of worship, and in some cases the contact has produced "new" syncretic religions. Some Africans live in widely dispersed homesteads, others in compact villages, and still others in densely packed urban areas. House types consist of simple lean-tos, many shapes and forms of wattle and daub, mud-brick, scrap metal, and packing crate enclosures, suburban style ranch houses, and high rise apartments. It would be possible to continue the recitation almost indefinitely.

When faced with diversity, a reaction inevitably is to classify, to bring order to seeming disorder so that rational discourse and analysis are possible. The present chapter will present several of the more common classificatory schemes of African peoples and then attempt to discuss their relative values for interpreting contemporary events.

RACE

The recognition that not all people are alike physically undoubtedly dates before recorded history; there were occasional attempts by the Greeks and Romans to explain the variable distributions of certain features, particularly skin color. It was not, however, until the 18th century that "race" emerged as an important concept in European-American thought, and over the past 250 years or so, numerous books and articles have been written defining and classifying the races of humankind.[1] Many of these are honest, straight-forward scholarly studies that apply the available anatomical and genetic data, though there is still great debate over what constitute the most appropriate criteria for assessing racial differentiation, and consequently there is no classification that generally is accepted as definitive. Unfortunately, much of the rest of the literature is flawed by ulterior motives, especially sensationalizing "strange and mysterious" peoples for popular consumption or justifying policies of inequality by supposedly showing how races can be ranked along an inferior-to-superior scale.

Because of these problems, race must be considered virtually useless as a social scientific concept. From a descriptive standpoint, about all that can be said confidently for Africa is that it is inhabited by peoples from diverse genetic pools, including those of African, European, and Asian origin. Analytically, the limitations are even more severe, in that so far as is known, race explains nothing. Consequently, for the foreseeable future, race should be left to the biological sciences where hopefully the human race's genetic characteristics can be studied in a rational manner.

Of course, race-thinking or racism is another matter. It is operative in Africa today and both shapes and is shaped by social and political processes, as will be demonstrated in Chapter 31.

LANGUAGE

Africa is characterized by such a great diversity of languages that early attempts at classification presented an almost bewildering array of families and subfamilies. Fortunately, in recent years the picture has been clarified and simplified to a considerable degree, especially

[1] For a discussion of race as a concept in Western thought see Barzun, (1970).

by Joseph Greenberg. His work over the last three decades has led most linguists and Africanists to adopt his terminology and classification (Figure 2.1 and Table 2.1).

Greenberg's method is genetic, linking together languages that are related historically, and as such his scheme is extremely valuable in helping to interpret the historical geography of the continent. It is a necessary starting point in the study of the migration of peoples and the diffusion of goods and ideas. Also, it can be useful in

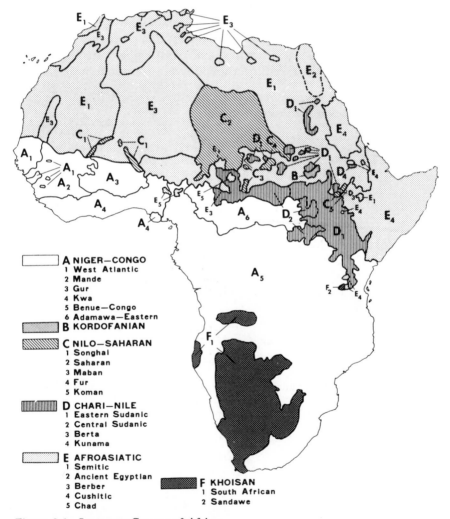

A NIGER—CONGO
1 West Atlantic
2 Mande
3 Gur
4 Kwa
5 Benue—Congo
6 Adamawa—Eastern

B KORDOFANIAN

C NILO—SAHARAN
1 Songhai
2 Saharan
3 Maban
4 Fur
5 Koman

D CHARI—NILE
1 Eastern Sudanic
2 Central Sudanic
3 Berta
4 Kunama

E AFROASIATIC
1 Semitic
2 Ancient Egyptian
3 Berber
4 Cushitic
5 Chad

F KHOISAN
1 South African
2 Sandawe

Figure 2.1 Language Groups of Africa.
Source: Greenberg, 1966, with permission of Joseph H. Greenberg and Indiana University Research Center for Language and Semiotic Studies.

identifying people who have much in common, since sharing a language often means sharing a culture. In fact, this correspondence has been so frequent that linguistic labels are employed more widely than any others in designating the peoples of Africa, for example Kikuyu, Beja, Herero, and Nuer. The correspondence of language and culture, however, is far from perfect. Sometimes a common language hides considerable cultural diversity, as occurs among the Tutsi, Hutu, and Twa of Ruanda. In addition, language differences can obscure fundamental cultural similarities. The Baamba of Uganda speak two mutually unintelligible languages but share the same basic culture (Kasfir, 1972). Finally, it must be emphasized that it is only at the local level that one can use language as a surrogate for culture and identity. Language families and subfamilies are high-order aggregations and abstractions; they do not represent indigenously

TABLE 2.1 Languages of Africa

Family	Subfamily or branch	Examples
Niger-Congo	West Atlantic	Serer, Wolof, Fulani, Temne
	Mande	Soninke, Bambara, Mande, Mano, Kpelle
	Gur	Mossi, Dagomba, Tamprusi, Lobi
	Kwa	Kru, Ewe, Akan, Yoruba, Nupe, Ibo
	Benue-Congo	Bantu, Tiv, Jukun, Biram, Ibibio
	Adamawa-Eastern	Teme, Mono, Mbaka, Zande
Kordofanian	Koalib	Koalib, Kanderma, Moro
	Tegali	Tegali, Tumale
	Talodi	Talodi, Masakin
	Tumtum	Tumtum, Krongo, Miri
	Katla	Katla, Tima
Nilo-Saharan	Songhai	Songhai
	Saharan	Kanuri, Teda, Zagahawa
	Maban	Maban
	Fur	Fur
	Koman	Koman
Chari-Nile	Eastern Sudanic	Dilling, Murle, Shilluk, Acholi, Dinka, Jie, Nandi
	Central Sudanic	Bongo, Sara, Lugbara, Madi, Mangbutu
	Berta	Berta
	Kunama	Kunama
Afroasiatic	Semitic	Hebrew, Arabic
	Ancient Egyptian	Ancient Egyptian
	Berber	Tuareg, Ghadames, Beraber, Kabyle
	Cushitic	Beja, Somali, Galla, Sidamo, Iraqw
	Chad	Hausa, Mandara, Logone, Fali
Khoisan	South African	Nama, Naron, Korana, Kung, Hiechware
	Sandawe	Sandawe

Source: Greenberg (1966)

perceived reality. It is highly unlikely that, for instance, the Wolof of Senegal and the Temne of Sierra Leone recognize that they share a linguistic heritage, much less that they belong to something resembling the West Atlantic subfamily of the Niger-Congo family.

It also must be realized that any classification is an instantaneous pattern representing numerous, interacting processes. In Africa, there are several of these processes now operating that portend rather substantial modifications in the language maps. First, there are languages that are being actively displaced. Examples are the various Khoisan dialects in southern Africa. Their area already is much more circumscribed than that shown on Greenberg's map and it is conceivable that they could disappear completely in the near future. Second, there is the continuing spread of former colonial languages, especially English and French. These have tended to be used primarily by the elite—academics, civil servants, scientists—but they are spreading more widely because of increased educational opportunities. Then, too, there is a variety of pidgin forms of English and French that are used in everyday conversation, particularly in West Africa. Third is the development and diffusion of such *lingua franca* as Malinke and Hausa in western Africa, Bemba in central Africa, and Swahili in eastern and central Africa. Both Tanzania and Kenya have declared Swahili as their official national language. Finally, Arabic has continued to spread in the wake of conversions to Islam.

Overall, then, though displacements may work in the direction of simplifying the language maps of Africa, the other processes point towards highly complex patterns of multilingualism. Africans have generally been multilingual because of the necessity to communicate across group boundaries, but now the trend seems to indicate an even more intensified use by individuals of several languages, with the purposes of the communication specifying which language is chosen. In Kenya it is already common to find people who have retained their local language for informal conversations; use English for much reading and for conversations on national and international affairs; listen to Swahili radio broadcasts; and, depending on religious predilictions, worship in Arabic. Somehow, future language classifications and maps are going to have to take this kind of language diversity into account.

CULTURE

In an endeavor to provide for more comprehensiveness in delineating similarities and differences among peoples, anthropologists and geographers frequently have constructed what are known as either culture areas or culture regions. Though the precise procedures of construction vary somewhat, the basic framework inevitably includes some sort of aggregation of cultural characteristics into areal units so that every space on the map becomes part of a definable culture area or perhaps transition zone (Newman, 1971). Occasionally, statistical procedures are used in the aggregation, though estimating the areas and boundaries is more characteristic.

Several culture-area schemes have been devised for Africa,[2] but by far the best known is that by Melville Herskovits (1930, 1962a). Herskovits recognized ten areas (Figure 2.2)—North Africa, Desert,

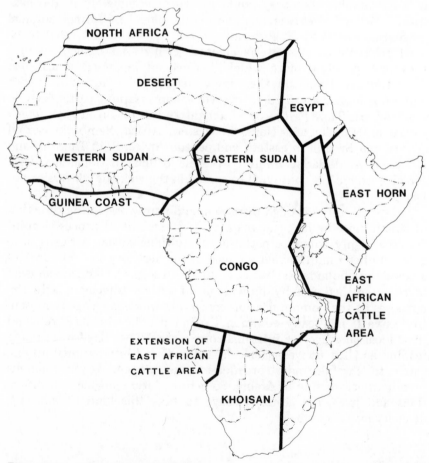

Figure 2.2 Culture Areas of Africa.
Source: Herskovits, 1962a. Reproduced with permission of Alfred A. Knopf, Inc.

[2] See, for example, Murdock (1959).

Egypt, Western Sudan, Eastern Sudan, East Horn, East African Cattle, Khoisan, Guinea Coast, and Congo—and each is described in terms of various predominant cultural traits and complexes.

Such culture-area schemes can be useful introductions in the study of unfamiliar parts of the world, particularly when compiled by an observer having skill and experience equal to Herskovits. Beyond this, however, their use can create problems, especially for the novice. No matter how carefully constructed, an impression of uniformity that is not in accord with reality is bound to be given. No one group of people is likely to possess all the characteristics that are enumerated, and, in fact, some people in the group may possess virtually none of them. Then, too, culture is much more than the aggregation of traits and complexes, but this more has proved to be an illusive entity in building culture areas. Enlarging the scale does not make these problems disappear; it only reduces them somewhat. Finally, the dilemma of imposed versus recognized reality once again is encountered. As Herskovits (1962:58) himself has stated, "As far as the people of an area are concerned, they have no awareness of the unities imposed by the student."

ETHNICITY

One way of getting around this problem of recognized identity, while at the same time making group labels more pertinent to an understanding of contemporary Africa, is to employ the concept of ethnicity. Here the central issue is how the people define themselves; how a differentiation is made between "We" and "They." The exact criteria used, such as language, religion, eating habits, initiation ceremonies or what-have-you, are important and need to be enumerated, but they really are only secondary to the simple act of identifying, of setting off one's own group from others.

In Africa, as elsewhere, groups with very strong, long-standing identities can be found. These often correlate with the existence of a former centralized conquest state or empire, as is the case with the Ganda of Uganda, the Ethiopians, the Zulu of South Africa, the Songhai of Mali, and the Bemba of Zambia. In other instances a sense of identity has emerged from an outside threat and the desire for self-preservation. One example of this is the Sotho of Lesotho who were formed from a number of fragmented peoples fleeing the expansions of the Zulu and Boers during the nineteenth century. Still others coalesced in response to economic opportunities. This seems to have occurred among the Ibo of Nigeria when European trade began penetrating up the Niger River and among the Dahomey during the height of the trans-Atlantic slave trade.

How much of Africa was covered by large, well-defined groups when the colonial era began is uncertain; but in all likelihood it was less than half. Nevertheless, European administrators assumed such groups were the norm and in their zeal for demarcating administrative units they began naming "tribes"[3] and appointing rulers to fill up the spaces on the map (Levine and Campbell, 1972). This was particularly true in British-governed areas under the policy of indirect rule, where locating indigenous leaders and specifying the prevailing social-political traditions were essential. What happened was the creation of many new self-conscious groups. A case in point would be the Sandawe of Tanzania who, despite their unique language and many customs that set them off from surrounding peoples (Newman, 1970), never seem to have possessed a sense of solidarity and separate identity until they were organized into an administrative subchiefdom and virtually told who they were.

The colonial powers imposed boundaries that both consolidated and created ethnic identities, a process that will be discussed further in the next chapter. Each country became compartmentalized into so-called tribal areas that were supposedly different from one another. In some cases, one or at most two or three very large groups were dominant, such as in Dahomey, Upper Volta, and Swaziland. In others, several large groups were interspersed among more numerous smaller ones—Kenya, Nigeria, the Congo (Zaire). And in still others, many small groups predominated, for example, in Tanganyika (Tanzania), Mozambique, and the Cameroun. But no matter what the particular pattern might be, it was continually reinforced by government actions, especially those related to law enforcement, taxes, and project funding. Academics, most notably anthropologists, also seem to have played a reinforcing role, because they generally accepted the designated labels as givens for their analyses (Levine and Campbell, 1972).

This ethnic legacy has been inherited, and indeed accepted, by the present independent African governments. Politicians in Kenya play off Kikuyu against Luo and against Kamba and against the various minority groups. Sierra Leone must contend with a Creole-indigenous split, with the indigenous peoples being fragmented by a Temne-Mende conflict. Nigeria worked to bring the Ibo back into national life, and Zaire, despite a recent proclamation declaring all its citizens as equal, regularly has to play politics with over 250 recognized ethnic groups (Turner, 1972).

---

[3] Because of its association with colonialism and its implications of relative primitiveness, the term tribe has fallen out of favor.

, Ethnic conflict and competition are realities in contemporary Africa and in all probability they will continue, and perhaps even increase in intensity, as competition for jobs and resources increases. At this moment ethnic groups are the most logically-based political pressure groups, an observation that inevitably is made by aspiring politicians. Perhaps someday class or generational conflicts will emerge as the most salient political facts of life, but it is doubtful that ethnicity will ever disappear, as the United States is witnessing today.

SUMMARY

The peoples of Africa exhibit a great deal of diversity in a variety of ways, as should be expected given the size of the continent and its long and complex history of settlement. How to classify these diversities has posed a continuing dilemma to scholars. Quite obviously, no system of classification will find universal acceptance, since a classification's usefulness depends upon its purposes. Unfortunately, one of the most commonly employed classifications—race—is clouded by questionable purposes as well as by conceptual uncertainties. A genetic classification of languages is very useful for historical studies but seems to break down for descriptive and analytical purposes under conditions of rapid change. Culture areas are valuable pedagogical devices, though such devices tend to oversimplify. Consequently, for studying contemporary social, political, and economic events in Africa, ethnicity would seem to provide the key for the most appropriate labels. It allows people to define themselves and is a fluid enough concept to incorporate changes in definitions. Of course, this means that it will be virtually impossible to construct neat, logically ordered classifications and maps, but investigators simply will have to learn to live with such a fact.

3

The Impress
of Colonialism

BURTON O. WITTHUHN

After limited contacts through the Mediterranean coastal fringe, persistent interaction between Africa and Western Europe began with the Renaissance voyages of exploration of the fifteenth through early seventeenth centuries. The causes of the upsurge of interest in exploration were many. Advances in shipbuilding technology and navigation were taking place, and commerce was being systematized by merchant companies and governments, particularly for procuring critical metals and meeting the demands for spices (to make spoiling foods palatable!). Christianity provided an impetus for exploration in its search for converts, and it added a special psychological zeal to the desire to reach new lands. Finally, the occupation of the Middle East by the Ottoman Turks created a need to find alternative trade routes to India and China.

Relying largely on knowledge derived from Arab mathematicians and cosmographers, the Portuguese mastered the art of sailing the open ocean, and thanks to the patronage and inspiration of Prince Henry, the so-called Navigator, and the support of Lisbon's commercial interests, Portugal's navigation and cartographic competence quickly surpassed all of its European competitors. The coast of northwest Africa was contacted in the early 1400's, and systematic coastal exploration continued until the end of the century. Despite the fact that Portugal attempted to keep its seafaring technology secret, it soon began to spread as, in turn, did European contact with Africa. Spain entered the competition by mid-century. English and French adventurers appeared in the last decade of the fifteenth century, and the Dutch joined in a century later. The Danes and Swedes embarked upon an African quest in the 1640's and the Brandenburgers set sail in the 1680's.

As the number of European states operating in Africa increased, the competition between them grew, and each found it desirable to operate from specific territorial bases. Coastal fortresses were built as collection depots for the dried fish, pepper, ivory, beeswax, hides, amber, indigo, sugar cane, gold, and, of course, slaves brought from the interior. Thus began the European presence in Africa.

SETTLEMENTS AND COLONIZATION

Efforts at European settlement and colonization, however, were not actively pursued during this early period of exploration and trade. Coastal fortresses functioned only as spatial isolates of European activities. Even their immediate hinterlands remained virtually unknown until well into the nineteenth century. As many trader's diaries clearly indicate, the Europeans were in their fortresses at the discretion of the local African peoples. They could have been dislodged at any time.

As the decades passed, the slave trade began to dominate Europe-Africa relations. By the time of its century-long height (from the middle eighteenth to the middle nineteenth centuries) thousands of able-bodied men and women were shipped each year across the Atlantic (Curtin, 1969). The deplorable conditions aboard the ships and the dehumanizing experiences of servitude in the New World were obvious disasters for those who were impressed. Equally disastrous were the impacts on the social-political order of many parts of Africa. Some regions were virtually depopulated by continual raiding. Diseases spread in the wake of disorganization. Autocratic rulers came to power with the aid of guns and ammunition. Arts and crafts disappeared from some cultures. The commercial and social rape of Africa had begun.

As opposition to the slave trade grew, European industrialists were forced to take a new look at Africa. They began to see Africa as a source of primary raw materials and as a marketplace for manufactured goods. To control trade effectively, it was necessary for the European powers to know, in some detail, the interior of the continent. Travelers and explorers were backed by governments and varied interest groups. Mungo Park, Richard Burton, David Livingstone, Henry Stanley, John Speke, Heinrich Barth, Rene Caillie, Paul Soleillet, Emin Pasha, Samuel Baker are but a few of the notables who undertook the task of augmenting the sketchy knowledge of Africa available to the outside world.

It is unfortunate but this new period of encounter produced new tragedies for the African people. Impoverished by the loss of manpower and material wealth and in a state of disunity because of slavery-prompted internecine wars, Africa was ill-prepared to resist the "benefits" of imposed Westernization.

Typical of the arrogance, deceit, and self-serving legal fiction of the new contact is the following treaty agreed to by Henry Stanley on behalf of the African International Association and the King and Chiefs of a site along the Zaire (Congo) River near Kinshasa (Boyd, 1889: 113-14):

> The Chiefs of Ngombi and Mafela recognize that it is highly desirable that the "African International Association" should, for the advancement of civilization and trade, be firmly established in their country. They therefore now, freely of their own accord, for themselves and their heirs and successors forever, do give up to the said Association the sovereignty and all sovereign and governing rights to all their territories. They also promise to assist the Association in its work of governing and civilizing this country, and to use their influence with all other inhabitants, with whose unanimous approval they make this treaty, to secure obedience to all laws made by said Association, and assist by labor or otherwise, any works, improvements, or expeditions, which the said Association shall cause at any time to be carried out in any part of the territories.

> The Chiefs of Ngombi and Mafela promise at all times to join their forces with those of the said Association, to resist the forcible intrusion or repulse the attacks of foreigners of any nationality or color.

> The country thus ceded has about the following boundaries, viz: The whole of the Ngombi and Mafela countries, and any tributary to them; and the Chiefs of Ngombi and Mafela solemnly affirm that all this country belongs absolutely to them; that they can freely dispose of it; and that they can neither have already, nor will on any future occasion, make any treaties, grants or sales of any parts of these territories to strangers, without the permission of the said Association. All roads and waterways running through this country, the right of collecting tolls on the same, and all game, fishing, mining, and forest rights, are to be the absolute property of the said Association, together with any unoccupied lands as may at any time hereafter be chosen.

> The "African International Association" agrees to pay to the Chiefs of Ngombi and Mafela the following articles of merchandise, viz: one piece of cloth per month, to each of the undersigned chiefs, besides presents of

cloth in hand; and the said chiefs hereby acknowledge to accept this bounty and monthly subsidy in full settlement of all their claims on the said Association.

The "African International Association" promises:

1. To take from the natives of this ceded country no occupied or cultivated lands, except by mutual agreement.
2. To promote to its utmost the prosperity of the said country.
3. To protect its inhabitants from all oppression or foreign intrusion.
4. It authorizes the chiefs to hoist its flag; to settle all local disputes or palavers; and to maintain its authority with the natives.

Agreed to, signed and witnessed, this 1st day of April 1884.

One can only suspect that the 450 independent African chiefs who signed similar agreements with Stanley were inadequately appraised of the content of documents bearing their marks. Whether these men held trust to the lands by undisturbed possession, ancient usage, or divine right, their anguish and remorse upon learning the true nature of the agreement must have been substantial.

By the fall of 1884, the mutual hates, the fears, and the conflicting claims of the several European powers precipitated a conference hosted by Prince Bismarck in Berlin. In attendance were representatives of Austria, Belgium, Denmark, France, Germany, Great Britain, Norway, Portugal, Russia, Spain, Sweden, Turkey, and the United States.

By February of 1885, the conferees decided that any power wishing to claim a colony or protectorate anywhere in Africa would need to notify formally the other signatories and back its claim with demonstrable effective authority in the area concerned. The Berlin Agreement set the rules for partitioning Africa, but more importantly, the Agreement guaranteed the foreign occupation of virtually the whole of the continent. Whereas 90 percent of Africa remained under African rule in 1880, by 1900 only Ethiopia and Liberia remained in sovereign possession of their territories (Figure 3.1).[1]

COMPARTMENTALIZATION

The Berlin Agreement serves as a benchmark for colonialism. During the periods of coastal and internal exploration, the European political space of Africa remained a set of loosely connected nodes of

[1] The colonizers did not share similar philosophies or policies. This review will consider Africa in gross generalizations, referring to colonizers as if unitary in purpose and performance. In reality, there were distinct differences in the European colonizers. Each left its own spatial impress that is still reflected in spatial patterns of modernization (see Sections VI and VII). Development planning in each African nation must build from (or overcome) this legacy.

Figure 3.1 Africa in 1910.
Source: Redrawn from Stamp and Morgan (1972:30) with permission of John Wiley & Sons, Inc.

commercial activity. But the mandated institution of demonstrable effective authority changed all this. The European notion of sovereignty brought with it a total compartmentalization of political space in which there were no empty areas. From the ownership of a landholding through a hierarchy of political administrative areas such as the community, county, state, and nation, all pieces fit together with neither overlap nor extension. The resulting pattern contains homogeneous administrative units and clearly defined boundaries.

All this seems to have contrasted markedly with prevailing African territorial conceptions. Bohannan and Curtin (1971) have observed that community relationships within Africa are not seen within a context of ownership, but rather in terms of social relations and the juxtaposition of social groups. Boundaries were not rigidly drawn and all land did not have to be effectively occupied in a legalistic manner.

It is quite possible that the African rulers did not see any threat in relinquishing the requested boundaries in the treaties made by Stanley and others, for they had the promise that the alien power would not interfere with the occupied or cultivated lands. On the other hand, it is unlikely that any westerner would misconstrue the significance of Stanley's intent except in that ceding areas tributary to a defined boundary even oversteps the basic limitations of the western bias of territorial jurisdiction.

For the colonist, the lines of delimitation also often proved to be very illusory. Lacking maps or detailed descriptions of African societies, the divisions that seemed so natural and necessary in Berlin proved almost meaningless in terms of prevailing African physical, cultural, economic, and political realities. Note, for example, all the straight-line boundaries. These usually were drawn from divides between the coastal nodes of competing powers and extended inland until they conflicted with other extensions. Whereas the reality of a straight line drawn across the Sahara or the Kalahari may be of little consequence, the impacts of similar delimitations across populated areas, such as between Kenya and Tanzania, Angola and Zambia, and Ethiopia and the Somali Republic, obviously has social-political implications.

Another example of European boundary ignorance is the use of waterways. The Zambezi, Cunene, Zaire (Congo), Limpopo, Ruvuma, Senegal, and many other rivers were used as divides based on the ease of demarcation rather than upon an awareness of their central, unifying role for societies present along their banks. Similarly, lakes Chad, Mobutu (Albert), Amin (Edward), Tanganyika, Nyasa, and Victoria proved useful to the boundary delimiters in Europe. Little did it occur to them that river and lake basins serve more as spatial integrators than as territorial divides.

Discovering their lack of homogeneous and functional polities, one might have assumed that the European colonists would have attempted to correct their specious boundary definitions. Indeed they did, but not by correcting disruptive international demarcations or by changing their conceptions of boundary to better fit the African experience. Rather they set about to impose unification and interaction from within. The new boundaries came to demarcate the extent of a particular coin usage, the jurisdiction of a given governor, the limit of a tax, and the end point for a colonial language.

The shapes of many African countries that resulted from the various manipulations of the European colonial overlords often have proved to be something less than administratively efficient. The barbell of Zambia, which is infringed upon by protrusions of both Zaire and Mozambique, is defensively unsound and spatially unrealistic. Equally inefficient to administer are the elongated shapes of the Congo, Cameroun, Dahomey, and Togo, each of which has its capital city on or relatively near to one end of the elongation. Although it is naive to suppose that the realities of any environment can, or should, dictate the configuration of a state, it is equally foolish to overlook the impacts of predetermined shapes on future defense, communications, and governance.

Just as shape can affect administrative efficiency, so too can size. Comparison of Sierra Leone and Chad illustrates the consequences of size differences. Sierra Leone has an area of 72,500 square kilometers, whereas Chad includes some 1,285,000. The costs of developing and maintaining an infrastructure of communication links are positively correlated to size; these costs grow geometrically with increasing area. Similarly, the cost of regularly spaced border installations, either for defense or administrative control, are functionally related to size (boundary length) and not to the resources of a country. Some might argue that as the size increases, so too, do resources such as arable land. Chad, with 71,000 square kilometers of arable land, does surpass the 37,000 square kilometers in Sierra Leone. But, while the arable land of Chad is less than twice as large as that of Sierra Leone, the total area of Chad is nearly eighteen times larger. The geometry of size and the efficiencies that accrue to political areas as a consequence thereof rarely have been studied empirically. Too often, the assumption is that whatever the size, it is just right.

Size has aspatial implications as well. In a meeting of nation states, Chad and Sierra Leone have equal representation, or do they? Then too, psychological advantages may accrue to individuals who perceive in their nation's size a lessening of external threat or room to grow regardless of the realities upon which such perceptions are based. Although it is too soon to know the full impact that territory perceptions will have on future citizens of Zaire or Cabinda, it is unlikely that their outlooks will be similar unless they are both members of a larger confederation or republic.

Complicating the geometry of the political subdivision of Africa is the restructuring of large Empire units into smaller national units. As the twentieth century began, the European powers had no way of knowing that less than sixty years of tenure remained for most of them. Rail lines, developed to meet Empire needs, established patterns of accessibility which are today as tenuous as they once were expeditious. Examples include the Dakar, Senegal-Bamako, Mali railway; the Abidjan, Ivory Coast-Ouagadougou, Upper Volta linkage; and the Mombasa, Kenya-Kampala, Uganda connection.

Most lacking in the current political structure of Africa is the development of a well defined spatial hierarchy. Partially to blame has been the imposition of the alien compartmentalization unto an already weakened human spatial organization. As Haggett (1966:18) has suggested, spatial structure requires an open system based upon movements, networks, nodes, and hierarchies. Unfortunately, the defined boundaries created by the Europeans closed both the boundaries and the system to alternatives in the evolution of hierarchical development.

If we assume, for argument's sake, that the development of a spatial structure is in response to local needs, then movements of individuals, messages, and goods will energize the system. The movements, in turn, define a network or grid of nerve endings for the structure. The focusing of activity and interaction by movements along the network causes some locations, or nodes, to gain functional significance. Nodes may refer, therefore, to urban places, markets, post offices, or any functionally specific location. Depending upon uneven energizing effects, various nodes will become differentiated into a hierarchical organization. But, what if the system and its boundaries are closed? Can a structure be imposed which will later come to operate as if it were energized at the grass roots level?

Over much of Africa, colonialism froze societies within fixed boundaries, but the dynamic quality of ethnicity did not fit well into the rigidity of these new boundaries. Forced to accommodate both a new territorial limit as well as a centralized political administration, many of the traditional societies expanded into new supralocal assemblages. These new structures came to be the "tribes" of European reference. The Ewe in Ghana and Togo, the Ibo in Nigeria, the Kikuyu in Kenya, and the Soga in Uganda are typical of such altered societies.

An institutionalized chieftainship, especially where such organization promoted centralization and amalgamation of overlapping authority groups, connotes a stratified society (Soja, 1971). The Ganda in Uganda and the Nangodi of Northern Ghana are two examples of peoples having this kind of societal organization at the time of the colonial penetration. These stratified societies were particularly amenable to the self-rule (indirect rule) policies practiced by the British—often with the effect of reinforcing a politico-military strata to the detriment of other traditional sectors. Since the colonists were not interested in preserving lineage or indigenous spiritual bases, their selective reinforcement was self-serving and most disruptive of the encountered mixture of territorially and societally based legitimization factors. While the colonist clearly understood the realities of chiefdom hierarchies and territorial limits, there was little inclination to understand the other societal-spatial relationships operating in a given region.

In retrospect, it is increasingly clear that the explorers and early colonists frequently took inappropriate actions because they did not understand the implications of what they were observing. Land standing idle was assumed unused. Weakly defined territorial bounds were considered evidence of poorly articulated political systems. Spatially separated political areas were clearly a sign of backwardness. These and other incorrect judgments made the external impress of alien impact all the more burdensome to the peoples affected. It is not surprising, therefore, that the modifications and reorganizations of society, forced by the contact, prompted the emergence of new African territorial states.

4

Colonial Officials and Socio-Economic Development

ROBERT HEUSSLER

Among the better known and widely believed clichés about British colonialism in Africa is that it was absent-minded in conception and so minimal in scope and actual performance that it did little more than keep the peace. According to this view, colonial regimes were either unconcerned with such dynamic questions as economic development or incapable of doing anything about them. By extension, the economic difficulties of new African states are ascribed to European neglect. Some critics go farther and accuse Britain and her fellow colonial powers of having exploited their African dependencies, leaving them weaker than they found them. The first of these notions contains elements of truth; the second is a caricature; together they give an impression that is partial, inaccurate, and misleading.

The subject of Britain's aims and activities in Africa is best approached through study of the role of local officials—district officers (D.O.s) and their colleagues in the professional and technical services. These men were the cutting edge of government, the implementers of policy from above in times when there was money for large-scale projects; but more often they were the facilitators of small schemes which they themselves frequently conceived, which were paid for out of local revenue, and which were personally supervised by officials at the grass roots.

In Africa, Britain acquired enormous new colonial responsibilities. Unlike other colonial areas, most African territories were not suited to emigration and rapid self-government (in contrast to Australia and Canada); were not well endowed with natural resources and self-sustaining administrative and commercial potential (compared with Malaya, Ceylon and parts of the West Indies); and were not strategically important (like Gibraltar and Aden) with expectation of military expenditures. The scramble for Africa was an aberration from previous norms. Territories were taken over for reasons of competition in international power rather than their particular value. Even potentially rich areas like Northern Nigeria required priming from London to get their administrations going.

From the start, the objectives and accomplishments of the new colonial governments were subject to three main influences: London's traditional insistence on cheap government; the ethos of administration within the territories; and a deep cultural ambivalence about Europeanization and modernization, particularly in relation to economics.

Parsimony from the imperial center was of long standing. Grants in aid were not unheard of, but the universal, long-term rule was self-support.[1] Up to 1945, when the *Colonial Development and Welfare Act* became operative, this meant living off local taxes in poor countries. Civil services were small in relation to land area and population. Communications, already primitive, improved but slowly. Each place tended to prosper according to its own inherent wealth and the talents of its people.

The average British official found himself in charge of a vast area with a large and widely scattered population. He had neither the staff nor the budget to work miracles. Yet his isolation from superior authority and his prestige with local peoples gave him opportunities for the exertion of personal influence that far exceeded anything available to civil servants in advanced countries. At the same time it put a premium on his own personality, values, and capabilities as vital forces in day-to-day administration.

During the early stages, officers were drawn from military units or from the staffs of chartered companies, whereas later on they

---

[1] There were important exceptions. For example, a loan of four million pounds, raised by the Gold Coast government on the London market to support a ten year development program (see R. E. Wraith, *Guggisberg*, London, 1967, p. 123). But these served to prove the over-all rule that colonial regimes had to be supported by local revenue and that such projects as the building of railways were aimed at enabling colonies to pay their own way rather than providing the kind of development that came after 1945.

came from universities in England as had the members of the Indian Civil Service. Despite differences in education, experience, and even social origins, most officers shared basic assumptions about government. Political order, embodied in a nation state, was so primordial as to be taken for granted, as was the desirability of stable, honest, and efficient regimes.

By the same token, D.O.s felt concern and affection for the common people in their areas. They were constantly uncovering cases of abuse of authority on the part of chiefs and lesser office holders, and the courts that were set up by colonial governments soon had their dockets filled with complaints that took long hours for harassed D.O.s to look into and resolve. The logic of the situation—culturally self-confident Europeans ruling over African leaders viewed as incompetent and irresponsible and arbitrating between them and their subjects—rendered paternalism inescapable.

But paternalism to what end? Should indigenous peoples be protected from exploitation but otherwise left to develop on their own lines? Or should they be led deliberately towards a culture and society not their own but presumed superior by the alien elite that now ran their country? Throughout the whole of the British period in Africa, the debate went on; secretaries of state in London, governors in colonial capitals, and officials down to newly arrived cadets talked about the dilemma and about the moral dictates of one course or the other.[2] Policy statements were issued and sometimes acted on, with varying effects. Meanwhile each district, province, and colony changed quickly, or slowly, or hardly at all depending on its own special blend of human and material traits. Influences tending to inhibit growth sometimes were overcome by imagination and strong leadership. In other instances natural advantages were not seized upon and opportunities were lost. Elsewhere material progress was made or not made according to the value judgments of British and African leaders, without reference to other factors such as mineral resources or the presence of marketing centers.

---

[2] Harold Ingrams, one-time acting governor of Aden and former chief commissioner in the northern territories of the Gold Coast, laments a tendency of the English in tropical countries to try to make local peoples behave like Anglo-Saxons, an effort that was foredoomed in his opinion (letter to author, January 5, 1965). An officer in Uganda observed: "These people possess a genius of their own... we don't want to turn out third rate copies of ourselves . . ." (Acting Collector, Toro District, to Commissioner, Western Province, 28 July 1908, District Files); "I always thought our job in Tanganyika was to make the Territory fit for heroes to live in . . ." (F. Longland, formerly of the Tanganyika service, interview, February 2, 1965); "I was very parochial in my outlook . . . and . . . regarded 'federal' (i.e. a united Nigeria in which local custom would be submerged) as rather a dirty word." (C. Hanson-Smith, formerly of the Northern Nigerian service, letter to author, May 22, 1967).

Many officers opposed any scheme that might interfere with the established patterns of traditional life. The sensibilities of such men formed a natural counterpart to those of African leaders who were suspicious of European enterprise. On the British side these views were often the lineal descendents of the nineteenth century anti-slavery movement. The Aborigines Protection Society in England and, later, its equivalent in the Gold Coast kept constant pressure on the British government in support of causes that interested them. Attempts by the colonial government to regulate mining in the interests of African landowners and of sound economic practices were frustrated by Society lobbying, as was an early plan for the building of a harbor at Takoradi. A Tanganyika D.O. many years later successfully opposed a graduated tax designed to help the economy of the whole territory because, though development-minded in other respects, he did not feel that his constituency was ready for it.[3] Some officers were actuated by a deep-seated conviction that materialism was not the most valuable or attractive aspect of European civilization and that their duty was to spare Africans its dehumanizing effects.[4] A good many had gone to Africa precisely because they did not want commercial careers.

It would be wrong to suggest an invariable correlation between class-imbued bias against trade in England and administrative postures in the colonies. But often there did seem to be a connection. When disputes arose between D.O.s and business firms, it was only natural that officials would think of the rights of Africans in broad, social terms, whereas businessmen would concentrate more narrowly on sales and profits.[5]

Conditions, attitudes, and tendencies that conspired to edge the colonies forward economically presented a picture of similar complexity. Improvements in communications came early, despite the lack of money, since the very survival of new regimes and their military units depended on overseas links. Coastal, river, and lake navigation had gained steadily during the nineteenth century. With the arrival of permanent administrations, roads were pushed into the interior and railways followed.

---

[3] J. J. Tawney, memoir of service in Kasulu District, Tanganyika, 1940s, mimeo, p. 37 (privately provided).

[4] H. Hignell, an early Tanganyika District Officer, was notoriously of this view. (See his letter of October 4, 1934, File 41/2A, Dodoma, Central Province, National Archives, Tanzania).

[5] D. A. Pott, a Northern Nigerian D.O., complained in the 1930s that peasants were lured into United Africa Company canteens where they spent more money than they could afford, having little or nothing left over for buying seed or paying taxes (see his letter of May 9, 1939, written from his post at Rijau to the D.O. at Kontagora, Colonial Records Project, Oxford).

As always in human affairs, natural evolution and spontaneous responses to unforeseen opportunities played a major part in the whole development process. There were thousands of *ad hoc* plans and time tables, with widely varying results and nothing approaching a grand scheme, conceived at an early date and applied systematically in all the colonies. At first, financial weakness and a determination not to burden Africans with heavy taxes resulted in a stand-off in which neither system, African or European, could prevail. The earliest stage was one of establishing an order that was bound to be unfamiliar to the people and would be resisted by many. Formidable obstacles had to be dealt with before a basis could be built for anything like European-style prosperity. Formerly, government in parts of Africa had meant war camps run by warrior castes whose main function was raiding neighboring peoples for slaves or cattle. It took time to stop this.

Once pacification had been completed D.O.s worked on demographic assessment and on a rational system of taxation that would allow British-supervised local authorities to make regular expenditures in what was considered the public interest. Since the average African was a farmer, primary emphasis was placed on agrarian development at a pace determined by local capacities. At first D.O.s did the best they could on their own, handing out seed and performing rudimentary experiments. In central Tanganyika soon after the British conquest, an officer launched his own scheme for promoting cash crops, noting in his diary, ". . . if it comes off it will revolutionize the district. . . ."[6] Later on, administrators were joined by professional agricultural and forestry officers and in some cases by veterinarians. New projects begun by the specialists were then watched over by D.O.s when the former had moved on.

Coffee growing in northwest Tanganyika was started in this easy-going way during the late 1920s.[7] By the 1930s it was well enough established to raise local purchasing power and to provide work for men who had formerly migrated annually to Uganda.

In parts of Tanganyika, Kenya, and Southern Rhodesia, development was complicated by the presence of white settlers. Alienation of some of the most valuable tracts put additional pressure on land, especially in such areas as Kilimanjaro and Meru where heavy indigenous settlement was already creating problems.

[6] F. J. Bagshawe, diary, October 25, 1921, Colonial Records Project, Oxford.

[7] See "Memorandum on Native Coffee Development in Bugufi, Biharamulo District, Tanganyika, 1936," Colonial Records Project, Oxford, by J.F.R. Hill. I am grateful to Mr. Hill for his observations on this and other cases (interview, April 19, 1965).

District officers and European employers of African labor took very different views of things: the former trying to build up local institutions and emphasizing local rights; the latter struggling to support themselves on small profit margins in a fluid labor market. The D.O. wanted a strong African chief because this meant widespread improvement: more efficient tax collection, better local courts, sound budgets, progressive efforts in education, road building, public health, and special projects such as bush clearance and irrigation. But to the settler, a strong chief was a strong opponent. Progress was made in the face of the difficulties posed by settlers. It was fortunate from the standpoint of Africa's needs later on, however, that white settlement did not become an important phenomenon throughout British Africa.

Comparable in importance to agriculture was the raising of livestock. Vast stretches of upland were devoted to pastoral economies that extended thousands of miles from the great savanna of the western Sudan to the hills of Nyasaland and the Rhodesias. Cattle-owning peoples who kept their herds on the move, season by season, in search of pasture were suspicious of any government and were correspondingly harder for colonial officials to deal with than were villagers. Nevertheless, an attempt had to be made to bring them into some ordered relationship with the rest of society. Otherwise there was a tendency for them to prey on settled communities which they exploited for their own benefit rather than for mutual well-being. In northern Nigeria D.O.s concentrated on getting more accurate counts of herds for tax purposes and on keeping track of seasonal movements so as to reduce intertribal disorder and to control rindeperpest and other cattle blights.[8] The process was slow. But by the 1930s the advantages of government-provided disease prevention and treatment were coming to be appreciated by such pastoralists as the Fulani in West Africa and the Masai in Kenya and Tanganyika. Grazing routes were changed voluntarily to include veterinary clinics. Sometimes, to the chagrin of local authorities, whole herds would be moved permanently so as to be nearer to regular medical advice and help.

In general, the trends of these years favored pastoralists: better and more secure communications; a higher standard of living among farmers and villagers with whom they dealt; a steady improvement in the health of their cattle and in the condition of pasture lands caused by such measures as erosion control; and a slow but unmistakable rise in the quality of local government. The end result was more

[8] *Cf.* L. C. Giles, touring diaries, Zaria Province, Northern Nigeria, 1930s, loaned by the author, and C. Hanson-Smith, "Notes on the Sokoto Fulbe," typescript, 1955, loaned by the author.

prosperous herdsmen who were less introverted socially. In addition to working on improvements in the agrarian and pastoral economies, D.O.s undertook thousands of personal projects and special assignments that had cumulative effects. One was maintaining good relations between European enterprises and local communities. The United Africa Company (UAC), the largest in British West Africa, had been on the scene under various names since the middle of the nineteenth century. Its importance to Nigeria's economy was great, a fact that administrative officers could hardly ignore. Yet, as always with giants, there were abuses, especially in areas where UAC agents dealt with commercially inexperienced peoples. During the groundnut production campaign of World War II, the D.O. in Gwandu was continually uncovering malpractices such as the cheating of peasants by UAC clerks who did large scale buying for the Company in local markets.[9] The D.O. and the Emir's staff worked together to thwart this by seeing that peasants knew what the going rates were and that clerks paid them. The assistant district officer (A.D.O.) in Yauri did what he could to improve relations with the UAC's officers while helping local businesspeople at the same time. He and the Emir made river boats available for shipment of Company produce down the Niger, a mutually profitable arrangement that gave seasonal employment to local boatowners and kept down the UAC's transportation costs.

Starting cooperative societies was a small thing at first, but they were to grow into national institutions of wide-ranging importance to farming communities and their market towns. In northern Nigeria, British agricultural officers won the confidence of many farmers by selling them new implements at reasonable prices and loaning them cattle for plowing and fertilizing. Seed and salt were sold on account, with terms the peasants could afford, a reversal of the age-old state of affairs whereby tenants were exploited by landlords and kept permanently in debt. Regional plans grew from these promising beginnings and administrative officers spent weeks patiently explaining to farmers in village after village how the proposed loans would work. Some villagers thought the idea ". . . too good to be true," and the much discussed inhibitions of Islamic ideas proved to be less powerful than was supposed.[10] Even so conservative a chief as the old Emir of Zaria remarked to a British officer that just as his predecessors had given in to the Europeans on abolishing slavery, so now he and his local officials would cooperate on

---

[9] *Cf.* Letters written by the then D.O. to his family in England, November 13 and 18, 1943, kindly loaned to author by the writer, Sir Arthur Weatherhead.

[10] *Cf.* "The Hausa Village and Co-operation," L. C. Giles, typescript, 1937, loaned by the author, and interview with Mr. Giles, London, March 23, 1965.

economic reform whether or not particular moves seemed to be in accordance with tradition. The British, thought Emir Ja'afaru, tended to overestimate the practical force of religious and social prescriptions. When cooperative societies finally got going in the 1940s, they received great popular support and were found to be enormously helpful in promoting self-reliance.

Such was the down-to-earth work of British officers—numbering first starting with the Scramble of the 1890s and lasting until most the colonial period. Roughly, their labors fell into two stages: the first starting with the Scramble of the 1890s and lasting until most administrations had become firmly established shortly before World War I; and the second continuing up to independence and involving various kinds and degrees of development based on the new order. For the most part there were no large outlays from London until after World War II. British officers did provide the proximate discipline and the daily example of efficiency and planned action that were essential for primary development in each territory. Slowly the money economy took hold, in local treasuries, in small private businesses, and in the minds of the people. The consumer mentality spread as its tangible accoutrements increased: roads and bridges, cash crops, market industries, savings, investments, education. The adoption by Africans of these European things and thoughts was first hesitant, then enthusiastic. Africa became more Europeanized because the natural tendency of the British to recreate their own civilization resulted in new options, and because Africans sometimes preferred these to the old ways.

London's policies and actions show a fairly consistent pattern of limited commitment and deference. There is truth to the characterization that the British were reluctant imperialists. Places taken over in the Scramble were not passionately wanted; they never claimed Britain's attention as India did in its heyday; they were not economically profitable (Clarke, 1936). Furthermore, the notion that colonial administrators should guide indigenous peoples to a higher civilization was not accepted in the British territories in anything like the degree it was in those of France, Portugal, and Belgium. The old antislavery idea that Africans should control their own destiny never really died out. And in any case, most officials were not convinced that Englishness was exportable.

When nationalism developed, British officials had mixed feelings. Many thought Africa was not ready to go it alone and that the departure of European supervisors would signal a breakdown in standards of public service, a decline in honesty, efficiency, freedom, and wealth. Some have felt that events since independence confirm this view.[11] Others were more sanguine and small numbers stayed on

[11]J.F.R. Hill, letter to author, July 3, 1971.

to help bridge the divide between colonial and national government.[12] While conceding that Africa had a long way to go, such people welcomed Africanization in the last years of colonial rule and thought that things moved faster and more imaginatively with Africans in charge. "We made much more progress in the last few years under regional Nigerian ministers . . . than (we had) under a central European secretariat."[13]

These two attitudes are reminiscent of that earlier division between officers, especially administrators and educators, that hung on the question of whether or not outsiders had a right to determine the course of a people's future. Many were sure, all through colonial times, that they had no such right and that their duty was to protect the traditions that Africans already had and seemed to want preserved. Others, with equal sincerity, were persuaded that Africa's past was dead and gone and that no one wanted new ways more than the Africans themselves. Looking back on the era of Europe's intervention in Africa it would seem undeniable that alien ideas and techniques have triumphed over indigenous ones, especially in government and in the economic area. It is true that African regimes have been increasingly concerned in recent years to deemphasize outside influences by reverting to original place names and by encouraging literary and musical forms that owe their inspiration to precolonial cultures. But such efforts coexist with and do not diminish the unmistakable thrusts towards material well-being on Western models that continue to dominate virtually every African horizon. Psychological and social stresses and political and economic upheavals, similarly, have brought to mind the growing pains of European states in their own formative years and not the kinds of difficulties that African and other preindustrial societies went through before the nineteenth century.

There can be no doubt that Africa has embarked on moderniza-tion. The function of colonial governments during their brief hegemony in Africa was to act as stewards and guides, sometimes unknowing and usually spontaneous ones, in the beginning stages of that process.

---

[12] Two of the most prominent of these are D. A. Anderson and Sir Bruce Greatbatch. Anderson began as a member of the Gold Coast service in the 1940s, stayed on after Ghana's independence to specialize in Africanization of the civil service, and then did similar work in Tanzania and Kenya. Sir Bruce, an officer in northern Nigeria, became secretary to the premier of that region after independence, then moved on to Kenya to serve the new African government there.

[13] F. J. Lattin, formerly of the Nigeria and Uganda services, letter to author, July 17, 1960.

II

*PARAMETERS
OF CHANGE*

Change pervades Africa, as environment, economy, and society are responding to the pressures of population growth and to the exigencies of development and modernization. Some change is planned; some is inadvertent, reflecting the impact of commitments of people and resources to increased productivity and to new modes of livelihood. In the next eight chapters, important change-related parameters are discussed. These include population, human physical well-being, and environmental resources.

Human beings are the logical starting point for the analysis of changing man-environment systems. In Chapter 5, Thomas outlines some of the basic population characteristics of Africa, noting both the continent-wide commonalities and the important regional variations. Particular attention is drawn to the impacts of rapid growth rates, which make severe demands upon scarce resources in serving an increasingly young population.

Physical well-being is an important parameter of change, both in terms of population as a resource and for the general quality of living. In Chapter 6, Newman discusses some of the general features of food consumption and dietary quality. During drought or other catastrophes, starvation has been no stranger to Africa, but even

Rural clinics and mobile health services supplement the work of urban hospitals and research institutes in providing health care to Africa's people. This mobile tuberculosis facility in Ghana helps combat one of the continent's more persistent diseases. (Photograph provided by the Ghana Information Services Department)

An expanding population and increased rural modernization are written on Africa's landscape. Bananas, maize, taro, and livestock are raised on this Sebei farm on the slopes of Mt. Elgon in Uganda. Notice the newer style of roof material, purchased from the proceeds of coffee sales, the major Sebei cash crop. (Photograph from P. W. Porter)

Akosombo Dam on the Volta River in Ghana provides hydroelectric power for development of industry and consumer needs. With 40 percent of the world's hydroelectric potential at hand, Africa's planners place strong emphasis on tapping this natural resource. (Photograph from the Ghana Information Services) during less calamitous times, many African diets are deficient in critical nutrients, especially protein. Though some positive changes have taken place in recent years, unfortunately population growth and urbanization have not enhanced dietary quality. Absent in many areas is the kind of social and health "wholeness" that Wisner defines in Chapter 7. Diseases, both nutritional and pathogenic, must be seen in that ecological context, including the question of the degree of harmony or dissonance among people and with nature.

Climate most definitely is an environmental resource. Indirectly it influences the other environmental conditions that in turn affect nutrition and disease; directly it relates to the degree of physical comfort an individual experiences. Ojo, in Chapter 8, outlines some basic considerations of human physiological climates in Africa. He highlights the marked variation of these climates and demonstrates that popular images of Africa's climates largely are erroneous. Many mid-latitude summer climates resemble African conditions, the major difference being in duration rather than in inherent qualities.

From the standpoint of agricultural productivity, the important climatic elements are solar energy and water. In Chapter 9, Porter explains how these elements interact to limit agricultural production. Human societies must cope with such limitations, and Porter suggests some ways in which East Africans have chosen to structure their environments in order to do so.

Chapter 10 continues the theme of human interaction with the environment, this time focusing on the vegetation of Africa. From Adejuwon's analysis we see that it would be erroneous to attribute present vegetation patterns to climate alone. Extrapolating from detailed studies in Nigeria, the author is able to document the degree to which people have influenced the structure and evolution of Africa's vegetative communities.

Many savanna and grassland areas of Africa are marginal for human occupation except at very low density and with highly mobile technologies—hunting and gathering and pastoralism. Yet, these environments are among the world's most productive in animal protein. The wild herds could produce meat yields that humans seldom can approximate with domestic livestock grazing unimproved pastures, and, indeed, the multiple use of the savannas and grasslands for meat production and tourism may be both economically and ecologically more sound than allowing crop and animal husbandry to continue their expansion. These issues are examined by Knight in Chapter 11.

In the final chapter in this section, Beyer discusses the problems and prospects associated with mineral, energy, and water resources.

It is clear from her analysis that many vital mineral resources are in abundance, but that most of these have been exploited for export rather than for national or regional consumption. This is an imbalance that will have to be corrected if Africa is to derive the maximum benefit from its minerals. On a continent-wide basis, water for domestic and industrial use also is plentiful, though there are numerous problems with reference to location, timing, and quality that must be resolved. Lastly, though coal is in short supply, other energy sources are promising—petroleum and natural gas, nuclear fuels, hydroelectric power, and solar radiation. Overall, then, Africa does seem to have its share of mineral, water, and energy resources, but, like the rest of the world, it faces crucial management decisions in attempting to allocate these resources for the collective good.

5

Population Patterns, Projections, and Policies

IAN D. THOMAS

As a result of the slave trade, for several hundred years prior to the twentieth century the total population of Africa seems to have remained constant (Table 5.1). During the present century, however, the increase in population has been great, so that Africa now shares with Latin America the highest rate of population growth of the world's continents. Moreover, it appears that this increase will continue into the future for at least one generation and probably for much longer. One estimate, for instance, places the population in the year 2000 at 768 million, or about twice the 1975 size. In addition, Africa has the world's highest rate of urban growth, though the proportion of the population urbanized remains small.

It must be stressed at the outset that historical data on Africa's population are meager, and even the figures cited for recent years are likely to contain a large error because of the many problems encountered in census enumeration. Some of the more significant of these problems include poor communications, lack of trained personnel, limited finances, suspicion of enumerators and regional political rivalries. Indeed, several African states have not even yet attempted to take a complete census, most notably Ethiopia and Somalia. Nonetheless, sufficient information does exist to demon-

54

TABLE 5.1   Estimates of the Population of Africa
and of the World 1650-2000

Year	Population (mil) World	Africa	Africa as % of World Total
1650	470	100	21.7
1750	791	106	13.4
1800	978	107	10.9
1850	1,262	111	8.7
1900	1,650	133	8.1
1920	1,860	143	7.7
1940	2,295	191	8.3
1960	2,982	270	9.1
1970	3,632	344	8.5
2000	6,130	768	12.5

Sources: Wilcox, 1940; Durand, 1967; United Nations, 1968, 1970.

strate that Africa has complex population patterns no matter what the characteristic (absolute numbers, sex, age, fertility, mortality, mobility) or the scale (continental, regional, national, local).

POPULATION PATTERNS

Considering its land area, the total population of Africa south of the Sahara, the unit of analysis for the remainder of this chapter, is relatively small and overall is sparsely distributed (Figures 5.1 and 5.2). Nevertheless, there are some marked regional variations. In West Africa two discontinuous belts of population concentration are discernible. First, along the coast are population clusters from Senegal south to Liberia, and from Abidjan, Ivory Coast, east to Cameroun and beyond to the Congo estuary. Second, there is the inland belt of the "Sudanic zone" from Lake Chad through northern Nigeria to the Upper Volta basin, to the inland delta of the Niger and thence to southern Mali. In East Africa coastal and inland clusters are again distinct. In Ethiopia there is concentration on the Abyssynian Plateau, and southward there are major clusters around Lake Victoria and Lake Nyasa and in the upland regions of Kenya, western Uganda, Rwanda, Burundi, and northern Tanzania. The coastal populations of East Africa are not so dense nor extensive as those of West Africa, but a belt of higher density from Mombasa south to the mouth of the Zambezi and including Zanzibar and Pemba is discernible.

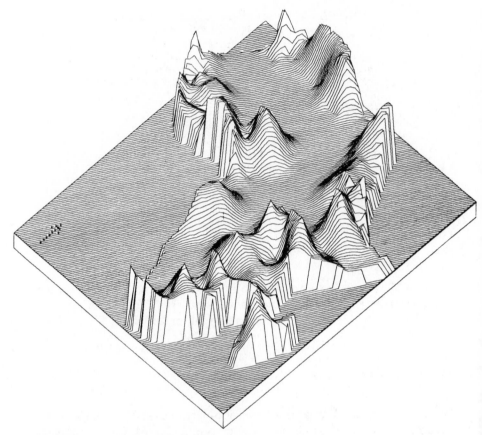

Figure 5.1 Population of Africa. A computer-drawn map of Africa's population density provided by Katharine L. Fuess.

Southern Africa similarly demonstrates the attraction of coastal
locations with population concentrations from southern Mozambique to Cape Town, and of favored high plateau and mountain
areas. Dumanowski (1968) has argued that the distribution of the
population of Africa is clearly related to the occurrence of
transitional conditions in the physical environment, especially
coincident boundary zones of climate, surface waters, and relief.
Variations between these settled areas in the level of population
density and internal density differentiation are believed to result
primarily from such extra-environmental factors as history, culture,
and economy.

Allan (1965) has suggested that each traditional economy,

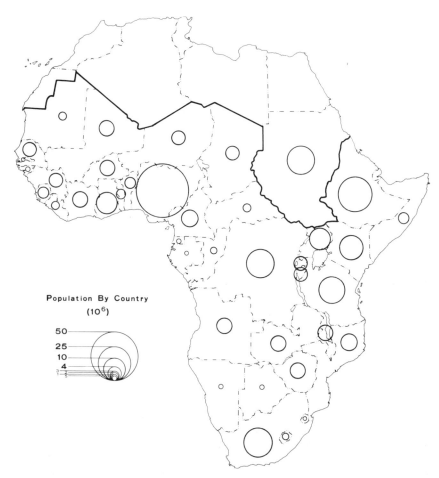

Figure 5.2 Population Number, 1970.
Source: U.N., 1971a.

comprising methods of food production characteristic of climatic-vegetation zones, has its own critical population density which in the long run can only be exceeded at the expense of environmental deterioration. Collecting and hunting societies require 25 square kilometers per head; traditional pastoralism supports no more than 3 persons per square kilometer; and the critical density for subsistence small grain cultivators in the savanna lands is less than 8 persons per square kilometer. In more favored areas where systems of permanent cultivation prevail, critical densities may range from 25 up to 160 per square kilometer. Population growth without agricultural intensification will lead to soil depletion, although cash cropping may raise supportable densities, if it provides income for purchase of more foods than could previously have been raised.

There are two major areas of very low density at the continental scale: the Sahara in the north and the Namib in the southwest. Smaller low-density areas, nonetheless significant within national territory, occur throughout a belt extending from the southwest Sudan through the Central African Republic, northern Congo, Gabon, and South Cameroun. Much of eastern Africa (covering East and South Ethiopia, Somalia, northern Kenya, the plateaus of Tanzania, southern Zaire, and much of Mozambique and Zambia) also is sparsely peopled. Fitzgerald (1955) regarded climatic aridity as the principal barrier to an extension of the settled area, but attention also has been called to the role of the rain forest and of sleeping sickness in fostering low numbers of people in an area (Gourou, 1961). It is clear, however, that within nations, historic, cultural, and economic experiences have contributed almost as much to the occurrence and location of sparsely populated tracts as to densely populated ones. Controversy still active on the origin of the sparsely populated "middle belt" of Nigeria is illustrative of the continuing need for careful investigation of the factors associated with varying population densities (Mason, 1969).

Particularly marked variations in the degree of clustering and in the pattern of density are related to the occurrence, frequency, and distribution of towns. An estimated 1.5 million lived in cities of 100,000 or more in 1900; by 1960, 20 million lived in cities throughout Africa, and by 1970, the figure had jumped to around 40 million. Not all the countries of Africa have shared equally in this process. South Africa is the most urbanized, with over 40 percent of its population in towns of more than 40,000, with Senegal having about 30 percent, Ghana 25 percent, and Nigeria 20 percent. At the lower end of this scale are countries such as Mauritania, Ethiopia, Malawi, Tanzania, and Cameroun with less than 10 percent of their population in urban centers. Overall, Africa still remains the least urbanized of the continents.

People are not the same size, sex, or age. Distribution maps seldom portray these variations, but as detailed census and survey findings become available, it is possible to depict, describe, and analyze the patterns of population characteristics. Of particular interest and importance for understanding the dynamics of the population are the variations by sex and age and differences in the level of mortality and fertility.

Data on the Afro-American population of North America and fragmentary evidence from African countries suggest that the ratio of males to females (sex ratio) at birth is rather smaller, 103 to 100, than is the case in non-African populations of the world, 106 to 100. Within Africa, variations from one country to another in the sex ratio are likely to be the result of three factors:

1. differential mortality of males and females—probably higher male deaths at young ages but higher female deaths during the childbearing years;
2. sex differentiated interterritorial migration;
3. differentials in the completeness of census recording—with a possible underreporting of male infants and males of the young adult years (Van de Walle, 1968: 43, 46).

Five countries of Africa south of the Sahara have very low sex ratios (Figure 5.3)—Congo, Lesotho, Gabon, Ruanda, and Malawi— largely a result of high rates of labor migration to other states. Eight other countries have low sex ratios—Guinea, Togo, Mozambique, Swaziland, Zaire, Central African Republic, Cameroun, and Chad. The plateau lands of eastern and southern Africa have moderate sex ratios, as do the Sudanic states of West Africa. Areas where the recorded number of males exceeds that of females occur widely throughout West Africa, as well as in Angola, Namibia, South Africa, Rhodesia, Uganda, and the Sudan. While some of these cases are attributable to immigration—Gambia, Ghana, Rhodesia, and South Africa—others are not so readily explained. For instance, Upper Volta is an area of out-migration. Much work remains on the collection, analysis, and interpretation of data on sex balance and the causes of geographic and age-specific differences.

The general characteristics of the age structure of an African population are demonstrated by the age-sex pyramid of Tanzania (Figure 5.4). These characteristics may be contrasted with those for the United States. The outstanding features are:

1. a very high proportion of children;
2. a small proportion of people aged 15-45 years in comparison with the numbers aged 0-15 years;
3. a small proportion aged 45 and over;
4. slightly more males than females in the higher age groups.

Thus, the ratio of consumers to producers is high; there are many mouths to be fed, and the need for educational and medical facilities is great. One further feature requires comment. Irregularities in the

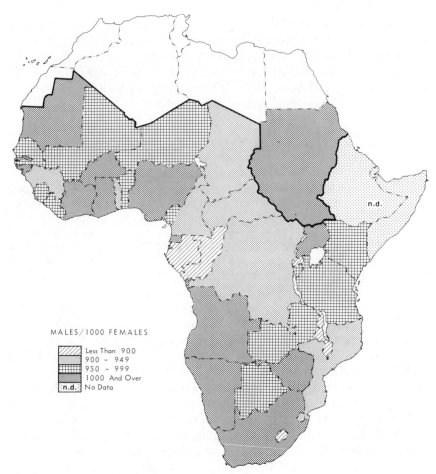

MALES/1000 FEMALES

Less Than 900
900 - 949
950 - 999
1000 And Over
n.d. No Data

Figure 5.3   Sex Ratio.
Source: U.N., 1971a.

shape of the pyramid are likely to reflect inaccuracy in reporting. Ignorance of exact chronological age is widespread and constitutes one of the major hindrances to demographic analysis of the population of Africa.

The shape of Tanzania's population pyramid is characteristic of most African countries. Nevertheless, within Africa, national and regional variations do exist. Though the proportion aged less than 15 years is high throughout Africa (Figure 5.5), it is particularly so where infant and early childhood deaths have been diminished and where fertility remains at a high level (as in Rhodesia, Kenya, and

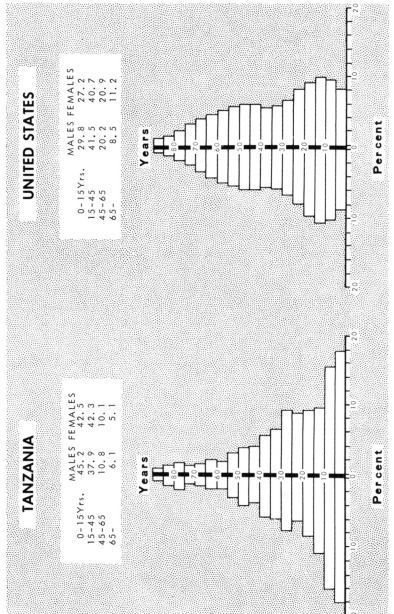

Figure 5.4 Age-Sex Pyramids for Tanzania and the United States.

Mali). The proportion is less where fertility is lower (as in middle Africa) and especially if this coincides with high childhood mortality (as on the West African coast).

Data on fertility and mortality are fragmentary and all national estimates are subject to wide margins of error. Recent work has begun to provide comparable estimates of fertility for subnational areas (Page and Coale, 1972:57-61), data which have been generalized to produce a continental isopleth map (Figure 5.6). The general level of total fertility—which may be interpreted as the average number of children borne by women who have completed their

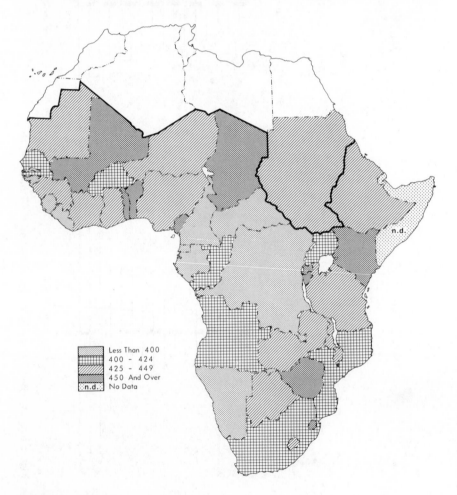

Figure 5.5 Proportion Aged 0-15 years.
Source: U.N., 1971a.

childbearing years—is six to seven children. Regional differences reflect cultural and environmental factors, the elucidation of which remains one of the major challenges to research in demography, medicine, and geography.

Many factors affect fertility level. It is useful to distinguish direct factors such as age at marriage, proportion who ever marry, and extent of birth control practices, from those social and economic factors which operate less directly, for example the level of education of women and the occupation of husbands (Davis and Blake, 1956). Bourgeois-Pichat (1965) has examined direct factors in

Figure 5.6 Total Number of Children Born.
Source: Compiled by author from data in Page and Coale, 1972.

Africa and identified broad regional differences in the proportions married by successive ages. In Black Africa, the percentage married at young ages is very high by comparison with North Africa. There are also regional differences in the incidence of sterility after successive births. A combination of high marital age-specific fertility and patterns of sterility and marriage are sufficient to account for the major regional differences in crude birth rates—North Africa, 50 per 1000; West Africa, 50 per 1000; and Africa south of the Equator, 40 per 1000. Studies of the relation between birth control programs and the level of birth rates, of the causes of sterility, and of factors affecting marriage patterns are limited in both number and geographical coverage.

The study of patterns of mortality is seriously hampered by the inadequate available data. Much of southern and eastern Africa has life expectancy values over 40 years and the states of southwest and middle Africa have values less than 40 years (Figure 5.7). In West Africa the pattern is more fragmented. It is certain that mortality varies greatly within national areas with the level being affected by a very wide range of factors, among which the lack of medical facilities, the prevalence of epidemic and endemic diseases, and the incidence of droughts and famines are important. The generally low life expectancy at birth is largely the result of the high rate of infant and early-childhood mortality. The median value of infant mortality (before reaching one year of age) of the 27 states for which the United Nations gives an estimate is 156 deaths per 1000 live births. Errors of reporting are likely to make this an underestimate. Reported crude death rates range from as low as 16.6 per 1000 (South Africa) to 30.2 per 1000 (Angola), with the largest number of countries in the range 20 to 25 per 1000.

A tentative characterization of the regional demographic situation is:

Eastern and Southern Africa—moderately high to high fertility, and moderate to low mortality;
Middle Africa—low fertility and high mortality;
Western Africa—high fertility (lower on the coast), variable mortality.

It is important to stress that the comparative terms "low," "moderate," and "high" apply to the range within Africa. On a global basis Africa has high mortality and very high fertility.

POPULATION PROJECTIONS

As already indicated, Africa south of the Sahara has high rates of

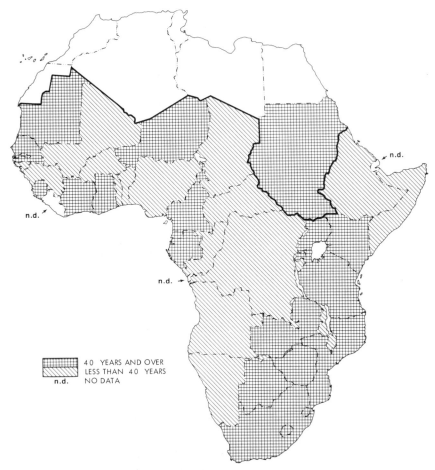

Figure 5.7 Life Expectancy at Birth.
Source: U.N., 1971a.

population growth: out of thirty-nine states only ten have an annual rate of increase less than 2.0 percent, whereas fourteen have rates of increase above 2.5 percent. The most rapidly growing areas are in the east from Botswana to Uganda and Kenya and in the states of eastern West Africa—Togo, Dahomey, Nigeria, Niger (Figure 5.8). Areas of relatively slow growth are more dispersed. The present age structure and prevailing levels of fertility ensure that population growth will remain high for the remainder of this century, unless there is widespread, catastrophic disaster.

Van de Walle (1967) has prepared projections based on trends in the level of vital rates for the major regions of tropical Africa. In

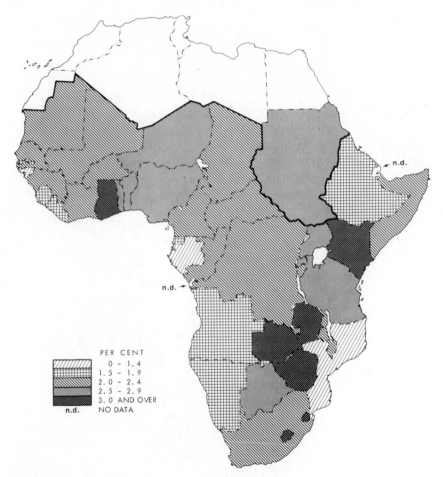

Figure 5.8 Annual Rate of Population Increase.
Source: U.N., 1971a.

establishing a base population for the projection, he assumed that all estimates published were underestimates. Those derived from administrative sources alone were inflated by 10 percent; those from full censuses were inflated by 5 percent. In each region all the available information was used to estimate levels of fertility and mortality (Table 5.2). It was assumed that in western and eastern Africa there would be no change in the level of fertility between 1960 and 1980, and that in middle Africa there would be a linear increase in the gross reproduction rate from 2.6 to 3.0.[1] Mortality rates were projected to

---

[1] The gross reproduction rate is a measure of population replacement. It may be interpreted as the number of daughters replacing each mother.

TABLE 5.2 Regions of Tropical Africa: Estimates of Total Population, Fertility, and Mortality for 1960[a]

Region of Tropical Africa	Total Population 1960 (mil)	Gross Reproduction Rate	Expectation of Life at Birth (yrs.)
Western	75	3.1	32.0
Middle	29	2.6	38.4
Eastern	48	3.1	38.7

Source: Van de Walle, 1967.
[a]Regions are defined by the following boundaries:
Western: Mauritania, Mali, Niger, Nigeria;
Middle: Chad, C.A.R., Zaire, Angola;
Eastern: Kenya, Uganda, Rwanda, Burundi, Tanzania, Zambia, Rhodesia, Mozambique, and Malagasy.

continue to decline, such that life expectancy at birth would increase annually by a half year (Table 5.3). Overall, the three regions combined have a projected population increase in the twenty year period of 56.6 percent. Eastern Africa has the greatest increase; middle Africa the least. The increment in western Africa amounts to 41.1 million people, eastern Africa excluding Ethiopia and Somalia 33.1 million, and middle Africa 11.6 million.

The average population density increases appear moderate—an increment of five persons per square kilometer in twenty years for the continent as a whole. Because this increase is through natural growth *in situ*, and because population distribution is very uneven, with high concentrations in a few areas, the actual pressure of people on resources can easily be underestimated by overall densities. Again, extra numbers even in areas of low density can create serious

TABLE 5.3 Regions of Tropical Africa: Estimates of Total Population and Population Increase 1960-1980

Region of Tropical Africa	Total Population (mil) 1960	1980	Population Increase 1960-1980 Percent	Density psk.
Western	75.0	116.1	54.8	6.7
Middle	29.0	40.6	40.0	1.8
Eastern	48.0	81.1	69.0	7.4
TOTAL	152.0	237.8	56.6	5.0

Source: Van de Walle, 1967.

ecological problems unless adjustments in land use systems are rapidly introduced and accepted.

The high rates of increase make difficult the maintenance of education, health, and service provisions because considerable increases in the number of schools, teachers, hospitals and doctors, wells, water pipelines, etc. are necessary to keep a constant ratio of facilities to people. If, simultaneously, a country is attempting to provide more widespread services (for example, universal primary education, and pre- and post-natal clinical care for all mothers), then the high rate of population increase imposes a severe burden indeed.

Difficulties in providing social services are exacerbated by the changing age composition of the population as long as fertility remains at a high level (Table 5.4). The proportion in the labor force ages will *diminish* between 1960 and 1980. Correspondingly, the proportion in the younger age groups will increase. Not only is the total population growing but there is a shift in the relative proportions at each age so that productive age groups comprise a smaller proportion and the younger age groups a larger proportion at the very time when these countries are trying to divert greater social capital towards provision for the young.

POPULATION POLICY

National governments are increasingly taking account of projected population figures as awareness develops of the important implica-

TABLE 5.4 Regions of Tropical Africa: Age Structure for Major Age Groups, 1960 and 1980

Regions of Tropical Africa	0-4 Years No. (mil)	%	5-14 Years No. (mil)	%	15-64 Years No. (mil)	%	Over 64 Years No. (mil)	%
Western								
1960	20.8	17.1	18.2	24.3	41.9	55.8	2.1	2.8
1980	20.8	17.9	30.1	25.9	61.6	53.1	3.6	3.1
Ratio								
1980:1960		1.047		1.066		0.952		1.107
Middle								
1960	4.5	15.5	6.8	23.4	16.7	57.4	1.1	3.7
1980	6.5	15.9	9.7	23.8	22.9	56.5	1.6	3.8
Ratio								
1980:1960		1.026		1.017		0.984		1.027
Eastern								
1960	8.6	17.9	12.3	25.6	25.8	53.8	1.3	2.7
1980	15.1	18.6	21.7	26.8	42.0	51.8	2.3	2.8
Ratio								
1980:1960		1.039		1.047		0.963		1.037

Source: Van de Walle, 1967

tions of current demographic rates for even short-term development. The need for improved estimates of contemporary levels of fertility and mortality—and thus, of natural increase—and of the size of the national population at a base date is emphasized by the number of occasions on which countries have discovered that their current population estimate in a census year falls short of the enumerated total. Nigeria provides a prime example [estimated mid-year 1962: 36.5 million; 1963 census: 55.7 million, although 45 million is thought to be a more valid figure (Okonjo, 1968:83-4, 90)]. Others, such as Tanzania, Kenya, and Uganda have experienced similar surprises, though of a lesser magnitude (mainland Tanzania 1967, estimate—10.6 million, census—11.9 million; Kenya 1962, estimate— 7.5 million, census—8.6 million; Uganda 1969, estimate—8.3 million, census—9.6 million).

All of the countries of Africa have laws which indirectly affect family size, population growth, population distribution, and population movement. In addition, the plans of many governments for economic and social development have sections that relate to these aspects of population. Yet an explicit population policy is the exception rather than the rule. By 1973, ten nations in Africa south of the Sahara had an official family-planning policy (Ghana, Dahomey, Nigeria, Sudan, Uganda, Kenya, Rhodesia, Botswana, South Africa, Tanzania), but only three (Botswana, Ghana, Kenya) had an official policy to reduce population growth (Nortman, 1973).

The laws that constitute a population policy are as varied as those affecting the import and sale of contraceptives, the system of maternity leave, income tax and family allowances, the appropriation of rural land, and the zoning of residential areas in towns. Caldwell (1968) demonstrated that in 1965, francophone areas had more restrictive legislation than anglophone areas in terms of the importation and supply of birth-control equipment and the availability of abortion. Certain African governments were opposed to family planning since they wished to have larger national populations— Tanzania, Zambia, and Sierra Leone. Since Caldwell wrote, there has been a reaction in these African countries against institutions and foreign governments allegedly attempting to curb population growth, but also an increasing acceptance of family planning for maternal and child health reasons.

Another important area of population policy is migration. International migration is subject to regulation, and the laws relating to immigrants have tended to become more restrictive in recent years as countries have tried to replace foreigners by nationals in industrial, service, and administrative occupations, and have attempted to alleviate unemployment. Internal migration is more usually the object of social and economic restraints than of legislative action. Attempts to relocate populations within the rural area, or to redirect the flow of rural-to-urban migrants back to the land are common throughout Africa. Resettlement schemes of one sort or another have been developed in Zaire, Senegal, Upper Volta, Niger and Ghana on the western side of the continent, and in Kenya, Uganda, Tanzania, and Zambia on the eastern side (see Chapters 17 and 18). The reserved-land policies of Rhodesia and South Africa represent a more rigid form of internal control. Most countries are now more aware of the need to take direct account of population factors in their planning, but much research remains to be done before the relationship between birth rates, migration, and particular forms of government policy and control are fully understood. But this knowledge is basic to formulation of the demographic components of national plans for social and economic development.

6

Dietary and
Nutritional Conditions

JAMES L. NEWMAN

For individuals to function properly, diets that regularly supply adequate amounts of calories and nutrients are required. During the years of childhood, it is especially important that the needs of both physical and mental growth be met, otherwise serious, irreparable damage may result; a poor childhood diet can leave its mark throughout the lifetime of a person. In the adult years, a variety of nutritious foods must be consumed to help maintain health and to keep the body performing at a high level of strength and energy. People who regularly subsist on an inadequate diet not only risk nutritional deficiency diseases, but they are more susceptible to various parasites and infections. The reverse process also occurs and together the two illustrate what in biomedical parlance is known as a synergism, or "an interaction that is more serious for the host than would be expected from the combined effect of the two working independently" (Scrimshaw, Taylor, and Gordon, 1968:16).

Because of such widespread ramifications, diet is intimately linked to the issue of social and economic development. Only a well-fed population can be expected to carry out the many essential and difficult associated tasks. In the words of President Nyerere of Tanzania:

72   PARAMETERS OF CHANGE

We have said on many occasions that the three enemies are poverty, ignorance, and disease. By learning about better diet and by using this knowledge, we shall be reducing our ignorance, overcoming many of our diseases, and getting ourselves in a much better position to overcome our poverty. We shall be building up the nation's most important asset—that is, ourselves as human beings (Latham, 1965:3).

In Africa, as throughout most of the rest of the world, grains are the primary staple food (Figure 6.1a). Wheat, barley, and rice prevail in North Africa, whereas south of the Sahara, maize, sorghum, millet, and occasionally rice are predominant. Throughout the tropical forest areas, root and tree crops, especially the yam, taro, and the plantain, replace the grains, with the highly adaptable cassava

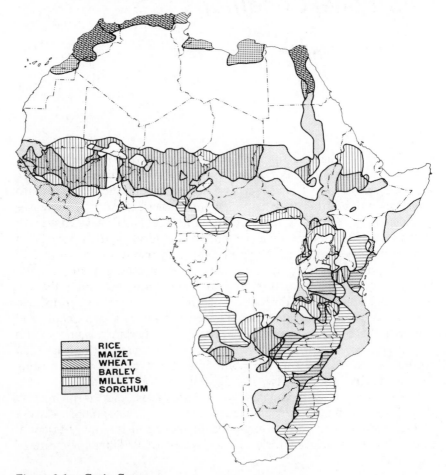

Figure 6.1a Grain Crops.
Source: Adapted from Murdock, 1960, with permission of the *Geographical Review*

being found increasingly as a staple or co-staple crop just about everywhere (Figure 6.1b).

Whether made from a grain, tuber, or fruit, the dominant African food is a stiff porridge-like substance that is widely termed *ugali* in the eastern portion of the continent and *fufu* in the western. It is made by processing the crop into a coarse flour, which later is sifted and boiled until the desired consistency is reached. Invariably the porridge is served with one or more relishes (side dishes), most commonly the green leaves from sweet potatoes, cassava, and a variety of wild plants, groundnuts, Bambara nuts, several types of peas and beans, peppers, onions, tomatoes, and less often meat or milk. These relishes either are boiled, fried, or roasted, depending on

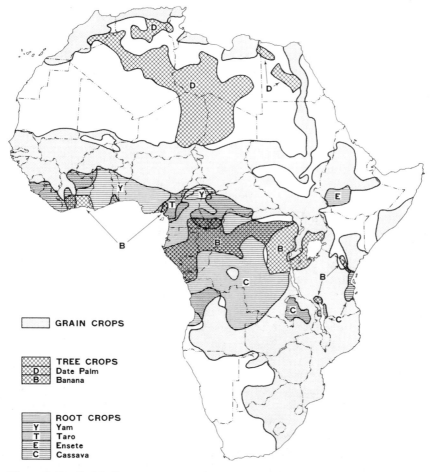

GRAIN CROPS

TREE CROPS
D Date Palm
B Banana

ROOT CROPS
Y Yam
T Taro
E Ensete
C Cassava

Figure 6.1b Stable Subsistence Crops.
Source: Adapted from Murdock, 1960, with permission of the *Geographical Review*

local preferences. Milk frequently is drunk soured rather than fresh. Several other important foods are worth noting. One is *couscous*, a fine grained flour that is made into a paste and then steamed in a double boiler. It is an Arab food and occurs wherever Arabs or their legacy are located. Another is a pancake fried in oil. It is termed *injera* in Ethiopia where it constitutes the national dish, but it is widespread all across the northern portion of the continent. Unleavened bread is a staple in parts of North Africa, and in the Sahara dried dates and figs often are the mainstay of the diet.

Meat is uncommon at most African meals. Once per week would be a high frequency of occurrence, and, indeed, for many individuals it virtually is never available except perhaps at major feasts and celebrations. Fish consumption, though increasing, is still restricted to peoples along the seacoasts, lake shores, rivers, and in the urban centers. Fish traditionally have been subject to a variety of restrictive taboos, as have eggs, which are just now beginning to enter African diets to any appreciable extent. Milk consumption is quite variable. It is common in the northern, eastern, and southern portions of the continent. Among some pastoral groups milk assumes the role of a staple, appearing as the only food at many meals. In the forest areas of western and central Africa, however, sleeping sickness and other diseases severely restrict the keeping of livestock, and thus little or no milk is available. Interestingly enough, in these same two areas the populations exhibit high rates of lactase deficiency. The enzyme lactase breaks down the lactose in milk so that it can be absorbed. Without it, milk simply passes through the digestive system, producing stomach aches and diarrhea in its wake. Milk is not always the good and natural food that it is advertised to be.

As a rule, two meals are eaten per day, one either in the morning or at noon, the other during the evening. Snacking between meals is common, especially for children who regularly will pick up wild fruits and nuts. The men of a household usually eat apart and are given the largest portions of the most nutritious foods. When served, little meat or fish is left for the women and children after the men have had their fill.

Special mention must be made of beer drinking. A low alcohol content beverage fermented from one of the grains or from plantains is drunk by just about everyone in Africa outside of the predominantly Islamic areas. It is served at most social occasions and contains important calories and large quantities of vitamin C plus small amounts of protein, calcium, iron, phosphorus, niacin, B_1, B_2, and B_{12}. Subsistence farmers normally plant more than enough crops to meet their minimum food needs even in relatively bad years, and it is this "normal surplus" that is used for brewing and sometimes in commerce (Allan, 1965). Palm wine is popular wherever palm trees can be grown, and distilled beverages and bottled beer are being consumed in ever-increasing quantities.

The result of these food consumption practices is a carbohydrate dominant diet. For example, in the Gambia, out of a total daily per capita food intake of 769 grams, 562 grams (73 percent) come from carbohydrate sources (May, 1970). In Sierra Leone, it was found that 74.4 percent of daily caloric consumption came from carbohydrates, with only 17.4 percent from fats and 8.2 percent from protein sources. A survey of the Kwanga area of Zaire showed 89 percent of the calories being derived solely from cassava (May, 1965).

Because of a high carbohydrate intake, caloric consumption in Africa is typically adequate, except for occasions when natural and man-made disasters intrude. Although estimates of caloric need are somewhat varied, mainly because of uncertainties surrounding the impacts of age, sex, physiology, activity level, and climate, a total of 2,000 calories per day per capita probably is reasonably close to a minimum level for proper bodily maintenance. At a national level of aggregation (Figure 6.2), only Algeria, Angola, Mauritania, Ruanda, and Somalia fall below this figure.

National averages, however, almost always obscure considerable internal variations. For instance, it was found that daily caloric intake in various locales in Kenya ranges from as low as 1,487 to as high as 2,498 (May, 1970). In Togo, a range of 1,601 calories to 2,183 calories was recorded (May, 1968). A study of the Serenje District of Zambia showed that in two of three villages the men had more than an adequate intake of calories and that in the third village they were only about ten percent short of requirements. But for the women and children the picture was entirely different. Women averaged only 65 percent of the requirement and the children a mere 45 percent (May, 1970).

There are significant seasonal variations in food availability with which to contend. Particularly in the savanna areas of West Africa, a phenomenon known as the "hungry season" occurs each year. This is a time just before the early maturing crops are ready for harvesting, when the grain bins are at their low ebb, when foods must be rationed carefully in order to insure a minimum quantity for survival. In consequence, caloric intake drops sharply. Studies in the Central African Republic, Chad, and the Congo reveal per capita caloric consumption per day can dip to 1,400 on a widespread basis, with totals as low as 850 being fairly common (May, 1965). As Hunter

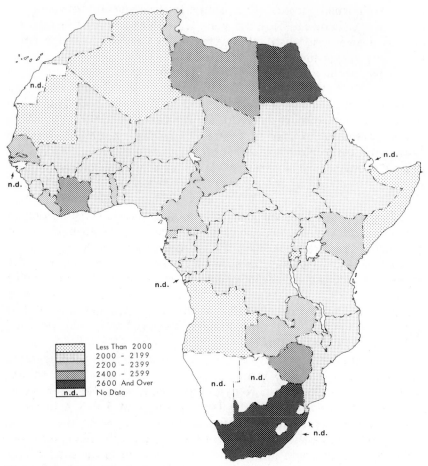

Figure 6.2 Daily Caloric Consumption.
Source: FAO, 1970.

(1967a) has shown, this decrease manifests itself in significant losses in body weight. If the population is underweight to begin with, then the "hungry season" has severe long-run implications for the health of the community. In most cases, however, the deprivation is short-lived as the harvest once again brings adequate quantities of food to most households.

Occasionally food shortages persist and lead to famine. Though the historical record of famine in Africa is highly incomplete, it is known that famine is no stranger, particularly to the semiarid portions of the continent where droughts, locusts, and floods have paid regular visits. Indeed, the world has just witnessed such an event in the Sahel region of western Africa, that border zone between desert to the north and savanna to the south. For six years, from

1968 to 1973, the rains failed, and, coupled with a host of economic, social, and political problems, produced a tragedy of the most profound kind (Newman, 1975). The human death toll reached at least 100,000. Millions of head of livestock perished, ecosystems were profoundly and perhaps irrevocably altered, and whole societies essentially were destroyed. Another recent famine took place in eastern Nigeria during the Biafran secession, indicating that political disasters can be as deadly as national disasters.

More persistent than calorie shortfalls are various nutrient deficiencies, many of which can have serious health impacts. Here attention will be focussed on those dietary-deficiency diseases that are particularly widespread and chronic: vision impairment, anemias, and kwashiorkor.

There are various forms of vitamin A deficiency that can lead to vision impairment. The mildest is *night blindness*, with more critical shortages leading to keratomalacia (softening, ulceration, and eventual extrusion of the cornea) which can produce total blindness. Vitamin A deficiencies are most common among children in the rapidly growing slum areas of the major African cities, where the richest sources of vitamin A—milk, cheese, butter and eggs—are too expensive for many families to afford.

The majority of anemias are produced by iron deficiencies. They are most severe among pregnant and lactating women, who require especially large quantities of iron, and among very young children, who may inherit anemia from the mother or contract it because of an iron-poor diet. Mothers' milk is a poor source of iron and thus it must be supplemented after about six months of age with other foods if anemia is to be avoided (Robson, 1972). In most instances, anemias are not caused strictly by a lack of sufficient iron in the diet, but rather by the synergistic interaction of diet with parasitic diseases, notably hookworm, bilharzia, and malaria. Unless taken in super-abundant quantities, supplies of iron are consumed quickly by parasites, with little left for bodily sustenance.

Kwashiorkor, or protein malnutrition, is present to some extent in every country on the continent and is, without doubt, Africa's most serious nutritional disorder. It normally affects children between the ages of six months and three to four years, the time of onset usually corresponding to when the child is weaned from the breast onto the normal carbohydrate dominant diet. After four years of age, the requirements of protein relative to body size fall off appreciably and consequently the probability of contracting protein malnutrition declines markedly.

Kwashiorkor is hard to diagnose in its early stages. Caloric intake usually is sufficient, so the afflicted child appears deceptively fat. It is not until the disease is well developed that the primary symptoms of growth failure, edema, reddish-brown hair that is easily plucked from the scalp, pallor, and digestive problems appear. If untreated, kwashiorkor often leads to death, although the final cause of death is more likely to be parasitic diseases or infections such as measles, whooping cough, and dysentery. And, unfortunately, kwashiorkor is difficult to treat because of the child's lassitude and disinterest. As one authority has observed:

> The misery of the child suffering from kwashiorkor may be one of the most distressing aspects of the disease. Frequently the child curls up in a corner and shuns all forms of attention and appears to want nothing but to be left alone to die (Robson, 1972:59).

For those who do survive a serious attack of kwashiorkor, the effects are usually carried for a lifetime. Stunted physical growth long has been recognized as an outcome, and increasingly, evidence is accumulating to suggest that mental harm is done as well, harm that later affects learning and behavior (Scrimshaw, 1967).

Kwashiorkor is a classic example of the ecology of nutritional disorders. Numerous aspects of a people's environment and culture come into play. These include the physical environment conditions that affect protein production and the social-cultural factors that specify eating habits; the economic conditions that allow for purchasing foods and the population dynamics that relate to pressure on resources; the prevailing knowledge of alternative foods and their respective protein values and the governmental policies that affect food production and consumption. Consequently, attempts to alleviate kwashiorkor must be comprehensive. It was a failure to recognize just this that has led to much of the disillusionment now surrounding the prospects of the Green Revolution for resolving mankind's food problems (Brown, 1970). It is quite apparent that there is considerably more to improving diet and nutrition than supplying high-yield, nutrient-fortified crops.

CHANGING FOOD PATTERNS

Diets, like much else in contemporary Africa, are presently in a state of considerable flux. For analytical purposes, these dietary changes can be broken down into those that seem to be nutritionally positive and those that seem to be nutritionally negative.

Most positive changes in diet center around an increasing awareness of food quality, brought about largely through government-sponsored nutritional education programs. Dietary improvement is encouraged on radio and television, child and maternal-care clinics are becoming more numerous, and mobile health units, often including educational films, are used in many countries to reach remote rural populations. As a result, many traditional taboos and avoidances are being overcome, particularly those centering on protein-rich fish and eggs. Additionally, mothers are being made more aware of the nutritional demands of children after weaning, and three meals per day are becoming fairly common.

Also important are improvements in transportation and marketing systems that allow for more efficient flows of such foods as meats, dairy products, fruits, and vegetables. Regions subject to periodic crop failure now can be reached with relief much more quickly.

One of the most serious negative changes is the rapid spread of preference for highly refined maize, rice, and wheat. These have become status foods, associated with upward mobility, and they run the risk of turning pellagra and beriberi from minor, localized disease problems into widespread, major ones. Another status-related example is the increasing popularity of pale-leaf vegetables such as lettuce and cabbage at the expense of nutritionally richer dark-leaf vegetables, including the leaves from such cultigens as sweet potatoes and cassava. Nutrient-poor cassava also is increasing its range as a staple or co-staple food, though not because of its high status. Rather, rapidly accelerating population pressure in some areas requires the use of cassava because of its higher caloric yield per acre than grains. Also, it offers the additional advantage of requiring little labor for cultivation and harvest.

As elsewhere throughout the world, bottle feeding of children is becoming more popular because of its convenience. For well-to-do families who can afford high-quality formulas, this trend presents no health hazard. For families, however, who can afford only cheaper substitutes, a definite threat of lowered diet quality for children is posed.

Wild food products such as fruits, nuts, and insects once provided valuable supplements to the diets of many Africans. Increasingly, though, these are falling into disuse without adequate substitutes taking their place. Frequently this decline in use has resulted from the press of population on the land and the consequent destruction of habitats providing these products. In other instances, status considerations once again emerge as prominent factors. Bush products are gaining the image of being "primitive" and thus are not thought of as fit foods for modern people.

Finally, there is an association between increasing rates of urban population growth and negative dietary changes. Food becomes an expensive commodity in urban areas and must compete with expenditures for other items such as housing, clothing, and transport. Children undoubtedly suffer the most, because it is the high nutritional value but also high cost foods like milk and meat that are sacrificed first. As more urban families become headed by women who must work as well as see to the welfare of their children, it is certain that diets will continue to suffer. There is no doubt that as a group in Africa, it is the urban poor who have the worst diets. And unfortunately, the number of urban poor is increasing rapidly.

7

Health and the
Geography of Wholeness

BEN WISNER

A few years ago this chapter might have been called "Disease in Africa." It would have described the distribution of malaria, hookworm, and sleeping sickness over the continent, pointed out the wasting impact of these diseases on the "development" process, and bemoaned the shortage of medical manpower. Such a chapter probably would have been squarely in the tradition of environmentalism that has characterized European writing about Africa since the earliest despairing reports of missionaries and travelers whose colleagues and families died so frequently of "fever" in the "white man's grave." A belief in the innate unhealthfulness of the tropics and of Africa in particular is neither a relic of the European's first contact nor a journalistic image to quicken the reader's pulse. Respected scientists continue to present the same description in similar terms. For instance, Pierre Gourou (1953:6) has written:

> In physical and mental activity and in the reproduction of his kind, man is restricted in the tropics by serious maladies whose existence is entirely due to the hot, damp climate. We who live in temperate lands find it difficult to realize how baleful Nature can be to man or to understand that in unreclaimed regions water may swarm with dangerous germs, myriads of blood-sucking insects may inject deadly microbes into the human body and the very soil may be harmful to the touch.

Such pictures of "baleful Nature" lack all perspective on the role of human behavior and social organization in the transmission cycles of the parasitic and infectious diseases so common to Africa. If these descriptions lack an ecological viewpoint, they are even more lacking in historical perspectives, which recently have implicated colonial importation of pathogens in the present pattern of many diseases (Rodney, 1972).

Clearly disease is an obstacle to national and human liberation in the countries of Africa. My approach, however, will be to focus not exclusively on disease but on health as well—that state of social wholeness which indigenous African medicine strives to maintain and which political organizations in some parts of the continent are succeeding in reestablishing. What is needed is *a balanced view of both the health potentials of Africa's physico-social environments as well as their health hazards.*

HEALTH AS WHOLENESS

The human strength and social potential of health are summarized and symbolized in the traditional African definition of health as wholeness—*"uzima"* in Swahili. An anthropologist with much experience among the coastal people of Tanzania puts it very well:

> . . . health is *uzima*. It is wholeness; man is never alone as an individual but always as part of a whole, a part of his kin, his clan, lineage, family past and present which again through an elaborate symbolic framework related the human race with the nature around and with the whole universe. Health is to retain that *uzima*, wholeness, and to be a part of it in such a way that the basic balance is not disturbed. Man's wholeness was essentially preserved when he remained as an integrated part of the whole and lived in harmony . . . If there were problems between groups of people or individuals with varying interests in the group, it resulted in shaken health . . . (Swantz, 1970).

This view of health and health care contrasts vividly with the mechanistic, biochemical, technical definitions that seem implicit in Western hospital medicine. It is true that the World Health Organization (W.H.O.) speaks of "a state of complete physical, mental, and social well-being" (Mechanic, 1968:49), but even here the emphasis is on the adequate function of an individual in society, without questioning the wholeness of that society itself.

Wholeness is not a concept totally foreign to Westerners. Virchow probably meant very much the same thing when in 1948 he described politics as "medicine on a large scale" (Rather, 1958). Alfred E. Miller (1972) recently revealed a striving toward such a wholeness concept over the past few decades in European medicine by bringing the reader through the history of public health and stressing "community medicine" as offering a "model for looking at the community itself as a patient."

Things Fall Apart, says the Nigerian novelist, Achebe. If the social or medical geographer mapped patterns of social fragmentation, he would have a community medicine tool as valuable as any map of mosquitos or tsetse. In a continent so large, undergoing such a rapid change, there are many different ways for things to fall apart. The fracture of wholeness can take place slowly as leprosy eats not only at hands but also at family bonds, condemning the long-time sufferer to wander and beg because rehabilitation has not yet been organized on a large scale. It can take place swiftly in the death of an infant from neonatal tetanus or of a child from cerebral malaria—both tragically preventable.

The fracture of wholeness is also historical. Several works (Segal, 1966; Fanon, 1965) document the strain on family bonds and human relations that accompanied labor migration and forced introduction of cash crops into preexisting African economies, an historical situation which for millions in the settler minority states of southern Africa is still a daily reality.

Where governments attempt increases in well-being through large scale irrigation, industrialization, and pioneering settlement of under-utilized lands, the concomitant stresses on the wholeness of the peasant's knowledge and ability to manage ecosystems is shattered and new wholenesses must be created.

Everywhere shattered wholeness cries out for new forms of social organization that will break the cycle of uncertainty which is a more general and pervading problem than disease alone. Severe malnutrition in the small child of a delta rice farmer was traced ultimately to the father's inability to cultivate enough land following an operation he had for hydrocele, a common and debilitating condition caused by blockage of the lymphatics of the scrotum by small parasites transmitted from man to man by mosquitoes. The child's condition was complicated by diarrhea from water contaminated by human feces. This child might die, but others in the delta community may not since collective farming and nucleated residence is presently being introduced. These two social initiatives attempt to reestablish a wholeness that would support the farmer as he convalesces, provide a central day-care school where children can be screened for early signs of malnutrition, and where intensive educational campaigns and socio-political pressure can enforce the protection of water sources, the use of latrines, and the elimination of mosquito-breeding sites.

Nearly a thousand kilometers north of that delta, nomadic cattle herders have been hit hard by drought and famine. Wholeness is shattered. The dwelling units disperse. An old man eventually finds his way to a small town, where, nearly blind from trachoma, he begs and sleeps under cardboard in a back street among pieces of trucks and Land Rovers that have succumbed to the long, corrugated roads of the dry country. Some of these pastoralists have been recruited onto self-help, small-scale irrigation schemes; others into fishing schemes. A host of other problems of adjustment of diets and behavior have arisen, but the outline of a new wholeness is appearing.

A young man, just married with one child moves to the city with his elder brother, and with help from an uncle, raises enough money to begin a small carpentry shop. The early months are very hard. Everyone lives in two dark, unventilated rooms. All of the brother's four children are discovered to have tuberculosis. The wife goes into the hospital with the children. Months of worry pass during which the brothers must press ahead with the carpentry just to stay afloat. The strain is too much for the younger one. He becomes depressed. He drinks and begins to lose weight. Just outside town the Ministry of Lands has opened a new "site and service" scheme where members help one another build homes and add to them as they save money. It represents an attempt to tackle improvement in the residential environment through a form of wholeness, the self-help community—but will these brothers ever manage to find a place in the scheme?

The concluding sections of this chapter will provide more examples of the health promotive potential of African innovations and social wholeness, but before this is done, it is necessary to highlight those diseases that are of the most immediate concern.

DISEASE PATTERNS

What are the most frequently seen illnesses in Africa? Which are the greatest killers? A report of the World Health Organization's first ten years of activity in the "African Region" (all of Africa south of the Sahara except Sudan, Ethiopia, and Somalia) emphasized programs against communicable diseases, especially *malaria, yaws, bilharzia,* and *tuberculosis,* and programs for the general improvement of *maternal and child health* and for *environmental sanitation* (W.H.O., 1958). A similar report on the second ten years sums up the situation as follows:

> Available data showed that over most of middle Africa malaria infected
> virtually every child by its third year of life, accounting for probably one

third of those who failed to survive that critical hurdle; that although human trypanosomiasis had been largely contained, its reservoir in animals and the ever-present tsetse posed a constant threat of resurgence; that schistosomiasis would probably spread even further as hydro-agricultural and industrial schemes developed; that onchocerciasis continued, unchecked, to create human suffering, while forcing the abandonment of extensive fertile areas the loss of which, even temporarily, the countries could ill afford; that tuberculosis and leprosy pursued their course among a heavy proportion of the population; that although considerable progress had been made in reducing yaws endemicity, the goal of eradication had become more difficult to achieve; and that other diseases such as measles, smallpox and cerebrospinal meningitis added each year to the toll of morbidity and mortality. In addition to this heavy load, the prevalence of kwashiorkor and other manifestations of protein deficiency was also known, as was the general inadequacy or total absence of sanitation facilities and safe water supplies, particularly in the rural areas (W.H.O., 1968:4).

The pattern of importance varies from country to country and within countries, but these same diseases appear, if only in a different order (May, 1955; Hall and Langlands, 1968; McGlashan, 1966; Schaller, 1969; Vogel *et al.*, 1974).

African Trypanosomiasis (sleeping sickness). Sleeping sickness is the pathological state caused when either of the protozoans *Trypanosoma gambiense* or *T. rhodesiense* invades the human blood stream and later the cerebrospinal fluid. Human beings are the chief reservoir of these protozoans; however, wild game, especially bushbuck and antelope, and domestic cattle serve as animal reservoirs. Transmission begins when one of several varieties of tsetse (*Glossina* spp.) feeds on the blood of an infected human or animal host. The parasite then develops in the fly. Transmission is complete when the fly, which remains infective for life, feeds again on a susceptible host. Infection with both trypanosomes is usually fatal if untreated, and *T. rhodesiense* can kill in just a few months.

The disease is ecologically complex because of the large number of different tsetse varieties that act as vectors, their widely differing preferences for habitats, different feeding habits, and because several other trypanosomes exist which, while not infecting human beings directly, severely affect their livelihoods and settlements by infecting their domestic animals, especially cattle.

Tsetse now inhabit 4-5 million square miles of tropical Africa. Point prevalences as high as 26 percent and 79 percent have been reported (Hughes and Hunter, 1970).

Onchocerciasis (river blindness). River blindness is a chronic, nonfatal filarial disease in which the female worms (*Onchocerca volvulus,* a nematode) inhabits fibrous nodules in the skin and discharge microfilariae (small worms) that migrate through the skin, frequently reaching the eye, where they can produce blindness. The reservoir is the infected human, and transmission takes place via the bite of an infected black fly, especially *Simulium damnosum* and *S. neavei.* Like trypanosomes, the onchocerca undergo an extrinsic stage of development in the body of the insect vector. During this period the microfilariae picked up by a black fly during its blood meal become infective larvae, migrate to the fly's salivary glands from where they can be implanted in the skin of another human. The female fly lays her egg in swiftly flowing water, and since such a breeding place is necessitated by the fly larvae's large oxygen requirement, the maximum range of the adult fly is seldom more than twelve miles from such water.

River blindness is endemic in the vicinity of running water in the entire savanna belt south of the Sahara, from Senegal in the west to Uganda and Kenya in the east. The Institute of Malaria and Vector Borne Diseases at Amani, Tanzania, estimates there are about 350,000 infected persons in East Africa alone. Hunter (1966) refers to prevalences in northern Ghana ranging from 31 percent to 83 percent and averaging 60 percent.

Schistosomiasis (bilharzia). Bilharzia in Africa is a disease caused by the blood flukes called *Schistosoma haematobium* and *S. mansoni. S. haematobium* is the more common and eventually lodges itself in the pelvic veins and gives rise to urinary problems. *S. mansoni* lodges in the veins of the intestinal wall. Both parasites produce eggs that exit from the body in the urine and feces respectively. The eggs, if deposited in water, hatch, and liberated larvae enter a suitable snail who becomes its intermediate host. After several weeks of development in the infected snail, free swimming larvae reenter the water and can penetrate human skin while the new host is bathing, wading, playing, or drawing water. The larvae enter the blood stream. They develop to maturity in the liver, from where they migrate to urinary or intestinal veins to share the person's daily bread and produce eggs, beginning the cycle anew.

S. haematobium is highly endemic in the whole valley of the Nile and over practically all of Africa. *S. mansoni's* distribution is more restricted, including the Nile delta north of Cairo, East Africa from the Upper Nile to Zimbabwe, the Republic of Congo, West Africa east and southeast of Senegal, with several foci in Natal. Prevalence in many areas reaches 75-95 percent.

Bilharzia often has been used as the textbook example of an untoward effect of "development" projects in water management, especially the large-scale irrigation projects that have sprung up in the last few decades in tropical Africa. Highly endemic bilharzia has accompanied such famous irrigation schemes as the Gezira in the Sudan and the Volta Dam development in Ghana as well as smaller projects in Nigeria, Tanzania, Angola, and Namibia. The minimum requirements for transmission are to be found at Lake Kariba, and infection could develop explosively as it did with construction of the Akosombo dam and creation of Lake Volta.

Malaria. Malaria is endemic in virtually all of Africa. As with both sleeping sickness and river blindness, malaria is a water-related, insect-vectored, communicable disease. The specific agents are the four protozoans *Plasmodium vivax*, *P. malariae*, *P. falciparum*, and *P. ovale*. The arthropod vector in this case is the anopholes mosquito, especially *Anopheles gambiae* and *A. funestus*. Humans are the only important reservoir, and transmission takes place via the blood meals of infective mosquitos. The developmental cycle of plasmodia both in the human body and in the female anopheles is complex and varies from parasite to parasite. Such variation is strongly influenced by temperature while the plasmodium is in the mosquito. Besides temperature, other factors combine to produce the complicated mathematics of transmission, endemicity, and epidemics. Some of these other factors are the longevity of mosquitos, their frequency of feeding, their choice of blood meal, and the degree of immunity existing in the human population.

Malaria is a notorious killer of children in infancy and, acting synergistically with intercurrent infection and other parasites, contributes to much anemia and malnutrition. Placental malaria has been mentioned in connection with other factors producing low birth weight in Africa (Williams and Jelliffe, 1972).

Tuberculosis. Another disease noted for its debilitating interactions is tuberculosis. The bacillus *Mycobacterium tuberculosis* is the responsible agent of the disease, the only bacillus to be mentioned among the various forms of life (protozoans and helminths) that have so far characterized our discussion. Infection occurs generally by inhalation of air-borne bacilli, although a significant amount of non-pulmonary TB arises from drinking milk from infected cows. Air-borne droplet infection is characteristic of crowded conditions, as in many sections of the fast-growing cities of Africa. Unfortunately, only half of the active TB sufferers eventually seek help; half do not and continue to infect those around them, both in the cities and in the countryside when they return.

Shennan (1968) notes considerable variation in the prevalence of TB in different countries of Africa, with the highest rates in the south and west. Representative rates (only roughly comparable) are Nigeria (urban) 5 percent; Sierra Leone (urban) 5 percent, (rural) 4 percent; Ghana 3 percent; Gambia and Liberia 2 percent; South Africa and Transkei 5 percent; Botswana 4 percent; Swaziland 3 percent; Lesotho 2 percent; Kenya, Uganda, Tanzania (mainland) and Zanzibar (urban) 2 percent; and Zanzibar (rural) 1 percent.

DISEASE CONTROL

The "balanced view" between hazards and potentials announced as the goal of this chapter might seem lost already in the wealth of information on human-environment relationships over which people appear to have so little control. Further reading in medical ecology and the geography of disease probably would weight the balance even more toward environmental dominance (May, 1958, 1961). Management and control of disease, however, are being effectively pursued. There are new curative and preventative technologies on the scene and most importantly, there are innovative patterns of person-to-person and person-to-nature relations that promise to bear the fruits of improved health. The "balanced view" can be upheld.

Control of sleeping sickness. The major means to control sleeping sickness include population evacuation, the killing in large numbers of the wild animals that serve as tsetse food supply, hand catching of the fly, selective brush clearance, areal defoliation, and large-scale attempts to poison tsetse with DDT and Dieldrin (Knight, 1971). Various legal restrictions on human and livestock movement in tsetse areas as well as compulsory medical examination and regulation of land use also have been tried, as have insect repellents and mass chemotherapy.

Although clearly some moderate combination of approaches probably gives results in each situation, the pattern under colonial rule, which unfortunately seems to have been inherited by the present generation of control officers, was to attempt to control too much land, to attack the problem with too much force—a strategy satirized by Forde (1971) as "the Pax Brittanica theory of the epidemiology of trypanosomiasis." Thus wild hosts were eliminated and the tsetse simply altered their feeding habits. Areas were evacuated, allowing foci of game-borne trypanosomiasis to prosper unchecked. Large areas were cleared where there was neither the population nor the land potential for the intensive settlement (greater than 80 persons per square kilometer) needed to maintain a habitat uncongenial to the tsetse. It would seem that in the long run, control of sleeping sickness must employ a full ecological approach. In Forde's view, existing information about the agricultural/pastoral potential of various endemic areas can be used to give a reasonable indication of the density of settlement they can be expected to support, and the control measures can be instituted only at a pace and on a scale which subsequent settlement can maintain. He notes:

> What ought to be avoided are all forms of mass treatment, whether by mass injection of curative or prophylactic drugs, or by blanket spraying with insecticides, or by large-scale felling of vegetation, or destruction of wildlife. All sorts of biological as well as mechanical bulldozing may, on occasion, control the spread of disease but at a cost to future generations that cannot be fully assessed (Forde, 1971:492).

What Forde envisions are control techniques adapted to the settlement potential of a range of environments, with intensive irrigation schemes at one extreme and game parks on the other.

Control of river blindness. The World Health Organization estimates that over 10 million square kilometers of fertile African land is denied to agriculture and stockraising because of sleeping sickness. Allowing for overlap, additional millions are rendered uninhabitable by river blindness. An important difference is that the foci of river blindness transmission are the river valley lands of the savanna belt. Thus, relatively speaking, the land in question is even more valuable because of its irrigability and its potential role in famine prevention in areas of rainfall variability, a point that cannot be overemphasized in view of recurrent Sahelian drought. The value of this land might partially explain the ambitious plans which UNDP, FAO, IBRD (World Bank), and WHO have made in agreement with the countries sharing the Volta River Basin. The plan is to kill the larvae of the Similium fly in their waterway breeding places with larvicides. However, WHO's Onchocerciasis Advisory Team for the African region dates only from 1966, and, in fact, so little is known about the disease that it is not fully understood why the *Onchocerca volvulus/Similium damnosum* complex of the Guinea savanna results in few eye lesions, whereas the same *O. volvulus/S. damnosum* complex in the more northerly Sudan savanna produces much blindness. Also, some caution must be exercised in the massive chemical intervention in ecosystems, given some of the recent studies that reveal frequent unforeseen and disastrous consequences (Gillet, 1970).

Bilharzia control. With bilharzia the problem is less how to control the disease than to answer the question, at what cost? There are basically four modes of control used in Africa (Essex, 1972):

a. Control of the parasite by means of mass treatment;
b. Improved sanitation;
c. Control of contact with water and the provision of safe water supplies;
d. Snail control by means of modified water use in agricultural practice or chemical control using molluscicides.

Mass chemotherapy alone will not control bilharzia because the available drugs have a cure rate of only 35-65 percent. Reinfection is easy and nearly inevitable, and certain people at any given time may be unsuitable for treatment, including pregnant and lactating women.

The combination of improved sanitation and controlled water management seems to give the highest benefits for unit cost, although this depends, of course, on how one does the calculations. Improved sanitation can break the transmission cycle of dozens of other helminthic infections as well as bilharzia, and a protected water supply can reduce the threat of even more numerous water-borne, water-bred, and water-dependent diseases. An attack on the snail hosts of the schistosomes may achieve its purpose in breaking the chain of transmission without altering the potential of irrigation or other waterworks to breed malaria or to transmit typhoid and amoebic dysentery.

Malaria control. Malaria must be eradicated from the face of the earth, according to the Eighth World Health Assembly (1955). On a global scale, WHO has had considerable success in this aim, but not in Africa. After some experimentation with mass chemoprophylaxis, even dosing salt with malaria-supressing drugs in Ghana, and larvicidal attacks on the breeding places of anopheline mosquitos, control methods have settled down to the approach of residual chlorinated hydrocarbon applications to the interior walls of houses. Only half of the adult anophelines need die from contact with residual DDT, Dieldrin, or BHC to bring down transmission rates to a critical threshold below which malaria disappears, unlike larvicidal attacks, which must kill 95 percent of the larvae to be effective.

Some success has been achieved in South Africa, Ethiopia, the highlands of Zimbabwe, southeastern Uganda, and in the forested zones of Liberia and Cameroun. Otherwise, the program for Africa seems to have persisted in a "preeradication"-control infrastructural-preparation phase.

The point of preeradication programs is to build up the manpower and health infrastructure needed to carry out an eradication program that demands:

a. An attack phase of at least three years during which all interiors are sprayed twice a year (at least 200 spraymen per million of population needed);

b. A consolidation phase where case-finding takes place and cases are treated, thereby allowing anophelism without malaria;

c. A maintenance phase where imported cases are controlled.

Prothero (1972) describes well the difficulties of consolidation and maintenance under a system of heavy migration and noncoordination across national frontiers, a great hazard especially where success in phases a and b have lowered immunity and created the possibility of epidemic reintroduction of malaria. Coverage, of course, must be complete, and the whole eradication campaign must continue speedily to avoid chemical resistances in the protozoans or mosquitos. All in all, the sheer organizational, manpower, and financial requirements are very heavy and such demands must be met in a multiplicity of physico-social environments.

There are also biological reasons why eradication is particularly difficult:

> *A. gambiae* and *A. funestus*, the vectors in tropical Africa, typically produce stable malaria. *A. gambiae*, in particular, has every quality required for the successful transmission of malaria. A strong, long-lived mosquito, which bites man in preference to any other animal . . ., it takes large blood meals and is likely to acquire infection from minimally infective humans; its eclectic breeding habits make antilarval campaigns against it difficult; it tends not to rest for a lethal length of contact on insecticide-treated surfaces; in several areas it has developed a practically complete resistance to the effects of some insecticides . . . its extermination in Africa south of the Sahara and north of the Union of South Africa is probably impossible. Malaria eradication in the area in which *A. gambiae* is the carrier is a problem of much greater difficulty than anywhere else in the world (W.H.O., 1958:180-81).

It is not surprising that malaria eradication has seldom passed beyond the control phase in Africa.

Tuberculosis control. The theoretical aim of tuberculosis control is to remove infectious persons from the population as soon as possible by means of supervised domiciliary chemotherapy, supported by a network of screening, case-finding, and defaulter follow-up when someone discontinues treatment within TB's 1 to 1-½ year duration. Attempts are underway over much of Africa to execute control schemes on these lines, but because of cost, vaccination of infants and children against tuberculosis (giving much slower results) is also practiced on a large scale, especially in combination with smallpox vaccine in WHO-sponsored campaigns.

Many characteristics of tuberculosis make it difficult to counteract. It takes numerous forms; some are infectious; some are not. Its curative demands can place excessive burdens on underdeveloped health systems. To treat one child with TB meningitis equals the cost of vaccinating thousands! Its long period of latency and the possibility of relapse after years of dormancy make epidemiological prediction difficult.

Like bilharzia, tuberculosis is a disease intimately associated with the general standard of living of a people. It is not surprising that TB is often found in association with other diseases of poverty and childhood. For instance, 38 percent of the cases of malnutrition admitted to pediatric care at Dar es Salaam's (Tanzania) Muhimbili Hospital in 1972 also had tuberculosis (personal communication, Dr. T. Okeahialam).

Control of this disease is as imperative as it is difficult. A main stumbling block to the approach of mass chemotherapy of sputum-positive cases is defaulting: people often stop treatment before they are cured, become infectious again, and relapse. A repetition of three times in this cycle may cause the bacilli to resist antituberculosis drugs. This is a classic case of a "social constraint" which, unfortunately, is on the increase.

It has been said that three types of epidemiology are needed to facilitate any control program:

a. Circumstantial epidemiology, which describes in essentially historical, geographical, and sociological terms the conditions in which disease occurs;

b. Aetiological epidemiology, which defines the causal organism and describes its transmission from person-to-person;

c. Mathematical epidemiology, which shows how the various factors concerned in transmission interact with each other to build up a composite picture of endemic or epidemic conditions. (Forde, 1971:493-94)

Geography has clearly had a role in the circumstantial epidemiology of all five diseases discussed. Human-density mapping, vector range and habitat descriptions, studies of human migration, water-use patterns, and settlement patterns all have been useful. We could argue, however, that geography's role is not exhausted there, nor are there only three sorts of epidemiology involved in the control (or more properly—*management*) of disease. Note that in all five disease-control programs, little attempt has been made to change human behavior or to mobilize human energies on a large scale. So many references are made in the literature of disease control to the necessity of raising the general standard of living (especially for bilharzia and TB), yet programs continue to stumble over such social phenomena as TB defaulting. Something must be missing. We should term the study of this missing link *political epidemiology*, and we will now return to an account of the geography of wholeness.

THE GEOGRAPHY OF WHOLENESS

Our hopes for a radical improvement in the health status of Africans are pinned to an establishment of social wholeness. Here lies the root of "health potentials" of a magnitude comparable to the sizable "health hazards" already described. Here lies the social means for breaking the cycle of poverty-disease-debilitation-low productivity-poverty which emerges from the tangle of endemicities holding back development.

As the argument progresses, we will cite examples of more and more comprehensive and disciplined communal life. For now, however, let us consider a rudimentary form of cooperation—the self-help water supply. Literally thousands of shallow wells have been constructed with self-help labor in the past two decades, often with material aid from outside organizations. Have these wells made people more healthy? Do they reveal health potentials latent in African social organization?

The answer to the first question should be yes. If the homemaker can avoid traversing disease infested habitats to fetch water she will be healthier. If her journey is shorter, she might produce more, and the family might eat better. If the water source is protected with a simple cement sleeve protruding above the ground, a cover, and a hand pump, risks to her family of typhoid, hepatitis and dysentery are reduced. Unfortunately several studies agree that many self-help projects *have not* had such health benefits.

The reasons are two-fold. First, as White, Bradley, and White (1972) argue, beyond a basic level of water quality (security against cholera and typhoid in low-cost projects), most remaining health benefits accrue to increases in *quantity* of water consumed per person per day. Many self-help water projects have not encouraged increases of consumption above 10 liters per capita per day, which is the East African average for rural non-piped sources, because they have usually not brought water near enough to homes. Thus "water washed" diseases such as scabies, skin sepsis, and trachoma remain unaffected. In addition, kitchen hygiene and child care are not affected, with little reduction in childhood diarrhea.

The second problem to come to light is that while villagers often cooperate in constructing a water source, its maintenance and protection is so intimately associated with other health practices and the general level of cooperation in a village that pumps often remain broken. Frustrated users open protecting covers and draw water with contaminated ropes and containers, and children continue to defecate near the water source (Wisner, 1973).

In Tanzania, an attempt has been made to go beyond single project self-help to attack these problems through a mass health education campaign designed to raise political consciousness at the same time that substantive health information is imparted. The campaign involved over two million persons in weekly radio-dis-cussion-action groups all over the country. The core of many of these groups were preexisting "functional literacy" groups. The campaign covered water supply and dysentery as well as latrine construction, bilharzia, malaria, hookworm, and tuberculosis. Although evaluation of this campaign—called *Mtu ni Afya* (Man is Health)—is still underway, it is obvious that the response in some areas of the country has been explosive. Hundreds of new latrines have appeared in villages, and in some areas groups have refused to disband at the end of the broadcast series, but continue to meet and work on supplementary reading material produced at their request on such topics as trachoma and venereal diseases. Arrangements are being made for more elaborate training of village members in pump maintenance and incremental improvement of existing water works such as construction of communal washing slabs.

In other words, the "Man is Health" campaign began to fill in gaps in the previous program of self-help water management. It began to construct a wholeness. But the story becomes more complex at this point since social precondition and potential become entangled.

The unique condition that allowed the mass health campaign to work as it did was another Tanzanian innovation—the *Ujamaa* (cooperative/communal) village. Since 1967, there has been a very rapid establishment of nucleated producers' cooperative villages in the country. Leaving aside the much debated questions of whether the villages are (a) economically viable and/or (b) leading to a truly socialist economic organization, a single fact remains. The villagers do consume services in common and have generally been motivated to carry individual self-help forward to the point where many villages are engaged in continuous and integrated surveillance and improvement of their environment. The "village health committee" takes on a new role in this context and can tap long established social sanctions to enforce proper refuse disposal, latrine use, etc.

The village health worker will be the Village Medical Helper (VMH) who tends to be educated to the primary level, a young person, whom the village chooses to send to the district hospital for a 3-6 month course. The VMH's ultimate role, if preventative, can reinforce mass health education, self-help, and the increasing trend toward communalism. The similarity with the Chinese "barefoot doctor," while not to be overstressed, must be pointed out.

Such developments also should be viewed in the light of the overall health manpower situation in Africa. Wood (1972) recently concluded a review of the situation as follows:

> The first inescapable conclusion is that we have very few people with which to undertake the enormous task of coping with the health needs of all people. . . . Within this overall shortage there is a particular shortage of the more highly skilled, and this is made even worse by their maldistribution in relation to population. Some of the reasons for this maldistribution are described by Gish in terms of effective economic demand in relation to private and public medical care.

> The second inescapable conclusion is that considering the relation between the probable economic and population growth rates and the cost of training and employing highly skilled health workers, we are not going to reach any order of staff/population ratio, for the whole population, which is compatible with current target patterns for delivery of medical care so long as these include such features as primary consultation with a graduate physician, universal access to hospital care and the availability of a variety of super specialties.

> Manpower studies for various countries and regions of Africa . . . each spell out in detail that the existing shortage of skilled manpower is unlikely to be greatly relieved in the next 20 years or so.

> These two conclusions, the existing shortage and the widening gap, pose a crucial choice. Either we continue to aim at a type of medical care which cannot be extended to cover all in need, or we revise our ideas on types of medical care and delivery systems . . . . The only direction in which these considerations lead us is toward the greater use of paramedical and auxiliary staff. . . .

As this century concludes we are likely to see a greater divergence of specialists, "more highly skilled" medicine, and various forms of "people's health service," the former treating mostly the growing middle class in large urban complexes, the latter more or less autonomously working in rural areas containing peasants with rapidly increasing political awareness. One extreme form of such a people's health service is seen in the former Portuguese colonies in Africa (an important example to which we will soon return). Its seed is also seen in the increasing involvement of "lay" people—parents—in the health care of their own children.

Perhaps the most exciting health potential that is now emerging in the communal villages of Tanzania concerns child health. Most people are aware of the shockingly high mortality rates for infants (under 1 year) and preschool (up to 5 years) children in Africa. The latter rate can approach 500 per 1000 in some localities, and national statistics are not comforting. A recent estimate for Tanzania as a whole had 139 of each 1000 live-born children failing to reach their first birthday (Thomas, 1972).

Most child health problems are preventable. Below one year these tend to be *respiratory tract infection* (especially pneumonia), *diarrhea*, and *marasmus*. In the preschool child, the chief diseases are *protein-energy malnutrition* (especially kwashiorkor), *diarrhea*, *malaria*, *intestinal worms*, *tuberculosis*, *anemia*, and *accidents*.

All of these insults to the growing body interact, especially malnutrition and infection. I have already cited the frequency with which one encounters tuberculosis and malnutrition in the same child. Malaria and worm infection both produce anemia. Burns, a very common childhood accident in Africa, diarrhea, tuberculosis and other infectious diseases such as measles can combine in various ways to debilitate and lower the child's resistance. A deadly combination seen all over Africa is undernutrition and lowered resistance preceding measles, which rapidly deteriorates into gross malnutrition.

In order to attack these problems day-care centers are being established in Tanzania. Their essential tasks are to (1) offer a basic venue for immunization (against TB, whooping cough, diphtheria, tetanus, small pox, and measles) and periodic health screening; (2) provide an opportunity for communal feeding of children with mixed vegetable protein/animal protein supplements as locally available; and (3) raise the general level of child care, environmental control and communality in the village. The day-care centers combine well-established health benefits with the continuity, intensity, and discipline of communal life. In many ways their success hinges on the political development of Tanzania's village communities and their urban/periurban equivalents. Indeed, political awareness is Africa's *major health priority* during the remainder of this century, and nowhere is the politicizing process taking place so fast as in the territories liberated from Portugal.

Angola presents a difficult test of the balanced view of health in Africa. If any country fits the nineteenth century stereotype of the "heart of darkness," Angola does. It is vast: Larger than South

Africa; as extensive as Malawi, Zimbabwe, and Zambia taken together; about four times the size of the British Isles. Its environments run the gamut from rich, cool highlands to tropical forests, to dry woodlands, to virtual desert. Climate, vegetation, soil, groundwater, and insect vectors would seem to have dominated for centuries the human life scattered over this territory, firmly rooting such causes of human suffering as malaria, skin diseases, parasitic infections and malnutrition.

Is this truly a case of environmental dominance or is it so by human default? Portuguese colonial administration was infamous for its stingy provision of services. Angola is no exception. Most health facilities are concentrated in the maritime zone that represents the one-quarter of the national territory where the European population was most dense. Toward the interior, in the vast region embracing five districts (Malanje, Bie, Lunda, Mexico, and Kuando Kubango), with an area exactly that of France, the number of health facilities is very small: 5 regional hospitals, 16 rural hospitals, and 60 field dispensaries. Yet the Angolan population in that region numbers about two million. There was one doctor for every 1000 white settlers, but only one doctor for every 75,000 Angolans (MPLA, 1970, 1971).

Given such neglect, it is not surprising that the Popular Movement for the Liberation of Angola (MPLA) has sought as a top priority the establishment of health services. Each region they control is divided into a number of zones and these in turn are subdivided into sectors. The regional "medical assistance service" is headed by a director, in most cases a doctor or medical assistant; the zone by a medical assistant or qualified nurse; the sector by a nurse or a nursing assistant.

These health services have undergone considerable growth during the early 1970's. As an example, let us take a zone that stretches from the border with Zambia westwards deep into Angola (Personal communication, 1974). It is divided into a northern medical subregion and a southern subregion, and in the former as of January 1974, there were six stationary medical centers—a main hospital on the Zambian border and five dispensaries in base camps in the interior—serving some 50,000 people. The border hospital is headed by a doctor and is composed of both inpatient and outpatient tents and a small laboratory. The doctor has close contact with the nearest Zambian health facility, making referrals for laboratory confirmations and critical care, and sees Zambian as well as Angolan patients. Periodically he tours the other five centers in his subregion.

The dispensaries are staffed by medical assistants except for one headed by a doctor. They have large outpatient demand and are assisted by first-aid orderlies and nurse-midwives. These latter two cadres are trained in batches of 20 at the border hospital, where they also return for refresher courses. The first-aid orderlies usually are trained for six months initially and then set to work under supervision. They are the backbone of mass outreach. They help at the dispensaries, but are basically mobile. They teach villagers the rules of hygiene and give health education wherever they go. The training of first-aid orderlies emphasizes the recognition and treatment of the most common diseases. It also includes study of some anatomy, physiology, and pathology. The course is for six months with a six month refresher after a year of service. In all, the northern subregion has two doctors, four medical assistants, twenty nurse-midwives, and 90-100 first-aid orderlies.

Guiné-Bissau may have suffered even more colonial neglect than Angola in the health field. When PAIGC opened its military fronts in 1963, there was not a single trained African doctor, medical assistant, or medical aide. There was a handful of African nurses, but essentially the *Partido Africano para a Independencia de Guiné e Cabo Verde* (PAIGC) was starting its health services from scratch. Guiné-Bissau declared itself independent on September 24, 1973. At that point, the party's health services had to face the imminent burden of caring for all of the country's 700,000 people. The emphasis of the health system is first on *decentralization* and second on *paramedical staff* (in 1974, there were only 12 doctors and 11 medical assistants). A third emphasis is on *preventive care*.

PAIGC gives the following three points as the foundation of their preventive health action:

1. The creation of "brigades sanitaires" (health brigades) in each sector (there were only seven as of Independence);
2. The realization of vaccination campaigns;
3. The generalization of chemoprophylaxis against malaria.

Health brigades generally are composed of three health workers. They move from village to village, holding meetings and discussions during which they emphasize the importance of latrines, boiling water, giving locally available supplementary food to children from six months onwards, early and continuing attendance at antenatal clinics, and regular use of antimalaria tablets. They also visit schools, where iron supplements are becoming routine, and help with vaccination campaigns.

Of the three liberation movements, PAIGC has probably had the greatest success with vaccination since its territory and population are much more manageable. Despite enemy action, PAIGC was able to organize two cholera campaigns covering 20,000 people in total and managed to exclude cholera from its territory. This reflects with tragic irony on the "civilizing mission" of Portugal, which between April and September 1974, suffered 1959 cases of cholera with 32 deaths!

There have also been annual campaigns against smallpox and yellow fever since 1971, and localized use of TAB and tetanus toxoid. There are plans for universal smallpox and yellow fever coverage soon as well as universal vaccination of under-fives with BCG against tuberculosis (PAIGC, 1974). PAIGC health cadres have also been active in relief activities in the Cape Verde Islands, where the Portuguese had neglected a drought and famine situation for many years very similar to the Sahelian crisis.

In Mozambique, FRELIMO (*Fente de Libertação de Moçam-bique*) also has a strong political orientation towards health service. Its basic philosophy can be seen in the following:

> . . . It was found, that most of the cadres . . . apply the principle that in the relationship between politics and technique, politics come first. In the past, lack of understanding of this point gave rise to purely administrative attitudes and behavior among health cadres, which made it difficult for them to communicate with the masses. Without the people's support and cooperation, the health services found it difficult to do their work within the framework of the popular and revolutionary struggle we are waging. Now there is proper understanding of the political role of the health services, the main pre-occupation of our comrades in the health services being to cultivate love for the masses with whom they are in direct contact and among whom they represent our movement and political line. (FRELIMO, 1973a:17-18.)

Materially it began very poor in the health sphere. In 1968, for Cabo Delgado province there were only 11 district hospitals and 56 first-aid centers staffed by 315 people (FRELIMO, n.d.). Nonetheless, the early emphasis was on prevention and mass involvement in campaigns against infectious diseases. As early as 1967, localized campaigns against typhoid, tetanus, and tuberculosis were underway, and in that year 100,000 people in the liberated zones had been vaccinated against smallpox (Mondlane, 1969). By 1971-72, the number of health workers had increased to 420 at 40 district hospitals and a much greater number at first-aid centers (FRELIMO, 1973b).

LESSONS

A balanced view of health and disease in Africa can gain a great deal from the examples of the liberation struggles (Wisner, 1975). Here the *social and historical context of health and disease* stand out as starkly as the physical context must have appeared to an early explorer engulfed in a cloud of mosquitos!

We learn in these extreme cases how materially poor people can build up a health service on the premise that the cadre is not elite, that *the peasant can teach* as well as learn, and that health, education, production, and political activity are all inseparable elements in a common struggle to create a truly free, independent, prosperous, and enduring national social structure. We learn how *wholeness* is constructed through anti-elitist attitudes. We can learn, in short, a bit about the *political epidemiology* which we claimed earlier seeks a missing link in the tableau of success and failure of disease control programs in Africa.

8

Physiological Climates

OYEDIRAN OJO

The significance of the four climatic elements of temperature, humidity, wind, and radiation, in influencing the physiological system of an organism, forms the basis for the study of physiological climates. Of these, the effects of temperature and humidity are the best known. For instance, at high temperatures, an organism's heat loss through radiation and conduction/convection is disturbed, and high humidity in conjunction with high temperature interferes with evaporative heat loss. Residents of middle latitude areas with cold winters are well aware of the effects of wind, but the influence of wind is only occasionally mentioned for tropical areas. There is generally very little information on the influence of solar radiation, which in contrast to temperature, humidity, and wind, imposes a heat load on the organism by transferring energy to it from outside. The significance of heat and solar radiation are reflected in the fact that different organisms react differently to incoming insolation and heat. The organisms may be unable to suppress or eliminate these stresses at a sufficiently rapid rate when they are excessive. Overheating may lead to death. Thus, the four major climatic elements each have important impacts. In reality, however, they act in combination. Physiologically there are no completely isolated reactions.

SOLAR RADIATION

Response to solar radiation is instantaneous so that absolute values during a daily cycle significantly affect the comfort of the organism. Such cumulative processes as growth, activity levels, appetite, and nervous-system functioning depend on the amount of incoming radiation. The temperature of the organism itself, which significantly influences biochemical processes, is also a function of the instantaneous incidence of radiation.

In addition to knowing the instantaneous amount of insolation received, it is necessary to measure absorbed insolation, a factor which depends on both the total insolation as well as the reflectivity (albedo) of the organism. *Albedo* is a function mainly of the color of the reflecting surface, but it also depends on the nature of the surface and the spectral quality and angle of incidence of the radiation. For example, the amount of insolation absorbed by humans depends partly on the thickness of the corneum (the dead layer of the epidermis) which varies widely throughout the body, being particularly thick on the palms of the hands and the soles of the feet.

When the body is exposed to solar radiation for a sufficiently long time, sunburn (erythema) may result. This can be followed by blistering or peeling of most of the superficial layers if conditions are severe. After one or two days, the redness may fade away and may be replaced by a brown coloration usually known as "suntan." The process operates on both light and dark skinned persons, though obviously it is more dramatic on the former. Skin cancer is another direct effect of solar radiation. It is induced by the same wave lengths that produces the sunburn-suntan complex. The incidence of skin cancer is greater among whites than among blacks probably because of a less thick corneum (Blum, 1954). When skin cancer occurs among blacks, it is distributed without reference to exposed parts, suggesting a nonsolar cause. Solar radiation also can harm the eye, causing pain, visual disturbances, excessive excretion, and swelling. Such effects are most common in areas with high-surface reflectivity—deserts and shores.

HEAT AND COLD

As already emphasized, temperature, humidity, wind, and radiation jointly influence the thermal balance of any organism. To maintain the balance, various mechanisms operate to regulate heat gain or heat loss. Probably the first reaction to increased heat load is a rise in body temperature. This may lead to a decrease in metabolic heat production, increased respiratory activity, and an increase in perspiration, which in turn may adversely affect the efficiency of some regulatory systems of the body. For example, increase in perspiration, particularly by an unacclimatized person, can result in an excessive loss of salt, thus producing dehydration, which in the early stages reduces the blood volume and promotes heat exhaustion. In more advanced stages, heat exhaustion can cause disturbances of the cell functions, muscular inefficiency, loss of appetite, difficulty in swallowing, acid accumulation in the tissue, and nervous irritability. A net gain of heat may even reach a sufficiently high level to produce depression, heat stroke, and death.

Another possible consequence of heat is the reduction of blood supply to the upper portions of the nervous tissues (especially the cerebral cortex), which are most sensitive to lack of oxygen. The effects of this may range from lassitude to loss of consciousness, depending upon the degree of the circulatory insufficiency and the sensitivity of the cerebral cortex at the time.

Because of the prevalence of tropical climates in Africa, all of the various effects of excessive heat must be taken into account. Cold, however, plays a role in many parts of the continent, particularly in the highland areas and in the extreme northern and southern latitudes. The effect of cold is also significant during the nights, particularly in the desert areas during low sun periods. Even in humid areas with comparatively high night temperatures, the excess of body heat loss over gain may be such that night conditions are chilly.

One of the first physiological reactions to cold is the constriction of the blood vessels in the fingers, cheeks, toes, and ears. The result is reduced heat transfer from the interior of the body to the surface. The insulative value of the peripheral vessels is significant to the body heat economy because the stored heat is conserved and the demand for metabolic heat production is reduced. However, the cold may be so extreme that vasoconstriction can no longer sufficiently retard the heat loss from the body. Still higher thermal inbalances may lead to shivering, which increases metabolism, although at the same time it may decrease the insulative value of the peripheral tissues by lessening the degree of vascular constriction. Cold may result in frost bite, making the affected body parts become red, swollen, and painful. If cold is very severe, the depth of the affected body shell is increased, and eventually, the internal organs are affected. Cerebration is retarded when the internal body temperature is less than 92°F (33.3°C), with definite clouding of consciousness occuring when a value of 88°F (31.1°C) is reached. Death usually results at a temperature of 80°F (26.7°C).

PHYSIOLOGICAL CLIMATIC INDICES

A number of indices have been developed for assessing the degree of sensation of animals and humans to heat and cold conditions. Among these, the Effective Temperature index (ET), the Wet Bulb-Globe Temperature (WBGT), the Heat Stress Index (HSI), and the Thermal Acceptance Ratio (TAR) have been employed specifically for humans. For animals other than humans, the Heat Tolerance Test, the R-Value Heat Tolerance Test, the Felting Test, and the Cooling Efficiency Test are widely employed. Two others, the Relative Heat Strain index and the Thermal Index based on the energy balance approach have been used both for humans and animals. Because of the space available only the ET index will be discussed here.

The Effective Temperature index (ET) is the best known scheme for indicating the thermal significance of the environment and is the most widely applied to Africa (Terjung, 1967; Laddel, 1949, 1957; Peel, 1952, 1954, 1961). It was developed by exposing volunteer subjects to different atmospheric conditions of temperature, humidity, and air movement and by asking them to rate their comparative sensations of warmth or coolness. From their reactions, two nomograms were drawn indicating the combinations that produced sensations on normally clothed persons and on persons stripped to the waist.[1] Comfortable values for test subjects vary with their accustomed environment, with values between 68°ET and 78°ET being most comfortable in areas such as the southern United States and tropical Asia (Terjung, 1967).

Terjung (1967) has mapped the ET index in Africa for January and July (Figures 8.1, 8.2). In January, the Effective Temperatures range from below 45°ET in the north to above 85° ET in certain southern regions. There is a series of islands of above 80° ET which are strongly latitudinal from eastern Gambia to southern Mali and to northern Dahomey. Another high ET region extends from southern Chad, through the northern Central African Republic to Lake Rudolf. In southern Africa, pockets of high ET occur in the Zambezi and Limpopo valleys and in the southern Kalahari. The Effective

---

[1] In the first approximation, the ET index may be written in the form ET = 0.4 $(T_d + T_w)$ +4.8 where T_d and T_w are dry and wet bulb temperatures respectively.

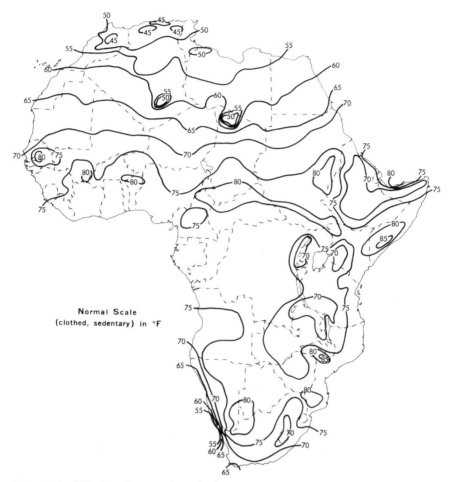

Figure 8.1   Effective Temperatures in January.
Source: Terjung, 1967. Adapted with permission of the *International Journal of Biometerology.*

Temperature map for July shows that small outliers of 80° ET occur in the Moroccan Meseta and inland southern Somalia. The 85° ET is found in large sections surrounding the Djouf Basin, the Bodele Depression, and the Nile Basin. The influence of such highland massifs as the Ahaggar, Plateau du Tademait, and Tibesti Massif is reflected in comparatively low figures. ET values above 85° appear around the Red Sea. Large portions of the southern hemisphere exhibit ET values of less than 75°. The highlands of Ethiopia and East Africa drop below 65°ET, with the coldest temperatures on the continent being experienced in the Drakensberg and high plateau areas of South Africa.

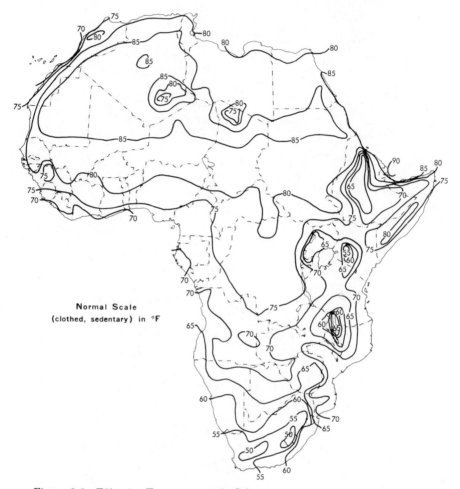

Figure 8.2 Effective Temperatures in July.
Source: Terjung, 1967. Adapted with permission of the International Journal of Biometerology.

PHYSIOLOGICAL CLIMATES

In an attempt to summarize the degree of climatic sensation experienced by humans, Terjung (1966; 1968) has developed a classification that uses the ET index, wet and dry bulb temperatures, and relative humidities. The various zones of sensation are shown in Figure 8.3, and maps for January and July are presented in Figures 8.4 and 8.5.

In January, only a few isolated areas experience *Extremely Hot* climates, while *Sultry* climates occur along the Guinea coast. Hot climates appear in a wide belt latitudinally oriented from Gambia to

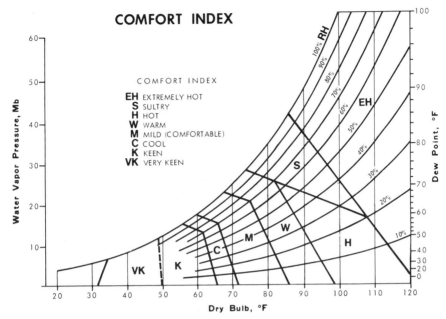

Figure 8.3 Comfort Index. The curved percentage lines represent levels of relative humidity (RH).
Source: Terjung, 1968. Adapted with permission of *Geografiska Annaler,* Stockholm, Sweden.

Somalia with projections into Tanzania and Kenya. They also occur in a compact region in southern Africa. There are four major occurrences of *Warm* climates: an east-west belt in the north; areas adjacent to the Ethiopian highlands; the east-central interior; and a crescent-shaped region in southern Africa. *Mild* climates occur in four major areas: a latitudinally oriented belt in the north; the Ethiopian highlands; the uplands of Kenya, Uganda, and Rwanda; and along the Benguela coast of southwest Africa. Finally, *Cool* climates are observed in an irregularly shaped bend across northern Africa, and *Keen* climates occupy parts of the Maghrib, the Tibesti Mountains, and the Ahaggar.

The northern two-thirds of the continent changes markedly in physioclimatic stress in July. *Extremely Hot* climates occupy the entire western and central Sahara and the Red Sea shore. Just to the south are the *Sultry* climates. *Hot* climates prevail from Rio de Oro to near the Red Sea and in many smaller pockets and a semicircular shaped area from Angola, through Zaire to East Africa. An eastern coastal belt stretches to Lourenço Marques. *Mild* climates appear in the highland areas of East Africa and large areas in southern Africa. *Cool* climates are confined to southern Africa.

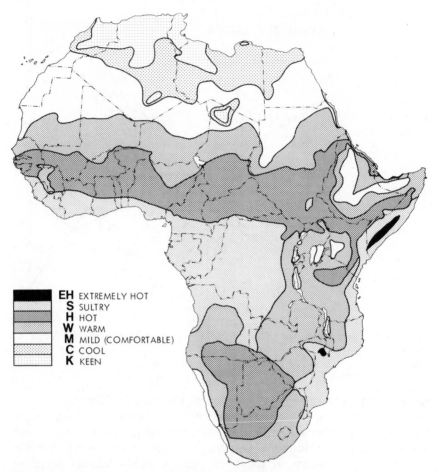

Figure 8.4 Daytime Physiological Climates in January.
Source: Terjung, 1968. Adapted with permission of *Geografiska Annaler*, Stockholm, Sweden.

    African data belie many of the images residents of middle latitudes have about tropical climates. The daytime physiological climates of Africa are quite similar to climates experienced over much of the United States during the summer. The major difference is the duration of warmer climatic types in Africa rather than their qualities. African climates can be experienced *in America* by selecting the right place and season! Marston Bates wrote a book entitled, *Where Winter Never Comes* (1952), an apt description of African climates compared to summer climates familiar to middle-latitude residents. With many African areas lacking extreme winter temperatures, nonclimatic factors intervening between people and climate—such as clothing—are less significant in overall

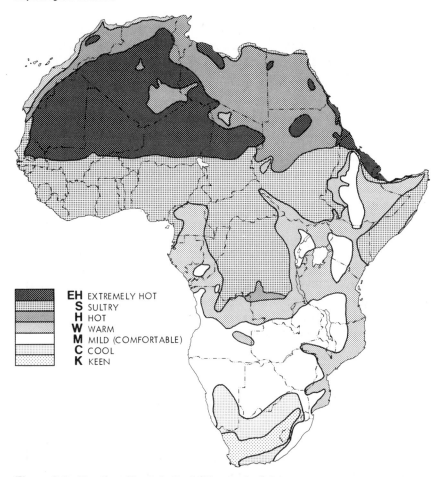

Figure 8.5 Daytime Physiological Climates in July.
Source: Terjung, 1968. Adapted with permission of *Geografiska Annaler,* Stockholm, Sweden.

adaptation in Africa than in middle latitudes, but they still are important for comfort.

One of the most significant nonclimatic factors is the degree of adaptability of organism physiology. This in part depends on the hereditary characteristics of individuals as well as on the environment. Thus, there are various reactions to different environmental stimuli. If removed from one environment to another, it is possible that certain individuals will succeed better than others in adapting to new conditions. The degree of acclimatization is another factor influencing adaptability. Generally, it results in the development of functional and structural changes that positively influence one's ability to live in cold or hot conditions without distress. Acclimatization may result from several causes. For example, the organism may have the ability to decrease the metabolic heat production or there may be facilities for an increase in heat loss such as increasing the sweating ability. Also, the organism may develop an ability to accept physiological discomfort and disturbances, and thus increase its tolerance of heat or cold.

Clothing is another significant nonclimatic factor influencing the degree of adaptability to hot or cold conditions. With clothing, the rate of heat exchange by conduction-convection is reduced. In addition, the rate of evaporation is reduced because the skin experiences virtually still air instead of the movement of ambient air. Thus, with clothing the amount of unevaporated water and consequently the wetness of the skin is increased. This is why it is necessary that in hot environments, interference by clothing be kept at a minimum for comfort. Clothing additionally influences the radiative transfer between the surface and the environment. With clothing, there is a new surface that exchanges radiation with the skin at a rate depending upon the relative temperatures of both the skin and the clothing. If, for example, the skin receives less radiation from the surroundings than from clothing, more heat will be gained by the skin surface from clothing and less outgoing radiation will be lost from the skin surface.

LIVESTOCK RESPONSES

Up to now physiological climates have been discussed from the perspective of human comfort. But livestock comfort also must be considered, given the importance of livestock in many African societies and the need for increasing animal production in order to improve human nutritional conditions. Though much of what already has been said is applicable to livestock, a few special observations are in order. Individual characteristics such as age, body structure, and weight are significant variables in determining livestock adaptability. For example, metabolic heat production is a function of age, with younger animals tending to be more sensitive to heat (Bianca, 1961). The levels of physical activity and productive processes such as lactation in cattle, egg production, and wool growth add to metabolic heat production. Various structural features also affect the heat balance and consequently the degree of sensation to temperature. Animals with relatively large body surface and such structural characteristics as short glossy coat usually are associated with high heat tolerance.

Another factor affecting the degree of climatic sensation is the level of nutrition. For high quality breeds of livestock, it is essential to have adequate nutrition. But, a high level of nutrition is associated with high resting metabolic heat production which in turn depresses heat tolerance. Thus, well fed cattle are usually less heat tolerant than poorly fed cattle. Furthermore, when food is consumed, heat is generated by the various processes involved (prehension, mastication, digestion, absorption, and metabolism of food), which then depress heat tolerance. Food intake can also act as a body temperature regulating mechanism because with a rise in environmental temperature the intake of food is naturally reduced; the reverse occurs at low environmental temperatures.

Many economic, social, and behavioral factors also play a significant part in the tolerance of livestock to heat or cold. Management is important in producing microclimatic environments and consequently in regulating the heat load on an animal. Shelters alter the components of the energy balance. While shelters can produce a shading effect and reduce the incoming heat load, they may adversely restrict effective outgoing radiation since temperatures in unventilated or badly ventilated shelters may be higher than the average outside.

CONCLUSION

Africa's climates and their sensations are highly varied, ranging from hot and humid to cold and dry. Only a few areas, such as along the West Coast and the Red Sea, possess truly uncomfortable conditions, but unfortunately it is these very areas that were popularized in early writings and so have formed the stereotype of Africa as a steaming, sultry place. Actually, over most of the continent, the stress factors are not appreciably different from elsewhere in the world, and, in fact, are less severe than in the midlatitudes with its hot summers and freezing winters. Traditional clothing and shelter have dealt with most discomforts and future technologies should be able to ameliorate others.

9

Climate and Agriculture
in East Africa

PHILIP W. PORTER

In this chapter, we will look at things from the plant's point of
view. For our purposes, the plant is "life's delicate child," the central
character in this study. We hope to show that understanding of
agricultural practices, and of agricultural climates comes only through
examining processes that occur in both the biophysical and social
environment in which people and plants live. Our exploration will try
to do three things: (1) explain the processes operative in the
relations between plants and the climatic milieu in which they grow;
(2) describe and compare the geographical patterns of climatic
elements and agriculture in East Africa, to show how the latter strongly
reflects the former; and (3) illustrate ways in which farmers
understand, adjust, and adapt their crops, techniques, labor schedules,
and agricultural strategies in the light of the requirements both of the
biophysical and social environments.[1]

[1] At times, this chapter refers to the farmer as male: He, him, his fields, his
decisions. This may be justified on the grounds than men in East Africa
dominate farm management. Although women do much of the work and make
many important decisions, still it's a "man's world." Since the object of the
chapter is to relate the farmer's understanding of the environment to his
intervention on behalf of the growing crop, it seems appropriate to describe
these relations on a one-to-one basis: the farmer and the crop.
    I thank Richard H. Skaggs, Department of Geography, University of
Minnesota, for the helpful editorial review of this chapter.

We can do this best by focusing on the features of the climate that affect the well-being of the plant. In the following section we build a picture of the spatial and temporal distribution and variability of the major elements affecting the growth of plants in East Africa. These elements are then combined and interrelated with the life processes of plants by treating them within the framework of the energy and the water budget.

RAINFALL

Water is the most important environmental variable in East Africa. The role of rainfall is paramount in creating differences from place to place in vegetation, soils, disease vectors, agriculture, and livestock keeping. We need to look at rainfall at several temporal and spatial scales to get through the obscurities of averages to the realities of a resource whose next move is unknowable, except in terms of different kinds of probabilities. Rainfall is an exceedingly complex phenomenon. Overall it has a high degree of unpredictability, though there are these regularities:

1. The higher the elevation, the higher the rainfall on slopes exposed to moisture-bearing air streams. It is a common feature of air streams in equatorial regions to be divergent at low levels and convergent aloft, which leads to increased stability and absence of rain. The air at the surface is fed from above and its moisture content is continually diluted by drier air. Rain may occur when such air streams are forced aloft by land masses and, in general, the higher the elevation, the greater the rainfall.
2. In addition to the orographic triggering of rainfall, heating of land surfaces leads to convectional rainfall, particularly during the predictable "high sun" periods in East Africa. Although convectional storms may yield high rainfall amounts in short periods, they are often small in geographic extent, sometimes a matter of a mile or two across.
3. Low pressure systems develop annually well to the north and south of East Africa, in southern Africa in its summer—December-January-February—and in Sudan, Ethiopia, and India in their summer—June-July-August. These systems are fed by air streams which, in travelling across the Indian Ocean, have been warmed and have taken on a heavy burden of moisture. Low level convergence leads to decreased stability and a high probability of precipitation. The air streams that pass over East Africa en route to low pressure sinks are convergent; that is, they are "jostling" one another for space. As they converge, warmer air masses are forced aloft leading to general rain over large areas and during periods of several months.

The several effects of these regularities is to give a unimodal (November-April) rainfall distribution to the bulk of Tanzania, a

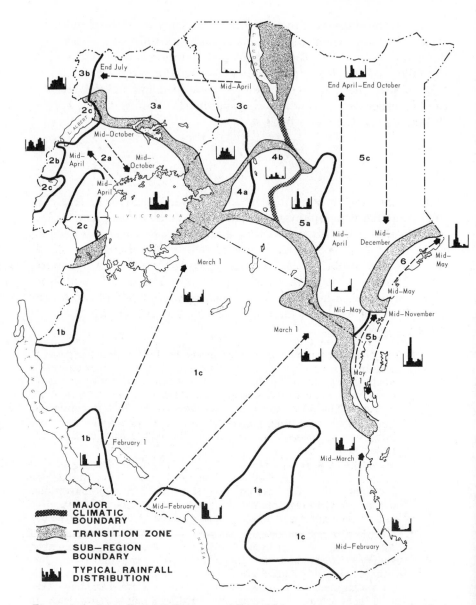

Figure 9.1   Basic Rainfall Regimes of East Africa, based on Harmonic Analysis
Data.
Source: Potts, 1971. Adapted with permission of *The Journal of Tropical
Geography.*

unimodal distribution to northern Uganda and west-central Kenya
(April-November), and a complex bimodal distribution to the most
populous parts of Uganda and Kenya between Nairobi and Mombasa
(Figure 9.1). The regularity in the transformation from unimodal to

Main Characteristics of Major Rainfall Regimes in East Africa

Region	Type of Distribution	Temporal Position of Maximum	Mean Annual Rainfall (mm)	Amplitude of Dominant Harmonic (mm)
1a	Unimodal	Mid-February-Early March	1000-2000+	100-190
1b		Early February	1000-1400	80-140
1c		Mid-February-March	>1000	50-110
2a	Bimodal	Mid-April/Mid-October	1000-1600+	40-70
2b		Mid-April/mid-October	>1400	50-60
2c		Mid-April/Mid-October	>1000	>50
3a	Unimodal	Late June	1000-1600	50-80
3b		Late July	>1200+	40-70
3c		Mid-April/Mid-June	<1000	<50
4a	Trimodal	April/August/November	>1000	25-30
4b	Trimodal	April/August/November	<1000	60-100
5a	Bimodal	Mid-April/Mid-October	1000-2000	60-100
5b		Mid-May/Mid-November	800-1200+	50-80
5c		Late April/Late October in north; Mid-April/Mid-December in south	<800	<50
6	Unimodal	Mid-May	800-1000	60-90

bimodal regimes is related to latitude and high sun period. At the equator there are two times a year when the sun stands overhead, March 21 and September 21. As one moves north or south, the dates of overhead sun approach one another, converging on June 21 (or December 22) when at $23\frac{1}{2}°$ north (or south) latitude the sun stands overhead at noon. This annual march of the sun results in bimodal and unimodal curves for radiation as well as in rainfall.

A map that attempts to display the distribution of one and two peak rainfall patterns is shown in Figure 9.1, based on an analysis by Allan Potts (1972). He used a curve-fitting device called *harmonic analysis* to make a best fit of rainfall regimes. This technique does well for the assuredly unimodal regimes and for those bimodal regimes whose peaks are about six months apart; but where the peaks have migrated toward one another to any appreciable extent, the pattern, though still effectively bimodal from an agricultural point of view, may be classified in some other way. Nonetheless, this map gives us a first look at the timing aspect of the rainfall resource in East Africa.

Figures 9.2 and 9.3 display the *amounts* of rainfall the farmers have to work with, using two sets of expectations. Figure 9.2 shows average annual rainfall in East Africa, which is an approximate "50-50" rainfall probability; about half the years will be wetter and half the years drier. A histogram of annual rainfalls will show the pattern to be positively skewed, giving more years with values below the mean than above it. For example, Dwa Plantations in Kenya shows 29 years below and 24 years above the mean, and an uneven distribution of rainfall totals. Ten years are in the 300-400 mm and in the 500-600 mm ranges, but only three years in the 400-500 mm (millimeter) range. The skewness becomes even more marked when one looks at individual months on the rainfall dispersion diagram for Dwa Plantations (Figure 9.4). The bimodal distribution of the rain is clear, with the "grass rains" in November somewhat more reliable than the second rains which normally peak in April.

It makes more sense for farmers to plan agriculture around conditions they can be sure of attaining 80 percent of the time (which one can think of as four out of five years in the long run) rather than only about 50 percent of the time. Further, it should be obvious that the rainfall expectation during the agriculturally significant period is likely to be a more useful time unit than the entire year. However, at present we have probability maps only for annual values. Figure 9.3 shows the amount of annual rainfall which will be exceeded 80 percent of the time. The meaning of these rainfall patterns to the farmers has to be interpreted in the light of how much moisture crops need in their season to meet the demands of evapotranspiration (water need), and it is clear that 300 mm (or

Figure 9.2 Average Annual Rainfall.
Source: Tomsett, 1969.

12 in.) concentrated in one three-month span may be useful whereas 400 mm (or 16 in.) shared in two separate rainfall seasons, as in Dwa Plantations, may not be useful.

With regard to the variability of rainfall, nature has still another trick up its sleeve; the amount of rain that comes in one month is no

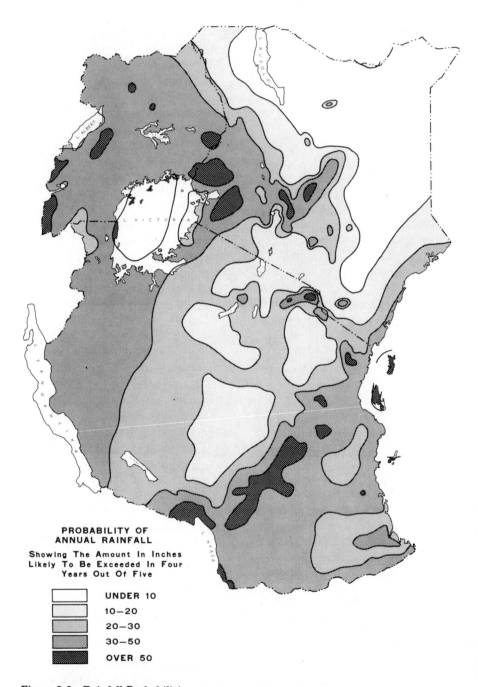

Figure 9.3   Rainfall Probabilities.
Source: Morgan, 1972. Adapted with permission of Oxford University Press, Eastern
Africa Branch. 118

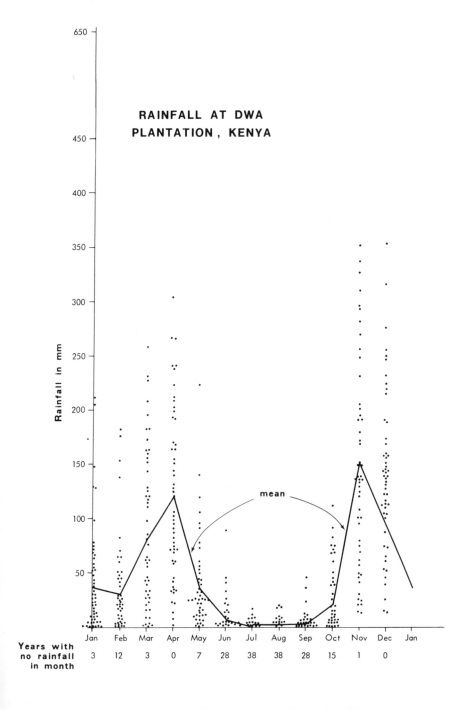

RAINFALL AT DWA
PLANTATION , KENYA

	Jan	Feb	Mar	Apr	May	Jun	Jul	Aug	Sep	Oct	Nov	Dec	Jan
Years with no rainfall in month	3	12	3	0	7	28	38	38	28	15	1	0	

Figure 9.4 Dispersion Diagram. Rainfall at Dwa Plantation, Kenya.

guide to the amount of rain that will come in the next month. Thus farmers face a truly unknowable resource that is ambiguous, uncertain, and inscrutable. As we will see, their planning must take into account this fact of agricultural life. There are places in East Africa where the rainfall is ample, reliable, and even partly predictable from month to month, but by and large rainfall is a puzzle to East African farmers.

Of all the climatic aspects that trouble farmers in East Africa, the variability in the amounts of rainfall and when the rain comes are the two most serious. The rainfall dispersion diagram (Figure 9.4) suggests this, but let us look at it another way, by comparing evapotranspiration (about which we will say more later) with water availability. Over a run of 53 years at Dwa Plantations, there were only 51 *months* when rainfall exceeded evapotranspiration! Overall, in 28 years the first rains (November) failed; in 37 years the second rains (April) failed. In 18 of 53 years both rains failed; at least five times the rains failed two years running; and they failed twice for three consecutive years. It is generally true that the lower the rainfall, the greater the variability it exhibits; and thus another regularity in the variations of climatic elements can be added to those we have considered earlier. In Dwa Plantations we are looking at a situation close to the margins of possible agriculture.

ENERGY AND MOISTURE DEMAND

Solar energy is the basis for life. Indeed, life can be defined as a "delaying mechanism" against the long-term trend of the universe toward increasing entropy. "[L]ife postpones the effect of this basic law using the stream of sunlight to build highly complex assemblages of proteins, carbohydrates, lipids and other biological molecules" (Gates, 1971:89). In this section we consider thermal energy as it relates to temperature and evaporation, and light energy as it relates to photosynthesis.

Temperatures are conservative and highly predictable every-where in East Africa. Temperatures are so regular that they may be predicted within about $2°C$. For mean maximum temperature the equation used is $T(°C) = 33.9 - 1.7A$, where A is altitude in thousands of feet. Thus at sea level, mean maximum temperatures are $33.9°C$; at 1,000 ft., $31.2°C$., and so forth. For mean minimum temperatures the equation used is $T(°C) = 24.4 - 2.1A$, where A is again altitude in thousands of feet.[2]

[2] The respective equations in metric units are:
$T(°C) = 33.9 - 5.6A'$ (mean maximum)
$T(°C) = 24.4 - 6.9A'$ (mean minimum)
where A' = altitude in thousands of meters.

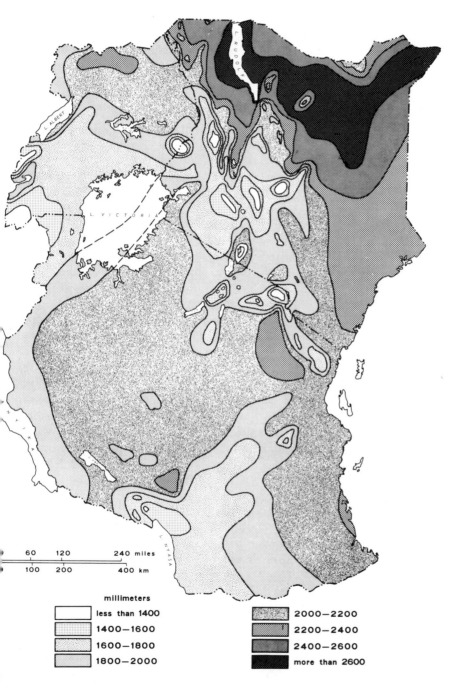

Figure 9.5   Annual Potential Open Water Evaporation (Penman Estimate).
Source: Dagg, Woodhead, and Rijks, 1970.

Temperatures do not vary much even from month to month, though the greater the latitude, the greater the variation in mean temperatures between warmest and coolest month. Further, the diurnal range varies more at higher elevations. As we will see, this has important agricultural consequences. In East Africa, altitudinal and latitudinal variations in means, maxima, minima, and range on daily, monthly, and annual bases are highly predictable. Year to year variations in these values are quite small. Except for microclimatological purposes, the researcher in East Africa can forget thermometers!

The hidden twin of sensible heat, or temperature, is latent heat, or evaporation. The relationships of evaporation and rainfall are the main determinants of the kinds of plants that can grow in an area. Roughly we can think of these terms as water need and water supply. Radiation income is measured in gram calories/cm^2 (or langleys). The amount 590 gm cal/cm^2 is sufficient to convert one cubic centimeter of water from a liquid to a vapor state. This process of vaporization, which includes both transpiration from plant (and animal) surfaces and evaporation from water and land surfaces, is our standard measure of moisture moving in a particular part of the hydrologic cycle—moisture moving from the ground and plant surface of the earth into the atmosphere. It is exceedingly useful that radiant energy can be expressed as an equivalent amount of vaporized water for it allows us to look at energy as a kind of reverse rainfall. Moisture income and outgo are expressed in the same units—millimeters or inches of water. As we will see, it is useful to view energy income as a moisture demand, and to compare it with rainfall income as a moisture supply. The pattern of radiation income sets up a demand for water which varies considerably in East Africa. Figure 9.5 shows the pattern of potential evaporation. The annual potential open water surface evaporation (E_O) varies largely with elevation. A high of 2,700 mm (106 in.) is reached in northeastern Kenya. Tanzania averages 2,000-2,200 mm/yr (79-87 in.). The southern half of Uganda and much of the Kenya Highlands have a general range of 1,600-2,000 mm/yr (63-79 in.). Such cool, highland areas as Mt. Kenya, Mt. Elgon, the Aberdares, Mau Summit, Kigezi, Mt. Kilimanjaro, Oldeani, and Tukuyu have annual evaporation levels of less than 1,400 mm (55 in.).

The transpiration of water through leaf pores, or stomata, is the way internal temperatures of plants are regulated. When water is freely available, the rate of transpiration is controlled by the rate of incoming radiation. However, if root and stem systems cannot transport moisture to the leaf at a rate equal to the potential transpiration rate, or if water from the soil becomes a limiting factor, the stomata will close, cells will collapse, and the wilting point will be reached. The importance of these facts is that plants themselves do not control their growth or the rate of transpiration of moisture to the atmosphere; they are the passive instruments of transpiration whose rate, when water is nonlimiting, is a direct function of radiation.

The radiation income can be expressed as potential evaporation (E_O, open water surface evaporation). The estimate of E_O which has been found most satisfactory in East Africa is that by Penman (1948, 1963). His model is derived from reasonable physical principles, using data on wind speed, ambient temperatures, absolute humidity, and radiation as well as a number of empirical constants. It consists basically of three terms: (1) incoming short-wave radiation; (2) outgoing long-wave radiation; and (3) wind and saturation deficit, the balance of which gives the potential evaporation. The third term considers the steepness of gradient in humidity of the air around the leaf, and the amount of energy advected to a place from adjacent areas. This can have a major effect on irrigated fields lying in the path of winds coming from semiarid areas.

ENERGY AND PRODUCTIVITY

Photosynthesis is the process in which chlorophyll uses the visible light to produce carbohydrate out of water and carbon dioxide. The geographic pattern of photosynthesis in East Africa results partly from interactions with other climatic regularities we have been discussing, for the amount of photosynthesis at a place is a result environmentally of how much radiation reaches the ground [which is governed by day length, sun angle, cloud cover, aspect (slope exposure), and slope], and the thermal regime. Although the fundamental patterns of rainfall and inherent soil quality are more important determinants of agriculture, the pattern of potential photosynthesis cannot be taken as given, despite the common belief that in the tropics, temperatures provide favorable, nonlimiting conditions for plant growth.

The plant is a living machine. It is, in fact, a small factory. In economic terms we can view energy, water, carbon dioxide, and various materials as *inputs*—the raw materials brought to the factory. The manufacturing process is photosynthesis—a process in which chlorophyll uses the visible light to produce carbohydrate out of water and carbon dioxide. The *output* is carbohydrate which can be measured in various ways: as $g/m^2/day$ (the rate at which a plant or an area of plants assimilates the products of photosynthesis); as accumulated dry-matter production (usually the above-ground weight of the plant); or as yields in quintals/hectare or lb/acre of the economically valuable part of the plant. At every moment in a plant's life the condition of the plant and the influences of the environment surrounding the plant affect the output.

The gross photosynthesis of an area in crop can be estimated if one takes into account the following: total daily light or radiation intensity; photochemical resistance; resistance in the plant tissue to the diffusion of carbon dioxide; the density of foliage; the fraction of light not intercepted by a given leaf layer which thus penetrates to the lower layers; the distribution of light within the canopy; spectral changes in the light after it passes through a leaf; day length; and variations through the day in radiation intensity. That is a formidable list, but the necessary facts have been determined for many crops, and data which vary geographically (radiation and day length) are known for enough places in East Africa to permit gross photosynthesis to be mapped. Monteith (1965) has developed a physically and botanically reasoned means of estimating gross photosynthesis. His model was used to estimate daily gross photosynthesis in mature maize for East Africa.

But a plant never accumulates all of its gross photosynthesis because some photosynthates are consumed by plant respiration. Respiration is the process whereby plants absorb oxygen from the air and release carbon dioxide. In respiration, plants burn up material to do the work. Whereas photosynthesis in a plant occurs in the leaves during daylight, respiration goes on at all times, and involves leaves, stems, and other parts of the plant. The higher the ambient temperature, the greater the respiration of the plant, up to leaf temperatures of about $45°C$. Respiration rates for different plants vary, but in all cases the relationship is positive—higher air temperatures result in higher respiration rates. Warm daytime temperatures correlate positively with photosynthetic rates; warm nighttime temperatures imply greater use of photosynthates for respiration. Thus the optimal conditions for potential (or net) photosynthesis (gross photosynthesis less the amount lost to respiration) are cool nighttime temperatures and warm daytime temperatures. In tropical areas, such temperatures are characteristic of the highlands. The amount of gross photosynthesis lost to respiration varies from around 50-60 percent at the coast to perhaps only 25 percent at elevations of 2,450 m (8,000 ft.) in the coolest month.

For illustrating contrasted East African situations, we have chosen February and August (Figures 9.6 and 9.7). The essential fact to be noted on both maps is the higher rates of potential photosynthesis in the highland areas, and the low rates in the persistently warm lowlands along the coast in Tanzania and Kenya, and to a lesser extent along the axis of the western rift valley, and in dry, hot northeastern Kenya. The highland-lowland contrast in rates of potential photosynthesis persists month after month throughout the year, though with higher potential photosynthesis rates occupying two core areas—the Kenya Highlands and the Tanzanian Southern Highlands—from which salients spread out to embrace adjacent areas of highland country, especially in interior Tanzania during the dry season.

February features much rain in southern Tanzania and very little in Kenya and Uganda, and potential photosynthesis, much affected by cloud cover, reflects this fact. February is a month of harvest in the bimodal rainfall parts of southeastern Kenya, and crops are in their vegetative growth stage in southern Tanzania, where planting begins mainly in December. The map for August shows higher rates of photosynthesis in central and southern Tanzania, especially in the highlands, where because of longer growing seasons and moisture stored in the soil some crops are still being harvested. In most places in southern Tanzania, however, crops have been harvested by then. But in Uganda and west-central Kenya, the harvest is in full swing in August, a time of high rainfall and considerably lower rates of potential photosynthesis compared with dry season months.

The greater potential photosynthesis of the highlands gives these areas a built-in potential, not dissimilar to the environmental advantage of mid-latitude areas over the tropics, though the effects are brought about mainly by differences in cloud cover and temperature rather than day length (Chang, 1968). This higher potential should be, and is, reflected in higher yields at these elevations. Higher yields are also obtained because plants after flowering tend to take longer to reach physiological maturity than in warmer, lower areas. Thus, a given crop will be filling seed at a higher rate for more days in the highlands than it will in the lowlands. The advantage, which these two attributes of potential photosynthesis combine to give, makes highlands potentially nearly twice as productive as lowlands for some grain varieties. Indeed, one of the tasks of crop-breeding programs is to create hybrids and composites that do well in a particular environment. Table 9.1 shows how several of the hybrid maize varieties have performed in the East African Maize Variety Trials. From this table we can note two things: (1) the increase in yields with elevation; and (2) that certain crops do best at a given altitude. SR52 has been especially bred for middle and low elevations and short rainfall seasons; H632 has been especially bred for the upper parts of middle elevations; and H611C for high elevations. Each does best in its optimal altitude range.

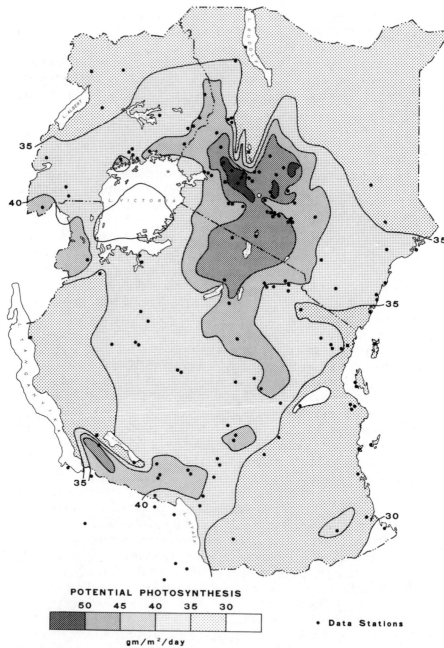

POTENTIAL PHOTOSYNTHESIS

50   45   40   35   30

gm/m²/day

• Data Stations

Figure 9.6   Potential Photosynthesis—February.

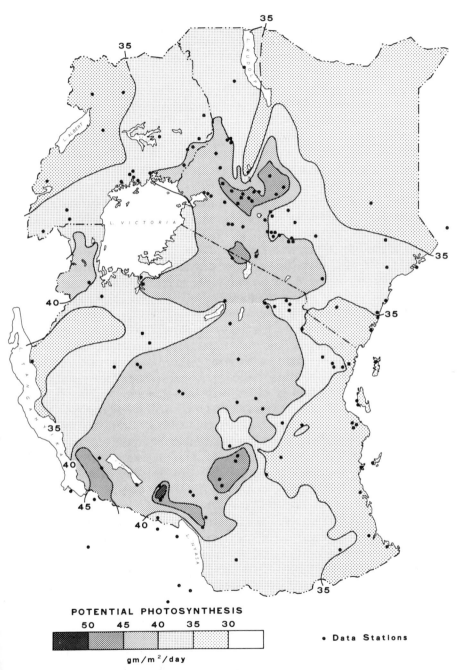

POTENTIAL PHOTOSYNTHESIS

| 50 | 45 | 40 | 35 | 30 |

gm/m²/day

● Data Stations

Figure 9.7 Potential Photosynthesis—August.

TABLE 9.1   East   African   Maize   Variety   Trial   Yields   at   Different
Elevation Ranges (in 100 kg/ha)

Elevation Range	H611C	H613B	H632	H511	SR52
0-850 meters	33.8	29.3	37.3	33.9	46.2
900-1,600 m	45.3	40.4	48.4	42.4	48.7
Over 1,650 m	71.1	69.6	58.3	51.1	53.1

MOISTURE AND ENERGY—CROP WATER NEED

It has long been known that plants transpire at different rates during different parts of their season. When plants are very young and small and a field consists mostly of dry, bare soil, moisture is transpired (and evaporated) to the atmosphere at a very low rate. As the plants gain in size and the surface area of the leaf increases, the rate of transpiration increases. When a plant reaches maximum size and vigor it may transpire at a rate well above E_O. This is caused partly by the geometry of the transpiring surface, its roughness, and partly by the greater areas of transpiring surface as compared to the area of ground underneath. The leaf-area index is a measure of this relationship.

It is common for fields with young plants to have an E_t/E_O (E_t = plant transpiration) ratio of 0.50. This ratio increases through a season as the plant reaches full vegetative vigor and declines in the latter part of the season when leaves become senescent and growth is concentrated in seed or fruit (Wangati, 1969). Table 9.2 gives a summary of values of E_t/E_O for a number of annual crop/season combinations as well as for certain perennial crops. The season lengths needed to bring an annual crop to maturity in East Africa tend to vary with altitude and radiation income, if there is no prior limitation because of water availability.

To be sure that we have clearly in mind the relationship between E_t/E_O and E_O as an expression of the moisture demand placed by the environment on the plant, consider Table 9.3. The distribution of the rainfall will, of course, have a lot to do with the timing of the season, but the fact remains that if a crop takes the same amount of time to mature (6 months, say), the water requirements of the crop started in May would be 8 percent less than the water requirements of the crop started in July. Against this must be balanced the likely higher rate of potential photosynthesis in the months with a higher radiation income. Figure 9.8 illustrates the potential trade-off between water requirement and potential yield, and contrasts a coastal and a highland station. The months actually used

TABLE 9.2 E_t/E_o Values for Crops in Different Months of Their Season

Crop	Month 1	2	3	4	5	6	7
Bananas	0.40	0.50	0.60	0.70	0.80	0.95	0.95
Beans	0.75	0.90	1.25	1.35	0.85	0.60	
Bulrush Millet	0.50	0.90	1.00	0.60			
Cassava	0.50	0.70	0.70	0.70	0.70	0.70	0.70
Finger Millet	0.50	0.80	1.00	1.00	0.70	0.50	
Groundnuts	0.50	0.80	0.90	0.90			
Maize	0.50	0.90	1.00	1.20	0.80	0.50	
Rice	0.65	1.30	1.30	1.30	1.30		
Sesame	0.45	0.70	0.90	1.10			
Sorghum	0.50	0.80	1.00	1.20	0.50		
Soybeans	0.55	1.05	1.10	1.10			
Sweet Potatoes	0.50	0.70	0.70	0.70			
Selected Cash Crop:							
Cotton (210 days)	0.55	0.70	0.85	0.95	0.65	0.55	
Sugar Cane	0.50	0.75	0.95	1.20	1.10	1.10	1.10
	1.10	1.10	1.10	1.10	1.10	1.10	1.10
	0.50	0.50	0.50*	0.70	1.10	1.10	1.10
	1.10	1.00	1.00	1.00	1.00	1.00	1.00
	1.00	1.00	1.00	1.50	ratoon harvest		
	* = harvest						
Tea (mature)	40 days after pruning:	0.00					
	40 to 70 days after:	0.50					
	thereafter:	0.85					

Source: Partly after D. R. Rijks, personal communication.

for crops in Mbeya are as shown by the asterisks. The most efficient months from a moisture-saving photosynthesis-adding standpoint are May, June and July—a happy combination. Ngomeni, in addition to a lower general level of potential photosynthesis, uses the lower half of the arc of months from mid-March through July (sometimes into August).

We have looked at a number of separate aspects of energy and rainfall as they affect plants. In the real world, of course, they act together. The natural vegetation "understands" the complex seasonal

TABLE 9.3 Moisture Requirements for Crops Planted Two Months Apart

Month:	May	June	July	Aug.	Sept.	Oct.	Nov.	Dec.	Total
E_o in mm	116	115	127	147	173	183	164	140	
E_t/E_o	0.50	0.80	1.00	1.20	0.75	0.50	—	—	
Water need	58	92	127	176	130	92	—	—	675
E_t/E_o	—	—	0.50	0.80	1.00	1.20	0.75	0.50	
Water need	—	—	64	118	130	220	123	70	735

and longer term variability in heat, moisture, and sunlight. The plant's presence in the environment is proof of that. The vegetation is an unparalleled climatic integrating instrument, which is why ecologists use it so extensively as a means of environmental assessment and classification.

GEOGRAPHIC PATTERN OF CROPS

We have explored some of the major climate-plant relationships and have seen how they are distributed in East Africa. We have also gained some idea of how they vary through the year and from one year to another. The ensemble of relationships is truly the environment of the plant. As it happens some plants are adapted to a variety of combinations of the climatic attributes we have been discussing. Maize probably has the widest range as a rain-fed crop, whereas a crop such as bananas has a highly restricted range as to where it can be effectively grown without special measures to

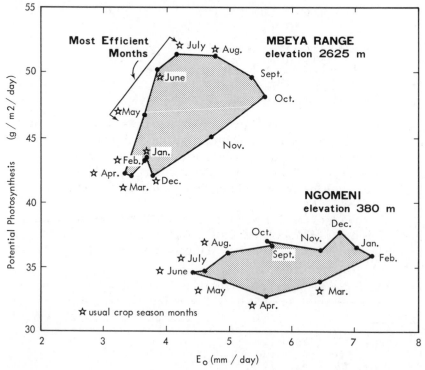

Figure 9.8 Contrasts in Potential Photosynthesis and Evaporation between Highlands and Lowlands.

provide water. The overall pattern of crops in East Africa is best visualized as an altitudinal transect.

At high elevations, over 2,000 meters (6,500 ft) where it is generally wet and relatively cool, one finds English (or white) potatoes and wheat, with finger millet and maize present, but less successful. From 1,250-2,000 m (4,000-6,500 ft) finger millet and maize are the best suited crops, with beans a common legume. Cassava and sweet potatoes, as well as bananas (if rainfall conditions are favorable) do well in this zone. As one moves to lower elevations, where the climatic regime becomes warmer, rainfall has greater variability, and the absolute amount of rain is less, maize and sweet potatoes, though still important crops, are increasingly ousted by sorghum, bulrush millet, pigeon peas, Bambara nuts, castor seeds, cowpeas, and cassava. Oil crops, such as sesame, sunflower, and groundnuts, occupy the better parts of these subhumid and semiarid areas. In many favored valley bottoms, rice assumes importance as a staple. Although livestock numbers per unit area decrease with lower rainfall, the importance of livestock in the economy of the people increases. In the semiarid areas of East Africa, where tsetse have not infested the vegetation, people rely heavily on the products of stock; and pastoralism, indeed, allows people to exploit environments from which crops are altogether excluded.

BEHAVIORAL STRATEGIES TO COPE WITH RISK

We can think of farmers as vegetation managers. In their crop domestication, plant breeding, use of fire, and replacing an area of forest or bush with a crop of their own choosing, they are upsetting an "equilibrium" established by nature, and substituting one of their own. Even herding livestock in an area is a form of vegetation management. If the farmers' understanding of the climate, soils, and other variables which make up their environment is good, the system may last indefinitely and continue to be productive. If they do not understand the climatic-soil-plant relationships, the environmental base may deteriorate—forcing them to move or to adopt a different way of using the environment.

Farmers generally have a remarkable understanding of their environment and ways to hedge their bets against a nature whose events are, as we have seen, unpredictable. There are many kinds of agricultural risks, some more related to climate than others. We will not consider agricultural vermin, like bush pigs, monkeys, baboons, and rats, or the elephants, buffaloes, hippos, and other game for which East Africa is famous. These, together with birds and insect pests, are threats to crops both while growing and after harvest when the crop is in storage (Mascarenhas, 1971). We concentrate here on the climatic hazards we have described in the first part of this chapter. What do farmers do to protect their plants; what are their methods of husbandry?

Who are the East African farmers? They cover a wide range of types from farmers whose operations are highly mechanized, such as the wheat farmers of Mbulu and Oldeani with their tractors, combines, and huge acreages, to those growing only subsistence crops and keeping a few goats. Most East African farmers combine crops for home consumption with crops for sale, sometimes the staple food itself—maize, rice, bananas, sometimes purely for cash income —cotton, coffee, tobacco, pyrethrum, cardamom, cashew nuts, and tea. Although much of what we discuss relates to food crops used for local consumption, the reader should not think of East African farmers as subsistence farmers. By and large they are not. They are tied in a variety of ways into local, regional, and international markets. With this qualification in mind, we turn to the question of behavioral strategies to cope with risk.

The first and almost self-evident method by which farmers protect themselves from environmental risk is selecting crops which are adapted to the conditions of the locality. Assume that the water requirements in the agriculturally significant period are 250 mm or more, 250 being the minimum amount at which crops just survive and give a small yield. Farmers would want to select a better than 50:50 probability of getting the rainfall needed; they might be able to live with an 80:20 or 90:10 probability of getting this minimum amount.

This leads to another very important feature of the agricultural system of subsistence farming—the concept of the normal surplus. The "normal surplus" is the phrase used by William Allan to describe the feature of overproduction in subsistence farming (Allan, 1965). There is a tendency, especially in areas of variable rainfall, for yields to be positively correlated with the amount of rain which falls in the season, one reason being that when soil moisture is exhausted, assimilation ceases, and the longer the rains carry on, the longer the period of assimilation in seed. Let us say that for a family of five, the farmer must ensure a production of 9 quintals of grain to meet family annual food needs and to supply next year's seed. In a poor year when the bare minimum of rainfall (250 mm) is achieved let us say that yields are only 2.25 quintals/hectare [about 1 bag (200 lb)/acre]. Farmers will regularly plant 4 hectares to ensure that the yield will be at least 9 quintals. But most seasons have more than 250 mm of rainfall and thus yields will usually be more than 9 quintals.

If, for sake of illustration, yields were 4.5 q/ha when the rainfall was 350 mm and 9.0 q/ha when the rainfall was 450 mm, much of the time the farmers would produce more than twice as much as needed, and in the long run once every 20 years they would produce 4 times more than their familys' need.

Something very like this is found in many African societies. The extra food produced is used in a number of ways, many of them social or economic rather than nutritional in object. Food is sold on local and national markets whenever possible. Much grain is converted into beer. Beer is commonly the reward at the end of work parties, and one can readily imagine the consequences on farm size and quality of husbandry in a current season if the farmer cannot afford, because of grain shortages from the previous season, to host such work parties. Food is used to meet social obligations, as political gifts, and simply to show hospitality. In western economic terms a planting strategy that results in normal overproduction, enabling farmers to produce enough food in all but the very worst years, is wasteful. The element of waste is built into any subsistence system using the concept of the normal surplus. The waste is both environmental and social. The land is overused. That is, if each farmer could get by with only 2 hectares each year, the land would get twice as much rest through fallow, thus improving its fertility. The labor invested in proportion to yield used is wasted. In good years harvesting may be indifferent, and food may be left to rot or be eaten by insects and birds, both in the field and the granary. Nonetheless, a normal surplus strategy makes excellent sense to farm families who must rely on their own efforts to provide their annual needs.

Choice of crops and planting an area with a view to creating a normal surplus are two ways to buffer the vagaries of nature. Three further ways involve: (1) care in the timing of agricultural activities; (2) mixing crops within fields; and (3) spacing fields far from one another. All are tactics to cope with variable rainfall. A good example of farmer behavior to cope with problems of drought hazard is found in Kilungu, Kenya, half a mile from Dwa Plantations, whose uncertain environment was discussed earlier. The bimodal, highly uncertain rainfall of Kilungu poses difficult problems for farmers. One practice is to plant new crops for the second rains (March-June) among unharvested crops planted earlier in the "grass rains" (November-January). Timing is a key element in agriculture, and it has been shown that to plant even a week late in this part of Kenya results in losses of potential harvest of 30-40 percent (Dowker, 1964).

The interplanting of crops and the complex schedule of

planting, harvesting, and planting for a second season give the field an appearance of chaos, but there are many ingenious and adaptive elements designed to ensure a moisture supply and a protective environment for the crops. The points listed below are not necessarily those made by the people of Kilungu, though they cite many of them; some of the elements have effects observed by plant physiologists and agroclimatologists. Nonetheless, these scheduling and interplanting practices work, and they are used by the people of Kilungu. First, visualize the sequence. A farmer plants maize, beans, cowpeas, sorghum, groundnuts, bulrush millet, red millet, cassava, pumpkins, calabashes and pigeon peas all mixed together in one large field. The crops come up all together in a riotous profusion of vines, leaves and stems. Weeds have no chance. The phosphorus flush in the soil that comes with the first rains is taken advantage of by these crops. Crops, such as maize, which might be rather indolent about putting down roots and strong tillers in a soil well supplied with moisture, have to compete with the other plants, and thus they put down roots to a depth of several feet. These deeper roots come into play later on in the season. Although the rate of moisture use of all these crops planted together is high, it occurs at the one time of the season when there is likely to be enough moisture available. Further, the interplanting provides a good continuous canopy within which photosynthesis can proceed. Since tropical areas have a relatively uniform radiation income all year around, a continuous leaf canopy, one with a moderate to high leaf-area index, is the most efficient user of radiant energy for photosynthesis (Chang, 1968). Both the farmer's interplanted field and the full-canopied, sometimes multi-storied, natural vegetation of many tropical ecosystems show adaptation to the uniformities of radiation in the tropics (Geertz, 1963).

After about seven or eight weeks some of the crops are harvested. Beans may be harvested as green vegetables. As the season progresses the millet is harvested; beans harvested for seed are taken and the vines pulled up. The number of plants per square meter of soil begins to decline and only crops requiring a longer time to mature are left. The bare weedless soil between the plants is dry, which forms a barrier to the movement of moisture to the surface. Evapotranspiration thus is reduced. The sparse plant population remaining is able to tap moisture from a larger volume of soil without competition from adjacent plants. This moisture, combined with the lesser amounts of rain which come at the end of the "grass rains," many times is sufficient to bring the maize and the longer growing millets to harvest. The plants also provide some shade for crops set out to get a start on the main rains. The thick mat of plant cover in the first weeks of the "grass rains" and the second rains also serve to hold the soil. There is also the adaptive fact that if the rains do give out, some crops will have been harvested and the agricultural effort will not have been a total loss. Another fact is that interplanting reduces the amount of work considerably by eliminating the need to weed, which often is the most serious impediment to agriculture and the management of larger acreages.

In the Kilungu area, farmers characteristically place fields far from one another. This dispersal of fields has the effect of ensuring that if the rains fail in one area, the farming effort for that season will not necessarily be a total loss. Storms, as we have seen, are often very small; and one good rain or its absence can make or break the crops in a particular field. Field dispersal is a form of insurance.

A good example of the way an East African people has evaluated the potentialities of the proximity of several different kinds of environment, and turned them to good account, is provided by the Pokot of west-central Kenya (Porter, 1965). Many of the Pokot live on the flanks of the rift valley where elevations range from 1,000 m on the rift floor to 3,350 m at the crest of the Cherangani Range. The Pokot live at all elevations in this transect, and what is more, a given Pokot family is likely to live in several zones, spanning a range of over 1000 m. The Pokot have words to describe different altitudinal zones (Figure 9.9). Two words divide the highlands (*masob*—cold country) from the lowlands (*keog'h*—hot country) and each is further subdivided. Upper masob becomes *tourku*, and *keog'h* divides into *kamass*—the lower steep slopes, and *touh*—the lower valley floor at the base of the *kamass*. Settlement is either in *kamass* or *masob*, but a family will likely have maize and finger millet fields in *masob*, *kamass* and *touh*. Some farmers of *masob* even grow English potatoes in the *tourku* zone.

The Pokot political and economic division of the land is designed to place different environments within the control of the community, and the individual family (Conant, 1965). The *korok* is a named political territory, which runs from the trunk stream flowing across the valley floor (*touh*) upslope to the forest in *tourku*, thus encompassing all four Pokot ecological zones. The side boundaries of the *korok* are normally streams, though sometimes a hillspur is used. A family whose houses are in *masob* would typically have four fields: a small irrigated maize field in *touh*, a larger finger millet field in *kamass*, and in *masob* itself, two fields—one of maize and one of finger millet, either of which might be irrigated. Figure 9.10 shows this arrangement according to altitudinal zones, and the way work is distributed over a nine month period with about nine separate planting, weeding, and harvesting times. Although it takes

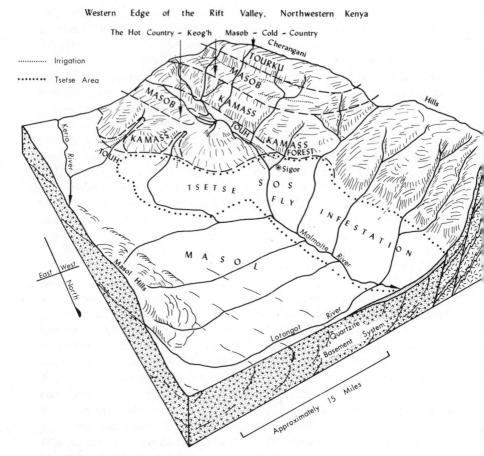

Figure 9.9 Pokot Environment. Western edge of the Rift Valley, northwestern Kenya. Keog'h-The Hot Country; Masob-Cold Country.

people up and down the mountain, this arrangement does distribute the work so that there is no intolerable load in any month. The timing of planting is consciously designed to make the best use of sun and rain. By a system of irrigation furrows, built long ago by the indigenous people, the Pokot have a supplemental source of water that can be brought into use anytime. It is used especially toward the end of the agricultural season as the rains begin to decrease.

The *kokwa*, a local council, is the decision-making body of the *korok*, in agricultural as well as other social matters. At its frequent meetings, the people discuss questions of when to repair and open irrigation furrows, who will use irrigation water on a given day and for how long. The *kokwa*, or smaller groups, decide where to open up new fields. Fields are worked as large communal units, though

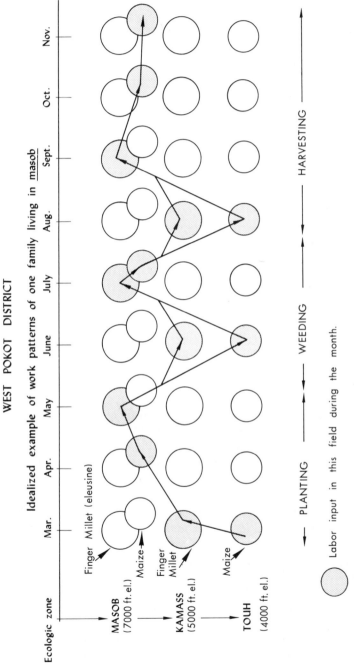

PLANTING, WEEDING, HARVESTING CYCLE IN TAMKAL VALLEY

WEST POKOT DISTRICT

Idealized example of work patterns of one family living in masob

Figure 9.10 Planting, Weeding, Harvesting Cycle in Tamkal Valley, West Potok District.

each wife has within the field one or more strips of land oriented with the slope which she plants, weeds, and harvests. Fields are used for several years and then allowed to fallow, during which bush is reestablished. Bush clearing and burning, fencing, and guarding are communal work.

In addition to using multiple environments within the *korok*, the Pokot take advantage of the proximity of tsetse-free plains of nearby *Masol* for livestock keeping. A mutually beneficial regional specialization and trade system has arisen wherein meat, milk, and hides are produced in *Masol* and traded for grain and other foods from the hills.

Space does not permit a detailed explanation of many other ways farmers try to adapt their livelihood to the possibilities which lie in the environment. We can, however, cite some of the more important ones. Livestock keeping is probably most important. Here is a resource that can be moved, traded, and sold. It can use environments not suitable for crops. It breeds fast in good years, but is a comparatively volatile form of wealth and source of food. Since stock are susceptible to disease, drought, and theft, it is common practice for farmers or herders to split up the herds, through an often complicated series of livestock exchanges, usually involving cattle, though they can apply to goats or sheep. The Pokot call it *tilia*. The terms of the exchange vary even within a particular community, but they usually specify who is to have the cow's milk, blood, and manure, and to whom male and female calves will belong. A time period may be set on the stock deal, but commonly it is open ended, until such time as the cow has produced a heifer, who in turn has proved fertile. In addition to the obvious environmental advantages of herd dispersal there are other advantages of a social nature. It enshrouds in mystery a person's exact wealth in livestock. Further, stock exchanges cement friendships; they bind people together and give them needs and goals in common.

Still other ways to buffer one's livelihood against the vagaries of the climate are food storage and food exchanges. The Pokot of *Masol* also say that one consideration in taking a wife is where she comes from; is it a place with a plentiful and reliable food supply? It is better, all other things being equal, to marry a second wife from an area whose harvest comes at a different time from that of the first wife's village. From the husband's viewpoint alone, the marrying of several wives is a way to ensure a large labor force and a large farm.

It is clear that we have moved from considering farmer practices in the biophysical realm designed to ensure the well-being of the crops, or insurance in the face of crop failure, to a discussion of farmer practices in the social realm. These practices, which focus on society, tend not so much to protect the crop from drought or other environmental threats as to protect farmers when the crop has failed. If farmers fail to save their crops, then they try to save themselves. Ties of kinship may enable them to obtain food from other areas. A farmer may send his wife and children back to her home temporarily. Increasingly in East Africa help is expected in the form of remittances from a son or daughter who has moved to a city and found a job. Also, the government is expected to provide relief, particularly during times of severe drought and food shortage.

CONCLUSION

To conclude, there are many kinds of farmers in Africa. We have concentrated on the problems that many in East Africa face in dealing with a complex, unknowable resource—the climatic environment surrounding their crops—and we have looked at these problems where they are most dramatic, on the subhumid and semiarid margins of agriculture. We must not forget that large numbers of East African farmers live in better watered areas where agriculture is highly productive and where the problems are less those of climate than those of population pressure, land shortage, and fluctuating or declining prices for crops sold on the world market.

We have seen that there is no simple way to describe the agricultural climate of East Africa. Our approach was a successive focusing on the climatic elements which make up the milieu of the growing plant. By and large, East Africa's farmers have a shrewd knowledge of what crops and practices will succeed in their area. But though the system works in its way, there are great pressures for change, for using better seed, fertilizers, fungicides, pesticides, and machinery—all with a view to increased production, better yields, and the creation of surplus income which can be used to finance other development. The real challenge to agroclimatology is to find ways to forge a bond between the western science understanding of the agricultural environment and systems of use of that environment that make sense, both economically and socially, to East African farmers. It is already possible to find optimal matching of crops/cropping systems and environments. Finding ways to match farmers with the functional requirements of the crops/cropping systems is a formidable task. It is, of course, the East African farmers themselves who will find the ways, just as they always have.

10

Human Impact on
African Environmental Systems

J. OLADIPO ADEJUWON

It is usual to identify four primary elements in the structure of
an environmental system: (1) nonliving substances including inor-
ganic elements and organic compounds, such as water, carbon
dioxide, oxygen, nitrates, and phosphates; (2) producer organisms
including green plants which harness solar energy to convert available
matter into organic food; (3) consumer organisms relying for
subsistence directly or indirectly on food from plant sources; and (4)
decomposer organisms, which are primarily microorganisms whose
chief function is to liberate energy and return matter to an available
state. Each of the structural elements in the environmental system
develops toward a qualitatively and quantitatively identifiable
standard, accommodating an optimum constant pattern of energy
flow. After such a standard has been achieved throughout the
system, a state of equilibrium has been attained.

In the context of human ecology, the environmental system
also includes specialized communication circuits such as the behavioral cues passing from one generation to another and the special
economic and cultural forms of information and material exchange.
Thus the structural elements of a human ecological system include
activities, institutions, and utilities such as farming, mining, houses,

factories, vehicles, and machines, among many others. These expend energy as well as promote or retard flows of matter and energy in the basic structure. In the geographical sense, an environmental system includes these facets, expressed areally: it can be described primarily as a unit area with a characteristic biome, economy, and culture, all of which are joined with the physical environment by pathways of matter circulation and energy flow.

In presenting a natural environmental system, we need to describe structural units such as soil and plant and animal populations as well as microorganisms and their activities. The scale of focus normally determines the level of detail described in each structural unit. Where a small pond is the object of study, presentation may require a determination of the chemical composition of the water and pond-bed material, and an estimation of the populations of all micro- and macroorganisms. From these, the functional and developmental characteristics of the system can be interpreted, including patterns of matter and energy flow in the entire biophysical complex, trophic (food) levels of the various biological populations, and courses of development toward the achievement of an equilibrium state. For environmental systems strongly influenced by humans, we would need to describe not only the associated human activities, but also the human institutions built upon the basic natural system.

As the scale of focus broadens and the environmental system increases in size, description must be generalized correspondingly. For example, rather than determining chemical composition of the abiotic substrate and estimating each biological population, the vegetation and the animal communities (the biome) as well as the soil are described in general terms. Thus, for discussing African environmental systems on a continental scale, we will consider: (1) the pattern of biological productivity; (2) the resultant differential accumulation of biomass in terms of the natural vegetation; and (3) the modifications of the latter resulting from various human activities.

BIOLOGICAL PRODUCTIVITY IN TROPICAL AFRICA

In an environmental system, energy is introduced through primary biological production, which can be defined as solar energy stored by photosynthetic and chemosynthetic activities of producer organisms. Part of the energy synthesized this way is used by the producer organisms themselves and the balance that is stored up in plant tissues (biomass) is apparent to us as vegetation. It is this balance that is made available to other living members of the environmental system.

Factors determining the rate of biological production include sunlight, carbon dioxide, water supply, and the fertility status of the soil. Since there is little or no spatial differentiation of carbon dioxide, its level of availability cannot be held responsible for differences in productivity on the earth's surface. Soil varies topographically. This means that within small areas (a few square kilometers) soils of qualities and capabilities as varied as those found throughout the world may be encountered. In considering an area as large as Africa, the soil becomes subsidiary as a factor of regional spatial differentiation. On the other hand, natural supplies of water, and to some extent sunlight, vary regionally and can be seen as the major basis of regional differences in biological productivity. In effect, the pattern of biological productivity is most related to basic climatic elements.

It appears that there is one single climatic parameter—actual evapotranspiration (AE)—that most broadly can be used in predicting net primary productivity. AE is the reverse of rain; it is the amount of water entering the atmosphere from the soil (evaporation) and the vegetation (transpiration) during any period of time. Evapotranspiration requires sufficient energy to make the phase transfer of the water from liquid to gas possible. Actual evapotranspiration is thus a measure of the simultaneous availability of water and solar energy in an environment during any given time period.

By assembling data on climate and productivity throughout the world, Rosenzweig (1968) has been able to derive a formula connecting actual evapotranspiration and net primary productivity. All data were transformed into common logarithms. Using the method of least squares, a linear regression of productivity on AE was performed. The productivity prediction equation, including 95 percent confidence intervals for the slope and the intercept is:

$$\log_{10} NAAP = (1.66 \pm 0.27) \log_{10} AE - (1.66 \pm 0.07)$$

where AE is the annual actual evapotranspiration in millimeters (mm) and $NAAP$ is the net annual above-ground productivity in grams per square meter (g/m^2). Using this equation and water balance data compiled for Africa (Thornthwaite, 1962), the annual productivity for approximately six hundred climatic stations in tropical Africa was calculated. The results have been used in compiling Figure 10.1 which shows a range of net annual above-ground productivity from zero to 4,500 grams per square meter. The

Figure 10.1 Net Annual Primary Productivity (g/m^2).

isopleth 500 g/m^2 seems to mark a break point enclosing areas of very low biological productivity. Such areas coincide, as expected, with the Sahara Desert, the Kalahari, and the Horn of Africa. Areas with very high *NAAP*—over 4,000 g/m^2—can be found in four main locations, the Congo Basin, southern Nigeria, a coastal area extending from Liberia to western Ghana, and a relatively small coastal area in Gabon. Over most of Africa, biological productivity decreases evenly from the four highly productive areas to the desert margins. However, certain areas also with steep gradients in productivity are worth noting. From western and central Ghana where *NAAP* is over 4,000 g/m^2, there is a sharp decrease within a distance of 80 kilometers to 1,200 gm/m^2 on the Accra plains in the southeast. This steep gradient marks the position of the Akwapim Hills. Similarly, other areas of sharp changes in biological productivity correspond to the position of the Cameroun ranges and the eastern edge of the African Plateau in Mozambique, Tanzania, and Kenya.

Actual evapotranspiration is primarily a function of energy supply and available water, and the pattern depicted on the map corresponds strikingly to that of rainfall. As a matter of fact, there appears to be an inverse relationship between biological productivity and solar radiation incident at the surface. For example, the average total radiation per day in Benin City (Nigeria) is 800 calories per square centimeter (cal/cm^2), whereas that of Fort Lamy (Chad Republic) is 1,100 cal/cm^2 (Oyenuga, 1971). This notwithstanding, mean annual biological productivity at Benin City is 3,493 g/m^2. This is a confirmation of the view held by Riehl (1954) that in the tropics, the thermal growing season lasts the whole year. Thus, the major limiting factor in Africa for biological production is not sunshine but moisture. It is the volume of rainfall that spells success or failure for crops, a fact poignantly brought to view with the Sahelian drought.

NATURAL ENVIRONMENTAL SYSTEMS

In a natural environmental system, the initial rate of net primary biological productivity as affected by green plants is higher than the rate of organic matter decomposition resulting from microorganism activity. The balance accumulates as biomass until a stage of equilibrium is reached. At such a stage, there is no net annual accumulation of organic matter. This means that annual production and import of matter are balanced by annual community export and consumption.

For a given climatic region, it is usual to recognize a single climatic climax in equilibrium with regional climate, while also recognizing a varying number of edaphic climaxes that are modified by local conditions of the soil substrate. The climatic climax is a constant against which observed conditions may be compared. Although dominant species will vary from place to place, similar physiognomy is found under uniform climate. The degree of deviation, if any, from the theoretical climax can be measured, and the factors responsible for the deviation can be more readily determined when there is a basic "yardstick" for comparison.

In addition to a number of edaphic climaxes representing modifications by local soil conditions, widespread activities of human beings have resulted in drastically limiting the area of

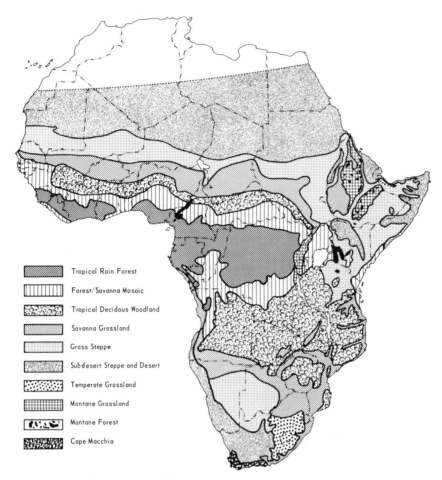

Tropical Rain Forest

Forest/Savanna Mosaic

Tropical Decidous Woodland

Savanna Grassland

Grass Steppe

Subdesert Steppe and Desert

Temperate Grassland

Montane Grassland

Montane Forest

Cape Macchia

Figure 10.2 Vegetation of Africa.
Source: Adapted from Keay, *Vegetation Map of Africa South of the Sahara,* Oxford University Press (Keay, 1959b).

occurrence of the climatic climax. Over large areas of the African continent, the vegetation seems to be either in equilibrium with humans or changing with various levels of intensity of human activity (Figure 10.2). With regard to the savanna vegetation that covers much of humid tropical Africa, the following propositions have now become generally accepted: (1) it is not a climatic climax; (2) the majority of the units of the vegetation can be considered as anthropic, existing because of human activities; and (3) the remainder can be considered as edaphic. In the case of the non-savanna, forest areas, human activities also have caused a widespread replacement and modification of the original forests. But in order to assess more precisely the impact of human activity, the nature of the climax vegetation in tropical Africa first must be determined.

There are four methods by which the climatic climax vegetation can be reconstructed. First, there is the experimental approach. This involves the removal of factors preventing development towards the climax. For example, cutting, grazing animals, and fire will be excluded. Under controlled conditions vegetation ultimately will emerge that is self-maintaining over a long period of time. The weakness of this method, of course, is the time taken by some climatic climaxes to develop, often more than the life span of an individual experimenter. In addition, the experiment may not produce the climax but rather suggest the direction and rate of development from which the climax can be interpreted. Second, the climax can be reconstructed from the distribution and nature of relic vegetation (Table 10.1) which may be found in inaccessible or undisturbed areas or in places specially protected for social, religious, or economic purposes. Because there is no difference in regional climate between the sites where the relics are found and the surrounding areas, such relics can be taken as an example of the climax. Third, an examination of the floristic composition of the existing secondary vegetation yields valuable hints in reconstructing the climax. Some species are faithful to the climax from which they have been derived. Finally, because climate determines the biological productivity that builds and maintains the climax, it can be assumed that similar regional climates produce similar climaxes. For example, if a climate similar to one at present supporting a grassland is known to support a woodland climax vegetation elsewhere, it is reasonable

TABLE 10.1   African Savanna

Macro-climate	Savanna Types	Forest and Woodland Elements			
		Rainforest		Woodland	
		High level relic sites	Low level wet sites	High level relic sites	Low level wet sites
Wet	Derived	Rainforest association	Rainforest association	—	—
	Guinea	Selected rainforest species	Gallery forest	Woodland associations	Gallery forest
	Sudan	Evergreen shrubs	—	Woodland associations	Gallery thickets
Dry	Sahel	—	—	—	—

to hypothesize that a woodland formation is the true climax. These techniques of reconstruction have been applied to the contemporary vegetation pattern in Nigeria (Figure 10.3). Keay (1959a) recognized a transition of the following types of vegetation from the coast northward towards the interior: mangrove swamp forest, fresh water swamp forest, lowland rain forest, derived savanna, southern Guinea savanna, northern Guinea savanna, Sudan savanna, and Sahel savanna. In the mangrove and fresh-water zones, plant communities are made up mainly of medium-to-large sized trees adapted respectively to brackish and fresh-water swamp conditions.

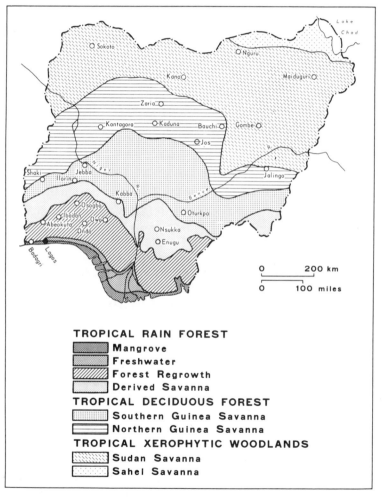

TROPICAL RAIN FOREST
- Mangrove
- Freshwater
- Forest Regrowth
- Derived Savanna

TROPICAL DECIDUOUS FOREST
- Southern Guinea Savanna
- Northern Guinea Savanna

TROPICAL XEROPHYTIC WOODLANDS
- Sudan Savanna
- Sahel Savanna

Figure 10.3 Natural and Anthropic Vegetation in Nigeria.
Source: Keay, 1959b.

Northward, the vegetation consists of forest and savanna. Savanna has been defined by Hopkins (1966) as a type of vegetation consisting predominantly of annually burned grasses. In addition to the grasses and herbs, trees and other woody plants normally are present. On the other hand, forest is a type of vegetation consisting predominantly of woody plants (trees, shrubs, herbs, and climbers) and from which grasses virtually are absent. From the lowland rain forest to the desert, the transition corresponds to the entire range of net biological productivity—from over 4,000 grams per square meter per annum to zero. Except that the dominant species vary from one place to another, and that distinct montane types are found in areas of higher altitude, the vegetation map of Africa south of the Sahara (Figure 10.2) follows a similar pattern. Thus there is justification for projecting the Nigerian climax types to the entire continent as an initial approach to suggesting the potential natural vegetation of Africa.

RECONSTRUCTING TROPICAL AFRICAN NATURAL ENVIRONMENTAL SYSTEMS

The true climax in the area of lowland rain forests in Nigeria is the tropical rain forest (Richards, 1952). Trees are dominant and their foliage forms layers (usually three), which are recognized with some difficulty. Below the tree layers is a shrub layer and also a sparse ground vegetation. The proof that the tropical rain forest is the climatic climax in the present forest areas can be found in the forest reserves that bear the same characteristics as those well associated with the suggested climax vegetation. Swampland forests may be seen as edaphic variants of the rain forest climax. Some swamp forest examples can be regarded as subclimaxes in that there is evidence indicating unimpeded development toward the climax.

Several lines of evidence suggest that the savanna zone next to the lowland rain forest areas (Keay's derived savanna) is derived from the tropical rain forest (Keay, 1959c). For one, the forest relics in the area are similar in essential characteristics to the tropical rain forest (Table 10.1). In addition, some derived savanna units occur on normal sites entirely surrounded by areas of rain-forest vegetation (Adejuwon 1971). Also, forest elements are present in the normal derived savanna vegetation. These include the oil palm (*Elaeis guineensis*) whose presence is one of the most faithful indicators of secondary vegetation in forested areas throughout West Africa. Finally, protection experiments show gradual development of the main characteristics of the climax vegetation and the elimination of such savanna features as a grass layer and dominance by fire-tolerant species (Charter and Keay, 1960).

The tropical rain forest is perhaps the only climax vegetation that has been established as characterizing the wettest parts of the intertropical areas. The climax or climaxes in the drier areas are yet to be described properly. From the floristic composition of the vegetation of these zones, it can be concluded that physiological conditions over normal sites are capable of supporting tree growth. Under natural conditions, in the absence of human activities and the menace of fire, one can expect trees to grow in number and size. An increase in number would lead to a change in physiognomy, with straight, tall poles replacing short and gnarled ones, and spreading crowns replacing rounded ones. The microclimate on the ground would change as thicker foliage develops, and so the dominance of grass on the floor would be threatened.

Considering the evidence provided by the relic vegetation in the Guinea zones, it is certain that the grass layer will be completely eliminated on normal sites under natural conditions. On poor sites such as ironstone escarpments, relic forests have been described by Keay (1960) as including an evergreen-shrub layer topped by a tree layer growing to a height of eight meters. It can reasonably be expected that on better sites, the tree layer would be more luxuriant. This is confirmed by the nature of the relic forests described by Jones (1963a, 1963b). These are found on normal, high-level sites in a zone noted in Nigeria for its sparse population. They, therefore, provide a good indication of the climax vegetation in the area. Certain parts of these forests have been described as well developed woodlands with a continuous canopy in which trees of typical savanna species are associated with rain-forest species. Below this is another continuous layer of small trees apart from a grassless ground vegetation.

The climax vegetation here could be given the name *tropical deciduous forest*. It is a forest in the sense that several tree layers are found in addition to shrubs and herbs on the ground. In fact, the structure is much like that of the tropical rain forest. It is different from the latter mainly because of its smaller stature and the predominance of deciduous elements in the highest tree layer. The smaller stature, however, should not be exaggerated. There are tall trees which apparently could flourish here, although they are now restricted to rain-forest areas, gallery forests, and relic forests in the Guinea zones.

The forest is regarded as deciduous because the characteristic savanna trees that dominate it as well as the rain forest species found in relic forests of the zones are deciduous. This characteristic constitutes the expression of the main feature of the climate—seasonality.

The relic vegetation found in the Sudan zone has been described as a tropical xerophytic woodland with a dense understory of deciduous, erect, and scandent shrubs limiting grass to occasional open patches (Keay, 1949). The vegetation has been recorded on rocky inaccessible sites, which means that it is virtually inviolate. This rock-site vegetation resembles the climax in areas drier than the Sudan—the Sahel zone, perhaps. Overall, the climax in the Sudan and the Sahel can be termed *xerophytic woodlands*. The term *woodland* is used to refer to a vegetation of small trees with light canopies. A ground layer of shrubs with some grasses is topped by a single storey of tree foliage. This simple structure makes it distinguishable from the forest climaxes in the humid areas. Also noteworthy is the significance assumed in the climax by hardy xerophytic thorn trees. The name for this climax vegetation has been chosen with a mind to the relative significance of these trees. In their physiognomy, they give expression to the main characteristics of the climate supporting them. At the boundaries with true desert formations, there is the possibility of a few or even one species dominating large areas or associations.

In areas drier than the Sahel zone of West Africa there is probably little difference between the present vegetation and the climatic climax. The climax here is made up of large bare patches with hardy trees and shrubs such as date-palms, tamarisk, and certain *Acacias* confined to the margins of wadis, playas, and other favorable locations where water is available at depth.

It appears, therefore, that in tropical Africa, there are four major natural environmental systems: rain forest, deciduous forest, xerophytic woodlands, and deserts. Each climatic climax type varies from one part of the continent to the other in its floristic composition, while maintaining a characteristic structure, physiognomy, and seasonality. In other words, each climatic climax is made up of associations that can be described and defined in terms of prevalent species. Apart from the differences in floristic composition, significant structural modifications result from local conditions of altitude, relief, and substrate.

From what has been said earlier about the relationship between climax vegetation on the one hand, and biological productivity and climatic elements on the other, it is reasonable to expect the boundaries between the various climax types to correspond to given magnitudes of biological productivity. Following this expectation Figure 10.4 has been produced showing a tentative distribution of

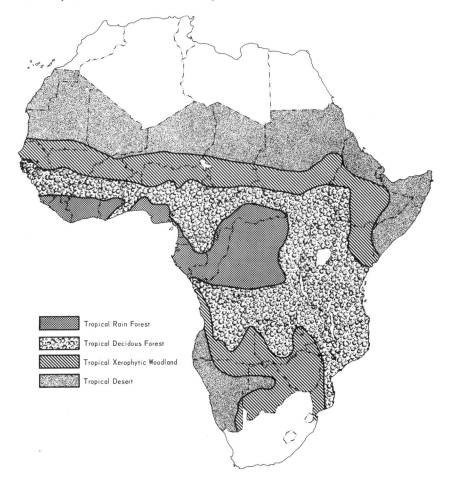

Figure 10.4 Potential Natural Vegetation in Tropical Africa.

potential climax vegetation in tropical Africa. It now becomes necessary to explain the differences between the potential patterns and the real vegetation patterns.

ANTHROPIC ENVIRONMENTAL SYSTEMS

There are several processes by which most of the present vegetation categories in tropical Africa have been derived from the original forests and woodlands. Each of these processes depends on human activities, including bush-fallow agricultural systems, generation of grassland by intensive recultivation and firing, cultivation of permanent crops, grazing, and forestry.

Many of the present secondary vegetation units exist as a result of rotational bush-fallow systems of cultivation. In these systems the farmer clears a small forest or woodland area of its ground vegetation and the lower story trees in preparation for cultivation of field crops. After a harvest or two, the plot is allowed to rest under fallow vegetation. With normal conditions, such a plot is recultivated after a period varying from five to ten years. It may, however, remain under fallow longer and have enough time to revert to high forest. This seldom occurs in areas with high densities of population except where, because of poor soils, field crops cannot be cultivated profitably. Rotational bush-fallow systems of cultivation account for much of the structural and floristic variations as well as the micropattern of the present plant cover of tropical Africa. Ross (1954) demonstrated that differences in vegetation are associated with the length of fallow in the forests of southern Nigeria. In the areas much affected by this system of cultivation, the vegetation becomes more herbaceous, and the "soft" stem plants assume an importance exceeding their role in the typical climax vegetation. Fast-growing tree species become more abundant, and the flora can become richer. Although some shade-loving forest floor species are eliminated altogether, the majority of the climax species are found in the anthropic derivatives, but invariably play much less significant roles. However, species specially adapted to the new open conditions are found in abundance. Stratification of foliage is reduced to a minimum, and the vegetation may become impenetrable because of the mass of thick herb, shrub, and sapling vegetation near the ground surface.

An area intensively used for agriculture over a long period of time is characterized by another process that leads to further vegetation degradation. The general trend can be noticed from the regrowth after cultivation, gradually changing from woodland fallow to grassland fallow and grassland. Grass becomes progressively more important whereas woody species become fewer. At advanced stages, forest woody species are eliminated, leaving new groups that are either fire resistant or fire tolerant. The process is initiated by the appearance of grass elements. Once established, these grassy fallows are liable to be burned, and the fierce fires progressively kill out fire-tender trees and shrubs. If fire tolerant savanna trees are available, they will colonize the grassland fallows. In time, the forest or woodland is replaced by savanna. The rate of degradation to savanna appears to vary not only with the intensity of human activity, but also with biological productivity. Thus, areas of xerophytic woodlands and deciduous forests have been more widely converted to savanna than the areas of tropical rain forest.

Fire is not only an agent of savanna derivation, but it has now become known as the chief equilibrium-maintaining factor. An experiment was initiated in 1929 in the derived savanna zone of western Nigeria to test the effect of protection from fire. Plots were laid out in an area of fairly open savanna vegetation. Some of the plots were protected completely from burning; some were burned annually at the beginning of the dry season; and others were burned at the end of the dry season. A visit to the experimental site 38 years later showed that the protected plot had become a type of rain forest. The grass layer not only was eliminated by the shade of the dense tree layer, but the typical savanna species in the vegetation had been overshadowed by typical forest species. On the other plots, the savanna vegetation was maintained, with those burned late in the dry season suffering greatest devastation. These are strong indicators that the savanna can be maintained by annual fire without cultivation. This means that cultivation is required chiefly to effect the initial conversion of an area of forest to savanna. After this, fire takes over as the agent of savanna preservation.

In the well-settled areas of West Africa, it is easy to accept intensive agricultural practice as the primary initiating factor of anthropic savannas. In parts of South and Central Africa, savanna sometimes occurs in areas where the density of population is less than two persons per sq. kilometer. What intensity of cultivation, one may ask, can result in vegetation degradation ending up in savanna with such a population density? For South America, Bennett (1964) solves the problem by accepting fire as an initiating factor. Even a small population can set fire to the bush, even though the incidence of fire, whether accidental or purposeful, may vary with the number of people. In drier areas of deciduous and xerophytic vegetation, the ground may be covered by conflagrable dry leaves that could lead to forest fires, especially toward the end of the dry season. In Nigeria, fire seems to be a rarity without a grassy ground layer. Even in areas of xerophytic woodlands, the ground layer is dominated by shrubs, not grasses. It has been demonstrated that in certain situations, fire set to an existing unit of savanna vegetation can invade the surrounding bush to allow the grass vegetation to extend its coverage (Adejuwon, 1971). The forest floor next to the savanna usually receives an abundance of light that would make it possible for a thick grassy ground layer to develop even if there were no cultivation. Such a situation will encourage fire to invade the forest margin, leading to the destruction of the fire intolerant elements that dominate the forest.

It is probable that long before the arrival of agriculture, the inviolate forest of tropical lands included patches of natural savanna. Fire set to such patches could have extended their coverage. In the drier parts of the tropics, extensive occurrence of anthropic savannas may have predated the arrival of agriculture. In more humid regions, extensive occurrence of savanna must have awaited agricultural populations.

The third process by which some of the present vegetation categories have been derived from the original forests and woodlands is the cultivation of former forest land with permanent crops, especially cocoa, kola, rubber, oil palm, and fruits. In addition to the fact that a general uniformity is imposed by the dominance of the crop plants, permanent tree crop lands must be recognized as a major vegetation type for two reasons. First, permanent tree crops cover extensive areas in the rain forest zone. In parts of the Nigerian cocoa belt, more than one-fourth of the land area is under cocoa and several sq. kilometers may be covered almost exclusively by cocoa or kola. Second, other plant elements such as weeds, epiphytes, and parasites found with the crops are widespread characteristic features. Thus these plots have a distinct physiognomy and floristic composition.

Grazing by domestic animals can be added as a process in vegetation modification. Over extensive areas cattle, goats, and sheep have become a force rivaling fire in the maintenance of the savanna. The heterogenous composition of the animal population ensures wide use of natural foods and holds the potential for great devastation of plant cover. When periods of above average rainfall encourage heavy exploitation of savanna and Sahelian environments, subsequent overgrazing during drought periods may exacerbate normal climatic variability and initiate major disaster, such as the Sahelian drought of the late 1960s and the 1970s.

A final process of vegetation alteration is timber felling, in that modifications (especially to the rain forests) can occur from selective felling of larger trees. This process considerably changes forest structure and brings about changes in soil characteristics as well. The closed tree canopy is broken, and full sunlight reaches the floor to encourage the growth of seedlings of particular species. Thick epiphyte tangles are formed and the forest becomes impenetrable.

ANTHROPIC FOREST SYSTEMS

As a result of these processes, the vegetation of tropical Africa has

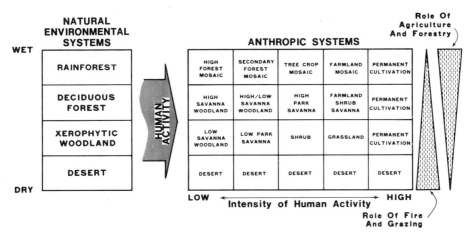

Figure 10.5   Human Impact on Vegetation.

been altered with varying intensity (Figure 10.5). In the areas where the rain forest has successfully resisted deterioration to savanna, four landscape types can be recognized—high forest, secondary forest, tree crop, and farmland mosaics. The high forest mosaic is characterized by little or no degradation. Two main topographical types can be identified in the mosaic. The first, the high forest, has a closed, tree canopy at least 20 meters in height, and resembles the natural or climax vegetation in the humid, tropical lowlands. In recent time, many such areas have been incorporated into forest reserves. A second topographic high forest type is the broken high forest, consisting of mature forest growth in which a few trees have either been felled or blown over by wind. Broken high forest also may indicate the presence of elephants. Moving in herds, these large animals can cause enough damage to result in pronounced modification of even the tropical rain forest.

The secondary forest mosaic has characteristics intermediate between high forest and fallow vegetation in that some stratification of tree foliage can be noticed. Apart from a lower stature, the presence of certain tree species such as the oil palm in West Africa differentiates the secondary forest mosaic from the high forest. Secondary forest mosaic normally is found in sparsely populated areas with fairly rough terrain or poor soils unsuitable for rotational bush-fallow cultivation, but near enough to areas of high density population to suffer from human activity, such as cutting of timber and firewood.

The farmland mosaic might be called the oil palm-bush in view of the abundant growth of these trees. Oil palms sometimes single-handedly form an upper stratum of tall trees under which cropland and fallow foliage are found. Four vegetation subunits can be differentiated. Cleared land that has been freshly cut from forest, thicket, or bush regrowth, but on which crops have not yet been planted is the first type. The upper vegetation is made up of the remnant of the recently lopped or defoliated trees as well as the characteristic oil palms, whereas the surface may be clear or covered by a thick growth of herbs. Plots that can be described in this way will be found only during the dry season when new areas are being brought under cultivation. Cropland vegetation is found on plots that currently are being cultivated. Especially during the first year of cropping, these plots may be covered almost completely by many crops planted together, including yams, cassava, rice, cocoyam, and maize. Where cultivation runs into the second year, cassava or cocoyam are usually left as single crops. Bush regrowth vegetation includes fallow of less than five years of age, although a similar vegetation may be older on poorer soils. Cassava, traces of yam heaps, and old yam poles often are seen. Herbaceous species are dominant as a group. Finally, thicket consists of vegetation with a predominantly woody growth, less than fifteen meters in height. This unit represents the normal limit reached by the secondary succession from cultivated plots back to forest before clearing and recultivation takes place. Sometimes it develops into secondary forest, but usually the land is cleared before the thicket vegetation is properly established.

The tree crop mosaic includes tree crops planted in the forest areas of tropical Africa. Most significant are cocoa, coffee, kola, banana, citrus, and rubber. The vegetation units in which these are found are not restricted to the large plantations maintained with modern agricultural techniques but include small peasant plots. Where found, the tree-crop mosaic could be viewed as having a geographical rather than a taxonomic connotation.

The anthropic basis of the derivation of the present units of forest vegetation in Africa is reflected in the facts that (1) units of farmland mosaic dominate areas of high density of population and the environs of towns and large villages; (2) areas covered extensively by tree-crop mosaic correspond to the parts with a moderate density of population and are located far from the larger settlements. In the forest areas of southern Nigeria, it has been observed that high population densities in the home regions of the Ibo, Ibibio, and Yoruba peoples correspond to the areas of farmland mosaic. The relatively less populated areas of Yorubaland and the Mid-West State are extensively used for cocoa, kola and rubber, whereas the sparsely peopled areas of southern Mid-West State, and the greater part of

South Eastern State, include the larger forest reserves (Adejuwon, 1968).

ANTHROPIC SAVANNA TYPES

Contemporary savannas may be viewed at a regional or local scale. Regionally, each of the savanna zones may be recognized as a unit. These include going from the wetter margin in West Africa, the derived savanna, the Guinea savanna, the Sudan savanna, and the Sahel. Each of the zones occupies areas within given ranges of biological productivity. In their distribution ranges, most of the typical savanna trees in Nigeria (about 190) are zonal. Only 16 species are found throughout the savanna areas in the country. Apart from these strictly zonal species there are plants found in the southern wetter zones that are not in the northern drier zones and vice versa. About 25 species are found exclusively in the Sudan and Sahel zonal systems, whereas 34 are exclusive to the three southern zones.

There are other plant-life characteristics that add to the distinctiveness of each zonal system. First, there is a general reduction in the stature as well as in the foliage density toward the north. This should be expected in view of the pattern of biological productivity. Tall stands dominate large areas of woodland in the southern zones. In the Sudan and Sahel zones, such woodlands rarely are encountered. In their places, one can find low savanna woodlands. The dominant trees, including species of *Acacia*, hardly ever reach heights of 10 meters. Individual species occurring throughout the savanna also demonstrate similar physiognomic differences. *Anogeissus leiocarpus*, a component of savanna woodlands, often reaches 35 meters or more in the derived savanna zone, whereas in the Sahel zone, it occurs as a small tree. Second, the savanna trees in Nigeria as a whole consist of both broad and narrow leafed plants, but there is the tendency for the latter group to increase in significance on the drier margins. Finally, each zone can be recognized by the significance of forest units and species. In the derived savanna zone, rain-forest units are found both at lower (edaphic) and at higher (relic) level sites. In the Guinea zones, rain-forest units occur as gallery forests along the river valleys. Even though they are not found at high level sites, relic vegetation includes species characteristic of rain forests. Nongrassy vegetation, which can be described as thicket rather than as forest, is also found at stream sides in the Sudan zone. At high level sites, rain forest units and trees are absent, whereas some evergreen shrubs may be found in place of grass on the floor of the relic vegetation. Neither rain-forest units nor elements have been reported in the Sahel zone. At a local scale, the density of human population has had marked impact on the nature of the savanna. The approach to any large town in the savanna zone is indicated by the replacement of woodlands by the more "open" types of savanna. In central Nigeria, Ramsay (1963) recorded a zonation of physiognomic types around the major towns. In areas most remote from towns are found high savanna woodlands. Toward the towns, these give way initially to the low coppice growth of low savanna woodland, then to parkland savanna, and finally to shrub savanna in which stands of *Adansonia digitata* (baobab) can be found. In the Ilorin division of Nigeria, high savanna woodlands are very rare and are found only on extremely shallow soils not suitable for cultivation (Taylor *et al.*, 1962). In the adjacent Borgu division, these woodlands are prevalent, covering almost all the land except immediate village vicinities. This situation corresponds closely to a striking population difference between the two divisions. In 1952, the population density in Ilorin division was about 60 per square kilometer, and that of Borgu only three.

CONCLUSION

Before the development of agriculture in tropical Africa, the environmental system produced climax communities varying from the high forest in the perennially humid regions to low woodlands in semiarid regions. Human intervention has led to a reduction of standing biomass resulting in a replacement of the original vegetation in the drier areas and a modification of the forests of the wetter parts. In the drier areas, invading savanna vegetation is now more extensive in areal coverage than any other type. The characteristic savanna species are adapted to fire, which is the means by which the vegetation is maintained, although its derivation may have included local systems of agricultural production. In the wetter areas, the original forests have been modified structurally to give a mosaic in which unstable units making up secondary successions back to high forest are dominant. There are large areas under semipermanent tree crop mosaics within the forest and continuous deviation of savanna at its more arid boundary. Development of the ecological resources of tropical Africa must include an awareness of human impact on the environment in premodern time. Contemporary activity will surely accelerate this impact in the absence of decisive countermeasures.

11

Wildlife

C. GREGORY KNIGHT

Most of us have seen African wildlife, and for an increasing number of us, our view has expanded beyond the caged, artificial environment of the zoological garden to the pseudo-natural environment of "wild animal safari lands." The importance of the continent's fauna greatly exceeds these attractions, however. It represents an important resource for future social and economic development, but possesses a number of management challenges in terms of favorable allocation and use.

Wildlife provides many of the following benefits: meat supply, trophies, skins, live animal exports, and tourism. In Ghana, some 80 percent of the fresh meat consumed is derived from wildlife (Riney, 1967), and in Nigeria, Olayide and Idachaba (1973) have calculated the value of "bush meat" at over $100 million per year. Tourism is now Kenya's major "export," with that nation having a Permanent Secretary for Tourism and Wildlife (see Chapter 29). But for many traditional societies, game also constitutes an environmental hazard. It competes with domestic livestock for pasture resources and may damage or destroy field crops. Wildlife also acts as a host for insects (vectors) capable of transmitting diseases (ticks, biting flies), and is a noninfected reservoir of human and livestock diseases. However, wildlife constitutes a critical reserve of genetic material for future generations.

South of the Sahara, grazing resources have been estimated at over 40 percent of the land area (Rattray, 1960). These resources include both grass pasture and grass and herbaceous browse materials in areas of mixed vegetative structure. Few African areas are purely grassland; most are a savanna mosaic of grasses and bush or tree vegetation. Here, the grass component represents a subclimax vegetation stage whose normal ecological succession has been arrested by fire, grazing of both wild and domestic animals, cultivation, and collection of firewood (Whyte, 1962). Many of these areas are ecologically marginal for human occupation. Attempts at cultivation during wet periods are thwarted by drought, and settlements are limited by the absence of permanent surface water supplies. Pastoralists must undertake seasonal as well as long-term migration to assure fodder and water for their herds. Tropical grasses become fibrous and decline in vital protein content as they mature, and eventually they dry out. In consequence, human populations are sparse and prospects for long-term development in these areas seem limited. Yet the African savanna and grassland areas do constitute an important spatial, ecological, and genetic resource, and in this chapter we will describe some of the prospectives to understanding alternative strategies for their use. Basic to our understanding will be discussion of the ecological functioning of the "natural" grassland environment, the comparative production efficiency of wild animals and domestic livestock populations, grassland and animal management problems, and the benefits from alternative management strategies.

ECOLOGICAL ADAPTATION

The grazing resources of Africa are characterized by plentiful solar energy but extremely seasonal water resources, with long dry seasons. Plant productivity, basic to support of animal life, is limited by lack of water. Rainfall may be widely distributed in space and time. This sparsity means limited photosynthetic productivity and, frequently, too little precipitation for domestic crops. How, then, do wildlife and humans harvest environmental energy in this kind of environment? Solar energy fixed by photosynthetic plant activity cannot be directly used by man, since our digestive systems are not adapted to grassy diets. In the absence of plentiful seeds and fruits, we can harvest environmental energy indirectly through animals whose digestive systems are efficient in using grass and whose mobility allows them to gather sparsely-distributed fodder resources by local grazing and seasonal migration through the year. The hunting of wild-animal populations or milking and slaughter of livestock make a portion of the solar energy finally available to humans. Energy losses at several steps along the way—in the photosynthetic efficiency of plants, in the use of plant calories by the grazing animal, in the animal's metabolism, in the proportion of the animal that is actually edible—are a necessary price for tapping solar energy incident in these areas.

Wild-animal communities cope with their environment in numerous ways that are superior to domestic herds. One of these is the interdigitation of species in space and in use of resources. Each occupies a distinct and often complementary ecological niche. This means that the place of each species in the web of ecological relationships (in the flow of energy and materials) is not fully competitive with others. The food preferences of each species, for example, are largely complementary. Grasses providing a major nutritional component for one variety may be ignored by others. Large species trample down deep grasses, making low-level food resources available to smaller species (Bell, 1971). The use of complementary resources means that the standing biomass of wild-animal populations is much greater than livestock under similar conditions, sometimes exceeding livestock by a factor of five! Therefore, the carrying capacity of grazing resources is much higher for wildlife than for cattle. An East African acacia savanna carrying 19.6-28.0 kg/ha. of cattle (11,200-16,000 lb/mi^2) can carry from 65.5-157.6 kg/ha. (37,400-90,000 lb/mi^2) of wild ungulates (Talbot, 1963). Note here that carrying capacity is measured in weight or biomass rather than in animal numbers, because measuring by numbers becomes meaningless when individual species vary from five kilograms (dik dik) to five tons (elephant). Wild animals use grazing resources which are too coarse for livestock. They also exploit grasses in a catenary succession, using upland grasses during the rainy season, then moving downslope to moister sites as the dry season progresses (Bell, 1971).

Wild-animal populations also are more ecologically adaptive than livestock because they often use water resources more efficiently and are more tolerant of stress and disease. The physiology of African ungulates incorporates specialized water conservation metabolism. The gemsbok, impala, hartebeest, and springbok can live six to nine months without drinking water (de Vos, 1969). The eland and oryx can survive using only water consumed while eating grasses and browse (C.R. Taylor, 1969). Heat stress is more easily tolerated by wild species than livestock (see Chapter 8). Diseases have less effect on survival and productivity in wildlife, and *nagana* (sleeping sickness or trypanosomiasis) is carried by wildlife as an intermediate host without ill effect. This disease, fatal in cattle, can be transmitted by tsetse feeding on infected wildlife. Thus, only inoculation of livestock or tsetse eradication make wildlife and cattle compatible in the same area. Wild-animal tsetse hosts also pose a sleeping sickness risk to humans.

MEAT PRODUCTION POTENTIAL

Not only are wildlife populations more adaptive than livestock populations, but they hold considerably greater potential as sources of animal protein for humans under natural environmental conditions. For most African ungulates, maturity is earlier, gestation period shorter, and growth rates more rapid than cattle. The impala and wildebeest reach maturity in slightly over one year (compared to 30 months for African cattle); the impala has a gestation period of 195 days (281 for cattle) and reaches marketable size in 18 months (5 years for cattle). The eland (largest of the wild antelopes, roughly the same size as African cattle) reaches maturity in 2 years, has a gestation of 260 days, gains 0.25 kilograms (0.55 pounds) per day (compared with 0.14 kilograms or 0.31 pounds for cattle), and is a marketable 360 Kg (800 lb.) in 4 years (Talbot *et al.*, 1965).

An eland-cattle comparison also illustrates typical meat yields of wild versus domestic animals in Africa. The eland has a 59 percent killing average (carcass weight as a proportion of live weight) whereas the African cattle has 50 percent (Talbot, 1963). The eland, as other antelopes, has less than 2.5 percent fat; cattle have 7 percent (emaciated) to over 30 percent (Talbot *et al.*, 1965). Thus the wild animal provides more meat per live weight and more of this is protein-yielding lean meat rather than high calorie fat.

Given the greater standing biomass, earlier maturity, more rapid gestation, earlier marketability, better carcass yield, and greater protein content, it is obvious that wild animals are a far more ecologically efficient source of meat protein than traditional domestic cattle under African conditions. Maximum yields from either population requires careful harvesting with reference to maturity, sex, and numbers taken. The flavor and texture of wild meat varies among species, but is not "gamey" under suitable conditions of slaughter, butchering, cooling, and aging (Talbot *et al.*,

1965). Game meat is less succulent than domestic beef, but possibly desirable for its lower caloric and fat content, although careful inspection and processing may be required to minimize disease and parasite risks. In countries with problems of malnutrition, game meat represents an important potential source of protein supply that increases short-term and long-run environmental productivity. Humans become the predators in the food chain, and they harvest by careful design rather than happenstance.

MANAGEMENT PROBLEMS

Use of the production potential of wild-animal populations creates a number of problems. Among them are maintaining breeding populations, poaching, competition with pastoralists, animal migration, low animal densities in arid areas, and grassland management. Already some African species are threatened with extinction.[1]

Maintenance of breeding populations and poaching are interwoven. Uncontrolled hunting for meat and trophies would certainly continue in the absence of regulation, and control of poaching is a perennial problem even under strict game management. Animals threatening fields and farm settlements must be controlled, and encroachment of farmers and pastoralists into game lands is incompatible with maintaining game populations.

Game reserves and national parks are a territorial solution to prevent human encroachment, but boundaries set under political constraints may not be compatible with ecological reality. If, during annual migrations, animals leave the reserve, they become "fair game" for local populations in the absence of enforced hunting laws. As human populations grow, delimitation of reserves and parks will be increasingly difficult. Thus in spite of the excellent game and national park management record in many African areas, still only 1.7 percent of the land area south of the Sahara has been allocated to national parks and major game reserves (Swift, 1972).[2] There is clearly a great need to expand this figure before it is too late, and to do so in ecologically rational ways by including whole *ecounits*, the land required to support the wildlife ecosystem during its seasonal fluctuations (Myers, 1972; Sullivan and Shaffer, 1975).

Although wild game is a rational allocation of grazing resources

[1] Guggisberg (1970) lists nine African species now extinct, and 40 mammals and birds in danger of extinction.

[2] Maps and brief descriptions of the national parks and game preserves in Africa are available in Guggisberg (1970).

on the arid land fringe, here animal densities are so low that costs of game harvesting—hunting, dressing, cooling, transportation—may become financially prohibitive. Yet such an allocation could be the only viable solution for society if drought conditions make human occupation untenable.

Finally, management of game requires management of grazing resources. Protection from fire leads to bush encroachment at the expense of grasses. Controlled burning at times appropriate to each locale is one solution, as is careful monitoring and control of the numbers and balance among grazing species. Equally important is environmental management to decrease erosion and to maintain perennial stream flow as a water resource for game reserves. Conscious reclamation efforts may be required to prevent further damage by wild animal or livestock overgrazing (Riney, 1967). As modern society maintains an active interest in wildlife populations, it must recognize the need for scientific study of ecosystems and the requirement for active intervention to maintain those systems.

ALTERNATIVE STRATEGIES

Existing range lands in Africa are used predominantly for subsistence production by pastoralists, largely at the expense of wild-animal populations. Only a small proportion are incorporated into commercial beef production units or into national parks and game reserves. What, then, are the alternatives for future allocation of grazing lands? They range from allowing traditional hunting, agriculture, and pastoralism to take their toll under a "do-nothing" policy to full range land management for domestic livestock, national parks, or game ranching (Table 11.1). Each strategy has benefits and costs, and each possesses certain incompatibilities among potential benefits.

Although most African nations require licenses for hunting major wildlife, provisions of such regulations are difficult to enforce in isolated rural areas. Expansion of cultivation and pastoralism inevitably means gradual decline and eventual elimination of wildlife populations. Such expansion can have a short-run benefit in mobilizing land resources for growing populations, and it even provides a meat supply, control of wildlife damage, and possibly trophies and skins, but only for the short run. The long-term costs of a *laissez faire* policy may be devastating. Overgrazing may be extended into undamaged areas, leaving major reclamation tasks for a later period. Agriculturalists enticed toward arid margins invite disaster when normal environmental variability brings periods of

TABLE 11.1 Benefits of Alternative Strategies of Grassland Management

Management Strategies	Potential Benefits[a]									
	Meat Supply	Damage Control	Disease Control	Live Animal Export	Trophies Skins	Tourism	Economic Development	Employment	Conservation	Research
None[b]	(C)	C	C	(C)	(C)	I	I	I	I	I
Livestock Ranching	N	C	C	I	I	I	N	N	N	I
Game Preserves	N	C	I	C	N	C	C	C	C	C
National Parks	N	C	I	C	N	C	C	C	N	C
Game Ranching	C	C	C	C	C	N	N	N	N	C

[a]Symbols: C, compatible
(C), compatible, but limited duration
N, neutral
I, incompatible

[b]Allow traditional hunting, agriculture, and pastoralism to continue development in grassland areas.

drought. The long-run costs strongly weigh against the short-term gains of such a policy.

Improved systems of pastoral activity, including potential pasture improvement, are one alternative for the grassland areas. It is not inconceivable that such schemes, whose viability has been demonstrated on Kenyan and Rhodesian ranches, would be economically viable. But productivity certainly would be greater under a game-ranching scheme, and more economically beneficial once a firm market in game meat has been established. Thus livestock ranching has a comparatively lower potential for meat production, but it would eliminate wildlife damage and threat of disease, even providing a short term supply of trophies and exportable animals during the period of establishment. It is by no means certain, however, that traditional pastoral societies will be receptive to ranching programs, nor that the most modern technologies can be successfully instituted over wide areas of grazing resources. Also on the debit side is the elimination of animal populations for conservation and research purposes.

Game preserves and national parks provide an attractive opportunity for multiple uses which are compatible with the many benefits from livestock (Myers, 1972). Controlled harvesting to maintain ecological viability would also provide meat, trophies, and exportable animals. Although game preserves and controlled areas typically allow hunting under strict license control and parks are largely for "hunting" with binoculars and telephoto lens, the necessity for active population control in national parks means that officials rather than safari hunters will harvest game here. The meat production potential of this game cropping is not yet well developed, but mobile abattoirs and refrigerated transportation will enhance this use of parks.

Tourism is a major benefit of game protection, providing important foreign exchange, economic development, and employment tying traditional and modern economic sectors together (Myers, 1972). It is doubtful, however, whether tourism induces modernization. Certainly urban tourist centers prosper, but much of the income may flow out of the host country toward sources of capital investment in hotels and resorts and toward the "just like home" products that tourists expect. In addition, tourism can create a local impression that parks are only for rich foreigners, whose behavior may be antagonistic to local mores and income levels. Tourism impedes animal behavior and ecology; automobiles moving off park roads interfere with grazing resources; and only a small proportion of tourist-derived revenue accrues to the benefit of wildlife (Myers, 1972). Nevertheless, the tourist resource is certainly a compelling reality backing up idealistic conservation commitments. Without tourism, game populations would be in greater danger.

National parks and game preserves do not provide disease control except through prophylaxis or treatment of people at risk. The probability of a casual tourist sustaining sleeping sickness in an East African game park is remote (Knight, 1971), but nearby permanent residents and their livestock demand greater concern.

A final alternative is full game ranching, merging technologies from livestock ranching, and game management to rear wild animal populations. Experiments have been undertaken in developing game ranches for meat production (in Kenya and Rhodesia, for example), and African antelopes have been domesticated for research and selective breeding purposes. Whether game ranching could be made compatible with tourism is uncertain, and such a strategy still would use grazing resources once available to noneconomic wildlife species and threaten the existence of some, especially natural predators (leopard, lion). Thus game ranches provide many, if not more, production potentials than livestock ranches or national parks, but compared with parks they are only partially compatible with economic development, tourism, and animal preservation.

CONCLUSION

Development and maintenance of game preserves and national parks represents a major investment by African nations. Nevertheless, it is a task that has only begun when broadened to larger questions of using game populations as renewable food resources and of preserving and enhancing the African environment. It is unrealistic for those of us in the industrialized world to expect African countries to give high priority to preservation issues in the face of other development concerns. Tanzania, for example, already spends a larger proportion of national income on national parks than does the United States (Myers, 1972). As individuals, there are organizations through which we may express our concern and commitment to African wildlife; at a minimum we can support legislation controlling trade in products from game species threatened with extinction (such as the Endangered Species Conservation Act of 1969). As more is learned about wildlife and grazing ecology in Africa, we will certainly see greater attention to wildlife as a resource vital for human sustenance.

12

Mineral, Energy, and Water Resources

JACQUELYN L. BEYER

If it were possible to discuss and understand mineral, energy, and water resource issues in Africa only in terms of measurable quantities available in particular places, the task for this chapter would be comparatively easy (Figures 12.1 and 12.2). However, there are several factors that complicate matters considerably. For one, the process of establishing the precise quantities of such earth materials as iron, copper, petroleum, coal, and water is on-going, so that it is necessary to work with varying degrees of uncertainty (Lovering, 1969). Uncertainty is increased further by the problems of understanding the present contributions to human welfare of resource availability and exploitation. If we wish to extend that understanding to the future, assessment becomes even more difficult. The difficulties are especially true for stock resources such as minerals and mineral fuels. These can be summarized as follows (adapted from Buck and Elver, 1971:17):

1. Mineral resources are subject to physical and economic depletion and are thus nonrenewable, unlike biotic, water, or solar resources. Minerals, however, are recyclable, as contrasted to mineral fuels, and can be included in the general stock of resources available over time for human use.

As – Asbestos
B – Bauxite
Be – Beryl
C – Copper
Ca – Cadmium
Cr – Chrome
D – Diamonds
G – Gold
I – Iron
L – Lead
M – Magnesium
Ma – Manganese
Ph – Phosphate
S – Silver
T – Tin
Tu – Tungsten
Z – Zinc

Figure 12.1   Minerals.

2. The unequal distribution of supply and demand means that trade policies, economic growth policies, and international or interregional tensions are focused on the places where unusual quantities of desired materials are located.

3. Even though it is apparent that the demand for and use of minerals and mineral fuels will continue to grow over the long-term, localized short-term overproduction will continue to cause problems. Extraction is not an easily adjustable operation.

4. Multinational corporations, a growing phenomenon of the late twentieth century, are very much involved in the minerals industry. As yet, it is not clear how sovereign national entities can effectively deal with foreign ownership and capital mobility.

5. New technology and new discoveries frequently cause major perturbations in the competitive position and trade patterns of producing companies and countries. These problems of cyclical instability, dislocation, and shortages require adaptive capacities that are not always easy to achieve.

6. It may be a major problem, especially for a developing country, to resolve in an optimal way the conflicts of resource management where mineral resource exploitation affects other natural resources.

7. There may be socially undesirable environmental effects, or the efforts to avoid such effects through regulation may inhibit or prevent mineral extraction or make it extremely costly.

For renewable resources the problems are not associated with depletion but rather with timing irregularities, geographic irregularities, and quality. Water, for example, moves through the hydrologic cycle at different rates during different times of the year. In addition, there are fluctuations from year to year. More often than not the place of demand is not coincident with supply. Water must not contain bacteriological impurities when used for domestic consumption. It cannot be too saline for agriculture, and it must be the right temperature and free of mineral impurities for most industrial processes.

Clearly there are aspects of human behavior and institutional organization that also affect the ways in which such resources are developed and managed. Political boundaries cut across rivers or a river may be the boundary, so that integrated river-basin management is difficult (United Nations, 1969a; Lepawsky, 1963). Attitudes toward and perception of hazards such as drought, pollution, or floods varies from place to place. Often, because of failure to take into account such perceptions, planning is made difficult. Demographic change, including population growth itself, may outpace the ability of managers to satisfy changing expectations and demands, a result of which could be an acceleration of social pathology. Anachronistic administrative systems may inhibit innovations in satisfying human needs. Multiple-purpose conflicts, as between water storage for irrigation or power generation and the need for flood runoff capacity, must be resolved by technology and management techniques which are expensive and complex.

The ways in which these interacting factors affect resource management decisions, whether private and governmental, over time presents an ever-changing challenge to human skills, ingenuity, and adaptability. There is no shortage of African human capability for positive responses to such challenges, which in a sense are only modern versions of age-old problems, but there is a shortage of time—time to develop the human potential, time to generate the capital and technical resources, time to establish demographic and political stability, time to experiment, time to reduce the long list of developmental and social change problems.

Certainly one way African decision-makers at all levels can reduce the stress of time is to use the experience of others as a means of avoiding costly errors. It is important, however, especially for those of us in western, industrialized societies, to remember that our techniques will not always be acceptable or even suitable (Farvar and Milton, 1972). It should not surprise us if particular modes or strategies we propose are perceived as crude or inappropriate tools to aid in reaching African societal goals. Neither should it surprise us if our perceptions of the value of African resources, especially minerals, should clash with African perceptions. We may see Africa as a

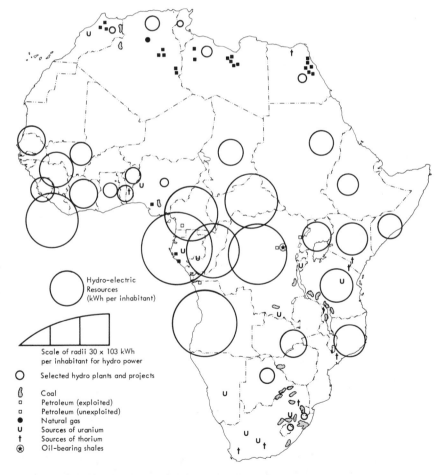

Figure 12.2   Hydroelectric Resources and Fuel Reserves.
Source: United Nations Economic Commission for Europe.

cornucopian pool of wealth waiting to be exploited to serve our material, economic, and strategic purposes. Africans will see that these are ends to be served only insofar as such contributions become a means to their own ends. There is no better example than the crisis in western and Japanese economies generated by Arabian leaders' determination to use their countries' natural wealth to serve political goals. The outcome of such conflict can continue to be violence-inducing "grabs" for such wealth, or they can be, if we can mentally accommodate divergent values, an impetus toward cooperative efforts to resolve mutual problems.

Future scenarios must take into account the ways in which these conflicts are resolved. For example, at present the geographic pattern of mineral and mineral fuel deposits is such that only a few countries in Africa represent, to outside investors, attractive opportunities. The economies of these countries may benefit, at least in the short run, while mineral and energy poor countries continue to lag. One future scenario may be written to show industrialized countries and multinational corporations exploiting this gap by using the poor countries as a model of what might happen if foreign interests in the mineralized enclaves are not protected. Another scenario, however, might show these "islands" of economic wealth becoming nodes for wider material improvement in the lives of all Africans through interregional cooperation and integration.

One of the myths associated with general western views of Africa and the African experience is that without European (and in the twentieth century, American) expertise, capital, and willingness to take risks, Africans would have been long delayed in their introduction to the wonders of a minerals-based society. The truth is, of course, that metallurgy is very old in Africa, with a chronological gradient from the Nile Valley to southern Africa (Figure 12.3). Archaelogical research has revealed a diffusion pathway from the metallurgical hearth in Anatolia to the Nile Valley and to West Africa, the latter reached by the Iron Age about 2,000 years ago. The Bantu brought iron-working techniques and iron tools as they migrated to central, eastern, and southern Africa (Wrigley, 1960; Oliver and Fage, 1966; Pelletier, 1964).

As a consequence, early European intruders found mining of gold, iron, tin, and copper, frequently in large quantities. Trade was sometimes extensive, especially through Arab and Portuguese entrepreneurs. These indigenous "ancient workings" became the nodes that attracted Europeans, who initially depended on local knowledge for guidance, and from which further geographic exploration was pushed, especially for industrial age minerals such as lead, zinc, chrome, manganese, coal, and oil.

Workings for Copper — **C**

Workings for Tin — — — **†**

Iron — Widespread

Gold—Belt Schists – – 🔴

Major Cities — — — — — o

Figure 12.3 Minerals: Ancient (pre-European) Workings.
Source: Adapted from Pelletier (1964) with permission of Oxford University Press Southern Africa.

Gold, and rumors of gold or in some cases silver, along with slaves, were early magnets for European interest in Africa south of the Sahara (Curtin, 1973). Interest in other minerals developed slowly, and only rarely were such minerals as iron or copper important as

exports to Europe. Local development needs, especially in South
Africa, were a spur to expanded mining in a few cases. Only in the
twentieth century, especially with the surge of industrialization after
World War II, was there increased interest in mining for export.

MINERALS AND FUELS

Several aspects of the current minerals and mineral-fuel picture for
Africa began to emerge more clearly in the post-World War II period.
First, even the most optimistic predictions about the outcome of
more intensive exploration will not change the general pattern of
geographic concentration of materials. Only a few countries now
have confirmed reserves of coking coal, iron ore, petroleum or other
important industrial minerals. One authority notes that ". . . it must
be remembered that mineral output is highly concentrated, with
three African countries accounting for about three-quarters of the
continental production and only eight or nine countries having an
output above the world average either on a per capita or per unit area
basis" (Hance, 1967:6). Such concentration is reinforced by the
colonial legacy of political fragmentation and export oriented
single-product economies. The primary goal of most colonial
administrations was to encourage investment to generate revenue
through taxes and royalties to support the costs of government, but
this was not widespread until the pressure of World War II stimulated
concern over resources.

Rarely, however, were governments *per se* before World War II
directly involved in mineral exploitation and processing activities. It
was left to private entrepreneurs to provide capital and skills, recruit
and train a labor force, develop markets, and plan expansion.
Principal exceptions included areas of white settlement in southern
Africa and the Belgian Congo. In South Africa a consistent policy has
been to use economic development, based upon expansion of
primary production and a rural economy into a diversified, modern,
industrialized state, as a means to the political goals of a minority
white population (Horowitz, 1967). Minerals always were seen as
means to achieve various political and social ends by the officials of
the Belgian government in the Congo after 1908. For various reasons,
then, South Africa, the Rhodesias, and the Belgian Congo became
major sites for European settlement of mineralized areas and of
investment.

There were, of course, wide-ranging social, economic, and
political impacts from resource conversion activities in these terri-

tories. Africans were brought directly from largely subsistence agricultural activities into an urban-oriented wage-based economy. Because the system of migrant labor, with limited periods of work by single males, was so widespread, the impact of modern ideas about society were equally widespread. An African labor proletariat rapidly emerged—in some cases to provide a base for anticolonial independence movements and in others to present a continuing dilemma with reference to traditional social policies (Horowitz, 1967).

Railroads and roads were built to isolated deposits and new towns emerged from the bush. Wage differentials were great between whites and blacks, but Africans introduced to a money economy were not likely to want to return to barter or subsistence. A major change, especially after 1941, was the emergence of powerful multinational corporations. The individual risk-taker, whether writing checks or proving out a claim, gave way to the carefully organized, structured corporation whose officers solicited investment funds in the money markets of Brussels, Paris, London, and New York. The need to have such elaborate organization to pay the costs of the tools, skilled personnel, and capital equipment to find, mine, process, and deliver to markets at a profit large quantities of bulky materials generally is conceded. The problem is, for post-independence African governments, one of balancing out these needs in the face of local shortages of trained people, transport, capital, and markets and the need of a growing population to make use of all available resources, including "wasting assets".

Africans now have many twentieth century models of how to handle this problem, including expropriation and state control. These have not yet been seen as major alternatives by most African governments. Other means include renegotiation of pre-independence agreements with private investors so that company policies and obligations with respect to training of management personnel, developing local manufacturing, supporting educational goals, and more generous payment schedules are revised. The Zambian experience since independence is an especially relevant case study of this process (Elliott, 1971; Hall, 1965).

In addition there are now international institutions, especially the United Nations agencies, whose personnel can provide objective assessments of a proposed resource development project. Technical information and guidelines can be given by the World Bank (International Bank for Reconstruction and Development), the United Nations Development Program, the Economic Commission for Africa, the Organization of Petroleum Exporting Countries and other agencies. No government need be isolated in dealing with a mining firm or minerals processor wishing to invest in a particular country. The willingness to make such an investment and to carry out development in such a way as to increase the long-term benefit to the country itself is increasingly a part of the changing relationship, especially as governments become more involved in planning for economic and social change.

In theory even a nonrenewable asset can generate the kind of economic wealth that can make it possible for a society to improve and maintain its material well-being over the long run (Petterson, 1951). The problem of managing nonrenewable resources is obviously different from renewable resources such as hydroelectric power or climate. The difficulties of implementing a management policy can be demonstrated by listing the elements necessary for a minerals policy that can help to solve the problems of depletion, competition, and transition to more complex, less dependent economies. These elements include (adapted from Buck and Elver, 1971: 18-20):

1. Maintain an adequate domestic supply of all minerals at reasonable prices—increasingly important as domestic industrial markets are developed.

2. Establish standards of land tenure, pricing, safety, processing, degree of domestic ownership and control, employment, conservation and rehabilitation.

3. Encourage increasing amounts of domestic processing and manufacturing insofar as this is realistic in the face of marketing realities.

4. Encourage and expand domestic ownership and control of mineral resource industries, taking appropriate account of the continuing need for foreign capital, while optimizing benefits derived from foreign capital invested in the nation's mineral industry.

5. Maintain and improve the nation's international competitive position in world mineral markets.

6. Ensure that infrastructure necessary for rational mineral exploitation is provided, either by government or by industry.

7. Ensure that requirements are met for technical and economic information systems, including the development and dissemination of data such as geological and mineral maps and reports, statistics and technical information.

8. Optimize any potential that mineral exploitation offers with respect to economic development in disadvantaged regions and thus to alleviate regional economic disparities.

9. Forecast problems related to mineral depletion and declining regions in order that the unfavorable impact on employment and local economic activity is minimized.

10. Conserve mineral resources in the sense of achieving optimum recovery from given deposits and minimizing waste.

11. Establish standards of environmental quality and minimize costs external to the mineral project itself.

12. Minimize external or foreign discriminatory actions affecting the nation's mineral trade.
13. Ensure that mineral exploitation contributes an equitable share of the tax revenue of the nation.
14. Increase the development and use of domestic skills.
15. Ensure that mineral resources and mineral industry activities contribute to and reflect general governmental social, economic, developmental, strategic, and sovereignty policies and goals.

Implementation of such a comprehensive set of principles necessarily would mean more involvement by governments in mining decisions than has been the case. This in turn requires policy-makers to decide, amid all the pressures for improvement and change, on the priority to be given to investment in training of managers and workers; to mapping, measuring, and exploration; and to the direction and pace of constructing infrastructure.

The need for a transition to a more stable, long-term production base through the multiplier effect of mineral and mineral-fuel exploitation primarily for export also suggests a need for a parallel development of energy systems for local needs. One of the most dramatic indices of the difference between relatively rich, developed societies and poor, developing ones is the *per capita* use of inanimate energy (Harper, 1966). Inanimate energy can be seen as the application of "energy slaves" to necessary tasks, releasing humans from onerous back-breaking labor and providing the surplus production over and above basic needs, and stimulating the spiral of growth. The "energy crisis" that hit in 1973 and which adversely affected the industrialized world, except for the U.S.S.R., as well as developing nations, has sensitized many millions to the nature of energy resources management problems. These problems have long been noted by conservationists and include the finite nature of fossil fuel deposits, the "entropy trap" associated with the second law of thermodynamics, and the need to reassess wasteful consumption practices. As this crisis of supply, costs, neomercantilism, and reduced standards of living continues it will be necessary for resource managers everywhere to become concerned with energy strategies. Such strategies will incorporate local exploitation of geothermal, solar, and wind sources to supplement the standard industrial age sources of hydroelectricity and fossil fuels. The equation will also include nuclear sources at some level, but until technological innovation provides for fusion power there will be more problems in fission power than human societies have yet demonstrated the capacity to solve.

African sources will become increasingly important in the global energy calculus. Libya and Nigeria already have become common place names in European and North American periodicals. The search for industrial age fuels began as early as the 1850s, especially in South Africa, but again it has been only in the last decade or so when exploration and discovery have changed the energy map so dramatically that major recalculations have taken place for the continent. Again, the pattern is spotty with only Algeria, Libya, and Nigeria producing major quantities of petroleum and natural gas for export. South Africa, short of oil (none has yet been discovered in spite of massive exploration efforts) but strategically placed, also plays the geopolitical oil game. For fuel-exporting countries, the double problem remains of balancing their pressing short-term needs for revenue and their long-term development needs that will eventually call for an increased *per capita* energy use.

The inability to achieve such a balance will result in a widening of the gap between a domestic economic sector within which masses of people remain caught in a traditional archaic and achingly poor condition and a dynamic, modern sector externally controlled. The indices to look for in examining whether this gap is being reduced or was not allowed to develop in the first place, include rates of domestic consumption, the refining capacity, and the growth of ancillary petroleum-consuming industry.

Africa has limited coal reserves, especially coking coal for steel manufacture, and it will continue to face problems in developing a strong metals-based industrial sector. Rail transport is inhibited by deficiencies in coal, although electrification with the development of hydroelectric resources will help. It is not necessary, however, to assume than an *in situ* shortage of resources is necessarily an obstacle to economic development—the experience of Japan in instructive. The problems of dependable sources of supply at acceptable costs in a highly competitive world probably will ensure that countries with reasonable local supplies will lead in the development race.

The pattern of petroleum deposits is brighter than was thought possible just a short time ago. Again, only a few countries are presently or potentially favored and production for export is still the main goal. Petroleum is more easily transported than is coal and interregional transfers may become more common in the future. Uranium reserves are ample for nuclear developments but, except for South Africa and possibly the U.A.R., widespread development of nuclear energy production is still far in the future.

For conventional energy sources, the brightest picture is hydroelectric power. This is true not only because of the quantity of the potential but because development of hydroelectric power has to be for African consumption. There can be interregional transfers, as will be the case with most of the power generated at Cabora Bassa dam in Mozambique, but no export to other continents is feasible. Progress in developing major hydroelectric resources, usually in conjunction with large multiple-purpose projects, will inevitably generate improvements in transportation and industry.

Nonconventional energy sources also hold promise for local and regional strategies—Africa is well-placed with respect to solar potential and for exploiting the difference in temperature between surface and subsurface waters of the tropical oceans (Zimmermann, 1951). Geothermal supplies have been tapped at Kiabukwa in Katanga (Zaire) and many coastal areas have persistent winds. It may be that the pressure in Europe and North America to find alternatives to the heavy dependence on petroleum will produce technological shortcuts to assist such strategies in Africa. One of the problems is that an elite minority, modeling their lives on the European example, will set standards of energy use that may not be feasible for the African masses. Enlarging energy resources to increase productivity and improve material well-being is not only a physical or managerial issue. It represents a basic, fundamental problem of distributional justice.

In any case, there are many uses for inanimate energy from pumps in rural areas to electrified railroads and petrochemical industries. The significant fact about energy in Africa in the latter part of the twentieth century is that the politics of oil, uranium, and industrial minerals will have to be dealt with in sophisticated and innovative ways if benefits are to accrue to ordinary Africans.

WATER

A useful starting place for a review of water resource management issues in Africa is the examination of the three variables that are significant—place, time, and quality.

Geographic discontinuity is a factor for every continent and region. Delivery of water through natural processes is highly uneven, as a glance at a world map of precipitation distribution will show. Africa is no exception and shows a range from extremely low or intermittent water supply to continuous high inputs of moisture. Both extremes lead to adjustment problems which help to explain, in part, low population densities in both the arid and wet zones. One of the historic characteristics of water management programs has been the transfer of surplus water from places of high supply to places otherwise more desirable for human activities but which are water deficient. The technical process for such transfers has altered little, except in magnitude, over time—barrages, dams, tunnels, canals, and aqueducts. Such discontinuities are essentially problems of matching supply and demand for a particular place or, in other words, of ensuring adequate quantities of water.

Quantity constraints in particular places can be reduced in a number of ways. The rather large range of choice theoretically available is illustrated in Table 12.1. Questions about the appropriateness of American, European, or Soviet technology should always be kept in mind, but it is clear from national and international efforts across Africa that the possibilities for transfer and application of diverse techniques is clearly recognized. It will become increasingly imperative for these kinds of measures to be implemented as population increases, demand for goods and services grows, and more Africans live and work in cities. Water is a basic need, and concern for its management as a resource component in all forms of economic activity from food production to tourism will require growing allocations of money, talent, and organization. In addition, hazard aspects of water, availability or quality (drought, floods, hail, health) will have to be dealt with as socioeconomic and demographic changes alter traditional forms of coping.

Even places with a comparatively high total year's supply of moisture may present management problems because of discontinuities in the timing of delivery. The rhythms of human activities associated with food production have to be keyed to diurnal, seasonal, and periodic fluctuations in water supply. The onset of a rainy season triggers a whole set of responses as does the onset of periodic drought. Strategies of crop combinations, mobility, ritual, division of labor, and storage and allocation of reserves evolve as a base for survival (see Chapter 9). Such adjustments are disrupted by modern technologies which smooth such discontinuities, especially large scale dams, reservoirs, and deep wells. It is probably fair to say that agricultural populations are more likely to deal with such fluctuations by the *in situ* strategies suggested above, whereas management of urban water supplies calls for more determined attempts to even out supplies over time in order to provide clean, dependable amounts for domestic and industrial uses (although some industrial uses, such as food processing or processing of agricultural raw materials will have high seasonal demands).

Long-range fluctuations leading to recurrent but noncyclic drought also are coped with by various traditional strategies (Mbithi and Wisner, 1972). These become more difficult to implement as population increases and, as the severe early 1970s drought in the

Sahel region demonstrates, such environmental stress is likely to result in total breakdown of traditional socioeconomic structures as well as in a tragically high loss of life. Parenthetically, if such breakdown persists and leaves millions of former farmers and herders in permanent need of outside help, we may be on the verge of the implementation of the "triage" principle with respect to such aid, especially in the face of rising costs for food and diminishing world surpluses (Paddock and Paddock, 1967).

Storage of water in some form will remain the most universally accepted technique for such management, along with transfer from places of concentrated surplus to places of concentrated demand. In addition, as demand for food increases, there will be increasing pressure to maximize solar energy inputs by supplying water for irrigation during dry seasons. In some cases, especially in South Africa, the pressure will be to shift water from high-consumption irrigation agriculture to urban and industrial uses (Kokot, 1967).

Water quality in terms of sediment and dissolved-solids load, bacteriological content, and potential disease vectors is of universal concern. High mineral content affects fisheries, agricultural lands, and industrial processes. Frequently mineral content will be perceived by domestic users as dangerous or unpleasant (White, Bradley, and White, 1972). Human use requires bacteria-free and disease-free water not only for ingestion but also for bathing and laundry, since only skin contact is needed for invasion in tropical waters by organisms such as schistosome larvae or the spirochetes that produce a form of jaundice. Water sources, especially in tropical and subtropical zones, are the habitat for disease causing organisms such as the malarial mosquito. The irony of water management is that the benefits of extending water supply projects to provide irrigation water or improved domestic supplies, are frequently counterbalanced by the penalties of extending the impact of water-borne diseases to new territories.

Frequently sedimentation during floods can be beneficial in renewing riparian agricultural lands, but penalties accrue in the forms of crop destruction during flooding, filling of reservoirs, and harm to water-supply systems.

For the near future, the largest percentage of effort with respect to quality control in Africa will be focused on water for human use. Clean, potable supplies will have to be delivered to increasing numbers of urban dwellers, but the more dispersed rural peoples also will need access to quality water if the age-old impact of water-borne diseases on human capabilities and potential is to be reduced. That such a task remains enormous and complicated can be inferred by a

TABLE 12.1 Methods of Increasing Water Supply or Reducing Demand*

I. Collection and transportation	II. Conservational consumption	III. Substitution of resources
A. Engineering for collection, storage and transport foggaras, dams, aqueducts	A. Reduction in the disappearance of water drought resistant plants water budgeting for irrigation evaporation control cropping practices natural vegetation management	A. Waste disposal-settling soil filtration combustion by product manufacture
B. Groundwater collection techniques, foggaras, tubewells, fracturing consolidated aquifers, well-drilling, pump design	B. More efficient withdrawal lined canals recycling reclamation closed circulation	B. Transport pipelines highways railroads
C. Transport technology, tunnel design and construction, cement and concrete technology machinery for tunnels, ditches, canals, canal lining		C. Power thermal and nuclear
D. Water-derived services electricity transmission		D. Recreation scenic travel indoor

TABLE 12.1 Methods of Increasing Water Supply or Reducing Demand* (cont'd)

IV. *Multiple-use*	V. *Expansion of supply units*	VI. *Reconnaissance discovery and evaluation*
A. Storage reservoir	A. Underground storage (recharge) spreading spraying wells and trenches for recharge	A. Surface geophysical methods for groundwater discovery seismic refraction and refraction sensitivity surveys induced electrical polarization
B. Design of reservoir rule curves for water retention and release	B. Water recovery improved drilling techniques increase rates of flow acidizing fracturing horizontal collectors improved pumps	B. Non-geophysical surface techniques for groundwater discovery
C. Reconciliation of competing uses and increase in complementary uses	C. Disease control	C. Subsurface geophysical methods resistivity and spontaneous potential logging gamma ray logging and neutron radiation measurement temperature logging borehole diameter logging flow meter logging fluid conductivity logging
D. Alleviation of hazards flood control disease vector management	D. Use of sea and saline waters demineralization	D. Prediction of aquifer productivity and storage capacity
	E. Use of sea and saline water (untreated) corrosion resistant alloys reduction of marine organism growth salt tolerant processes and plants	E. Appraisal of natural underground movements of water chemical dyer radioactive isotope tracers computer analog
	F. Increasing supply in local water budgets weather modification to reduce hazards of thunderstorms, hail, lightning	

*E. Ackerman and G.O.G. Löf, *Technology in American Water Development* (The John Hopkins University Press, 1959), pp. 79-105, 334-406. © 1959 by the Johns Hopkins University Press.

comparative look at a more "advanced" post-industrial society. People in the United States take pride in high quality water-supply services, but it is apparent that some areas of the country have never really been incorporated into a minimally health-protecting system, most often because many municipal water-supply systems were built before adequate knowledge about removal of toxic chemical or biological contaminants was available (McDermott, 1972). There is also clear evidence that the stress of increasing additions of chemical toxicants is such that many large systems may not deliver adequate quantities of safe water in the future. The United Nations has concluded that too little is being done to close the gap between the present—and developing—demand for water in African urban areas and the availability of quality water. It should be noted that this study deals only with urban water supplies and the figures show that the total number of people expected to need improved water supplies by 1977 will still be only 12 percent of the whole population (Dieterich and Henderson, 1963).

Such activities as drilling boreholes on farms, training sanitation engineers, installing municipal standpipes, photo-mapping, or the establishment of a Ministry for Water Affairs may all, in sum, produce necessary changes over a long period of time, but visible landscape changes are few and undramatic. There is a more visible and dramatic sign of change—the multiple-purpose river basin project, or reservoir. This has come to be a twentieth-century development technology analogous to the nineteenth century railroad. Water, and its control through engineering works, has become the tool for transforming landscapes, harnessing energy, and changing the lives of people in villages and cities. The dam has replaced the steam engine as the awesome symbol of power at work to make life better. From Aswan to Cabora Bassa, from the Orange River to Kainji, construction crews and engineers are at work. The cooperation of the United Nations through the United Nations Development Program and the International Hydrological Decade has been added to the work of other international and national agencies. "The significance of dams for any consideration of the problems of African modernisation hardly needs to be emphasized. With the possible exception of railways, there have been no projects in Africa of comparable size and implications to the giant dams, involving as they do such unparalleled commitment of resources, with corresponding social, political and legal consequences" (Warren and Rubin, 1968:ix).

There is no better example of the way in which minor changes in a system can result in major perturbations in the workings of that system, or indeed the evolution of a completely new system. Build a dam and one clearly affects stream flow, rates of erosion, ground-water supply and depletion, wildlife habitats and, in cases of large reservoirs, riparian microclimates. Other ecological impacts include the extension of water-borne diseases and aquatic perturbations such as the bloom of *Salvina auriculata* in Kariba. Also significant are changes in occupation patterns with the need for resettlement and solution of new social frictions, and the dislocation of traditional authority systems. The shocks of such socioeconomic changes are often much more difficult to cope with than are the physical and ecological changes. Intricate strategies have to be designed and frequently these are accepted only after painful trial and error (Brokensha and Scudder, 1968).

Sometimes adverse ecological and social impacts are caused, or worsened, by insistence on using a project as an end in itself or for purposes which are political or prestige-oriented rather than for development. Kariba on the Zambezi is a symbol of the lost dream of Federation when it was thought that such a dam would be a magnet for investors, giving them confidence that the neat complementarity of copper, labor, and entrepreneurship could override the political objections of Africans to continued European rule. In a sense, the Orange River project in South Africa has some of the same elements. Hastily proposed at a time of lowered prestige and increasing world political pressure, this project overemphasizes the delivery of water to white farmers for internal political advantage. It does not involve integration with planned projects in Lesotho because of an effort to ensure against use of headwaters control as political leverage. And it focuses on pride in the comparative technological superiority, in Africa, of South Africa (Simons, 1968).

It is not surprising that the age of major dams should have come so dramatically to Africa. Dams are very old as a technique for water management, but the notion of integrated river basin management is a twentieth-century dream that evolved in the United States (White, 1957). The Tennessee Valley Authority became a prototype experiment in the use of multiple-purpose storage facilities to stitch together a comprehensive plan for controlling all the waters of a river basin for purposes of regional economic and social development. By 1960, this idea had diffused widely, although nowhere is there an example of comprehensive implementation of planning for an entire basin; everywhere international boundaries remain as strong constraints on the concept. There are 54 international rivers in Africa and only the Niger, Gambia, Senegal, Chad, Nile, and Zambezi are covered by any kind of international agreement. All of these are very loose arrangements with sovereign riparian states that are still very jealous of their perceived interests.

Many projects in Africa are, or were designed as, single-purpose reservoirs either because of costs or because physical and economic conditions called for focusing on one goal: Kariba was designed essentially to produce power; the Nile dams (until construction of the High Aswan) were designed for irrigation purposes; and even the major Orange River project in South Africa is predominantly for irrigation. It is nevertheless clear that the ramifications of even a single-purpose installation are widespread. Workers gain new skills during construction. At the peak of construction over 8,000 workers had come to Kariba, most of them directly from rural villages, and they learned about concrete, earth moving machinery, surveying and electrical installation—to say nothing of life in a boom town. Hydroelectric power, developed for mines and railroads, may improve productivity in other areas. Byproducts of Kariba have been a developing fisheries industry and recreation, at least for affluent whites in southern Africa. The problems of resettlement, especially where anticipated by government planners as is the case with the Kafue project in Zambia, can be a stimulus to organization of new forms of village and rural community services. As noted in a United Nations survey: "The scope of such efforts is demonstrated by listing the subjects on which research is currently being undertaken at these reservoirs: biological and limnological surveys and studies, programmes of development of fisheries, public health problems arising from environmental changes including epidemiological studies and vectors of water-associated diseases, studies in connection with resettlement, the study of utilization of shore areas, climatology, hydrology, wildlife resources, etc." (Economic Commission for Africa, 1972:95.)

AFRICA AND RESOURCE MANAGEMENT

Africa is changing with respect to resource management problems in profound ways. Across the continent traditional resource conversion techniques are being altered under the stress of increased numbers of people, new aspirations and expectations, and rising consciousness of possibilities for a full life. Universally the educated elite have accepted the Western model of scientific rationality with respect to understanding and manipulation of natural systems. This model accommodates the idea of growth, reductionism as an approach to knowledge, and exploitation of materials through applied science.

But just as Africa changes so does the world, and one of the ironies of current development struggles is that acceptance of the Western ideas of growth, change, and betterment is gaining just as that way of life is brought into serious question by critics who note that a more reasonable world view must incorporate the "spaceship earth" notion. New problems have arisen that were only dimly foreseen, if at all, at the height of political change from colonies to sovereign nations, led by people determined that Africans would share in the fruits of technological and economic efficiency. Now the familiar divisive issues between rich and poor—the fact of wealth disparity, the "neocolonialism" of raw material export dependency, racism, cultural attitudes—are compounded by concern, based in the wealthy nations, that humans will destroy the earth as a habitat.

Experts vary in the strength of their convictions about the degree of trouble the world faces, but there is general agreement that there are signals that human political, economic, and cultural institutions are out-of-phase with life-support systems. Most are willing to admit that at least in theory it is possible for human action to disrupt the network of natural processes. Beyond this level of argument there is rapid divergence. Some experts tend to view the situation with so much alarm that they have come to be known as "doomsday prophets." Hardly any representative of this viewpoint is to be found outside Western Europe or North America. In the case of other industrial nations, the reason is either ideological or preoccupation with growth. Lesser developed societies are skeptical— limiting growth or increasing the costs of development through environmental protection might forever freeze the pattern of poverty their members are trying to reshape.

Whatever the scope of views about the long-range consequences of continued environmental stress, it is clear that the world community, through its scientific and political organizations and citizen-action groups, has launched a serious effort to understand the nature of the problem and to anticipate large-scale impacts before their effects become irreversible. The United Nations Conference on the Human Environment, held in Stockholm during June, 1972, was a watershed for this effort (Ward and Dubos, 1972). It was the first such international conference on the environment, but it also operates as a reference point for designing a new model of the kind of world both developed and developing countries may find necessary to cooperate in building. Components of such a model might include:

1. Lessening of political fragmentation exemplified by rules of national sovereignty in order to provide for global monitoring, standard-setting, administration, and enforcement.
2. Recognition that acceptance of limited-growth models may need to vary spatially—developed countries will have to accept some burden of

compensation to the lesser developed. Otherwise pollution will simply be exported (Russell and Landsberg, 1971).

3. Production-consumption systems need to be converted to stock-maintenance wherever possible with maximum recycling.

4. New models of progress and human welfare with less emphasis on material goods and more on service and support of knowledge accumulation.

5. Internalization of production costs which have environmental impact so that debts to the environment will not pile up.

6. Review of linkage between production systems of the industrialized world and population-resource-development imbalances in the lesser developed countries.

7. A change in the role of governments for many open societies. More intervention will be necessary for environmental protection but this will bring problems of legitimacy of government action in the face of citizen pressures and the need to check the power of the monitors and controllers.

8. Regenerative structures and cities—e.g., architecture and landscape design which provides for recycling and reuse rather than exploitation and resource drain.

Imagine yourself as a decision-maker in Africa—a farmer resettled after a dam has been built and your village inundated; a college student wishing to help the home village; a paramedical worker in a small city with no sewerage facilities; a United Nations special projects officer faced with recommending a minerals-exploration plan; a government official discussing grant proposals with World Bank representatives. How would you feel? What would you want to learn? What advice would you give? How would you determine priorities? How secure would the future look? Questions like these in the hundreds are being asked—and answered—by thousands of people in Africa day in and day out. Their answers and actions are part of a process which is changing the landscape of Africa.

RURAL CHANGE

Africa's population is predominantly rural. In the countryside, the direct linkage between man and the physical environment remains salient, in marked contrast to the many indirect linkages that characterize urban life. Because most African agricultural systems were subsistence oriented, tradition (which might be interpreted as conservatism) is particularly important. Life itself depends on success of the crops or survival of the livestock. Therefore, change in rural areas is frequently, and perhaps wisely, slow and tentative. Nevertheless, rural areas of Africa have experienced marked transformations. These transformations are typically a result of population growth, development of a market orientation, or their joint influence. Rural change depends upon both traditional and imported crops and technologies. It may involve the slow and careful evolution of production or, more rarely, agricultural colonization and large-scale development schemes.

In Chapter 13, Knight describes the nature of traditional African agricultural systems, exploring some of their dynamics in the recent past. Use of the term "peasant" connotes the increasing envelopment of the traditional farmer into the larger economic milieu dominated by urban areas and the market economy. Weighing

Students at an agricultural college in Ghana learn the operation of mechanized farm equipment, one direction for potentially increasing production of food and cash crops. (Photograph from the Ghana Information Services)

A young coffee plantation in Tanzania reflects the diffusion of cash cropping from large colonial estates to African smallholders, providing a modest basis for rural development. (Photograph by C. C. Knight)

Contour plowing of valuable farmland in the Machakos area of Kenya represents one technique for maintaining the productivity of valuable soil resources. (Photograph by P. W. Porter)

Rural primary schools in Kenya and other African nations have an increasingly important role in fostering rural development. (Photograph by Kenya Information Services)

the recent patterns of agricultural productivity in Africa, Knight suggests probable transitions of African agriculture in the early twenty-first century.

Berry, in Chapter 14, examines in more detail the dynamics and processes of rural change in Africa, citing many specific examples. Population stress and economic opportunity are seen as the major dimensions of rural change. This change has become manifest through changes in space (community migration or expansion), agricultural systems, and individual migration. Breakdown of agricultural systems due to overstress also occurs.

According to Ojo in Chapter 15, much of the initial evolution of agricultural production and development of market economies occurred in areas of relatively high population density. Trade focused on these areas, and along with the greater relative concentration of nonagricultural craft activities, modernization was given an early impetus. Low-density areas have remained relatively isolated in many African nations, bypassed by transportation routes and other allocations of development facilities.

How does government facilitate agricultural change? Berry answers this question in Chapter 16 by looking at the way in which African governments have responded to local initiatives for change and to imperatives of increasing agricultural production. Technology, crops, water supply, animal husbandry, credit, marketing, communications, information services, education and agricultural schemes are some major dimensions of induced change leading to development and modernization.

Among the most radical approaches to rural change is the process of instituting agricultural settlement projects. Silberfein (Chapter 17) suggests that such settlements may result from many circumstances, but with a common ultimate goal of agricultural development. Examining the successes and failures of various settlement schemes in Africa, she proposes smaller projects that will have the greatest potential for success.

Migration as a component of rural change in Africa is explored by Udo in Chapter 18. Whereas rural-to-rural migration is only one part of the whole pattern of human movement in Africa (see also Chapter 23), it has played an important role in the evolution of important cash-cropping regions and in the settling of frontier areas. Many of these migrations cross the international frontiers imposed during the colonial era, creating national and ethnic minorities important in the host countries. Udo weighs the positive and negative impacts of labor migration, suggesting that the pattern is likely to persist into the future.

Rural areas are, of course, not isolated from urban centers but are inextricably tied to them in the modernization process. After gaining an appreciation for the nature of rural change and development, we will turn to the urban centers and subsequently to the linkages tying city and countryside together.

13

Prospects for
Peasant Agriculture

C. GREGORY KNIGHT

The vast majority of Africa's labor is expended in agricultural activity. Within African nations having a substantial base for industrialization, a persistent agricultural sector must produce necessary food to support both farmers and those living in urban areas. For African nations with severely circumscribed industrial potentials, most citizens will continue to till the soil, seeking suitable nutrition and a modicum of cash income. In no country of tropical Africa are we likely to see a massive draining of agricultural population to urban areas in the next few decades.

One useful direction for undertaking discussion of change in peasant agriculture is hypothesizing future patterns. Organizing our discussion toward this goal, we will draw upon a set of complementary perspectives for examining African agricultural production. Then we can turn to the contemporary pattern of peasant agricultural production, looking at the performance of African agricultural systems in recent years. We shall see that there have been distinct regional patterns of food productivity with respect to population, ranging from some nations now producing more per capita than a decade ago, whereas others have fallen considerably behind earlier levels of per capita food supply. The necessity of feeding a growing population is obviously one impetus to agricultural change, but what are others? Expansion of the market economy and adoption of new technologies also are important. If these pressures toward agricultural change are to provide means for meeting expanding needs and desires of African peoples, what constraints to production must be removed or abated? Finally, given the pressures toward change and ecological, economic, and cultural constraints upon evolutionary processes, what patterns are likely to emerge in peasant agriculture in tropical Africa in the early twenty-first century?

PERSPECTIVES ON AGRICULTURAL PRODUCTION

Agricultural practice in Africa as well as elsewhere is a set of systematic interactions between man and environment. Agriculture may be viewed as an ecological channeling of environmental resources (see Chapter 9). It may be seen as a set of human activities, with certain kinds of behavior creating a cultural landscape that is an enduring portrait of human interaction with the environment. It also may be seen as a set of relationships between factors equated in terms of a common monetary denominator, measuring the performance of the system in economic costs and returns. Ecology, culture, and economy are thus the three major perspectives we can bring to any agricultural situation.

There is an additional perspective cross-cutting these three that is frequently neglected. When we look at agricultural practice in our own society, we share many of the same cultural attributes and outlooks as farmers. To a large extent, we "speak the same language." When we look cross-culturally, we may erroneously assume the same kind of commonalities found between ourselves and farmers in our own culture. In fact, ignoring cultural differences between themselves and Africans with whom they interact has proven to be a major cause of "failure" of well-intentioned schemes of agricultural development experts. Thus, this cross-cutting perspective is one that requires us to address ecology, culture, and economy in two modes—a view from outside the culture in question and a view from within it. This "two view" perspective simply says that the analysis we bring to an agricultural situation may differ considerably from the viewpoint of the African farmer. Our scientific expertise can have meaning only if we understand potential differences in outlook. The alternative is either a naive assumption that everyone thinks the way we do (and the high probability of failure) or a very big stick (which few of us would espouse, even if it was "for their own good"). Let us look at ecology, culture, and economy from the "two view" perspective.

African agricultural systems function within the realm of universal ecological processes, but they may seem foreign to us in the way environmental energy and matter (water, soil nutrients) are actually manipulated. Many contemporary African agricultural systems still use centuries old techniques. Characterized by the term "shifting cultivation," an African farm is typically composed of a homestead and several widely scattered fields, some near the home, and some located among older, abandoned fields in various stages of regrowth. Having been cultivated for several years and abandoned in the face of declining soil fertility, increased weed competition, and greater productivity potentials of newly-cut and burned fields, former fields will regrow toward the natural vegetation until opened again for production (Nye and Greenland, 1960). Before we erroneously attribute this kind of agricultural activity to tropical conditions and/or cultural attributes of African people, we must turn to other times and places where similar agricultural practices have occurred. Shifting cultivation remains important in tropical areas where land resources are sufficient to support this comparatively extensive form of land use. In addition, shifting cultivation occurred in wooded mid-latitude areas up until the recent historical past. American Indians and colonial settlers "slash-and-burned" their fields; in Sweden, burned-field agriculture persisted through the 1920s. A common denominator of shifting cultivation seems to have been sparse to moderate population with respect to rates of woodland regrowth—where natural fertility could be reestablished in lengthy fallow before recultivation. Shifting cultivation still remains an extremely efficient agricultural system, providing from 10 to 15 calories of food output for every calorie of labor input to production, in comparison with an estimated two to as low as one-fifth calorie output per calorie input in modern, mechanized agriculture. The difference is, of course, massive energy requirements for manufacturing machinery, producing fertilizers, running tractors, and the like. So long as land resources that can be managed by hand cultivation or animal-drawn plough produce a crop sufficient to meet the demands of the farmer, simple technologies are more energy efficient than modern, industrial farming.

The kinds and mixtures of crops in traditional agricultural systems are extremely diverse. In Africa, indigenous crops (sorghum, finger millet) are supplemented or replaced by crops from many world areas including maize, beans, and cassava (tapioca or manioc) from the New World; rice and bananas from Asia; and taro and yams from the Pacific (Murdock, 1960). The fields themselves may consist of an *apparent* hodge-podge of intermixed crops, a structure quite alien to us who are accustomed to one crop in a field planted in straight rows. Mixed fields are ecologically efficient under non-mechanized agriculture, with various plants sharing different water, nutrient, and solar energy requirements. In addition, a multiplicity of plant forms decreases potentially available niches for weeds and helps to limit the spread of diseases and pests. Multiple crops are also a form of insurance; if one fails, another may succeed.

We already have used the phrase, "agricultural system" in describing tropical African agriculture. Although the phrase potentially indicates application of modern systems analysis to the study of farming activities, it has a more general and significant meaning. A farming system incorporates the environment and culturally-based knowledge, technologies, and implements for channeling environmental resources into and through crops and livestock (Duckham and Masefield, 1970; Ruthenberg, 1971). An agricultural system is the fundamental linkage between farmer and environment, indeed between all societies and environments for producing food and other agricultural commodities. Maps of land use, aerial photographs, and other graphic materials are useful *indicators* of the nature and distribution of agricultural systems, a kind of signature of human activity or landscape artifact. But an agricultural system is essentially behavioral; it is part of the cultural heritage and contemporary learning and behavior of people. Farmers are decision makers, and as such, farming systems incorporate relevant frameworks upon which the myriad of farming decisions are made. These frameworks include environmental knowledge (often incredibly detailed and empirically valid in the local setting); the socio-cultural milieu; and, increasingly, local, regional, and world-wide economic realms. Anthropologists, geographers and others have come to recognize the importance of understanding systems of knowledge and decision making in studying or implementing agricultural change. Indeed, attention to ethnosciences, ethnogeographies, ethnobotanies, and similar aspects of traditional thought may provide useful paths for cross-cultural understanding of agricultural systems. This may be one important means toward increasing the farmer's understanding of the agent bringing new ideas and of enhancing the agent's appreciation of the knowledge and sophistication of the farmer.

Opportunities (travel, education) and material amenities (radios, bicycles, improved housing, purchased goods) of the modern world are, for the traditional farmer, accessible largely through the money economy. Many traditional African societies were subsistence oriented, trading little of their production in comparison to the vast proportion allocated for local consumption. Access to the wares of the world requires a commitment beyond this limited scale of production, and it may involve sale of traditional crops or incorporation of new crops and technologies specifically designated for sale. The burden of taxes, the opportunities of school fees, and the existence of the normal surplus (see Chapter 9) that could be mobilized was frequently the first step into the money economy. Once initiated, progressive development of local agricultural production moved rapidly in many parts of Africa, so that today one would be hard-pressed to find any society uninvolved in the cash economy. Still, most family production units allocate most of their land and labor to producing their own food, with those who devote time primarily to cash crops like coffee, cocoa, or kola supplementing a cash income with limited food production.

Frequently outside planners have viewed agricultural development and change as an economic matter—the provision of credit, farm inputs, marketing systems, and the like. This viewpoint is erroneous by omission rather than by commission. Economic rationality of new systems and infrastructure to support cash-crop production are clearly requisite for successful development (Chapter 16). However, this economic perspective must be set within local economic aspirations as well as ecological and cultural milieus. For farmers in some areas, provision of credit, opening of new roads to market, and other inducements may initiate a strong commitment to development. For other farmers, and most strongly for pastoralists (Schneider, 1974), modern economic opportunities have yet to prove desirable.

PEASANT AGRICULTURAL PATTERNS

Inventory and mapping of peasant agricultural systems is difficult. No universally accepted system of nomenclature describing agricultural systems has been accepted; even for Africa, various investigators have used similar but not identical terminologies and criteria for their application. A range of typical terminologies applicable to African peasant agriculture (Table 13.1) reveals a broad concurrence on *intensity of land use* as a primary criterion of description, supplemented by different *kinds of activity* as a secondary factor. Upland agriculture, floodland agriculture, and pastoral activities are differentiated, whereas integrated crop and livestock (mixed) farming may be components of certain categories (for example, Allan's [1965]

TABLE 13.1   Peasant Agricultural Systems

Allan[a]	Boserup[b]	Benneh[c]	Morgan[d]	Ruthenberg[e]
Pastoral	—	—	Pastoral	Grazing
Shifting cultivation	Forest fallow	Shifting cultivation	Shifting cultivation	Shifting cultivation
Recurrent cultivation	Bush fallow	Bush fallow	Rotational bush fallow	
Semi-permanent cultivation	Short fallow	Planted fallow	Semi-permanent cultivation	Semi-permanent cultivation
Permanent cultivation	Annual cropping	Permanent small-scale cultivation[f]	Permanent cultivation	Ley farming / Permanent rain-fed cultivation
—	Multi-cropping	—	—	Perennial cultivation
—	—	Floodland cultivation	Floodland cultivation	Irrigation farming

[a]Allan, 1965
[b]Boserup, 1965
[c]Benneh, 1972
[d]Morgan, 1969a
[e]Ruthenberg, 1971
[f]Includes compound farming, mixed farming, specialized horticulture, and tree cropping.

permanent cultivation and Boserup's [1965] annual cropping, and multicropping). Given the great difficulty of reconciling different data, a map of contemporary peasant agricultural systems is certain to err in many details. Nevertheless, the basic distribution of these systems is known (Figure 13.1).

A review of several other chapters will reveal the strong relationship between agricultural systems, environmental complexes, and human population densities. More intensive forms of agriculture occur in areas of greater potential environmental productivity (East African highland areas, for example) and of human population pressure (coastal West Africa). Shifting cultivation and pastoralism

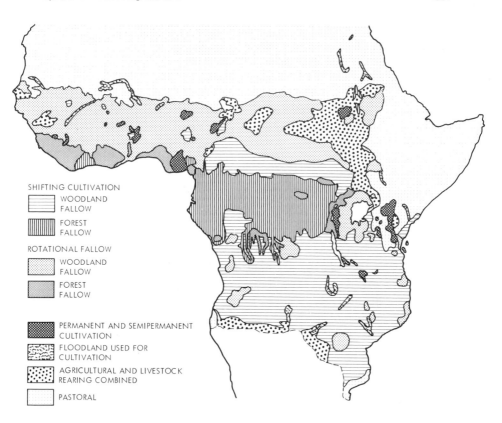

SHIFTING CULTIVATION
☐ WOODLAND FALLOW
▥ FOREST FALLOW

ROTATIONAL FALLOW
☐ WOODLAND FALLOW
▨ FOREST FALLOW

▦ PERMANENT AND SEMIPERMANENT CULTIVATION
▤ FLOODLAND USED FOR CULTIVATION
▥ AGRICULTURAL AND LIVESTOCK REARING COMBINED
☐ PASTORAL

Figure 13.1 Traditional Production Systems.
Source: Adapted from Morgan (1969a) with permission of Methuen & Co., Ltd.

are the least intensive agricultural systems. Rotational bush fallow represents an increment in intensity wherein field boundaries are commonly preserved between clearings. That pastoralism and mixed farming systems have not penetrated into the more humid areas of Africa may be attributed to a disease environment that severely limits livestock production. The use of preventative drugs and continued clearing of potential tsetse habitats may significantly decrease the problem of animal sleeping sickness, permitting the development of fully integrated mixed-farming systems in areas where cattle now are largely excluded (Knight, 1971). The map does not indicate the degree of contemporary market commitment by peasant cultivators, but surveys, censuses, and possibly space photography revealing cash-crop distribution may make such a mapping possible in the future. Certainly, most African cultivators have some commitment to the market economy, although production of export crops is still quite localized (Hance, Kotschar and Peterec, 1961).

Given the continuing dominant role of the small holder in African agricultural production, what has been the current productivity of this sector of African economies? The Economic Research Service of the U.S. Department of Agriculture periodically compiles estimates of agricultural production in African nations, both in absolute terms and in proportion to previous production levels. Remembering that statistical reporting services in African nations will be less accurate than formal agricultural censuses and other detailed data compilation typical in the industrialized world, these indices still portray recent dynamics of agricultural productivity in Africa (Figure 13.2). Most African countries substantially increased their total agricultural production as well as food production during the decade 1961-1972. When these figures are expressed on a per capita basis, however, most nations barely maintained productivity with respect to population. This is especially true of the West African Sudan-Sahel belt plagued by drought in the early 1970s. Even favorable national productivity figures may hide serious regional disparities in production within countries. Only very significant increases in production suggest improvements of diets likely to have been deficient in the 1961-1965 base years. Indices near 100 suggest a perpetuation of past conditions rather than any improvement.

Given this discouraging, mixed record of productivity improvement in the face of population increase, what factors have induced agricultural change, and what do they portend for the future?

PROCESSES OF CHANGE

Population growth, the impetus of a money economy, and innovative technology have combined to bring change to African peasant agricultural systems. Rural response to population growth has taken several forms. Agricultural systems have intensified to enable production of needed commodities from increasingly limited land resources. New areas have been settled, or out-migration has occurred from rural areas. In some cases, near-disaster has occasioned government intervention. A range of responses to population growth are explored in Chapters 14 and 15, and here we focus on two general perspectives of this facet of rural change.

Allan (1965) and Ojo (1968) have viewed population change in relationship to the ability of land resources and agricultural technologies to carry populations of varying densities. The concept of *critical density of population* integrates human numbers, kinds of

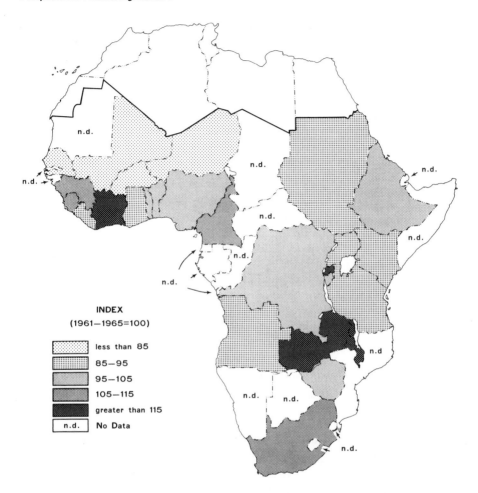

Figure 13.2 Food Production Per Capita (1972).
Source: U.S. Department of Agriculture (1973).

agricultural activities, and qualities of local resources. Beyond a specific level, a potential spiral of disaster is initiated—proper fallow lengths cannot be maintained, so land is fallowed for shorter periods; shorter fallow means less productivity, necessitating larger fields to be cultivated per capita; larger fields further decrease land in fallow and regeneration time, decreasing fertility; and so on. Cash cropping and other land allocations may accelerate pressure on land resources by removing land from basic food crop cycles.

The alternative to this kind of spiral is the evolution or introduction of agricultural systems able to sustain higher population densities. Boserup (1965) has examined a range of agricultural responses to population growth through history, suggesting that

there exists a common evolutionary sequence of agricultural intensification in response to population growth. The transition from forest
fallow to bush fallow, short fallow, annual cropping, and
multicropping historically was accompanied by improved tools,
increasing integration of livestock with agriculture, more stable
settlements, evolving transportation networks, increasingly complex
social and political systems, transition toward permanent forms of
land tenure, and greater labor specialization (Table 13.2). Without
modern forms of mechanization and use of inanimate energy sources,
productivity of human labor decreased in order to secure increasing
returns per unit area of land. As Ojo suggests (Chapter 15),
precolonial agricultural patterns reflect population density. Cities
and towns, even farmsteads, are often surrounded with zones of land
use of varying intensities (Morgan, 1969b). Most accessible areas are
intensively used, whereas those more distant may remain in forms of
shifting cultivation.

The Boserup model does not exemplify the majority of recent
agricultural changes in Africa. Allocation of land to cash crops, in
conjunction with accelerated population growth in the colonial and
post-independence period, has meant that traditional agricultural
systems have not always been able to respond to the need for
intensification in ways that might have been possible over a longer
time period. If viable intensification strategies were available, local
people may have remained unaware of them. Nevertheless, African
cultivators are cognizant of the implications of decreasing fallow
periods and land availability, larger field sizes, shifts to more
calorie-productive but less nutritionally complete crops such as
cassava, and the disappearance of the normal surplus. Once these
issues become critical, there may be great receptivity to change.
Finally, the Boserup model does not incorporate contemporary
industrialized alternatives, dependent on machinery and massive
energy inputs, combined with a major shift of population out of
agriculture to urban-industrial occupations. Nevertheless, it is instructive to view current agricultural change in Africa within the broader
context of world experience rather than as a unique process.

Embarkation into the European-focused money economy was
sometimes spontaneous, but most often it was forced upon African
peoples in the early colonial period by the advent of taxes. The
arrival of imported material goods, the desire for providing access to
education for children (which in Africa usually entails payment of
school fees), and opportunities to mobilize the normal surplus and
later to adopt new cash crops all initiated a cumulative commitment
to the market system that has become increasingly pervasive.
Traditional products slowly give way to manufactured substitutes;

luxuries become necessities; mobility and communication reinforce new definitions of the good life. Today's economic backwaters tomorrow become places where farmers have carefully calculated income potentials from their land holdings. They begin to feel a frustration rooted in a persistent disparity between their incomes and those achievable in urban areas. Increased commercialization is a second dimension of change in rural Africa, but this change is most often a veneer overlying a persistent traditional food-crop economy.

Innovations in technology frequently accompany change induced by population growth and economic development. Within the realm of traditional expertise, there may simply be an evolutionary change in emphasis among extant agricultural techniques for managing different environmental resources. Among woodland shifting cultivators, for example, agricultural techniques for management of grassland resources that were once subsidiary assume new importance as grassland, short-fallow agriculture develops. Changing emphasis among traditional crops also may occur, particularly from grains to root crops. Former crop sequences may be developed as fertility-maintaining rotations. Beyond traditional abilities, new technology may include implements (plow and oxen), fertilizers and pesticides, new crops, improved varieties of traditional crops, new management techniques, and irrigation. The ways in which these technologies are introduced and interact with traditional practices are discussed in Chapter 16.

CONSTRAINTS TO CHANGE

Plant ecologists refer to the "Law of the Minimum" that states that the productivity of biological systems is controlled by factors most near critical minima. Planners of agricultural development often have taken an analogous approach, asking what factors constrain the process of change. These factors may be found in ecological, economic, or cultural realms.

The African environment offers both potentials and perils for development. Capitalizing on Africa's assets may mean removing ecological constraints to change. Among these constraints are plant and animal diseases, problems of soil productivity, excessive or deficient water resources, pests, and indirect constraints such as human disease and uncomfortable climates (Chapters 7 and 8). Because many similar restraints have been circumscribed by technology in the developed world, it may be tempting to assume that in tropical areas they are somehow intractable. Most experts agree that this is not the case. Tropical problems are different in *kind* rather

TABLE 13.2   Agricultural Intensification[a]

Dimensions of Change	Stages Forest Fallow	Bush Fallow
Population density	Very low	Low
Fallow: cropland ratio	10+	4 - 10
Tools	Fire, ax, digging stick, hoe	Fire, ax hoe
Livestock	Incidental	Possible manuring on some fields
Settlements	Unstable, dispersed	Stable, larger
Transportation	Paths, trails ⎯⎯⎯⎯⎯⎯→	Evolution of road network
Social Infrastructure	Little formalization ⎯⎯⎯→	Increasing complexity
Land tenure	General use right without permanent interest ⎯⎯⎯→	Increasing tenacity of tenure; Persistent rights to cultivation land
Labor specialization[b]	Little division of labor	Some division of labor crafts
Output to labor	Very high	Moderate
Output to land[c]	Very low	Low

[a]Modified from Boserup (1965) and Porter (personal communication).
[b]Except by sex, age, which is common at all stages.
[c]Output to all land in the system, not just cultivated land.

	Stages	
Short Fallow	Annual Cropping	Multicropping
Moderate	High	Very High
2-3	Annual	2-3 Year
Hoe, plow, fire, draft animals ———→	Plow draft animals, hoe [Irrigation, tractors, chemicals may occur] ———→	
Stock for plow and manure ———→	Increasing provision of fodder; Increasing conflict between grazing and cultivation rights ———→	
Permanent settlement ———→	Permanent settlements Increasing link to urban system ———→	
——————————————————————→		Urban-focused road network
———→	Social organizations, health, water, other services ———→	Greater elaboration
———→	Individual tenure ———→	Permanent ownership possible fragmental landlord/tenant
Some non-agricultural full-time craftsmen ———→	Greater specialization; increasing labor inputs; emergence of wage labor ———→	
Low ———→	Moderate to high (industrial economies) Low (traditional, Oriental economies) ———→	
Moderate	High	Very high

than in *magnitude* compared to those of middle latitudes (Hodder, 1968). Specific solutions used for managing resources in mid-latitude areas may not apply to the tropics, but the same scientific techniques used in discovering and experimenting with solutions there do have validity in Africa. This application of Western research techniques that have proven profitable in the development of "Green Revolution" crops in Mexico and Asia is now being undertaken in Africa. Given reasonable time, the product may well be solutions to problems that appear to be uniquely tropical.

We already have criticized a singular focus on economy as insufficient in development, but economic rationality is *necessary* even though it may not be *sufficient* to sustain agricultural change. The unavailability of capital, for example, may mean that particular critical labor bottlenecks remain as significant limitations to productivity. Lack of hired labor or suitable machinery during a critical period of planting or harvesting may impose a limit on the amount of crops cultivated, leaving farmers only partially employed during the rest of the year. Other economic constraints include lack of markets, poor transportation, fluctuating prices, unavailable banking facilities, lack of input materials, and a limited fluidity of land resources.

Land tenure arrangements are a particularly difficult dimension of economic constraint. Many African countries want to prevent the emergence of a landlord-tenant situation and actively impede the development of permanent, individual land-holding systems. This may mean, however, that land as a basic agricultural resource is not available to enterprising farmers who would put it to good use. Solutions to this dilemma have been sought at all extremes, ranging from true freehold tenure to a maintenance of traditional communal systems of access to land. Forms of "right holder" tenure have been proposed as a compromise alternative, with the individual maintaining strong control over land resources and their disposal through inheritance or sale, but with well-defined social restrictions imposed by government when it appears that undesirable landlord-tenant relationships are developing (Makings, 1967).

Cultural constraints to change may be manifest in any society, particularly when change forbodes undesirable repercussions beyond agricultural activity. The rationality for change lies ultimately in the recipient rather than in the agent of change whose exhortations go unheeded until they assume cross-cultural relevance. Basic cultural configurations at variance with rural change are most marked among pastoral peoples. Schneider (1974) has argued that pastoral peoples are receptive to development, if this is defined as growth in their traditional economy. What they resist is change, a shift from one kind of economy to another. Costs to the existing social system of change in economy are unacceptable. If development among pastoralists means increasing numbers of cattle, overgrazing, and long-term destruction of resources, environmental costs may force change, in spite of the cultural costs involved. Agricultural peoples have been more receptive to change. Indeed, it is remarkable that most African societies have survived rates of change virtually unrivaled elsewhere in the world. Modernization undertaken over many generations in the industrialized world has occurred in one or two generations in Africa. Given this impressive history, it is likely that rural African societies will respond favorably to change that is locally meaningful and rational.

PEASANT AGRICULTURE IN THE TWENTY-FIRST CENTURY

Though fraught with difficulty, the writing of a scenario for peasant agriculture over the next half century is a profitable exercise forcing us to articulate the parameters that will control its dynamics. Probable transitions of each of the existing agricultural systems can be suggested in tabular format (Table 13.3). Population growth, economic development, and technological innovations each contribute to patterns of change. Alone, population growth will alter traditional production systems toward more intensive alternatives. New farming technology will facilitate this intensification, and acceptance of the new technologies undoubtedly will be enhanced by attractions of modernity—commodities from the marketplace and such social amenities as schools, reliable water supplies, community centers, and the like. For example, rotational bush fallow may be expected to move toward a commercialized form of short-fallow agriculture as a result of all three processes. Whether the idealized transitions will be realized depends on the functioning of the ecological, economic, and cultural constraints mentioned.

What spatial patterns might result from these probable transitions? Clearly, contemporary patterns of population density, environmental productivity (most particularly, availability of water resources), existing market orientation, and economic infrastructure (roads, railroads, urban centers) provide spatial foci for rural change. The following might be *reasonable* assumptions from which to build a scenario of peasant agriculture in the twenty-first century (but you might alter them and suggest the ways in which predicted patterns would change):

1. A moderate short-run success of governments in spreading economic development from existing foci;
2. A dominant role of urban centers and transportation networks in

TABLE 13.3   Probable Transitions of Traditional Agricultural Systems

Traditional Systems	Potential Transitions Under:		
	Population Growth	New Technology	Market Orientation[a]
1. Pastoral	1	Ranching	Ranching
2. Cultivation and livestock	4	4	**4**
3. Floodland cultivation	3	3	**3**
4. Permanent & semipermanent cultivation	4	4	**4**
5. Rotational bush fallow	4	4	**4**
6. Shifting cultivation	5	4	**4**

[a]Boldface equals market-oriented.

amplifying market orientation;

3. Most rapid and widespread intensification in existing areas of high population density and in areas of rapid population growth;

4. Severely limited change in areas with climatic handicaps, especially vulnerability to drought; and

5. Emergence of new crop varieties and agricultural strategies to support intensification, and local verification of their applicability leading to acceptance.

Figure 13.3 moves from the pattern of traditional systems (Figure 13.1) along the transitions suggested and across geographical space following patterns of existing and proposed transportation development (Chapter 22), population pressure (Chapter 5), resources (Chapter 12), and urban influence (Chapter 19). Intensification occurs almost everywhere; the notable exceptions are pastoral areas in both West and East Africa. Market orientation spreads outward from rail and road networks and from cities; cash cropping in the various export commodities is intensified in existing production areas and diffuses outward. Cash production of staple commodities grows to satisfy the needs of expanding urban populations. Isolated areas, however, experience little increased market orientation. The resulting spatial pattern evokes guarded optimism liberally sprinkled with pessimism. Some areas, such as coastal West Africa and central Africa and the East African highlands, will emerge strongly in the early twenty-first century. Other areas, including the semiarid fringes and isolated portions of virtually every African nation, will remain as

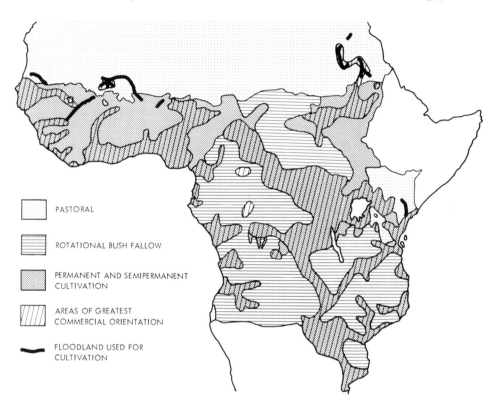

PASTORAL

ROTATIONAL BUSH FALLOW

PERMANENT AND SEMIPERMANENT
CULTIVATION

AREAS OF GREATEST
COMMERCIAL ORIENTATION

FLOODLAND USED FOR
CULTIVATION

Figure 13.3   Evolved Production Systems.

economic backwaters with human and environmental resources largely untouched for at least another generation. Hope for these areas may lie in the fact that predictions such as this elicit decisive remedial action. This might take the form of greater investment in the rural areas or allocation of resources to expanding urban-industrial employment opportunities.

The future of peasant agriculture in Africa is moderately bright. However, potentials for agricultural modernization which now seem favorable will be meaningless if population growth absorbs most increases in productivity or if enlightened responses to rural aspirations are not forthcoming from African governments and foreign benefactors.

14

Dynamics and Processes
of Rural Change

LEN BERRY

Challenge to agriculture in traditional societies has come about
in two important ways, through *stress* and through *opportunity*.
The chief cause of stress has been increasing population pressure,
the most significant unplanned change resulting from European
influence. Population growth was compounded by the alienation of
land to European farming and settlement in some areas and by the
fixing of ethnic boundaries for administrative purposes by the
colonizers, who thus "fossilized" what had before been a flexible and
adaptable system. In many cases there was a parallel increase in
animal numbers, resulting from improved veterinary services, which
added to the stress on traditional subsistence bases. Opportunity
came with the development of the market economy. The main
evidence of response is the remarkable and widespread smallholder
production of cash crops which is one of the most striking
achievements of African agriculture over the past three decades.
There has been long continued government promotion of cash crop
production in many areas, but the current level of output largely
represents a spontaneous response to expanding markets, improved
transportation, and improvements in the general economic infrastructure.

In terms of both stress and opportunity, the effect has been to upset traditional balances, and the contemporary picture is one of societies in transition as readjustments take place. These readjustments to both adverse and beneficial effects of "modernization" are an important part of the dynamics of change.

Contemporary processes of change may be either spontaneous, that is generated within the system, or specific, planned changes operating from outside. These two forms may be termed *internal* and *external* changes. This distinction has practical use in terms of understanding the dynamics of change for planning purposes. External changes will be discussed in Chapter 16.

The pattern of response to internal change in any one area and for any one group is a function of many variables, including the existing traditional system, environmental constraints, pressures on the system, the opportunities available for beneficial modification of the system, opportunities for alternative employment, and local initiative.

Adjustment and adaptation can take place in any one of the following ways, or, as more often happens, in a combination of ways:

1. Through *space changes*, where a group shifts its base or expands from an existing base;
2. Through *system changes*, where a group adopts different methods, and/or different crops within the same area; and
3. Through *migration of individuals*, where some part of the group moves, either temporarily or permanently, away from the traditional base.

Sometimes a traditional group is unable to make any of these adjustments. When this happens we witness the adverse effects of *overstress*, with economic hardship and environmental deterioration. In the following sections we outline specific examples of the ways in which these changes have occurred.

ADJUSTMENT THROUGH SPACE CHANGES

Mobility is part of African history. To a large extent, the customary solutions to problems of land shortage and land deterioration have been group migration (Prothero, 1968). The Sukuma of Tanzania are a people who have made adaptations to their traditional system over long periods of time. Initially this came about through the introduction of cotton as a cash crop under the German administration. Cotton set in motion a number of modifications in the land-use pattern and in methods of husbandry, but the most recent changes, over the last twenty years, have resulted from movement into new areas. The Sukuma number over a million people whose original settlements were south and east of Lake Victoria. As a result of increasing population pressure on the existing land resources, they have spread from this area, both south and west. They have continued cotton cultivation in these areas, adapting their methods to take account of the greater availability of land and the changing soils and topography. In these flatter areas away from the lake are found larger, more rectangular fields associated with the ox-drawn plough in contrast with the traditional ridged fields of hoe cultivation in core areas. Thus some system modification has accompanied space change. This has not been very fundamental, however, because most of the farming operations are still manual and the plough does little to mitigate real labor constraints in the system (von Rotenham, 1968; Collinson, 1963, 1964).

The Kikuyu of Kenya are another large group of people whose traditional system has long been subject to stress. The original area of cultivation for the Kikuyu was the Kikuyu plateau adjacent to the Aberdare Mountains (Figure 14.1), one of the most favorable agricultural areas in Kenya. By the 1920s, population increase had led to an extension from this favorable base both into the higher areas and lower areas. The higher areas were colder and wetter, and the lower areas were much hotter and drier, so that both were less optimal for traditional food crops, especially millets. Even so, this movement did not solve the problem, and pressures continued to the point where grazing and fallows both were reduced. Land was fragmented into uneconomic holdings as families tried to provide in

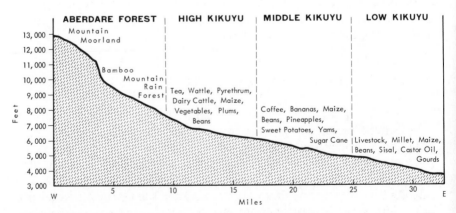

Figure 14.1 Agricultural Cross-section of the Kikuyu Plateau.
Source: Redrawn from D.R.F. Taylor (1969:485) with permission of Methuen & Co., Ltd.

the traditional way for the next generation. By 1939, it was estimated that no new land was available within the system, but there was nowhere else to move. "The Kikuyu were surrounded on all sides by land alienated to Europeans" (D.R.F. Taylor, 1969).

Official records bear witness to the growing distress of the people, but show an unsympathetic lack of appreciation of their difficulties and adjustments already made. District commissioners complained about the subdivision of the plots and about the misuse of steep slopes for maize growing, while ignoring the root cause of the problem until violence erupted in the form of the Mau Mau Rebellion. Present solutions such as land consolidation were either imposed or induced following Independence, but these are external.

ADJUSTMENT THROUGH SYSTEM CHANGE

System change is seldom abrupt, even when induced from outside, but there are examples of effective changes that have occurred spontaneously in some regions over a long period of time, where the adaptive capacity of the system has been able to meet the pressures of an expanding population by making changes in crops and in husbandry practices. Changes in crops, however, are not always for the better. When cassava, for example, has to be substituted for more nutritious millets to feed growing numbers or to gain crops from impoverished soils, dietary quality suffers.

In the original settlement areas of the Sukuma, system modification has occurred as a result of opportunities offered by the government promotion of rice as a cash crop and the high prices paid for it. Lower elevation clayey soils, formerly used as grazing areas, have been brought into cultivation for rice. Similarly, the growth of Mwanza has stimulated the provision of milk and vegetables for the urban market. Here, as near other urban centers, there is a zonation of agriculture around the town area (Morgan, 1969b; Prothero, 1953). These are, of course, all cash crops, and no fundamental change has occurred in the traditional food-crop pattern. This division between cash and subsistence food crops is characteristic of present day Africa.

The Kara are an ethnically mixed group of people living on an island in Lake Victoria. They have a long history of population growth and land shortage, during which, it is thought, there has been a progressive intensification of the agricultural practices on what is essentially a very unfavorable resource base. The Kara are exceptional among African farmers in their use of manure for crops and fodder for animals. Careful terracing and irrigation techniques are based on family labor and traditional methods of hand cultivation (Figure 14.2). This development is thought to predate European influence and to be a spontaneous response to population pressure on a very small land area—84 square kilometers. The present average agricultural density is about 250 people per square kilometer (Ludwig, 1968; Malcolm, 1953). However, there is evidence that this intensive subsistence agriculture with its high output per acre but low output per worker is not a Kara ideal. Many now are migrating to the mainland and reverting to more extensive practices as semipermanent cultivators of cash crops, which give a higher return per hour of work (Ludwig, 1968).

System change among some Ewe people in the Lower Volta region of Ghana is an example of spontaneous response to external change in environment. The Ewe are a riparian farming and fishing group. As a group they were greatly affected by exogenous circumstances in the form of the Volta River Project, which involved the construction of a dam upstream from their settlements, depriving them of traditional fisheries and naturally irrigated, fertile agricultural land. An official report concedes that the minimum loss to this community was 25 percent of direct earnings without subsidiary or linked effects.

A study by Lawson (1972) shows that in spite of this adversity, these communities were able to adapt their traditional methods to the changed circumstances and were, in fact, better off at the time of the study than previously. It is interesting to see how this came about and what kind of changes were made.

Almost immediately, advantage was taken of the lake fishery provided by the dam. Fishermen moved temporarily upstream for fishing and returned with high earnings, bringing a sudden increase in the availability of cash. This did not in itself represent a new pattern of activity, for upstream fishing and temporary migration for that purpose were traditional. What was new was the large increase in rewards leading to an increase in the numbers engaged in fishing. By 1967, fishing had become dominant over farming as the main occupation and the main source of income, although most families combined the two operations. Subsistence farming remained the basis of the economy. Whether fishing will continue to be so important will depend on the continuing productivity of the lake fisheries, a factor that cannot be guaranteed.

Two interesting factors were revealed as a result of this sudden influx of cash into a community that before had a low standard of living. One was the attitude to investment and the other was the

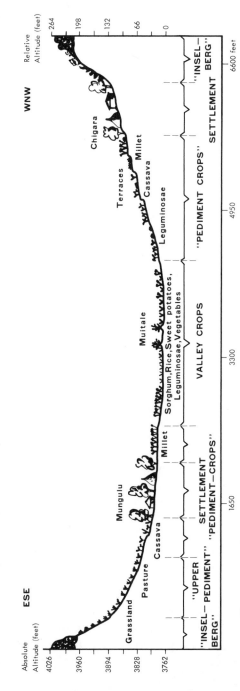

PROFILE OF A TYPICAL VALLEY SHOWING THE LAND USE WITHIN A CATENA (UKARA)

Figure 14.2 Profile of a Typical Valley Showing the Land Use in Ukara.
Source: Ludwig, 1968, with permission of Weltforum-Verlag Gmbh, Munich.

discovery that savings from "normal surpluses" were a regular part of the economic pattern. It was the display effect of the high incomes from fishing which led to the savings being revealed, as cultural constraints were relaxed. Savings were clearly an important part of the subsistence economy, as an element of security. To some extent, the level of consumption was controlled by this need for security, even when the new fishing incomes became available. Apart from some initial unproductive investment in prestige housing, a form of spending which was culturally acceptable, most of the increased income went into investment in cattle or education, or was simply hoarded as cash. The increase in the demand for consumables was small. What was particularly interesting was the lack of investment in agriculture. The returns on investments in agriculture were known to be small, given the existing constraints within the traditional system, and the decision to invest in cattle and in education (leading some family members to better jobs which would benefit all) was quite a rational one in the circumstances. Improvements in agriculture could only bring in high returns if good markets for cash crops existed. Improvements in subsistence farming could bring only marginal returns.

The traditional rural economic system remained basically the same, and the needs of the farm were still paramount as the basic support system of the community:

> Labor demands of the farm, especially for subsistence, take priority over all other work . . . where full-time wage employment was taken it was not unusual for the employee to take time off for farm work at the period of peak labor input *i.e.* planting time (Lawson, 1972:28).

Certain adjustments had to be made in the agricultural land use pattern, as a result of the dam construction, to compensate for the loss of the fertile riverine lands. These riverine areas were the best lands in the system and had been continuously farmed from year to year, whereas the upland areas were used in a much less intensive way, commonly being left to fallow for ten to fifteen years. The effect of the dam was a reduction in the length of the fallows, often below the economic margin, said to be about four or five times the length of the cultivation period. No extra inputs were made to compensate for the reduced fallow so that there was some deterioration and loss of fertility. The total area under cultivation, however, doubled as land formerly considered marginal because of its distance from the villages came into the farming system. No change was made in the farming pattern or in the methods of cultivation, traditionally hand cultivation using the hoe and the axe. The same crops continued to be planted—cassava, maize, groundnuts, and sweet potatoes. Cassava remained the staple, although previously its cultivation was confined to the flooded lands. It is interesting to note how conservative subsistence farming is, and how separate the cash element appears to be in such systems.

The Akwapim are a group of migrant cocoa farmers in southern Ghana, notable for their positive response to the opportunities presented by the successful production and marketing of this crop. Although today they are going through another period of readjustment following the infestation of much of the cocoa area by a virus disease, there is no sign of a decline in the commercial enterprise that was generated. Changes that occurred in the cocoa-growing regions remain of great interest in the study of rural change in Africa (Hunter, 1961). Basically, these changes were related to the commercialization of agriculture, rather than to modernization in the sense of improved farming methods and techniques. The introduction of cocoa farming involved the addition of a semipermanent tree crop to a traditional bush-fallow farming system, and a good deal of the reason for success had to do with the fact that it could be accommodated easily into that system without disturbing the ways in which the basic food needs could be met. Traditional agricultural practices remained the same, with the cutlass being the common implement for all operations, from land clearing to planting and weeding. Cocoa simply became an extension to the existing farming system. Perhaps one of the more revolutionary changes was the involvement of men in the cultivation process, for their traditional role was to prepare land but not to share in the cultivation work, which was the responsibility of women. Here, as elsewhere in Africa, with the advent of lucrative cash crops, the men became involved in their cultivation. Food crops, however, continued to be in the care of the women (Kamarck, 1966, 1967).

The successful spread of cocoa farming, sometimes quoted as an example of "rural capitalism," brought a number of significant changes within the farming system. The accumulation of savings and, more significantly, the reinvestment of such savings in agriculture, marks a "new frontier" (Lawson, 1972). African farmers are not accustomed to invest in agriculture, which seldom appears to give an adequate return. In this case the returns were both adequate and highly visible, and the farmers responded to the economic incentives to expand a profitable business. The expansion involved an areal movement westward into the forest lands, including the purchase of land from other groups. This was not a space change because it did not involve the whole group, but it consisted of a kind of extension of the system. Even for th se farmers who spent most of their time in the forest areas, "home" remained the towns of the Akwapim ridge. Something of the pattern of this system was recognized by early map makers, who designated the forest farms "camps." The establishment of cocoa farms in the forest areas did not represent in any way an abandonment of the traditional system. Rather the "migratory process" derived "much of its strength" from being based on the "traditional organization" (Hill, 1963), which was heterogeneous and flexible; it was adaptable to change and could absorb it.

It has been suggested that the whole question of land purchase which was associated with the spread of cocoa farming was something new in Africa, but Hill (1963) demonstrated that this was not so. The selling of land to "strangers" had long been common practice, including outright sales without reversion conditions. Conditional selling, with ultimate rights of reversion to the group, is a more common form of sale in Africa. Nevertheless, the type of land purchase made by "company groups" did give rise to distinctive patterns of land use which can be contrasted with the more traditional matrilineal forms. The company lands were organized in the form of strip farms, reflecting individual purchases, whereas the family lands reflected the mosaic of traditional relationships and usufructuary rights. The existence of company groups was merely for the convenience of negotiating purchases and was not a cooperative farming group. Farming remained an individual concern in the traditional fashion.

The agricultural landscape was also modified by the practice of monoculture in the cocoa areas, contrasting with the customary African fields of interplanted crops. Interplanting of cocoa with food crops was common at the nursery stage of the farms, but as the trees matured the food crops were grown on different fields, and the cocoa farms remained separate from the rest.

Another notable change in the system which suggested both ambition and success was the use of hired labor, uncommon in Africa on a large scale. In the early stages of farm establishment, farmers depended on customary family labor. As the farms expanded, seasonal contract labor was employed, and eventually permanent farm labor became a feature of the system. The use of labor was part prestige, part necessity, and part investment since it facilitated the establishment of new farms.

In seeking some of the reasons for the successful "peasant" production of cocoa, which was entirely a local enterprise and was not organized by trading companies who were concerned solely with the export side of the business, it is clear that the establishment of preconditions played a part. The farmers in this region already were accustomed to producing cash crops, such as rubber, oil palm, and some food crops for the market. Consequently, changes had been made in adapting the traditional structure. Incentives for change existed as a result of changes in awareness brought about through contact with the markets. The farmers thus were ready and able to seize economic opportunities which the introduction of cocoa farming provided.

ADJUSTMENT THROUGH MIGRATION

Individual permanent, temporary, or seasonal migration is a feature of many African countries at the present time, and is so widespread that general comments will be more useful than specific examples.

Employment for cash wages outside traditional agricultural systems began in the pre-independence period and involved mainly African men. They were employed on European farms, in European houses, and in European mines. Later they also became employed in low-level jobs in offices and in small factories, and in the developing service industries of the towns. Sometimes this led to a permanent migration, including the movement of families, particularly to mining areas, but more often the migration has been temporary or even seasonal. Families usually remain in the traditional home areas, cultivating their subsistence farms, and receiving help in the form of cash remittances from migratory members. Migrants keep close and continuing ties with their home areas, returning whenever possible for festivals and ceremonies of traditional life. Cultural and linguistic bonds are still very strong in Africa.

Search for cash employment is thus an important aspect of the present dynamics of change, and its effect on the rural system is both positive and negative. Cash becomes more available in the home areas, through remittances made to families. People in the home areas learn of the greater amenities of the towns from the migrants and develop new expectations and ambitions. This can lead to improvements in crops and techniques, but it can also lead to disaffection in the rural areas. Returning migrants may have lost the desire to do agricultural work. The social fabric of the group may have changed through the alteration of the sex ratio, which can cause a serious problem. Since the amount of land that can be cultivated in the traditional systems is closely correlated with the size of the labor force, the loss of able-bodied men (and increasingly of young women) often leads to a decline in agricultural activity. "This movement from village to town is not a case of the transfer of the surplus poor and illiterates of the rural areas. It is highly selective in terms of age, education, and to some extent sex" (Caldwell, 1963). This quotation relating to Ghana would be equally true for almost all instances of rural-urban migration. Migration in Ghana is, however, of a very high magnitude, and has led to some gross imbalances in the sex ratio. Hunter (1965) notes that in migrant source areas of the north, the sex ratio is a low 59. In some southern areas, the ratio reaches over 150.

OVERSTRESS: FAILURE IN ADJUSTMENT

System breakdown as a result of changes in external circumstances and problems of population growth in relation to the systems of land use that lead to land hunger is not uncommon in rural Africa. Sometimes problems become so acute that outside help in the form of government intervention has to be summoned. Sometimes small communities, unable to command sufficient notice, are left to struggle on with difficulties that lead to chronic malnutrition and real deprivation.

Reports of famine in Ndola District reaching the government of Northern Rhodesia in 1940 brought attention to the sad plight of the Lamba people. The immediate cause of the food shortage was a poor season for sorghum, the staple, but the root cause was much wider ranging, resulting from the combination of a number of factors. The development of the Copperbelt had led to a reduction in the land area available to the Lamba, and at this time they were confined to a reserve of about 400 square kilometers, which was about one-tenth of their original range. The result of increased population in the reserve had been a reduction in the woodland fallows, to allow more land annually for cultivation. This led to some deterioration. At the time of the famine, the area under cultivation was too small to ensure adequate food supplies in a bad season. There was also a shortage of labor caused by the migration of many young males, especially to the copper mines. Together these factors had led to the critical situation of 1940. Fortunately, the administration was able to respond with immediate relief in the way of food supplies, seeds for the next year's harvest, and a resettlement scheme to the south of the existing reserve where there was vacant "Crown Land." Like most resettlement schemes this was not wholly successful, but it served to avert real danger for the Lamba. The whole story is told by Allan (1965), including the efforts made at that time to determine the critical population density for the system.

Few people will have heard of Kisanjuni village in North Pare District in Tanzania, but the problems of the people who live there, the Magweno, are as difficult as any of those which have gained more notoriety. Their history over the last few years is one of increasing deprivation as land has become scarcer, plots smaller and less fertile, and food scarce to the point where malnutrition is evident (Mywangavo, 1969). Migration has resulted in the removal of the ablest part of the labor force from the village, contributing to the continued agricultural decline (63 percent of the village population of 378 is female). Attempts have been made to alleviate the land shortage by the cultivation of plots outside the village, but these lands are marginal and in that they are some four or five miles away, they entail more labor time in order to cultivate them. Such is the need for land, though, that thirteen of seventeen families in the village have to work these distant fields which represent one-quarter of the total cultivated area. The staple crop is banana. There is a little coffee and cardamom, but it is clear that chronic land shortage means that cash cropping is not likely to relieve the situation.

Land in the plains below Kisanjuni village is not yet used permanently for cultivation. It is possible that in the future this group may be forced to move in order to retain their cohesion, but this would clearly mean a considerable environmental and possible systems change which it seems they are not yet prepared to accept. The environment of the plains is very different from the mountains; the Magweno feel that it is unhealthy. Eventual control of malaria may change their attitude to the plains area. Alternatively, more could be done in the existing region by government help with irrigation. For the present, the Magweno exist with a low standard of living marginally alleviated by remittance of cash earnings from migrant members of the community.

The Gogo people of central Tanzania are an example of a semipastoral group suffering the twin handicaps of growing human and stock numbers. Their semiarid home is a harsh environment of repeated droughts and famines (Brooke, 1967; Mascarenhas, 1967b; Berry, *et al.* 1971). In spite of this, their population has continued to grow, and some parts of the area have shown a 50 percent increase in density between 1957 and 1967 (Berry *et al.*, 1971). Information on cattle numbers is more difficult to obtain, but Rigby (1969) suggests that there is an average 1.5 stock units per person. Estimates of cattle numbers for the whole of Tanzania show a steady growth over the past thirty years, and it is thought that the Gogo area may now sustain more than three times the stock rate of the 1930s, when it was already judged to be under stress (Staples, 1938).

A study of one large catchment area near Dodoma showed a

density of 1.9 hectares per livestock unit in an area where 2.5 hectares is considered to be the minimum safe density. Since this figure does not take into account the fact that part of the catchment is not used for grazing, it is an understatement of the problem. The actual amount of grazing is even less than 1.9 hectares per unit.

The results in terms of the environment are abundantly clear, both from a casual inspection of the bare eroded soils of the area and from detailed studies of soil erosion (Rapp, et al. 1973). Years of less than average rainfall have compounded the problem, and massive government aid has been required to avoid a disaster. Attempting to tackle the problems in a more fundamental way, the Tanzanian government is trying to reorganize settlement patterns in this region and to introduce new crops and a new way of life. Unexpectedly, wine production has proved to be one somewhat successful agricultural enterprise, but it involves relatively few people.

There are similar problems in semiarid areas elsewhere in Africa, notably in the central Sudan where the provision of improved water supplies for stock in the 1950s had the adverse effect of concentrating increased numbers around new water holes, with the result that zones of bare ground and nonedible grasses developed rapidly. This was a case where the resource base was actually depleted by "improvement" through insufficient attention to the working of the traditional rural system in planning for change (Graham, 1969; Lebon, 1965). It is the system that must be understood, as well as the land base.

It is more difficult for the pastoral peoples to accept change than it is for the cultivators, since their traditional systems are less easily modified and change is necessarily more abrupt. Crop farmers are able to add cash crops to their existing work patterns without greatly altering their way of life, but for pastoralists to become either cultivators or stock ranchers involves a radical change in life style and attitude.

Extensive cultivation in pastoral areas is generally precluded by the nature of the land, although there is almost always some crop cultivation associated with pastoralism. The part played by cattle in these traditional systems is so essential and so particular to the systems that methods of modern stock management inevitably clash with fundamental ideas and are consequently very difficult to introduce. Cattle represent both social and economic wealth: they represent income, savings easily convertible into cash, insurance, and social prestige. These factors, plus the fact that individual ownership of stock is combined in the system with communal ownership of grazing land, means that quantity is preferred to quality, an attitude completely at variance with efficient herd management. It may be that modern ranching will be better introduced by the establishment of large scale enterprise, rather than by any kind of modification of the traditional stock rearing systems. Pastoral peoples are among the more conservative of the rural communities in Africa. For them change threatens the very core of society.

15

Rural Production
in High Density Areas

G. J. AFOLABI OJO

Traditional African economies were characterized by their variety and diversity. Only very broad generalizations about all of them can be accurate to any degree, and specific details can hold only for particular cases within relatively small areas. As aptly described by Dalton (1970:64):

> ... traditional Africa comprised thousands of small economies. If we examined them separately without comparing them to the familiar economies of present-day Europe and America, we would be struck by their diversity. They differed with regard to the quantity and quality of natural resources at their disposal, and therefore the principal foodstuffs they relied upon. Some were hunters, gatherers, or fishermen precariously depending on natural environment for livelihood. Others were herders living off their herds and flocks; more were agriculturalists. Most combined several of these subsistence activities. Many of the hunters, gatherers, and herders moved with the seasons, and some of the shifting agriculturalists moved every few years. Others were permanently settled.

In spite of the kaleidoscopic and variegated patterns of these economies, there has been a fairly well defined distinction between those occurring in rural areas of low population density and those found in regions of high population density. Probably more than any other variable, the population factor accounts for many differences

226

in the nature of traditional economies. Scarce land must be used more intensively; careful nurture of limited resources requires labor and techniques that are unnecessary when resources are more abundant. In short, the evolution of local production over the centuries was a major reflection of the density of population in the different parts of the continent.

Until recent decades, local production over most of Africa was basically for subsistence in areas both of low and high population density. But unlike low density areas, the production systems in high-density areas often contained a greater volume of nonagricultural activities, especially craft-making, and were characterized by forms of internal and external trade. Many populous areas have nourished urban populations for centuries (see Chapter 19), and thus there were incentives to produce above the basic subsistence level. Farmers were receptive to methods that would increase productivity and consequently were primed for an early transition to market-oriented agriculture.

The main systems of agricultural production that have evolved in high-density areas are rotational planted fallow, compound farming, mixed farming, commercial tree farming, and the plantation. Rotational planted fallow is a skillful modification of ordinary bush fallow through the use of "special types of fallow plants which have the advantage of restoring nutrients to the soil faster than the natural fallow vegetation" (Benneh, 1972:248). Compound farming, a kitchen gardening system, is adopted in circumstances where it becomes necessary to use all available land, even the small spaces at one's door steps. The nearness of cultivated land to residential location makes it possible to depend on domestic manure for improving the fertility of the soil. This dependence explains why "the fertility of the soil declines from the area immediately around the compound house toward the outer boundary of the farm" (Benneh 1972:249). On the whole, compound farming is more commonly practiced in nonurbanized, high-density areas, as in Southeastern Nigeria among the Ibo.

Mixed farming is a recently adopted system of agricultural production in some high density areas of Africa. It involves the integration of arable farming with livestock rearing, a process requiring advanced techniques of farming including animal and mechanical ploughing and also the production and use of animal manure. The high-density areas, also being the areas where capital, labor, and managerial resources are relatively more available, have provided the conditions that are obviously more conducive for the introduction of mixed farming.

Commercial tree farming and plantation systems of agricultural production are not, strictly speaking, confined to high-density areas. In fact, these systems have been adopted in low-density areas where the conditions necessary for their establishment could be found, including availability of land, skilled labor, capital, and managerial enterprise. Quite clearly, these conditions are not evenly or equally available. Although land is abundant in sparsely populated areas, other factors may be relatively scarce. The converse is true of regions of high density: although land is scarce, the other factors may be relatively abundant. Hence, most of the major developments in commercial tree farming and plantation systems have taken place in populous regions. Furthermore, since these systems of agricultural production are adopted in response to overseas demands, the handling of the external trade generated by them has been focused on the urban centers that are already in a network of commercial and communication relationships with counterpart centers in overseas countries.

A concomitant development of colonialism in many parts of tropical Africa was the demand for agricultural products required as raw materials for manufacturing industries in the metropolitan countries. The trade that flourished during that era consisted mainly of a one-way movement of raw agricultural products from Africa to Europe and a one-way reverse movement of manufactured products from Europe to Africa. Colonial governments made strenuous efforts to stimulate large-scale cultivation of certain crops such as cotton and groundnuts. Representative of these efforts are the Inland Niger Delta Scheme, the Sudan Gezira Scheme, and the East African Groundnut Scheme, all of which typify the grandiose plans that colonial governments devised in an attempt to exploit the resources of Africa for their own needs. The dismal failure of the East African Groundnut Scheme, in particular, is illustrative of the rather hurried attempts, which the colonial governments made in those early days of acquaintance with the tropical environment, to exploit its apparent wealth (Wood, 1950).

Major changes in the agricultural patterns of the continent were made when the local inhabitants began to respond to the financial stimuli of cultivating export crops such as cocoa, oil palm products, rubber, coffee, and tea. This led to a rapid transition from local exchange production to an export-oriented production more or less in the form of the tradition established by Roman Africa, which grew wheat and later produced olive oil and wine for export to Rome (Mabogunje, 1968). These agricultural export products along with those of mining account in large measure for bringing the economies of tropical Africa into the orbit of the world economy, and their effects have been felt most in the urban centers and neighboring areas of high density of population. Although some of the local production of export crops took place in low-density areas, the benefits have accrued almost exclusively to the high-density urban-influenced regions.

In many parts of Africa, the transport network expanded in response to growth in the economy as well as to concentration of urban centers (Chapter 22). Populous areas were, from the beginning, nodes of transport networks. To cope with the increasing local production of agriculture and manufacturing industries, ports emerged along the coastlines in areas favored by natural conditions and also by a fairly large population. Considering the totality of their operations, such ports depended on centers of commodity collection and forwarding in the interior, which invariably were high-density areas or those that had the potentiality of becoming so. At a later stage of the development of the transport network, some hinterland nodes expanded and maintained links with ports as well as with other emerging centers of the region. This process of expansion leading to a sequence of transport development in underdeveloped countries has been demonstrated by Taaffe, Morrill, and Gould (1963). What should be stressed here is that the high-density areas lend themselves to becoming centers of the expanding transport network and also of a high level of local production. Moreover, although the last few decades have witnessed the rapid development of transportation networks and their extension to most nooks and corners of Africa, it is true to say that the high-density areas have benefitted most from the transport revolution. In turn, there has been an increasing concentration of economic activities, especially of production, in the urban high-density regions with their special locational as well as transportational advantages.

Most of the changes in form and volume of local production in Africa have direct and indirect effects on the land. With increasing technology, with the constant redistribution of the population (especially the paradoxical drift to some areas of high density), and with the expanding character of the transport network, more pressure is being brought on the land especially in the areas of already high-density population. The carrying capacity of the land is being threatened in many densely populated areas where, with any further increase in population, the density level may approach the critical. The significant result of the pressure on land in high-density areas is that land has acquired substantial value thereby leading to a modification of the land tenure system. The high value being set on land has put a new emphasis on local production in the sense that most people are now willing to use land only for productive purposes. Certainly as land values rise in the future, the availability of land for local production will become more and more significant. Similarly, systems of land holding will continue to change to meet the needs of the time by becoming owned and used more on an individual than a communal basis.

In recent years, many national governments have shown increasing interest in local production and have actually participated in ensuring several modern forms of production, both agricultural and industrial, especially on a large scale basis. It is significant that even though, in theory, governmental interest and participation are meant to affect all production, in actual practice efforts have been concentrated in high-density areas. This is brought about by the fact that the foci of human activities, and therefore governmental involvement, are normally in populous areas.

Governmental interest and participation derive mainly from the grim fact that the economies of many parts of Africa, caught in a vicious circle of low input, low throughput and low output, required intervention of external factors to bring change. The inhabitants, as individuals, were capable of only limited change toward making the economies rise beyond subsistence levels. Even at the early stage of response to the external stimuli of overseas demand for various agricultural crops, most individual farmers merely adopted the cultivation of the new crops without necessarily modernizing methods of production. Modern agricultural education that could influence the adoption of the methods of production was not within the reach of most farmers. It fell on the governments as primary agents of change to introduce agricultural experimental stations, farm institutes, and farm settlements as part of the overall design to bring about changes in agricultural production. In addition, the governments initiated different types of agricultural practice, each of which represents substantial development on traditional types. For instance, the modern types introduced in the eastern region of Nigeria include "commercial plantations, nucleus plantations, settlement schemes, small-holder investment schemes, and small-holder improvement schemes" (Fogg, 1965). These schemes were sponsored by the government as a means of providing at least one alternative that might be acceptable to farmers depending on their resources.

For a fairly long time, governmental efforts remained confined to the agricultural farms and stations. The efforts of agricultural extension officers charged with the duty of spreading the practice of modern methods used on the government farms were limited. More important still, government farms required an initial input of substantial capital and technical skill which make it rather impossible for the vast majority of traditional farmers to follow suit. By and large, there was a distance decay pattern of adoption away from the high-density areas to the low-density areas. A few exceptions of modern farms can be found here and there in low-density areas, where they take advantage of the large extent of agricultural land available. Examples include the wheat growing areas of northern Tanzania, the coffee producing districts of the Ivory Coast, and cattle ranching in the Rift Valley of Kenya.

The effects of governmental interest and assistance are now widely felt in each country. Many governments have established agricultural credit corporations or similar organizations through which money is loaned to farmers on very favorable terms. Although such loans are made available to all who are able to demonstrate that they can put them to good use and who are at the same time probably credit-worthy, farmers in high-density urban regions are at a considerable advantage in joining credit schemes. Similarly, farmers in high-density areas where scarce land resources severely circumscribe potential income may be more easily persuaded to join cooperative farming groups than those in low-density areas where other farming factors than land are most limiting to productivity.

Already in many parts of the continent, groups of farmers have begun to organize themselves into Cooperative Farming and Produce Marketing Societies. This development generally is regarded as a salutary supplement to the government-inspired Cooperative Unions which have farming as one of their major activities and also to the farming institutes and settlements which are strictly managed by government.

The pattern of concentration of production in populous areas within each of the national territories of Africa has highlighted the general imbalance between high- and low-density areas. This imbalance, a feature of regional disparity, is reflected not only in production but also in all the numerous facilities that accompany modernization. There are fears that the imbalance could worsen and the gap widen if it is not controlled with equity and imagination. However, up to a point, "some degree of regional imbalance in levels of economic development is a normal state of affairs . . . where the pattern of imbalance is strong, national planners should proceed with caution in attempting to redress the imbalance which may generate inefficiency in the national system and thereby slow down the national rate of national growth" (Logan, 1970:117).

The trend of population movement set in motion by imbalance is in itself fraught with many socioeconomic dangers. Thus the constant drift from the already poor low-density areas poses serious dangers to the social and economic life of the different countries. The low-density areas are being drained of their youth; the economies are being robbed of their vitality; and whatever is left behind, whether person or resource, becomes stagnated. The high-density areas, on the other hand, are being choked and stifled; congestion has made many of their basic amenities inadequate and many have become fertile breeding grounds for crime and political disorder. Yet, the economies of the high-density areas wax relatively strong, definitely at a much faster rate of growth than in the low-density areas. Thus local production is constantly tending towards a lop-sided development which favors the high-density areas. Governments are well aware of this phenomenon as can be seen in many of their economic policy statements and particularly in the development plans. One of the cardinal objectives of many development plans in Africa has been to normalize the disparities between populated core areas and low-density peripheries. But inertia is a very intractable foe; significant new growth poles outside the already densely populated parts of Africa are likely to be few and far between.

16

Facilitating Rural Change

EILEEN HADLEY BERRY

In both the colonial and post-independence periods, development agents have encouraged agricultural change beyond the
spontaneous changes already occurring in African societies. Since
pre-independence times, there has been an acceptance in Africa of
the need for rural change to raise living standards. The motivation
and perspectives of the "modernising" agents have been very
different at different periods. In the past these agents were European
settlers and missionaries, large commercial companies, and eventually
the colonial governments.

The colonizers and settlers and the colonial governments had
three major agricultural aims: to provide food for themselves; to
grow export crops for their overseas markets; and to "improve native
agriculture." Toward these ends, Africans found themselves recruited
to a new type of wage-earning labor force, became aware of the new
forces of the market economy, and were introduced to new crops
and methods of cultivation. These marked the beginning of rural
change, although in the early part of the colonial period, modern and
traditional activities were often separate and coexisted as two
distinct systems. The colonizers strengthened this separation by
arrangements which prohibited the growing of certain crops by

Africans, since it was thought at the time that the African farmer was not capable of maintaining the quality of production required for the export market.

The colonizers (and the missionaries, who were also very active in Africa at this time) nevertheless began to take an interest in traditional farming. They saw what they considered to be the "primitive" forms of "native" agriculture: scattered fields without hedges or "proper" boundaries; mixtures of crops in the fields; a prevalence of weeds; and primitive instruments of cultivation, the hoe, machete or cutlass, and the digging stick. With all good intention, they set about to "improve" the African farm as well as the African farmer. They introduced soil conservation methods and irrigation techniques and attempted to encourage tidier ways of planting. But their measures were often coercive and associated with an alien government. Emphasis was on land rather than on system. What they failed to appreciate was that they were dealing with integrated socioeconomic systems well adapted to and efficiently using available resources and factors of production. The association of alien coercion with new methods led to a hostility which persists to this day in some areas, such as the Usambara and Uluguru Mountains of Tanzania, hindering successful modernization.

Rural change had, however, begun during the pre-independence period, brought about by the gradual introduction of cash crops and by many indirect and often unintended consequences of intercultural contact. The positive incentive of cash-crop farming was, in fact, a major agent of change, disproving some of the myths of the "lazy African farmer." The African response to the introduction of a lucrative cash crop was nearly always favorable: sometimes it was remarkable, leading to such large increases in the production that marketing problems arose. This was the case with coffee cultivation in Uganda, Kenya, and Tanzania (McMaster, 1968; Baker, 1971; Knight, 1974).

It is significant that those new crops that best fitted into the traditional farming year were the most successful. An example is cotton which easily could be integrated into the basic maize/millet economy, and indeed in some areas is inter-planted with maize. Similarly, coffee became successfully adopted into a banana economy. In these cases no radical system change was required. System modification rather than system change was sufficient, establishing preconditions for more fundamental changes as crops needing greater adaptation were introduced.

Contact with the colonizers led to other changes. On the positive side were the changes in communications, transport facilities, and the opening of markets. There was also the establishment of services such as schools, hospitals, agricultural research stations, extension facilities, and improved rural water supplies. On the negative side were unintended demographic changes which led to pressures on traditional subsistence systems, alienation of land, and land restrictions imposed upon Africans that reduced resources available to them.

The present, independent governments and the agencies working with them in rural development projects have inherited both the practical forms of the agricultural advisory services and the prejudices formed in farmers' minds against many improvement measures. As the colonial governments before them, they look at land only in terms of its productive capacity, rather than in terms of its function in the traditional rural subsistence systems. There is now a greater awareness of the need to understand the traditional systems and to educate the farmers in the need for, and the possibility of, making changes which will raise their living standards (Schultz, 1964).

In the post-independence phase of development which we are now witnessing, many of the same problems persist, but motives and perspectives are different. The aims of the new governments are no less than a new national well-being. Among specific goals are: an increased standard of living in the rural areas, and a reduction of inequalities between town and country; a reduction of migration to towns not yet having the capacity to employ large numbers seeking work; a maintenance and improvement where possible of export cash-crop earnings, often the main source of national income; and an improvement of food production and development of better internal markets and communications to improve food supply and distribution. Even where goals are less precisely formulated, there is a growing recognition of the importance of the rural sector as supporting most of the population and holding an appreciable potential for development. In some cases this represents a major shift in thought and policy—industrialization had been thought of as the "engine" of growth, and agriculture was to be left to itself, to await modernization once an industrial base was established. Constraints on industrial development are now better known, and many governments are beginning to consider what kinds of investments can be made in agriculture as well as industry (Schultz, 1964; Eicher and Witt, 1964; Robinson, 1971). Facilitating rural change, in this context, means promoting the rural sector for major growth in the national economy.

Except for the coordinated schemes of agricultural development, which have been limited to certain geographical regions (and have not been entirely successful), the more usual approach to rural improvement has been through the search for "missing links" or critical "bottlenecks" which are thought to be the barriers to progress. Attempts to facilitate rural change have, therefore, often focused on a single factor, failing to give adequate attention to repercussions of this factor on the rest of the system. While single factor inputs may sometimes have the catalytic effect intended, they also can cause serious imbalance. One common example is provision of new water points for stock without clear consideration of the likely effects in a society which will attempt to maintain as many animals as water and grazing lands will support. Overgrazing in these situations frequently has led to serious land deterioration. Understanding of the total agricultural system is necessary if external inputs are to be effectively applied. The involvement of local people in their own development plans is also important. Too often, decisions have been made that are unacceptable to the group whose interests are at stake. In the end, all change depends upon the willingness and ability of the people to adopt innovations. Their cooperation is vital. Freedom of decision making at the local level is coming to be accepted in some countries as an important policy element.

Most African governments now have continuing agricultural advisory services available to farmers. These generally deal with the promotion of new crops and with advice on the use of insecticides and fertilizers. They may involve attempts to introduce ox-ploughs or tractors, and they also may help with such things as flood control, irrigation, and other aspects of water management. The encouragement of marketing cooperatives may become part of this kind of extension service. Frequently there are attempts at increasing the farmers' general awareness through educational programs. Rural credit facilities exist in some cases to encourage the farmers to make more inputs into their farm land.

The question is, then, how can such external inputs be made in such a way that change is facilitated without disorienting local production systems? African response to rural change has been varied, and it will be useful to examine rural modernization under various headings: technology, crops, water supply, animal husbandry, credit, marketing, communications, information services, education, and coordinated schemes. We then will appreciate some of the potentials and complexities of rural change in Africa.

TECHNOLOGY

The low level of much agricultural technology in Africa has led to a major focus on this element. The hoe and digging stick are still the most commonly used implements, and it was once thought that the introduction of modern technology in the form of farm machinery was a necessary prerequisite to increased productivity. However, there are many obstacles to mechanization on the African farm. Some problems are physical—soil conditions are often unsuitable for mechanical cultivation, and soil erosion may be increased where large areas have been prepared for cultivation by tractors and subsequent planting by hand has not been sufficiently fast to stabilize the soil. This is a common situation, for most of the farm work of planting and weeding is still done within the labor constraints of the existing system. Economic problems are more widespread than physical problems of mechanization. Most African holdings are too small and fragmented to enable efficient tractor use, and the returns for low-priced crops are insufficient to justify the capital outlay necessary to purchase or rent a tractor. Some degree of success has been achieved under a cooperative basis of enterprise for wheat farming on the Mbulu plateau of Tanzania, where both tractors and combine harvesters are efficiently used, and local skills have developed to maintain and repair the machinery.

Approaches to technological change must cover a wide range of options focused on particular situations. Much available farm equipment is designed for conditions in different parts of the world and is unsuitable for Africa. In some cases, better types of hand tools could lead to profitable intermediate changes, and in others the ox-plough has already proven more useful than the tractor. The whole question of an intermediate technology for Africa, and for other similar developing areas, is of great importance for progress in rural development (Dumont, 1966; Vail, 1975).

The possibilities of improving farm transport, now most often the human head or back, are somewhat brighter, since inadequate use has been made of animal transport and simpler forms of handcarts and bicycles, the production of which might be encouraged as a form of local industry. Trucks are often a sound investment in areas where there has been successful cash crop production over a considerable period of time, as in West Africa (Hill, 1963).

The maintenance of soil fertility in traditional agricultural systems generally was managed by field rotation rather than crop rotation, although mixed cropping may have had some beneficial effects on the soil. The use of fertilizers was rare, and although there has been a steady increase in the use of such inputs, the practice is far from being universal. The cost element would seem to be one constraint upon fertilizer use, for we find that farmers are often unwilling to employ it even for a lucrative cash crop. There is good evidence that in some regions the use of fertilizers is uneconomic because of existing husbandry not making the best use of them. The application of fertilizer alone cannot increase yields unless it is accompanied by more attention to soil preparation and weeding.

African Departments of Agriculture have as high priority, promotion of the use of fertilizers and pesticides for the encouragement of better land-use management. Part of the problem is the inexperience of those using these methods—many have not yet learned the importance of proper timing of the application or the required strengths to be prepared. There are also other factors which can easily negate fertilizer use. These include climatic hazards and problems of harvesting, marketing, or storage. Ambition is reduced by the fact that investment can be lost so easily.

In some cases where good agricultural extension work has been coupled with positive financial returns, farmers have shown themselves willing to respond to these "improvements." There is an example of this in Tanzania, where subsistence maize farmers participating in tobacco growing in cooperation with the Tanzanian government have been found willing to use six or seven sprays of fertilizer application on their new tobacco plots, and even on their food crops, when the returns from their holdings reached 1,000 shillings per acre, incomes much in excess of those previously obtained. There are many other important exceptions to the generally poor level of response to fertilizers, including the Wakara in Tanzania and many Nigerian farmers, such as those near Kano (Mortimore and Wilson, 1965).

African yields of most crops are well below potential, but it is probable that real changes will depend upon improvements in whole farming systems, including incentives to produce surpluses, rather than upon single inputs such as fertilizer. The same kinds of factors apply to other farm inputs. Farmers are unwilling to make cash outlays for pest control when crops are later destroyed through vermin or other animal attack in the fields and in storage centers. Statistics are difficult to obtain but it is known that a high proportion of food crops is lost in these ways. As much as 25 percent of the potential yield of cereals, and 30 percent of harvested crops in storage is lost in Tanzania (Mascarenhas, 1971). Storage losses are a constant problem. The use of insecticides thus is only a small part of the war against pests.

CROPS

Because of the importance of agricultural exports in earning foreign exchange, most African governments are now playing a major role in establishing crop priorities by promoting or discouraging particular crops. World-market conditions are vital to the economic production of most cash crops. Where there is strong international competition and formal or informal agreements to control markets, the role of government in regulating production is very important. This is the case for coffee, tea, sisal, sugar, cocoa, and pyrethrum. The search for new kinds of cash crops is also vital in view of the long term marketing problems associated with some of these crops. For example, tea, which has better marketing prospects than coffee, is being encouraged in Tanzania, Uganda, and Kenya. The government of Tanzania also is encouraging the production of fruit and vegetables for the European markets, now that rapid and frequent air transport is making this possible, and it is giving support to a specialized project for the growing of winter vegetables for the local expatriate market, the hotel business in Dar es Salaam, and export (Heijnen, 1972).

The production of certain food crops is being encouraged as a means of reducing import needs. Rice commonly is imported into African countries which are climatically suited to its production. Farmers are now being encouraged to grow rice and are being given special advice to help them. For example, in Tanzania Chinese agricultural teams have been engaged in this task, and teams from both Taiwan and the Peoples Republic of China have assisted rice-growing programs in West Africa. In traditional maize-growing countries, there is frequently a select but increasing proportion of the population which prefers wheat bread, creating needs for the import of this cereal. There is now a tendency for some African governments to attempt wheat production wherever suitable climates exist in order to curtail the use of foreign exchange for unnecessary imports. Growing urban populations are creating new markets for a wide variety of foodstuffs.

Government policies with respect to crop changes are brought into being through price manipulation (protective tariffs and price inducements), simple exhortation (cassava as a famine insurance crop), and creation of special schemes to facilitate production (rice on irrigation schemes and wheat on mechanization schemes). The response to these policies on the part of the African farmers has, on the whole, been positive and has demonstrated price responsiveness and rational economic decision-making. Attempts at changing priorities for food crops have, however, met with much less success. Traditional preferences dominate here. Maize frequently is grown in regions which are far below optimum for its successful cultivation, because it is the traditional staple for the community. Only the establishment of national markets and national distribution systems will allow the development of an ecologically rational production pattern for crops. In the case of seed selection and the new hybrids, costs in relation to returns within the constraints of the peasant farming system are again relevant factors in decision making. The problems relate to both production and marketing. There are critical planting times for the new hybrids, for instance, which the peasant farmer cannot always meet. The application of fertilizer and insecticide are essential if the promised yields are to be achieved. Planting in pure stands makes a significant difference to yields, a practice involving difficult adaptations for some farmers. Where the required cultivation methods are not followed, the increase in yield given by the hybrid is seldom worth the extra expense of obtaining the seed. The African farmers' response to the introduction of improved varieties of seed, particularly the new hybrid strains of maize, is as cautious as the response to any other inputs involving cash outlays. Yet awareness of the importance of seed quality in improving yields is growing, and demand for the new seed is increasing.

Another difficulty concerns the marketing of surpluses where the introduction of hybrids has been successful. In Kenya, the program for introduction of hybrid maize and extension work was exemplary, but a glut of maize resulted which could not be sold locally and which was produced at costs that made international marketing uneconomic. If wider use is to be made of the new high-producing strains in Africa, attention must be given to the first wave of effects in other areas. Significant changes in levels of production have been demonstrated in Asia and in Latin America, but what we need to know is the effects of such increases on the rural systems involved and on the market prospects for the crops. Experimental approaches need to be concerned not only with the cropping aspects but also with the social and economic ramifications of the introduction of this kind of change (Brown, 1970).

WATER SUPPLY

Availability of water is a key factor in all agricultural systems. Apart from its importance in relation to crop production, it is also essential for the use of sprays in fertilizer and pesticide application. Improved water use, however, generally has been focused on highly capitalized irrigation schemes involving completely new techniques and often new crops, since high quality crops are necessary to justify the costs of capital inputs. Irrigation therefore has been associated with what is called the "transformation" approach, because it has involved radical changes, and the response can only be assessed in the context of the "scheme" approach to change (see Chapter 17).

Water provision has been a frequent focus of improvement policies for the rural sector. Because there has been a strong tendency for water programs to be conceived and executed at a high technological level with engineer-designed supply systems and elaborate storage tanks, cost has inevitably restricted the scale of such projects. As a result, provision of improved supplies has not been extensive and has been insufficient to keep pace with the existing demands. In fact, in many areas the number of people supplied amounts to less than the population increase over the last ten years. The maintenance of large scale sophisticated systems already installed is an additional problem. There is an obvious need to develop simpler systems which can be cheaply installed and locally maintained, if the current national goals of widespread rural development are to be met.

ANIMAL HUSBANDRY

Animal husbandry is one of the most conservative sectors of agriculture in Africa. It is in this sector that the disastrous effects of the single-factor approach to change have been most clearly demonstrated. The first impact of modern ways upon the pastoralists usually has been a program of veterinary care, aimed at improved stock management through the use of inoculation and dips to control disease and the use of better foodstuffs. There also have been successful attempts to improve livestock breeds, particularly cattle breeds, and there has been a high degree of technical success in improving the quality of both milk and meat production. However, with few exceptions, there has been little increase in the number of animals sold for meat and only limited progress in the development of a dairying industry. Partly this is because of the role of livestock in the traditional system, where emphasis is on the number of animals kept rather than upon quality, and partly it is caused by limited markets (Rigby, 1969).

Cattle play an important role in the socioeconomic system, and it is clear that there are many ways in which this conflicts with attempts to introduce modern herd management and the commercialization of this sector. Farmers are ill-disposed to selling cattle unless the cash incentives are very strong, and this seldom being the case, livestock contribute far more to the subsistence part of any national economy than they do to the market sector.

Dairying still is limited, and there is competition to be faced from tinned and dried milk which have the advantage of not souring, and which often are cheaper. Local cattle give poor milk yields, and there are problems of storage, distribution, and hygiene. Also, improvement in this market has to overcome consumer resistance in populations unused to buying fresh milk, and with some justifiable prejudice against it (Chapter 6). Demand has so far been mostly from expatriate populations in towns. In East Africa this demand has been met by the Kenya dairying industry, formerly with produce from the European farms in the highland areas, but now partly from African smallholder dairy farms.

Because of the nature of meat and dairy products, marketing for this sector is more difficult to organize than the marketing for cash crops, but there appears to be great potential for these products in the future. They will prove critically important in developing higher nutritional standards.

CREDIT FACILITIES

Lack of capital and adequate rural credit facilities often have been cited as barriers to progress in rural Africa (Yudelman, 1964). Lack of capital reduces the farmers' ability to invest in land, and constrains the input of fertilizers, insecticides, and farm machinery which might lead to a "take-off" in agricultural production. Lack of title to land hinders the provisions of loans for investment, since there is no security for the lender. This particular concern has led to an emphasis in many programs on the establishment of a credit base through the promotion of individual land tenure (Swynnerton, 1954; IBRD, 1960).

Neither the accumulation of capital, nor the provision of credit, has had the hoped-for catalytic effect on farm improvement. The reasons for this relate, at least in part, to an alien conception of their importance as factors of production in traditional systems. Other factors appear to be more important in terms of constraints in the present stage of development.

In Ghana, the Ewe people had an unexpected increase in incomes which added significantly to their capital stock (Lawson, 1972). Even with this increase they preferred to invest in cattle or education for their children or to hoard the money for future use rather than to invest it in agriculture. This decision made good economic sense in terms of their opportunities and needs. Why should they put money into farms which give adequate economic returns on existing labor and cash investments, and would be unlikely to give more? No lucrative cash crop existed to guarantee favorable returns, and there were few markets for the sale of surplus foodstuffs. In these circumstances, "depositing" the money in cattle, or using it for education satisfied the need for good, secure investments, an important element in the system for subsistence farmers.

In Kenya, provision of credit facilities has led to some problems. Farmers do not always place high priority on the repayment of government loans, and governments find it politically difficult to carry through with foreclosures even when they hold deeds to the land as mortgage. Security of land tenure may mean very little for either farmers or governments in such situations. An example of this kind of problem is the situation which is developing on the High Density Schemes in Kenya, where a "mountain of debts" is accumulating (von Haugwitz, 1972). Here finance is provided by government loans bearing an annual interest rate of 6-1/2 percent to farmers who have been resettled from areas of "land hunger" and are consequently without capital assets. Land title is, therefore, the only security for the loans. Very little repayment has been made, for several reasons. Farm budgets drawn up by the Department of Settlement, intended to allow for repayment, were unrealistic: farmers were unaccustomed to handling commercial matters; levels of production were well below the targets set out in the farm budgets; and repayment of loans was secondary to the payment of school fees and other household expenditure (von Haugwitz, 1972). Some official resolution of this position will have to be made eventually, but meanwhile the debts increase, and provision of credit can hardly be said to be contributing to increasing the efficiency of the system nor rates of production.

Where specific cases of credit need can be identified, the introduction of a new crop may be facilitated or an existing area of cash cropping may be successfully extended. However, the farmers' position must be carefully analyzed to make credit generative. Very frequently, one of the most important credit needs is to bridge the gap between the time of outlays in the producing cycle and the harvest and sale times. In this case, a system where the cooperative buying agency supplies advances against the value of the cash crop can be workable if it is managed efficiently and if the interests of the farmers are adequately represented (Berry et al., 1971).

MARKETING AND COMMUNICATIONS

The importance of markets and of access by good roads can be observed along almost any newly built road in Africa. Within a year or two at most, settlement will have moved to the road, and familiar little stalls for the selling of local produce, and frequently of charcoal, will have sprung up. It is now generally considered that markets may be the most fundamental problem in terms of economic growth, since if provided satisfactorily, other improvements usually follow (Schultz, 1964). This is one single input which has been proved to have a catalytic effect.

Markets exist at three levels—international, national, and local. At the present time the national markets are the weakest because of the continuing widespread existence of subsistence agriculture. Agricultural produce is either an important cash crop destined for an overseas market, or local food crops which find their way only to the local periodic or permanent markets. Only a limited amount of produce consists of crops such as rice or cotton which go into the new national agricultural processing industries.

There are, of course, many well-known problems relating to the position of the African countries in world markets. Agreements on prices for tropical produce, and the whole question of price balances between natural products and synthetic products are vital to the economies of many African states. These are problems which can be solved only at the international level, and frequently the African producers feel at a grave disadvantage in their dealings with the consuming countries.

Policy decisions can be made nationally about choice of crops in the light of world prices, though this often is difficult. There are many examples where the market is the most difficult link in terms of planned change, particularly where heavy capital investment is involved and the choice of crop has to be satisfactory as a return on investment, taking into account world prices (Baker, 1971; Chambers, 1969).

Inter-African markets are small and few. Most African countries are oriented towards overseas markets, frequently associated with former colonial ties, rather than toward African neighbors. Both the institutional infrastructure and the physical infrastructure of roads and railways reinforce this situation, and rationalization of these networks is a necessary step in promoting development (Taaffe, Morrill and Gould, 1963).

The small size of the consumer markets within African countries is another reason for the limited amount of inter-African trade. Per capita incomes are low and spending power meagre. Yet the potential exists and such interchange could reduce dependence on the overseas markets (Green and Seidman, 1968).

One international market that has not been exploited but that has a long term potential is meat, and a number of African countries are in a good position to serve this market eventually, but first there are substantial problems to overcome. At the production level there is the question of how to develop efficient livestock units in countries where the people are unaccustomed to think of meat and milk marketing in relation to cattle owning, and where animals have a particular socioeconomic role that is incompatible with this type of endeavour (Rigby, 1969). At the commercial level, there is the problem that African meat has been thought of as "unsafe" because of the number of cattle diseases known to be endemic. This image needs to be changed by the demonstration of good management and high standards of hygiene.

At the national level, markets are related quite closely to the existing pattern of roads and railways. Those areas which have the densest communication networks also have the greatest amounts of commercial activity. Road building has, in fact, been one of the most significant forms of development aid in Africa, and the construction of "feeder" roads that facilitate the movement of local produce to market centers is a vital stimulant to rural change and development (McKay, 1971, 1972). Government organization of pricing, and also the role of the middle man in price fixing and market control, are important factors in their effects upon production (Mbilinyi and Mascarenhas, 1969).

Large increases in production as well as profitable production of new crops consequently depend on increases in the scale and type of marketing organization. There is no doubt about positive farmer response to the provision of good marketing facilities. In some cases where special projects are organized on the basis of a particular demand and facilities are made available to the farmers for collection and marketing, response has been so great that project membership has had to be restricted. (Heijnen, 1972).

Marketing cooperatives have operated with varying degrees of success in many parts of Africa. There is good reason to believe that the organization of efficient marketing procedures, coupled with the development of more rational road networks, will be one of the key factors in promoting rural economic development. Setting up of the marketing organization itself, however, is not enough. The organization has to be efficient. There are, alas, many examples of inefficient, even corrupt, cooperatives, and where these exist the farmers wisely attempt to sell elsewhere. Farmers become frustrated by the wastage resulting from inefficient collection services, and discouraged by low prices.

INFORMATION AND EDUCATION

In the past, education has had a rather negative effect on rural development. The expectations of those who went to school, and of the parents who sent them, were for employment outside the rural sector. The education they received, often in an alien tongue, did not fit them for farm work. Previously, too much emphasis had been placed on nonagricultural subjects. A system preparing students for nonexistent white-collar jobs was clearly out of phase with the new development objectives for rural progress. Tanzania, in particular, has restructured educational programs with these objectives in mind (Nyerere, 1967), and many other countries are watching for results with interest. An alternative view is taken by Forster (1970) who suggests that it is unrealistic to attempt to reorient education programs toward an agricultural content, and that there has been no real success where this has been tried.

This reemphasis on the importance of the rural sector also has led to direct efforts being made to reach the farmer through the establishment of information services, adult-education programs linking literacy to the dissemination of agricultural extension literature, and radio programs which have similar aims and complement literacy drives. In the short run, it is likely that the dissemination of information by radio will be most effective in reaching the existing adult population, whose standards of literacy are very low. Increased awareness of the modern sector and increased expectations can be stimulated through radio contact as an important way of raising national consciousness and explaining national goals. In the long run, one must expect that improved levels of literary skills will contribute to rural development by increasing farmers' knowledge and abilities.

COORDINATED SCHEMES

The "scheme" is a common method of planned change in Africa. The earliest schemes were initiated by the colonial governments. Schemes are usually, but not always, large scale and comprehensive, involving some degree of planning and control. Farmers lose their independence as decision makers and become participants. Reorganization of the land area in terms of usage or tenure also is involved, as are changes in techniques, especially if new crops are introduced. Marketing strategies are incorporated in many schemes. Schemes often involve resettlement, but can be directed to the reorganization of existing settlements (Chambers, 1969; de Wilde, 1967; Dumont, 1966).

Schemes have been set up for a great many different purposes, and have involved many different peoples and environments. They vary tremendously in size, from 50 hectares or so (Uganda's Farm Settlement Schemes) to over a million (Gezira-Managil Scheme in the Sudan and the "Million Acre Scheme" in Kenya). They vary also in the amounts of capital invested, although large investments are characteristic.

Some idea of the diversity might be demonstrated by listing some of the many reasons for their inception: famine relief; tsetse clearance; soil conservation; resettlement of war refugees; resettlement of peoples affected by dam construction; resettlement of people affected by land shortages and land deterioration; settlement of nomads; settlement of urban unemployed; "villagization" or grouping of scattered farmers into nucleated villages; promotion of particular crops such as cotton, sugar, rice, tea, or tobacco; and even ideological schemes based upon imported models such as the kibbutz. There has been a great mixture of goals, aims, and methods.

In general, and with a few notable exceptions, the coordinated approach as represented by the schemes has a low record of achievement. The most notable exception is the Gezira Scheme, and its later extension into the Managil, in the Sudan, which is held up as the model for agricultural improvement and has had a vital and demonstrable effect on the whole economy of that country (Shaw, 1964). As a model for agricultural improvement elsewhere in Africa, the Gezira Scheme proved less successful. Other large scale irrigation projects, in particular the highly capitalized scheme of the *Office du Niger* in Mali, have had, at most, a very limited achievement. The reasons are many, but they illustrate the difficulties of generating agricultural change through planned programs on this scale. In the case of the *Office du Niger*, de Wilde (1967) lists technical-planning deficiencies, lack of labor, lack of sufficient settlers, distance from markets and sources of supply, high costs in relation to value of output, shortage of well-trained staff, and lack of coordination as a result of the fact that both finance and technical assistance have come from many different sources—France, China, Soviet Union, and the European Development Fund.

The Swynnerton Plan and the Million Acre Settlement Scheme in Kenya were set up to solve problems of "land shortage" and involved considerable reorganization and resettlement. Success has not been general, but there have been some substantial increases in output and income (D.R.F. Taylor, 1969) and some genuine agricultural improvements.

While it is difficult to compare diverse projects for agricultural improvement in Africa, it may be useful to try to isolate some crucial factors of success. These seem to be:

1. *Type of management.* In the Gezira this was very competent and acceptable to the participants, even in the initial colonial period of the scheme. The need for control was understood, and incentives in the form of cash returns for cotton were sufficient for it to be tolerated. In many cases the management was alien, both before independence and after, and controls sometimes exceeded those which were necessary to the farm operations. For example, in the Mwea Irrigation Project in Kenya, farmers were expected to be back at their farms by four o'clock in the afternoon, and certain prison-like attitudes developed (Chambers, 1969). As expected, management was resented. In some cases the management hierarchy was not clear and there was conflict between administrators, managers, and technical advisors, who were all pursuing different goals (Chambers, 1969).

2. *Economic viability.* In the Gezira, cotton had a good international market, and the national organization of marketing facilities was skilled. In many cases the marketing aspect was not properly considered, or it was subordinate to other considerations. Crops were sometimes ill chosen and unsuitable. An example is a sugar-cane scheme in the Kilombero Valley in Tanzania, where the costs of the scheme created farmer returns lower than those achieved outside the scheme (Baum, 1968).

3. *Social factors.* In the Gezira, farmers were already familiar with irrigation techniques and were able to accommodate the new enterprise into their socioeconomic system. In many other cases, the primary purpose of the scheme had been "welfare" or "rehabilitation" rather than a strictly economic or commercial proposition. Consequently, economic incentives had not been sufficient to overcome the initial disadvantages experienced by urban unemployed who were expected to become farmers (Kilombero, Tanzania); school leavers who were not prepared for agricultural work (Uganda); and resettled people who found themselves in unfamiliar farming situations (Volta in Ghana; Khasm el Girba in Sudan; and also the *Office du Niger* in Mali). Chambers (1969) points out that preliminary surveys almost always were physical surveys, directed to questions of soil fertility or soil suitability, or else to matters of landholding and land tenure. Seldom, if ever, were market assessments carried out, or surveys made of social and farming systems.

4. *Unexpected or insufficiently considered outside factors.* The political nature of some of the projects made economic feasibility take second place, as for example the kibbutzim-type projects in Uganda. In other

cases the channeling of investments and services to schemes created privileged groups within the rural communities with adverse effects. Incentives were reduced for farmers for whom houses and food supplies were provided, even though the intention was to give settlers a start rather than an ongoing subsidy. Farmers outside the scheme were naturally resentful. There are a number of examples of this situation in Nigeria and Ghana; in Tanzania the Villagization Scheme has had this kind of problem. On the other hand, there are cases where farmers have been overburdened by loans, causing financial difficulties which then caused them to modify their cultivation procedures unfavorably, interfering with the planned system of the scheme. Another problem has been competing claims of subsistence and commercial agriculture for scarce cash and labor inputs. This has affected economic returns, particularly where increases in population since the inception of the scheme have increased the demand for food supplies.

Commercial farming will eventually have to proceed on a larger scale than the average African individual farm generally provides. Whether this comes about through the various forms of cooperatives or through the directed coordination of the scheme, two things seem to be essential if African farmers are to be successful in commercial enterprise, either as individuals or as participants in planned schemes. First, incentives in the form of cash returns must be sufficiently high and demonstrably certain. Risks cannot easily be taken where capital is scarce and subsistence is at stake. Second, cash crops must fit into the farmers' basic subsistence work plan, for in a subsistence economy it is this base level which largely controls change. Food crops come first.

In general, it seems that initiative is best stimulated and maintained where production is an individual responsibility. Farmers will accept certain controls over production, even "close supervision," where the advantages are clear and where they are voluntary tenants, not "settlers" or "selected tenants." They will more readily accept controls over the marketing of cash crops. It may be worth noting that the most common form of cooperative in Africa is the marketing cooperative, not the production cooperative.

It would be a pity, however, if attempts to encourage large-scale farming in Africa were to suffer from the discredit often attached to the existing schemes. There is obviously a place for large-scale, capital-intensive projects in Africa. Certain crops, such as wheat, are most profitable when grown on the large scale which mechanized farming allows. Others, such as sugar cane and tea, require the nearby establishment of processing factories, and this in turn demands some organization of collection and delivery procedures, best carried out on a large scale. It may be that the establishment of large-scale *fully-commercialized* farms, state farms, parastatal, or private, depending on the political circumstances, could be a successful way of organizing modern agriculture *outside the subsistence sector.*

If modernization of production methods, as distinct from modernization of marketing, is to proceed more rapidly, governments hardly can expect the African small-holder, tied by the constraints of his traditional subsistence needs, to be the spearhead of rural change. Most African farms are too small for mechanization and the kinds of investment and planning that go with it. Even where this is feasible through amalgamation into cooperative farms, the subsistence factor is still a controlling factor in the acceptance of change. The cooperative, no less than the individual farm, is still *semicommercialized.*

Economists (Robinson, 1971) have begun to think in terms of a two-tier approach to progress in agriculture, basically large scale commercialized and small scale semicommercialized retaining the subsistence base. The two thus would complement each other. Agriculture as the vital sector for development in this transitional period in Africa has two important functions—to increase national wealth and to support the majority of the population. A two-tier approach may be the best way of integrating these functions. Alternatively, is a modernized subsistence agriculture possible? Or will real modernization have to await growth in the industrial sector and the evolution of national internal food markets?

Induced change has become policy in almost all African countries. Positive responses on the part of the rural population, essential to success, can be encouraged by realistic assessments of their needs and of possibilities for improvement, together with enlistment of local people in effecting change.

17

Settlement Schemes
and Rural Growth

MARILYN SILBERFEIN

Resettlement involves the relocation of selected participants within schemes that have been planned and executed by some agent or agency. The existence of an external agency differentiates resettlement from the self-initiated migrations that have been undertaken by various African groups in order to realize new opportunities or to escape overcrowding or other ecological and sociopolitical problems.

There are many circumstances that may lead to resettlement. The procedure has been used to alleviate overpopulation or to evacuate areas struck by natural disaster. It has followed in the wake of insect infestation, declining soil fertility, and the construction of large dams that inundate long established farming areas. Sometimes economic growth has provided the impetus. The existence of a sparsely populated area has motivated planning agencies to promote resettlement as a vehicle for using the land to its "full potential."

Although resettlement schemes have been introduced as solutions to a wide range of problems, nearly all schemes have as their ultimate goal the successful promotion of agricultural development. The rationale is this: if traditional cultivators can be grouped together in a new setting where the social and physical constraints of their home territory are not present, and if they can be provided with credit, training programs, and economic incentives, then a flourishing commercial enterprise should emerge from this reordering of human and physical resources.

Past resettlement experiments are useful in illustrating some of the difficulties emerging when relocation is adopted as a panacea for a host of social and economic ills. The most renowned pre-World-War-II project was the Gezira Scheme, the successful irrigated land settlement for the production of cotton near the confluence of the White and Blue Nile in Sudan. None of the many imitations that have been attempted since have been able to duplicate the economic viability of Gezira. Critical factors of Gezira's success may have been its completely commercial orientation and the favorable position of cotton in the world market of that period (see Chapter 16).

An example of resettlement on a much smaller scale took place in Tanzania (1924) in response to a sleeping-sickness epidemic that was spreading within the infested north-central part of the country. This situation was brought under control by the clearing of a large area of brush and woodland for the resettlement of the occupants of the affected area. Many of the families involved remained unconvinced that the tsetse was responsible for sleeping sickness and were reluctant to leave their traditional holdings. There were also complaints that the concentrated arrangement of buildings at the resettlement site were an inadequate substitute for the small, scattered villages that were being abandoned. Finally, as in the case of a comparable tsetse-clearing scheme at Anchau, Nigeria, it was necessary to employ the threat of punishment in order to complete the resettlement process (Hatchell, 1949).

There was a hiatus in all projects of this type until the late 1940s when colonial governments began to recover from the world-wide depression of the 1930s and the economic deficits of World War II. However, it appeared that little had been learned in facilitating innovative pioneer settlements and that newly created agencies were destined to repeat past mistakes. For example, at the Zande Scheme (a project designed to bring commercial cotton to the southern Sudan in the 1950s) farmers were forced into villages where their agricultural activities could be supervised (Reining, 1966). The hostile reaction of the Zande to being manipulated and the indecisiveness of the government officials responsible for the scheme led to the decline and ultimate abandonment of this unpopular project within four years of its inception.

A similar sequence of events occurred at a northern Nigerian project initiated in 1953 to upgrade and increase agricultural productivity (Baldwin, 1957). The members of this scheme were to be recruited by a program of incentives and a well-organized publicity effort. However, a very low level of response from the local population led to an intensification of the enlistment campaign; farmers who considered the resettlement site too remote from their home villages and from dependable water supplies were pressured and sometimes forced to participate. The scheme eventually was closed after many of the reluctant volunteers returned to their original homes following equipment failures and increasing social breakdown.

Another hiatus in the planning of African settlement schemes took place after these and other similar failures, including large scale undertakings such as the Tanganyika Groundnut Scheme. The settlement approach was not attempted again until the 1960s when several dramatic projects were initiated in conjunction with African independence. The agents of political change involved in this most recent stage of development were determined not to repeat past errors, eschewing the use of force in obtaining scheme members while acknowledging the need for careful physical and socioeconomic planning. The survey (sometimes including a social survey to supplement the evaluation of the land base) and pilot scheme(s) became the precursors of a resettlement program.

It was typical of these projects of the 1960s that goals were spelled out clearly and in great detail. The Volta Resettlement Program, originally designed to evacuate the area to be inundated by the Volta (now, Akosombo) Dam, developed several additional objectives: (1) to use resettlement to enhance the social, economic, and physical conditions of the people; (2) to improve the agricultural system and speed the change to a cash economy; and (3) to locate new settlements in a rational way (Brokensha and Scudder, 1968).

Similar broad ranging objectives accompanied many other schemes. Resettlement in western Nigeria, for example, was expected to prevent the migration of young farmers to urban areas by providing them with rural options that might be equally attractive. It was postulated that if settlements were carefully planned and executed, with provisions made for adequate compensation for one's efforts, then young people with some education might be tempted to apply (Roider, 1971). The social and economic justifications for the Tanzanian resettlement program included bringing dispersed farmers into central villages where they would be provided with such modern amenities as health and educational facilities, pumped water, and possibly electricity. These same farmers also would receive a substantial income from the high yields they were to achieve cultivating under expert supervision. Finally, each settlement, with the mixed population it was expected to assemble, would become a small-scale experiment in interethnic cooperation and nation building.

Those independent African states that envisioned a substantial resettlement program usually devised a spatial strategy for the distribution of schemes. A typical national plan might be organized as follows: (1) one scheme would be sited in each major region of the state; (2) the schemes would be accessible to the major transportation arteries; (3) the schemes also would be close to existing marketing and/or processing facilities; and (4) each new settlement would be centered within an area of high-agricultural potential.

The more goals that were contained within the initial strategy, the more that idealized plans conflicted with real situations. One such discrepancy was the conflict between the need for high-quality land and the fact that better land invariably was occupied by traditional farmers. To extricate these holdings from their owners would create legal complications as well as generate ill-will. Political considerations also undermined the goal of concentrating schemes in areas of high potential; regional officials contended that even the most remote and unpromising areas deserved at least one pilot scheme. Many of these differences finally were dealt with when settlement programs shifted from the drawing boards to the implementation stage. Theoretical models usually were replaced by more pragmatic pilot projects that took into account political conditions and economic constraints.

The most ambitious master plans were those that emulated the Israeli program of composite rural structure. This approach made settlement schemes a part of a newly created, four-order central place hierarchy. The schemes or agricultural villages (A level) with 60 to 100 families provided for only basic services. These were supplemented by nearby B and C level rural centers which served 300-400 families located in 5-6 farm villages. Several centers focused in turn on a town of 15,000-20,000 inhabitants which offered a higher standard of goods and services (banks, hotels) and included industrial plants for processing local products (Frank, 1968).

The closest approximation of the Israeli model in Africa is represented by the Volta Resettlement Program. Here 739 separate hamlets that had characterized the pre-Volta dam situation were regrouped into 52 locations within a central place hierarchy (Kalitsi, 1965). The new centers included: (1) agricultural villages (A level); (2) satellite villages with less than 5,000 inhabitants (B level); (3)

service centers of 5,000-8,000 inhabitants (*C* level); and (4) a central town with 8,000-10,000 inhabitants (*D* level).

The four-level hierarchical settlement program with its potential for rural development and the provision for high-quality rural services was not developed elsewhere in Africa because of a lack of the requisite resources. Some attempts were made to create a two-level hierarchy as in an eastern Nigerian program where six schemes focused on a common center. Most settlement programs, however, were forced to rely on two alternative options: (1) insuring that individual schemes were large enough to sustain certain basic services; or (2) tying the schemes to preexisting services centers and other facilities. In order to take advantage of the first option, the average settlement should include 200 families. Programs based on settlements which were initially smaller than this usually expanded their membership in order to provide better services. For instance, the original Niger scheme plan of 20 families per village was later redefined to include a minimum of 80 families so that shops, a primary school, and a dispensary could be sustained (Baldwin, 1957).

Tying schemes to preexisting centers and facilities was more difficult to implement, especially in terms of integrating settlements into regional systems of agricultural extension, marketing, administrative structure, and other facilities. The best example of an attempt at regional coordination can be taken from the Tanzanian experience. The settlement planning agency had initiated the experiment by dividing the country into eight economic zones, each of which was also an administrative region and each of which was to contain one pilot scheme. In every region, an official known as the "assistant director of development" would devise a plan to coordinate the settlement with other regional activities. Within two years, this plan was indefinitely postponed, partly because the original eight regions of the country had been subdivided to form a total of seventeen units. The final policy placed economic considerations (the elimination of time consuming, costly surveys) and political expediency (response to the demands of local leaders) ahead of the initial intent to distribute settlements in a regular and systematic mode. After these new priorities were established, a pattern emerged which was characterized by a peripheral distribution of settlements. This outcome had several disadvantages. Schemes were so widely scattered as to make centralized control difficult, and they were not always accessible to areas of potential recruitment. Even more critically, elaborate regional plans that would have supported the settlement in the role of "service center" were deferred because of shortage of funds and personnel. As goals were scaled down to economic realities, the possibilities of developing schemes as regional centers through coordinated planning became more remote (Silberfein, 1971).

Similar reevaluations of distributional strategy occurred in Nigeria, producing significant departures from the planned geometries. In the Eastern Region, an original program called for one farm settlement in each of twelve major political subdivisions; only six such divisions ultimately became settlement sites (Floyd and Adinde, 1967). Similarly, in western Nigeria, an initial plan called for the distribution of thirteen settlements so that each of the eight provinces of the country contained at least one. The plan was later superseded by an agreement to use whatever suitable land was offered to the government by traditional village authorities (Roider, 1971). In both cases it proved to be difficult, using monetary inducements and persuasion, to acquire appropriate land in contiguous blocks. As a result, some settlement sites were distorted in shape, departing substantially from the neat arrangements that had characterized the original designs.

The plans for structuring the settlements themselves were more frequently implemented than were the plans for scheme distribution. One critical question had to be resolved during the early stages of settlement planning: would a clustered or a scattered settlement pattern provide the best possible arrangement of households? There are both positive and negative aspects to each approach. Bringing together previously scattered individuals in a village setting allows for the provision of centralized services and encourages social interaction. On the other hand, such a concentration of households invariably implies a cost in travel time to the fields. According to Chisholm (1967), the relative advantages and disadvantages tend to cancel each other out. He recommended scattered holdings during the initial stages of development (to minimize production costs) with a subsequent transfer of the dispersed population to a more socially desirable clustered settlement. The change would occur when technology allowed a reduction in travel time to the fields.

Most African settlement designs were not evaluated according to efficiency criteria. Instead, the typical scheme stressed the importance of cooperation and access to services. It was based on centralized homesteads with small food-production plots surrounded by cash-crop cultivation fields. One of the earlier models for the clustered-village homesteads would front on three roads or paths—the largest of which would be a focus for scheme services (Figure 17.1). Problems in the implementation of this design, including that of surveying an area of irregular terrain, caused the *H*-plan to be

**PLAN OF H-PATTERN UNIT
WITH FIFTY HOUSEHOLD PLOTS**

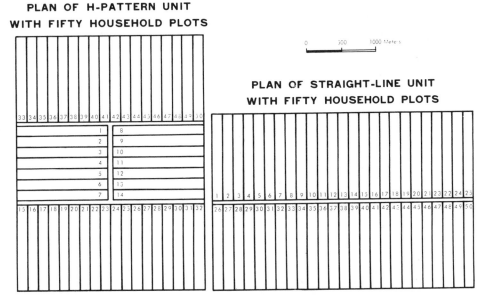

**PLAN OF STRAIGHT-LINE UNIT
WITH FIFTY HOUSEHOLD PLOTS**

Figure 17.1 Evolution of Zande Scheme Settlement Pattern.
Source: Redrawn from Reining (1966:105) with permission of Northwestern University Press.

gradually replaced by a simpler linear arrangement. Neither of these designs approximated the coherent village structure envisioned by the planners, primarily because the facilities that would have functioned as a village focus were not provided. Virtually no community centers, schools, or dispensaries were constructed due to lack of funds compounded by waning government interest, and the settlement pattern eventually reverted to a scattered form.

Eastern Nigerian schemes used a more complex design with six complete villages focusing on a "nucleus center" (Floyd and Adinde, 1967). The villages consisted of homesteads arranged around several basic facilities and surrounded in turn by land for cash-crop cultivation. Higher level facilities such as the senior primary school, processing mills, and a cooperative headquarters distinguished the nucleus center from the smaller service centers at each village.

The internal structure of the Tanzanian schemes also provided for a service area with school, dispensary, shops, and accommodations for the staff. Surrounding this area were three residential sections where settlers built homes and cultivated one-acre food plots. Fields used for cash crops formed the outer perimeter of the settlement and were allocated to individuals or groups according to an overall farm plan (Figure 17.2). In other African settlement

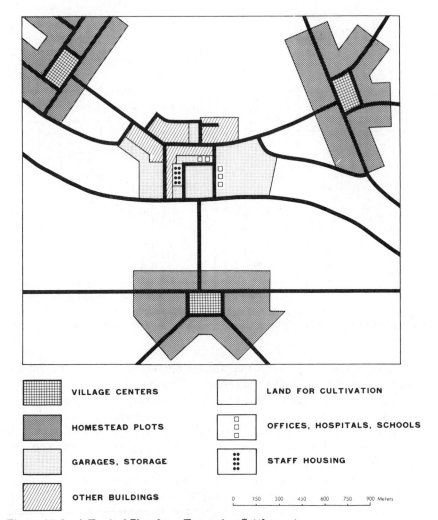

VILLAGE CENTERS

HOMESTEAD PLOTS

GARAGES, STORAGE

OTHER BUILDINGS

LAND FOR CULTIVATION

OFFICES, HOSPITALS, SCHOOLS

STAFF HOUSING

0   150   300   450   600   750   900 Meters

Figure 17.2 A Typical Plan for a Tanzanian Settlement.

programs the nucleated farm village was replaced by a linear or
scattered pattern. The rationale for this plan was usually specific to
the particular enterprise (Charsely, 1968; Watts, 1966).

Once a clustered-scattered option was resolved, relatively little
attention was paid to other aspects of scheme design. The structure
of the houses tended to be functional rather than attractive. Similar
basic house types could be found at most schemes, although some
variation occurred in construction materials and numbers of rooms.
After a model was devised, it usually was applied throughout a

settlement program unless local circumstances made such uniformity impossible. Only the Volta resettlement planners seem to have been interested in the aesthetics of the villages. Modest efforts were made to group several houses around small open spaces and to place houses at varying distances from the road. It thus became possible to avoid the typical monotonous rows of uniform houses that characterized most settlements (Huzlar, 1970).

The establishment of post-independence settlement programs was followed by an evaluation process. In general, however, the application of economic and sociopolitical criteria to judge scheme success have been less then satisfactory. The economic achievements of the schemes have been disappointing as reflected in higher initial costs and lower returns to investment than originally anticipated. In part these results can be explained by:

1. Declining prices for certain agricultural exports;
2. Cash crop yields that have not reached projected levels; and
3. Cost overruns in the acquisition of capital goods.

The first factor was, of course, beyond local control. The second factor has been the result of such circumstances as a breakdown in scheme organization, an unsatisfactory settler work output, or vagaries of weather. The third factor has emerged when scheme planners have opted for expensive equipment and high-cost personnel. Often this type of excessive capitalization has been used in support of the "showcase function" of the settlement.

Economic success also can be examined from the point of view of returns accruing to individual settlers. Although there has been considerable variation in the profitability of scheme participation, the factor that has most discouraged potential scheme members has been a perceived lack of economic potential. The settlers themselves usually have been dissatisfied with their annual income and some even have reported a decrease in material possession during the first three years of scheme participation and a reluctance to await the long term results of their efforts. Alternately, settlers have responded favorably to improved levels of services. The new facilities (such as schools and dispensaries) have been widely acknowledged as superior to those characterizing prescheme situations, although they have not offset disappointing financial returns.

The ultimate economic criticism of the settlement is this: Are capital intensive-settlement projects the appropriate vehicles for modernization in a typical African country where land and labor are relatively abundant and capital and skilled manpower are scarce factors of production? Opponents of resettlement have argued persuasively that money invested in other types of programs would produce higher returns or, at the very least, encompass significantly larger components of the population. Certainly, the number of people directly benefiting from resettlement has been limited to a small fraction of the national population of each country which has initiated such a program, and the cost of relocating and capitalizing each family has been substantial (from $30 to $2,000). Scheme members have been assessed for as much as 90 percent of these initial costs, but the vast majority of settlers have been unable to make more than a token repayment during the first three years of their membership. Critics have offered comparative-cost assessments and cited the substantially lower sums needed to support more broadly-based agricultural extension programs. These programs have reached a much larger segment of the population, but they have moved much more slowly in bringing about technological change.

Supporters of resettlement have argued that their approach has been the only viable choice to convert traditional cultivators into modern farmers. They underscore the heavy financial investments required to transform sparsely settled land into highly productive agricultural enterprises. These advocates also have observed that premature assessment of scheme success is unfavorable because most schemes have not been in existence for a sufficient period of time to permit full development. There is some validity in this point of view; many of the national resettlement programs had been terminated after only three to four years of operation. Little consideration was given to experiments with crop selection and the allocation of crops to specific fields. The first few years of operation are required to determine the best land use arrangement, the most desirable marketing system, and the ideal job assignment for specific members of the permanent staff. Long-term evaluations would probably cast the settlement in a much more favorable light, especially in the case of schemes specializing in cash crops requiring three to five years to mature, such as coffee or cocoa.

The high cost of establishing settlements sometimes has been justified on the basis of the expected "demonstration effect." For example, Malawi settlement planners referred to the anticipated spin-off from functioning scheme operations and in eastern Nigeria, "communities bordering on the settlements were already watching the new institutions with deep interest" (Floyd and Adinde, 1967:219). In each case there was the expectation that farmers living in the vicinity of planned settlements would observe and eventually adopt the advanced agricultural technology demonstrated by the schemes. Consequently, the original investment could be justified on the basis of increased production norms for both the scheme enterprise and the rapidly increasing population of neighboring cultivators.

Few evaluations of the "scheme demonstration effect" have been undertaken (Morris, 1967). Three studies have shown surprisingly little transfer of modernized agriculture from schemes to the surrounding areas. These studies, two in western Nigeria (Roider, 1971; Adegboye et al., 1969) and one in Tanzania (Silberfein, 1971) suggest that neighbors are aware of the physical presence of the scheme, but adopt few, if any, practices. The major exception is the use of fertilizers. Many of the African schemes were merely islands of agricultural change rather than diffusion centers of innovation and increased productivity. Although outsiders were allowed free access to scheme property, they often regarded these projects as foreign intrusions in a traditional setting. Some local farmers became jealous of the privileges granted to scheme members whereas others were antagonistic toward nonlocal staff and settlers. The availability of scheme facilities was supposed to counteract these kinds of suspicions but such advantages often were lost when scheme participants attempted to monopolize a dispensary or school. Thus the edge of the schemes frequently became a boundary effectively separating two technologies, and ultimately, two systems of farm organization.

When the evaluation of strictly economic criteria have presented settlement programs in an unfavorable light, resettlement agency planners have pointed to the role of schemes as agents of social change. When this approach is used, analysis begins with the success or failure of the recruitment program. The acquisition of a permanent membership lies at the heart of each successful project, but recruitment efforts seldom have attracted a large body of aspirants to support any kind of selection process. This deficiency in part can be traced to the failure of scheme officials to acknowledge the significance of links between a would-be recruit and his home area. Most of the individuals exposed to the opportunity of scheme membership were bound by a strong traditionalism, lack of mobility, and personal communication limited to the immediate environs. Interaction typically was limited to the immediate neighborhood (village, hamlet). This localized communications web rarely was penetrated by the mass media or even by the flow of information from government sources to local officials.

Many examples can be cited that indicate that settlement officials ignored the restrictiveness of a traditional society. These constraints centered on the active participation of an individual within a localized extended family or a larger group. The Chipangali

Scheme (Zambia) required that some of the cultivators who occupied a densely populated reserve move a distance of 50 miles to an area outside of their traditional territory. This transfer was resisted by the local Ngoni as being tantamount to breaking off all relations with friends and relatives (Kay, 1965). The traditional leadership found little compensation in the fact that overpopulation was resolved by the out-migration of potential scheme members.

Resettlement programs that were directed to developmental goals encountered similar problems in delineating catchment areas for their recruitment campaigns. In some cases, publicity was directed to a limited zone within 15-30 miles of the scheme. This restriction in the size of the recruitment area sought to overcome various cultural barriers by appealing to a fairly homogeneous population susceptible to easy integration within the structure of the new enterprise (Watts, 1966).

A more typical approach was adopted in Tanzania. Individuals of diverse origins were recruited so that each settlement program represented an exercise in interethnic cooperation. To accomplish this goal, publicity sessions were organized by agricultural extension agents throughout a given region to stress the positive facets of social integration. This technique was singularly inappropriate. Most cultivators paid no attention to the government message (of improved quality of life and increased economic rewards) beyond the immediate vicinity of the schemes. They tended to associate the settlements with all of the negative qualities that the "unknown" can generate: a new environment that might be unsuitable for familiar cash crops; problems of water and firewood supply; a potentially hostile indigenous ethnic group; and finally, the inscrutable vagaries and regulations of government control. The latter consideration produced several real concerns: the government could reoccupy the land at any time, impose restrictions on the activities of scheme members, or create additional tax obligations. Clearly, the traditional sociopolitical institutions provided greater security for the majority of farmers than could a systematically organized government enterprise.

Narrow definitions of suitable settler characteristics have compounded the problem of recruitment at many schemes. Among the qualities of the ideal settler that have been set forth are youth (under 25), unmarried status, married with children, literacy in French or English, excellent health, and an aptitude for agricultural work. Such lofty standards invariably were reduced for want of sufficient recruits or because of a shift away from arbitrary values. One particular bias has remained, however. Some schemes have encouraged the participation of young men who have completed four to six years of schooling and who would otherwise be unemployed. In Malawi, for example, initial enrollment in any scheme was confined to the Young Pioneers, an organization which was founded to encourage agricultural development among participants ranging in age from 18 to 35 years (Phipps, 1970).

In summary, almost all of the recruitment programs encountered difficulties in meeting selection criteria when they sought recruits in areas where there were no land shortages to motivate inhabitants to migrate. The secure traditional farmer, working a small acreage of cash or subsistence crops, regarded settlements with suspicion and preferred to reside in a familiar linguistic and social setting. The most successful recruitment programs occurred among farmers with extensive education or an urban experience and, more importantly, among farmers in poor economic straits because of overcrowding in their home districts. Unfortunately, many of these potential recruits chose alternate options to scheme membership and were not available or susceptible to any inducement.

Failure to accomplish changes in the life style of scheme participants constituted yet another disappointment to advocates of scheme development. In part this has been the fault of settlement staff who failed to implement an upgrading of the educational level of scheme participants in such areas as adult literacy, health, and child care. Scheme members often remained ignorant of the relative values of different foods while continuing a traditional and frequently unbalanced diet. Most did not make use of latrines, nor did they boil water or take other precautions to avoid diseases in new areas to which they had not adapted. Thus, the main area of behavioral change seems to have occurred in the conversion to modernized cash-crop production with little ancillary change in life style.

We have emphasized the limitations of resettlement as a developmental technique. When the approach gained adherents in post-independence Africa it was sometimes touted as the panacea for curing a whole gamut of agricultural ills. The enthusiasm for this type of agrarian reform all too frequently resulted in overcapitalization and a disregard for the human factor in effecting the relocation process. Considerable variation existed in the goals and objectives of the various schemes and some were smoothly functioning enterprises with the potential to become self sustaining. Yet, a sufficient number of problem schemes were generated to disillusion most planning agencies with the efficacy of heavily-endowed scheme development. By the early 1970s, many settlement programs had closed down or

264 RURAL CHANGE

were in an arrested stage of development. In order to judge the real impact of schemes developed in the 1960s, it will be necessary for another decade to pass.

Meanwhile, the Ministries of Agriculture of various African states have been exploring other mechanisms for upgrading commercial cultivation in the aftermath of scheme failures. One approach has been to continue traditional programs with a larger extension staff bringing about gradual change through persuasion. A compromise between extension and resettlement has provided a further approach to agricultural development, using certain desirable aspects of the old settlement programs but on a more modest scale. For example, groups of five to twenty close associates may begin to farm cooperatively—those that make modest progress qualify for limited government assistance to purchase building materials, equipment or other needed inputs. Alternatively, the government itself may initiate new settlements, but with a minimum of capitalization and an emphasis on self-help.

In Tanzania these policies have been activated in the creation of *Ujamaa* villages which can be instigated simply by several farmers moving their homesteads closer together (Cliffe, 1971). Ideally, a communal organization of production will emerge when members of the group recognize the advantages of working together. The goals which can be achieved through this system include improved levels of services, economies of scale, and ultimately material benefits. Special criteria must be adopted to evaluate *Ujamaa* settlements because of the motivations used to elicit participation and sustain communal membership. These measures would include: (1) the availability of group (as opposed to individual) wealth; and (2) the degree to which cooperative activities (agricultural and otherwise) have become the basis of scheme organization (Kates, McKay, and Berry, 1968-69). These and other criteria have shown that *Ujamaa* settlements generally provide a more satisfying social environment than the earlier village settlement schemes.

Geographers have been concerned with the role of concentrated activities that can stimulate economic growth in surrounding areas (Harvey and Greenberg, 1972). Among the possibilities are urban centers, various types of commercial enterprises (mines, plantations, state farms), and resettlement schemes. However, resettlement schemes have largely failed as "growth poles" in generating agricultural change beyond their immediate environs; small scale schemes, on the other hand, tend to be less complex in operation and their technology is much closer to the level of traditional farming procedures. As a result, the transfer of a modicum of technology and innovation is now a reality and larger audiences seem more responsive to these demonstration units. It is feasible that small schemes in Tanzania and elsewhere may become the most practical vehicles for expanding and improving commercial cropping in areas of traditional agriculture.

18

Migration and
Rural Change

REUBEN K. UDO

Pre-colonial migrations in Africa were essentially of the colonization type, with people moving into "empty" areas or displacing
previous inhabitants. Such migrations have continued into the
present, but on a much reduced scale. Rather, today's migration
patterns are largely the result of processes initiated during the
colonial era, when Africa was to serve as a primary producer for the
factories of Europe as well as a market for some European industrial
products. The new colonial economy created a great demand for
labor to work the mineral deposits and large commercial plantations
and timber concessions. In addition to these large-scale foreign-
owned mining and agricultural enterprises, the new economy also
featured the adoption of new industrial crops such as cocoa, cotton,
peanuts, and rubber. The demand for wage labor by local farmers
cultivating export crops arose partly because their scale of operation
was greater than that of the peasant food-crop farmer who depended
largely on family labor, and partly because more and more children
were going to school instead of helping on the farms.

The demand for labor in the growing industrial, mining, and
agricultural districts constituted a major pull factor in colonial
migrations in Africa, but there were also some push factors which

"forced" potential migrants to move. These include shortage of farmland or the periodic occurrence of famine; the desire to earn money to pay taxes, school fees and for buying imported goods; and the desire to escape from kinship obligations. But in spite of the strong desire for money by some groups, the demand for labor always exceeded the supply. The shortage of labor during the first two decades of this century was caused largely by the reluctance of many people to migrate to work in distant places, and partly by the adoption of export crop production by African farmers. In Uganda, for example, the strong desire to earn cash to pay for imported goods forced the Ganda to migrate to work in various parts of East Africa until about 1907 when most Ganda found that cotton growing (introduced in 1904) at home was paying more than wage employment outside their home territory. The result was that by 1908, government found it difficult to recruit labor for construction and maintenance of essential services (Powesland, 1954), and since then, Buganda has remained a net importer of migrant labor to work on the cotton fields.

In various parts of the continent, attempts were made to solve the labor situation by importing workers from abroad, an action which was to create the Asian population in South and East Africa. In order to obtain workers to construct roads, railways, sea ports, or to work on plantations, most colonial administrations also resorted to direct forced labor through penal and impressed labor as well as indirect forced labor through the imposition of poll taxes payable in cash. In French West Africa, for example, every male between 18 and 60 years of age was required to contribute a certain number of days on any project to which he was assigned (Thompson and Adloff, 1958). Writing about Mossi migration, Skinner (1965) has observed that men who were unwilling or unable to obtain European money to pay taxes had their goods seized and sold by chiefs or French administrative officers, and that those who had neither taxes nor goods were compelled to migrate to work in Ghana or face punishment by the administration.

By 1950, forced labor had been abolished in the French and British territories but not in the Portuguese territories of Mozambique and Angola where the system continued into the early 1960s (Bailey, 1969). The abuses associated with forced labor brought about much publicity and it is necessary at this point to stress that during the colonial period the vast majority of people who migrated to work for wages were not forced, at least not directly, but did so in order to "better themselves" materially. Many people were attracted to the growing port towns, a number of which became the political as well as the commercial capitals of the various territories. Mounting unemployment of school leavers in some of the cities featured prominently and tended to mask the continued shortage of wage labor to work on the large plantations (Ivory Coast, Liberia, Zaire) and the smaller African farms in western Nigeria, Uganda, and Ghana. The vast majority of migrants during the colonial period, however, went to rural districts to work for wages or as independent tenant farmers and mining laborers. The situation today is not very different, although the proportion of rural-urban migrants has been increasing more rapidly since 1960. In Ghana, for example, as many as 70 percent of internal migrants, numbering over 600,000 in 1960, went to rural areas to work on farms and mines, and a vast majority of the 850,000 aliens who lived in Ghana in that year also settled in rural areas (Addo, 1972).

Figure 18.1 illustrates the pattern of modern migration in Africa south of the Sahara. A few regional contrasts deserve mention. Starting with the directions of movement, we notice that in West Africa, most migrants go to the more accessible and better developed coastward areas where the mines, commercial plantations, peasant tree-crop farms, and timber concessions are located. The most important, in terms of numbers involved, of these coastward migrations include the Mossi into Ghana from Upper Volta (Skinner, 1965; Cornelisse; 1972), the Hausa into southwestern Nigeria and southern Ghana (Prothero, 1958), the Ibo and Urhobo into the Nigerian cocoa belt (Udo, 1970b), and the seasonal migrations of *navetanes* (stranger farmers) from Mali and Guinea into Senegal and Gambia (Jarrett, 1949). There are, however, a few cases of migrations into interior locations such as to the Jos tin mines and the peanut and cotton growing areas of Kano and Katsina provinces in Nigeria.

In South, Central, and East Africa, most migrants go to landlocked locations, the only coastward areas attracting migrant labor being the sisal estates of Tanzania and the sugar-growing districts of Natal. Important components of modern migrations in these regions include labor migrations from Ruanda and Burundi into the cotton belt of Uganda (Richards, 1954), migrant labor from Mozambique into South Africa (Bailey, 1969; Harris, 1959) and labor migrations from Malawi into Rhodesia and South Africa (Barber, 1961; Van Velsen, 1960).

A more fundamental contrast exists between areas like the Uganda cotton belt or the cocoa belts of Ghana and Nigeria, where migrants settle to work for African planters or to lease farmland for cultivation, and areas like the South African mining districts or

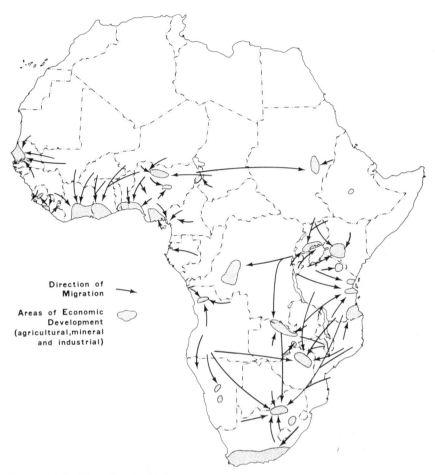

Figure 18.1   Migration in Africa.
Source: Adapted from Prothero, 1965. Reproduced with permission of Long-man Group Ltd.

Rhodesian farms where the migrants work for a European settler group. In Rhodesia and South Africa, the migrants are essentially wage-earners, and there is no question of them settling down permanently as tenants or purchasing land outright for cultivation. In Uganda and most of West Africa, on the other hand, many migrants who originally worked for wages have since acquired some farmland to cultivate on their own. The rapid increase in the number of these self-employed migrants has created a problem of continuing shortage of labor as well as problems of adjustment. The numerous small squatter settlements built by these migrant tenant farmers has introduced a new element into the cultural landscape of areas like the Nigerian cocoa belt where the indigenous people live in large, compact towns.

MAGNITUDE OF INTERNAL AND INTERNATIONAL MIGRATIONS

Although the direction, character, and problems of migrant labor in Africa are well-documented, the data available are neither adequate nor sufficiently reliable to permit a precise statement on the magnitude of population movements. The data situation is particularly poor with respect to internal migrations within each country, since migration usually has not been enumerated in national censuses. International movements are much better documented owing to border immigration checks and the use of government-sponsored as well as private labor employment agencies to handle the recruitment and transportation of migrant labor. Unfortunately, such agencies do not operate in most countries and in countries where they have been established—Mozambique, Malawi, Nigeria, Upper Volta, Zambia—only a small fraction of migrants take advantage of the services provided. The vast majority of migrants prefer to make their own arrangements for travelling and for securing jobs to avoid the delays and formalities of having to use a recruiting agency. Large-scale smuggling of agricultural workers across international borders has been reported in Upper Volta (Cornelisse, 1972) and Mozambique (Bailey, 1969) and has given rise to disputes between the labor-exporting and labor-importing countries. Among other things, these cases of illegal emigration compound the problem of computing the magnitude of international migrations. Therefore, the figures given in the paragraphs that follow are based on estimates made at different times for different countries, and although the coverage is incomplete, they do give a fair indication of the number of people involved in these migrations.

One of the examples of large-scale movements of people from one rural area to another is the long-distance migration of West Africans to the Sudan Republic. In 1956, there were about 600,000 West Africans in that country, and this increased to about 750,000 in 1963 (Davis, 1964). Most of these West Africans were from Nigeria, Chad, and Niger. They had settled permanently or temporarily while on their way to or returning from the pilgrimage to Mecca. But although this was originally a religious-motivated migration, the economic factor is very important today and according to Davis the sedentary agricultural elements among the West Africans constitute a considerable force in the economic growth of the Sudan. The survival of the Gezira Scheme during the Great Depression has been credited to the industry of these migrants, who took over vacant tenancies abandoned by local Sudanese farmers in addition to their own tenancies (Davis, 1964).

In a recent study of the migrant labor system in West Africa, it has been estimated that about 75,000 *navetanes* or "stranger farmers" are involved in the seasonal migration into the groundnut growing areas of Senegal and Gambia (Berg, 1965). Some of these migrants, most of whom originate from Mali and Guinea, work for wages, although the vast majority of them are employed on terms which provide time for them to cultivate farmlands allocated in lieu of cash wages. About 90,000 Hausa take part in seasonal migration into the cocoa belts of Nigeria and Ghana, while another 150,000 Ibo, Igbira, and Urhobo settle as self-employed migrant tenant farmers in the cocoa and rubber growing districts of southwestern Nigeria. There are also about 45,000 Nigerian migrants, mainly of Ibo and Ibibio origin, working in the cocoa and other farms on Fernando Po.

The two West African countries which depend heavily on migrant labor from neighboring countries for the development of export agriculture and mining are the Ivory Coast and Ghana. In the Ivory Coast, where about one-half of the total wage labor force in 1965 was made up of foreigners (670,000 Africans and 30,000 non-Africans), a large proportion (about 70 percent) of the unskilled laborers in the coffee and cocoa plantations originated from Mali (220,000 workers), Upper Volta (200,000) and Guinea (150,000). Since about 1910, the mines and cocoa farms of Ghana have depended on migrant labor from Nigeria, Togo, and Upper Volta and until 1969, when the Ghana government ordered a massive expulsion of aliens, migrants from Nigeria and the Middle East were in control of the trade in manufactured goods. According to the 1960 census, over 850,000 persons or 12 percent of the 6.7 million people in Ghana were of foreign origin, and almost 68 percent of these aliens were born outside the country. As would be expected, the vast majority of these migrants originated from the neighboring countries of Togo (280,670), Upper Volta (194,570), and Nigeria (190,780).

Labor migration in East Africa is directed mainly towards the cotton growing districts of Uganda, which support well over 150,000 migrants working for wages or settled as self-employed tenant farmers (Richards, 1954). Most of the immigrants to Uganda originate from Ruanda and Burundi and a large proportion can be considered to be permanent residents.

The magnitude of the migration in both Central and South Africa is greater and often the migrants travel much longer distances than in West and East Africa. In South Africa, the main destinations of labor migration are the gold and coal mines of the Transvaal, Orange Free State, and Natal. In 1958, these mines employed 361,400 African workers, about 235,700 of whom were drawn from outside the country (Green and Fair, 1962). According to another estimate, the Witwatersrand mining and industrial complex attracts about 300,000 migrant workers every year (Kimble, 1960). Looking at the problem from Mozambique, which is one of the major source regions for migrants to South Africa, Bailey has pointed out that in addition to the 100,000 contract workers that the Mozambique government has agreed to provide to South Africa every year (since 1900), "there has always been a large number of illegal emigrants, at times reaching a figure three times that of the legal workers" (Bailey, 1969:173). The relatively high wages paid in the mines help to attract numbers of migrants who journey "on foot, on horse back, on bicycles, by dug-out canoes, steamers, lorries, train and even by air," often traveling a distance of up to 2,000 miles!

In Central Africa, the main economic islands employing migrant wage labor are the Rhodesian highlands and the Zambian and Katanga copperbelts. Migrants employed in Rhodesia originate predominantly from Malawi, Mozambique, and Zambia, with Malawi supplying over 40 percent of the total number of 280,000 nonindigenous males employed in 1956 (Barber, 1961). In 1961, about 300,000 or nearly half of the total African labor force of 660,000 were classified as immigrants. Rhodesia, like the Ivory Coast and Ghana, depends very much on migrant labor to develop her mineral and agricultural resources, and as with the Ivory Coast, only a few of its citizens ever seek work outside the country (Yudelman, 1964). Rather, the migration of Rhodesian Africans is essentially internal, involving up to 50 percent of the young adult male population. Katanga attracts about 56,000 workers from Burundi, Ruanda, and Angola, and the Zambia copper belt employs about 45,000 workers from Malawi, Angola, Tanzania, and Mozambique.

Incomplete as the picture presented in this section may be, the figures will leave no doubt about the magnitude of the flow of people from one part of the subcontinent to another. The influx of hundreds of thousands of migrants from various ethnic groups with different cultures has created significant social and administrative problems in the centers where they settle. Those source regions which lose a substantial proportion of their adult male population have also suffered social disruptions and basic economic changes, a topic which will be discussed in more detail.

MAJOR SOURCE REGIONS OF MIGRANTS

The facts presented so far show clearly that it is the localities and regions where economic activity is expanding that are attracting migrants from other parts of Africa. It is hardly necessary to observe that regional economic inequality existed in precolonial Africa, but it was during the colonial period, which brought about the emergence of economic islands producing minerals and export crops for the metropolitan markets in Europe, that the differences became very marked. The fixation of boundaries between ethnic groups prevented the precolonial method of acquiring farmland by conquest and colonization and thereby created excessive population pressure on the land resources of some districts. Today poverty is by far the most important reason why many Africans migrate to farms or work for wages in areas outside their homelands. The case of the Ganda cotton farmers shows clearly that improvements in the economy of the home districts could reduce or even halt emigration to other rural areas.

As a general rule, the rural areas exporting large numbers of workers are very densely populated. The pressure on available farmland is great, often resulting in soil impoverishment and soil erosion, and in almost all cases shortage of farmland is the main push factor in these migrations. In southern Ghana for example, Krobo and Shai migrant cocoa farmers came from the dry and infertile Accra Plains, whose unproductive soils had compelled the people to move to established food farms and later cocoa farms in the more productive humid forest areas of the southwest (Field, 1943). Other major source regions for migrant cocoa farmers in Ghana include the narrow Akwapim Ridge district whose steep-sided slopes do not provide adequate farmland for the local population and the densely settled northeastern district where the ravages of river blindness have forced the indigenous people to abandon up to 40 percent of their territory (Hunter, 1967b).

Pressure of population on land also accounts for the high incidence of emigration from the Kikuyu areas of Kenya, the African Reserves of Rhodesia and South Africa, Burundi, Ruanda, the Mossi district of Upper Volta, parts of southeastern Nigeria, and southern Malawi. In the most populous parts of the latter two areas, densities exceed 750 persons per square mile and family holdings rarely are more than two acres. Continuous cropping is now common and in southeastern Nigeria, the compound land has almost replaced the main farmland, just as grazing land has been replaced by continuous cropping in southern Malawi. In both areas, crop yields are poor (Udo, 1964; Barber, 1961), and therefore, it is not surprising that over 300,000 persons from Malawi and more than 600,000 from the congested districts of southeastern Nigeria migrate to work outside their districts of origin.

Land shortages in the Mossi district of Upper Volta, the African Reserves of South Africa, and southeastern Nigeria have been aggravated by soil erosion. In the drier areas of Sokoto Province of Nigeria, Mali, Niger, and parts of South Africa, poor harvests and famine, caused by unreliable rainfall, have resulted in the seasonal and permanent emigration of young adults.

There are, however, many sparsely settled areas which also export population. Often such areas have no source of earning cash income except through cultivating food crops, and thus labor migration offers the easiest method of obtaining money for meeting various expenses.

The major source regions for migrants, therefore, are characterized by a relative lack of wage-earning opportunities. Often the head of the family does not earn enough money to pay his tax and feed his family for the whole year. It is the mounting poverty of such regions that has induced the more enterprising and able-bodied man to migrate to work in the mines, plantations, timber concessions, and industrial centers.

MIGRATION AND RURAL CHANGE

As might be expected, changes occasioned by migration are most obvious in the areas that attract migrants. The increased tempo of activities and the resultant changes in the economy and society of the areas which attract migrants are not difficult to identify. The benefits, if any, that the areas exporting labor derive are not so obvious; as a matter of fact, many writers argue that migration is often detrimental to the economy and disruptive to the social organization of the source areas. It appears, however, that the migration process continues today because it is mutually beneficial to both the exporting and the receiving districts.

Starting first with rural destinations the most obvious change appears to be increasing economic activity as evidenced by rising production figures in mining and agricultural exports from such areas. Also, migrant labor has played a leading role in the complete replacement of extensive areas of tropical forests, by man-made forests of cocoa, rubber, oil palms and even forest plantations of teak. Plantation villages and camps have been built in areas that virtually were uninhabited or that supported a small number of hunting groups or shifting cultivators. In the areas where self-employed migrant farmers are found, the traditional settlement patterns have been radically modified by the establishment of numerous camps and farming villages that are basically different from the larger and more compact villages and towns occupied by the indigenous population. This is the case in the Nigerian cocoa belt and the Uganda cotton belt where migrant tenant farmers tend to squat widely throughout the territory.

As a general rule, the migrant population of a given district has a much larger proportion of active adults (15-45 years) as compared with the indigenous population and in districts where the migrants outnumber locals, the demographic characteristics of the rural population have changed. Most self-employed migrants who depend heavily on family labor are married and usually live with their wives. Wage-earning migrants, on the other hand, tend to leave their wives behind in their village of origin. This is particularly so in Central and South Africa where African workers are not allowed to settle permanently in the farms and mines located in "European Reserves."

Migrants or returning locals may bring lasting change. No one who knows western Nigeria can doubt the impact which kola nut production has brought. Although a wild variety of kola (*Kola acuminata*) grew locally, it was not until the commercial variety (*Kola nitida*) was introduced by returned migrants from Ghana that production began. Today, kola has displaced cocoa as the major cash crop in Ijebu Province and has attracted thousands of Hausa migrant kola traders, many of whom can be found settling in the large villages.

It is in connection with the development of mineral resources, the products of which have influenced the types and location of manufacturing industries, that migration has created a most impressive and lasting change on the rural landscapes of Africa. The complete transformations that have taken place in the Witwatersrand and the Katanga and Zambian copper belts, and similar but less pronounced changes that have occurred in the Jos tin fields, the Udi coal mines, and the Sierra Leone diamond fields, have been caused exclusively by mining and auxiliary activities and the large numbers of migrants they have attracted. At the beginning of this century, most of these mining districts consisted of uninhabited or sparsely-settled land occupied by pastoralists or cultivators. Now these same areas support towns with many manufacturing and service industries. Some of the premining era villages that existed in the neighborhood of the mine fields have been completely transformed into dormitory settlements for those workers who do not live in the camps. These settlements have begun to receive electricity, piped water, and medical facilities.

The effects of the loss of manpower on the economy and society of the districts where the migrants originate feature prominently in the literature on migrant labor. Many writers maintain that although these migrations are induced by economic conditions at the source regions, the loss in population suffered by such regions has often affected adversely the local economy as well as the family life and civil authority in traditional societies. Some writers, however, argue that for seasonal migrations, the benefits far outweigh the cost (Berg, 1965) and that on the whole permanent emigration is still beneficial to the economy of the source regions. We now examine the evidence for these two viewpoints.

The age selectivity of the migrant population is considered to be the cause of some of the economic problems, whereas sex selectivity is thought to be a major factor responsible for some of the social problems prevalent in districts that export population. Since most migrants are able-bodied adults of 15 to 40 years of age, it is reasonable to expect a fall in local food production if the proportion of emigrants is high. It also has been observed that the absence of many young men has created a serious labor shortage with respect to certain jobs such as making yam mounds, roofing houses, or pounding oil palm fruits, all of which are traditionally considered men's activities. In parts of South Africa, it is reported that some families are no longer able to produce enough food because of the absence of the men (Schapera, 1956; Southall, 1954).

Detailed studies of the labor situations in source regions suggest, however, that the assumption of labor shortage resulting from emigration is not supported. For example, among the Esu of Cameroun, Ardener and Ardener (1960) report that although about 40 percent of the active adult population was absent during the period of their investigation, there was no noticeable drop in food production. A similar observation has been made for the Thonga of Mozambique. At any given time, over 50 percent of the economically active Thonga males are absent from the home area, but such a loss never has seriously threatened the "ability of the population to survive or reproduce" (Harris, 1959:57).

The fact is, that in many rural situations, there seems to be considerable underemployment, and the loss of some population should lead to a fuller use of manpower. Also, since much migration is seasonal, productive capacity in the home area will not be lessened as long as the timing of the migration does not interfere with local labor demands. The major contribution of women in food production throughout Africa may be little affected by male absence.

Many writers consider the social disadvantages of migrant labor to be more serious than possible economic disadvantages. Among other things, labor migration is said to have contributed to a weakening "tribal cohesion" and the authority of chiefs in the villages. It is also argued that it has brought about a greater incidence of broken homes and has had the effect of reducing birth rates in the villages that export population.

Critics who have written at length about the "evils" of the migrant labor system appear to ignore the fact that broken homes, lack of respect for elders, sexual immorality, the drop in food production in districts that export population, and so on are not necessarily caused by migration. Rather, they can be said to be part of much broader processes of social and economic change, in which traditional values and authorities are being replaced by those emanating from the urban-industrial way of life. Halting labor migration would not halt these changes.

THE FUTURE OF MIGRANT LABOR

The great demand for labor to develop the mineral deposits, commercial plantations, private farms, and timber concessions has been responsible in large measure for the movements of people from one rural area to another. Today, the demand for labor to work in many rural areas remains high despite mounting unemployment in the cities. In Liberia, labor shortage has been the main factor limiting the expansion program of the Firestone Rubber Company, and in 1957, the Liberian government had to close down some new diamond mines so as to stop a diamond rush that threatened to worsen the labor situation in the plantations and iron ore mines (Jurgen, Tracey, and Mitchell, 1966). In countries like the Ivory Coast, Equatorial Guinea, and South Africa, which depend heavily on migrant labor from internal and external sources, production would be drastically curtailed if the migrant labor system were disrupted. Thus, although the authorities of some of the labor-deficit countries are very concerned about their heavy dependence on foreign labor, it is quite clear that the free flow of labor is indispensable for continued economic growth. Stricter immigration controls in West Africa since independence in 1960, culminating in the expulsion of about 500,000 aliens from Ghana in 1969-1970, have only worsened the labor situation. It appears, therefore, that whether or not the advantages outweigh the disadvantages, labor migration is likely to continue for many decades.

Labor migration has persisted for over seventy years in most parts of Africa. Since the system is rooted in the essentially open colonial economy of the subcontinent, it is only a complete transformation of that economy that can result in a drastic reduction in the volume of rural-rural migrations. Such a change appears to be out of the question in South Africa where the official government policy of apartheid has endorsed migrant labor from the Bantu homelands to the White Settler Reserves as a permanent feature of the economy. Over the remainder of the continent, structural changes in the economy are likely to result in a decrease of rural-rural migration and a corresponding increase in rural-urban migration, a topic which will be covered in Chapter 23.

IV

URBAN CHANGE

Although it is the least urbanized of the continents, Africa is in a period of highly accelerated city growth. Everywhere major cities are getting larger, at growth rates two to three times those for population in general. Cities have acted like magnets, attracting to their environs those individuals who (1) are seeking permanent or temporary wage employment; (2) desire the diversions of the urban way of life; (3) wish to break the social and behavioral bonds of traditional rural society; (4) hope to find wealth and power; and (5) are dispossessed, with no place else to go.

In the wake of this rapid influx of people has come a number of serious social and economic problems. Adequate housing is scarce, so that it is necessary for many to put up hastily erected structures made from any available material. These soon proliferate on suitable sites, giving rise to the so-called shantytowns or *bidonvilles*, which are without even minimum urban services—piped water, sanitation systems, paved roads, and electricity. Jobs are not being created fast enough and, in consequence, the ranks of the unemployed are swelling. Crimes against both persons and property are frequent. Certain diseases are reaching chronic proportions: tuberculosis in the crowded, unsanitary shantytowns; childhood malnutrition in circum-

Major arterial routes link central city areas with residential suburbs in Accra, Ghana. Nevertheless, congested urban housing areas serving recent migrants and the urban poor challenge planners throughout Africa. (Photograph from the Ghana Information Services Department)

One solution to the urban housing dilemma has been construction of low-cost housing projects such as Eastlands in Nairobi, Kenya. Persistent poverty plagues such developments throughout the world, and such consequences as malnutrition and crime are unfortunately well-known in Africa as well. (Photograph from Kenya Information Services)

stances where mothers cannot afford nutritious foods and cannot supervise eating habits; venereal disease as prostitution becomes the only way of making a living; mental illness when the stresses and strains of urban life become too great. Then, too, there are the problems of urban structural imbalance. It is only the large cities that are growing; most of the small cities and towns are either stagnating or declining. These and other related urban ills are well documented in a variety of sources, ranging from social science monographs (Hance, 1970; Hutton, 1971; Caldwell, 1969), to such novels as Ekwensi's *People of the City* and *Jagua Nana* and Achebe's *Things Fall Apart*, and to virtually every issue of Africa's major newspapers.

But a listing of the problems of city growth must be counter-balanced by a listing of the prospects. As indicated in Chapter 1, cities are the centers of modernization. They are the nodal points for the diffusion of new technologies to the country-side, and thus future rural development depends on present and future urban development. And, of course, they are the places where new ideas are formed and created. In particular, the cities are central to the whole process of breaking down old, narrowly defined loyalties and creating new, wider identities. Finally, the recency of African city growth means that many planning alternatives are still open. There is a real possibility of African planners' learning from mistakes made elsewhere and consequently their taking a lead in creating more humane urban environments.

The next three chapters will probe some of these problems and prospects in more detail. Chapter 19, "Urban Economic Development," is a macroscale analysis which Harvey begins with an overview of the history of African urban development and builds into a discussion and classification of cities based on present economic characteristics. In Chapter 20, Sommer models the general growth patterns of urban areas. In Chapter 21, "The Urban Housing Challenge," Brand focuses on the growth of uncontrolled settlements and the responses to them in Accra, Ghana. Both Sommer and Brand examine alternative urban policies for the future.

19

Urban Economic Development

MILTON E. HARVEY

The history of African urban economic development shows that the strong association among industrialization, a decrease in agricultural population, and increased urbanization as experienced in Western societies is indeed tenuous. Admittedly, Africa has had a long history of urbanization, and in more recent years this process has been immensely accelerated. But rather than secondary (manufacturing) activites, African urbanization seems to be related to tertiary (service) employment in commerce, construction, education, the civil service, religion, and the military. In a historical perspective all these functions were not significant simultaneously. Religion and administration came first, followed by the military, commerce, and finally education and construction. More recently, manufacturing on a limited scale has added to the functional complexity of African cities. This chapter traces the development of African urban economies. It also considers an existing economic dualism, and the economic implications of city primacy.

URBAN ECONOMIC DEVELOPMENT—A HISTORICAL PERSPECTIVE

The central theme that permeates this historical overview of African urbanization is the changing role of towns in response to: (1) changes in the internal and external linkages of states; (2) the transformation from belligerent to agricultural trading societies; (3) the shift from animate to inanimate modes of transportation; and (4) the move from a barter to a monetary oriented medium of exchange. The central belief is that the evolution of the African economic base reflects changes in interdependencies between states, the nature and number of externalities, and the economics of agglomeration. Although cities arose quite early in Egypt and Roman North Africa, attention here is focused on developments in the south.

The savanna state era. Urbanization in western, central, eastern and southern Africa was characterized by the emergence of centralized states, the intensification of external linkages, and international trade between geographically different environments. Because of differences in regional resources, the commodities involved in these transactions naturally differed, resulting in varied spatial organizations. Historical evidence indicates that West Africa entered the Iron Age around 300 B.C. with the Nok culture around the confluence of the Niger and the Benue. The importance of iron in the evolution of urban centers in West Africa cannot be overestimated. With iron tools and weapons the inhabitants could produce more food and could better protect themselves. With increased food production, there was spatial expansion and the initiation of urbanization. It was this mutually interdependent process that caused the creation of states in the West African savanna, and the emergence of occupational groups other than farmers. As Davidson and Buah (1967:20) note:

> With iron tools there could be more and better farming. With more farming there began to be enough food to maintain specialists who worked at making tools, weapons and other hand-made things. This division of labor encouraged trade, at first local and then long-distance, by producing a wide range of goods. All this, together with the growing size of populations, called for more complex forms of political organization.

As was the case in the Nile valley, agricultural surplus and the establishment of long distance trading stimulated urban development and influenced the type and nature of the urban economic base. In western West Africa, these changes were related to centralized states such as Ghana and its successors; in the east, they were associated with the Hausa city states.

The state of Ghana and its successors were strategically located for trade with both the forested gold-producing south and the North African coast. The important trading centers were the southern termini for trans-Saharan caravan trading routes, and the northern termini for trading routes from the more forested south. Between North Africa and West Africa, for example, gold, ivory, ebony, hides, and skins were exchanged for salt, manufactured goods, silver, copper, rum, mirrors, and cowries; a trading system that was considerably intensified after North Africa was conquered by the Muslims in the eighth century A.D. (for trading routes see Davidson and Buah, 1967). This increased trade resulted in the growth and development of centers in North Africa and the Sudanic savanna as well as along the trans-Saharan routes. In North Africa, examples include Fez (809 A.D.), Kairovan (800 A.D.), Oujda (944 A.D.), Algiers (950 A.D.), and Cairo (970 A.D.). Other centers include Sijilmasa, Tripoli, Tunis, Rabat (1160 A.D.), and Marrakesh (1060 A.D.). In the Sudanic region we find Kumbi, Saleh, Jenne, Timbuktu, and Gao as caravan-route termini, Niani and Tekrur as gold-mining centers, and Walata, Audaghost, and Segou as caravan confluents. Along the routes, the specialized centers included Taghaza (salt), Taodeni (salt), and the oasis ports of Wadan, Tichitt, and Tuat.

In the eastern section of West Africa, trans-Saharan trade also developed among the ancient and powerful empire of Kanem-Bornu, and Libya, Nubia and Egypt. Other political organizations involved in this trans-Saharan trade were the Hausa city states centered on the trading and defensive towns of Zaria, Kano, Katsina, Biram, Daura, Gobir, and Rano. In general, these cities were centers of defense and administration, marketing centers for contiguous rural farmers who exchanged agricultural products for handicrafts and imported products, and centers for long-distance trading. Indeed, "expansion of long-distance trade by the techniques of currency and credit went hand-in-hand with the growth of learning, and with valuable advances in handicraft industry" (Davidson and Buah, 1967:108).

The only section of the West African rain forest where the ingredients of urbanization were present on any large scale was the Yoruba area of western Nigeria. From the two earlier established nuclei of Ile-Ife and Old Oyo, the spread of the Yoruba into the relatively uninhabited forest ultimately led to the founding of numerous urban centers such as Ketu, Owu, Ijebu-Ode, Ogbomosho, Oshogbo, and Ibadan. Functionally, the Yoruba towns were centers of administration, commerce, trade, and domestic crafts.

Urbanization in the West African savanna was paralleled by a similar settlement transformation in East Africa. Here the diffusion of the Bantu, the spread of southeastern East Asian foods such as the banana, and the use of iron tools in agriculture all occurred during

the period 1000-1400 A.D. Prior to this time, there was trade among
East Africa and Egypt and the Mediterranean. Generally, this trade
involved ivory, rhinoceros horns, tortoise shells, palm oil, iron ore (at
Sofala), and gold. It resulted in the emergence of coastal trading
centers like Mombasa, Malindi, Zanzibar, and Kilwa. These were
autonomous city states that had a complex system of social,
political, and economic interdependence. Commenting on the trading
importance of this area, Kirkman (1966:106-107) writes:

> The coast of East Africa towards the end of the last millennium B.C. was
> brought into the Asian commercial system, to provide raw materials and
> curiosities for the more sophisticated countries across the sea. The
> commodities which first attracted the outside world to Africa were
> aromatic gums, ivory, slaves, tortoiseshell, leopard skins, rhinoceros horn,
> gold, and the more prosaic hides, palm oil, cotton, copper and iron . . . .
> For payment were brought spears, knives, axes, cloth and later beads and
> porcelain.

Although all these towns were important general-trading centers,
some were more associated with certain commodities: Sofala with
gold, Kilwa and Mombasa with slaves.

Early urbanization in southern and central Africa also can be
associated with the migration of the Bantu and their new iron
culture. But with the exception of the famous stone walled towns of
Monomotapa of which the Great Zimbabwe is the most famous,
town development in this region was only intensified after European
colonization.

Were these pre-European centers actually towns? Such a
question should be answered against the background of the economic
base of today's urban centers. Presently, most centers in Africa are
functionally associated with education, administration, commerce,
defense, and handicrafts. In general, these same functions were found
in many pre-European centers. In West Africa, Kumbi Saleh, the
capital of Ghana, covered over a square mile area and had a
population of about 30,000:

> This city consisted of two sections, the first, the king's residence, was a
> fortress with many rounded walls. In the other it had a dozen mosques,
> and was "the market city of the Muslims" (Davidson 1959:85).

El Bekri asserted that Aoudaghast was "a very large city with several
markets, many date, palm, and henna trees as big as olives . . . [and]
filled with fine houses and solid buildings" (quoted by Davidson,
1959:84). The importance of Timbuktu as a center of precolonial
trade is known even to the nonspecialist. In that city, El Bekri writes,
"there are numerous judges, doctors, and clerics, all receiving good

salaries from the king" (Davidson, 1959:93). This town became an important entrepot, and because of its location, it gradually absorbed the trade of the neighboring centers like Walata. When Leo Africanus visited the city in the early sixteenth century, Timbuktu had a population of about 25,000, smaller than Gao, the capital of the Songhai Empire.

Similar examples of pre-European urbanization are found in East Africa. Great Zimbabwe, a capital of the Rozvi Mutapa Empire was an important urban center south of the Zambezi River. Functionally, it was the headquarters of a ruler and the distributing center for gold. Other important trading and commercial centers included the coastal Islamic city-states like Kilwa, an important trading center for gold in the thirteenth and fourteenth centuries, and Mogadishu, an important cultural center.

Up to the end of the fifteenth century and the beginning of the sixteenth century, African urbanization was highly affected by the rise and fall of centralized states and the periodic disruption of transcontinental trade. In the sixteenth century, as these states disintegrated, foreign European influence, notably Portugal and Spain, started transforming the human surface of the whole continent. In a very general sense, this influence changed the axis of interaction from north-south across the Sahara Desert, to an interior-coastal orientation. As the trans-Saharan trade routes decayed, the budding savanna interior centers slowly declined. New urban centers geared towards maritime trade with Europe developed at advantageous geographic locations such as estuaries, protected bays and inlets, and easily defensible sites such as capes and isthmuses. Examples of such coastal settlements included Bissau in Portuguese Guinea, Porto Novo and Ouidah in Dahomey, Lagos in Nigeria, and Benguela and Luanda in Angola. In the interior, at heads of navigation and important caravan termini, examples include Kumasi in Ghana, Zinder in Niger, Abeche in Chad, Sikasso and Segou in Mali, Bobo-Dioulasso and Ouagadougou in Upper Volta.

An intensification of the urban pattern occurred in the latter part of the eighteenth and the earlier part of the nineteenth century. Some of the coastal centers—Freetown in Sierra Leone, Monrovia in Liberia, and Bathurst (now called Banjul) in Gambia—were founded as homes for freed slaves. In the interior we find Ibadan and Oyo in Nigeria, and Ardra in Dahomey.

Interest in Africa as a source of slaves and raw materials for the Industrial Revolution in Europe led to competition and conflict between various European nations for territorial control. To help settle all the issues involved, the Berlin Conference was convened in

1884-1885. As noted in Chapter 3, this partitioned the continent into spheres of influence, and the Colonial period in African history was begun.

The colonial urban pattern. From the above analysis, we can see that before the Balkanization of the African continent, only the riverine belts of the savanna, the coastal-based city states of East Africa, and a few isolated pockets of the forest zone, such as Yorubaland, had distinct urban nodes within an otherwise rural settlement matrix.

Clearly, the colonial era had certain economic, political, and sociological evils. However, we must concede that it did initiate forces that have altered the socioeconomic landscape of much of the continent. The main characteristics of this era were the institution of centralized administrative systems over heterogeneous ethnic and linguistic groups, the introduction and gradual diffusion of Western medicine and education, of postal service and a monetary system of exchange, of cash crops and mining, and above all, of rails and roads. In various parts of Africa, the propagation of these impulses has been studied under the rubric of modernization, diffusion, and social change, topics that are treated in Chapters 25, 26, and 27.

In aggregate, these innovations caused many changes in the traditional system. First, the resultant tranquility and political stability considerably reduced internecine fear and suspicion; people could move through and live in areas where they formerly were regarded as strangers. Second, the concentration of educational, administrative, and medical facilities in a few nodes induced the inception of a new type of urbanization, the creation of new centers, the decline of many existing centers, and the mercurial growth of others. Third, the introduction of mining and cash crop production, coupled with the gradual evolution of a road-rail network, resulted in constant changes in the pattern of urbanization and the urban economic base. Finally, many local communities in Africa had some form of currency in precolonial times, but it was during this era that a more structured, less bulky monetary system was introduced in the new, culturally diverse states. These last two factors caused changes in the employment and occupational structure of many African towns. Such modifications either involved alteration of traditional economic structures or the complete abandonment of others that could not be easily modified in the light of the transformation. New values, new occupations and new economic activities were adopted.

The colonial period essentially affected traditional crafts in three ways. First, the importing of manufactured and aesthetically more pleasing alternatives slowly undermined the market for locally-produced cloth, shoes, and household goods. In many instances it was even cheaper to purchase the imported varieties. Second, and as a direct result of the first, many Africans abandoned subsistence agriculture and either found jobs with regular incomes, or concentrated on cash-crop production to get the money required for purchasing new amenities. Third, Christianity was introduced resulting in the rejection of African religions. The first two factors naturally caused a drastic reduction in the number of people employed in domestic crafts, whereas the last attempted to strip traditional crafts of their magico-religious ramifications. Thus, Christianity seriously undermined the social and political importance of craft organizations.

Although the decline in the number of people working in crafts has continued, during the last decade tourist and growing domestic demands reflect an expanding interest in Africa's traditional crafts. There has been an evident revitalization of craft industries. In many African countries, governmental organizations designed to encourage crafts have been established. This process of craft rehabilitation often has involved either the use of imported substitute materials or the use of Western instruments and appliances.

The occupational structure of Bamako, the capital of Mali, clearly shows the employment composition of males in a typical colonial urban center (Meillassoux, 1968). Only 10 percent remained in agricultural employment. Of the 42.5 percent wage earners, only a small proportion was at or above the level of junior executives. Also nearly one half of the gainfully employed were either unskilled or employed in other low paying jobs. One half of the men were independently employed and of these, 50 percent were associated with trade. Generally, a large proportion of the urban entreprenuers were petty traders who often sold their commodities at some centralized market (Chapter 24).

Although colonial censuses of African countries do have among their occupational categories one for those working in manufacturing industries, in the majority of cases the figures reflect those employed in crafts and the preparation of foodstuffs. Modern manufacturing industries were very few indeed. For example, in Nigeria, there were no manufacturing industries before 1939 and few before independence. In the Ivory Coast, to give another example, industrial development began only after the port of Abidjan was opened in 1952.

Yet another major consequence of the colonial period on the economic structure of African cities was the large scale migration of

Asians and Middle Easterners into various African countries. Understandably, they settled largely in the more important urban centers.
Attracted through their trading contacts with the French in the ports
of the Mediterranean, the Syrians and Lebanese came first to French
West Africa before the end of the last century, and then gradually
spread to the British colonies. Between 1921 and 1931, their number
slowly increased and by 1951, there were over 15,000 in West Africa.
Partly because of the land-tenure system, whereby land is vested, and
partly because of their low education, most found retailing very
rewarding. Another reason for the majority of Lebanese and Syrians
being engaged in retailing has been adduced by Morgan and Pugh
(1969:414):

> In each territory the nationals of the occupying power have predominated,
> but only in a few cases have they been willing to undertake socially
> "inferior" work even where this is remunerative. In consequence,
> opportunities have existed in commerce, particularly in retail trades, for
> other non-Africans.

Before independence there were very few Asians in West Africa.
Where they were found, they worked either as retail traders as in
Sierra Leone and Ghana or as clerks and skilled workers as in some
parts of Nigeria. It was in East Africa that the Asian influence on
trade and entrepreneurship was most marked. The history of Indians
in East Africa goes back to antiquity, but their major influx dates from
the construction of the East African railways (1895-1904) when
Indians were introduced as construction laborers. Despite the
attempts by European settlers in 1902 to discourage Asiatic
immigration, the Indian population steadily grew, partly because of
economic pressures in India. Although many Indians worked as
laborers, for the most part they returned home when their contracts
expired. It was, rather, the traders from Gujarat and Bombay
following in the wake of the railway, who formed the nucleus for the
settled population. In addition to trading, they also began to work in
construction, transportation, and agriculture. In addition to trade,
the Asians also became important in plantation agriculture and the
processing of raw materials, especially sugar cane (Ehrlich, 1965).

The post-independence era. During the post-independence era,
four basic changes in the urban economic base have taken place. First
is the relative increase in African industrialization, especially manufacturing. Many African leaders have come to believe that industrialization is a panacea to developmental problems. They generally agree
with Dumont (1966:103) that:

without factories, an economy cannot get off the ground and effect rapid growth in labor productivity, nor can it provide for the massive demands of modern agriculture. Industrialization is also a symbol of economic progress, not a negligible factor in inspiring enthusiasm for development.

Closely related to this process of post-independence industrial development are the detailed formulation of long-term development plans and the emergence of state-financed industries. Indeed, few Africans presently have enough money to invest in industries. However, as was the case with the colonial developmental pattern, most of the new industries are located in areas of labor supply and market potential, namely urban centers. The structure and processes of manufacturing and industrialization will be discussed in more detail below.

Second, there has been a conscious attempt to encourage African entrepreneurship by legislation and governmental subsidies, sometimes channeled through a development bank. Of these two, the first has been more effective. Briefly, it has involved legislation restricting the commercial adventures of nonindigenous people to wholesaling and other specified types of trade. They are prevented from becoming involved in retail trade, transportation, real estate, and the buying and exporting of raw materials. However, all these measures have not immediately transformed many indigenes to entrepreneurs. The results of survey research in East Africa by Marris and Somerset (1972:149) suggest that lack of business ability and commitment are important factors in business failures: "the successful transfer of commercial and industrial opportunities involves entrepreneurship as much as innovation does. It cannot be guaranteed by redirection of capital, training, and licenses, any more than sustained development can be guaranteed by investment" (Marris and Somerset 1972:12-13).

A third change has been the establishment of industrial estates and other conscious attempts at spatial reorganization. Characteristically, these industrial estates have been located near an urban pool of labor and a potential market. West African examples include the Wellington Industrial Estate near Freetown; Tema, just east of Accra; the Apapa section of Lagos; and the area behind the wharves of Petit Bassam Island in Abidjan. In East Africa examples include the industrial districts of Nairobi, Dar es Salaam and Entebbe. This type of developmental process has reinforced the existing colonial spatial structure.

Finally, partly as a reaction to the above, and partly because of the desire to integrate national space by a systematic developmental process, many countries are consciously decentralizing activities, creating a new spatial structure designed to complement ideology. The Ujaama villages of Tanzania are an example in point (Chapter 17). At a different level, the feverish construction and upgrading of roads, as well as the extension of railways, also are attempts at producing a "more" efficient spatial structure.

URBAN ECONOMIC DUALISM:
INDUSTRIALIZATION VERSUS DOMESTIC CRAFTS

Having traced the emergence of a technological based economic system from the traditional nonmarket oriented system of pre-colonial Africa, we may have created an impression that there has been a transformation of African urban economic structure from the traditional to a new and more efficient status. Actually dual economies, with distinctive traditionai and modern sectors, still exist and functionally intersect (Rivkin, 1970).

The relative importance of these two sectors in the urban economic structure of Africa has been investigated by many scholars. In most studies, the paucity of modern manufacturing industries has been emphasized. For example, of the 233,947 persons employed in manufacturing in Ghana in 1960, the majority were self-employed artisans who provided carpentry, tailoring, and other local services. Many practiced their trade in the dry season as an adjunct to farming (Peil, 1972). Similarly, Kilby (1962) showed the preponderance of small-scale domestic crafts in eastern Nigeria. Of the 10,728 firms in the region, only nine percent possessed any automated tools, whereas 58 percent used simple hand tools. Over 34 percent were one-person operations. In contrast, there were about 686 modern industrial establishments in the whole of Nigeria in 1964!

The number of establishments does not necessarily reflect the relative importance of traditional and modern manufacturing sectors of the economies. However, it indicates the extent of traditional craft in the African economic scene. Table 19.1 shows the relative contribution of certain industrial sectors to the gross domestic product in Nigeria. It is evident immediately that initially, crafts contributed more to the Gross Domestic Product than manufacturing. In recent years, however, the contribution of crafts has remained relatively constant whereas that of manufacturing has continuously increased, surpassing that of crafts from 1958 onward.

The traditional and modern sectors of the economy do interact, with money being remitted from the modern sector to help sustain the traditional sector. In Ghana, Peil (1972) observed that about

TABLE 19.1   Sectoral Output as a Share of Gross Domestic Product of Nigeria (at 1957 prices), in Percent

	1950	1957	1961	1964
Agriculture	56.0	52.7	56.6	53.6
Livestock	8.7	6.3	6.3	5.6
Fishing	1.4	1.5	1.5	1.8
Forest products	1.4	1.6	1.3	0.9
Mining and oil	1.1	1.0	1.4	2.8
Manufacturing and utilities	0.6	1.4	3.9	4.7
Transport and communications	4.5	8.5	4.6	4.7
Building and civil engineering	3.0	4.7	2.7	3.2
Crafts	2.3	1.9	2.0	2.4
Government	2.2	3.4	3.6	3.5
Other services	18.8	17.0	16.1	16.8
	100.0	100.0	100.0	100.0

Source: Kilby, 1969:11. Reproduced with the permission of Cambridge University Press.

25 percent of sampled factory workers sent money home. Part of the remitted funds sustain local crafts. This indicates that without the assistance of either the government or individual families, traditional handicrafts may, like the wildlife in certain parts of Africa, ultimately disappear. Because of the historical and cultural value of crafts and more recently because of the value of their products as tourist artifacts and momentos, governmental efforts have increased that are designed to revive these activities by retraining the artisans in the uses of modern technology. Adult-education programs and courses in technical institutes or colleges designed to reequip and give these people the requisite management skills are examples in point. Some African countries, like Sierra Leone, have established a Ministry of Tourism and Cultural Affairs. For other countries, such as Kenya, an Industrial Development Corporation has been established with the aim of aiding African businesses with loans. Kenya has also developed both a Small Industry Research and Training Center (1965) and a Management Training and Advisory Center (1966).

MANUFACTURING INDUSTRIES

Outside the Republic of South Africa and the Arab countries of North Africa, large scale industrial development in Africa resulted from development strategies in the post-independence era. The change in development priorities after independence meant that the African countries had to draw up industrialization plans to basically answer the following questions: Where will the industries be located? What types of industries are ideal? How large should these industries be? And, above all, what are the aims of industrialization?

The basic aim of all the African countries has been export valorization and adequate import substitution. The former involves the initial processing of commodities before export; that is, intermediate manufacture. The economic bases of this type of manufacturing have been well summarized by Kilby (1969:137):

> The advantages of industrialization based on export processing as compared to import replacement are: (a) it is not limited by the size of the home market, (b) its import-content of intermediate inputs is typically lower and (c) the likelihood of subsidized uneconomic production is significantly less. On the other hand, such industrial development is limited by the quantity of exports and the extent to which they can be processed; moreover, its potential growth inducing effects are frequently less than for the import-replacement.

By their very nature, valorization-type industries are related to the natural resources of individual countries. Within each resource belt, these industries have been located in the urban centers, especially the ports and break of bulk points. In the African context, the main industries in this category are: oil milling, cotton ginning, and the processing of other fibers, grain milling, sugar refining, tobacco processing, timber mills, and the beneficiation of mineral ores.

Valorization industries were the first industries in Africa. In fact, many of them were established very early in the colonial era. For example, the first mills for groundnuts were set up in Senegal as early as World War I, and during the 1940s in Mali and Upper Volta. Groundnut processing in Nigeria dates from 1941. The history of the processing of the oil palm fruit follows the same pattern. The Dutchscher screw-press was first introduced in the late 1920s. By the time the larger and more expensive Pioneer mills were introduced into Nigeria in 1946, there were roughly 1,300 of the screw-presses in operation. Finally in 1963, the more efficient Stork hydraulic hand press was introduced. These industries were concentrated in the Sapele-Calabar area.

In addition to their long establishment, valorization industries are more widespread, and in many countries of tropical Africa they are indeed the only industries. This is especially true in monocultural economies of countries like Gambia, Mali, Niger, and Upper Volta. Unlike export-substitution industries, which are mainly dependent on either agricultural or imported raw materials, valorization industries also use minerals as raw materials. The concentration of iron ore in the Bomi Hills of Liberia and at Marampa, Sierra Leone, and the beneficiation of copper ore in Zambia by smelters and electrolytic refiners are examples.

Most valorization industries are privately owned. This is particularly true in former British colonies. For example, in East Africa, most of the cotton ginneries are very small and often cost less than $3,000. The locational strategy of these gins is indeed interesting. "Numerous ginning firms, competing for the crops, located works as close as possible to the source of supply to avoid being intercepted by others" (O'Connor 1966:88). In general, the locational strategies for various valorization industries may be different, but the major manufacturing centers are usually large urban centers in the belts of raw material production.

In the last few decades, African countries have developed industries aimed at import-substitution. Usually, import-substitution occurs through certain growth stages. The first stage often is associated with simple consumer goods, and the second stage with intermediate and capital goods. As expected, the size of most African states and the recent nature of industrialization means most of the industries produce only basic consumer goods such as food, textiles, lumber, footwear, cigarettes, beer and spirits, paper, and cement. These consumer industries are sometimes divided into those based on local raw material and those using imported materials. It is difficult, however, to divide existing industries into these two sets because, as in the cigarette industries, some countries do produce the raw material whereas others have to import. Consequently, such a distinction will not be stressed in our analysis of these industries. A more meaningful distinction is that between intermediate and final manufacture (Mabogunje, 1970a). The former includes textiles, paper and paper products, printing and publishing, rubber products, chemicals, petroleum and coal, basic metal and metal products, excluding machinery; the latter includes food products, beverages, tobacco, footwear and apparel, leather, wood products, furniture and fixtures, machinery (excluding electrical), and transport equipment.

These industries are concentrated in urban areas. One of the basic locational considerations is cost of labor and other services. A distinction should be made, however, between unskilled or semi-skilled manual labor and skilled clerical or technical workers. The former are essential, for example, to cotton spinning; the latter for more specialized and complicated industries such as oil refining. These examples imply that the type and cost of labor are highly dependent on the type of industry. In general, however, the different labor requirements only can be found in large urban centers.

In addition to labor availability, other factors, termed *centripetal forces*, have also encouraged the concentration of industries in the cities. The major centripetal forces in African industrial location are adequate transportation and sources of power, water, and other public utilities. Because of these considerations Pearson (1969:91) concludes that:

> The analysis of the influences which bear upon the choice of industrial location in developing countries shows that, with the exception of supply-based industries, in whose cost structure the importance of transport costs on raw materials is overwhelming, the pressures are generally centripetal. Not only are there cost advantages in situating a manufacturing plant in an urban rather than a rural area, but there are also benefits to be gained from being in a larger rather than a smaller town.

Table 19.2 clearly indicates the dominance of urban centers in the location and concentration of industries in tropical Africa.

A CLASSIFICATION OF AFRICAN CITIES
BASED ON ECONOMIC DEVELOPMENT

In spite of the paucity of information about African towns, and the difficulties associated with the collecting and reporting of data, in the last few years attempts have been made to classify African cities. Such attempts have been either in terms of the important agencies of change (Hance, 1970), or in terms of the degree of transformation of the original system (Mabogunje, 1970a). Rather than attempt to replicate or verify these classification systems, an assessment based on kinds of industrialization will be presented here.

A selected list of 79 centers ranging in size from 2,000 for Villa Cisneros, the capital of Spanish Sahara, to Cairo with a population of 3,525,000 was compiled. In this list are the capitals of all African states as well as other principal cities in each country. For each of these places, 33 variables about economic composition, the importance of selected industries (scored on a comparative scale of 3 for large, 2 for intermediate, 1 for small, and 0 for none), and population in 1960 and 1966 were collected. These variables were designed to calibrate economic development and to reflect the changes in the traditional economies (Table 19.3).

The 79 X 33 matrix of centers and certain indicators of industrial development was subjected to a principal component analysis. Eight manufacturing components associated with greater-than-unity eigenvalues and accounting for 72.5 percent for the total variance were extracted (Figure 19.1). These divide into three broad categories reflecting increasing complexity, increase in amount of capital

TABLE 19.2 Percentage Share of National Manufacturing in the Capital Cities of States in Tropical Africa

City	Percentage
Banjul (Gambia)	100.0
Monrovia (Liberia)	100.0
Bangui (Central Af. Rep.)	100.0
Libreville (Gabon)	100.0
Bukavu (Rwanda)	100.0
Dakar (Senegal)	81.48
Bujumbura (Burundi)	80.00
Freetown (Sierra Leone)	75.00
Blantyre (Malawi)	72.73
Abidjan (Ivory Coast)	62.50
Dar es Salaam (Tanzania)	62.50
Khartoum (Sudan)	60.00
Conakry (Guinea)	50.00
Douala (Cameroun)	50.00
Addis Ababa (Ethiopia)	47.09
Nairobi (Kenya)	41.67
Lagos (Nigeria)	35.00
Lusaka (Zambia)	35.00
Brazzaville (Rep. of Congo)	33.00
Accra (Ghana)	30.43
Kinshasa (Zaire)	30.28
Kampala (Uganda)	27.78
Cotonou (Dahomey)	16.67

Source: Mabogunje, 1973:11. Reproduced with permission of *Economic Geography*.

investment, and increase in the minimum scale of output. These groups are the valorization industries, the basic consumer industries, and industries that produce both intermediate and capital goods.

Components 3, 6, 8, and to a limited extent, 7 are largely valorization industries, reflecting the regional distribution of raw agricultural and mineral resources. The identification of the centers with the highest scores (Appendix 19.1) showed the strong geographical bias in valorization industries. While the third component is strongly associated with the North African cities of Casablanca, Fez, Oran, Benghazi, Alexandria, Cairo, and Khartoum, the sixth component identifies the main ground-nut and oil-palm producing areas of tropical Africa. The major centers are Monrovia, Accra, Port Harcourt, Addis Ababa, Dakar, and Kano. The first three centers are associated with oil-palm processing; the last three with ground-nut processing. Sugar refining, component 8, is largely associated with the larger urban centers of central, eastern and southern Africa.

TABLE 19.3   Urban Economic Variables

A. Locational and Size Factors
  1. Population in 1960
  2. Population in 1966
B. Population Composition
  3. Africans (3, 2, 1, 0)
  4. Europeans (3, 2, 1, 0)
  5. Others (3, 2, 1, 0)
C. Raw Materials
  6. Petroleum (3, 2, 1, 0)
  7. Diamonds (3, 2, 1, 0)
D. Intermediate Manufacture
  8. Vegetable oil milling (3, 2, 1, 0)
  9. Cotton ginning (3, 2, 1, 0)
  10. Iron and steel (3, 2, 1, 0)
  11. Chemicals, plastics, and matches (3, 2, 1, 0)
  12. Grain milling (3, 2, 1, 0)
  13. Tobacco (3, 2, 1, 0)
  14. Timber mills (3, 2, 1, 0)
  15. Tanning (3, 2, 1, 0)
  16. Rubber (natural and synthetic) (3, 2, 1, 0)
  17. Cotton textiles (weaving, etc.) (3, 2, 1, 0)
  18. Woolen textiles (weaving, etc.) (3, 2, 1, 0)
  19. Making up of textiles and sacking (3, 2, 1, 0)
  20. Textiles undifferentiated (3, 2, 1, 0)
  21. Printing and publishing (3, 2, 1, 0)
E. Final Manufacture
  22. Sugar refining (3, 2, 1, 0)
  23. Wine/spirits production (3, 2, 1, 0)
  24. Brewing and mineral waters (3, 2, 1, 0)
  25. Canning (3, 2, 1, 0)
  26. Paint and varnish (3, 2, 1, 0)
  27. Glass and pottery (3, 2, 1, 0)
  28. Petroleum refining (3, 2, 1, 0)
  29. Footwear (3, 2, 1, 0)
  30. Cement production (3, 2, 1, 0)
  31. Electrical engineering (radios, etc.) (3, 2, 1, 0)
  32. General engineering (cables, etc.) (3, 2, 1, 0)
  33. Building materials (3, 2, 1, 0)

Examples of such centers are Kinshasha, Lubumbashi, Luanda, Bulawayo, Beira, Lourenço Marques, and Durban. Except for Lubumbashi and Bulawayo, the remainder are also ports.

Component 7, which is better correlated with diamonds and glass, relates to three different urban concentrations. The North Africa cluster which includes Rabat, Casablanca, Algiers and Oran is associated with petrochemicals and glass, and the Equatorial cluster consisting of Accra, Lagos, Bangui, Khartoum, and Dakar is associated with chemical industries. The third group, the southern African cluster, consists of Pretoria, Johannesburg, Bulawayo and Kimberley. These towns are largely associated with one or more of the three industrial types constituting this factor.

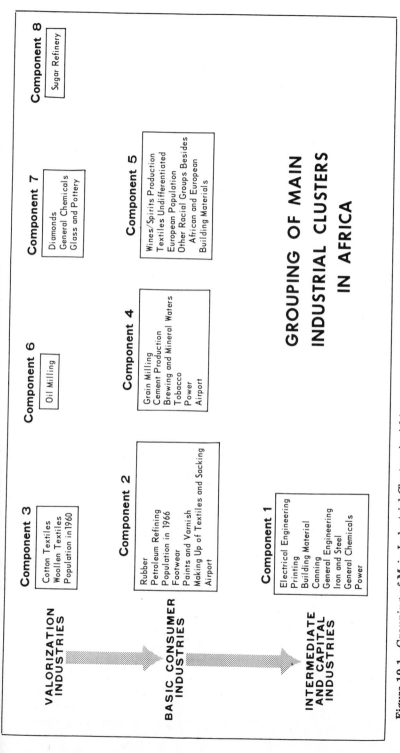

Figure 19.1 Grouping of Main Industrial Clusters in Africa.
Variables loading positively on each component are listed (calculated by the author). African population loaded negatively (−0.73) on component 5. The number of each component indicates its contributing rank in differentiating African cities.

Two of the remaining components, 2 and 4, are associated with basic consumer goods. These components reflect the type of industries related to the first stage of import-substitution. Specifically, component 2 comprises a group of relatively cheap industrial products, a few of which can be found in the fast growing urban centers with international transportation linkages. Although 33 of the 79 places used in this analysis had high scores (> 0.60), a few centers were far more important, with scores greater than 1.00 on component 2. These places tend to fall into four broad groups. First, is the North African subsystem centered on Algiers, Tunis, Alexandria, and Cairo, with secondary concentrations at Oran, Bône, Bizerte, and Tangier. Besides Alexandria and Algiers, not all these centers have large rubber industries. They are, however, important for certain types of petroleum-refining industries, paints and varnish, footwear, and the manufacture of textiles. Second is the West African cluster centered at Lagos with secondary concentrations at most capitals and important regional centers. Here examples include Dakar, Bangui, Bamako, Bissau, Conakry, Freetown, Monrovia, Abidjan, Kano, Ibadan, Fort Lamy, and Libreville. Third is the Central African subsystem centered on Kinshasa, Lubumbashi, Zomba, Luanda, and Bulawayo. The final cluster is the southern African subsystem centered on Lourenço Marques, Durban, Cape Town and Johannesburg. Secondary centers include Windhoek and East London. In terms of total industrial production, the first and last groups are the most important.

Two interesting qualities of the industries in component 4 are their fast growth in the post-independence era and their dependence in some cases on imported raw materials. The most important centers for the industries in component 4 are Casablanca, Algiers, and Cairo in North Africa; Dakar in West Africa; Kinshasa, Lumumbashi, Benguela, and Luanda in central Africa; Dar es Salaam, Nairobi, and Bulawayo in eastern Africa; and Lourenço Marques, Durban, Cape Town, and Pretoria in southern Africa.

Component 5 essentially is similar to the last two, but the high negative loading of the African population component suggests that it is associated with the urban centers of southern Africa. The two industries are basic consumer goods that are usually located in areas of potential markets. Understandably, the main centers are Cape Town, Durban, Pretoria, Johannesburg, and East London.

The industries in component 1 are designed to produce intermediate and capital goods, rather than the simple consumer goods associated with the last three components. These industries are, in essence, a higher stage in the process of industrialization and are indeed necessary for significant structural changes in African economies. As Ewing (1968:12) observed, "the real issue remains the need, if serious development is contemplated, to launch a programme for the production of capital and intermediate goods, what de Bernis . . . has called the production of machines which produce machines, with a view of changing the structure of the economy." Because of the present level of economic development, small populations and low income per capita, economies of scale make it impossible, without the grouping of countries, for most areas of Africa to have the industries in this component. The minimum scale of output for many of these industries are fairly high for most existing markets in Africa. For example, Ewing estimates that a modern integrated iron and steel works concentrating on the production of light steel ingots needs a minimum of 500,000 ingot tons per year, ammonia needs a minimum of 50,000 tons, and an integrated pulp and paper mill a minimum of 40,000 tons. Because of these reasons, it is not surprising that the centers with the highest scores on this component are largely in southern and northern Africa.

This analysis of industries in Africa shows that there are regional variations in the concentration and type of industries, and that African industrial development is largely related to the pattern of urbanization. The basic pattern of industrial distribution shown in Figure 19.2 indicates (a) that there are more kinds of industries located along the coast or near navigable waterways than in the interior and (b) that there are definite industrial clusters separated by belts of no industries. In general, the areal distribution of manufacturing in Africa is conditioned by consumer demand, local materials, service activities, and other urbanization economies. The basic clusters are Casablanca-Algiers, Alexandria-Cairo, Dakar, Accra-Lagos, Addis Ababa, Kampala-Nairobi, Lubumbashi-Lusaka-Salisbury-Bulawayo-Pretoria-Johannesburg, Durban, and Cape Town.

ECONOMIC IMPLICATIONS OF CITY PRIMACY

The foregoing analysis of industrialization clearly shows the dominance of a few urban centers, especially the capitals. Besides the overwhelming importance of the capital in industries, these cities also have a greater share of public services, employment opportunities, and better medical and educational facilities. For example, Bamako, the capital of Mali, has 54 percent of all wage earners in the country, 62 percent of national production, about 49 percent of all salaries and wages, 33 percent of the profit from all businesses, and it also consumes 45 percent of all imported oil products, 33 percent of all imported cement, and about 50 percent of all imported goods.

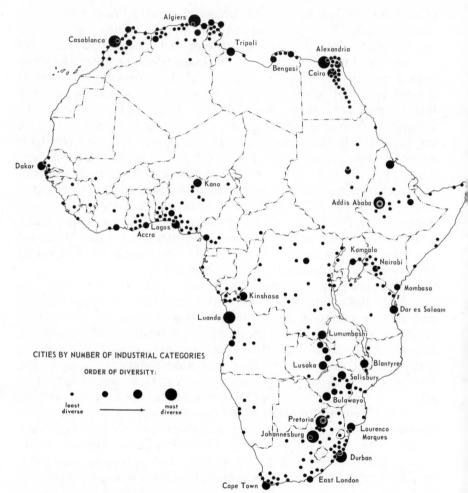

Figure 19.2   Urban Industrial Development.

Similarly, Nairobi has about 48 percent of all wholesalers in Kenya, and Addis Ababa has about 48 percent of the doctors, 59 percent of the nurses and 31 percent of the available beds in hospitals in Ethiopia; Douala in the Cameroons has about 33 percent of all commercial banks, 50 percent of all hospital beds and about 80 percent of all business establishments.

The concentration of resources in the capital and other large urban centers has been regarded by certain regional economists as essential in the early stages of economic development. Reiterating Hirschman's view on the necessity of such disparities, Alonso (1968:9) writes:

... polarization, regional inequality, or primacy are normal aspects of the early stages of development, corrected by natural processes (a form of negative feedback) with the achievement of development. Primacy, over-urbanization and gigantism are not diseases but growing pains.

Unfortunately, the effect of such cumulative causation has resulted, in most African countries, in increasing primacy, and the expected "trickle down" effect of growth in certain selected nodes on the periphery has not occurred; articulation has not replaced polarization between the core and periphery. Few scholars working on African economic and regional development share the opinion that given time, the system may generate growth in the periphery (Hance, 1970). Most have concluded that an equilibrium model cannot work in Africa because "disequilibrium is built into traditional societies from the start ... (Thus) regional convergence will not automatically occur in the course of a nation's development history" (Friedmann, 1966:14). For example, in Ghana, Darkoh (1971) observed that concentration of manufacturing in existing urban areas has failed to institute a chain of growth in the relatively undeveloped hinterland.

In general, most African countries are attempting to decentralize industries and services, and thus replace the colonial dendritic interaction pattern by a locational matrix that is based on a new pattern of central places with a commensurate transport network. In 1968, the Ghana government decided to encourage decentralization of industries from the Accra-Tema area by tax rebates. Companies which establish in certain approved areas will be given a 20 percent tax rebate, authority to carry forward losses against three years of assessments, a reduction of 50 percent in excise and sales tax, and exemption from the Excess Profit Tax (National Liberation Council, 1968).

In tracing the processes of urban economic development in Africa we have seen the significant role of urban centers in societal and spatial reorganization. Because of the colonial pattern of trade and resource utilization, few centers emerged as the focal points for the concentration of modernizing agencies and instruments of economic development. It may be necessary for African countries to reorganize their geographic space so as to remove the economic and political strangle-hold of the few prosperous cities. Presently, these evolving systems can be modified and restructured with minimum social, political and economic cost. However, if the present spatial structure persists and economic dominance increases, the cost of massive change will become increasingly prohibitive.

APPENDIX 19.1   Industrialization Component Scores[a]

Locale	Scores on derived components[b]							
	1	2	3	4	5	6	7	8
Rabat	−0.18	0.22	0.23	−0.21	−0.35	0.38	0.85	0.06
Tangier	−0.08	0.66	−0.14	0.11	0.11	−0.60	−0.08	−0.27
Casablanca	0.22	0.46	7.38	1.15	0.82	−0.04	1.17	1.15
Fez	−0.56	−0.40	0.72	−0.36	−0.36	−0.11	−0.03	0.31
Colomb-Becher	−0.46	0.04	−0.33	−0.38	−0.38	0.13	−0.21	−0.26
Algiers	0.71	1.34	−0.64	4.07	4.07	−2.30	1.25	−1.35
Oran	−0.31	0.92	0.85	−0.17	−0.17	−0.70	1.72	0.01
Bône	0.15	0.66	−0.59	0.25	0.25	−0.79	0.06	−0.01
Tunis	0.40	1.29	0.02	−0.24	−0.24	−0.06	−0.03	0.24
Bizerte	0.00	0.70	−0.30	−0.35	−0.35	−0.62	0.06	−0.01
Tripoli	0.10	−0.75	0.63	0.06	0.06	0.22	−0.41	−0.65
Benghazi	−0.58	0.18	1.08	−0.10	−0.10	0.75	−0.46	−0.96
Alexandria	0.40	3.39	1.51	−0.12	−0.12	0.27	−0.60	−1.84
Cairo	−0.84	5.39	0.70	2.10	2.10	−0.59	−1.64	−1.54
El Aiun	−0.47	−0.33	−0.18	−0.84	−0.84	−0.63	−0.18	−0.18
Villa Cisneros	−0.42	−0.26	−0.18	−0.56	−0.56	−0.48	−0.25	−0.32
Nouakchott	−0.48	−0.21	−0.24	−0.55	−0.55	−0.17	−0.27	−0.30
Dakar	−0.09	0.95	−0.19	1.32	1.32	4.03	−0.44	−0.65
Banjul	−0.31	−2.55	−0.28	−0.02	−0.02	0.00	−0.11	−0.03
Timbuktu	−0.57	−0.15	−0.25	−0.61	−0.61	0.14	−0.34	−0.33
Bamako	−0.35	0.77	−0.18	−0.38	−0.38	−0.03	−0.02	−0.36
Bissau	−0.48	0.64	−0.20	−0.34	−0.34	−0.01	−0.38	−0.48
Conakry	−0.21	0.87	−0.32	−0.16	−0.16	−0.04	0.13	−0.25
Freetown	−0.13	0.78	−0.34	0.13	0.13	−0.08	0.04	0.05
Monrovia	−0.08	0.69	−0.11	−0.60	−0.36	1.39	0.04	−0.43
Abidjan	0.06	0.64	−0.13	−0.36	−0.20	0.50	−0.07	−0.90
Ouagadougou	−0.60	0.37	0.03	−0.52	−0.30	−0.14	−0.37	−0.64
Accra	0.21	0.68	−0.60	−0.35	−0.52	1.69	2.37	−0.49
Lome	−0.44	−0.14	−0.25	−0.47	−0.28	−0.18	−0.23	−0.30
Porto Novo	−0.43	−0.30	−0.32	−0.68	−0.22	−0.34	−0.11	−0.09
Niamey	−0.48	−0.17	−0.23	−0.54	−0.26	−0.17	−0.28	−0.32
Agades	−0.57	−0.15	−0.25	−0.61	−0.38	0.14	−0.34	−0.32
Kano	−0.30	0.72	−0.25	−0.78	0.49	4.50	−0.09	−0.03
Ibadan	−0.21	0.77	−0.05	−0.74	0.19	0.24	0.38	−0.66
Lagos	0.31	1.14	0.54	1.89	−0.99	0.07	1.19	1.89
Port Harcourt	1.02	0.43	−0.07	−0.68	−0.59	1.27	−0.15	−0.27
Fort Lamy	−0.45	0.69	−0.02	−0.26	−0.34	−0.15	−0.34	−0.48
Bangui	−0.45	−0.09	−0.57	−0.94	−0.48	0.03	2.26	−0.59
Yaounde	−0.46	0.03	−0.19	1.20	−0.47	−0.25	−0.30	1.20
Libreville	−0.28	0.45	−0.08	−0.37	−0.23	0.19	−0.36	−0.47
Port Sudan	−0.34	−0.24	−0.32	−0.36	−0.32	−0.21	−0.23	−0.09
Omdurman	−0.37	0.39	−0.30	−0.56	−0.28	−0.37	−0.13	0.05
Khartoum	−0.20	−0.25	1.10	−0.36	−0.12	−0.20	0.71	0.39
Mongalla	−0.52	−0.52	−0.34	−0.75	−0.35	−0.03	−0.18	−0.11
Addis Ababa	−0.11	0.35	0.35	−0.47	0.14	2.88	0.53	−0.14
Massawa	−0.48	−0.49	−0.39	−0.67	−0.38	−0.03	−0.13	−0.06
Djibouti	−0.48	−0.18	−0.22	−0.55	−0.26	−0.17	−0.27	−0.31
Mogadiscio	−0.29	0.30	0.25	−0.96	−0.06	1.13	−0.43	−0.36
Nairobi	0.77	−0.90	−0.49	3.59	−1.33	1.25	0.99	0.38
Kampala	−0.04	−1.03	−0.26	0.74	−0.06	−0.23	0.25	0.46

APPENDIX 19.1   Industrialization Component Scores[a] (cont.)

	\multicolumn{8}{c}{*Scores on derived components*[b]}							
Locale	*1*	*2*	*3*	*4*	*5*	*6*	*7*	*8*
Kigali	−0.48	−0.19	−0.23	−0.55	−0.26	−0.17	−0.27	−0.31
Bujumbura	−0.35	0.67	−0.29	0.95	−0.61	−0.41	−0.33	−0.42
Kinshasa	−0.22	1.99	−0.13	3.82	−0.08	−0.17	−0.36	3.82
Mbandaka	−0.25	−0.19	−0.34	−0.27	−0.41	−0.20	0.12	0.04
Kisangani	−0.06	0.29	−0.53	0.67	−0.32	−0.59	−0.07	−0.10
Brazzaville	−0.22	0.24	−0.34	−0.19	−0.44	−0.20	0.16	0.03
Lubumbashi	−0.39	1.12	−0.76	2.41	−0.48	−0.30	−0.27	2.41
Dar es Salaam	−0.15	0.30	−0.42	3.17	0.01	−0.27	−1.20	−0.04
Zanzibar	−0.47	−0.64	−0.38	−0.09	0.17	−0.36	−0.31	−0.10
Luanda	−0.23	0.99	−0.34	1.17	−0.23	−0.70	0.13	1.17
Benguela	0.49	−0.24	−0.30	1.54	0.02	−0.29	−0.13	1.54
Lusaka	1.21	0.70	−0.36	0.57	−0.56	−0.06	−0.40	−0.20
Zomba	−0.07	0.69	0.37	−0.54	1.99	−1.50	−1.16	−1.28
Salisbury	5.60	−0.81	−0.45	−0.14	−0.81	0.14	−1.27	−2.30
Bulawayo	5.11	0.75	−0.22	1.17	−0.91	−0.43	−0.32	1.17
Beira	−0.30	−0.79	−0.39	0.89	−0.10	−0.19	−0.60	0.95
Lourenco Marques	−0.59	1.21	−0.06	2.25	0.24	1.12	−0.51	2.25
Windhoek	−0.26	0.93	0.04	−0.26	1.28	−1.08	−0.66	−0.87
Walvis Bay	1.14	−0.45	0.47	0.20	1.28	−0.98	−1.66	0.09
Gaberones	−0.48	−0.48	−0.34	−0.53	0.01	−0.42	−0.18	−0.03
Cape Town	0.21	−0.64	0.46	1.87	6.29	1.47	−1.26	−0.67
Grahamstown	−0.51	−0.39	−0.21	−0.45	0.92	−0.86	−0.39	−0.19
Durban	1.62	1.89	−1.12	4.10	1.90	0.27	−1.12	4.10
Kimberley	−0.41	−0.67	−0.49	0.59	0.98	−1.28	−0.57	−0.09
Pretoria	−0.70	−1.13	−0.26	2.37	1.01	−0.21	3.20	−0.33
Johannesburg	1.64	2.43	−0.61	−1.48	3.02	−0.82	5.42	−0.49
East London	−0.39	8.95	0.33	0.09	1.07	−1.30	−0.21	0.38
Maseru	−0.43	−0.67	−0.38	−0.45	−0.01	−0.43	−0.13	0.01
Mbabane	−0.47	−0.52	−0.37	−0.53	0.02	−0.43	−0.17	−0.01

[a]Calculated by the author using principal components analysis. High positive values mean more contribution by variables loading positively on the component.
[b]See Figure 19.1 for component identification.

20

The Internal Structure
of African Cities

JOHN W. SOMMER

African cities need as much study as possible as soon as possible, and they also need a rapid input of coherent policy by bold administrators. Early attempts at urban policy making in Africa often meant the adoption of planning programs ill-suited to the majority of the urban residents, and these worsened the problems of spatial organization of the city. The creation of European and African residential reserves, so characteristic of the early part of this century, is one example.

Planning programs either may result in new spatial structures that promote, or facilitate, the articulation of new spatial processes, or they may be instituted to freeze a spatial structure and the processes that give it life. Furthermore, some planning has resulted in structures far in advance of still incubating processes. As a consequence, there has been under-utilization of the structures and enormous waste. An example of this is the investment in magnificant multilane boulevards linking low density suburbs with the city center. At other times, the rapid occurrence of a spatial process, such as a population implosion on a capital city, has left planners without structures or even designs of structures to cope with the problem. Generally, these incidences of disequilibrium do not cancel themselves out; instead they reenforce one another to the dismay of Africa's city dwellers.

In this chapter we shall examine some of the facts of the internal structures of cities on the African continent; relate these to processes that use, abuse, extend, and demolish these structures; and cite specific examples of structure and process in African cities.

ORIGINS OF THE AFRICAN CITYSCAPE

In West Africa a large number of towns and cities date back hundreds of years (see Chapter 19). Although the following passage refers specifically to Yoruba towns, it holds for other indigenous towns in this region as well:

> Irrespective of the way they developed, most Yoruba towns approximated to a given town-plan. The most salient physical elements in this plan were those related to the administrative, the trading and the defense functions of the town. Centrally placed within most Yoruba towns was the palace of the Oba, the head of the city administration and the symbol of its urban status. So important was the palace that its grounds, in general, occupied an extensive area of land. The palace grounds, apart from containing the palace, also provided ample open space for recreation and for public religious or social occasions (Mabogunje, 1968: 96-97).

Other elements of the city related to us by Mabogunje are a major market opposite the palace, other smaller markets often in association with the residences of minor chiefs, religious shrines near the markets, and roads radiating from these centers of activity. An added element of the indigenous African city was the protective wall surrounding it; in the case of Ibadan the wall was eighteen miles in circumference. These features and others, such as the organization of residential space into ethnic quarters (each with its own social organization) and guild-like craft organization, evoke the classic image of a preindustrial city (Sjoberg, 1960).

These cities developed through trade and administration and were, thereby, partially prepared for the elaboration and extension of these same functions under the colonial aegis. Outside of West Africa, we find few indigenous towns that retained their importance unless they were adopted as centers for colonial administration. One such center, Kampala, Uganda, developed from an indigenous fortified capital into a modern city whose chief function is still administration, both for traditional institutions of the Ganda people and those of the state (Gutkind, 1963).

We are faced, then, with a vast land mass where the main impetus for extensive, dense, and persistent nucleated settlement came from outside, both from Europe and from the Islamic world. Aside from the obvious general locational effect on Africa's cities (coasts and at the head of river navigation), these cities bear the spatial imprint of alien cultures. Only in recent years, particularly during the post-colonial period, have the colonial urban structures been modified. Let us examine the layout of the colonial city in Africa to understand how spatial structure was designed to guide desired processes. Afterwards we shall try to understand what are the consequences of these structures for the life styles of urbanites in contemporary Africa.

THE COLONIAL CITY

Dotting the shores of tropical Africa from St. Louis, Senegal to Lobito, Angola, and from Port Sudan, Sudan to Beira, Mozambique, we find many of Africa's cities and most of its capitals. Furthermore, much of Africa's industrial capital and most of its educated elite are also at the periphery of the continent. These facts are more *occidental* in their making than *accidental!* They are the result of the contact of different civilizations at convenient break-in-bulk points— a product of an exchange economy featuring the division of African space by colonial powers from the shore to the interior (see Chapter 3). Even the indigenous urban centers of West Africa did not escape European hegemony and spatial reorganization. Indeed, traditional centers such as Kumasi (Ghana) and Ibadan (Nigeria) took on European trappings, but they were outpaced by the European creations of Accra and Lagos respectively. In East Africa, cities stimulated by Arab trade, such as Mombasa and Mogadiscio, received another cultural veneer when European powers took control.

Each of these colonial cities is unique, of course, but this hardly denies us the opportunity to generalize about their typical structures and functions. What was the composition of these cities? What characterized them? What does the inheritance of colonial structures mean for the post-colonial era?

Most of Africa's cities during the colonial era were ports and they served as entrepots between the mother country and a diffuse hinterland. Manufactured goods from the mother country, or another of its colonies within the empire, were shipped to the African port where the goods passed through a repackaging process for marketing. Similarly, raw products of agriculture or mining were shipped from the countryside to the African city for loading on ocean freighters. Several structural elements may be discerned immediately: a port, warehouses, railroad depot, a truck park, and roads. Little industry was encouraged in the colonial city so as not to compete with those in the mother country. However, as population increased around these ports, the need for local processing became compelling, hence the growth of light industries such as bakeries, breweries, and bottling plants adjacent to the port.

Nearby were the buildings of officialdom—a customs house, public health offices for quarantine, and often military emplacements overlooking and protecting the harbor. With these basic elements already named we may begin to construct an image of a colonial city whose core is adjacent to the sea and indeed, is the focus of land and sea transport routes. The core is made up of a mixture of private commerce almost entirely in the hands of non-Africans. Some light industry flanks the core where it has access to transportation.

But this is an incomplete image because people and their services are not yet part of the picture. In the earliest days of the development of the African colonial city, African and non-African were not as spatially separated as they were in later stages of development. European and Asian traders lived in commercial compounds literally at their places of business, whereas European administrators lived in government houses in hilly or coastal sites outside the urban core, to take advantage of sea breezes. Usually the lower, less well-drained areas near the core were left for Africans. Not uncommonly there were strings of residential development, often traditional African huts, along the main arteries radiating from the core toward the periphery. Little thought was given to water supply and waste control in these cities prior to the twentieth century when population increase forced these on colonial administrators.

Such considerations led to the increasing separation of residential areas on a racial basis. Administrators, with few funds for urban amenities like water supply and waste control, created separate dwelling areas for Africans and Europeans and even went so far as to create "no man's lands," or *cordons sanitaires*, between them. Several serious epidemics among African city dwellers early in this century hastened the administrative decision. New suburbs were extended in sectoral, or estate fashion, providing for the continued spatial separation of Europeans and Africans. Transplanted village craft industries engaging one or two workers speckled the African residential areas.

Provisions for the colonial city's population generally came from a central market in the core, displaced a distance from the port toward the main population centers. Fresh produce brought from the hinterland could be sold along with imported goods at the market. These markets were often large and diversified purveyors of all manner of goods for the whole city. Later as residential areas spread, satellite markets and small retail establishments began to spring up away from the core.

Near the port, either in the core itself or on its periphery, were points of commercial entertainment. Bars, brothels, eating places, and hotels developed as the town grew and trade became more active. Little thought was given to public recreational facilities until the last years of colonialism. European needs were provided in private sporting and social clubs. For that matter, little attention was given to the pressing need for education, which was left to religious missions whose arrival often preceded the first administrators. These missions, of all faiths, provided schooling and some public health care as well as religion. The churches and their associated schools were located at the fringe of the commercial core. Public education did develop and the educational buildings were located in residential areas.

Many of the colonial cities developed along the lines of basic plans prepared by colonial administrators. These plans were effective for the core but frequently the formal plan was ignored by the African urban migrants who built shelters near kinspeople who preceded them as urban residents. In the French and Belgian colonies, large blocks separated by wide streets contained a helter-skelter of dwellings made from various materials. In British Africa the large block layout was absent outside of the core. It is true that British colonial administrative policy was not as focused on the spatial layout of these cities spawned by empire as was French policy, but it would be incorrect to state that the British let growth occur at will. Regulations for urban administration were adopted by colonial governments and by the mid-twentieth century, most colonial territories had an office concerned with town planning. The public efforts may be recalled as being too little, too late, but the geometric layout of streets in the core of the African city lent more coherence to movement than no spatial planning would have done. Similarly, the emplacement of essential facilities such as power-generating plants and public-works yards aided the transition to post-colonial life.

These descriptions suggest a simple spatial model (Figure 20.1) of the colonial city in Africa. We shall examine the model again at the conclusion of the next section. Although highly generalized, the

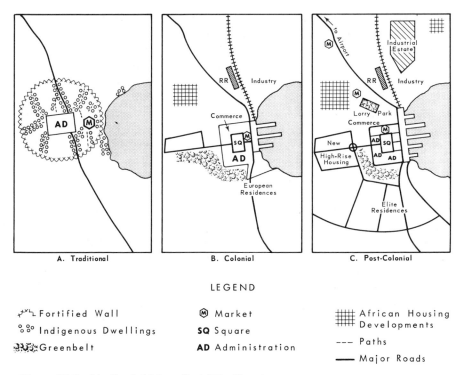

A. Traditional   B. Colonial   C. Post-Colonial

LEGEND

ﾑﾑ Fortified Wall   Ⓜ Market   ▦ African Housing Developments

°°° Indigenous Dwellings   **SQ** Square

Greenbelt   **AD** Administration   ––– Paths

—— Major Roads

Figure 20.1 Idealized African Port City Structure.

arrangement of activities portrayed was repeated time and again on Africa's shores.

THE POST-COLONIAL CITY

With the advent of political independence for most African states by the early 1960s, changes occurred in the processes underlying the spatial structures of their cities. Some of these changes, such as the removal of foreign administrative authority and its supporting military personnel had little immediate effect upon spatial structure: African elites moved into the work and residence places previously occupied by Europeans. Indeed, it is more to the point to examine the addition of new structures than the alterations of the old. Recognition of the essential inertia imbedded in heavy capital investment suggests that we should turn our attention more toward newly created spatial structures than toward those resistant to change.

The most obvious change has been the extension of dwelling units, which, when taken together, cover much more space than did housing a decade or so ago. Furthermore, there has been an increased use of vertical space. Most colonial cities had been relatively compact, but with only a few multistoried buildings. The post-colonial city has spread out and up! Naturally, many high-rise structures are placed in or near the core, but a surprising number have relaced the African huts that lined the thoroughfares extending from the core to the periphery. There are even a few high rises amidst the sprawling suburbs.

Underlying this growth of structure has been the exceedingly rapid growth of urban population (see Chapter 21). Structural response to the hyperpopulating of the city has taken several forms, and these forms have followed a characteristic sequential path. Rural migration to the city had been occurring for some time prior to independence, but these streams of migrants increased as the rural individual perceived new economic promise in the city. The use of the media by African leaders during the last days of the fight for independence, its increased use to urge national unity afterwards, and the extension of improved transportation into the rural areas each brought the promise of a better life and new economic freedom; it was clear to many that the first fruits of independence would be picked in the capital city.

The early migrants contributed to the growth of shantytowns, or *bidonvilles*, as close to the city core as possible. When no room was left near the center these tin-roofed urban villages spread to the edge of the city and beyond. In or near Lusaka (Zambia), the number of shantytowns jumped from 9 to 32 in the period 1967-1970, housing 100,000 of the city's 270,000 people (Simmance, 1973). Such residential areas had even fewer amenities than the large bloc African residential areas built during the colonial era. Fetid conditions, coupled with high unemployment, have been perceived by African leaders to be unbearable for their countrymen and, of course, potential political dynamite.

Political response to these potentially explosive conditions was relatively rapid; housing authorities were formed (or reformed) and extensive public works undertaken. But no matter how fast the housing went up, the numbers of unsheltered increased more rapidly, especially as news reached the countryside that the government provided good housing in the city. A circle of cumulative causation became established and the population of the primate city of each African state skyrocketed.

The increase of industrial nodes has not kept pace with the need for jobs, thus, there has been an increasing emphasis in industrial structure in post-colonial Africa. In some African countries industries have been spurred by real processing and marketing potential; in others, protective tariffs on competing foreign goods have allowed the development of industries where none would otherwise exist (Ewing, 1968). We have witnessed a major change in the structure of most of Africa's large cities where private foreign enterprise has been active and where national industries have been authorized. The process that has wrought this change has been the desire for economic independence as well as political independence from the former colonial power, and, of course, the desire for economic growth. It is important to realize, however, that industrialization is taking place in only a few of Africa's cities, usually its ports and/or capitals (see Chapter 19). This locational concentration is also contributing to the focus of migration streams on already over-burdened cities.

Characteristically, the new industrial areas have either been linear extensions of the pre-existing industries along rail sidings, or they have been new industrial parks, or estates, set away from the city near new migrant settlements. The development of entirely new industrial towns such as Tema (Ghana) which are separated from the country's major city are more an exception than a rule.

A third major structural change has been the extension of the route system to accomodate increased traffic flow. New routes have been extended to the hinterland from the edge of the city, and new routes have penetrated from the edge (usually from the airport) to the urban center. Although proportional ownership of vehicles is not great in African cities, automobiles, minibuses, buses, trucks, and bicycles combine to congest the arteries around the core.

The spreading of the city has meant an increase in the journey to work for many employees as well as a general extension of movement patterns. Three characteristic kinds of movement account for much of the traffic in the African city. First, there are many displaced urbanites whose previous residences near the core were destroyed by slum clearance projects. Their new residences are now at the periphery or even in new towns, but their work, or their search for work, is carried out in the industrial zone or near the commercial core. Common-laborer jobs require early arrival and one may observe trucks and minibuses packed with workers heading toward the center, crowding the streets at dawn. A second wave of movement comes from the suburbs later in the morning when government employees, who often make up more than half of the city's salaried workers, mount bicycles and any other vehicles for their trip to the offices at the center of the city. Joining this movement of the bureaucracy are the employees in commerce. A third major movement is that towards the markets at the center and in the residential areas. This movement has a mixture of origins and destinations; the vendors come first from their market gardens beyond the built-up area in the early morning and later the shoppers begin their purchasing activities. There is major movement to the central market near the core, but there is also substantial local movement to smaller, or more specialized markets in different parts of town.

Along with the increase in automobiles in African cities, there has come a rising demand for paved roads. Most of the newer suburbs built for government workers have well articulated route systems to service the houses. Even in the periurban resettlement schemes often there are more formalized route systems (often unpaved) than exist in the shantytowns of the inner city.

To add to this complexity of increased movement and congestion are the increased demands for public services. Among the most important of these are water supply and waste disposal. Simply stated, in the African city there are too many people concentrated in too small an area to rely on wells and pit latrines. Banjul (formerly Bathurst), Gambia, highlights waste disposal and water-supply problems. Planners there have even speculated on the residential abandonment of the city's site on St. Mary's Island.

A classic example of this outpacing of urban structure by the process of urbanization is Lagos, Nigeria. A Ford Foundation study reported:

> In Metropolitan Lagos, for example, chaotic traffic conditions have become endemic; demands on the water supply system have begun to outstrip its maximum capacity; power cuts have become chronic as industrial and domestic requirements have escalated; factories have been compelled to bore their own wells and to set up stand-by electricity plants; public transport has been inundated; port facilities have been stretched to their limits; the conditions have degenerated over extensive areas within and beyond the city's limits, in spite of slum clearance schemes; and city government has threatened to break down amidst charges of corruption, mismanagement and financial incompetence (Green and Milone, 1973: 14-15).

The structural response to pressures such as these has created an African city quite expanded and somewhat different from what preceded it. Figure 20.1 attempts to capture the essence of this new configuration.

EXCEPTIONS TO THE POST-COLONIAL CITY

It is obvious that much is lost in any general model, hence it is important to establish what are the major exceptions. Two of these come immediately to mind: the African city which is not a capital (or primate city), and those cities which may not be located on the sea coast. In these exceptions, aside from an expansion in tourist facilities, an increase in light industry, and more controlled population increase, the remaining colonial cities in Africa are not much different from the model presented in Figure 20.1.

During the 1960s, 16 of 57 cities with over 100,000 population "were coastal ports or river ports, and almost all the others (apart from the Yoruba group of towns), owe their dramatic growth to their location on the port-linked colonial railway systems. . . ." (Rosser, 1973:25.) The strings of these cities leading from the port to the interior are numerous and the major nodes on these strings are often centers for extractive activities in agriculture and mining. Other nodes are often the capitals of land-locked states such as Bamako, Mali, or Ouagadougou, Upper Volta.

Many of these interior cities have experienced painful withdrawal from colonial life, particularly those whose primary *raison d'etre* is trade with surrounding agricultural areas. Agriculture suffers the vicissitudes of erratic climate and uncertain world markets and thus leads to an unstable economic base. Traders formed the core of these interior cities and were often Asian or Middle Eastern. The addition of political uncertainty to the uncertainties of climate and markets caused many traders to leave the interior for the capital city, or to leave the country entirely. Kaolack, Senegal for example, with its dependence on the groundnut trade has suffered economic deterioration in recent years. Other, smaller towns, whose base is fundamentally agricultural, suffered actual losses in population. Smaller towns in the Republic of Sudan are cases in point (United Nations, 1964). Nairobi and Salisbury are two cities that have been successful in making the transition from an agricultural to an industrial base.

Agriculturally-based cities, with their associated processing activities, are a marked contrast to Africa's mining centers, which have continued to be focal points for migration. The "copperbelt" towns in Zaire and Zambia, and the coal and ore centers of Nigeria, Liberia, and Sierra Leone have continued to grow and to spread. Basically, the spatial organization of these cities differs little from their seaside counterparts, the obvious exception being that the city tends to be circular since there is no constraint on building due to a water barrier. The result is that more people can be close to the center, thereby reducing, relatively, the need for urban spread. There were and are fewer Europeans in these smaller mining cities compared to the ratio existing in the capital city or at the port, and this has affected the kinds of structures which have been built. Recreation places are more oriented toward the indigenous population, which means fewer sidewalk cafes in the former French areas, or less likelihood of a golf course in a former British area. Instead of public housing for Africans, the private mining companies initially put up "barracks" or row houses for their workers. As these towns grew and as more workers came from various parts of the country, the residential areas developed along ethnic lines. In the sense of ethnic heterogeneity, the mining towns are more like the capital cities or the ports than they are like other towns of the interior which have an agricultural base.

The commercial pattern is much the same in all of the cities: a central market, Asian shops at the center, and a sprinkling of African and Asian shops in and around the residential areas. The mining towns have acquired commercial functions that serve the surrounding rural population as well as the people who work in the town. Craft industry also exists in the mining towns, but to a much lesser degree than in the capital city where access to tourist trade continues to stimulate traditional manufacturing.

Some studies of these newer urban centers suggest that the problems of urban growth we have noted already are repeated in mining towns such as Enugu, Nigeria; Lunsar, Sierra Leone; and Bibiani, Ghana (Jennings, 1959; Mills, 1967; Darko, 1963). Population is drawn to these places in search of employment, crowding occurs, the town spreads, and eventually population growth surpasses the economic potential of the town. If the supporting mines are exhausted, a severe problem of displaced workers develops. In general, the mining centers have not received the same level of ameliorating financial inputs from public funds as have the capital cities.

Considering these exceptions, what may we conclude about the spatial dimensions of the cities of contemporary Africa?

The largest cities have grown larger and a number of smaller towns have stagnated. This is not a universal phenomenon, but only in countries with strong economies, such as the Ivory Coast, Zambia, or Kenya has the primate city become larger without causing the rest of the towns in the urban system to deteriorate. Africa of the 1960s and 1970s also has witnessed increased interregional migration, and this migration has been focused on the countries and cities of greatest economic promise (Caldwell, 1969; see Chapter 23). The results of this migration are represented in the ethnic composition of the major cities. A point of major importance is that the ethnic mosaic of the cities is becoming more complex, and to a certain degree, the ethnic residence quarters are decomposing. In dimensional terms we may characterize this changing residential phenomenon as a breaking up of a complex surface (of ethnic homogeneity), or set of surfaces (linguistic uniformity, cultural attributes, or whatever), and a reformation of these into a new, more heterogenous surface. This kind of transition, so evident in Africa's cities, may be thought of as a structural representation of the progress toward a more integrated society (Sommer, 1974).

Industrial activity has increased in a number of cities, sometimes encouraged through the building of industrial estates. Public administration employment has increased, especially in new public buildings built near the centers of the towns (Mascarenhas, 1967a). Commerce has spread out with the residential suburbs where small shops and produce markets have sprung up to serve the increasingly dispersed population.

The spread of the suburban areas and the increase in nodes of activity in different parts of the city have created a different surface of interaction and movement which is straining the existing lines of communication. More movement is required to get people where they are going. In Lagos, "many workers have to leave their homes for their work places as early as one or one-and a-half hours for a journey of less than five miles distance" (Mabogunje, 1974:22). More people are moving across existing paths as well as along them. Travel is slow. Accident rates are high. New route systems are being constructed with all of the attendant turmoil as heavy construction occurs. This turmoil is increased in the lucky suburbs where water and sewer lines are being laid.

Our impression of the city in contemporary Africa is that of an active, expanding, structure of human settlement. Most cities do have generalized features, which we have seen, yet each city is an exception to some general rule. Dakar, Senegal, for example, illustrates many of the commonalities of African cities modified by particular historical experiences and site characteristics (Figure 20.2).

THE PURSUIT OF PROPINQUITY

It can be argued that many problems concerning the organization of African urban space will dissolve in the long run if, unimpeded, population redistributes itself to take advantage of the environment

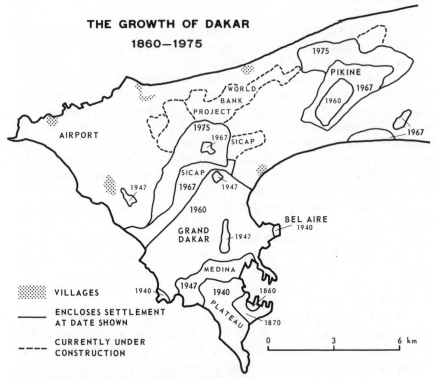

THE GROWTH OF DAKAR
1860—1975

Figure 20.2   The Growth of Dakar, 1860-1975.

in which it is located. There are many individuals, however, who would like to create short cuts to this slow-working redistribution procedure by trying to look to future urban needs and to create structures that will serve the needs of the city's population and guide growth toward positive ends. A group of statesmen met at Addis Ababa in 1971 to prepare recommendations for the Stockholm Conference on the Human Environment in 1972. Among their recommendations to governments were the following, concerning the planning of urban and rural settlements in Africa:

a. Land-use planning and control so as to ensure optimum utilization of the land and to minimize speculation as well as to enable the less privileged people to have the necessary land for the construction of suitable housing.

b. Rational distribution of development activities, employment opportunities and public services.

c. The planning and development of housing for the greatest number of people with maximum use of local architectural concepts and local materials . . . .

In this way a solution to the problems of shanty towns and squatter settlements may, at least, in part be found, but it is essential, at the present time to improve the conditions of people living in the slums as an initial step (United Nations, 1971b.).

The question of what is "optimum utilization of the land" or "rational distribution of development activities . . ." was left unanswered at the conference. One hopes the question will be answered by the urban planners in time to prevent misdirection of the slim resources which can be set aside for the development of the internal structure of the city.

In general, it seems the enthusiasm for transforming crowded urban settlements into cities filled with green spaces and sprinkled with public squares and monuments, which so characterized the planning goals in the early post-colonial period, are being rethought as economic realities present themselves. The pursuit of propinquity, or nearness, must become an important goal for the less wealthy African countries. Very few African states can afford the sprawling metropolis as a settlement form. The residence-work separation should not be allowed to increase dramatically. This may be a bitter pill to swallow for those who had hoped for low density, highly mobile settlement systems. Furthermore, it may be a pill not worth swallowing unless something can be done to stem rural-to-urban migration. The continuance of this process of concentration presents political problems that may promote increasingly authoritarian solutions. It may be more important now to direct public assistance to the villages and smaller urban centers in the national hierarchy than to continue to put this investment in or about the primate city. Once again there is no guarantee that this will be a successful strategy, but it may aid in the attempt to reach a balance between economic development and political turmoil.

There is a further question of subtle importance that the African city planner must address. The filling of once European residential areas by the African elite has, in fact, separated the leaders from their former neighborhoods. Will this separation of leaders and masses in the political surface of the city be viewed symbolically as a separation of political goals as well? The conflict over spatial needs for minimizing the journey to work and for having open spaces in the city is dramatized in the former *cordons sanitaires* that now separate the elites from the crowded urban imigrants who need space for shelter. Can the planners, employed by, and themselves members of, the elite, hold these spaces open in the face of crushing needs? Should they? These are questions the African city dwellers must decide for themselves, and they must be decided upon soon to prevent the implantation of structures that will direct growth instead of follow it.

On an even larger scale there is the serious question whether the contemporary African city is more of a "consumer innovation," living off the countryside, than it is a productive unit generating economic growth (Mabogunje, 1974). One must wonder if the marginal productivity of government employees justifies their subsidy as urban residents.

There are few universals that hold between different cultures and certainly the perception of space is a matter that seems to vary from people to people around the world (Hall, 1969). What is invariate is the actual geometry of space that allows us to estimate optimal organizational structures for the use of space under specified conditions. This is not a trivial exercise. When one tries to account for different attitudes by people and different goals among societies, and then to understand that these are changing constantly, the question of the organization of space becomes exceptionally complex. Yet there is no reason to shy away from this complexity if it is the reality that must be confronted. With thought and effort, African urban space can be arranged to allow for interaction with the least possible cost. Lines of communication can be created that extend possibilities for interaction. Areas can be separated from each other when interaction is not desired, and transportation can be organized to have benefits of access while minimizing the threat of accidents. These things are possible, yet they should be undertaken to facilitate the goals for the particular society rather than to constrain it in an undesired or unworkable structure. Discovering what is desired is probably easier than discovering what is workable.

Despite its urban dilemmas, Africa is blessed in being the last continent to come under the heavy impact of urbanization; it is able to draw on the experience of other nations and it has at its disposal an increasingly developed body of knowledge concerning the organization of space.

21

The Urban
Housing Challenge

RICHARD R. BRAND

The explosive character of urbanization in Africa has produced a monumental challenge to orderly development, particularly in terms of the quality of urban dwelling environments. African cities have mushroomed and now defy most traditional planning remedies. This unprecedented challenge calls for an unprecedented response, thus the need for radical alterations in institutional attitudes toward housing for the urban poor.

In studying urban dynamics the relationship between urbanization and urban growth is fundamental. In the aggregate, the level of urbanization in Africa remains the world's lowest, but urban growth rates are unexcelled; moreover, the low level of the former insures the continuance of rapid urban expansion through migration for some generations to come. Figure 21.1 depicts the precipitous rise in urban population that took hold about a generation ago. It is probable that African urban populations have expanded at about 4½ to 5 percent per annum since the mid-1940s. When it is recalled that European and North American urban growth rates averaged only about 2.1 percent during the nineteenth century phases of peak industrialization and immigration (Davis, 1969), the African experience is even more significant. Moreover, urban growth rates in some

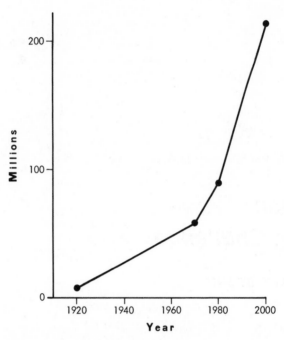

Figure 21.1 Urban Africans, 1920-2000.
Source: United Nations, 1969b.

countries, notably Kenya, Liberia and Ivory Coast have ranged well above the regional average, with their capitals having doubled in population in the last six to ten years!

Available data suggest that urban fertility in most of Africa is somewhat lower than village levels (Pool, 1971). However, urban mortality has dropped substantially, so that rates of natural increase are almost as high in the cities as in the countryside. With overall population increasing at 2.5-3.0 percent, urban growth rates exceeding this range can safely be ascribed to migration. This means that in cities like Dakar, Conakry, Abidjan, Kinshasa, and Dar es Salaam whose post-war growth rates have ranged upwards of 6 percent per annum (Davis, 1969), about two-thirds of their growth has stemmed from net migration.

In terms of the socioeconomic composition of the urban-directed migration streams and the impact on their destination nodes, Turner's description of urban populations in developing countries is particularly well suited to the situation in Africa. In his view, "the city, in the urbanizing world, is increasingly the refuge of large numbers of the poor and it is the poor who now determine a great part of its physical growth" (Turner, 1968:108). Difficulties of absorbing these people and providing opportunities for employment and housing at levels commensurate with their skills and earning power are among the greatest *challenges* facing the architects of the new nations of Africa.[1] According to Safier (1970:36):

> In a growing number of (African) countries the observed rate of urban growth has appeared to persistently exceed the capacity of the economy and society concerned to "accommodate" the increase. By accommodation is here meant not simply the provision of urban shelter and other physical amenities, but also the generation of productive employment opportunities, and community facilities of all kinds, that would assist new immigrants to make openings for themselves in an "urbanized environment." There are growing symptoms of gross deficiencies in the economic and social organization of larger cities around the continent—high rates of under- and un-employment, poor housing and worse environmental conditions for rapidly expanding low income groups, social maladjustment and delinquency, and so on.

UNCONTROLLED URBAN SETTLEMENTS

If the burgeoning growth rates of cities in developing countries constitute developmental challenges or stimuli, autonomous (or uncontrolled) urban settlements represent popular responses. Recognizing the pervasiveness of these phenomena, the United Nations Interregional Seminar on Improvement of Slums and Uncontrolled Settlements met in 1970 "to alert Governments to the magnitude of the current crisis in housing and urban development, and the deterioration of the environment" (United Nations, 1971c:4). Though the meeting was at least a decade late as an "early warning system," it did accomplish spreading awareness of the problem beyond a limited circle of informed persons. The vast documentation assembled for the conference was positive proof that few large cities in the developing world are without slums and shantytowns.[2] Statistics produced for the seminar corroborated what urban specialists have

[1] The choice of the word "challenge" in lieu of "problem" or some other term with a negative connotation is purposeful and underlies the argument developed below that a new attitude must be adopted toward the role of the poor in urban development.

[2] The terms "slums" and "shantytowns" are used throughout the essay although it is recognized that alternative terms designed to eliminate the pejorative connotations of the former are also available. These include such terms as "autonomous urban settlement" and "transitional settlement." The problem here is that these assume certain tendencies or characteristics that may or may not be present in the African context. For an overview of the debate surrounding the terms to be applied to the general case of uncontrolled urban growth see UNICEF (1971).

been saying for a decade or more, namely that "the housing situation in most African countries is characterized qualitatively and quantitatively by an utter inadequacy. . ." (United Nations, 1965:1). Though still very sparse, data on the subject do suggest that the magnitude of uncontrolled populations averages from a quarter to a third of total city populations (Table 21.1). The demand for low-cost housing in African cities simply has outstripped the supply.

Many local variations make it difficult to compare low status settlements with each other. Clearly, definitional issues are important and until satisfactory classification schemes are developed, it will be hard to generalize about whether uncontrolled settlements constitute housing problems or interim solutions. Stren (1972:493) points out a major perceptual cleavage that stems in part from a lack of clear definitions and criteria for analysis:

> Attitudes toward slums often depend on the vantage point of the observer. Government administrators generally try to control or prevent them, and official reports and studies stress the dangers of the physical and sanitary deterioration accompanying their growth. Until recently, almost all African governments with a visable slum problem took the position that the major solution was demolition and redevelopment of the slum neighborhoods. . . . By contrast, studies undertaken by social scientists have been almost unanimous in emphasizing the positive aspects of life in urban slums, and in criticizing government policies which have aimed to demolish them.

The point is that the administrator and the academician have not been addressing the same issues and applying the same criteria; no wonder interpretations diverge!

Having seen evidence of the pervasive nature of uncontrolled settlements in African cities, our attention now turns to an examination of the salient factors contributing to the formation of

TABLE 21.1 Uncontrolled Settlements in Selected African Cities

City	Year	City Pop.	Pop. in slums and shantytowns	
			Total	Percentage
Accra (Ghana)[a]	1970	633,900	ca. 200,000	ca. 30/35
Dakar (Senegal)[b]	1969	500,000	150,000	30
Dar es Salaam (Tanzania)[b]	1967	272,800	93,000	34
Lusaka (Zambia)	1967	194,000	53,000	27
Nairobi (Kenya)[c]	1969	500,000	170,000	40

Sources: [a]Estimated by the author.
         [b]United Nations 1971c:21.
         [c]Haldane, 1971.

the most common variants, unplanned innercity slums and uncontrolled settlements on the periphery, using Accra as an example (Figure 21.2).

ACCRA, GHANA: A CASE STUDY

Broadly speaking, conditions affecting the composition and growth of slums and peripheral shantytowns in Accra can be grouped into those that are largely external to the city and those that originate within it (Figure 21.3). The former include such things as the low level of economic development in many parts of the country, the rapidity of the urbanization process, and the continuing flow of poorly skilled urbanward migrants. The latter group is composed of a range of more immediate conditions, some affecting slums, others affecting shantytowns, and still others affecting both.

In the last analysis it is the transitional state of the Ghanaian economy and spatial organization that lies at the root of the urban housing challenge. Like other landscapes at similar levels of economic development, that of Ghana is markedly imbalanced. Its lagging regions (such as the Northern, Upper, and Volta Regions) and moribund towns (such as Cape Coast, Winneba, Kita, and Kete Krakye) generate labor migrations to cash-cropping areas and mining towns, but the largest flows have been directed to the regional capitals and the rapidly growing Accra-Tema area. Conceptually, Ghana's leading cities represent a handful of distinct peaks in an otherwise moderate to low-lying residential desirability surface (Gould, 1972).[3] Expanding educational opportunities, here as elsewhere in Africa, enlarge the awareness space of the rural population and act as catalysts in the rural-urban relocation process (Remple, 1971; Todaro, 1971a; Caldwell, 1969). It follows that increases in rural education without commensurate employment expansion will reinforce the existing sex, age, and ability selectivity of out-migration from depressed rural areas least able to afford the loss. Continued concentration of economic activity in a few leading cities is certain to reinforce their "bright-light" effects, thereby increasing the propensity to migrate. This can be seen in Ghana where value-added per capita in 1960 was some six times higher in Accra than in the Northern Region, and four times as high as that in the Volta Region (Birmingham, Neustadt and Omaboe, 1966). Not

[3] Similar findings depicting a concentrated pattern of residential desirability have come from Nigeria (Gould and Ola, 1970) and Uganda (Tinkler, 1970).

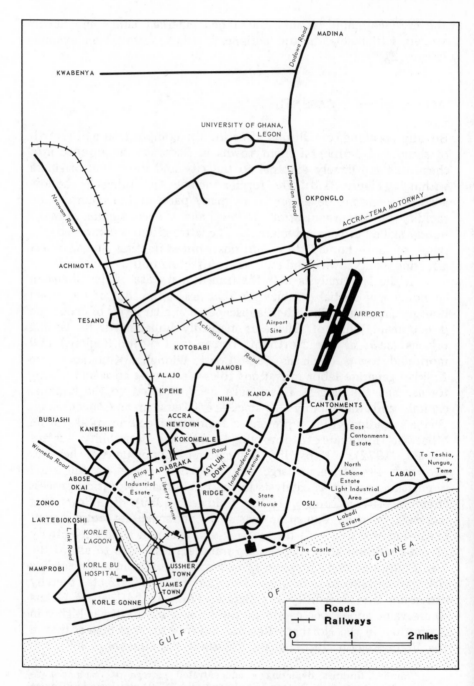

Figure 21.2 The City of Accra, Ghana, ca. 1970.
Source: Redrawn from Peil (1972), with permission of Cambridge University Press.

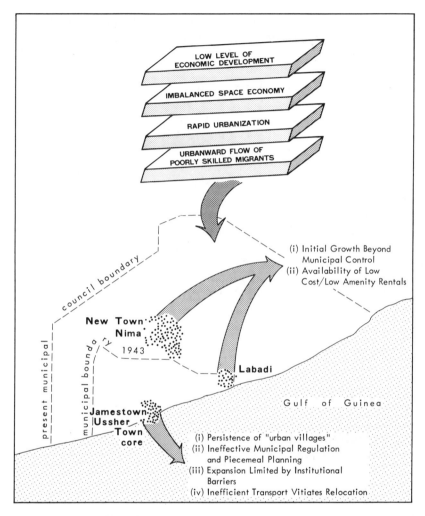

LOW LEVEL OF ECONOMIC DEVELOPMENT

IMBALANCED SPACE ECONOMY

RAPID URBANIZATION

URBANWARD FLOW OF POORLY SKILLED MIGRANTS

(i) Initial Growth Beyond Municipal Control
(ii) Availability of Low Cost/Low Amenity Rentals

council boundary

New Town Nima
1943

Labadi

present municipal

municipal boundary

Jamestown
Ussher
Town core

Gulf of Guinea

(i) Persistence of "urban villages"
(ii) Ineffective Municipal Regulation and Piecemeal Planning
(iii) Expansion Limited by Institutional Barriers
(iv) Inefficient Transport Vitiates Relocation

Figure 21.3 Factors contributing to the Formation of Uncontrolled Settlements in Accra, Ghana.

surprisingly, migrants from those relatively depressed regions ranked first and second among all migrants in Accra in that year. Housing successive waves of poorly skilled migrants inundating Accra is a Herculean task which has not been met with great success in the past (Abrams, 1957). Without effective regional development planning designed to encourage alternative growth centers, even the most ambitious city plan and capital investment will fail. Urban and regional planning are interdependent and must be coordinated.

Central slums. Among the factors contributing to the formation and persistence of central city slums in Accra, four stand out in importance: the existence of protomodern "urban villages" in the core; a history of uncoordinated and generally ineffective municipal management; institutional barriers to spatial expansion; and a failure to decentralize the urban space-economy.

Unlike most colonial cities in East Africa, Accra grew up encapsulating a series of indigenous coastal villages. Two of these, Jamestown and Ussher Town (Figure 21.3) were the sites of the earliest of these settlements and now contain some of the oldest and most dilapidated housing stock in the metropolitan area. In contrast with large western cities where residential land in the core was all but eliminated by expanding business districts, the central business district in Accra remained small until after World War II. Consequently, there was little commercial-residential competition, and a tripartite mix of land use developed so that central Accra still retains a sizable population of low status residents in juxtaposition with a "bazaar type" retail area and a modern central business district.

The blighted conditions that now characterize much of Jamestown and Ussher Town are not recent. Indeed, nineteenth century accounts of congestion and general deterioration would not be entirely inappropriate today.[4] Minor efforts at slum clearance in central Accra date from the 1880s, but the first project of any consequence was that begun in 1908 in response to an outbreak of plague. Subsequent programs were mounted in the 1920s, and again in the aftermath of the 1939 earthquake, but in each case plans were hurriedly drawn in reaction to a natural calamity; no continuous planning program existed.

In the post-war period the competition for space in central Accra increased sharply as in-migrants arrived in greater numbers and the central business district required additional space for newly-acquired functions (Brand, 1971). The effects of living conditions were twofold. First, the value of land in all parts of the core increased (Amoah, 1964), with the result that the poor are now living on relatively expensive land. Second, the volume of residential space diminished under the thrust of commercial invasion, thus producing a classic example of a blight-ridden zone of transition. Since new land was not available and vertical development of more than three stories was rare, various forms of space-packing developed. Most common was the extralegal subdivision of properties and houses by clever landlords. Analogous processes have been described for Ibadan by Mabogunje (1962:60) as growth by "fission," meaning

[4] For vivid accounts of 19th century conditions see Stanley (1874:79-80), Henty (1874:252-61), Kingsley (1897:29-30), and Great Britain, Colonial Reports (1886 and 1887).

"the replacement of simple, large structures by more complex and more numerous smaller units." In central Accra, rooms were partitioned, occupancy regulations were ignored, sheds appeared in alleyways, courtyards were packed with flimsy shacks, and street-sleeping became more common. Population densities in several of the most congested tracts in Ussher Town rose to over one thousand persons per hectare and greatly increased the pressure on physical facilities (Brand, 1972a). All of this happened under the not-so-watchful eye of the Municipal Council.

The problems of central Accra were explicitly addressed in the Town Plan of 1959 and large tracts were designated as slums for either demolition or remedial treatment, but by this time population levels were very high and the political power of the indigenous Ga community blocked large scale renewal. The upshot of these combined factors has been the maintenance of a protomodern form of land use in the central city. Economically, some of the city's most valuable land remains under-utilized in the form of urban villages, frequently in the shadow of high-rise office buildings. Neither colonial authorities nor post-independence administrators have been able to control the quality of residential environment in the core, a condition contributing to the advanced stage of congestion and physical blight over much of the area today.

In addition to the foregoing, there also have been institutional barriers to expansion in central Accra rooted in the polarized nature of society itself. Not unlike other societies in developing countries, the gap between the elite and the masses is extreme and has been translated into bold spatial terms. The elite in Accra traditionally have controlled a large tract of high quality land close to, but not contiguous with, the high density core. Very little functional interaction developed between these regions; instead, the government area and elite zones of residence have effectively blocked any easterly or northeasterly expansion of the high density core.

The segregation of the elite began when the European popula-tion enlarged in the 1890s; prior to that everyone lived in the Jamestown-Ussher Town core (Henty, 1874), the only built-up section of the little town (Figure 21.4). When Victoriaborg was constructed in the mid-1890s, government functions and European residences were withdrawn from Jamestown and a rigid spatial separation was begun. As the preindustrial friction of distance lessened with the introduction of motor cars and telephone communications (Brand, 1972b), the wealthy removed themselves farther from the crowded core along a well-defined sectoral path, today's Independence Avenue (Brand, 1972a).

When the institutional barrier of government and elite land use

ACCRA AND CHRISTIANSBORG, ca. 1895

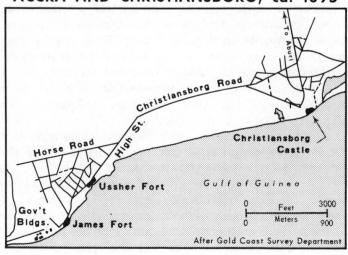

ACCRA, ca. 1900

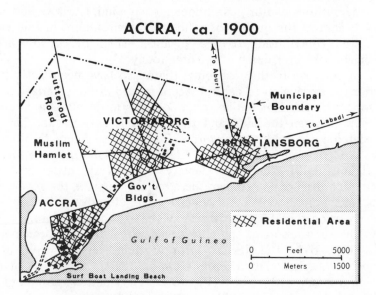

Figure 21.4   Early Development of Accra.

accentuated the physical barriers presented by the sea and the Korle
Lagoon, only two paths were open to the expanding community,
west across the lagoon and due north. Although the lagoon has been
bridged at several places and a movement north beyond the

commercial core has occurred, expansion has been limited and congestion in the core remains a serious problem.

A fourth influence on slum conditions in central Accra, partially related to the previous factors, derives mainly from the highly centralized pattern of urban economic functions. For the majority of its inhabitants, Accra has been and continues to be a pedestrian city wherein access to central markets and trading opportunities sets constraints on the range of residential locations. Because of the historical lack of inexpensive means of municipal transport (Dunyoh, 1968) and the scarcity of large-scale markets and wage employment nodes beyond the central city, the poor have traditionally been drawn to blighted inner-city neighborhoods in proximity to their jobs. Decentralized locations of the Industrial Estate, the Light Industrial Area on Ring Road East, and several new markets (Figure 21.2) are steps in the right direction, but the need for an efficient but inexpensive municipal bus system has grown considerably with the post-war increases in urban population.

Perhipheral shantytowns. Among factors affecting the growth of peripheral shantytowns in Accra (Figure 21.3), two are singled out for comment here, the veritable saturation of living space in the center and the lack of municipal control beyond the city limits. While it is true that the strangers community of Sabon Zongo was set up as a Muslim exclave beyond the municipal boundary some fifty years ago and squatter huts appeared in what are now Abose Okai and Labadi in the 1930s (Brand, 1971), the occurrence of massive areas of substandard dwellings is largely a post-World War II phenomenon. Accra absorbed one-half million people between 1948 and 1970, over three-quarters of them migrants. With 23,000 additional people to house each year, difficulties of finding low-cost space in the core increased and many newcomers were forced to look elsewhere. The only other sizable areas of inexpensive rentals were located on the urban margin beyond the working class districts of Osu to the east and Adabraka/Kokomemle to the north (Figure 21.2; Peil, 1972; Brand, 1972a). Beginning in the late 1940s and continuing through the 1950s and 1960s huge quasi-squatter communities grew up in New Town/Nima-Maamobi, and Labadi swelled by the infusion of low-status migrants (Harvey and Brand, 1974). While more definitive studies of the role of intraurban migration in growth processes are high-priority research needs, there is no doubt that the city has passed through the stage of growth by space-packing. Central Accra appears to have reached a residential saturation point about a decade ago; since then the major growth process has been that of areal expansion. Spearheading the urban sprawl are the uncontrolled, low-income settlements on the periphery.

The second influence on the development of peripheral communities is the urban boundary itself. Political geographers distinguish between antecedent, subsequent, and superimposed boundaries according to the state of the cultural landscape at the time of demarcation. In the case of Accra the various boundaries always have been antecedent, that is, demarcation took place in relatively unpopulated territory outside the existing cultural landscape of the city. However, in many cases the boundary gave rise to settlement just beyond. This was the case with the squatter beginnings of Abose Okai in the 1930s, and of the enlarged population of Labadi during the same period. The most dramatic instances were those of Accra New Town (formerly Lagos Town because of the large number of Nigerians who settled there) and Nima. Neither of these were in existence when the 1943 boundary was demarcated, but arose when masses of poor migrants arrived in response to economic growth following World War II. By the time that the boundary was next adjusted in 1954, an entire community had formed, unplanned and without motorable roads or most urban amenities.

In each of these cases, uncontrolled communities spawned close enough to the urban economy to be accessible, but just beyond the potential reach of municipal authority. The effect of the boundary on the settlement pattern of Accra and other African cities is striking. Taxes, building codes, and police interference ended here, and title to land could be secured by traditional means without need of the expenses and complications usually accompanying transactions within the built-up perimeter.

Actually, Nima is not a squatter settlement because it originally developed on land that was leased by local headmen to Hausa chiefs. It is more appropriately referred to as an "autonomous settlement" or simply an "uncontrolled settlement" because unauthorized building and subdivision continued even after the municipal limits were extended to encompass it in 1954. In this respect, Nima is a prototype of many similar settlements in Africa and several of its attributes have wider applicability.

PLANNING FOR THE FUTURE

It seems quite clear that the growth of autonomous settlements and the general inability of governments to exercise significant control are not going to diminish in the near future; rather they will most certainly enlarge as urbanization proceeds. Implicit also is the recognition that the transition underway in African countries cannot be totally controlled in the short term, save by the most stringent of population control measures such as those employed by the autocratic regimes of Rhodesia and South Africa. There are, however, a number of planning alternatives that have been developed elsewhere and are now being introduced to Africa. Undoubtedly, their success will depend upon the right combination of these schemes at national, regional, and municipal levels of operation.

In general, there appears to be growing support for a closer coordination between urban and regional planning in Africa. Kenya and Tanzania, for example, have already taken steps designed to reduce the population flows to their leading cities. Basically, it is intended that a decentralization of political and economic power will tend to anchor more of the rural population in place (Mascarenhas and Claeson, 1972; Taylor, 1972), but little hope is held for short term results. What is needed *in addition to* such schemes at the regional level is a resolution on the part of these and other African governments that an urban crisis exists and that the standard remedies (such as slum clearance and rehousing), palliatives (such as urban renewal and rehabilitation) and cosmetics (such as government sponsored housing estates) are very expensive and, at best, partial answers to the challenge. It is abundantly clear that most urban planning and housing schemes in Africa have traditionally catered to those who were prepared to pay, namely the middle and elite classes (Stren, 1972), but today this is no longer a viable emphasis. The challenge to orderly growth comes not from these groups but from the masses. No government in tropical Africa can hope to house people at public expense and even if this were possible, such a move would be self-defeating because it would inevitably attract more migrants than it possibly could accommodate.

If this reasoning is valid, then a perspective on development called "progressive improvement" and a package of land and housing development strategies generally known as "sites and services" might follow. Basically, the philosophy of progressive improvement begins with the explicit recognition that the urbanization process is inevitable and that the growth of low-income areas can be guided by government and converted into a positive development force. The argument is as follows:

> People living in transitional urban settlements have demonstrated remarkable vigour and ingenuity in improving their living conditions despite enormous obstacles, including strong initial institutional opposition to the very existence of these settlements. The current evidence from the

developing countries indicates that when these population groups obtain minimally secure employment and a measure of security of tenure to the land they occupy, they act to improve their environment through the investment of substantial "popular sector" resources, money and labour, in the gradual improvement of their dwellings and surroundings. In a number of cities, these communities have evolved to become significant social and economic assets to their cities. The physical facilities developed through this process constitute an important contribution to the capital assets of their country, developed at little or no expense to government. (United Nations, 1971d: 21-22).

This is the wrapping within which a "sites and services" package is offered. A complete package might include programs of land acquisition, employment generation, physical planning, community services, finance and credit, administrative reorganization, and technical assistance. Plans in suitably modified forms are actively being promoted by the United Nations Center for Housing, Building, and Planning which stands ready to offer the technical assistance needed to formulate such multisectoral programs (United Nations, 1972b). Presently, Senegal, Ghana, Kenya, Sudan, Tanzania, and Zambia have "sites and services" programs underway and have included the same in their national development plans (United Nations, 1972a). Since the approach is flexible and depends largely upon the existing circumstances in a particular city, no patents for guaranteed success come with the package; nevertheless certain features appear to be constant.

Essentially, "sites and services" proceeds from the willingness of government to improve the welfare of the urban poor by taking over tracts of land, demarcating them, providing them with minimal sanitary and social services, and offering them to low-income groups according to their capacity to pay. By implication this amounts to government *direction* of land use development; land so designated ceases to be a speculative commodity and is acquired, subdivided, and offered for lease with secure tenure and *minimal subsidies.* The success of these schemes seems to pivot on this latter factor. A gradation of services ranging from none to many also is possible depending upon the local circumstances and effective demand in a particular place; however, the choice of what kind of house to build and how to build it is guided only by minimal health and safety standards and is largely up to the tenant. Implementation can take many forms but usually development corporations are empowered to organize the land development program.

According to United Nations experience, household expenditure studies indicate that low-income households in a sample of less developed countries spend between 5 to 13 percent of their income for housing.

> Given the fact that developed land is only about 20 percent of total housing costs, repayments or ground rents could go as low as ½ to 3 percent of household income. If project standards are designed on this basis and households can actually afford more on housing, they have the choice of amortizing their debt more quickly or rapidly improving their dwellings. (United Nations, 1972b:19).

The experience of most African countries is as yet too recent to assess the degree of success along these lines. However, several years experience with "sites and services" in Zambia appears to have resulted in an arrangement whereby the rich are offered fully serviced plots and are required to pay in full. With these funds the government is able to finance loan subsidies for the poor (Zambia, 1972). In Ghana the winds of change also appear to be flowing with the completion of a pilot cooperative housing scheme in Tema which demonstrates the feasibility of economically and technically sound self-help programs. The project produced houses whose economic rent was within reach of most regularly employed low-income workers and long lists of interested tenants are on file for future houses to be built under this hire-purchase scheme. In contrast, hundreds of publically constructed houses meant for the same target population stand unoccupied just adjacent to the cooperative site because their economic rents range to three times those of the latter. Whether the success of the Tema cooperative can be replicated in Accra and the other large Ghanaian cities is yet to be determined, but the potential is surely there and the need has never been greater. Beyond this only time will tell whether this planning alternative will be widely adopted in Africa.

V

RURAL-URBAN SYSTEMS

Linkage intensity between urban and rural areas is a key variable in the modernization process. The two must be tightly interwoven in order that the rural areas efficiently provide their food, mineral, manpower, and other physical resources, and that the cities exercise their cultural, political, and intellectual leadership, plus develop the necessary secondary and tertiary economic activities. In other words, a fully integrated system of activities is an imperative of modernization.

In Chapter 22, Filani deals with the important linkages created by transport and communication. On the whole, transport is still in an early phase of development in Africa. Though rivers have been used since time immemorial in spreading people, goods, and ideas, it is only in recent decades that significant improvements have been made in river-channel navigation. Similarly, most ports are being upgraded to handle more and bigger ships. Railroads were begun in virtually every country during the colonial era, but with the exception of South Africa, the rail nets tend to be poorly integrated both nationally and internationally. As elsewhere in the world, the most rapidly expanding mode of transportation is the road. A

Ebute Ero daily market
,agos, Nigeria, is one of
,unted thousands of rural
urban markets that bring
and countryside together
Africa. (Photograph by
. Good)

railroad in Sierra Leone
s bulk commodity trans-
to the countryside by
.s cheaper and less sub-
to vagaries of weather
over-the-road haulage.
.ograph by J. B. Riddell)

casting House of the
of Kenya in Nairobi
ts the important role
.unications media have
 nging people together in
.n nations, whether to
rage national conscious-
or to provide agri-
al extension services.
.ograph from Kenya In-
tion Services)

number of all-weather roads are in existence and many more are under construction. In the near future, the most pressing need is for a more extensive system of rural feeder roads to open up new producing regions and allow for better interregional exchange. Airlines effectively link Africa to the outside world. Each country has an international airport, and connections to and from Europe and America are quite regular. However, intra-Africa air travel is another matter, especially to areas away from the large cities. There, airports are few, and the expense for the movement of people and products by air is presently too great to warrant investment and development.

Modern communications systems are extremely important to Africa. Multiband portable radios can be found everywhere on the continent, and they have become significant not only for recreation but also for education. Governments use the airwaves to spread their respective national ethos and to present information on such topics as better health and nutrition, improved agricultural methods, how to build a house, how to respond to a census enumerator, and so on. Newspapers in a variety of languages are widely available, although only special weeklies are to be found in the countryside. Television is beginning to take hold but so far it is restricted to the cities. Finally, as with air travel, telecommunications are good with the outside world but most inadequate inside Africa. Lines radiating from the large cities are few and often it is necessary to go through London or Paris before connecting with another African country.

Closely associated with transport and communications is "Population Mobility," a topic discussed by Prothero in Chapter 23. Africa long has been characterized by the mobility of its populations, dating back to such major migrations as those by the Bantu and the Nilotes. In more recent times, as Chapter 18 noted, migrants have trekked to the mines, plantations, and cities. Some of this movement is seasonal, some semipermanent, and some permanent. But no matter what the duration, an enduring characteristic is the contacts kept up with the home area. Very seldom are ties cut completely, and visits back and forth regularly are made. Many cities seem virtually deserted on weekends as people flock back home, and a common topic of conversation among city dwellers is which relative is coming to visit next. Thus, face to face channels are kept open for the exchange of information and ideas.

Important communications also characterize one of Africa's most dynamic and exciting institutions, the market. Virtually every corner of the continent now is tied into some sort of market structure, but as Good in Chapter 24 shows, there is great variability in such market characteristics in regard to location, size, extent of trade area, physical form and arrangement, the types of goods available, and timing. Yet no matter what their exact nature, the markets are places where different people mingle, making the kinds of contacts so vital to national integration and modernization.

22

Transport and Communication

MICHAEL OLANREWAJU FILANI

Africa stretches about 8,000 kilometers from the Mediterranean Sea to the Cape of Good Hope and 3,200 kilometers from west to east at the Equator. Tropical Africa alone is almost three times as large as the United States. On such a continent, where vast distances separate one region from the other and where the economically productive areas are scattered widely, the importance of transport and communication systems cannot be overstated. It is not surprising that up to 1959, about one-third to two-thirds of all expenditures in the various national development plans went into the building of roads, railways, and harbors; in recent years between 15 and 20 percent of total public expenditures have gone into improving these systems.

Most African countries inherited a pattern of transportation systems specifically designed by the colonial powers to assist in the exploitation of national resources. The systems also were designed to encourage the importation of merchandise and foster effective administrative security. Thus, in the wake of independence, the various countries found themselves looking more towards Europe than to neighboring African countries. Even today, a glance at a transport map of Africa still shows this "colonial" pattern.

TRANSPORT SYSTEMS

Before the colonial era, transport for trading activities and social contacts was restricted to human porterage or pack animals. The paths worn by human feet usually were narrow, winding, and obstructed, broken by flooded rivers during the rainy season and by quickly` regrowing vegetation in forest areas. Today in many parts of the continent human porterage is still a prevailing means of transport. It is widely used between farms and other centers of agricultural production and is an important method for distributing goods, especially in rural areas. In a study of commodity flow patterns in Bawku in northeast Ghana, on one market day over 66 tons of local produce came into the market. Of this, 81 percent was carried by headloading, 11 percent by truck, 5 percent by bicycle, and 3 percent by donkey (Gould, 1960).

The prevalence of human porterage is both a function and a factor of rural poverty. Existing roads often are untarred and have wooden bridges easily washed away during the rainy season. Moreover, the plots of individual farmers generally are small and outputs often insufficient to justify motor vehicle carriage. Petty trading activities prevail in the rural areas and profits accruing from these are so small that the traders could not afford to spend part or all on vehicular transport. As a result, freight movement from isolated villages to the nearest market must be by head porterage or at best by bicycle.

This traditional system of transport has a limiting effect on the amount of trade goods that can be carried over great distances. It is also time consuming and quite expensive in terms of opportunity cost to the user. The time lost in traveling between production and initial marketing centers can represent an important loss in productivity. When farmers use themselves or hire porters, the economic cost of porterage is mainly the opportunity cost of labor otherwise needed in various operations on the farm.

River transport is another means of movement of great antiquity in various parts of Africa, and it has played a significant role in the economic development of some countries, notably Zaire, Gambia, and Nigeria (Figure 22.1). The Congo and its tributaries form the most extensive river navigation system on the continent. Other major navigable waterways include the Niger and Benue, the Volta, the Nile, and the East African lakes. Rivers like the Zambezi, Rufiji, and Tana, which flow into the Indian Ocean, are navigable for short stretches. The Senegal River is useful not only to Senegal but also to Mali and Mauritania, and the Gambia River provides the main outlet for its country's products.

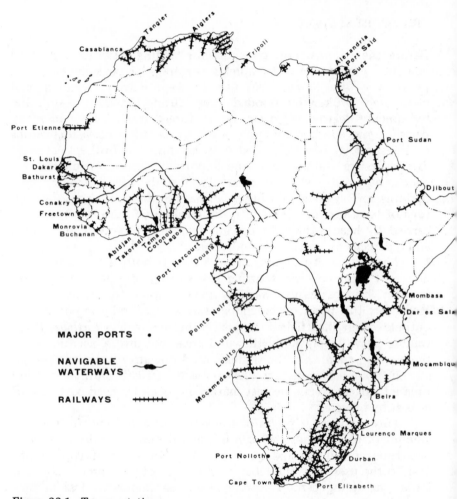

Figure 22.1 Transportation
Source: Compiled by the author. Maps of basic transportation features can be
found in such sources as the *Oxford Regional Economic Atlas of Africa* (1967),
Hance (1975), and the Michelin maps of Africa (no. 153, 154, 155).

Although river transport provides the cheapest means of
movement, rivers today are generally of local importance and are
contributing little to the process of economic development in most
parts of the continent. River transport suffers from severe seasonality
in river volume, the silting of deltas obstructing ports and access to
the sea, and the presence of many cataracts that impede continuous
navigation on long river stretches. In some countries such as Zaire,
rail links have been built to complete the river transport systems at
points where navigation is broken by rapids. In Nigeria, the recent

completion of the Kainji Dam is assisting navigation on the Upper Niger River.

Although the traditional means of transport are still important, railways, roads, and air transport have developed significantly in recent years. The spatial structure of these modern systems has been determined historically by several factors. Foremost among these are the political and military considerations of the various former colonial powers; the diversity in the spatial distribution of agricultural and mineral resources of the continent; and more recent attempts at developing links both within and between African countries. The first two factors were particularly important for railway and harbor development, the bulk of which took place during the colonial era; the third factor is increasingly influencing road and air networks. The origins of most of the transportation systems lay in the needs to exploit resources in a way most remunerative to the colonial interests and to establish "effective control" as designated by the Berlin Agreement of 1884. Thus, the haphazard and uncoordinated picture of the African transportation map today largely can be attributed to the artificial pattern of development and integration imposed by past colonial rule—the pattern of links between the interior and the coastal ports (see Chapter 3). This structure has not been altered significantly since independence.

The "railway era" in tropical Africa began shortly after the partition of the continent among the various European powers, with the main period of rail construction lasting from 1885 to about 1935. At the beginning of this era, strategic factors were stronger than economic ones in determining which lines were built. It was not until after effective territorial administrative machinery had been established that economic considerations replaced strategic ones in determining routes. The numerous railways that link the hinterland with seaports still reflect the heavy dependence of the greater part of most countries' economies on overseas trade and the low level of trade among African countries themselves (Figure 22.1).

The total length of African railroads in 1968 was put at 75,842 kilometers (ECA, 1968), but some 29.1 percent of this total is in South Africa. In relation to the size of the continent, this figure is very low, a factor that must have prompted Hance to assert that the railway map of tropical Africa is notable chiefly for its emptiness (Hance, 1967). Most of the railways consist of single track routes with a few branch and connecting lines.

With the exception of South Africa, railway systems generally are unconnected, since there are tremendous variations in such technical characteristics as gauge, couplings, brake systems, and

RURAL-URBAN SYSTEMS

buffers. Most of the railways in North Africa are 1.435-meter gauge, except in Sudan where the entire route is 1.067 and in Tunisia where 80 percent of the track is 1.000-meter gauge. Railways in Kenya, Uganda, Tanzania, and Ethiopia have 1.000-meter gauge. In West Africa, Nigeria and Ghana have 1.067-meter gauge, but 1.000-meter gauge predominates in Senegal, Mali, Guinea, Ivory Coast, Upper Volta, Togo, and Dahomey. Differences in gauge reduce the efficiency of links within and between many African countries and undoubtedly retard progress toward interterritorial railway integration.

These shortcomings notwithstanding, railways account for a significant part of the freight haulage in most African countries. In 1960, they accounted for 57,609 million ton-kilometers of freight traffic. Of these, the South African rail system carried 30,885 ton-kilometers, or more than half of the total. In 1968, Africa's total rail-freight traffic increased to 87,164 million ton-kilometers with South Africa still accounting for over half (United Nations *Statistical Yearbook*, 1970). Generally, the traffic density of rail freight in Africa is low. In 1968, this density (excluding South Africa) averaged only 0.7 million ton-kilometers per kilometer-length of route compared with 1.0 to 3.0 million ton-kilometers recorded in Western Europe and in the United States. Freight movements on most of the rail lines have been growing faster than passenger travel partly because competition from the road is less intense for freight than for passengers. In some countries rail-passenger traffic increased between 1965 and 1968, but in most it declined. Countries recording an increase of 5 percent or more in rail-passenger traffic included Algeria, Angola, Mali, Cameroun, and Congo. Nigeria registered the largest decline in passenger traffic, over 12 percent per annum. This may be attributed largely to the civil war that disrupted the railway system. Passenger traffic also declined significantly in the U.A.R., Morocco, Tunisia, Ghana, Senegal, Dahomey, and Zaire.

The fragmentary structure of much of the railway system and the limited scope of inland waterways make road transport of particular importance in Africa. Road transportation first developed as a complementary system to the railways. Between 1900 and 1930, the railways were virtually unchallenged as the major means of long distance transport for both passengers and goods, but since the end of the Second World War road traffic has increased at a tremendous rate and most existing railways now suffer from road competition.

Today road transport is the fastest growing means of transportation in Africa. Its inherent advantages include speed and regularity of service, flexibility in terms of the size of load, ease and speed of transshipment, and door-to-door conveyance. This minimizes handling costs, risk of damage, and the need for packaging. It provides a much quicker service than rail, particularly for short-distance traffic. Moreover, where goods and passengers are transported by rail, inland waterways, or air transport, the beginning and end of the journey often are made by road. In this sense, road transport provides feeder services for other transport systems.

It is difficult to assess the development of road transport in Africa.[1] This is because of the lack of comprehensive and comparable data on road traffic—a factor that makes it impossible to use the standard transport indices of ton-kilometers and passenger-kilometers. Available data concern road network density and numbers of vehicles. In the late 1960s, the total length of roads in Africa excluding South Africa was put at 1,125,000 kilometers. The density of this network averaged 39 road kilometers per 1,000 square kilometers of land area, less than one-third of average world density. Road density varies greatly between and within countries. In the West, Central, and East Africa road density averaged 42, 43 and 54 kilometers per 1,000 square kilometers respectively, but North Africa recorded an average density of only 22 (ECA, 1969). As might be expected, countries with deserts such as the Sahara and the Namib and those with mountainous areas have the lowest road densities. The lengths of all-weather roads (paved roads) was probably less than half of the total length of all roads. A large proportion consists of dirt roads often impassable during the rainy season.

African road systems consist mainly of a large number of separate local and national networks, similar to the railway situation. Interregional or interstate networks are few, the notable exceptions being links between Botswana and Rhodesia, Zambia and Tanzania, Tanzania and Kenya, Ethiopia and Sudan, Mauritania and Senegal, Senegal and Gambia, Ghana and Togo, Dahomey and Nigeria, and Nigeria and Chad. All these lines are *ad hoc* connections rather than planned regional and subregional networks (ECA, 1968).

One of the most outstanding developments in African transport systems within the last two decades has been the growth of air lines. Since independence, significant efforts have been made in the development of air networks both for domestic and international services. In 1960, only 12 countries in Africa had national airlines, but this number has increased to 35. Consequently the total air traffic as measured by ton-kilometers of passengers and cargo flown

[1] The excellent Michelin maps of Africa cover the continent in three sheets (sheets 153, 154, and 155). At a scale of 1:4,000,000 only major roads can be shown.

by all scheduled carriers h:.s grown very rapidly, both increasing by about one half from 1967 to 1970. This rapid increase of African air transport is explained, in part, by the low level from which the rise took place and the increasing importance of international communications since independence.

Air transport shares with road transport the advantages of flexibility and speed. It is not only the most rapid and convenient mode of transport between African countries and the rest of the world but also in many cases the only form available for inter-African movement.

Air routes linking one African country with another are still not well developed. There is a heavy predominance of international traffic in African countries in contrast to Latin American countries where there has been intensive development of domestic air transport. Comparatively few routes serve Africa in the trans-continental east-west direction, although most of the countries are well linked with Europe, North America, and the Soviet Union. The routings of European airlines frequently make it necessary for Africans to fly from North or East Africa to West Africa by way of Europe.

As is common with all other modern means of transport on the continent, air traffic is concentrated in areas of intensive economic development and high population densities. Traveling by air is still largely restricted because of expense; the majority of passengers on African planes are diplomats, government officials, and business executives.

COMMUNICATION SYSTEMS[2]

Africa lags behind the rest of the developing world in telecommunications. Personal word of mouth and face-to-face contacts are still the most common means of communication between individuals and groups. Interpersonal telecommunication systems—telephones, telegraphs, postal, radio and television services—are still very much underdeveloped. In contrast to places such as the United States and Europe where telephone ownership is more or less a necessity, it is still a luxury and "status symbol" in most parts of Africa.

The total number of telephones in Africa in January 1970 was 3.14 million, only 1.2 percent of the world total. In 1970, for every 100 of its people, Africa had only 0.9 telephones compared with 1.5 telephones for every 100 inhabitants in Asia, 2.6 in Central and South America, and 54.7 in North America. Telecommunications also have grown comparatively slowly in Africa. For example, the

---

[2] This section relies heavily on data from the *United Nations Statistical Yearbook*, 1970 and ECA *A Survey of Economic Conditions in Africa*, 1971.

growth rate of telephone installations is about 7 percent per annum as against 10 percent in Latin America and 30 percent in Asia. The distribution of telephones varies from one subregion of the continent to another and between individual countries. In 1970, North Africa accounted for 59.1 percent of all telephones in Africa excluding South Africa. This was followed by East Africa (20.3 percent), West Africa (16.3 percent), and Central Africa (4.3 percent).

In many countries inland trunk networks are poorly developed. In Africa, it is often easier to get a line to Europe than to a neighboring country. Even between countries that have some form of direct telephone link, it is still more satisfactory to route calls around the two long sides of a triangle via London or Paris. Thus, when an African country communicates with another African country by telephone, the connection often must be made through transit centers situated outside the continent. These circuits are consequently slow, expensive, technically unsatisfactory, and politically risky.

Some curious anomalies exist in the telecommunication systems of most countries. For instance, telephone subscribers in Lagos (Nigeria) can make international telephone calls to Europe and the United States fairly easily through the newly completed INTELSAT earth station near Ibadan, but they cannot speak to other parts of the country for weeks on end. When lines are operating, calls have to be booked, with frequent annoying delays.

As in the case of the telephone system, postal communications between African countries still suffer from systems developed during the colonial era. Most investments in telecommunications went into providing international links suitable for the needs of the metropolitan powers. Airmail, in particular, was routed via European capitals, a structure that has not changed significantly during post-independence years.

Postal services also are retarded by the lack of efficient transportation links within and between African countries. Air transportation which could play a great role in intercontinental mail transportation is not being fully used. Indeed, few air connections are used for exchanging mails between neighboring countries. As a result, most African countries still route mails meant for other African countries through their former colonial capitals such as Paris, London, Brussels, and Rome. This inevitably results in delays and high costs. Sometimes delays of up to three or four months occur for correspondence between the various parts of the continent and delays of several weeks are experienced within individual countries.

Radio and television broadcasting services have grown substantially in the post-independence period. In 1970 the number of radio receivers was 15.5 million, or more than twice the level of 1963. Television services have also been developed, but the number of receivers is still quite low—1.2 million in 1970. The ratio of television per population was 0.34 receivers per 100 inhabitants in 1970.

Satellites are the newest telecommunications media, offering many channels for radio and television transmission. At present there are four satellite earth stations operating in Africa: one each in Morocco, Nigeria, and Zaire focused toward an Atlantic satellite and one in Kenya oriented toward an Indian Ocean satellite. However, these satellite facilities are not well developed for internal communication. For example, it was possible for Nigerians in and around Lagos to watch an Apollo moon landing and the Olympic games live on television screens, whereas millions of other Nigerians, especially in rural areas, still do not know what television is.

IMPACT OF TRANSPORT AND COMMUNICATION SYSTEMS

The degree to which transport and communication systems can exert spatial influence on a region's economy cannot be overemphasized. The present pattern of economic development in the different parts of Africa clearly illustrates this influence. The colonial experience of most African countries strongly influenced the spatial and structural patterns of the transport and communication systems, and in consequence the patterns of economic development. The location of economically important resources largely determined the routing and extent of the transport networks in individual countries. Thus, a transportation system developed that focused the flow of commodities on a few selected termini, especially in coastal areas. Relatively frequent interaction occurred between the termini and the hinterlands, with few or no lateral connections within the boundaries of each colonial power. Inter-territorial movement was virtually nonexistent.

Consequently, the coastal towns and the urban centers along the networks developed out of proportion to the rural areas. These centers are now commonly referred to as "growth poles" and they continue to draw the resources of their hinterlands, producing the regional inequalities predominating in the African space-economy today (see Chapter 19). Although it might be argued that inequalities in regional development stemmed from the initial uneven distribution of Africa's natural resources, the subsequent increased perpetuation of the inequalities has resulted mainly from the nature of the transportation network. The initial locational advantages on the "colonial" transport networks enjoyed by certain areas have been reinforced and extended even after nearly two decades of independence by African countries. As O'Connor aptly noted, "a circular process is at work whereby the colonial transport network has greatly influenced the spatial patterns of economic development and this in turn determines where most of the demand for improved transport facilities (and indeed communication systems) arises" (O'Connor, 1971:156).

Despite the shortcomings of the transport and communication systems that have developed from the colonial era to the present, the significant roles these systems have had in inducing social and economic changes should not be overlooked. They played a vital part in the establishment of colonial administration. Railways and roads broke down the friction of distance and ethnic isolation and facilitated the free movement of traders. Settlement patterns have altered as villages relocated along roadsides to take advantage of ease of movement and the possibilities of trade. Radical changes have taken place in patterns of land use as new cash crops were introduced.

In many countries the colonial transport systems traverse diverse agricultural regions and thereby provide the basis for subsequent interregional trade. In Nigeria before the advent of rail and road transport, the market for any given product was limited to the village or town of its origin and its immediate environment. When railways and roads were constructed, markets for such products as yams, cotton, groundnuts, cocoa, palm oil, and cattle were extended. It became possible for the producers of livestock in the northern part of the country to supply the much needed meat to southern markets; various other commodities followed a similar pattern. The most significant impact of transport systems has been felt in the cash economy of the individual countries. In the 25 years before World War II the railways in Nigeria enabled exports of groundnuts to increase 200 times and those of cocoa 30 times (Harrison-Church, 1949). Groundnut export from Kano region in northern Nigeria showed an increase within two years of almost 1,000 percent—from less than 2,000 tons in 1911, before the arrival of the railway, to about 20,000 tons in 1913 a year after the railway reached Kano (Mabogunje, 1968). In Ghana, export traffic in cocoa and mahogany increased 600 percent and 500 percent respectively between 1904 and 1905 following railway construction (Gould, 1960). The spread of cash crops in Ghana has been traced in terms of transport development (White and Gleave, 1971). For example, cocoa cultivation started in Akwapim within reasonable headloading distance to the port of Accra. In the 1920s, it spread along the new railway from Accra to Kumasi via Koforidua and Juaso. The subsequent development of road transport also affected the spatial distribution of the product in the country. Similar histories can be traced in various West African countries such as Senegal and Sierra Leone where agricultural developments have followed the lines of transportation.

Travel time, human labor, and transport costs have been significantly reduced by the advent of modern means of transport. For instance, in Dahomey before the construction of the rail line, carriage of goods from Cotonou to Niamey was said to have required 70 days by human porterage. When the line reached Parakou in 1934, the time was reduced to three days, and air service now covers the route in one-and-one-half hours (Hance, 1967). In his study of tin-mining on the Jos Plateau in Nigeria, Hodder (1959) showed a remarkable shortening of travel time. Before the railway reached the plateau in 1927, the road journey from the tin mines to the coast took 35 days. With a connection to Port Harcourt on the coast, not only was the journey reduced to less than 35 hours but the cost came down by nearly three-quarters. Many other examples demonstrate the significant impact of transport on the cash economy of individual countries (Gould, 1960; Soja, 1968; Riddell, 1970).

The impact of roads on the process of social and economic development of the various countries has been equally pronounced. Road transport exerts a spatial influence on the opening up of undeveloped rural areas. It is used to carry produce of regions not reached by railways either to railheads or directly to the coast in the case of export products. Road transport also affords substantial investment and employment opportunities not only in the maintenance of the roads but in the assembly, servicing, and operation of vehicles and provision of supply facilities for fuels and lubricants. For example, Gould (1960) discovered that in Ghana in the 1950s, the motor transport industry came second only to cocoa farming in amount of money expended.

The effects of rail and road developments largely have been concentrated within individual countries, but those of air transportation and telecommunications have been international in scope. With emerging airline and communication systems, major African urban centers have come into relatively easy contact with one another and with the outside world. It has become possible to hold conferences that would not have been possible without long delays. Both air and communication links have created to some extent a "time-space-convergence" among African countries, the political and economic benefits of which cannot be overstated.

THE FUTURE ORIENTATION OF TRANSPORT AND COMMUNICATION SYSTEMS

Although many social and economic changes have been induced by transportation and communication, it has become increasingly obvious that these systems are not adequate for the present needs of African countries. Nowhere in tropical Africa is there a fully integrated transportation and communication network. Various African leaders have begun to realize the shortcomings of the spatial and structural patterns of the systems and their implications for the continued process of development both at national levels and inter-African integration. It is too easy to shift the blame of the present structure on former colonial powers; unfortunately some countries after independence have concentrated mainly on the improvement of established patterns with little or no significant attention paid to the development of rural-urban or farm-to-market linkages. Even after many years of independence, the inadequacy of transport systems from the point of view of national economic integration and the amelioration of rural poverty is still quite obvious. There are, however, serious attempts in some countries to correct the bias of the "colonial" transport patterns by building new roads and improving existing ones so as to promote intraregional trade, mobility, and interaction.

Significant progress has been made towards international cooperation in transport and communication systems under the auspices of the Organization of African Unity. Economic integration is now one of the accepted objectives of the OAU, and this will require among other things the establishment of effective transport and communication links. To facilitate this objective various road projects have been developed throughout the continent. These include the Trans-Saharan Highway from Algeria through Mali to Niger, the Tanzania-Zambia road, the Nairobi-Addis Ababa road, and the road link between Freetown and Monrovia. Work already has begun on the projected 6,500 kilometer East-West Highway which will run from Mombasa, Kenya to Lagos, Nigeria cutting across Uganda, Zaire, the Central African Republic, and Cameroun. These roads undoubtedly will stimulate inter-African trade and, it is hoped, will promote closer understanding and relations among African peoples.

Considerable investments continue to be made to improve railway operations by replacing and increasing rolling stock, and by extending the railway networks. During the last two decades many new rail lines have been built. Some of these, however, still follow the "colonial" pattern of a simple line leading inland from the coast to tap mineral deposits. Typical examples include the Mauritania line stretching from Port Nouadhibou to the iron deposits of F'Derik and Tazdit and the Liberia rail line running from Buchanan to the iron mines of Mount Nimba. Other new lines include the extension from Kuru near Jos to Maiduguri in the northeast of Nigeria; the Sudan rail line from Khartoum and Sennar to El Obeid has been extended far to the southwest; and the Pointe Noire—Brazzaville line now stretches to the mining areas in southern Gabon. Some lateral rail links also have been built, with notable examples being the Kotoku-Achiasi line linking eastern Ghana to the west and providing a direct connection between Takoradi and Accra, and the line across Tanzania opened in 1963 to link with the northern Tanzania-Kenya-Uganda railway system. Some new railways are under construction and many more are planned. The Trans-Cameroun Railway was extended to Ngaoundere in 1974. The railway project linking Tanzania and Zambia was financed and constructed by the People's Republic of China. This line, apart from its economic significance, is politically important to Zambia because it reduces the country's import-export dependence on Rhodesia.

In the field of air transport considerable efforts now are being made by the Economic Commission for Africa to discuss possibilities of multinational air-transport systems. The proliferation of national airlines following independence can be explained only in terms of political prestige. In the late 1950s and early 1960s, the ownership of national airlines became a "status symbol." Thus, the West African Airways Corporation jointly owned by Nigeria, Ghana, Sierra-Leone, and Gambia as a subsidiary of BOAC disintegrated in 1958, becoming national airlines. The Central African Airways was dissolved in 1967, and replaced by three national airlines. Other countries such as Mali, Senegal, and Guinea have launched their own national air services. Given limited local markets for freight and passenger traffic and the inability to compete effectively with well established international services, most of these national airlines have run at a loss and become a drain on limited development resources.

Emphasis now is shifting from the creation of individual

national airlines to that of multinational cooperations. Losses suffered as a result of earlier ventures seem to have had a sobering effect. Considerations are being given to the possibility of reintegrating the former West African Airways, and Ghana and Nigeria already have agreed to pool their technical resources to operate coastal services. East African Airways, embracing Uganda, Kenya, and Tanzania, still remains intact. Apart from these efforts, much recent investment has been devoted to the improvement of international and domestic airports. Runways have been extended to take jumbo jets. Terminal buildings continue to be built or improved.

The future of Africa's telecommunications seems bright in the light of recent developments. With the work now being done by the International Telecommunication Union, a series of projects have been or are being investigated. A preliminary survey of the Pan-African Telecommunications Network was completed in 1969. The project is expected to provide about 16,000 kilometers of telecommunication links among thirty-three African nations at an estimated cost of 80 million dollars, with planned completion in 1975. Although comprehensive data on the telecommunications developments of individual countries are not readily available, there are ample indications of considerable expansion and improvement in networks and services.

Developments of transport and communication systems show that African countries themselves are not satisfied with the present situation. More efforts are still needed; success will not be achieved without great difficulties in terms of physical environmental problems, inadequate capital, and shortages of equipment and personnel (Hance, 1967). Further developments also require a peaceful and stable political atmosphere, not only for the transport integration of individual countries but also of a whole continent where mobility of goods and people, thoughts and ideas, are of vital importance to social and economic progress.

23

Population Mobility

R. MANSELL PROTHERO

Rural-urban relationships may be viewed in the context of total contemporary mobility (Figure 23.1); Gould and Prothero, 1975). Population movements may be distinguished that occur exclusively within rural areas, between rural and urban areas, and within urban areas. The last two of these categories are relevant to the present discussion. Rural-urban mobility is two-directional, with movements from towns to rural areas being important in the total context of mobility. Urban mobility includes both interurban and intraurban movements.

			TEMPORAL					
			CIRCULATION				MIGRATION	
			Daily	Periodic	Seasonal	Long-term	Permanent	Irregular
SPATIAL		Rural-Urban						
SPATIAL		Urban-Rural						
SPATIAL	Urban	Inter-Urban						
SPATIAL	Urban	Intra-Urban						

Figure 23.1 A Typology of Rural-Urban Mobility in Africa.

In addition to the spatial dimension in mobility, there is also a temporal one. This involves recognizing a basic distinction between movements that may be classed as circulation and those that may be described as migration, though the latter term is sometimes used in a general sense to include all types of movements. Circulation is used to describe movements that do not involve a permanent change of residence, but where absence from place of residence is for varying periods of time with subsequent return. Such absences may be repeated frequently. On the other hand, migration involves a permanent change of residence. However, the distinction between circulation and migration may not necessarily be related directly to time, for some circulation may exceed migration in duration of movement. Also, the definition of permanence may involve not only a conventional measure of time but also the migrant's social and economic commitment to the home area compared to the new destination (Van Velsen, 1963). Because it is impossible to achieve a universally acceptable definition of permanence (Mangalam, 1968; Petersen, 1968), the problem of defining what constitutes "permanent" may be such that there is sometimes a blurring of the distinction between circulation and migration.

Circulation and migration each may be subdivided further in temporal terms about which it is possible to be more specific. Daily circulation includes movements of less than 24 hours duration. Periodic circulation may vary in length from no more than 24 hours to a maximum of one year. Seasonal circulation is a special category of periodic circulation which deserves distinction because the duration of movement is defined in terms of marked seasonal variation in the physical environment with resulting economic response. Long-term circulation involves absence from place of residence for more than one year and possibly many years, but with subsequent return. Two subcategories of migration may be recognized depending on interpretations of permanence in movement. Permanent migration is that which is understood in the conventional use of the term, to move from one place of residence to another and to remain there for more than one year. However, there are those who move from one place of residence to another without the immediate intention of permanence. Such movements may be described as irregular migration.

RURAL-URBAN MOBILITY

Population pressures manifest themselves in a variety of ways. They have been responsible for "push" factors in some rural areas with resultant movement to other rural areas and to towns (Zelinsky,

Kosinski and Prothero, 1970). These pressures have been expressed in terms of relationships among resources, population, and economic expectations; combinations of these at various high and low levels give rise to situations in which migration pressures may be present or absent (Mabogunje 1970c). The Ibo of eastern Nigeria have been subject to severe population pressure coupled with high economic aspirations but low availability of resources to meet them. In this and other comparable circumstances, those most under pressure have sought relief elsewhere. They have also been influenced by "pull" factors of attraction to rural areas with little population and abundant land available for settlement, or by urban areas with advanced economic development and employment opportunities. Towns have become increasingly important during the present century as destinations for those forced to leave congested rural areas. Not only do they offer, or seem to offer, opportunities for economic improvement, but there is the attraction of other amenities associated with urban life.

While factors motivating movements from rural areas have been shown to be primarily economic, it has been argued that there is need to differentiate between "necessary" economic factors conditioning potential migration and "sufficient" factors, often of a personal, social, or psychological nature, that actually precipitate a move. In the case of migrant laborers, the necessary causes affect the rate of migration, whereas the sufficient causes influence the individual incidence of these decisions (Mitchell, 1959). More recently, the balance between these factors has been questioned (Gugler, 1969). Explanations of rural-urban movements in terms of rural-urban economic differentials have been sought by economists (Beals, Levy and Moses, 1967; Todaro, 1971b). These are difficult to measure, particularly with the problems of ascertaining what constitutes a wage in the rural areas of Africa. The data available are, for the most part, of a crude and aggregate character.

Until recent decades much of the rural-urban mobility occurring in Africa south of the Sahara was periodic, seasonal, or long-term circulation, and there were marked differences between one part of the continent and another. Seasonal circulation, to rural areas as well as to towns, was most common in West Africa, with its east to west zonation and consequent gradation from south to north in terms of decreasing amounts of rainfall and lengths of the wet season. From the northern parts of West Africa—Mali, Upper Volta, Niger, and northern Nigeria—where population/land relationships are delicately balanced in marginal environmental conditions, large numbers of adult males moved southward during the dry season in search of work in areas of cash crop production and in coastal cities like Dakar, Abidjan, Accra, and Lagos, and inland centers of growing economic importance like Bouake, Kumasi, and Ibadan (Prothero, 1962). In these towns they formed substantial groups of temporary occupants who in the latter part of the dry season moved northward again to their home areas to farm in the wet season. In terms of rural-urban systems their impact upon towns, other than in providing unskilled labor, was limited, as was the impact of urban influences upon them.

For those not going such great distances in the dry season, movements often involve whole families locating on the peripheries of both the larger and smaller towns, laboring or practicing some trade or craft (Prothero, 1957). This phenomenon is sometimes referred to as *cin rani* ("to eat away the dry season"). Reverse movements from towns to rural areas may take place in the wet season when labor requirements for agricultural work are high.

Not all movements between rural and urban areas are timed in such a seasonal pattern. In the past and continuing into the present, traders are involved in movements, the durations of which may be either periodic or long-term. In the latter case the length of residence in places other than their home settlements may be such as to seem to be permanent migration. But this is difficult to determine in view of the links that people maintain with their home areas, the frequent visits made to maintain social and economic ties, and the plans to return when they have become sufficiently prosperous or to retire at the end of their working lives (Mabogunje, 1972). Not only traders but people with education and other skills similarly move for varying periods to towns (Caldwell, 1969). A case in point would be the Yoruba and Ibo from southern Nigeria, who diffused during the first half of the century to urban centers throughout Nigeria and beyond, and in the process, developed areas morphologically distinct from the indigenous settlements in which they located. These "strangers areas" (*zongo sabon gari*) have been enlarged in the present century and provide housing and other assistance not only for long-term residents but also for periodic and seasonal migrants belonging to the same ethnic groups (Cohen, 1969; Harvey, 1968; Mabogunje, 1968).

Rural-urban movements in eastern, central and southern Africa have contrasted in several respects to those in western Africa. Circulation has been a major component of these movements, but it has been much less seasonal than in western Africa and characteristically more periodic and long-term. Furthermore, systems of control over movements have operated, particularly in central and southern Africa in contrast to the largely spontaneous movements in western

Africa. These contrasts were related to the more direct involvement of Europeans in economic development in these regions of the continent, their permanent settlement, and their continuing political and economic dominance in parts of southern Africa. Towns associated with mining and industrial developments have been foci for rural-urban movements in Zaire (Denis, 1958), Zambia (Kay, 1967), Rhodesia (Kay, 1970) and South Africa (Green and Fair, 1962), and administrative and commercial centers the foci for movements in Uganda (Elkan, 1960), Kenya (Ominde, 1968) and Tanzania (Claeson and Egero, 1972). Colonial regimes differed in their migration policies, particularly with respect to African mining and industrial labor. In the Belgian Congo, official efforts were made to stabilize the force by permitting laborers from rural areas to settle at their places of employment with their families, often with accommodation provided by the employing companies. Migrant labor circulating between rural areas and urban and industrial centers characterized employment on the Copper Belt in Zambia, and continues in Rhodesia and in South Africa. In areas with no indigenous urban traditions, towns were founded essentially for Europeans with Africans as temporary residents to serve their needs and with strict control over the nature and pattern of African residence. Thus, governments were much more involved in the processes of mobility than they were in western Africa (Heisler, 1974).

With independence in Zambia there has been some acceleration of factors to reduce periodic circulation and to develop a more stable urban population, either through long-term circulation or permanent migration. In Rhodesia and South Africa the discriminatory racial policies of minority European governments continue to exercise considerable constraint upon the movements of people. South Africa controls its African population through various severe measures, of which influx control is directed to limiting the residence of Africans in urban areas reserved primarily for Europeans. The Republic continues to depend for much of its economic developments upon migrant African labor both from within the country and from outside. Foreign migrant laborers come from Mozambique, Malawi, Lesotho, Botswana, and Swaziland to work for contract periods of between 10 and 24 months. Recruitment, transportation, employment, and repatriation are all under strict control. Migrants may not be accompanied by their wives and families. Although periods of employment are of limited duration, laborers may spend even shorter periods in their home areas before returning again to South Africa. This pattern is frequently repeated throughout their active working lives. Large-scale absences of males in the working age groups have produced considerable economic and social constraints upon rural societies. In some instances societies have been able through institutional changes to adapt relatively successfully to these absences (Van Velsen, 1960; Watson, 1958); in others the stresses have resulted in economic and social disorientation if not disruption.

INTERURBAN AND INTRAURBAN MOBILITY

Those who move from rural areas to towns in systems that are not subject to strict official control seem to do so more usually in one-stage moves, rather than by a step-wise process. The latter process has been identified in Latin America, in India, and in some other parts of the developing world. Some evidence for it has been advanced recently in Sierra Leone (Riddell and Harvey, 1972), but there is need for further investigation of step-wise migration in Africa. A limiting factor in its development may be the poorly developed urban hierarchy, particularly in the tropical parts of the continent. Interurban mobility may be found among professional groups and among those involved in trade and commerce at different scales and on various levels of sophistication.

Intra-city movements occur on a very large scale, though they too have received relatively little attention compared with other forms of mobility (Harvey and Brand, 1974; Roussel, Turlot and Vaurs, 1968). Rapidly increasing urban populations have produced high densities in expanding urban areas. The latter lead inevitably to the likelihood of increased separation between place of residence and places of work, resulting in increasing volumes of daily circulation. In some instances, the populations employed in urban occupations live outside of the urban area. In their daily commuting, they may be involved in a short-distance rural-urban circulation. In the larger cities of Africa the numbers of commuters put poorly developed transportation systems under great strain.

In addition to daily commuting, the other major category of intraurban mobility is that involving changes of residence (Brand, 1972a). These changes apparently are frequent among those who stay temporarily in towns before their return to a rural area and also among those who have moved to town for longer periods. Among the latter, in the earlier stages of their stay they may move frequently in the process of initial economic and social adjustment. Assuming that their economic circumstances improve, as their length of stay in town extends, their spatial mobility will be closely linked with associated social mobility.

CONTEMPORARY TRENDS AND PROCESSES

Although rural/urban circulation continues in all parts of Africa, the trend is probably towards longer absences from rural areas with increasingly longer periods being spent in towns, except where migration is controlled, as in South Africa. It is difficult to determine the extent to which this is a trend towards true permanent migration, involving a definite break with rural areas and settlement in urban places. It is probable that the majority of those living in towns, even though they may be second or third generation urbanites, still retain links with rural home areas, with grandparents, great grandparents, and more distant relatives. Such people must be considered essentially urban-based and their visits to rural areas involve urban-rural circulation that is predominantly periodic in nature.

The rural/urban and urban/rural system by definition constitutes a continuum and not a dichotomy, involving complex social, economic, and political linkages. These linkages are much greater and more powerful than they were in the past. Their nature, the factors and the processes involved, at various levels of individual and group interaction, have been indicated in a systems approach to rural-urban migration (Figure 23.2; Mabogunje 1970b). This approach indicates the importance of positive and negative feedback from urban to rural areas affecting the amount and nature of further migration from the latter to the former, and considers the processes by which the country person becomes a towns person. These linkages between town and countryside are important not only from the point of view of population movement but also from the point of view of the diffusion of elements of modernization from the towns. (Riddell, 1970; Soja, 1968). While virtually no part of Africa remains untouched by some aspect of modern development, the towns are by far the most dynamic with respect to social, political, and economic changes. These changes are having increasingly catalytic effects on rural areas, and are achieved through the movement not only of people but also of ideas facilitated by the development and improvement of communications in every sense of the term.

Those who constitute the urban population of Africa are a selected group whether they have moved to towns or have been born in them. They are a minority of the population of the continent as a whole and in no country do they form a majority. Although rural-urban movements leading to permanent settlement in towns are increasing, there is yet no massive rural depopulation such as occurred in Europe and North America in association with industrial development. Still, Africa is in the process of a well-established and accelerating urban revolution. This has resulted from a variety of

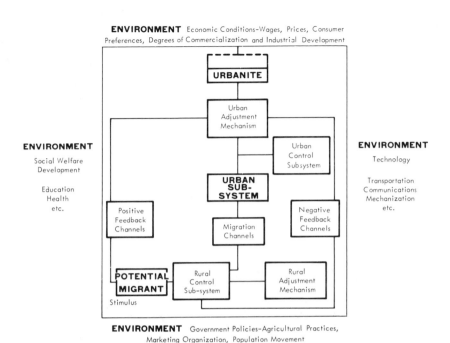

ENVIRONMENT Economic Conditions–Wages, Prices, Consumer Preferences, Degrees of Commercialization and Industrial Development

URBANITE

Urban Adjustment Mechanism

ENVIRONMENT

Social Welfare Development

Education Health etc.

Urban Control Subsystem

URBAN SUB-SYSTEM

Positive Feedback Channels

Migration Channels

Negative Feedback Channels

ENVIRONMENT

Technology

Transportation Communications Mechanization etc.

POTENTIAL MIGRANT

Stimulus

Rural Control Sub-system

Rural Adjustment Mechanism

ENVIRONMENT Government Policies–Agricultural Practices, Marketing Organization, Population Movement

Figure 23.2 A System Schema for a Theory of Rural-Urban Migration.
Source: Redrawn from Mabogunje (1970b), with permission of *Geographical Analysis.*

factors, of which population growth contributing to rural pressure is undoubtedly of major importance. Social and economic developments in the towns have been considerable, but the revolution in urban growth has not been complemented by a comparable revolution in economic development. As a result, urban economic and social resources are also under pressure. An industrial revolution of sufficient proportions to meet further increased demand for these urban resources is unlikely in the foreseeable future. There is an urgent need to reduce the rate of urban growth through some reduction in the rate and volume of movement from the rural areas. This is difficult to achieve. To have any hope of success it will require the reduction of population and the promotion of economic development and social improvement in rural areas. The motivation and organization for these changes must originate in the towns where the available resources in concepts and techniques of modernization are most advanced and where the decision-makers are located (Logan, 1972). This calls for continuing more closely integrated rural-urban systems, ones in which emphases and directions are different from those in the past. Needed now are outflows from urban cores to rural areas involving relatively few people but much in the way of ideas, knowledge, and economic opportunity.

24

Markets and
Marketing Systems

CHARLES M. GOOD

Markets are familiar and vital elements in the socioeconomic life of contemporary African peoples. In simplest terms markets are specific sites where sellers and buyers assemble on appointed days to exchange goods and services, and to participate in a variety of social activities complementing routine business transactions. Indeed, some observers stress that the social and political importance of markets is as great as their economic significance (Bohannan and Curtin, 1971; Piault, 1971). Markets are indigenous institutions both north and south of the Sahara, and today there are complex networks comprising thousands of markets distributed across the changing landscapes of rural and urban Africa. While greatly diversified in terms of size, locational attributes, timing, and principal economic functions, all market places can be conceptualized economically as mechanisms designed to rationalize the fundamental problems of collection and distribution posed by spatial and temporal variations in supply and demand (Good, 1975).

The economic profile of most African populations is such that only a small proportion of markets, apart from those located in urban settlements, can be supported on a daily or permanent basis. Consequently, a majority of rural markets are characterized by periodic meetings. The frequency of market meetings varies widely, reflecting historical and social factors as well as the interplay of economic forces on individual markets and market systems. Among the Yoruba of western Nigeria, a common periodic cycle is four days. This appears to be related to the traditional four-day calendar week in the area. Other market cycles are usually multiples of this four-day week. In essence, periodicity is probably the most conspicuous and fundamental feature of the marketing scene. The temporal space between market meetings is in part related to the nature and habits of production, consumption norms, and purchasing ability of predominantly rural populations. It provides a means of adjusting to the constraint of distance in areas where transport facilities are inadequate and costly. Timing is an important factor in the relative locations of markets and sets the rhythm regulating the circulation and convergence of people and goods. The distribution of market periodicities and market networks presents a complex picture of functionally separated, contiguous, and overlapping systems—a kaleidoscopic pattern of place-time interrelationships.

African markets typically perform one or more of four primary economic functions. They serve as centers for collection and local exchange of produce originating in the immediate hinterland of a market such as foodstuffs, livestock, and craft articles; they provide services such as cooked meals and locally-made beer, tailoring, barbering, and repair of bicycles, watches, and shoes; they are distribution points for goods *imported* from other areas of a country and from abroad, such as manufactured consumer items and dietary staples; and they are bulking points for goods to be *exported* from the local region.

Local exchange occurs in a majority of rural markets and operates at all levels of development. It features small-scale division of labor, offers a means for disposing of goods produced in excess of family needs, and can provide a hedge against periodic shortages of foodstuffs and utility items which are experienced in the household and locale. Places of production, marketing, and final consumption tend to be situated near to each other. Demand for local exchange alone is unlikely to stimulate the establishment of market places.

Importing, bulking, and exporting of goods are interrelated activities, each of which is represented in most market places in varying proportions and levels of significance. These functions focus our attention on the interconnections and external associations of markets: the movement and aggregation of people, goods, money, and information in and among specific groups of markets, and the linkages between town and country, areas of surplus and deficit, and the internal and world economic systems.

In comparing market systems within and between the major

regions of Africa, some striking areal contrasts are noticed in the origin, scale, intensity, and complexity of marketing activities. This would be demonstrated, for example, by even a casual inspection of rural markets in southern Ghana and south-central Uganda. In the former area, and throughout much of West Africa, market-place exchange is a traditional and vigorous part of commercial life that features a high proportion of professional traders and well-developed flows of commodities between specialized production areas. For instance, the Ghana census of 1960 disclosed that traders (many of whom were not of Ghanaian origin) formed one-eighth of the national labor force and accounted for 1 of every 22 persons in the country.

On the other hand, markets found in increasing numbers in every district of Uganda are, for the most part, a recent phenomenon superimposed on a loosely integrated national economic system characterized by a high degree of farm self-sufficiency. Apart from production of cash crops such as coffee, cotton, and tea, which are not sold through market places, regional specialization as a basis for internal trade is spatially restricted to a few areas and specific localities. Consequently, regional and market interrelationships are weak. The existence of markets, therefore, is based upon other considerations, most notably the demand for manufactured consumer goods and services among rural households that produce the bulk of their own food requirements. These Ugandan markets are mainly import points visited by itinerant African traders who often reside in rural or urban communities that are 50 or even 100 miles distant from a specific market. They obtain their stocks from wholesale and large retail outlets in towns or trading centers and then transport the goods to a series of periodic markets where direct contact is made with the rural African consumer.

If markets were intentionally closed down in rural areas of Uganda, many of the local communities *supporting* them, as distinct from those "full-time" traders who *depend* on them for a substantial part of their cash incomes, might feel disadvantaged, but probably would not be seriously handicapped. (Individual markets are, of course, always susceptible to a process of spontaneous spatial adjustment whereby the least economic enterprises are eliminated or relocated.) Despite these general characteristics market places are, together with small African-run shops, still one of the two most important mechanisms for formal exchange in the spatial pattern of Uganda's "grass roots" economy. Indeed, in several areas of the country markets are such an accepted element of the contemporary cultural fabric that they are perceived as "indigenous" institutions.

ORIGINS OF INDIGENOUS MARKETS

Why was organized market-place trade an outstanding feature of extensive areas in precolonial Africa, whereas other large areas were inhabited by essentially marketless societies (Figure 24.1)? This question has aroused increasing debate and speculation among geographers and other social scientists who feel that the presence or absence of market institutions is a key diagnostic variable in the analysis of historical and present-day patterns of socioeconomic development.

One approach to this problem is to identify, by means of comparative research on precolonial market areas, the circumstances that were apparently conducive to the emergence of market exchange and the processes by which markets were actually established upon the landscape. The generalizations derived then may be compared against knowledge, similarly obtained, of social, economic, and ecological patterns in marketless societies. The primary purpose of this procedure is to develop and organize the evidence in such a way as to construct a theory of market origins that can explain the observed differences in the institutional and structural arrangements for exchange among precolonial African peoples.

Achieving an explanatory model is complicated by the fact that indigenous African economies were neither static nor isolated from forces promoting change which penetrated even the most remote corners of the continent during the precolonial era. African societies exhibited many types of exchange arrangements and levels of economic organization. At one end of the scale were largely self-sustaining, spatially restricted communities whose exchange needs were met almost entirely by means of occasional barter and customary gift transfers tied to the structure of kinship and political obligations. Toward the opposite extreme were communities that maintained regular lines of external communication and featured specialized production, highly developed markets, professional traders, and complex currency systems. In the vast middle range were economies characterized by various phases of trade-related activities in which subsistence-oriented exchange coexisted with expanding intercommunity links and an evolving system of commerce.

Several different concepts, variables, and kinds of analysis have been employed in the search for an understanding of market development. One popular interpretation of market origin begins by assuming that people share an inherent tendency to barter; this

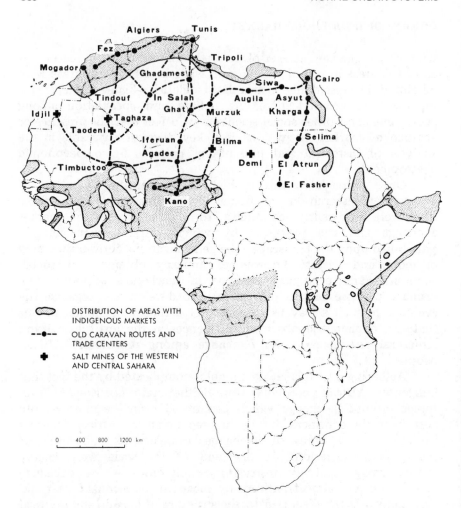

Figure 24.1 Distribution of Precolonial Market Areas.

generates a need for exchange within the local community which increases division of labor. Local market places follow, and eventually external trade develops. A second assessment reverses the order of events. Trade and markets can never arise out of the demands of individual or local exchange; instead, their emergence is related to the development of *external* contacts among different communities. Here the emphasis is placed on the stimulus provided by regional complementarity and on the characteristics of the societies who recognize and then exploit the advantage to be gained in offering mutually scarce goods to each other (Meillassoux, 1971).

If proof for the second proposition is found to be widespread, it still must be recognized that any attempt to explain why markets have or have not developed in particular areas will require knowledge of the regional conditions affecting many centuries of growth as well as consideration of a whole complex of other related factors. For example, there may be variable thresholds of population density below which markets do not occur, and empirical studies suggest that political stability and the organizational capacity of a society to maintain peaceful conduct of trade are also highly relevant (Hodder, 1965a; Good, 1970).

But in general terms, the spatial expression of economic complementarity (growth of regional interaction) is perhaps the most fundamental precondition for the emergence of indigenous market institutions. Markets are induced by an external demand that stimulates production of goods for exchange against imported goods. In precolonial Africa, they arose as mechanisms to expedite regular circulation of goods through different exchange cycles (producer-trader, trader-trader, trader-consumer, and producer-producer) *between* areas that were not economically self-sufficient. Moreover, extensive evidence shows that the genesis of many markets was clearly related to their location on or their accessibility to inter-regional or long-distance trade routes frequented by professional traders dealing in more valuable and exotic commodities (Jackson, 1971). Lack of markets in regions where exchange is dominated by person-to-person relations and where foreign traders are not present, and the fact that markets are often located on the boundaries of those regions with complementary economic/ecological zones, lend support for this thesis (Meillassoux, 1971). In northern Tanzania, for example, the traditional market of the agricultural Arusha and pastoral Masai peoples has been described as a "border institution." When the Arusha-Masai borderland shifted westwards in response to German penetration and changing patterns of land use, the market moved accordingly (Gulliver, 1962).

APPROACHES TO CLASSIFYING MARKETS

African markets present problems of classification because of the many characteristics they possess and the variety of functions they perform. Ideally, the classification adopted should be inclusive (account for all cases) and contain categories that are mutually exclusive (see, for example, Scott, 1972). At least seven criteria *might* be used. Among them are: (1) *location* (e.g., rural, periurban, and urban; or intrasettlement, extrasettlement, circulation nodes, and border points between complementary zones); (2) *size of market* (e.g., number of seller units, level of attendance, or level of revenues generated); (3) *size of trade area* (e.g., varying with market timing and local population densities); (4) *physical form and internal arrangement;* (5) *function in the chain of distribution* (e.g., local exchange, feeder, import, bulking and export markets, or retail and wholesale markets); (6) *order of or kinds of goods and services provided* (e.g., proportions of low order, cheaper, and commonly available items vs. higher order commodities; or personal service markets, food staples markets, livestock markets, and manufactured consumer goods markets); and (7) *timing* (daily and periodic).

Most of these criteria are of limited use for purposes of classification. For instance, a majority of markets perform at least two *distributional functions* such as local exchange, bulking, and export, or local exchange and importing; and in many situations it is not yet feasible to clearly differentiate retail from wholesale trading. A classification based on *kinds of commodities* is also unsatisfactory because several or all of the categories of goods and services available in one market are usually represented to some degree in most others. Use of the *locational* criterion would enable a distinction to be drawn between rural and urban markets. However, in western Nigeria and numerous areas elsewhere, a problem arises in differentiating between rural and urban settlements. Moreover, at any given time some rural markets are in the process of acquiring "urban" characteristics. Consequently, the development of a simple "either/ or" classification encounters difficulties because "rural" and "urban" represent the extremes of a locational continuum. In other words markets, with or without associated settlements, are subject to ongoing processes of adjustment in their structure, functions, and "location."

In geographic terms, two of the most fundamental attributes of markets are their *timing* and *locational* pattern. All markets can be said to meet either at specific intervals of time or on a daily (all-day, every morning, every night) basis. In the case of periodic markets, those in a given area can be expected to have evolved an accommodation whereby the potential conflict between the temporal and physical location of one market and the next (in time and space) is reduced or eliminated. The locational pattern of markets in space can be viewed as the outgrowth of a process. By analyzing market distribution we may be able, at least in theory, to sort out the process behind an observed locational pattern (Smith, 1971).

Periodicity of occurrence is an attribute of probably well over

three-quarters of all African markets. Whereas this temporal staggering of market meetings is most representative of the rural sector of
the economy, a decreasing proportion of general and specialized
markets in the rapidly expanding towns and cities also retain periodic
features. Smaller markets offering emergency items and perishables
such as fresh meat and fish on a daily basis are quite common in
many rural and periurban areas. Unlike many periodic markets, the
location and size of these daily markets tend to correspond with
the distribution and hierarchy of settlements. Indeed, the largest and
most important daily markets are distinctly urban phenomena and
owe their existence to the concentrated and collectively continuous
demand for foodstuffs, manufactured consumer goods, and services
by nonagricultural populations. In Ibadan, Nigeria, for example,
most markets are daily. As in other parts of Yorubaland, they are
differentiated into morning (feeder), all-day, and night markets.
Dugbe, one of the largest markets in Ibadan, is open seven days a
week from about 9 a.m. to 6:30 p.m. On an average day, it contains
between 5,000 and 6,000 sellers and is attended by some 30,000
people. Its main function is to supply foodstuffs and other products
to city-based consumers, particularly Nigerian middle-class people
and Europeans (Hodder, 1967).

Variety in the length of market weeks, their areal distribution,
and the persistence of these periodicity regimes are intriguing and
complex phenomena for which no generally satisfactory explanation
has been discovered. This diversity of market weeks is nowhere more
pronounced than in West Africa, where market periodicities are
frequently interspersed. For example, four-day markets may occur
with seven-day markets. In areas such as East Africa, where most
markets were established after the start of the colonial period,
markets generally are held on one or more fixed days of the
"Western" six-day work week (*e.g.*, every Monday or every Wednes-
day and Saturday) or once every 14 days or 28 days. Thus in Ankole,
Uganda, about three-quarters of all district markets occur weekly,
each meeting on the same day of the week throughout the year.
Excepting a few markets that meet every 14 days to handle a large
volume of cattle sales, most of the remaining market sites spring to
life only once every 28 days. However, in several cases "weekly"
markets are also held on the same sites in the three weeks preceding
each "monthly" meeting. In the Buganda region, immediately north
and west of Lake Victoria, 14-day markets are by far the most
numerous and also the most important as defined by levels of
attendance, order of goods offered for sale, revenues, and the
movements of professional itinerant traders. Interspersed with these

are smaller numbers of daily, weekly, and monthly ("cattle") markets, as well as several specialized daily markets held at major fish landings which convert to multifunctional markets (fish, produce, and manufactured goods) once every 14 days.

Recent research has permitted preliminary mapping (Figure 24.2) of areas of market periodicities in the great stretch of territory extending from Senegal to Cameroun. *Two-day markets*, separated by one marketless day, are relatively rare and largely confined to the four-day zone of western Nigeria and Dahomey. *Three-day markets* are most prominent among the Mossi people of Upper Volta and in northeastern Ghana. *Four-day markets* dominate a nearly continuous zone extending across southern West Africa from the lower Volta River to Cameroun. *Five-day markets* seem to be highly localized, occurring in and around the Tiv country south of the Benue River in Nigeria, and among the Dogon of Mali and Lobi of the Ivory Coast and Upper Volta. *Six-day markets* are found among the Diola of Senegal, in northern Ivory Coast, among the Dagomba and Konkomba peoples of northern Ghana and Togo, and in the Jukun country of eastern Nigeria. The *seven-day market* week, which is also the length of the traditional Islamic week, clearly has the widest distribution. It dominates practically all of the territory situated north of the Niger and Benue Rivers in Nigeria, the Akan-Ashanti area in the forest zone of southern Ghana, the Songhai area along the middle Niger, northwestern Ivory Coast, western Guinea, the Wolof country of western Senegal, and the Malinke areas of the Senegambia, Mali, and eastern Guinea. *Eight-day markets* are spatially associated with the four-day zones in Yorubaland and the Ibo and Ibibio areas of Nigeria, occurring also in southern Ivory Coast and southwestern Cameroun. While there are isolated examples of even longer market weeks in West Africa, such as the indigenous 16-day Yoruba cloth and black-soap fairs at Oje in Ibadan, and the 24-day Aro trade fairs in eastern Nigeria, they appear to belong to a class by themselves in that they reflect specialized trade growing out of an unusual combination of local circumstances (Hodder, 1967).

How and why these different market weeks evolved remains a perplexing issue. Some periods coincide with ethnic boundaries, while others cut across them. In many areas of West Africa, and among the Konso of south-central Ethiopia, the names for the days of the week are the same as the names of the places in which the markets meet (Kluckhohn, 1962). Another system designates the first day of a three-day week as "market day," the second "the day after market day," and the third "the day of preparation for market" (Hill, 1966:305). Indigenous Ibo markets arose within the frame-

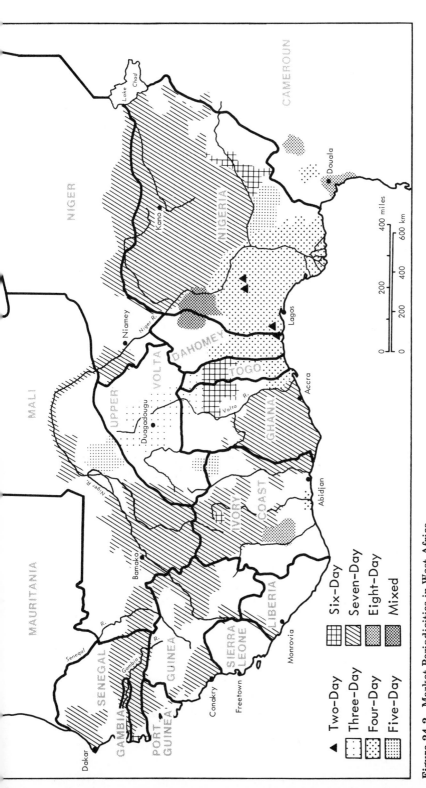

Figure 24.2 Market Periodicities in West Africa.
Source: Adapted from Smith (1971), with permission of the *International African Institute.*

work of a preexisting four-day week and are "widely believed to have developed out of the custom of the rest day" during which people do not work their farms (Hodder and Ukwu, 1969). Ibo markets are named by the days of this traditional week.

Support for an environmental explanation of market weeks remains in doubt. Whereas the ecological gradient in West Africa is generally one of transition from the humid forests of the south to semiarid steppe in the north, the seven-day week predominates in southern Ghana as well as in the savanna and steppe zones of Nigeria, Niger, Mali, and Senegal. Furthermore, if Muslim traders from the northern areas were responsible for the southward diffusion of the seven-day week into the Akan territory of Ghana, why was it not adopted in the other forest regions they entered? Shorter market weeks may indicate the need to quickly dispose of perishable foodstuffs where constantly high levels of heat and moisture prevail. Yet three- and four-day weeks also extend over a wide range of latitude, and seven-day markets are reported in the equatorial zone of the Congo Basin.

The tenacious quality of the indigenous market weeks is one of the more remarkable examples of the extreme stability of particular cultural traits and the continuity they provide between past and present. These regimes show little sign of yielding to the ordering of the "modern" Western week, which otherwise has such a pervasive influence on the temporal patterns of administration, education, leisure, and the newer kinds of commercial activity.

Sociocultural concepts and relationships clearly underlie differences in market periodicity schedules. A generalization that focuses on the role of society, custom, and tradition in market development is needed to counterbalance a tendency to rely too heavily on economic location theory. The economic rationale for periodicity draws on two concepts from Central Place Theory: *threshold* and *maximum range*. Threshold, designating the minimum range of a good, is defined by the population density and disposable income of an area. It is represented by the radius of a circle encompassing the level of demand an establishment must achieve in order to realize profit from producing or offering a central merchandise or service. The maximum range is a distance beyond which demand for a product available at a given place and price falls to zero. It signifies the farthest distance dispersed consumers will travel to purchase a product at a central place (Christaller, 1966; Stine, 1962).

Survival of an establishment offering merchandise at a permanent site on a daily basis requires that the maximum range must equal or exceed the minimum range, a condition allowing retail firms to conduct business from fixed locations. Failing this, the establishment will: (1) die out; (2) operate periodically but remain spatially fixed; or (3) become locationally mobile and move among a set of locations (market sites) according to a prearranged schedule. In the latter case, firms (traders) are itinerant and, together with other sellers, aggregate periodically to form a market. By staggering market meetings among a group of markets so that they meet on different days, each one can draw enough consumers to justify holding a market in an area where the disposable income of people is low. When demand is thus concentrated in place and time, traders can achieve viability by offering their goods to a much larger population than they could otherwise expect to contact. For consumers, the rotation of markets reduces the physical distance between them and the goods and services they want. They are able to "free themselves from the discipline of space" (costly transport) "by submitting to the discipline of time" (Stine, 1962:70).

The model outlined above suggests that the trader is a specialized professional whose livelihood is obtained almost exclusively from full-time market activities. Very often, however, the overall level of demand will be inadequate to enable the trader dealing exclusively in one line of merchandise to make a living. Alternatively, viability may be achieved by increasing the variety of commodities offered for sale. In Uganda, itinerant market traders who specialize usually sell high-value merchandise such as dress fabrics, new clothing, or used clothing. While purchase of these goods is subject to marked seasonal fluctuations (Easter and Christmas are periods of greatest turnover), often there is sufficient demand throughout the year to keep the opportunity cost low and enable the trader to survive. However, many other traders attempt to spread their overheads and profits over a greater variety of goods, combining items such as clothing, blankets, cutlery, enamelware, soap, and cosmetics. A similar accommodation is characteristic of rural shopkeepers, most of whom maintain small stocks of general merchandise, "specialize" in convenience goods such as sugar and kerosene, and may open for business only a few hours each day.

Part-time trading is an alternative and very widespread form of exchange in economies characterized by low levels of specialization, underemployment, and capital scarcity. Indeed, most individuals who sell in African periodic markets also are engaged in a variety of other economic activities. Examples include crop production, livestock herding, collection of produce from growers for resale, craft production (e.g., furniture, carpets, pots, and iron implements), and processing of goods. Under such circumstances the seller may decide to attend one particular market every nth day, or make regular visits to several markets operating on a rotating cycle (cf. Hay, 1971). In either case, the periodicity of markets facilitates a more efficient combination of sales with various other productive activities.

Several references in the literature on African markets point to the existence of integrated clusters or "rings" of periodic markets. Each market in a ring is temporally and spatially synchronized with the others in order to eliminate unnecessary competition and accommodate people who wish to attend several markets. Thus in Yorubaland, western Nigeria, indigenous market rings are described as logically and conveniently "composed of a complete and integrated sequence of markets taking place over four-day or eight-day periods," so that "the timing of marketing activities is evened out over the whole ring . . . and . . . no hamlet or other settlement is far from a market for more than three days" (Hodder, 1965b:55-56). This suggests that market rings are exclusive. If, on the other hand, the actual movements of itinerant market traders are used to define the pattern of market shift (the sequence of market locations in a ring), a trader who visits more than one market in a single day will participate in multiple rings. In this way individual markets can be assigned to several overlapping and interacting rings that form, in the case of Yorubaland, "a loose chain-mail pattern of rings" extending across most of the countryside (Eighmy, 1972; Hodder, 1965b).

In Uganda, the locations and schedules of weekly markets are fixed by parish and county officials in consultation with representatives of local communities. Additional coordination between counties reduces potential conflict between markets situated near their respective borders, and these are attended by people from both counties who live within convenient walking or cycling distance from the markets. This tends to "even out" marketing activities, but it is doubtful whether application of the market ring concept can do more than underscore the fact that competition between markets is both spatial and temporal (Hodder and Ukwu, 1969).

However, it would appear that the arrangement of markets in time and space is biased in favor of the consumer. This acts to the disadvantage of the itinerant trader seeking an optional or "most efficient" pattern of market visitation.

If the physical locations and periodicity of markets in an area do, in fact, complement each other, markets located near to each other and accessible to dispersed populations should be separated by a relatively long interval of time. On the other hand, markets meeting on the same day, or separated by a short period of time, should be physically farther apart from each other. In short, we might assume that "proximity in space implies separation in time" (Fagerfund and Smith, 1970:343).

Tests of this "efficiency" hypothesis have been made by geographers using data from three- through eight-day market areas in West Africa, and weekly markets in western Uganda. Distances between neighboring markets were compared with the number of days separating their occurrence. The findings tend to support the hypothesis for markets meeting on the same day, adjacent days, or separated by one complete day. However, in several cases the distances between markets separated by progressively longer time intervals were greater than anticipated, creating an inversion of the temporal-spacing relationship. These localized irregularities may be due to several factors not adequately accounted for, including incomplete or outdated information on market locations and schedules, functional differences (specialization) among markets, bias introduced by linear measurement of distances on maps (as opposed to measurement along the actual paths of movement), and anomalies produced by the juxtaposition of markets with different time cycles (Smith, 1971; Good, 1972).

In extensive areas of Africa, markets are regularly situated away from established settlements. Instead, they are located at points of convenient accessibility for several villages or population clusters. Such points are most often the nodes of local or regional circulation networks, including roads, footpaths, livestock routes, and river and lake crossings (Figure 24.3).

In areas of dispersed human settlement markets generally are located with respect to servicing as large a population as possible within the limits imposed by existing methods of local transport. For example, in the Ankole District of southwestern Uganda the rural settlement pattern consists of physically scattered single-family homesteads separated from one another by dense banana groves, subsidiary plots of field and garden crops, and fallow land; and in the pastoral zone by wild pasture and rangeland. The repetition of this pattern in the landscape means that although markets take the name of a particular loosely-grouped "village," the majority of persons attending are from villages other than the one after which the market is named.

In areas where settlements are compact (i.e., many individual units of occupance are clustered together), the locational orientation of markets may be within settlements, between settlements, or both. The pattern for any specific area or society will depend on several considerations. These include the extent to which settlements

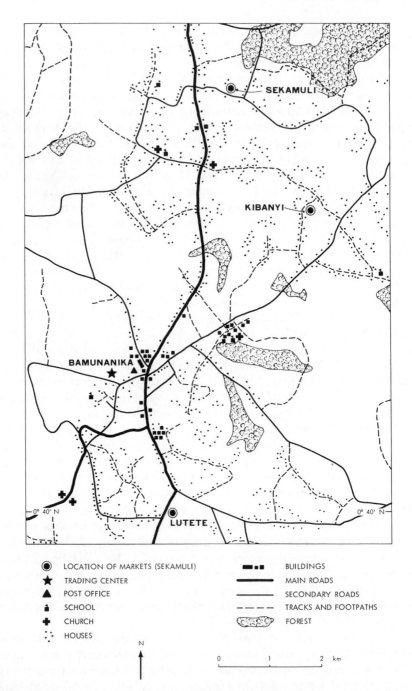

Figure 24.3   Fourteen-day Markets in Part of Bulemezi County, East Buganda District, Uganda.

function as important units of both social and economic organization, and antecedent factors such as the degree to which everyday relations between the various populations attending markets historically were peaceful. However, the most important point to be emphasized here is that market sites are always potentially responsive to changing economic, social, and political conditions that may induce fundamental alterations in their spatial association with other landscape elements.

SOME INTERNAL CHARACTERISTICS OF MARKET SITES

African market places are quite diversified in terms of size, mode, and quality of construction, facilities for market users, and physical maintenance. At one end of the scale are innumerable markets that are simply open spaces or clearings, perhaps only a hundred square yards in area, alongside a road where buyers and sellers (together with a fee collector!) customarily meet on a regular schedule. If any facilities do exist at such sites, they are usually crude shelters, constructed by the sellers themselves, consisting of a roof of thatched material supported by wooden poles. At the other extreme are the huge and often heavily congested urban markets operated by authority of city councils or similar bodies. The *mercato* in Addis Ababa, for example, which is reputed to be the largest open-air market on the continent, spreads over several square miles and includes retail stores, wholesale outlets, warehouses, truck depots, restaurants, hotels, bars, and *bordellos*.

Geographers are inclined to emphasize the spatial or situational aspects of markets, focusing on the interdependence of a market and its complementary region, or on the interrelationships among a group of markets forming a larger system. Although comparative studies of the nature and uses of market sites are practically nonexistent, the literature does contain a wealth of information on individual markets and suggests a number of general characteristics.

1. **Physical facilities.** Temporary (thatch, wooden poles, mud, plaster, cardboard) or permanent (concrete, corrugated iron roofing and siding) materials, or both, are used in the construction of stalls, shelters, food service establishments, display platforms, administrative offices, livestock corrals and crushes, and butcheries on a market site. The whole area is usually at least semienclosed with some type of fencing (wooden rail, barbed wire, mudbrick or concrete wall, hurricane mesh, or shrubs) to facilitate collection of market fees and general supervision.

In general, the physical facilities and upkeep in African markets are inadequate to meet the basic needs and aspirations of market users. Insufficient display space (which can act as an indirect constraint on an enterprising seller's scale of operation), lack of or insufficient water supplies (especially critical for butchers), lack of lock-up storage space, and poor sanitation are just a few of the more common problems. While these are relatively minor issues when compared to the need for improved marketing organization and increased specialization (the basic formula for economic growth), they are nevertheless relevant to the morale, incentive, operational efficiency, and well-being of market users. The worst physical problems tend to be associated with urban markets in cities where accelerating in-migration of population has far outpaced the capacity or concern of urban authorities to maintain basic social services. Ebute Ero, a daily market on Lagos Island, typifies the extreme congestion, lack of planning, and public health hazards existing in most markets in the Nigerian capital. Narrow streets and alleys, choked with motor vehicles, bicycles, pedestrians, domestic animals, and refuse, are lined with shops and residences in various states of deterioration which front on open sewers. At one location butchers are found selling fresh, exposed meat along the immediate perimeter of an open sewer. High temperatures and humidity, ubiquitous garbage, poor drainage, excrement, flies, and dead rats reflect conditions of environmental quality that are seemingly beyond redemption. Affluent Nigerians tend to shop in specialty or department stores in the central business district. Thus they are able to avoid regular contact with the city's traditional market places. Apart from butchers, and shopkeepers on the periphery of the market, the trade is almost totally dominated by women. Many of these women are obliged to bring their infants and preschoolers, who spend the day in the market's dark, dank, and unhygienic environment.

2. Market authority. In those areas of Africa with indigenous markets, there were usually appointed or heriditary authorities who had the duties of keeping the peace, preventing dishonest dealing, and maintaining the cleanliness and repair of the market. Some also had rights of levying a fee on goods entering the market and charging rents on market stalls. In the West African craft guilds there were authorities responsible for safeguarding standards of workmanship among the blacksmiths, brass and silversmiths, woodcarvers, weavers, potters, masons, carpenters, and many other specialized groups.

In some cases there have been, effectively, several market authorities. For example, the interest of a local chief might be largely financial (a proportion of the market revenues accruing to him directly), whereas other individuals would exercise their authority over political, jural, social, or ceremonial functions in the market (Hill, 1966). In the kingdom of Bunyoro-Kitara in western Uganda, precolonial market places were established or supported, and commerce encouraged, by the *abakama* (kings) principally to support their political goals and social values. All markets cutomarily "belonged" to the king. In the reign of Mukama Kabarega (1870-1899) four flourishing markets were located adjacent to the palace, one of which was supervised by a special detachment of the national army. The kings also had a deliberate policy of assigning their political agents/tax collectors (the king's "eyes and ears") as market masters throughout the empire—a lucrative and prestigious position commanding great respect. Trade in strategic goods such as ivory was a royal prerogative in Bunyoro (as in Buganda and Nkore). In essence, the king's economic role, which made him the largest receiver and bestower of material gifts, was an inseparable part and measure of his own political influence and, thereby, the social and areal coherence of the empire (Uzoigwe, 1970).

The regulation of indigenous market systems, or the introduction and control of markets in marketless societies, were important aspects of colonial policy influencing African economic development. Colonial administrators often encouraged the establishment of markets as a means of stimulating the use of money, generating revenue, and creating demand for consumer goods. Paradoxically, however, official attention to markets was all too frequently tempered with suspicion and the marketing process burdened with restrictions by enthusiastic administrators who felt they should protect Africans from the "evil" effects of competition and other "immoral" influences (Bauer, 1968; Good, 1970; Marris and Somerset, 1971).

3. **Internal arrangement and patterns of specialization.** The basic order underlying an African market is rarely obvious to a non-African visiting one for the first time. The most vivid first impression (apart from the realization of one's own strangeness) is really a fusion of many images and sensations—the milling crowd of people creating a noisy and often festive atmosphere, the brilliant colors of African trade cloth, the haggling of sellers and buyers, exotic produce, pungent aromas, and much more.

Initially, the internal structure and distribution of market activities may seem to lack organization, and the market site may be congested and sprawling well beyond its original boundary (this is a common problem of many older established markets). However, closer inspection on return visits enables one to recognize distinct, repetitive, and rational patterns in the location and conduct of market affairs. Sellers of various goods and services tend to group together and return to roughly the same spaces or stalls each market day, thereby creating patterns of areal specialization by commodities. To a greater or lesser extent there also are definite divisions of labor and patterns of specialization by sex, age, and ethnic group which vary areally with local cultural distinctions, and often between rural and urban markets.

In Ankole, Uganda, market surveys showed that nearly three-quarters of the part-time and over 90 percent of the full-time traders were male. This is in striking contrast to southern West Africa, where women monopolize much of the trade and own many of the legendary "mammy wagons" that carry people and goods to and from markets. Along the Guinea Coast of West Africa women have traditionally had an important role in market trade. The indigenous agricultural economies of this region supported relatively high population densities and produced significant amounts of goods beyond subsistence needs. These societies evolved far more specialized modes of production, including craft guilds, and elaborate exchange institutions, than were to be found in any other major region south of the Sahara.

> Perhaps the power of economic motivation traditionally found in these societies of western Africa accounts largely for the favorable economic position held by ... women. In much, if not all of the Guinea Coast countries ... a woman's earnings belong to her. Their traditionally sanctioned economic position made it possible for them to adapt to innovations that were in the nature of continuities. Thus they seemed easily to have grasped how credit, in the banking sense, could be a factor of importance in extending the scope of their dealings, after European currencies became the universal medium employed in effectuating exchanges (Herskovits, 1962b:xii).

The high degree of female participation in West African exchange is probably also accounted for in part by the longevity of the market place tradition in that region, whereas in large areas of East and Central Africa markets are innovations which have been in existence for less than four decades. Today in Uganda many women engage in part-time marketing, and growing numbers are adopting trade as their dominant activity and source of income. As such, their traditionally narrow roles (which essentially relegated them to food production and child-rearing) are undergoing slow but fundamental changes. Emancipation in this sense has progressed further in the urban areas such as Kampala, where opportunities for initiatives in small-scale trade are greater and where customary constraints regulating the scale and locus of social interaction are less binding than in the more conservative surroundings of the rural village.

4. **Markets as social institutions.** Rural markets, in particular, are multifunctional events that satisfy many of the social and cultural needs of the population. Anyone who has interviewed individuals in a market can attest that "noneconomic" purposes are often paramount in the minds of many people. Markets are an excellent example of the focal character of most human activities. They meet on a regular schedule and attract sizable populations that are varied in terms of family, village, ethnic, and regional affiliation. Therefore, it is not surprising that markets can be, and are, used for nearly every conceivable purpose that requires a large number of people gathered together under controlled conditions (Bohannan and Dalton, 1962).

Improved roads, modern forms of transport, increased literacy, expansion of *lingua francas*, transistor radios, and, in selected areas, television have all been instrumental in helping to overcome many factors that have traditionally impeded information flow in Africa. However, despite the often remarkable advances in communications over the past eighty years, the majority of rural inhabitants are illiterate, and most people outside the towns still do not own or have easy access to a radio. In this context, market places perform an extremely significant role as communications nodes. That a goodly amount of the information received and disseminated in a market may be of the informal "grapevine" or gossip variety does not dilute the social use of this basic function.

More specifically, markets are places "where, in the absence of traditional feelings concerning homestead privacy and interclan hostility, elders may gather, heterosexual liasions may be initiated, local people can come into contact with those [e.g., taxi, lorry, and bus drivers] who are passing through the area, [and] gossip may be passed on" (Levine, 1962:534). Chiefs and government officials often use the market as a forum for making important announcements, or as a convenient location for collecting taxes or convening a court. Veterinary and community development personnel may offer practical advice on animal husbandry and maternal and child care. One unusual but positive demonstration of how markets can be used to accomplish a variety of developmental objectives comes from Mali, where the U.S. Public Health Service Smallpox Eradication Program discovered that markets provided the most convenient and effective medium for ensuring high vaccination coverage of the country's sedentary villagers and nomads—populations with vastly different mobility patterns (Imperato, 1969).

As is evident from the examples given above, to adopt a strictly commercial view of African market activities is as naive as thinking that professors who attend the annual convention of their professions do so for the sole purpose of reading and hearing research papers. While the social dimensions of markets may contribute little to improving standards of material wealth, they clearly satisfy part of the basic formula for African living. For the geographer or other social scientist seeking to gain a deeper understanding of African social institutions and of the ways social behavior is channeled, organized, and patterned in space, the market place is an excellent laboratory.

CONCLUSION

In conclusion, it will be recognized that only a few of the issues that are basic to an understanding of African markets are examined in this essay. Several other questions are essential to any comprehensive view of markets as functional systems.

1. **Markets in the chain of distribution.** For any given area, how are different goods moved into and out of markets? Or, more generally, how do markets articulate the series of transactions and commodity movements (e.g., bulking-distribution: retailing-wholesaling) between the initial producer and ultimate consumer?

2. **Spatial economic organization and connectivity of markets.** To what extent are the markets of an area functionally differentiated from and interdependent with each other? In areas such as Uganda most rural markets have developed and remain essentially independent of each other's existence. They are basically import centers to which consumer goods are carried and sold by itinerant traders supplied from the towns. With the exception of cattle markets and those at major fish landings, there are few special-function markets where products of rural peasant origin are bulked for subsequent distribution to larger urban markets. The system is essentially one of "downward" vertical trade (urban to rural) with virtually no significant horizontal trade (rural to rural). Furthermore, in comparison with coastal West Africa, there is little "upward" vertical exchange (rural to urban). Most of the food supplies

imported from the rural areas by the towns do not pass through the rural market place.

3. Markets in the dynamics of regional economic and social change. What kinds and forms of adjustments do individual markets and market systems make in response to increasing or decreasing rural population densities, the growth of specialization among rural producers, a changing retail structure (e.g., expansion of rural shopkeeping with accompanying duplication of some market functions), higher regional incomes, changing consumer preferences, and accelerating urbanization? Each of these processes impinges on market places either directly or indirectly, and acts to induce changes in their distribution and/or relative importance in the hierarchy of market centers, in the level of marketing intensity (e.g., by promoting the insertion of additional dates in a periodic schedule), and in functional emphasis. In parts of West Africa the relative significance and functions of periodic and daily markets are undergoing a distinct transformation. Periodic markets are shifting to an emphasis on specialized wholesale trade, while more and more indigenous traders are becoming permanent shopkeepers around the perimeter of the larger daily markets in the main towns. It may be argued that the proliferation of permanent retail shops, which incorporate many of the functions associated with unspecialized periodic markets, is the end result of the conversion from periodic to continuous marketing. A similar process of functional and structural change has been noted in the case of London (Covent Garden) and Paris (the *Halles*) during the eighteenth and nineteenth centuries (Hodder and Ukwu, 1969).

Such changes raise another issue relevant to the process of commercial development. As African economies become more diversified and complex, does the economic importance of the market place increase or decrease? To date there is little statistical evidence directly available to assist in answering this question. In attempting to assess this particular issue it remains problematic whether the experience of the developed countries, including both those with capitalistic and socialist orientations, is an appropriate gauge.

VI

MODERNIZATION

The geographical patterns resulting from the interrelated processes of change and development focusing upon and emanating from urban areas are one aspect of modernization. In Chapter 1 we indicated that modernization connotes a development trajectory with commitments of individuals, communities, and space to Western models of economic behavior and structure. The role of the individual and community in modernization incorporates social, psychological, and economic changes from traditional patterns. Geographically, these changes mean an expansion of spatial interaction and interdependence, logical outgrowths of increased economic specialization and concentration. The organization of space is a critical dimension of modernization, and it may be traced to the focal importance of urban areas and the transportation networks that tie hinterland to city, and link city in a web of spatial and economic interaction.

In geography, the modernization concept has meant the spatial coincidence of various social and economic indicator variables. This coincidence suggests an underlying spatial dimension of the processes of change and development. Spatial correlation between income levels, population concentrations, transportation routes, communica-

388

Modernization and people. Three generations of a Wakamba family in Kenya have been born to different worlds as their homeland and nation become increasingly tied to larger scale economic and political systems. (Photograph by P. W. Porter)

Modernization and economic activity. A rural general store (*duka*) in Tanzania attests to the modest but increasing wealth in rural areas producing cash crops for national and world markets. (Photograph by C. G. Knight)

tion systems, educational facilities, and other development features points out the importance of spatial proximity and interaction, and the role of urban centers as growth poles in modernization.[1] As yet, geographical descriptions of the modernization pattern in African areas are only tentatively linked with the actual processes generating them. It would seem that these processes are the kinds of interrelated economic, social, and environmental changes described in earlier chapters, but in a spatial configuration where the sum becomes greater than the individual parts. This further suggests that creation of spatial linkages jointly tying together geographical regions and economic sectors are a critical prescriptive element in development planning. The major allocation of development funds in Africa to transportation networks underscores this importance.

Weinand (1972) has created an idealized model of the development process in a spatial context, merging separate perspectives on transportation, growth poles, and economic development into a single conceptual structure (Figure VI.1). At an initial stage, coastal settlements only begin to tap an undeveloped interior (A). The emergence of one of these centers as a growth pole (B) initiates backwash (polarization—demands by the city on the region) and spread (trickle down—benefits from the city to the region). The interior remains untapped. Development of regional service centers (C) extends the economic frontier upcountry in conjunction with further development of the transportation network. One or more of the regional centers may emerge as a growth pole itself (D), playing a role similar to that of the initial growth pole in stage (B). Spread effects at this later stage cause further growth in the regional centers between growth poles.

Though highly simplified, this model will be reflected in the three descriptions of modernization that follow. In Chapter 25, Riddell illustrates the complementary role of proximity, networks, and spatial hierarchy in the emergence of modernization patterns in Sierra Leone. Treating modernization historically, he is able to show the linkage between diffusion of modernizing institutions and the resulting patterns expressed as a modernization surface.

Maasdorp (Chapter 26) indicates the linkages in geographical space between various forms of dualism that have emerged as a facet of modernization in Swaziland, and, by extension, elsewhere. This dualism can be seen in the sectoral structure of the economy, in land tenure, in society, and in the organization of Swazi space. Maasdorp suggests that space is important in Swaziland at two scales—internally

---

[1] The spatial coincidence of indicator variables is usually measured by spatial correlation. Principal components analysis (or factor analysis) is used to extract the most important common, underlying dimensions shared by the variable set.

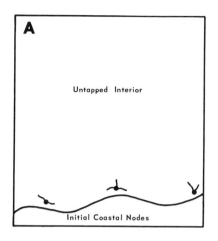

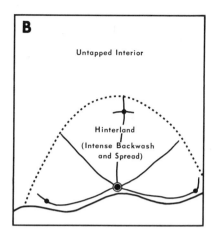

——— TRANSPORT ROUTE
◉ GROWTH POLE
● INTERMEDIATE SERVICE CENTER
● REGIONAL SERVICE CENTER

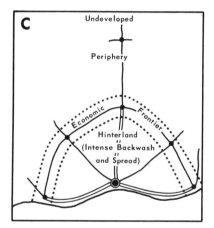

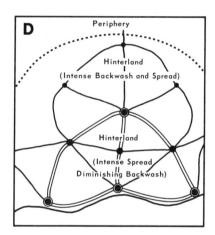

A Spatial Development Process.
Source: Adapted from Weinand (1972), with permission of *Australian Geographical Studies.*

in the dualism of modernization, and externally in relationships with other states in southern Africa.

In Chapter 27, Gould treats modernization as a spatial pattern portrayed through time. Arguing that we cannot understand modernization as a process without appropriate description of its patterns, Gould draws upon a number of variables to illustrate that pattern in Tanzania over five time periods from the early 1920s to the eve of independence. It is intriguing that the past remains salient: spatial patterns that emerged in the early colonial period prove a half-century later to have been virtually indelible.

The development of theory concerning economic development and modernization is an exciting application of modern social science to Africa and the developing world. The chapters in this section suggest profitable vantage points for the geographer's embarkation on this quest.

25

Modernization in Sierra Leone

J. BARRY RIDDELL

Africa presents a strange paradox to the geographer. In spite of the highly publicized programs of advancement, the talk of revolutionary schemes of economic development, Africanization and the removal of the colonial legacy, and the fairly remarkable increases in many indices gauging development, in many ways Africa remains much the same today as it was a half-century ago. Whole communities remain isolated, with social organization dominated by time-honored ways. Agricultural techniques and implements have changed but slightly. Disease, hunger, and malnutrition persist as daily problems for much of the population.

Yet within this traditional pattern, hints of change exist, and in some areas, especially in the towns and cities and along the roads and rail lines, revolutionary alterations have been made. Usually the changes are minor and not readily visible, although often they are profound, reaching to the very core of the social and economic structure. New roads, railways, and airlines serve aspiring nations, bringing new ideas, new methods, and new people to even the remotest corners. The beginnings of health and sanitary facilities have been provided throughout the countryside. The school has become a familiar institution over wide areas, and western education usually is highly esteemed. New organizations exist for the marketing of crops and the joint purchasing of daily needs. Information is disseminated by newspapers and radios and increasingly by television. National and local development plans have been formulated and implemented.

These changes, which affect all spheres of life—political, social, economic, and psychological—constitute the modernization process. This process is reflected by spatial diffusion dynamics, assuming patterns of varying intensity and rate. Its origins are often localized in specific regions or zones, where modernizing institutions create a cross-cultural contact situation, and the pattern of change moves from these foci like a wave across the map and cascades down the urban hierarchy as it is funneled along the transportation system. Thus, new ideas, new techniques, and new ways of life diffuse across geographic space according to three overlapping and interacting, yet conceptually distinct, rules. These rules may be specified as contagion, transport-oriented diffusion, and hierarchical spread. Together these three subprocesses characterize the spatial dimensions of change in the developing nations of Africa.

Spatial process takes place within a geographic framework. Earlier chapters have already provided an overview of the human, cultural, physical, and economic background of Africa. Our investigation of modernization is focussed upon Sierra Leone. Climatically, it is typical of West Africa, being constantly hot with a wet summer and dry winter rainfall regime. Because of its specific location and the steady onshore winds during the high sun period, monsoonal rainfall exceeds 500 cm annually along some parts of the coast and averages 200-300 cm in the interior. The primary tropical forest has been so distorted by human activity that the typical landscape today is grassland interspersed with secondary bush vegetation. The country is generally flat, with most of its land surface below 150 m and only a few peaks exceeding 1000 m. However, because of the heavy rainfall and its marked seasonality, the drainage network is exceedingly dense.

Culturally, the country is dominated by two ethnic groups, although there are at least fifteen other groups of significant size. In the provinces, people live in 146 chiefdoms, averaging in size between 250 and 500 sq. km.[1] The density of population (30 people per sq. km. in 1963) is high by general African standards, yet it varies from areas with less than 10 people per sq. km. in the northeast to densities exceeding 100 on the Freetown peninsula. Historically, a

[1] These chiefdoms constitute the spatial units for analysis in this chapter.

major distinction has been that between the former freed slaves who have emerged as a distinct Creole society on the Freetown peninsula and the peoples of the interior.

THE STRUCTURING OF GEOGRAPHICAL SPACE:
THE SPATIAL FABRIC

The spatial fabric of a country has three component parts: *proximity*, *network*, and *hierarchy*. The first, *proximity*, refers to the frictional effects of distance and need not concern us here other than noting that intervening distance between places (or people) hinders mutual interaction. This friction-of-distance has declined historically as transportation and communications have improved and as personal propensities to move have increased. As will be illustrated below, distance effects are a prime regulator of the pace and pattern of change.

Network refers to the transportation system of railway and improved roads and the communications networks which accompany them. Prior to the colonial period in Sierra Leone natural networks were used—the sea, rivers, and streams. Only bush paths represented improved forms of transportation. Clearly the frictional effects of distance were immense, because natural routes were subject to disruption by warfare, flood, and drought. Nevertheless, goods and people did move, often over great distances. However, personal mobility was restricted and trade was irregular, low in volume, and limited (except over quite short distances) to high value goods such as kola, gold, and ivory. In the absence of wheeled vehicles, goods were headloaded and officials and dignitaries were carried along the paths on suspended hammocks.

To provide for more effective administration and to act as a stimulus for trade, railway construction was begun in 1895 by the British at Freetown, with the line to run inland perpendicular to the coast and to extend to the south-eastern corner of the country. Its impact was immediate—the movement of colonial officials was improved and the volume of trade increased markedly. But the impact was limited to areas within a short distance of the line. Beyond a few miles it was simply too time consuming to move produce to the rail. The British then began a series of trials—feeder roads were constructed to expand the railway's hinterland, and experiments were made in the use of animal power, traction engines, barrel rollers, and tram lines. Gradually the roads were improved in quality, and by the early 1920s, a few trucks were using them, even though the road network essentially was a series of short, disconnected feeders barely suitable (economically or physically) to the use of motor vehicles. To encourage the use of trucks, the road network was expanded during the late 1920s to an interconnected system providing a thin areal coverage over much of the country (Figure 25.1). With the economic depression of the 1930s, no new construction was undertaken and the road network remained tributary to the railway. However, during World War II the road net, which was previously connected only indirectly by rail to the main port at Freetown, was linked to the capital. With the post-war expansion of trade, the road network took on increasing primacy in the transportation system and the railway's traffic fell not only relatively, but absolutely. Recently a few new links have been added to the road network and the more important roads have been paved; the railway is in the process of being phased out of existence.

Hierarchy refers to the urban-administrative system. Prior to contact there were no cities or even towns in Sierra Leone. The typical village settlement was a small agglomeration of houses whose inhabitants essentially were engaged in agriculture. Often these villages had smaller outlying settlements attached to them, and there usually was a hierarchy of importance to these settlements based upon the chief in residence. As trade gradually developed, a set of settlements at river mouths, heads of navigation, and on internal trade routes assumed increasing importance because of their role as trading centers or break-of-bulk points. With the British declaration of a protectorate over the hinterland in 1896, certain centers were designated as headquarters towns, and these assumed greater significance because of the associated package of administrative and service activities. Over time, the administrative system expanded and grew in complexity (Figure 25.2), a hierarchy literally was carved onto the map. These centers, in addition to those which developed in response to trade (or to mining activity in a few instances), evolved into Sierra Leone's urban system.

DIFFUSION REGULARITIES

Although modernization can be characterized and described, it is difficult to measure because it is composed of many separable aspects, with the whole process being greater than the sum of its parts. Consequently, we cannot discuss the spread of modernization *per se*, but must consider institutions or indicators of the process in

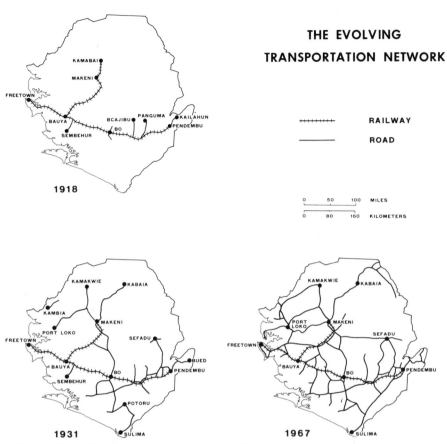

Figure 25.1 The Evolving Transportation Network.
Source: Riddell, 1970.

viewing its spatial diffusion. Thus we might consider the spread of schools as one aspect of educational modernization, whereas changes in cropping patterns or commercial intensity might describe part of an economic dimension. Here we will be concerned with certain indices mainly for what they can tell us of the spatial dimensions of change, although each process evokes its own interest. These indices will help to interpret the three ways phenomena diffuse across geographical space—by contagion, by movement along the transportation system, and by stepwise progression down the urban hierarchy.

Contagious diffusion can be illustrated by the spread of cooperative societies. These societies have been organized and encouraged in Sierra Leone both by the colonial administration and

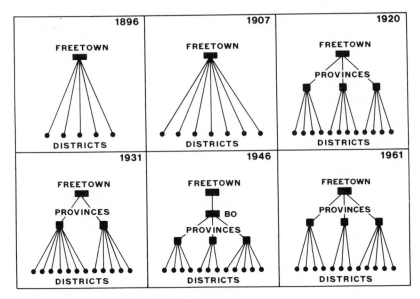

Figure 25.2 The Evolving Administrative Hierarchy of Sierra Leone.
Source: Provided by the author.

by the present independent government. Their function is fairly simple and basic, although their operations are quite complex. Essentially a cooperative society is a group of people living within a restricted geographic area who join together for the production and marketing of certain crops (or products), for the sale of general consumer items, or as a thrift and credit organization.

The cooperative movement has been a positive benefit to rural society. The quality of crops produced by members has improved as the marketing societies have offered prices higher than the existing marketing system. In addition, incentives have been provided for increased production, including generally higher prices and provision of means for owning machinery and transport and for buying tools and fertilizers. There also have been several peripheral benefits. People have been trained in democratic organizations at the local level. At the same time, by means of marketing and buying institutions, the societies are a vehicle for the Africanization of trade and for training in basic business techniques. The new meeting halls, stores, roads, and better drinking water attest to the fact that cooperatives have also served social welfare.

Cooperative societies originally were organized and encouraged by the colonial administrators, but once the idea took hold, it spread rapidly on African initiative. When a society was established in a village, quite often neighboring villages pressed for their own cooperatives. The positive benefits were many and usually highly visible.

The most important aspect of the spread was simple geographic proximity or nearness to what was an innovation. The earliest societies formed in the years preceding World War II were highly successful, but as the war cut off external markets and the government's energies were redirected, the societies disappeared. After the war, the desire for co-ops was expressed in many parts of the country, but because of the lack of supervisory and technical personnel, the government was unable to encourage formally the movement until 1949. The beginnings were, by necessity, small and localized, and by the end of the first year of operations six societies were under government supervision. From the original six, growth and spread of the movement was continuous (Figure 25.3). Several core areas developed, largely in response to the fairly distinct and separate cropping areas for rice, cocoa, and piassava (palm fiber). From these cores, societies began to spread outward through the areas ecologically suitable to each crop. Gradually the cores began to coalesce, becoming linked by the later spread of the thrift and credit societies which were free of any environmental constraint. The diffusion was contagious; existing societies acted as models for neighboring villages.

Primary education is an index of modernization whose diffusion has been very much influenced by the evolving transportation system (Figure 25.4). Its regulation and spread, although controlled in later years by the government, was initially in the hands of the several proselytizing mission societies. It is fair to say that without these Christian missions, educational opportunity in Sierra Leone would have been much delayed. Thus when we consider the spread of education, we must recognize that rather than representing the unified action of one corporate body, the growth of educational facilities depicts the effects of over 15 separate voluntary organizations operating over a time period spanning 175 years, and interacting with each other, and with varying degrees of government regulation and control. Yet the overall diffusion pattern is highly regular in its areal expression and quite strongly reflects the influence of the evolving transportation system.

Primary education in Sierra Leone dates from 1792, when a school was established by the Sierra Leone Company in Freetown and a schoolmaster was sent out from England. Education was quickly established in the colony and by the mid-1820s, there were 22 schools. Most of these schools were organized and supported by

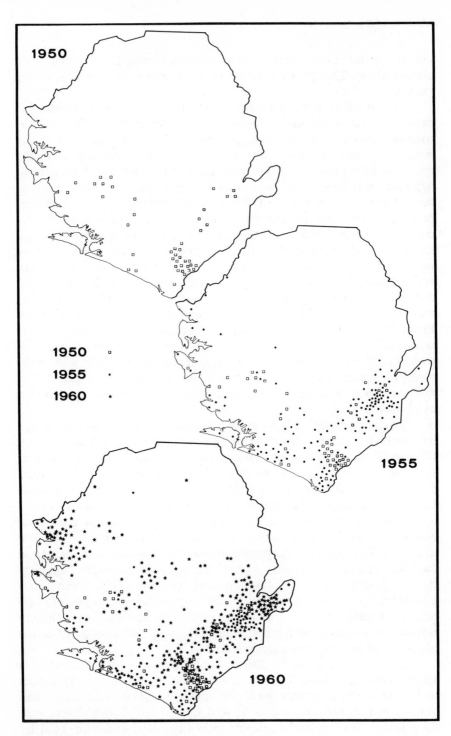

Figure 25.3 The Spread of Cooperative Societies.
Source: Riddell, 1970.

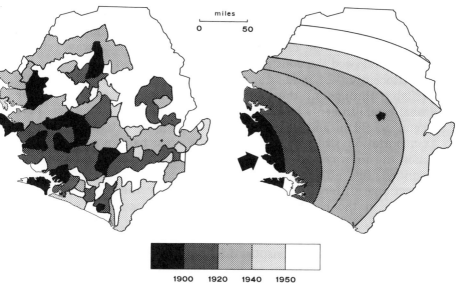

1900 1920 1940 1950

Figure 25.4 Diffusion of Primary Education.
Source: Riddell, 1970.

Christian missions, although the government provided some school-ing for the newly-landed freed slaves. However, the penetration of education into the hinterland beyond the colony lagged far behind. The harsh environment, which meant disease and death to the teachers and missionaries, and the presence of many Muslims effectively blocked the spread of mission schools inland for many years.

Gradually, a few mission stations were permanently established along the sea coast to the south of Freetown in an area unaffected by Islam. Although these beginnings were small and localized, the spread of schools into the interior and into traditional society had begun. The earliest stations were coastal as the sea offered the only means of relatively easy transport. Over time the missions expanded and a few schools were extended inland up the river valleys so that by 1898, there were 31 schools in the interior. But, the Hut Tax War of that year (a result of the British declaration of a protectorate over the interior in 1896) effectively wiped out the large part of the educational effort in the Protectorate. Missionaries, teachers, and their adherents were either forced to flee or were killed.

However, the effects of the rebellion lasted only a short time and many of the schools were reopened. At the same time, a transportation revolution occurred in Sierra Leone, and the railway the British were building inland from Freetown provided the first means of improved inland transport. The missions took advantage of the new link and opened schools all along the line; educational facilities began to appear hundreds of miles into the interior. Then, as feeder roads were extended to complement the railway, schools literally followed the construction crews up the roads.

Recently, as road transportation has become more widely available throughout the countryside, the linear pattern of educational establishments has been greatly modified. The interstices have begun to fill in and new forces have emerged, but the imprint of transportation still can be seen on the areal pattern of education. Since the railway and most roads were located in the south of the country, the effect has been a sharpening of the north-south educational differential, initially produced by the resistance of the Muslims in the northern half of the country to Christian mission efforts and thus to schools. In effect, Islam has acted as a semipermeable barrier to the spread of schools to the north, thus further modifying the transport oriented pattern.

Hierarchical diffusion occurs as the result of two distinct spatial frameworks. Certain modernizing institutions are locationally competitive, and their pattern of spread over time can be understood through principles of central place theory. Other institutions have been imposed upon the landscape as adjuncts to the spatial hierarchy of the colonial administrative structure.

The evolution of the spatial pattern of secondary schools illustrates the operation of competitive and central-place principles in the diffusion process. In addition to the obvious time lag, the underlying principles defining the locational pattern have been distinct from those described for primary schools. If we consider schools as central-place functions with specific thresholds (the number of students required to support a school) and ranges (the distance from which a school is able to draw support), then the respective values for secondary schools are much greater than for primary. Because of the generally low level of education and the very high drop-out rates, the secondary schools draw from wider areas, and their locations, rather than being ubiquitous, are highly localized, especially in the larger urban places.

The earliest secondary schools were opened in 1845 in Freetown, and they drew students from all along the West African coast. In fact, the first 17 secondary schools opened in Sierra Leone were located in Freetown, and only 92 years after the establishment of the first secondary school, the first Protectorate school opened (1937). Very gradually, and then more rapidly in the late 1950s and

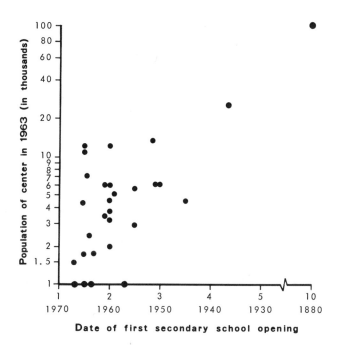

Figure 25.5 Hierarchical Diffusion of Secondary Education.
Source: Provided by the author.

early 1960s, secondary schools opened in many of the larger interior towns (Figure 25.5). With only minor exceptions, a map of secondary schools today is a map of the urban system.

The mechanism for the hierarchical spread of secondary schools is the competitive (or space-serving) nature of the institution. Additionally, competition for student support from the surrounding area is complicated by the fact that most of the schools are run by rival mission societies. Locations with a suitable threshold (*ie.* students trained through the primary system) are few and far between and are confined to the largest urban places where populations are denser, primary education is more widely available, and to which primary school trained young people have migrated. In the early years only Freetown had an adequate threshold for the support of a secondary school. Gradually, as primary education was extended throughout much of the country, the demand for such institutions increased and a school could be viable where a concentration of demand occurred in a limited area, in other words, in the second largest urban center. Then the threshold would appear at the third largest, fourth, and so on; thus schools appear to spread down the urban hierarchy.[2]

Quite a different force directed the expansion of medical and health facilities in Sierra Leone, although the spatial patterns were remarkably similar to those of secondary schools in that they exhibited hierarchical diffusion. Here, the colonial administrative system, with its capital and its provincial and district headquarters, was the determining, directional agency. The first hospital service was located in Freetown and gradually such services were extended over the countryside by the location of lower-order medical facilities at the district headquarters towns to serve the colonial administrative personnel posted in the interior. Eventually, these were upgraded to hospitals, the facility in the capital was expanded into a more specialized hospital, and lower-level services were established in the other small but important centers in the provinces. These low-level services functioned as health centers and dispensaries. Medical care began to be provided for the population of the country as well as the expatriate administrators. Thus medical facilities spread down the urban system, or evolved with it, as adjuncts to the colonial administration.

THE CONTEMPORARY PATTERN OF MODERNIZATION

The contemporary spatial pattern of modernization in Sierra Leone reflects the aggregate processes of diffusion of many modernizing institutions and processes. A number of variables were selected as indicators of the modernization process (Table 25.1). The high degree of interrelatedness among certain groups of variables is indicated by the high loadings on the first principal component extracted from the original data matrix. The principal components technique was chosen to aid in the search for the major dimensions of modernization and the overriding pattern of the spatial fabric of modernization in Sierra Leone.[3]

A mapping of the scores of the first component (Figure 25.6) indicates a very marked difference between Freetown and the provinces, with the Western Area assuming an intermediate position between the two. The areal pattern of modernization in the

---

[2] In some areas of Africa the mission churches and schools located in areas of dense rural settlement and formed the nucleus around which later settlements grew (see Johnson, 1967). Alternatively, missions and schools sometimes were located at markets (but not a village) and thus set in train the processes which added other services and activities.

[3] See Riddell, 1970.

TABLE 25.1   Modernization Variables and Component Loadings

Name	Description	Loading on First Principal Component[a]
DATESCHOOL	The date of establishment of the first primary school in the chiefdom	.72
DATEHEALTH	The date of opening of the first health facility	.36
DATEHOSPIT	The date of opening of a permanent hospital facility	.67
DATESECSCH	The date of opening of the chiefdom's first secondary school	.63
DATEPOST	Date of establishment of postal services	.51
DATEBANK	Date of opening of first bank	.68
DATETELEP	Date of establishment of telephone link	.71
DATETELEG	Date of establishment of telegraph link	.62
DATETRANS	Date at which chiefdom linked with the national transport network	.72
D.H.Q.	Dummy variable weighted by the number of years a district, provincial (x2) or Protectorate (x3) Head Quarters	−.83
DATEN.A.	Date of establishment of Native Administration form of chiefdom government	.69
EDUCAT	Percent attending school, 1963	−.73
LITER	Percent literate in English, 1963	−.88
URBGROW	Absolute increase in urban population from 1927 to 1963	−.80
URBPERCENT	Percent of chiefdom population residing in places over 2,000, 1963	−.73
TRADITION	Percent of labour force engaged in farming, fishing and hunting, 1963	.52
ROADDEN	Miles of road per square mile of chiefdom area, 1963	−.71
LGTOWN	Absolute size of largest urban place in chiefdom, 1963	−.79
MOBILITY	Percent of population residing in chiefdom, born elsewhere, 1963	.47
OUTMIG	Per capita rate of migration to Freetown, 1963	−.77
DATEELEC	Date of installation of electricity supply	.67
DATECOOP	Date of opening of first cooperative society	.30

[a]Eigenvalue = 10.00; percent of variance in original data set explained = 45.5

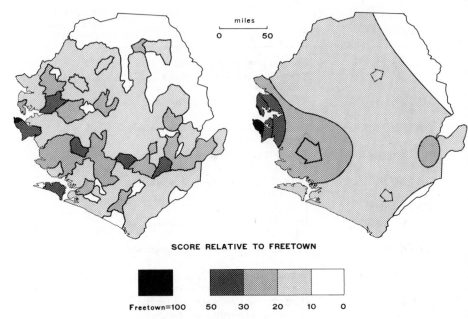

SCORE RELATIVE TO FREETOWN

Freetown=100   50   30   20   10   0

Figure 25.6   Modernization in Sierra Leone.
Source: Riddell, 1970.

provinces is not a smooth even surface, nor does it indicate a regular
decline in levels of modernization with distance away from Freetown. Rather, it depicts a generally low surface with local peaks
associated with the centers of the urban-administrative hierarchy, a
marked north-south differential, and a linear wedge of higher values
associated with the rail line. It is evident that this first, general
modernization component does reflect the fabric as defined by
spatial network and hierarchy in Sierra Leone.

  To filter the spatial regularity from the general pattern of
modernization, a trend surface analysis has been employed. The
sixth-order surface indicates a general progression of modernization
levels increasing inland from Freetown with a warping to incorporate
the effects of the wedge of development associated with the rail line
and to indicate the strong distance decay function from Freetown
inland. Thus it is evident that the process of modernization, as
summarized by the components analysis, is dominated and directed
by the network and the hierarchy, that define together the spatial
fabric of the country.

African nations are undergoing a complex process of change, but this change has a very regular spatial dimension. Once geographic space has been abstracted from the specifics of resource endowments, the pattern of change that can be observed is dominated by the three forces of proximity, network, and hierarchy. The diffusion of change is such that the patterns as they evolve through time are recursive, reflecting the spatial regularity and continuity of the process. As geographers, concerned with the spatial pattern of diffusion of modernization, we can add to the understanding of the interrelationships of its various subdimensions by indicating their interaction within the geographic framework, as well as by depicting the spatial impact of such change.

26

Modernization in Swaziland

GAVIN MAASDORP

Modernization, a term that was popularized by Lerner (1958), involves the transformation of traditional society. It is a multidimensional process requiring change on a wide front— economic, social, political, cultural and psychological—and as a consequence has been studied by many different disciplines. Although most approaches have focused upon a particular discipline, they appear to be characterized by attention to three common underlying processes—industrialization, urbanization, and rural change.

Economic development is accorded a high priority in the less developed countries, and a characteristic of modern economic growth is that it involves sweeping structural changes (Kuznets, 1966). These changes imply industrialization and urbanization, with the share of agriculture in aggregate output and employment declining and that of manufacturing and services increasing.

One approach to modernization stresses attitudinal and value changes as a prerequisite. This may be seen in the emphasis on "achievement" by McClelland (1961) and Hagen (1962), which had a forerunner in Schumpeter's (1934) entrepreneur. Another school stresses the removal of impediments to the productive processes as a precondition for the appearance of the appropriate attitudes and behavior (Weiner, 1966).

In fact, the elements of change are interrelated and interdependent and the precise relationship will vary from country to country. The elements of change are diffused through the population and through space by education, transportation, and communications media. An important feature of the process is that new ideas are communicated from outside sources (Lerner, 1958; Schultz, 1964: Salcedo, 1971).

Several important consequences stem from the fact that modernization in Africa has not been generated indigenously. Among these are the problems associated with rural-urban migration (Lerner, 1967), the educational bottleneck, the need to restructure spatial patterns (Soja, 1968), and political instability as new systems of government evolve.

Attempts have been made to produce a sequence of modernization (Lerner, 1958; Salcedo, 1971), while factor analysis has been used in quantitative approaches to a typology of development and modernization (Adelman and Morris, 1967; Soja, 1968; Riddell, 1970). However, the possibility of an element of spuriousness in such refined measures should not be ignored. Not only are the concepts themselves imprecise, but the variables are chosen arbitrarily, depending on the available data and the purpose of the study, and they are subject to conceptual and measurement problems. Although value judgments cannot be avoided (Seers, 1972) there is a danger of bias towards readily quantifiable factors.

Moreover, the concepts of development and modernization are themselves changing. Economists now tend to reject the emphasis on rising per capita income in favor of such welfare aspects as poverty, unemployment, and income inequality (Seers, 1972). Yet it is in precisely these spheres that data in developing countries are usually inadequate. Other disciplines have also shifted their focus; thus political scientists are tending to emphasize institutional order rather than democracy (O'Brien, 1972), and sociologists are concerned with ethnocentrism, which is most overt when modernization is regarded as synonomous with westernization (Bernstein, 1971). There is a recognition that development does not entail following the paths of the advanced countries, which no longer seem to provide really desirable models for the less developed countries (Seers, 1972).

SWAZILAND[1]

Swaziland achieved its independence in 1968. It is small both in area 17,365 sq. kilometers and *de facto* population (estimated as 494,000 in mid-1975).[2] There are four distinct ecological regions which run in north-south parallel belts (Figure 26.1). The climate is mainly subtropical and Swaziland possesses one of the best natural resource endowments in southern Africa, including areas of afforestation, irrigated agriculture, ranching land, and mineral deposits.

In the last census (1966) Africans comprised 97 percent of the *de jure* population; there were only 9,000 Europeans and 4,000 Eurafricans. There was a high degree of ethnic homogeneity, non-Swazi Africans numbering only 16,000. Only 14 percent of the population was urbanized.

In 1970/71 (the latest year for which data are available) Gross Domestic Product amounted to R72.8 million (or R168 per capita).[3] Agriculture and forestry accounted for 33 percent of GDP, manufacturing for 13 percent and mining for 11 percent. The economy is highly "open" and the respective shares of these sectors fluctuate from year to year depending upon world market prices for primary commodities.

Swaziland has a favorable balance of trade; for example, in 1973 domestic exports amounted to R72.8 million and imports to R68.2 million. The most important exports are sugar, iron ore, woodpulp, asbestos, citrus, wood and wood products, and meat and meat products. Britain, Japan, and South Africa together purchase about 75 percent of Swaziland's exports by value. In contrast, over 90 percent of imports either originate in South Africa or pass through South African commercial channels. Imports consist mainly of manufactured and processed goods.

Almost all development has been telescoped into the post-war period, especially from about 1960. Data constraints are particularly apparent, more refined statistics having been collected only since

[1] The author is indebted to Thoko Ginindza for her comments on a draft of this paper.

[2] Unless otherwise stated all statistics are quoted or calculated from official Swaziland publications. These are: *Annual Statistical Bulletin; National Accounts: Statistical News and Economic Indicators; 1966 Population Census: 1971/72 Sample Census of Agriculture; Annual Report of the Ministry of Agriculture; Educational Statistics; Employment and Wages Survey; Second National Development Plan 1973-77;* and *News from Swaziland.*

[3] In 1974, Swaziland introduced its own currency known as *emalangeni;* for foreign exchange transactions, however, it uses the South African rand. El = Rl and Rl = approx. US $1.40.

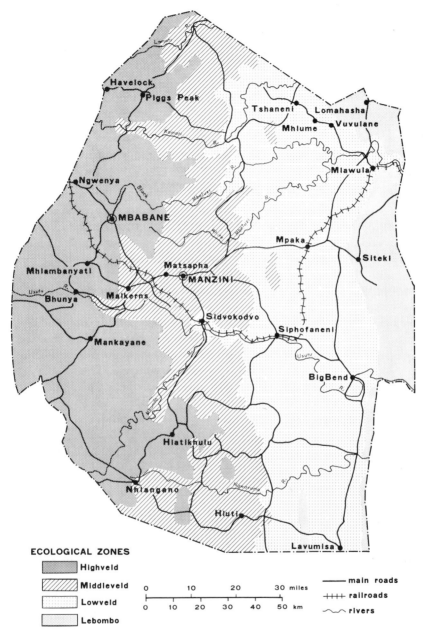

ECOLOGICAL ZONES

Highveld

Middleveld

Lowveld

Lebombo

0   10   20   30 miles

0 10 20 30 40 50 km

——— main roads

++++ railroads

〜〜 rivers

Figure 26.1 Swaziland.

1965. Many gaps still exist in the statistical system and although coverage and methodology are constantly being improved, comparisons over time are difficult. However, factor analysis has been applied to development in Swaziland mainly using 1966 Population Census results (Lea, 1972). Consequently, this chapter examines three factors regarded as particularly pertinent to the modernization process in Swaziland. These factors are:

1. the existence of dualism;
2. its position as a small developing country in a customs union with a larger more developed neighbor;
3. the persistence of a strongly traditionalist political structure.

By African standards, Swaziland's per capita income is relatively high; however, this masks the dualistic structure of the economy. Four types of dualism may be distinguished—sectoral dualism, spatial dualism, dualism of land tenure, and social dualism.

The well known phenomenon of sectoral dualism in an economy occurs when a modern sector exists side by side with a traditional sector based on subsistence agriculture. The roots of sectoral dualism in Swaziland are to be found in the economic history of the country. The traditional structure was that of a subsistence economy, but its foundations had been seriously undermined by the end of the nineteenth century. The Swazis were no longer self-sufficient. Land was lost to Europeans who also seized political control, and the introduction of a hut tax led to the flow of migrant labor to the gold mines of the Witwatersrand.

British administration was established in Swaziland in 1902 but many factors, both political and economic, militated against progress until 1945 when Britain made increased grants-in-aid available to the colonies (Fair, Murdoch and Jones, 1969). During the period 1945-1955 investment in Swaziland was directed mainly to modern sector agriculture, forestry, and mining (Leistner, and Smit, 1969). The following ten years saw almost four-fifths of public investment devoted to the physical infrastructure (particularly roads, the railway, and electricity). But the majority of Swazis had not been affected by economic development and therefore greater emphasis was placed on Swazi agriculture and education during the immediate preindependence period 1966-1968 (Fair, Murdoch and Jones, 1969).

Economic development has been confined largely to the modern sector, the traditional sector contributing only 14-15 percent by value of GDP during good agricultural years. It is important, therefore, to examine the role of the Swazi people in the money economy. Approximately 93 percent of those in wage employment (in both the public and private sectors) in 1972 were Swazi nationals. This proportion has increased appreciably since independence because of the "localization" of jobs. Altogether, some 59,000 Swazis are engaged in modern sector employment; in contrast, an estimated 149,000 (or 70 percent of "economically active" Swazis) are found in traditional agriculture.

Few Swazi farmers are engaged in commercial agriculture. The major projects to date which have aimed at bringing Swazi farmers into the money economy and in which fundamental innovations have been introduced, are two settlement schemes. A Pineapple Scheme comprising 26 farms was established in the Malkerns valley in 1965 and now produces one-third of total deliveries to the fruit cannery. The second scheme is that of Vuvulane Irrigated Farms (VIF), established by the Commonwealth Development Corporation near Mhlume in 1962. Ten years later 202 farmers had been settled on holdings mainly of 3-7 hectares in size. VIF produces 3 percent of Swaziland's sugar output (yields are as high as those in the estate sector) as well as seed cotton, maize, and vegetables. The scheme has proved so successful that a further 220 4 hectare plots are being prepared.

Outside of these schemes, cash incomes to Swazi farmers (whose holdings seldom exceed 2 hectares in size) accrue mainly from the cultivation of cotton and tobacco. The proportion of the cotton crop grown by Swazis has increased and they now account for one-fifth of total output. The number of small-scale Swazi tobacco growers—many of them women—has increased rapidly in recent years and they produce some 70 percent of the (admittedly small) total crop. Maize and beans are grown largely for subsistence but small quantities are sometimes traded locally.

In 1972 Swazis owned 83 percent of all cattle in the country. But the stock are of poor quality and because of their important social role, the numbers slaughtered is small as is their contribution to household income.

The migrant labor system provides an additional outlay for participation in a modern economy. In 1973, an estimated 10,000 Swazis were employed in South Africa.

The familiar center-periphery model refined by Friedmann (1966) is manifested in the Swaziland space economy by the presence of four cores of development in juxtaposition to an underdeveloped periphery. Fair *et al.* (1969) identified a primate core centered around the Mbabane-Manzini-Bhunya-Ngwenya area and three subsidiary cores focused on the Piggs Peak-Havelock, Mhlume-Tshaneni, and Big Bend areas respectively (Figure 26.2).

There is a wide economic disparity between the cores and the periphery. The core areas cover only 15 percent of the area of the country but account for some 90 percent of the total output of primary and secondary commodities, and 80 percent of wage employment. At the 1966 census they contained 9 of the 15 main towns and villages, 85 percent of the urban population, and 76 percent of the European population, but only 22 percent of the African population.

The primate core is the most diversified area in Swaziland. It contains the two largest towns, the main government, commercial and social services, and major industrial, mining, forestry and agricultural enterprises. The subsidiary cores are more specialized. They are based on asbestos mining, forestry, and citrus in the Piggs Peak-Havelock area, and sugar and citrus in both the Mhlume-Tshaneni and Big Bend areas.

The periphery tends to be less well endowed than the cores in terms of natural resources, although the soil and water resources of much of the area are good. Subsistence farming is the dominant economic activity in the periphery which contains 76 percent of the total population.

Functional linkages between the core areas and the periphery and among the core areas themselves are weak. The core areas are strongly oriented to centers in South Africa and Mozambique, whereas the periphery tends to be isolated from the mainstream of economic development. This occurs despite the existence of a relatively good road network. Functional linkages between the primate core and the rest of the country are perhaps strongest in the field of passenger traffic; this is largely a reflection of migration patterns, in that the primate core is the major employment center and attracts manpower from the rest of the country, especially the south.

Urbanization in Swaziland is a recent phenomenon. In 1945, there were only seven small villages, and even today only two centers—Mbabane and Manzini—have populations exceeding 10,000. Several "company towns" have developed since the war, but their growth is limited by their specialized functions (Whittington, 1970). Because of their lack of administrative and other facilities (Lea, 1972), they occupy a low position in the urban hierarchy in relation to their size.

Therefore the spatial integration of the economy is weak and economic development tends to be a localized phenomenon. The

○⊙   CITIES

•   TOWNS

⌒   CORE AREA

▨   SWAZI NATION LAND

▨   RURAL DEVELOPMENT AREA

| 0 | 10 | 20 | 30 miles |

| 0 | 10 | 20 | 30 | 40 | 50 km |

Figure 26.2 Modernization of Swaziland.

three main generators of internal links are (1) the supply of
government, professional, and other services and some commodities
from the primate core to the rest of the country; (2) the supply of

food and raw materials from areas of production to the primate core; and (3) the supply of labor from the periphery (Fair, Murdoch and Jones, 1969).

Land ownership has been an important issue in Swaziland ever since the granting of concessions to foreigners in the late nineteenth century following upon the discovery of gold. These concessions covered grazing, mining, trading, and other rights. In 1907, one-third of all land held by concessionaires was ceded to the Swazi nation (Swazi Nation Land). However, the Swazis have subsequently repurchased substantial areas and Swazi Nation Land now comprises approximately 56 percent of the total area. The remainder consists almost entirely of Title Deed Land which is owned either on a freehold or leasehold basis by individuals. Communal tenure prevails on Swazi Nation Land which contains 84 percent of the total population; nine-tenths of its area falls in the periphery (Figure 26.2).

Social dualism is manifested in the presence of a small European community which held administrative as well as economic power until independence in 1968. Since then political power has passed to the Swazis but the European community still dominates the economy.

The period of rapid economic development in the 1960s and the achievement of independence saw the emergence of a new Swazi 'elite,' mainly in the urban areas. The members of this group are those better-educated and better-trained Swazis who have secured good-paying jobs both in the public and private sectors as a result of the policy of localization.

There is a great discrepancy in incomes between the European and new elite group on the one hand, and the mass of the people on the other hand. In the public sector, for example, average annual earnings in 1971 for unskilled and semiskilled males were R324 and R744 respectively, compared with R4,500 for those in administrative and technical positions. The character of social dualism has changed in the last decade and today it is based on educational and occupational rather than on color lines.

There is a close spatial interrelationship among the four types of dualism. The modern sector of the economy is for the main part coincident with the four core areas. Almost all the major enterprises in Swaziland are found in these areas which, in turn, are coincident with Title Deed Land. The majority of Europeans and Eurafricans, together with the new Swazi elite, are found in the core areas. In contrast, the traditional sector of the economy shows a strong correlation with the periphery and with Swazi Nation Land. Lea (1972) found that Swazi Nation Land had the lowest factor scores on his modernization dimension.

During the last few years employment creation has emerged as one of the greatest problems facing developing countries. The Second National Development Plan (1973-1977) estimated that Swaziland needed to create 4,700 jobs each year to absorb new work-seekers, but felt that 2,500 would be the maximum possible. However, wage employment has increased more rapidly than envisaged in the plan, and neither open urban unemployment nor rural underemployment appear as serious as in some developing countries. That the government is aware of the social and political implications of unemployment may be illustrated by its approach to education and employment creation.

It is important that education in developing countries be related to the type of employment available. In Swaziland, 60 percent of those aged 10-19 years are at school but the quality of education is frequently low and the high dropout rate merely swells the ranks of the illiterate (which include 70 percent of the adult population). More importantly, however, there is a maladjustment between the academic orientation of the educational curricula and the job market. The requirements are for persons with training in mathematics, science, and agricultural, commercial, and vocational subjects. Therefore, policy is to restructure the educational system—school as well as post-school—along these lines. In addition, the importance of non-formal training is being stressed; this is often cheaper and more efficient than formal training and can be spread more widely, especially in rural areas.

The government is approaching the problem of employment mainly through schemes to improve Swazi agriculture and promote both large-scale industry and small enterprises. In this way it is hoped to extend the modern sector of the economy into the peripheral areas, thereby shrinking spatial dualism and redressing to some extent the urban-rural imbalances in income.

Swaziland is essentially an agricultural country and national development strategy emphasizes the improvement of agriculture in Swazi Nation areas where only 5 percent of the holdings produce mainly for the market. Agricultural exports emanate almost entirely from Title Deed Land, the relative contribution of Swazi Nation Land having declined since 1960.

Thus far, the settlement schemes mentioned above have been the major attempts to bring Swazi farmers into the money economy, but a two-pronged policy aimed at the modernization of traditional agriculture now has been adopted. This policy is based on Rural Development Areas (RDAs) and river basin schemes. The RDA program was adopted in 1965 and to date nine RDAs with a combined population of about 100,000 have been demarcated (Figure 26.2). Improvement in these areas is to be achieved by the reorganization of existing arable, grazing, and residential areas and by infrastructural development.

The river basin schemes perhaps hold out the greatest hope for the development of a modern Swazi agricultural sector. Possibilities for the development of large-scale irrigated agriculture exist in both the Mbeluzi and Usutu basins. Feasibility studies reveal that substantial areas could be irrigated, particularly in the Mbeluzi Basin where some 8,000 hectares of Swazi Nation Land could be used. These projects would involve the resettlement of Swazi smallholders and the development of new villages, while existing nodes such as Big Bend and Tshaneni would assume more important service functions.

These schemes are clearly of great importance in the eradication of dualism in Swaziland. Both areas adjoin subsidiary cores, and if the coal deposits in the Lowveld are exploited and industries processing the output of the schemes are established, the Big Bend and Mhlume cores could be fused into one. This would be a significant step in the elimination of spatial dualism in the Lowveld.

Small-scale industries and handicrafts can play an important role in job creation in developing countries (Hoselitz, 1968; ILO, 1970). They require, however, the provision of working capital and marketing arrangements. In Swaziland the government has established specialist organizations to promote small enterprises—small industries through the establishment of industrial estates in urban centers and the provision of technical and commercial training, and handicrafts through the provision of marketing and collection facilities.

In the existing modern sector and core areas the emphasis of government economic policy is on industrial development. The National Industrial Development Corporation of Swaziland (NIDCS), a statutory body formed in 1971, is charged with the promotion of industrial development, and it has been instrumental in attracting a number of new industries. The majority of these industries are being concentrated in the primate core, mainly at the existing Matsapha industrial estate. This conforms with the view expressed by many economists that in countries with small populations and areas it is unjustified to talk about diseconomies of scale and to squander scarce resources at several scattered growth points (Alonso, 1968).

Rather, regional policy should be concentrated in the first instance on developing economies of scale at one or two centers; once these have been achieved new growth points can be sought.

The exception to this policy of industrial concentration concerns material-oriented industries. In Swaziland the further development of industries processing forest products, byproducts of the sugar industry, fruit and vegetables, etc. would lead to the growth of the subsidiary cores.

An incipient fifth core may be identified in southern Swaziland where a large-scale afforestation program has been implemented. Nhlangano, which has recently attracted a large textile mill, will be the center of sawmilling and related activities. Therefore, it should expand as a service center, while the development of the southern RDA, the establishment of small-industry estates, and the recent extension of electricity transmission lines to southern Swaziland should further stimulate the development of this backward region.

Thus prospects for the gradual elimination of dualism appear to be good—sectoral dualism by the modernization of Swazi agriculture and the development of small enterprises, spatial dualism by the outward extension of existing core areas and the emergence of new cores, and social dualism by improved education and the further localization of posts in the public and private sectors. Dualism in land tenure will gradually be diminished by the land repurchase program.

As a consequence of their size, small countries face several developmental problems which are not usually encountered by large countries (Robinson, 1963; Demas, 1965; Benedict, 1967). The main problems are, first, their heavy reliance on foreign trade and especially on the export of a small range of goods, and second, the difficulty in industrializing because of obstacles in the way of achieving economies of scale. These problems, however, may be overcome by economic integration in the form of customs unions or common markets. But economic integration is usually proposed with neighboring less developed states and it is unusual for small developing countries to find themselves, as do Botswana, Lesotho and Swaziland (BLS), in a customs union with a developed neighbor (South Africa).

Problems arise in customs unions when member countries are at different levels of development. The major problem is that integration may, in fact, do nothing to lessen the polarization between the richer and poorer partners unless positive policy instruments are used to promote development in the less developed countries. Polarization arises from the generation of external economies in growth poles in one country of a union. It is particularly likely to occur where one member country has started its industrial development earlier than the others. In such circumstances, the advantages of integration will tend to accrue to the more highly developed partners, thereby generating a vicious circle with the rich countries attracting resources from the poor and becoming richer (Braun, 1971).

The four countries have been joined in a customs union since 1910. Although the new agreement of 1969 recognizes the problems arising from the polarization of development, it still contains defects so far as the small countries are concerned (Landell-Mills, 1971; Selwyn, 1972). In particular, it "cannot be regarded as adequately tackling the regional differences within the southern Africa geographical unit" (Landell-Mills, 1971:281).

What, then, are the nature and significance of these regional problems? The BLS countries cannot be examined in isolation; rather, they have to be viewed as part of the southern African space economy (Selwyn, 1972). From a spatial point of view, Swaziland is part of a prosperous development core, falling into two of the most advanced development regions of southern Africa. Therefore it has "prima facie advantages for growth over most African countries" (Fair, Murdoch and Jones, 1969:42). Swaziland adjoins what has been defined as the "principal region," i.e., the national core, of South Africa (Board, Davies and Fair, 1970), and this has important implications. From the higher surface economic area of the Witwatersrand a belt of upper surface stretches eastwards to the Swaziland border. This belt is part of the "inner peripheral economic space". The primate core of Swaziland is clearly an extension of the inner peripheral economic space belt. But a glance at the nodal service hierarchy shows that Swaziland lies beyond the influence of the major urban centers; the largest South African towns near the border are all "country towns" (Board, Davies and Fair, 1970).

Thus, although Swaziland is well situated vis-a-vis the major development core of South Africa, it is peripheral to the main urban centers and to the transport network between the Witwatersrand and the coast. Levels of economic activity and spatial integration decline with distance from the main nodes and belts of inner peripheral economic space. Thus it is argued that economic development would be facilitated if Swaziland were brought more effectively within the sphere of South Africa's major urban centers and growth zones (Fair, Murdoch and Jones, 1969).

However, there are several obstacles towards greater spatial integration within the customs union. Selwyn (1972) believes that the BLS countries present an extreme case of polarization in view of their weakness vis-a-vis South Africa and adduces several reasons which make it difficult for them to attract industry. In the case of Swaziland these reasons include high transportation costs, higher wage costs, the absence of agglomeration economies, the openness of its market to South African products, and its dependence on foreign capital, enterprise and management. Industrialists interested in supplying the customs union market tend to be South African-based and regard African countries as areas of high risk. Moreover, the BLS countries have to offer incentives to industrialists comparable to those offered by South Africa in its African "homelands" ("Bantustans"), some of which are closer to major markets than is Swaziland. The "homelands" are the linchpin of the policy of "separate development" ("apartheid"); because of its political and social characteristics, this policy impedes closer cooperation within the customs union.

In addition to the four types of dualism identified earlier, political dualism also existed in Swaziland. This was manifested by the coexistence of the parliamentary and traditional systems of government. Upon independence, Swaziland became a constitutional monarchy with a Westminster-type constitution. However, the Swazis are strongly traditionalists and much of the traditional power structure was retained. The Swazi National Council, a traditional body that advises the King (Ngwenyama) on all matters regulated by Swazi law and custom and connected with Swazi traditions and culture (e.g., Swazi Nation Land, mineral exploitation, etc.), continued to function. Parliamentarians were in fact also members of the Swazi National Council. Thus there was a degree of overlapping of personnel between the parliamentary and the traditional systems, the latter having adapted its institutions to the changed political situation brought about by independence. However, in 1973, the Ngwenyama suspended the constitution and appointed a Commission (reporting to him in 1975) to frame a new constitution paying special heed to Swazi customs and traditions.

The field of labor relations provides a good example of an attempt to introduce a local modification of a modern institution. Trade unions are regarded as foreign; instead a King's representative ("Ndabazabantu") is appointed at each large enterprise to liaise among management, worker, and government. (The government is a substantial stockholder in some of the major companies).

Three phases may be distinguished within the Swazi population: modern, traditional and transitional. The majority are still traditional—rural and conservative. Those in the transitional phase are the poorly educated, unskilled workers, akin perhaps to Lerner's (1958) "displaced persons." It is this group that is probably most affected by the social and other consequences of modernization. In Swaziland, for example, rural-urban migration leads to changing family structures, with changing age and sex structures in the periphery which affect agricultural productivity. Other social changes are reflected in the conflict between customary and Christian forms of marriage and in the growing substitution of cash instead of cattle as payment for *lobolo* (bride-price). Urbanization involves the appearance of socially undesirable activities (e.g., crime, gambling, prostitution), which are ignored in attempts to quantify modernization. Such attempts also ignore the urban informal sector; this sector is excluded from official statistics but could be an important source of productive employment especially in large cities. This is, however, unlikely to happen in Swaziland.

The study of the modernization process in Swaziland illustrates the importance of differing social science perspectives. The elimination of dualism implies an emphasis on the welfare aspects of economic development, the critical factor being to increase the proportion of Swazis active in the money economy. The political system illustrates how a traditional form of government is attempting to adapt to a changed situation. The disruptive effects of social change also have to be considered. The qualitative aspects of modernization—whether or not the techniques adopted in industry, agriculture, building, education and other fields are appropriate to the real needs of the country—are at least as important as the quantitative aspects in the assessment of the process.

27

Tanzania 1920-63 :
The Spatial Impress
of the Modernization Process[1]

PETER R. GOULD

It is difficult to see how we can write good theory illuminating the *process* of modernization before we have good descriptions of the basic spatial patterns that ultimately must be linked together through time. No social scientist, no matter what disciplinary viewpoint he assumes, will feel that his work is being disparaged when I say that our knowledge of such sequential patterns in Africa is slight, while our understanding of process is virtually nonexistent. Thus, from the spatially biased viewpoint of a geographer, I seek a sequence of measured descriptions characterizing the structure of an impressed, modernizing system at five points in time over the space called Tanzania. Such a descriptive sequence constitutes the first step on the road to modeling the *process* of change in Africa.

DEVELOPMENT TO 1919

After a series of diplomatic and military maneuvers typical of the late nineteenth century in Africa, blue lines were drawn across

[1] This chapter is reprinted, with modification, from P. R. Gould, "Tanzania 1920-63: The Spatial Impress of the Modernization Process," *World Politics* XXII, no. 2 (Princeton University Press, 1970), 149-70. Reprinted by permission of Princeton University Press.

poorly surveyed maps in the chancelleries of Europe to delimit the area now known as Tanzania. Such cursory delimitation brought an area of 890,000 square kilometers, nearly 1600 kilometers across its greatest diameter, under the control of a single colonial regime. Only seventy years later, in 1961, the independent nation of Tanzania was born from colonial and mandate rule.

The early years of such control are difficult to trace with a high degree of spatial resolution. From the turn of the century, German rule was a contradiction of enlightened economic and educational development in a few areas, with barbaric, punitive expeditions in others that slaughtered tens of thousands and laid waste whole countrysides. Political control demanded a system of communications, for it took up to sixty-five days to travel from Dar es Salaam to the farthest outposts of administration. Further pressure for roads and railways came from European plantation owners who had settled in the first years of the twentieth century around Tanga and Moshi. The latter were linked by rail in 1911, while the Central Line from Dar es Salaam to Kigoma was opened in 1914. However, it was not to serve German ambitions: from 1914 to 1918, development was not only stopped but reversed. Rail lines, roads, and telegraph wires, all the space-linking innovations built in the previous two decades, were sabotaged in the guerrilla campaign of von Lettow-Vorbeck, so that upon the assumption of British rule in 1919, administrative patterns and linkages had to be completely reestablished. For the most part, such renovations followed and consolidated those set up by the earlier German administration. Thus the pattern of the early twenties forms the starting point for this analysis and the first of five time-slices in which the structure of modernization is examined in its spatial content.[2]

THE EARLY TWENTIES:
CONSOLIDATION AND REPAIR

For the base period of the early nineteen-twenties, seven variables are available to index the spatial variation in the intensity of the

[2] For each time period, data were assigned to a hexagonal network of 289 cells covering the country so that the geographer's basic requirement of spatial assignability imposes an immediate limitation. We can no longer be content with regional, provincial, or other high levels of spatial aggregation in which single, and normally useless, values are reported for areas varying up to tens of thousands of square miles. Rather, our scale of observation is such that information becomes usable only when it can be assigned plausibly to equal cells. Because of the limitation imposed by the basic units of observation, and because methods of statistical reporting and degrees of aggregation change over time, comparability of all the measures from one time period to another is impossible to achieve.

modernization process (Table 27.1). The number of road-miles "fit for light-wheeled vehicles" per hexagonal cell (1) contained in this time period, as in all others, the greatest error. Road qualities are seldom precisely defined or recorded, and where dirt roads are concerned it is obvious that conditions vary markedly from season to season. I have used considerable subjective judgment in the definition of such roads, and we must be somewhat cautious where this variable enters the analysis. The Railway (4) is simply scaled as an attribute, since the network, or tree, remains rudimentary in form and the sheer presence or absence in a cell is all we require to measure. The number of Administrative Officers (2) indicates the locational intensity of the overall administrative impress. Ideally we could refine such figures by recording the number and routes of safaris by District Officers, but such data are available only in the old district diaries—many of which appear to have been lost or stolen. European Agricultural Officers and African agricultural instructors (22) index the availability of new agricultural practices and the possibility of agricultural innovation, while the number of Police (3) indicates the intensity of the ultimate power to enforce political decisions and control. Finally, the number of Hospital Beds (5) and the number of African Sanitary Staff (23) measure the availability of modern medicine and hygiene. Principal component analysis can be used to suggest interrelationships among these variables in geographic space.

A major component, accounting for nearly sixty percent of the variation, may be interpreted as a scale measuring the major aspect of the modernization process (Table 27.1). Note, however, the way in which both of the transport and communications variables document a second dimension at this time. Because their space-bridging, as opposed to space-organizing, functions were so critical, both road and rail appear only weakly related to the other measures, forming a distinct, though less important dimension to the modernization process.

If we calculate scores on the major scale of modernization for each cell and plot them cartographically, we can construct a modernization surface for the early twenties over Tanzania on which heights are always relative to the greatest value of 1,000 at Dar es Salaam (Figure 27.1). The phrases "Islands of Development" and "Islands of Modernization" are frequently used in the African context, but such verbal images are sharply emphasized by such a map. Only a little over a third of the country was touched, let alone impressed, by the process, and even this is an overgenerous estimate, for only the presence of roads serving as bridges between small nodes allows a large number of cells to be scored. Indeed, it is difficult to speak of a single surface at all; we have rather fragmented

TABLE 27.1 Modernization Variables and Principal Component Loadings[a]

| | Component loadings | | | | | | | | | |
| | Early Twenties | | Late Twenties-Early Thirties | | Late Thirties | | Late Forties-Early Fifties | | Late Fifties-Early Sixties | |
Variables	I	II	I	II	I	II	I	II	I	II
1. Total Road Miles	47	-69	54	24	56	45	83	26	78	40
2. Administrative Officers	91	06	88	-09	95	-16	73	-54	68	-69
3. Police	85	02	88	-32	93	-01	91	-35	88	-47
4. Railway	29	75	41	-11	44	32	46	14	42	22
5. Hospital Beds	92	07	75	-21			96	-18	95	-02
6. Piped Water			80	10			71	50	61	44
7. Telegraph			69	-29	76	30	75	40	68	43
8. Telephone			74	35	65	43	76	44		
9. Post Offices									85	18
10. Criminal Convictions			88	-10	88	14			94	-22
11. Electricity			62	-33			77	18	72	26
12. Other Government Officers					85	-46	80	-53	90	-38
13. High Court Circuits							86	-35	85	-25
14. Banks			83	-43	93	-01	88	-25		
15. African P.O. Savings			82	07	18	64				
16. Unskilled Wages			88	29			69	26	84	21
17. Tribal Dispensaries										
18. Total Economic Functions			20	48	83	-48			85	-51
19. Govt. Medical Personnel							80	-56	81	-56
20. Airfield Quality							80	39	71	43
21. Police Radio							65	11	87	-05
22. Agricultural Officers	72	-30								

TABLE 27.1 Modernization Variables and Principal Component Loadings[a] (cont.)

| | Component loadings | | | | | | | | | |
| Variables | Early Twenties | | Late Twenties-Early Thirties | | Late Thirties | | Late Forties-Early Fifties | | Late Fifties-Early Sixties | |
	I	II	I	II	I	II	I	II	I	II
23. Sanitary Staff	72	20								
24. Govt. Hospitals			74	46						
25. Designated Township			74	40						
26. Haulage License Applications									85	08
27. Commercial Estates			71	−16						
28. Development Loans									68	45
29. Criminal Cases					95	−19				
30. Doctors							85	−37		
31. Quality Stores							86	38		
32. Churches							78	38		
33. Cinemas							82	03		
34. Prison Population							78	−03		
35. Mission Hospitals									28	26
36. Teacher Training									62	31
37. Secondary Schools									65	18
38. Middle Schools									63	48
39. Bituminized Roads									73	00
40. Telephone Subscribers									80	−58
41. Asian Population									85	21
Eigenvalues	4.02	1.18	9.17	1.47	7.28	1.50	13.15	2.61	15.14	3.46
Percent Total Variation	57.4	16.9	53.9	8.6	60.7	12.5	62.6	12.4	58.2	13.3
Number of Variables Available	7		17		12		21		26	

[a]Calculated by the author. Loadings are shown for those variables for a given time period. Component loadings have been multiplied by 100.

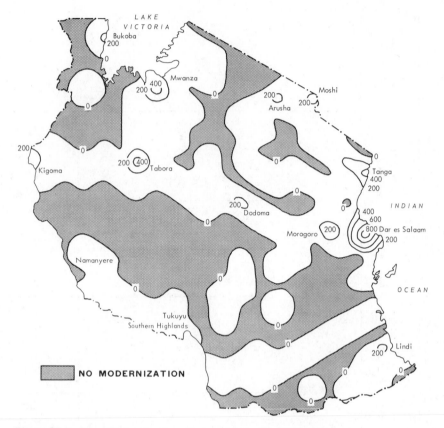

Figure 27.1   The Modernization Surface in the Early Twenties.

and disconnected pieces that appear to float in the still mill-pond of traditionalism (shaded pattern). The Central Railway forms a distinct axis on the map, with small nodes at Morogoro, Dodoma, and Kigoma. The Southern Highlands, remote and virtually inaccessible by modern transport at this time, have yet to show a distinct peak, although small detachments of police and rudimentary hospital facilities could be found at the administrative outposts.

THE LATE TWENTIES AND EARLY THIRTIES:
FIRST THRUST FROM THE CONSOLIDATING YEARS

The appointment of Cameron as Governor in 1925 brought a fresh point of view, new energy, and an air of optimism to the task of development. With its emphasis on communications and indirect rule, with commercial agriculture expanding rapidly to form a financial base, his era was marked by a surge of activity unequalled until the late forties. Such a thrust is reflected by the changes in the modernization surface (Figure 27.2), constructed from weighted combinations of seventeen variables (Table 27.1). The overall orientation of the vectors is still marked, with the first component accounting for fifty-four percent of the variation. Once again, only the transport variables Road Miles (1) and Railway (4), together with Tribal Dispensaries (17), load low, but both have increased over the first period. The increases are slight, and our interpretation must be cautious in view of the error component in the Road Miles, but there is some slight evidence that the other measures of modernization are becoming more strongly related to these fundamental space-linking and space-organizing variables. In addition to educational facilities (not included because their spatial location could not be accurately determined), roads and dispensaries were the first aspects of the modernization process to appear with any permanence in rural areas.

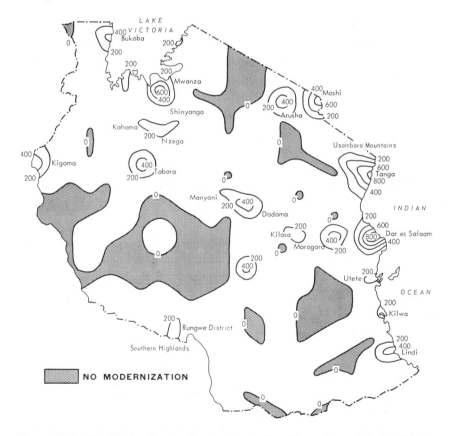

Figure 27.2   The Modernization Surface in the Late Twenties and Early Thirties.

Unlike the case in the earlier period, the transport and communication measures no longer define a distinct and separate dimension, but combine with other variables to index a possible second component to the modernization process. Such an interpretation must be severely qualified, for the evidence that the second component forms another independent scale is slight. The disparity between the first and second eigenvalues is large, and there is a clear break in the sequence of these measures describing variance absorbing capacity. Nevertheless, I shall interpret the second component as a weakly emerging scale contrasting measures such as Hospitals (24), Tribal Dispensaries (17), official Township Designation (25), and Post Offices (9) that are found in rural areas and smaller central places with Banks (14) and Electricity (11) that are exclusively attributes of a still rudimentary urban system.

The change in the modernization surface (Figure 27.2) is striking; sixty-five percent of the cells enter the analysis, and the large areas formerly untouched by the surface have been squeezed into smaller pockets. Despite such gaps, we can truly speak of a surface now, rather than of a series of fragmented pieces of the earlier period. Road-building activity has not only linked the bits together, but has also thickened the networks focusing upon the major urban nodes. The latter, however, still define distinct peaks, the greatest being at Dar es Salaam. Urban peaks have extremely steep gradients, implying that once the city is left, the decline in modernization is rapid. Little appears to have "trickled down" from administrative centers to the surrounding hinterlands.

As a whole, and relative to Dar es Salaam at this time, the modernization surface conveys an impression of considerable change from the early twenties. Though discernible earlier, most of the urban growth poles appear far more prominent as many aspects of the modernization process converge to these towns that provide the foci for small nodal or functional regions round about them. Note once again, however, that gradients are extremely steep in all directions.

THE LATE THIRTIES:
RECOVERY FROM DEPRESSION

Triggered by circumstances thousands of miles away and beyond the control of Tanzania, the Depression of the early thirties forced cuts in virtually every aspect of the development and modernization process. By the middle of the decade it became more a matter of keeping what had already been established, rather than of extending the surge of the previous ten years. However, by the end of the decade, and despite political uncertainties, most financial indices—exports, budgetary allocations, etc.—were back to previous pre-depression levels.

Only twelve measures are available for this period (Table 27.1), but an even stronger overall thrust is apparent with sixty-one percent of the variation being accounted for by the first component. The road and rail variables maintain their loadings, although these should still be interpreted cautiously, for their contribution to the major dimension becomes somewhat more complex. Road Miles (1) and Railway (4) also contribute to the second scale, together with Tribal Dispensaries (17) and Post Offices (9). As these are in contrast to Total Economic Functions (18) and Other Government Officers (12), we have further evidence for the appearance of a second relevant dimension in which essentially rural attributes are contrasted to those found mainly in the urban areas. Thus Road Miles (1) now contribute both to a major dimension of modernization and to a weak but emerging minor scale contrasting urban-rural aspects. They do this by virture of their space-organizing role, focusing the immediate hinterland areas upon the urban nodes, as well as their space-bridging or linking role that locates them in essentially rural areas still untouched by many other aspects of the modernization process.

When interpreting the modernization surface constructed from the scores on the first component (Figure 27.3), we must remember that it has been normalized with respect to the highest peak—Dar es Salaam. Thus comparisons to previous surfaces must be made with care, for a sudden, jolting surge in the capital can lower the other areas when they are scaled in relation to it. The contrasts are vivid, nevertheless, and indicate that in these relative terms the primacy of the capital increased substantially. Tanga, still second, cannot reach halfway to Dar es Salaam's peak, although it had a score eight-tenths as great ten years before. The process of "space-pinching" has proceeded, though at a far slower pace than in the twenties. Nearly seventy percent of the 289 cells enter the analysis, and the remaining blank pockets are practically devoid of population.

LATE FORTIES-EARLY FIFTIES:
THE POSTWAR SURGE

In the same way that the depression of the thirties thwarted the growth of the twenties, so the Second World War cut short the period of slow

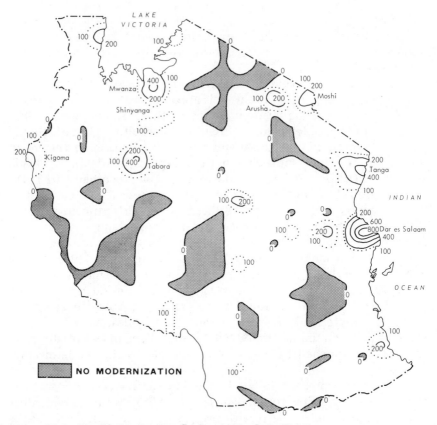

Figure 27.3 The Modernization Surface in the Late Thirties.

but steady recovery. After the war, however, the assumptions and attitudes of many trusteeship administrators differed considerably from those of their prewar colleagues. Many of the more sensitive felt the Winds of Change in the first postwar years, and planning horizons to the day of independence, while still seen dimly, shortened considerably from the vague estimates of a decade before. Furthermore, the attitudes of a small but growing group of Tanzanians began to alter, so that by the late forties and early fifties the pace of development began to be accelerated by views and values that had hardly constituted a force before.

Twenty-one measures of the modernization process are available (Table 27.1), with the first two major components accounting for 63 percent and 12 percent of the variation—figures virtually identical to those of the late thirties. One striking difference should be noted, however: whereas the road variable (1) contributed to both components in the immediate prewar years, it now loads strongly on the first, contributing at this time only to the major dimension of modernization. With their space-linking task completed by the war, the roads now take on much more strongly a space-organizing and space-draining function. Thus feeder densities thicken in the areas of expanded economic development—areas that focus, in turn, upon the modernization peaks and growth poles that assume to an ever greater extent the role of regional foci.

Nearly all the variables load highly and contribute to the major scale, indicating that modernization continues to be a strongly integrative process in which virtually all measures go hand in hand. No matter which aspect we choose—administrative, medical, judicial, economic, or communicative—all are reflected in the overall surge. Only the railway variable (4) loads weakly, defining a specific dimension almost by itself later in the sequential component analysis. Though a vital form of transportation upon which most of the export flow depends for its journey to the ports, the railway appears in areas of intense growth but must also traverse others almost bereft of modern attributes. Thus its overall relationship to other measures remains weak. Unlike the roads, with their cheap and flexible space-searching ability, the railway demands huge capital lumps, so that it is spatially inflexible and quite unresponsive to many forms of local transport demand that reflect modern developments in a regional as opposed to national, context.

Despite a lack of the "obvious" rural measures playing the same sort of key or indexing role as tribal dispensaries did in the late thirties, the second dimension may nevertheless be cautiously interpreted as a later manifestation of the rural-urban dimension that started to emerge in the earlier period. Most government functions (administrative, medical, and judicial) are concentrated in the towns, while the variables indexing and serving the private sector are not confined to the urban centers.

The modernization surface (Figure 27.4) reflects the remarkable changes that had come about during the first postwar period. While roughly the same number of cells enter the analysis, small changes appear in the shape of the empty areas as little-used road-links are abandoned and others added.

While strict and absolute comparisons are difficult, the general pattern resembles that of the late twenties-early thirties, providing some indication of the general stability and logical development of spatial forms inherent in the modernization process. Nevertheless, to use a photographic analogy, the latent image of modernization is far more developed by the late forties-early fifties. Particularly striking

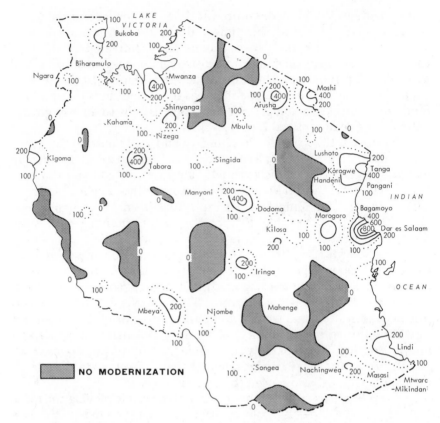

Figure 27.4   The Modernization Surface in the Late Forties and Early Fifties.

are the changes in the south as the ill-fated Groundnut Scheme sends
a jolt of development through the area. Dar es Salaam dominates the
country as usual, but the steep gradients from the peak indicate the
extremely local effect of the capital city upon its immediate
hinterland.

LATE FIFTIES-EARLY SIXTIES:
THE INDEPENDENCE YEARS

In the final time-slice of the analysis around the years of independence, 26 measures are available. In addition to a number of variables
used previously, there are also some indexing educational facilities
from the repetitive sequence of static patterns through time, is that
whenever we consider modernization we examine to a very high
(33, 36, and 37) and the economic service functions performed by

the towns (18). I have deliberately included Asian Population (41), for we have strong evidence that this population-group was a potent surrogate measure of local trade in East Africa at this time (Soja, 1968). Once again, the familiar spatial and structural patterns emerge, with all measures loading highly on the first component with the exception of the Railway (4) and Mission Hospitals (35). What is of particular interest, however, is the continuing strength of the second scale, which accounts for approximately thirteen percent of the variance. Thus the basic structure of the modernization process appears to be a major scale of considerable stability through time, to which virtually all indices contribute highly, together with a second, urban-rural scale that becomes more significant as time proceeds. Upon the latter, all government (2, 3, 12, and 19), economic (18), and local communication (40) measures are contrasted against the variables indexing modern aspects of developing rural areas such as Development Loans (28), Piped Water (6), Middle Schools (38), and the less intense communications facilities, such as Telegraph (7), Roads (1), and Airfields with good landing facilities (20), which increasingly supplement the poorer surface forms of transportation. Interestingly, the Asian Population variable (41), having made a substantial contribution to the first component, shows by its sign that it is on the side of the modernizing rural indices, an indication of the presence of Asian trade not only in the large cities but also in the smaller central places and nodes of modernization.

Because the intense concentration of all aspects of moderniza-tion in Dar es Salaam alters relative contrasts, additional isolines of one hundred and fifty have been added to the surface to accentuate the smaller, emerging humps (Figure 27.5). Dar es Salaam still towers as a peak over its immediate area, but so steep are the gradients that it still cannot link with the Morogoro node to the west. Other nodes, however, have coalesced into corridors of modernization, including Morogoro-Kilosa-Mpwapwa, and Shinyanga-Mwanza. Incipient corri-dors can also be found on the map.

TENACITY OF PATTERN AND THE DYNAMICS
OF CENTRAL PLACE SYSTEMS

Although we conclude on a somewhat predictive note, it would be foolish to imply that the analysis has illuminated the process, the actual dynamics of modernization in Tanzania. But what is clear, degree a deeper process of urbanization. Thought it pushes the question back a step, such a statement is nothing new: writer after

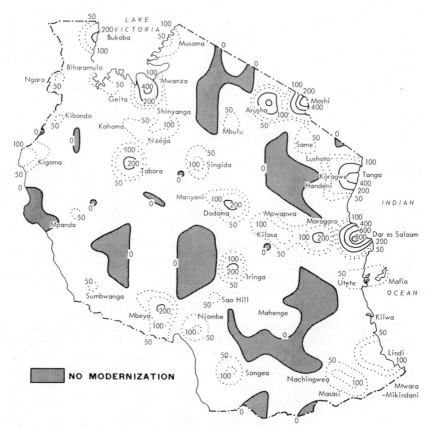

Figure 27.5 The Modernization Surface in the Late Fifties and Early Sixties.

writer has noted the way in which "the town is the door through which Africa is entering the modern world" (McCall, 1955:160). But although it is intimately linked with modernization, what we normally refer to as urbanization is itself only an intense aspect of a more general and continuing process of central-place development.

Thus, what we have seen emerging in the space called Tanzania between 1920 and 1963, and underlying the very modernization process we have tried to measure and structure, are the dynamics of that most spatial of systems—the central-place structure; a system of nodes of various sizes, at differing distances, linked with varying intensities, influencing areas contiguous and between, structuring, focusing, and serving their hinterlands, and acting as emergent poles of attraction for the surrounding population. For a crucial element in the development of central places is a rural-to-urban migration. In the African context this always means the breaking of old allegiances to extended family, traditional authority, unquestioned belief, own people, and familiar place, and the forging of new allegiances in the very process of questioning the old. And so, underlying any theory of modernization in space and time, there must be a deeper theory of the dynamics of central-place systems. But our existing theory is static and geometric, virtually ignoring the concomitant development of transportation and communication linkages, the very channels that allow the time-frozen patterns in space to become systems of human interaction and development. But there is increasing doubt that disaggregation of the spatial system into static patterns of nodes, linkages, and movement will lead to the writing of illuminating theory, for every piece of empirical evidence we have confirms the tightly interlocked nature of all these aspects.

Simply consider Tanzania in 1920, its people unevenly spread in clusters as the land, the rain, and the tsetse fly (themselves intimately related) allow more in some areas than others. Administrators are sent by the early colonial and mandate powers to the population clusters, not the empty areas, and the administrators themselves must move and communicate. Roads and railways link the administrative nodes and provide, in turn, channels through which modernizing innovations seep. From 1920 to 1963, the road vector loads 0.47, 0.54, 0.56, 0.83, and 0.78—ever higher upon the main dimension of modernization. What is happening, of course, is that the major cluster of modernization variables is moving ever closer to the single road vector, as in geographic, rather than geometric, space, modernization in all its innovative aspects is distributed from the major sources through the tarred arteries and laterite capillaries of the land and society. Some innovations have economic implications—coffee revolutionizes Kilimanjaro, sisal spreads around Tanga and Morogoro, cotton seeps through Sukamaland—and commodity flows swirl through the road network, feeding back information to the administrators who upgrade, realign, and tar the dirt tracks of the previous year. Other modernizing activities swell the small towns, and these in turn attract the surrounding people. Such human movements and interactions themselves become flows of messages feeding back new ideas and innovations to the villages. Roads and central places grow to serve the population, but the very pattern of the people is itself pulled and warped through time into greater conformity with the central-place structure and its network of linkages. Where demands of all sorts grow—administrative, medical, educational, economic— response is called forth. And so it is that the early patterns of the twenties (Figure 27.1), are still clearly discernible in the pattern at the time of independence (Figure 27.5), and will be seen still at the turn of the twenty-first century. But the why and the how still elude us. For description is not theory, and only theory is explanation.

VII

AFRICA IN THE WORLD

The phrase "world system" is becoming part of our common vocabulary. As travel and communication technologies grow, the fates of peoples and nations are being ever more closely tied together. Today, there really are no such things as isolated events; what happens in one place produces ramifications just about everywhere. Thus, the final section of this volume is devoted to Africa's involvement with the wider world. To discuss every facet of this involvement obviously would be impossible, and so attention will be directed to those issues that seem especially important to African developments now and in the near future.

For centuries Africa has been an exporter of raw materials, with gold-ivory-slaves forming a triad until after the middle of the nineteenth century, and an importer of consumer items. Colonialism eliminated slaves as an export commodity but added numerous minerals and agricultural products to the list and, at the same time, intensified Africa's reliance on imported manufactured goods. Unfortunately, as Lister demonstrates in Chapter 28, despite the proliferation of international and regional economic groupings to which African nations belong, this same pattern has continued and even intensified. Oil and other minerals now account for over 50 percent of exports, with agricultural-forestry produce not far behind. Coupled with a rise in consumer imports and an increasing reliance on outside capital to finance development projects, the result has been growing negative trade balances. A critical priority facing African

Investment from the industrial world may provide an impetus to development in tropical Africa. Similar interaction with southern Africa, such as this facility in South Africa, poses an important economic and political challenge to diplomacy between industrial nations and developing Africa. (Photograph from the Ford Motor Company)

Trade is still a dominant element linking Africa and the world, as the Mombasa, Kenya, harbor suggests. (Photograph from Kenya Information Services)

governments in the years immediately ahead is to reverse this process and place their respective economies on more diversified and solid footings.

Tourism, which has become an important generator of foreign exchange for some countries, is discussed by Williams in Chapter 29. Africa has much to offer the visitor, including a rich cultural heritage, impressive scenery, wildlife, plenty of sunshine, and uncrowded beaches. But the development of a tourist industry is fraught with uncertainties and dilemmas. First, a heavy financial investment must be made in infrastructure, particularly for lodging and transportation. Yet tourists are relatively fickle, and consequently there is always the potential for much unused capacity. Tourist facilities tend to add to already pronounced regional imbalances, in that most are concentrated in the large cities or in isolated country lodges. So far, it has not been an industry to generate spatial linkages. Then the question of possible tourist contamination must be faced—extreme wealth is often juxtaposed with extreme poverty; locals are placed in service-rendering positions; and possibly undesired social values are imported and diffused.

Though tourism has helped to widen the orbit of outside world contacts, the tendency is for African countries to be tied most closely to the former colonial metropole. This is well documented in the case of the Ivory Coast presented by Lister in Chapter 30. French administrators, technicians, and advisors are highly visible and continued dependency is insured by a series of "cooperation agreements" in political, economic, and legal spheres of activity. The details of these arrangements are a good example of what many refer to as neocolonial control.

Formal colonialism is very much present in southern Africa in the 1970s in the former Portuguese territories, and particularly in the white minority regimes in Rhodesia (Zimbabwe), South West Africa (Namibia), and South Africa. De Blij, in Chapter 31, traces the historical development of black-white confrontation and separation in this region, and outlines the intensified colonialism instituted to insure white dominance for as long as possible. This is the last outpost of a formerly world-wide phenomenon, and the shape of future events may very well hinge on actions taken by Europe and America, given South Africa's position in the world economy. In any event, "benign neglect" will not resolve the issue.

The final chapter deals with Africa-based assaults on these bastions of colonialism. McColl begins with a general discussion of revolutionary theory and traces developments in Guiné-Bissau and Mozambique and their ultimate success, thus linking African liberation movements with other struggles for freedom throughout the world.

28

Africa in the World Economy

DOUGLAS W. LISTER

Traditionally, Africa has played three main roles in the world economy: (1) a supplier of industrial raw materials and primary agricultural products to the industrial countries; (2) a market for the finished and semifinished exports of these countries; (3) a field for investment, both public and private. In all three capacities, the role of Africa compared to that of other continents has been small. Today, virtually all newly independent African states are dissatisfied with both the nature and extent of their role in the world economy. Much of their discontent has been focused on the world economic system which they believe generally is ill-suited to the needs of developing countries. This chapter will briefly describe the evolution of the world economic system, examine some of the more significant African attempts to reform it, and determine whether Africa's role in the world economy has undergone any meaningful changes since independence.

Since 1948, international trade has been regulated by a series of accords concluded within the framework of the General Agreement on Tariffs and Trade (GATT). As originally conceived, GATT was merely a temporary measure designed to bridge the gap between the end of World War II and the establishment of an international trade agency. Over the years, however, GATT has developed into something more than its signatories intended.

When GATT began operations in 1948, the organization had only 19 members, but by the mid-1960s, its membership had grown to more than 70 nations representing over four-fifths of world trade. The GATT has four main objectives: (1) reduction in import restrictions, including gradual reduction in existing tariffs and ultimate elimination of import-licensing restraints; (2) nondiscrimination by each member country in applying trade restrictions to commerce with other member countries; (3) settlement of trade disputes; and (4) granting of waivers from any GATT commitments on the basis of international consensus (Vernon, 1968).

The GATT has reduced tariffs at a series of multilateral bargaining sessions. Between 1947 and 1967, six such sessions were held. At the first five, tariff reductions for individual products were worked out initially between pairs of countries, and then extended by virtue of the nondiscrimination principle to the other members. A single tariff rate thus applied to imports of a given product, regardless of source. At the sixth session, the so-called Kennedy Round which began in 1964, the practice of negotiating product by product was abandoned in favor of an across the board approach. By the time the session ended in 1967, tariff rates imposed by the industrial countries on imports of industrial products had been cut in half. GATT's achievements in the area of quantitative restrictions, however, have been less substantial. The Tokyo Round of GATT talks begun in 1975 is expected to last 2 years.

The world trade system also has been influenced by GATT's procedures for the settlement of disputes and the granting of waivers. Several dozen difficult trade disputes have been settled during the life of the organization, usually with the aid of a group of experts whose task it is to study the problem at hand and suggest a solution on the basis of GATT rules. Member states also have obtained permission from the organization to retain or introduce restrictive measures that would otherwise have been illegal in order to protect certain sectors of their economies or establish customs unions or free-trade areas.

GATT's main thrust has evolved in the direction of a freer, more open system of world trade based on the principle of nondiscrimination. Until rather recently, GATT was practically the only international agency concerned with world trade. In 1960, however, the United Nations proclaimed the beginning of the First Development Decade, which prompted a number of inquiries into the effects of trade on development. The findings were disturbing. Between 1950 and 1960, it was discovered that for each one dollar increase of per capita income in the developing nations, income in the advanced countries grew by more than twenty dollars. Reliance on exports of unprocessed primary products was singled out as the principal cause of the relatively slow rate of growth of per capita income in the developing world. At the beginning of the decade, the total value of exports and imports for the developing countries as a whole registered a net surplus of 10 percent, but by the end of the decade this had turned into a 10 percent trade deficit. In 1960, one unit of primary products purchased 24 percent less manufactured goods than in 1950 (Goodspeed, 1967). The gap between "haves" and "have-nots" was obviously growing. The failure of GATT to spot this trend earlier and do something to check it prompted more than one observer to dub the organization a "rich man's club" that was only concerned with the problems of industrial countries.

Partially as a result of these findings, more than 2,000 delegates and observers from 119 nations gathered in 1964 for the first United Nations Conference on Trade and Development (UNCTAD). A second conference was held in 1968, and a third in 1972. At the first meeting, the slogan of the developing countries was: "trade *not* aid." But by 1968, this had become: "trade *and* aid." The change in rhetoric signified a growing awareness among developing nations that their problems were basically different from those of the rich countries, and that special measures in the form of commercial preferences and development aid would be needed, if the gap between rich and poor was to be narrowed.

While GATT and UNCTAD may appear to overlap, they are actually quite distinct. Essentially, GATT is an organ for the negotiation and administration of trade agreements, whereas UNCTAD is a forum for the definition of broad principles relating not only to trade, but to aid and development. UNCTAD also has a broader mandate by virtue of its larger membership, especially in matters involving countries at different stages of economic growth.

Flows of goods and services are only one aspect of international economic relations. Equally important are flows of money and capital. In July, 1944, a conference was convened at Bretton Woods, New Hampshire, in order to work out the future of the world's monetary and financial system. The meeting resulted in the creation of two key international organizations—the International Monetary Fund (IMF) and the International Bank for Reconstruction and Development (IBRD). Both organizations came into being in December, 1945, and they began functioning as specialized agencies of the United Nations in November, 1947.

As originally conceived, the central purpose of the IMF was to promote exchange rate stability, thereby facilitating payments relating to trade, aid, and private investment. Accordingly, each member pledged to maintain the "par value" of its currency as defined in terms of the United States dollar, within a narrow range or "band." Only in cases of "fundamental disequilibrium" in its balance of payments could a member change the par value of its currency, although objections were seldom raised if the amount of the change was less than 10 percent (Goodspeed, 1967). Until 1971, the dollar was tied to gold at a fixed rate which provided an anchor for the entire system. In that year, however, the United States abandoned this arrangement and allowed the dollar to move up and down or "float" in relation to market forces. By 1973, practically all the world's major currencies were floating, contradicting IMF rules. This new system of flexible exchange rates was legitimized at a meeting of the IMF in Jamaica, where a number of other important monetary reforms were also set in motion. Upon joining the IMF, members negotiate a contribution or "quota" which determines their voting power. Each member has 250 votes plus one additional vote for each $100,000 of its quota. The size of the quota also governs the extent to which a member can borrow from the IMF. As a result of the Jamaica meeting, the quotas of all nations are revised, raising the share of the developing countries, at the same time as total quotas are increased. Amounts available for lending under the IMF credit and other facilities will also be increased substantially. An aid package was also developed under which about one-sixth of the IMF's gold holdings would be sold for the benefit of the developing countries. This is also the first step toward the elimination of gold as a monetary standard. Eventually, gold will be replaced by a new unit, the SDR (Special Drawing Rights), based on a "basket" of key world currencies equivalent in 1976 to about $1.15.

The main purpose of the IBRD or World Bank, on the other hand, is to make or guarantee loans for productive reconstruction and development projects. As a rule, the subscription of member countries in the bank is based on its quota in the IMF. Upon joining, the country pays in 10 percent of its subscription. One percent of this amount is paid in gold or dollars and is freely usable in the bank's operations. The other 9 percent is paid in the country's own currency and is available for lending only with the consent of the member. The remaining 90 percent is not paid in, but may be called by the bank if required to meet its obligations arising out of borrowing or guaranteeing loans. Individual members' voting power is determined by the size of their subscription in the same way as in the IMF. Except in special circumstances, a World Bank loan must be for a specific project in a member country, or a territory controlled by a member. The project which the loan will assist must be technically and economically sound, and of high priority for the economic development of the country. The bank must be satisfied that the project will be well-managed both during its implementation and after completion. There must be reasonable assurance that the loan will be repaid, and the loan must not impose an undue burden on the economy of the borrower. The bank also ascertains that the perspective borrower cannot obtain finance on reasonable terms from other sources. The bank lends to governments of member countries or to public or private organizations which can obtain the guarantee of the member government controlling the territory where the project to be financed is located. The guarantee requirement is imposed by the bank's articles of agreement. The bank's loan usually consists of part or all of the foreign exchange costs of the proposed project but may in certain circumstances also cover some local costs.

In the early post-war years the emphasis of bank business was on reconstruction in Western Europe. After the Marshall Plan was introduced in 1948, the bank turned its efforts mainly to its other major task, develop lending. Today, the bank's main job is lending for productive projects which will lead to economic growth in its less-developed member countries. The bank does not fix rigid sectoral priorities; it lends on the basis of the needs of a particular country and time. Historically, relatively large amounts have been lent for transportation and electric power, reflecting the fact that in most developing countries the first need has been for improving infrastructural facilities, especially of the type for which private capital is not easily available.

As countries' infrastructure has grown, the scope for diversifying bank lending activities into other sectors has expanded. Thus electric power and transportation still account for a large proportion of bank lending, but the relative importance of other sectors such as agriculture has increased, the latter reaching nearly $2 billion in 1975. The value of loans is still small in some sectors such as telecommunications, education, and water supply, with lending beginning only a few years ago.

Since its creation, the World Bank has acquired two affiliate organizations, the International Finance Corporation (IFC) which became operational in 1966 and the International Development Association (IDA) which became operational in 1960. These two institutions and the bank itself form the World Bank Group. Membership in the bank is a requirement for membership in IFC, which works specifically with the private sector in developing countries, and in IDA, which operates in the same sectors and with the same policies as the bank, but with loans (known as "credits") provided only to poorer developing countries on easier terms than conventional World Bank loans. (By 1975, 116 countries had joined the IDA; its lending resources totalled nearly $1 billion. In addition to profitability and benefit to the host country, potential participation of local investors is an additional condition for IFC loans.)

The organizations described—GATT, UNCTAD, IMF, IBRD, IFC and IDA—have been the main components of the postwar world economic system. To be sure, other organizations such as the Food and Agriculture Organization (FAO), the World Health Organization (WHO), and the United Nations Educational, Scientific and Cultural Organization (UNESCO) also have been active on the world economic scene, but their importance is secondary.

During the first decade of independence, many African states became disillusioned with the world economic system. In particular, the nondiscrimination principle of GATT was considered incompatible with the creation of infant industries. African countries were unhappy over this organization's failure to stabilize the prices of their primary product exports. They also found themselves in the position of minority shareholders in IMF and World Bank.

Primarily for these reasons, African states have turned partly to regional arrangements for solutions to their problems of trade and aid. These arrangements fall into two broad categories: (1) those involving "vertical" links with rich countries; and (2) those involving "horizontal" links with other African countries.

One of the most prevalent forms of vertical ties is monetary in nature. Virtually all the French-speaking African states belong to the Franc Zone, which was largely administered from Paris. During the colonial period, the countries that made up French West and Equatorial Africa used a currency known as the CFA (colonies francaises d'Afrique) franc. But when the French-African colonies acquired independence around 1960, they split up into three separate monetary unions. One, composed of eight West African states (Ivory Coast, Upper Volta, Dahomey, Togo, Mali, Mauritania, Niger and Senegal), was headed by the Banque Centrale de l'Afrique de l'Ouest (BCEAO). Another, made up of five central African states (Chad, Congo-Brazzaville, Gabon, Central African Republic and Cameroun), was administered by the Banque Centrale des Etats de l'Afrique Equatoriale et du Cameroun (BCEAC). Both groupings continued to use the same currency as before, but the name was changed to communauté franco-africaine. Later, it was changed again to communauté financière africaine. The evolving nomenclature of the currency is significant, for it symbolizes the mixture of continuity and change that has characterized French-African relations in monetary matters as in others since independence. The third francophone African monetary zone was composed of the Malagasy Republic which in 1963 established its own central bank known as the *Institut d'Emission Malgache* (IEM). The IEM also issued its own currency, the *franc malgache* (FMG). Both the CFA and FMG, however, are tied to the French franc at a fixed rate of 50:1, making them equivalent to each other and to non-Franc Zone currencies.

The operations of these monetary unions are regulated by a series of accords known collectively as the Cooperation Agreements. Practically all the French-speaking African states signed such agreements with France almost immediately after independence. In each case, the agreement on monetary affairs was separate from other agreements on political, legal, and cultural cooperation, thus making it possible for the African parties to remain inside the Franc Zone while abrogating their treaty responsibilities in other areas.

In the case of the West African Monetary Union (WAMU), for example, the BCEAO initially was capitalized at $11 million, evenly distributed in the form of deposits to the eight member states. The management of the bank was entrusted to a board of 21 directors made up two representatives from each of the eight members and five from France. All decisions are taken by simple majority vote, except in certain cases where two-thirds is required. These include such important matters as changes in the rediscount rate and the fixing of ceilings on bank credit.

In each member state, a five-man National Committee also was set up to implement BCEAO's credit and rediscount policies. As a rule, this body includes the member's two directors and three others appointed by the government. Between meetings of the National Committee, a Director-General appointed by the committee is in charge of policy execution. The BCEAO's headquarters are located in Paris, but each member has a branch office in its capital city. The bank is the exclusive source of all legal tender in the eight member states.

The most significant feature of the Franc Zone from the standpoint of international economic relations, however, is the Operation Accounts which the BCEAO and the other francophone African central banks maintain with the French Treasury. By virtue of these accounts, the French-speaking African states are effectively relieved of the burden of managing their foreign exchange reserves. Under the Cooperation Agreements, these countries are required to turn over their holdings of foreign exchange to their respective central banks which, in turn, must deposit them with the French central bank. Some small deposits at banks outside the Franc Zone are permitted, and an amendment to the Cooperation Agreements passed in July, 1962, gave the francophone African central banks the right to invest some of their foreign exchange reserves in negotiable bonds having a maturity of two years or less (i.e. short-term IBRD issues). But most of their reserves must be turned over to the French. In return, they receive interest on their deposits at a rate equal to the rediscount rate of the Bank of France. The African banks also receive automatic overdraft facilities for use in times of foreign exchange shortages. Each time they avail themselves of these facilities, however, they must pay interest on their borrowings at a rate that increases from 1 percent for amounts up to 5 million CFA francs to two percent for amounts up to ten million. Beyond this point, the interest rate is the same as that of the French central bank (de Lattre, 1969).

What this arrangement amounts to is a mechanism for pooling foreign exchange reserves so that each subscriber is able to draw on the reserves of the group in times of foreign exchange shortages. Since France is also a subscriber, she too may use the reserves of her African partners to settle her balance-of-payments accounts with countries outside the Franc Zone. The contributions of the franco-phone African countries has been significant, especially in times of international monetary crises. In "normal" years such as 1962 or 1964, they accounted for between one-tenth and one-third of the total foreign exchange reserves of the Zone, but in crisis years such as 1966, when the French franc was under pressure, they accounted for nearly all of them (Siradiou, 1970). Monetary cooperation between France and her former African colonies is thus a two-way street which helps both parties to maintain the value of their currencies. Without the Franc Zone, it is doubtful that the francophone African states would have enjoyed "hard" currencies since independence, but by the same token their monetary policy has remained intimately tied to that of France. Similar, though less formal arrangements exist between the United Kingdom and many of her former possessions in Africa by virtue of the Sterling Zone.

Another organization of the vertical type is the association between the European Common Market (EEC) and the Associated African States and Madagascar (AASM). The main features of this organization are described in Chapter 30, and it is unnecessary therefore to say more than a few words about it here. Basically, the association provides commercial preferences on the European market for the main primary product exports of the AASM, and a modest amount of financial and technical assistance through the European Development Fund (EDF) and European Investment Bank (EIB). The organization also has a set of joint institutions where its European and African members meet periodically to discuss the workings of the commercial preference system and development aid program. At the moment, the association includes 46 associated states, including former African colonies, and the 9 members of the recently enlarged EEC. As a result of the commercial preference system, producers of tropical products in the associations have enjoyed a small competitive advantage over producers of similar goods in other parts of the developing world. The Community's aid has been a significant supplement to aid from other sources. It also has come predominantly in the form of grants. Here too, similar, though less formal arrangements exist between the English-speaking African countries and the United Kingdom by virtue of the British Commonwealth of Nations.

The other type of regional organization is "horizontal." Today, such entities exist in virtually every subregion of the continent. However, there is no Pan-African economic organization of any significance.

In East Africa, for example, regional cooperation dates back to the turn of the century when Kenya and Uganda formed a customs union. The modern-day successor to this organization is the East African Community composed of Tanzania, Kenya, and Uganda. Like its forerunner, the East African Community is a customs union; its members observe a common external tariff, and trade within the community is largely unrestricted. But the organization also aims to harmonize internal policies, especially in the critical area of industrial development. In addition, the three East African Community partners have attempted to equalize the gains from integration. In almost any regional economic entity, it is the richer states that derive the most benefits, especially at first. Their industries are usually more competitive, and once tariff barriers are reduced, they tend to drive out competitors located in poorer states. In the East African Community losses to these countries are minimized through the use of a "transfer tax." According to Article 20 of the new Treaty for East African Economic Cooperation, this tax is a charge imposed by one partner state on the exports of another into its territory where the state imposing the tax produces the goods in question in a certain amount or value. Only states with a deficit in total trade in manufactured goods may impose the transfer tax, the level of which may not exceed 50 percent of the *ad valorem* duty imposed on imports of similar goods from third countries. There is an eight-year limit on the duration of the tax. The East African Community also has established the East African Development Bank as a source of capital for its members (Mutharika, 1972).

Impressive on paper, the East African Community nevertheless has encountered certain obstacles in practice. Its ambitious efforts to distribute industries between members, in particular, have given rise to a certain amount of rivalry. Political animosity also has interfered with the workings of the organization. Still, the East African

Community is certainly one of the more successful organizations of its type. Several other African countries, in fact, had expressed interest in joining the organization, namely Zambia, Somalia, Ethiopia, Burundi, Rwanda, and Swaziland (Mutharika, 1972).

The main regional economic entity in southern Africa is the Southern African Customs Union, headed by the Republic of South Africa. The other members are the three former British High Commission Territories of Botswana, Lesotho, and Swaziland. The Southern African Customs Union actually is closer to an economic union. In addition to a common external tariff, its members observe certain common internal policies and coordinate their economic and social infrastructure investments. By virtue of the Rand Zone, the four member states are linked by a common currency (Mutharika, 1972).

In central Africa, the main economic organization is the *Union Douanière et Economique de l'Afrique Centrale* (UDEAC). Like the East African Community, the UDEAC developed out of an earlier organization known as the *Union Douanière Equatoriale* (UDE) which existed during the colonial period. The UDEAC also provides compensation to poorer members of the group for any losses incurred in the integration process. At the moment, the UDEAC includes the Central African Republic, Congo-Brazzaville, Gabon, and Cameroun.

In West Africa, there are three significant regional groupings. The first is the *Conseil de l'Entente*, composed of Dahomey, Ivory Coast, Niger, Upper Volta and Togo. While mainly a political organization, the Council has created a Mutual Aid and Loan Guarantee Fund that, as its name indicates, guarantees loans taken out by the members individually with the resources of the group. The other, more important West African organization is the *Union Douanière de l'Afrique de l'Ouest* (UDAO). Unlike its central African counterpart, the UDAO is only a customs union. The seven member states observe a common external tariff, and trade between them is relatively free of restrictions. But no steps have been taken toward the harmonization of internal policies. The UDAO presently includes the Ivory Coast, Dahomey, Upper Volta, Mali, Mauritania, Niger, and Senegal.

In May, 1970 at Bamako, these countries signed a protocol outlining a new organization, not unlike the UDEAC, known as the *Communauté Economique de l'Afrique Occidentale* (CEAO). Some observers regard the CEAO as a partial answer to some of the problems plaguing the UDAO since its inception in the early 1960s. By far the most severe of these has been the distribution of revenue collected on trade with third countries. Since most of this trade takes place through the ports of the coastal states, the landlocked countries have been dependent on their coastal partners for revenue they would otherwise have collected at their own borders. When several of the coastal states failed to turn over what the landlocked states considered a fair share of the revenue collected on behalf of the group, they began to reimpose duties on imports from their costal partners, thus negating the purpose of the entire arrangement.

In May, 1975 at Lagos, 15 West African nations, both anglo- and francophone, were signatories to an agreement creating the Economic Community of West Africa. As specific provisions are negotiated, there may be significant positive impact on the development of the region and on its spatial organization and interaction.

There are, of course, other important African regional groupings such as the *Organisation Commune Africaine et Malgache* (OCAM). The main achievement of this organization is the OCAM Sugar Agreement which regulates trade in this important commodity by means of quotas for both producer and consumer states. Another significant organization is the African Development Bank (ADB). Created in 1963 with an initial capital stock of $250 million, the bank has supplied its members with a variety of financial services including loans, loan guarantees, and venture capital. Finally, mention should be made of two of the smaller regional organizations—the Lake Chad Basin Commission and the Organization of Senegal River States. The Lake Chad Basin Commission is one of the few organizations including both English- and French-speaking countries, namely Chad, Cameroun, Niger, and Nigeria.

The efforts of African states to reform the world economic system have hardly been confined to the regional level. They have also put pressure on the rich nations to reform this system at the global level. Both at the 1968 meeting of UNCTAD in New Delhi and more recently at other forums, these countries have campaigned vigorously for a system of generalized preferences for their finished and semifinished goods on the markets of the rich countries. Nor have these efforts been entirely in vain. Limited systems of generalized preferences are already in effect on the important EEC, British, and Japanese markets. At the 1972 meeting of UNCTAD, the developing countries also proposed that Special Drawing Rights (SDR), which may be likened to a credit account with the IMF, be used as a means of aid. Specifically, it was suggested that the advanced countries contribute a portion of their SDR to the developing countries, thus linking international monetary reform to development aid. However, the "link" between this latest device for increasing world liquidity and development aid has not been fully realized.

Let us now see if these efforts, both regional and global, have produced meaningful change in Africa's role as a relatively minor producer of primary products and raw materials, a market for finished and semifinished exports, and a field for investment.

From 1960-1970, Africa's trade (excluding South Africa) with the rest of the world increased absolutely, but declined relatively. At the beginning of the decade, it was worth $11,860 million compared to $22,860 million at the end. Still, Africa's share in world trade declined, amounting in 1970 to only 4.5 percent (Africa Annual Review, 1972).

In recent years, Africa's balance of payments position also has deteriorated. Between 1969 and 1970, Africa's trade surplus (exports minus imports) declined from $2,100 million to $1,600 million. A worsening balance of payments position, however, is hardly peculiar to Africa. Since 1960, virtually all developing nations have faced declining terms of trade. African countries actually have been more fortunate than the rest, since their problems did not begin in earnest until 1970. Contrary to popular opinion, the prices of African commodity exports held up well over most of the decade. The unit value of these goods rose from an index of 101.0 in 1964 to 110.7 in 1969. This increase, in fact, was faster than that for manufactured goods produced in the industrialized countries. But with the onslaught of inflation in the developed world in 1970, the situation changed. In that year alone, the unit value of African imports rose by 7 percent, whereas that of exports increased by only 1 percent. Kenyan Finance Minister Mwai Kibaki found that during the first three months of 1971, the prices of his country's imports rose by ten percent, with export prices declining by two percent (Africa Annual Review, 1972).

Another cause of Africa's declining trade surplus is an increasing demand for imports. As the pace of development quickens, larger amounts of transport and capital manufactured goods are needed. These, in turn, generate more imports in the form of spare parts, fuel, and technical skills. Industrialization also creates its own class of managers, technicians, and advisers who frequently prefer prestigious foreign goods to goods produced locally. This has been evident in the rising proportion of consumer as opposed to investment goods in total African imports (Africa Annual Review, 1972). Thus, not only has Africa's share of world trade declined, but so have its gains from trade.

As for the nature of African trade, primary products and raw materials have continued to account for the bulk of African exports, while imports have been composed mainly of finished and semi-finished goods. As exports, oil and minerals have become increasingly important in recent years. Oil, which ranked fifth on the list of African exports in 1960, was in first place by 1970, accounting for over 30 percent of total African exports, in other words, more than twice as much as the next most important African export, copper. Together, oil and minerals made up 50.9 percent of the total value of African exports in 1969 (Africa Annual Review, 1972). For oil, 1971 was a significant year. In terms of production, there were no sensational gains. Nigeria's output leveled off after the post-civil war boom of 1970, and Libya's production actually declined in keeping with the Quadaffi regime's policy of not exhausting the country's oil reserves too quickly. Egyptian production increased somewhat, but otherwise no significant discoveries or dramatic increases in production were recorded, except in minor producers such as Congo-Brazzaville, Zaire, Tunisia, and Angola. In terms of price, however, there were important developments. Some price increases had already been won in 1970 for Middle Eastern oil, but in January, 1971, Libya took the lead in demanding price increases for African oil. This was followed almost immediately by price hikes for Nigerian and Algerian oil. As a result of these and other changes, the price of African oil rose by an average of 30 percent. Moreover, profits were no longer divided on the old fifty-fifty basis between the oil companies and the producer states. The new basis gave African producers 55 percent of the earnings (Africa Annual Review, 1972). Middle Eastern events of 1973-1974 drove oil prices even higher.

After oil, copper, iron ore, and diamonds are the most important African mineral exports. Copper alone accounts for roughly 10 percent of total African exports by value. African copper production, however, is heavily concentrated in a few countries, notably Zambia where it accounts for 95 percent of all foreign exchange and 30 percent of government revenue. Iron ore, representing approximately 5.7 percent of the total value of continental exports, is produced mainly in Liberia, Mauritania, Sierra Leone, and Algeria. Diamonds are produced primarily in Sierra Leone, Zaire, South Africa, and Namibia. Other African mineral exports include manganese, bauxite, platinum, gold, and chrome (Africa Annual Review, 1972).

Primary agricultural products still remain important exports from Africa. The chief commodity in this group is cotton, produced mainly in West and central Africa, the Sudan, Uganda, Tanzania, and Zambia. Of lesser importance are coffee, tea, and cocoa (Africa Annual Review, 1972).

To summarize, Africa has become *more reliant*—not less—on

exports of primary products and raw materials and on imports of finished and semifinished goods since independence.

As far as investment is concerned, the situation is similar. Instead of becoming less dependent on capital imports, newly independent African states have become more so. This is evident in the continent's rising level of international indebtedness. In 1965, Africa owed the world $7,297 million, but by 1970 this figure had jumped to $9,183 million. Africa's debt might even have been higher, if she had not received aid on "softer" terms than most other parts of the developing world. Aid to Africa has come mainly in the form of grants and long-term, low-interest loans. Still, Africa's aid, as a share of world aid, declined from 22 percent in 1965 to 16 percent in 1970 (Africa Annual Review, 1972).

The period since independence may well be too short a time to expect major changes in the economic role of a continent. But the fact that Africa's role in the world economy has undergone a relative decline at the same time as dependence on foreign markets, goods, and capital has experienced an absolute increase is evidence that the gap between Africa and the industrialized world is growing, despite the ambitious efforts of African states to close it.

29

Tourism

ANTHONY V. WILLIAMS

Africa has long attracted tourists seeking the exotic. They have ranged from the explorers of the sources of the Nile to the pampered big-game hunters populating treetop lodges in Kenya. While this aspect of African tourism still characterizes most people's images, parts of the continent may be on the verge of a boom in tourism rivaling that of some European countries in the 1950s and 1960s. There are many problems as well as promises with such development and some potential countervailing forces. Experience elsewhere, notably in the Caribbean (Bryden and Faber, 1971), suggests that mass tourism may *not* be desirable in developing countries. Before examining these points and ,delineating characteristics of tourism in Africa, a brief digression to describe some world aspects of international tourism may be useful. This is especially germane in that African experience with international tourism is still in an initial stage. Thus, perspectives gained from other areas may be useful.

There is no doubt that tourism is not only a significant component of international social and economic interaction but one of the most rapidly growing (Williams and Zelinsky, 1970). A survey of member countries by the Organization for Economic Cooperation and Development (OECD) in 1971 (*International Monetary Fund,* 1971) found tourist expenditures growing at an average annual rate of 11 percent per year in the 1960s, slightly faster than income from export goods and services. Growth in the early 1970s has been even greater, amounting to as much as 17 percent (Bank of Nova Scotia, *Monthly Review*, 1972). Marginal sensitivity of tourist expenditures to increases in consumer expenditure is great. Austrian citizens spend 2.5 percent more for international tourism with each 1 percent increase in consumer expenditure (*International Monetary Fund*, 1971). Tourist traffic already accounted for over three quarters of international air traffic density in 1970 (Canadian Imperial Bank of Commerce, *Commercial Letter*, 1970) and seems likely to go higher by the end of the 1970s—unless the energy crisis and world recession persist. Taking 1950 as a base, the number of international tourist visitors increased from 23,635,600 (Williams and Zelinsky, 1970) to around 181,000,000 in 1971 (*International Monetary Fund*, 1973), an increase of over 760 percent.

These gross figures, while adequate indicators of the overall development of mass tourism in the last two decades, conceal important geographical variations, especially pertinent to African countries. In discussing internal European tourist development, Christaller (1964) noted a tendency for increased flows to more peripheral and remote areas. For perhaps similar reasons, a desire to get away from the crowd and perhaps to save money, something of the sort also appears to be true in international tourism. The most notable examples in Europe are the rapid increases in international flows to Spain, the Balearic Islands, Portugal, and Greece (Williams and Zelinsky, 1970). There is still room for considerable expansion in intra-European tourism as witnessed by Greek government projections of an increase of 500 percent (from two million tourists a year to ten million) in Greek tourism during the 1970s (*International Tourism Quarterly*, 1971). This is a much more rapid increase than the threefold expansion that occurred during the 1960s. Whether these particular expectations are realistic is open to doubt, but there is little question that the expenditures generated by the tourist industry can be significant for smaller countries. Greek experience in the 1960s is similar to what some would postulate for various African areas in the 1970s, and revenues from international tourism amounted there to about $200 million in 1970, one third as much as the total export earnings of the country (*International Tourism Quarterly*, 1971).

It is necessary to mention here that while they are harder to measure, expenditures on *internal* tourism are much greater than international expenditures in developed countries. Pennsylvania, hardly thought of as a tourist haven by most persons, generated some

$4 billion in tourist revenues in 1969; that should be compared to total world tourist expenditures of about $20 billion for international travel during a comparable period. Even in Greece, not quite a developed country, indications are that domestic travel receipts are double those for international travel (*International Tourism Quarterly*, 1971). However, international receipts add to foreign exchange holdings and represent net external increments to the economies of small nations. Thus, actual monetary volumes understate the importance of international flows, especially in developing areas.

Large scale international tourism seems an attractive industry—free from the pollution associated with consuming natural resources, capable of absorbing unskilled labor, encouraging the retention and development of native arts and crafts, often focusing on remote or backward areas otherwise outside populous national core areas, and potentially avoiding foreign domination of a country's economy even though foreign investment may play a heavy role in the development of tourist infrastructure. Therefore, many of its problems are frequently overlooked. Bryden and Faber (1971) have criticized a conventional "booster" report by a research firm on the prospects for international tourism in the Caribbean, arguing the following points. First, much of the earnings from tourism goes to foreign owners—of hotels, transportation agencies, and suppliers. Then, to supply tourists with Westernized goods and services, they require mandates imports. These further draw down the net income a country receives from international tourism. In general, the increment to gross national income is much greater than the increment in income going to the native population. So while jobs are created and local products are bought, the amount of income generated by multipliers—that is, each dollar spent by a tourist generates income which is used to purchase something else and so on *ad infinitum*—is often less than unity in developing countries, perhaps 0.7 or 0.8 according to Bryden and Faber. Many optimistic research agency reports attempting to persuade governments to promote tourism cite income multipliers in excess of 2 (Bryden and Faber, 1971). The more an economy is internally capable of supplying its tourists' needs, the greater the multiplier and the consequential indirect effects of tourist expenditures. European countries are typically in a position to reap great benefits from these expenditures. But what may be good for an advanced industrial economy producing a variety of modern goods and services may not be good for an import-dominated economy.

There are other disadvantages to mass tourism. Aiming for the mass charter-flight market brings in many tourists who in turn require large investments in infrastructure—hotels, modern water and sewage systems, modern highway systems and so on. Large numbers of tourists may also "overload" the presumably limited number of facilities of interest to tourists, especially in peak periods, since tourism is still highly seasonal in most parts of the world. Furthermore, unless concentrated in remote areas of a country of little intrinsic interest to the indigenous population, massive tourism exposes members of underdeveloped societies to standards of living that are totally out of line with prevailing or reasonably expectable local standards. What effects this exposure has can only be imagined. It surely must engender some dissatisfaction with local conditions. Finally, tourists' actions and attitudes often fail to engender the kinds of cross-cultural understanding that are desirable.

Concentration on the economic elite rather than potential mass tourism lessens the need for widespread increases in infrastructure. Further, the income received per tourist is high enough to attract external investment, lessening the need for local expenditures. But this, too, has compensating costs. More of the income generated by tourism "leaks" from the economy because demands for imported goods and services are likely to be greater for high-income than middle-income tourists. And despite the lower incidence of indigene contact with elite tourists, their high individual visibility and their greater contrasts in wealth to the local populace are offsetting vices.

Most of these problems, especially notable in Caribbean countries at the moment, are not yet serious in contemporary Africa. But they need to be anticipated and if possible dealt with in advance. How African nations will judge the desirability of mass tourism versus attracting the elite, the level and direction of promotional expenditures, and investment decisions are still unknown. On the basis of recent evidence and experience elsewhere, the choice may well be for indiscriminate promotion of tourism with some constraints imposed by such desiderata as having the national airline get some assured share of tourist traffic (the situation with East African Airways *vis-à-vis* British tourists). There is an increasing tendency to demand majority or near majority ownership by indigenous groups or governments themselves in tourist enterprises started and financed by outsiders.

Travel industry promotion particularly in the United States and Canada, emphasizes the exotic and bizarre aspects of tourism in Africa; these include both cultural characteristics and natural attractions. A glance at the travel section of the Sunday *New York Times* or at the brochures of safari-oriented organizations confirms this judgment. In Britain and to a lesser extent in France and other former colonial countries, some attention also is directed at repatriates or those having friends or relatives in the former colonial areas. But in these countries and particularly in Germany and Scandinavia an increasing focus on chartered and relatively cheap sun and beach vacations has arisen in the last several years and the mass flows of tourists engendered by the lure of reasonable costs and still uncrowded beaches on both East and West African coasts may foretell the real future of African tourism.

With the possible exception of Kenya, African tourism is still undeveloped. A glance at the official and only readily available data for both pre-independence (Table 29.1) and recent (Table 29.2) years confirm this. Surprising for people used to the almost obsessively detailed statistical data available in advanced western countries is the absence in *both* periods of data for most African states and the relatively high number of "unallocatable" tourists. It is important to realize that absence of data does not necessarily (or even often) imply absence of the phenomenon being measured. In this case, accept on faith that *Homo Turisticus* is ubiquitous; only the concentrations vary. Were more recent information available, we would probably see two or three more countries enter the list, especially those West African countries such as Senegal now experiencing booms in mass tourism. South Africa appears to have about as great a tourist flow as Kenya. In this case the data are, however, a trifle misleading, in that many of South Africa's tourists come from neighboring Rhodesia.

The relative paucity of tourists in West Africa is evidenced by the fact that the international figures for *both* the pre-independence and recent period contain data only for Nigeria. This, it must again be emphasized, does not necessarily imply zero flows in the other countries. The American press, for instance, is replete with stories of black groups visiting Ghana, Sierra Leone, and other nations, and it is probable that considerable traffic is generated from the former colonial powers. But volumes are presumably small and this, coupled with inadequacies of the statistical reporting services, would explain their omission from the international compilations.

There is little doubt that spectacular attractions such as the East African mountain craters and gorges and the game parks of South and East Africa are absent from images of West Africa, although less-well-known, spectacular scenery here is not lacking and game preserves are present or planned. Major attractions for tourists are the cultural heritage of the area, particularly for American blacks but also for those curious about the old empires. In Senegal, to cite a promising example, the peculiar melange of African culture with

TABLE 29.1   "Pre-Independence" Tourism in Africa

FROM	Congo (Leopold.) 1958	Mozambique 1959	TO Nigeria 1961	South Africa 1960	Uganda 1959
TOTAL	12,246	51,230	57,278	169,493	7,454
Argentina	6			76	
Australia	48	182[a]		843	
Austria	44	74		130	
Belgium	2,667	377		468	
Brazil	9			57	
Bulgaria	1				
Canada	91	90	604	557	10
Chile	5				
China	3	41			
Czech.	3				
Denmark	92	90	387	155	
Finland	9			35	
France	1,082	549	3,196	584	
W. Germany	439	1,406	1,525	2,006	
Greece	254	204		177	
Hungary	3				
Iceland	1				
India	100		1,030	25[b]	227[b]
Indonesia	1			8	
Ireland	18		929	166	
Israel	34	45	772	363	
Italy	506	755	1,296	641	
Japan	27	103			
Luxembourg	21				
Mexico	3				
Netherlands	329	640	2,171	1,375	
New Zealand	3			583	
Norway	17			88	
Poland	14				
Portugal	583			145	
Romania	1				
S. Africa	850	25,851			141
Spain	50				
Sweden	123	153		333	
Switzerland	346	304	712	528	
Turkey	12				
U.S.S.R.	1				
U.A.R.-Egypt	6				
United Kingdom	2,431	18,562[c]	26,623	12,593	1,738
United States	1,826	1,334	5,573	4,585	73
Venezuela	2				
Yugoslavia	2				
Not specified	183	360	12,440	142,942	5,265

Source: *United Nations Statistical Yearbooks*, 1960, 1961, 1962.
[a]Includes New Zealand
[b]Includes Pakistan
[c]Includes Rhodesia and Nyasaland

TABLE 29.2   Recent African Tourism

FROM	Ethiopia 1970	Kenya 1970	TO Nigeria 1969	South Africa 1969	Uganda 1970
TOTAL	53,187	343,496	13,767	328,241	80,363
Australia	406	3,057[a]		9,185	
Austria		2,457			
Belgium		2,459		1,543	484
Canada		5,594	271	3,112	984
Denmark		3,962			584
France	7,154	7,548	188	4,166	936
E. Germany			⎱	10,018[b]	
W. Germany	2,880	22,771	431 ⎰		2,897
Greece		1,693		1,498	
India	1,785	17,604	308		2,333
Ireland				1,522	
Israel		3,591		1,831	408
Italy	3,561	10,291	187	3,425	1,788
Japan	756	3,031	144		611
Netherlands		5,110	267	5,433	738
New Zealand				1,770	
Pakistan					388
Portugal				2,611	
Sweden	1,191	4,180			537
Switzerland		9,289	144	3,639	1,005
United Kingdom	4,531	104,810	4,338	55,851	10,754
United States	11,239	49,138	1,556	18,389	10,940
Not specified	19,634	86,911	5,833	204,248	44,976

Source: *United Nations Statistical Yearbooks*, 1970, 1971e
[a]Includes New Zealand
[b]Data not separable

French ambiance and desirable beaches have created the basis for an attempt at developing a major resort system complete with a *Club Mediterranée* outpost that will cater largely to sun-hungry Europeans. Assuming the recently offered all-inclusive tours from Western Europe can be maintained from as little as $300 and can be extended to other areas, a number of countries with ocean frontage can be expected to develop touristically *if* the political climate is favorable to developers. The major country in the region, Nigeria, attracted a substantial number of tourists in pre-independence days, many of them British from neighboring colonies. In the late 1960s and early 1970s, the flow diminished sharply as an offshoot of the Civil War but they should soon increase. In terms of attractions, Nigeria's main assets to tourists are cultural, its role as the world's largest black state, the presence of the gateway international airport at Kano, and the reputed friendliness of its peoples.

In Central Africa, land-based tourism is undeveloped although some potential exists. Favorable factors include the presence of equatorial rain forests and game preserves. Zaire, for instance, has announced plans to set aside as much as 15 percent of its territory as nature preserves. In the absence of shore development, much of the actual tourist potential lies in the eastern and southern regions of Zaire, particularly the areas bordering Uganda and Ruanda, where beautiful lakes and majestic mountains are accompanied by a network of national parks left as a legacy by the Belgians. The physical attractiveness of these areas is great enough and Zaire is sufficiently prosperous to set in motion a tourist network that could in time overshadow that of Kenya, Uganda, and Tanzania combined.

The presence or recency of white colonial systems in southern Africa renders its tourist present and future somewhat different than those of other areas in the continent. The Republic of South Africa, in particular, has almost a West European ambiance despite the presence of the black majority population. Given cheaper transportation, its abundant tourist resources in the form of game parks, good tourist infrastructure, modern cities, and uncrowded beaches would make it a strong rival to Kenya for international tourism. But one must recognize that the reputation of South African policies might hinder such a development.

Potentially attractive areas for tourists abound in the rest of the southern region. These range from the Victoria Falls area on the Rhodesia-Zambia border, to the surfing beaches on the east coast, to the Latin flavor of parts of Mozambique. But given political unrest it is exceedingly risky to make any kind of prediction about the prospects for further increases in tourism in southern Africa. The most important present barriers are those of cost; even if these are overcome it may very well be difficult for tourists visiting colonial or white-dominated areas in the south to get permission to then visit the independent states to the north.

Apart from the Mediterranean Coast, East Africa offers the continent's most developed tourism. In this region there are the two major cities of Dar es Salaam and Nairobi, numerous national parks, game preserves and natural sights, and the Indian Ocean coast. The latter area in Kenya is the site of the first development of mass charter flight tourism in East Africa, largely originating in Germany. This is a rather peculiar development at first glance because the great majority of tourists continue to be British, American, and Canadian. But traffic-sharing agreements with the East African Airways have so far prevented the British from originating large scale charters; by default German and European operators have filled the gap. The

European tourists generally patronize the coast on sun and beach tours at cheap and all-inclusive rates, whereas Americans and British still focus on inland attractions such as Nairobi and the game parks and lodges. Given continuance of an approximate three- or four-to-one ratio of costs between the game park orbit and the coast's all-inclusive tour rates, the market for tourists in Kenya would seem to inevitably gravitate towards the coast. There is already, in fact, a German language newspaper circulating there. One great advantage of coastal tourism is that it is less likely to upset or compete with indigenous needs (Myers, 1972) in areas that are suffering from severe population pressures under prevailing conditions. The major disadvantage is that the infrastructure (roads, hotels, modern water, and sewage supply systems) needed for mass tourism is a heavy consumer of capital, which must either be diverted from other important allocations or be imported with the consequent danger of foreign control. But as an efficient generator of foreign exchange, and an employer of unskilled labor, international tourism has important benefits, and it has potential growth rates higher than those of most other likely exporting sectors of the economy.

At present, it seems as though Kenya will continue to tolerate and even welcome outside investment in tourist facilities. In Tanzania the picture is much less clear, but in all probability developments will be on a much smaller scale. The situation in Uganda is more problematic because of recent internal and international political difficulties.

Ethiopia has partaken of spillover effects from Kenyan tourism and from the heavy American military investment and Peace Corps involvement in the country during the 1960s, but its investment in tourist infrastructure is still small. However, given the presence of adequate natural attractions, convenient location on the air routes to East Africa from Europe, and a different and fascinating culture it has considerable potential for expanding its tourist trade.

If all the uncertain factors work out favorably one can predict that the 1970s and the 1980s will be the decades of the African tourist explosion—at least in terms of the European market. Whether competition from Latin American and Southeast Asian centers that offer somewhat similar attractions will develop is uncertain: if it does not, then American flows to Africa should show marked increases. Areas of particular promise would encompass the West African and Kenyan coasts and eastern Zaire. Other areas, notably in the South, have natural attractions for tourists but political problems make prediction even more uncertain than under normal conditions.

30

European Economic Presence in Francophone Africa: The Ivory Coast

DOUGLAS W. LISTER

One may say without excessive oversimplification that African states have tended toward one of two types of development. The first, often called "gradualist" or "conservative," is distinguished by an open, capitalist-style economy and close political-economic ties with one or more Western powers. Growth tends to be outward-looking, and the development potential of the export sector is appreciated. In economic decision-making, priority is given to individual incentive and the mechanism of the market; favorable treatment generally is accorded to private capital, both domestic and foreign. Membership in a world currency area such as the franc or sterling zone is maintained, and capital transfers are unrestrained. Heavy use is made of European personnel, often recruited from the former colonial metropole, in staffing the bureaucracy. A small role is assigned to the state in the development process, and there is generally more concern with growth and efficiency than with equity of income distribution.

An alternative approach, usually described as "structural trans-formationist" or "radical," is virtually the opposite on all these points. Its hallmarks are a closed, socialist-style economy and anti-Western neutralism. Little faith is placed in the export sector as an "engine of growth," and the reduction of dependence on the outside is emphasized. Ties with world monetary zones are generally severed, and a separate national currency is established. At the very least, strict currency controls are imposed. European personnel is used occasionally in the civil service, but it originates from more diverse national and political backgrounds. As a rule, the mechanism of the market is suspect, and a large role is reserved for the state in the mobilization and management of development resources.

With few exceptions (Guinea, Mali under Modibo Keita, and Congo-Brazzaville since 1963), French-speaking African countries have opted for the gradualist type of development. The purpose of this chapter is to explore some of the implications of this choice in terms of the domestic economic development and external economic independence of one such country, the Ivory Coast. In particular, attention will be devoted to the significant role which Europeans have played in the economic life of this newly independent African state.

Contemporary European economic presence in francophone Africa is basically a legacy of French colonialism. Unlike the British, the French never envisioned self-government as a legitimate goal for colonial peoples. Instead, they foresaw progressive assimilation with metropolitan France. Under the French Fourth Republic, territories like the Ivory Coast were integral parts of the French Union in which all citizens, regardless of color, theoretically enjoyed the same rights. This was, of course, pure myth for the vast majority of French-speaking Africans. In 1958, just two years before independence, the Ivory Coast had fewer than 20 high-level civil servants who were black (Berg, 1960). But the fact that a handful of African leaders such as Félix Houphouët-Boigny of the Ivory Coast, Diori Hamani of Niger, Léopold Sédar Senghor of Senegal, and Modibo Keita of Mali did serve in the Fourth Republic as Cabinet Ministers or Deputies to the French National Assembly is significant for the French concept of empire as an organic whole in which independence was anathema. Nor was the assimilationist urge forgotten when independence was granted in the early 1960s.

During colonial times, assimilation was particularly evident in the closed circuit of trade, aid, and private investment that existed between France and its African colonies. Trade between the center and periphery was regulated by a system of commercial preferences, the essence of which was special prices or *surprix* for the main exports of France and its overseas territories. Under this system, the prices paid in the colonies for imports from France were well above those for similar goods on the world market, and colonial exports drew higher-than-world prices in France. In 1954, it was estimated that the prices of goods traded under this system were 20-40 percent above world prices (Hayter, 1966).

For some commodities such as sugar, the *surprix* was achieved by a guaranteed minimum price for some or all of a colony's output. For others like palm oil, differential tariff rates were used between the French colonies and third countries. The French *Fonds National de Regularisation des Cours des Produits d'Outre-Mer* also offered short-term loans to colonial stabilization funds when prices fell below certain intervention levels. As a result of this system, French-African trade took place in an artificial environment characterized by guaranteed markets and inflated prices. In one sense, the French colonies were fortunate to have such a system because it eliminated the risks other producers faced on the world market. On the other hand, they were ill-prepared to assume the direction of their own economic affairs in 1960.

Not only did the French colonies carry on most of their trade with France, but they also received most of their capital for development from this one source. During the colonial period, the Ivory Coast and the other territories of French West and Equatorial Africa obtained most of their men and money from the French *Fonds d' Investissement de Développement Economique et Social (FIDES)* and *Caisse Centrale de la France d'Outre-Mer (CCOM)*. Between the turn of the century and the end of World War II, French West Africa received an estimated 46 billion francs, mostly in the form of long-term loans, from these two agencies. But the end of the war marked the beginning of a "New Deal" for French West Africa, especially the Ivory Coast. During the first ten years of the postwar period, more than four times as much aid was poured into the area as in the previous forty years. Approximately 70 percent of these funds came in the form of grants (Berg, 1960).

Hundreds of French administrators, technicians, and advisers were dispatched to staff the postwar development program. Here again, the French colonies were fortunate to receive this aid, but as a result they had little incentive to develop indigenous sources of capital and high-level manpower.

An equally important aspect of French aid during the colonial period was its sectoral and regional distribution. At least in the Ivory Coast, most funds went for infrastructure (roads, railroads, ports, electric-power facilities) and export agriculture, mainly coffee, cocoa, and wood. The most far-reaching infrastructure project was the dredging of the Vridi Canal in 1952 which made Abidjan a deep-water port capable of handling ocean-going shipping. The country's road network was expanded and improved during the first ten years of the postwar period, and production of export crops was increased by forest clearing. But little was done in directly productive enterprises. Moreover, since most infrastructure projects and plantations were located in the southeastern part of the country, the rest of the country, especially the North, remained relatively backward. The uneven allocation of French aid was evident in the gap between North and South in terms of per capita income and school enrollment. In the early 1950s, per capita income was estimated at 1,100 CFA francs in the North, compared to 7,100 in the South, and more than twice this much in the plantation areas (Stryker, 1971).

In 1957, the proportion of school-age children attending school for the country as a whole was 30 percent. But this figure was only 10 percent in the northern town of Korhogo, compared to 87 percent in the southeastern city of Abengourou (Zolberg, 1964). Even today, the Ivory Coast is characterized by a number of socioeconomic differences between North and South. Whereas the northern peoples (Malinké, Sénoufo) make their living mainly from subsistence farming (manioc, maize, sorghum, and some cotton), the southerners (Baoulé, Ebrié, Bété) make theirs from commercial agriculture (coffee, cocoa, bananas). A major problem all along has been the disproportionate growth of the capital city and the area around it. In 1910, Abidjan was a small fishing villlage inhabited by 700 people (Ebrié); by 1921 this figure had reached 5,400. In 1935, the Ebrié were "relocated" to make room for the French on the *plateau*, the site of the city's present downtown area, and by the end of World War II, the total population of the capital had reached 45,000. Ten years later, it was 127,000, and today is estimated at over half a million.

Private investment followed much the same pattern as public. Since restrictions existed on capital transfers outside the franc zone, non-French private investors were discouraged from investing in territories like the Ivory Coast. French private investors, on the other hand, faced almost no restrictions, which meant that private investment, like aid, was predominantly French. Most of this investment also was channeled into export agriculture, manufacturing, trading, and banking, all of which were centered in Abidjan or its immediate vicinity.

Given this close economic relationship with France, the advent of independence in the Ivory Coast did not mark the sudden and dramatic break with the past that is sometimes associated with African independence. To be sure, the young nation did acquire a greater measure of internal political autonomy, symbolized among other things by a set of political institutions, a flag, and a national anthem.

But in anything other than a formal political sense, the Ivory Coast was virtually as dependent as before.

In post-independence francophone Africa, European economic presence has two dimensions—bilateral and multilateral. The legal basis for bilateral ties between France and her former African colonies lies in a series of agreements concluded almost immediately after independence. As a rule, these "Cooperation Agreements" covered four fields: (1) political, including foreign policy, defense, and strategic raw materials; (2) economic, including monetary and financial policy; (3) legal, including the right of establishment for private investors and consular affairs; and (4) cultural, including aid to secondary and university education. The Ivory Coast signed nine Cooperation Agreements ranging over military, economic, financial, monetary, postal, telecommunications, civil aviation, merchant marine, and cultural affairs.

The general orientation of French-African *coopération* was to be worked out by "Mixed Commissions" composed of French and African representatives in equal numbers. Commissions were set up for each of the areas covered by the Cooperation Agreements, and meetings were held alternately in Paris and various African capitals. Aid and Cooperation Missions were established in each of the newly independent African states as antennas for the Cooperation Ministry. Their role was to assist in project preparation to keep abreast of any special needs or problems and supervise project execution. In each country, they were responsible to the French Ambassador. The degree of collaboration between these Aid and Cooperation Missions and their host governments has varied, but in the Ivory Coast it has been close. As a rule, only projects with a good chance of approval are proposed by Ivorian authorities.

All these organizations, however, receive their funds from two sources—the *Fonds d'Aide et de Coopération (FAC)* and the *Caisse Centrale de Coopération Economique (CCCE)*. The FAC was established in March, 1959, as a successor to the colonial FIDES, and CCCE was created out of CCOM. Both bodies are empowered to make loans, but only FAC is authorized to give grants (de Lattre, 1969).

The legal basis for European multilateral presence in francophone Africa lies in another series of accords known as the Association Agreements. Since 1957, seventeen African states and Madagascar have been linked to the European Common Market (EEC) by a series of three five-year agreements covering the main aspects of international economic relations—trade, aid, and private investment. The first, signed when most of these countries were still

French colonies, was contained in the same agreement which established the Common Market, the Rome Treaty of 1957. The second, concluded in 1963 after these countries acquired independence, was the subject of a separate accord known as the Yaoundé Convention. This agreement was later renewed in 1969 giving rise to the second Yaoundé Convention. The Lome Convention was signed in 1975 between the 9 members of the enlarged EEC and 46 associated countries, including Anglophone African states. These accords concerned economic matters only.

The idea of associating the colonies of the Six with the nascent Common Market was first proposed by Guy Mollet, Prime Minister of France, during the negotiations preceding the signing of the Rome Treaty. At the time, four of the EEC countries had colonies, namely: France (French West and Equatorial Africa, Madagascar and a number of lesser dependencies), Belgium (the Belgian Congo and Rwanda-Urundi), Italy (United Nations Trust Territory of Somalia), and the Netherlands (New Guinea).

From the outset of the Common Market negotiations, the Six were unanimously agreed that "special relations" with overseas territories were discriminatory and thus incompatible with the creation of a European customs union. But there was considerable disagreement over what to do with the colonies. For France, the problem was particularly acute because of the size of her colonial empire and the system of *surprix* under which producers in France and the French colonies enjoyed guaranteed markets and artificially high prices for some or all of their output. France was unwilling to abandon this system without some transitional arrangement to ease the shock of marketing at world prices.

For Germany and the Netherlands, the situation was altogether different. With long histories as free-trading nations, both were opposed in principle to commercial preferences. Moreover, they were reluctant to acquire any new colonial ties at a time when most Third World countries were seeking independence. Belgium and Italy, on the other hand, shared to a lesser extent the same problems as France. Both had colonies in Africa which they were reluctant to expose to free competition on the world market. When the question of association arose, they thus steered a middle course between France, on the one hand, and Germany and the Netherlands, on the other (van der Lee, 1963).

In the end, however, France was able to prevail by making her approval of the Rome Treaty contingent upon the establishment of a regime of association for her colonies and those of the other European imperial powers. Belgium and Italy readily accepted this condition, and Germany and the Netherlands regarded it as a necessary price to pay for French participation in the Common Market.

In the trade field, the main accomplishment of the Association Agreements was the creation of eighteen free-trade areas between the EEC and the Associated African States and Madagascar (AASM). For former French colonies like the Ivory Coast, this meant that commercial preferences previously accorded only to France were gradually extended to the other five members of EEC. In return, the former French colonies obtained duty-free access to an enlarged European market protected against outsiders by EEC's Common External Tariff (CET). By virtue of CET on tropical products, the Ivory Coast and the other Common Market Associates received a preference on their main exports (pineapples, coconut, coffee, pepper, cloves, nutmeg and cocoa). Thus a regime of "special preferences" was set up in the markets of the Six at the same time as a system of "reverse preferences" was established in the markets of the Eighteen. For a number of reasons, however, the "reverse preferences" provided for in the Rome Treaty and Yaoundé Conventions were never completely implemented. First, five of the Associates—Zaire, Rwanda, Burundi, Togo, and Somalia—were under previous international agreements to observe nondiscriminatory tariff regimes. Second, many of the Associates, the Ivory Coast included, invented new charges designed to compensate for budgetary revenue lost through tariff reduction with the Six. They contrived a number of duties known collectively as "revenue charges." In a formal sense, these were merely customs duties with another name, but since they were applied universally, they did not violate the principle of nondiscrimination between the Six. The AASM were also able to circumvent the requirement that internal taxes (or revenue charges) be no higher than those applied to like domestic products by claiming, with good reason in most cases, that no similar domestic product existed. Revenue charges thus became popular devices for meeting budgetary needs while technically complying with the Association Agreements. In the Ivory Coast, three such charges were invented, namely fiscal entry charges, special entry duties, and a value-added tax. For many imports, revenue charges amounted to more than customs duties. Finally, the Rome Treaty and Yaoundé Conventions contained escape clauses allowing the Associates to suspend application of these accords altogether if they interfered with the collection of adequate budgetary revenue, industrialization, or intra-African economic cooperation.

In the aid area, the principal achievement of the Association Agreements was the establishment of the multilateral European

Development Fund (EDF). Under the Rome Treaty, EDF was heavily capitalized and empowered to make grants for social and economic infrastructure investment. Additional funds were obtained from the European Investment Bank (EIB) which had previously been active only in Europe. The purposes for which EEC aid could be given were broadened to include agricultural diversification, industrialization and intra-African economic cooperation.

Although the initiative for all EEC-financed projects must come from the Associates, the final decision of whether or not to fund a particular project is made by the EEC. The responsibility for executing EEC-financed projects, however, rests with the Associates. The only requirement in this regard is that contracts be awarded on the basis of competitive bidding.

In the field of private investment, the main accomplishment of the Association Agreements was the placing of the Six on an equal footing in terms of the right of establishment and capital transfers. In former French colonies like the Ivory Coast, this meant extending the privileges previously enjoyed by French investors to investors from the EEC "Five." Nondiscrimination became the rule in this area, as in others. In the case of the Ivory Coast, however, the private investment provisions of the Association Agreements were of little or no consequence, because the country already had instituted a very liberal investment code in 1959 which made no distinctions between investors of different nationalities. Capital transfers outside the franc zone were also freed of restrictions in 1967.

Under the Ivorian Investment Code, foreign enterprises are divided into two categories: priority and nonpriority. The code lists six types of enterprises that may apply for priority status: (1) construction companies, (2) agroindustrial enterprises, (3) primary product processing units, (4) consumer goods manufacturers, (5) extractive industries, and (6) energy producers. Clearly, almost any foreign investor can apply for priority status. But in order to obtain it, the foreign investor must submit projects falling within the Ivory Coast's Five-Year Development Plan, and have them judged by the government as "of special interest to the country."

Provided this condition is met, any enterprise can become a priority and thereby take advantage of sizeable tax reductions and exemptions. In particular, the Investment Code provides for substantial reductions in import duties (customs duties and revenue charges), internal taxes (property taxes, profits taxes and registration fees), and export duties (fiscal exit charges). Priority enterprises may also be exempted entirely from import duties on raw materials and capital equipment simply by making their import requirements known in advance to the Planning Ministry's Office of Industrial Development. As for internal taxes, all enterprises, priority or not, are entitled to exemptions during the first five years of their operations, but priority enterprises often are given exemptions for a longer period, the duration of which is fixed by a special convention concluded between the government and the foreign investor. Finally, priority enterprises are entitled to a 50 percent reduction in export duties, unless their goods are destined for one or more of the other member states of the West African Customs Union (Dahomey, Upper Volta, Mali, Mauritania, Niger, and Senegal), in which case they are not required to pay any export duties.

In special cases, even more generous treatment is available. Under the Investment Code, priority enterprises are entitled to apply for what is called *le régime fiscal de longue durée*. Normally, this is reserved for investments with a slow rate of return (eg. oil palm) and therefore not all priority enterprises can obtain it. For those qualifying, no taxes are collected for a period of 25-30 years, after which the level of taxation is negotiated between the government and the foreign investor.

Beyond tax relief are very liberal rules governing reinvestment of profits. Priority enterprises are under no obligation to reinvest any of their earnings. For non-priority enterprises, however, there are several ways of going about the matter. Some enable foreign investors to recycle their tax payments into new investment; others merely require an investment of $2,000 or more in a project falling within the Development Plan that would be completed in three years or less. In no case, however, is the reinvestment requirement very high.

The final element in the Ivory Coast's regime for private investment is freedom of capital movements. Within the franc zone, capital transfers have always been free, but until 1967 this was not true for transfers involving third countries. Under the Cooperation Agreements, these were to be regulated by the Mixed Commission on monetary affairs. In 1967, however, the Ivory Coast passed a law which eliminated all restrictions on capital transfers outside the franc zone. In the words of this statute: "Financial relations between the Ivory Coast and foreigners are free." The law contained an escape clause authorizing the President to impose controls by decree, but this authority has seldom been used.

Since 1959, the Ivory Coast has made a deliberate effort to attract foreign investment through very generous tax exemptions and reductions and liberal rules governing the reinvestment and repatriation of profits (Ministère du Plan, 1971). Recently, however, there has been some talk of rationalizing the Ivorian Investment Code in such a way as to make the advantages offered to foreign investors proportional to the importance of their projects in terms of national economic development. At present, all the priority enterprises receive roughly the same treatment, and there are several high-ranking officials in the Ivorian Planning Ministry who believe that the country could secure not only more revenue, but also more valuable projects by making the Investment Code more flexible. Proportion-ately larger tax exemptions, for example, might be awarded to foreign investors whose projects are located in the underprivileged North. This sort of reform was in fact the subject of a lecture delivered by the Ivorian Planning Minister, Mohammed Diawara at Columbia University in 1970.

What, then, has been the impact of these bilateral and multilateral economic ties with Europe on the economic develop-ment and independence of the Ivory Coast? In the trade field, it seems that these arrangements have helped the Ivory Coast to expand its exports and to accumulate balance-of-payments surpluses on current account. From 1960-1970, the value of Ivorian exports grew annually by an average of 21.8 percent (United Nations, 1971e). This phenomenal record definitely was facilitated by the preferential access to the markets of the EEC "Five" made possible by the Association Agreements with the European Common Market. In 1960, France alone accounted for 72 percent of total Ivorian exports to the EEC countries, and 88 percent of Ivorian imports from the Six. But by 1970, these figures were 52 and 68 percent, respectively. Over the same period, the share of the EEC "Five" rose from 28 to 48 percent in the case of exports and from 12 to 32 percent in the case of imports. Moreover, it was primarily through trade with the EEC "Five" that the Ivory Coast accumulated its surpluses. Traditionally in a state of deficit with France, the country has maintained growing surpluses with the other EEC countries which have more than compensated for its deficits with France. In other words, the Ivory Coast probably would not have been able to achieve the surpluses that it has without the diversification of trading partners which has taken place under the Association Agreements. Of course, one could say that this diversification would have occurred anyway, and there is no definitive answer to this argument, since there is no way of knowing for sure what would have happened in the absence of the Association. But given the opposition of certain EEC countries—notably Germany—to the whole idea of preferential treatment for tropical products from EEC's African partners, it is extremely unlikely that the treatment enjoyed by this African country would have been as favorable as it has been if the Association had never existed. One must conclude, therefore, that this. arrangement has had a positive impact on the Ivory Coast's performance in the export sector.

Though Association with Europe has spurred the growth of Ivorian exports, it has done little or nothing to relieve Ivorian trade dependence on France. While important in development terms, the diversification of trading partners has been almost meaningless in terms of dependence. During the decade, France accounted for an average of 34.8 percent of total Ivorian exports and 54.3 percent of imports (United Nations, 1969c). If for some reason the French market were to disappear tomorrow, the economic consequences probably would be disastrous.

In the aid area, the situation is parallel. From 1960-1970, public sector gross domestic fixed capital formation in the Ivory Coast grew at an average annual rate of 22.6 percent (United Nations, 1969c). This magnificent achievement was facilitated by the inflow of capital, largely in the form of grants, from the multilateral EDF and EIB, and from the EEC countries individually. Taken together, EEC multilateral and bilateral aid accounted for approximately 84 percent of all foreign assistance to the Ivory Coast during the period (*Le Moniteur Africain*, 1971). Without the Association Agreements, it is doubtful that the Ivory Coast would have received the aid which it has from these countries. As noted earlier, France accounted for virtually all foreign aid to the Ivory Coast during the colonial period, and the significant achievement of the Rome Treaty and Yaoundé Conventions was that part of the burden of contributing to the development of the former French colonies was transferred to the EEC "Five" which had previously had little or no interest in francophone Africa. In fact, they still do not have much interest, but as a result of these arrangements, Germany in particular, and to a lesser extent, Italy, the Netherlands, Belgium, and Luxembourg all were forced to take an interest in order to obtain concessions from France, the first and most important of which was her signature to the Treaty of Rome. Like it or not, these countries have contributed two-thirds of a fund which, in turn, has supplied the Ivory Coast with 16.5 percent of its foreign aid over the decade 1960-1970. This does not include the additional 8.2 percent contributed by Italy, and the 3.8 percent contributed by Germany bilaterally (*Le Moniteur Africain*, 1971). Thus, Ivory Coast's multilateral and bilateral aid ties with Europe have obviously facilitated public sector fixed investment.

Here again they have done little to increase economic independence. France accounted for 55.1 percent of all Ivorian financial aid and 80 percent of all technical assistance during the decade 1960-1970. Without French aid, it is doubtful even today that the government could sustain the present level of public sector services.

Though less pronounced, the same pattern is evident in the field of private investment. During the decade 1960-1970, private sector fixed investment grew at roughly the same rate as public investment, namely 22.6 percent per year (United Nations, 1969c). This too is an impressive figure which was certainly facilitated by the inflow of private capital from Europe which was in turn facilitated by the Association Agreements. As noted above, these accords extended the privileges previously enjoyed by French investors to investors from the EEC "Five." Still, France accounted for 79.1 percent of all foreign direct investment in the Ivory Coast and 95 percent of all foreign high-level manpower during the decade 1960-1970 (de Lattre, 1969). Here, perhaps more than in any other area, loss of French support would be disastrous, since it would quite literally bring the Ivorian private sector to a standstill.

Thus the Ivory Coast's multilateral and bilateral arrangements with Europe have basically preserved an international political *status quo* in relations with its former colonial power France, while contributing to notable advances on the national economic front.

31

Persistent Colonialism
in Southern Africa

HARM J. DE BLIJ

Opinions differ, but in the present context the southern African region incorporates all the states and territories located to the south of Zaire and Tanzania. In terms of political geography, this area in the mid-1970s is still a region where decisions of white power structures dominate the course of events. In the economic geography of southern Africa, all the political units have in one way or another been tied together. The flow of trade, migration of labor, and development of ports and rail links all confirm the integration of the southern African region.

EVOLUTION OF THE COLONIAL FRAMEWORK

Southern Africa's colonial framework evolved in several distinct (though sometimes slightly overlapping) stages. The initial stage saw the Portuguese establish footholds along the coasts of present-day Angola and Mozambique, notably during the sixteenth and seventeenth centuries. The second stage witnessed the founding of Cape Town (1652) by the Dutch East India Company, and the growth of the Cape Colony attended by strife with the African population, especially along the eastern frontier. The third stage began with the permanent occupation of the Cape by the British (1806) and includes the acquisition by Britain of the Colony of Natal. During this period the Boers founded their republics on the South African Plateau, and Rhodes' Pioneer Columns secured the region then known as Zambezia (later Rhodesia) for the British Crown. The fourth stage involves southern Africa's participation in the "scramble," as Portugal pushed its still essentially coastal dependencies far into the interior, Germany claimed South West Africa, and the British and the Boers engaged in the Boer War. During this fourth stage, in the last quarter of the nineteenth century and the first decade of the twentieth, the main elements of the southern African boundary framework were defined, and the political status of the region's territories also was determined. Conquering Britain merged its victorious Cape and Natal colonies with the vanquished Boer republics into the Union of South Africa. Basutoland, Bechuanaland, and Swaziland became High Commission Territories, outside the jurisdiction of the Union Government. Angola and Mozambique remained Portuguese colonies; the differences between Northern Rhodesia and Nyasaland (to become British Protectorates) and Southern Rhodesia (developing into a British colony) were already evident.

TWENTIETH CENTURY MODIFICATIONS

Although southern Africa's politico-geographical framework at the beginning of the present century was essentially what it is today, a number of internal, organizational changes were to occur. Under the present heading we confine our discussion to the period prior to 1955, because at about mid-century the pace and nature of change in southern Africa took an entirely different course. Thus the first half of the twentieth century in southern Africa was one of adjustment and colonial accommodation. Major developments included not only the formation of a *Union* in South Africa, but also the termination of German administration in South West Africa and the establishment there of a South African *Mandate* under League of Nations auspices, and the formation, following lengthy preparations, of a *Federation* in the Rhodesias and Nyasaland, as well as the elevation of the Portuguese dependencies to *Provinces* of the Portuguese state.

Even before the Boer War ended, voices had been raised in Britain in opposition to London's campaign, which included concentration camps and a scorched earth policy. Britain's Liberal Party even then committed itself to a restoration of Boer rights in South Africa in the event of its assumption of power. When, in 1905, that party was indeed elected to office, the promise was kept. British Prime Minister Campbell-Bannerman's objective was far-reaching: he wanted to unite the vanquished highveld republics with the British colonies on the coast in order to create a Union of South Africa as a cornerstone of the British Empire. That the Boers could be persuaded to join in such a venture was largely the personal accomplishment of Campbell-Bannerman, who had termed the South African campaign as barbarous; his expressions of dismay and commitment to reparations had figured strongly in the Boer decision to give up the battle at the Treaty of Vereeniging in 1902. Prime Minister Campbell-Bannerman's objective was far-reaching: he formation of a South African Union could be implemented, but he was its architect, and the process he had set in motion could not be stopped despite strong opposition at home and in South Africa. And so, after a series of conferences, the Union of South Africa was inaugurated on May 31, 1910, at Pretoria, the old Boer capital. Its first Prime Minister was not an Englishman, but a Boer, General Botha. Another Boer, a lawyer named J. C. Smuts, attained prominence during the pre-Union negotiations. He, too, was to assume the leadership of the Dominion of the British Crown in the decades to follow.

South Africa's population, by the time Union was proclaimed, possessed all the heterogeneity it does today. The African majority had stood aloof from the Boer-British conflict, though Africans who were aware of all the ramifications of the events of the first decade of this century generally supported the British cause (Mansergh, 1962). Already confined to reserves and generally in a position of serfdom, the African population's position at the Cape and in Natal was somewhat better than it was in the Boer territories. The substantial Colored population at the Cape had been enfranchised for a half century, and the franchise had been extended to Africans as well. (This was not a universal franchise, but one achieved via a test). No provision for enfranchisement existed in the Transvaal or the Orange Free State; rather, there were specific ordinances against the granting of voting rights to Bantu and Coloreds. In Natal, always more conservative than the Cape, the Asian population originally brought to work on sugar plantations now numbered over 100,000 and they expected that the British, who would bestow self-government upon a defeated adversary, would also favor them. At least, the Asians hoped Britain would give them the option of British citizenship.

What emerged at the time of Union in 1910 was not a compromise but a confirmation of Boer doctrine. Even the timid moves toward a multiracial electorate that existed at the Cape were negated; the Union's government was to be a monopoly of whites.

Campbell-Bannerman's blueprint was to restore relationships among Europeans in South Africa, and there proved to be no room for negotiations relating to the involvement of non-whites, whether African, Colored, or Asian. Thus, in the half-century the Union survived in its original form, administration grew out of the principles for which, in essence, the Boers had fought their war. Party politics were the privilege of the white minority, and government its prerogative.

In 1919, following the end of the First World War, the Union gained control over neighboring South West Africa, the German colony whose forces it had defeated in a brief conflict in 1915. Thus the Union, only nine years after its creation, saw its sphere expanded by two-thirds of its original domain. The League of Nations' decision to award the former colony to South Africa was not based simply on proximity, however. The South African statesman Jan Smuts was active in the development of the League of Nations, and especially in the formulation of the League's Mandate System, whereby the colonial possessions of Germany and its allies were distributed among the victorious powers. It was largely due to Smuts' efforts that South West Africa became the ward of the Union, and subsequently Smuts devoted a great deal of energy toward the final incorporation of the territory into South Africa—not as a mandate, but as a fifth province.

World War II and the demise of the League of Nations tightened South Africa's grip on South West Africa. Although the United Nations placed the territory under its Trusteeship Council, South Africa pushed ahead with the integration of its fifth province. An attempt to deter the Union through the International Court of Justice failed, and during the 1950s and 1960s the South African presence in South West Africa became irretrievably entrenched. White residents of the territory were represented in the South African parliament and South African practices of racial-territorial separation were imposed. Occasional voices of opposition were quashed, though pressure from countries beyond southern Africa's sphere led recently to the adoption by the U.N. of the African-approved name for South West Africa, *Namibia*.

An African map is a reminder of South Africa's politico-geographic good fortune when it gained control over Namibia. Apart from its enormous size and its not inconsiderable productive capacity, Namibia's Caprivi strip carries the South African sphere of influence to the very banks of the Zambezi River, and to the border of Zambia.

The Zambezi River for a century has been more than a physiographic dividing line in southern Africa. In Mozambique, it separates the south, with its urban centers, rail and road communications to the interior, and substantial European population from the more frontier-like north. In the interior, it separates Rhodesia, where white rule still prevails, from Zambia and Malawi, today black independent states. In the past, too, the great river was a divider: Rhodesia was a British colony, then called Southern Rhodesia, and Northern Rhodesia (Zambia) was a protectorate. Nyasaland, also north of the Zambezi, similarly was a protectorate prior to attaining independence as Malawi.

As dependencies, Rhodesia always had a larger European population than Zambia and Malawi combined. Rhodesia was a part of the developing southern African plateau: its Great Dyke yielded minerals, its highveld contained areas of good soils, its lands were alienated and Africans confined to reserves. Salisbury, the capital, and Bulawayo, the second city, mirrored Johannesburg and Durban, albeit on a smaller scale. Rhodesia eventually attracted a quarter of a million whites. Zambia, on the other hand, experienced a later and slower influx of whites; the emergence of the Copperbelt as a major mining region notwithstanding. Zambia's white population never reached 100,000, and that of Malawi remained below 10,000. Aided by the protectorate status of their territories, the African inhabitants of Zambia and Malawi lost less than their southern contemporaries.

The growth and strength of Rhodesia, and the rather insular development of exploitive industries north of the Zambezi, led at an early stage to recommendations that the three territories be merged into a single political entity. In the 1920s, Rhodesian whites, then securing Self-Governing Colony status for their territory, were not enthusiastic about the prospect of taking on responsibility for the administration of the north, where African rights were to be respected much more strictly. During the 1930s, however, white attitudes began to change, and in 1938 the government appointed the Bledisloe Commission to investigate the possibility of a merger. The Commission's report, which argued in favor of closer ties between the Rhodesias but against an actual merger (on grounds of contrasting policies and practices toward African inhabitants which, it was felt, could not be reconciled), was lost in the chaos of World War II. But white Rhodesians had not forgotten the concept when, in the late 1940s, the possibility of federation again was raised.

Ostensibly the primary objective of federation in the Rhodesias and Nyasaland was economic: federation would enhance development, confirm the complementarity of the areas north and south of the Zambezi, and facilitate the distribution and consumption of electric power derived from the Kariba Dam, to be built in the Zambezi River. But the real goal was political: the extension of the kind of power the white minority possessed in Southern Rhodesia into Northern Rhodesia and Nyasaland. This was not lost on the African inhabitants of the area, who could see their small measure of progress endangered. Africans had secured membership in Northern Rhodesia's Legislative Council in 1948, and in that of Nyasaland in 1949. Their growing political consciousness was expressed by the formation of the Nyasaland African Congress in 1944 and the Northern Rhodesia Congress in 1948. In 1949 the African Mineworkers' Trade Union became a force in Northern Rhodesian politics.

In all three territories, the African population far outnumbered the white. In 1950, Southern Rhodesia's African population numbered slightly less than 3 million, that of Northern Rhodesia was about 3½ million, and that of Nyasaland, somewhat over 3 million. When the time came for the referendum on federation, however, only a few hundred Africans could not defeat a political scheme they overwhelmingly rejected. Thus the Federal State of Rhodesia and Nyasaland (also called the Central African Federation) was inaugurated in September, 1953. Salisbury became the federal headquarters. Representation in the Federal Assembly was overwhelmingly white and Southern Rhodesian. African spokesmen in all three territories vowed that the federal system would not survive for long. Elsewhere in Africa, the federal idea was tainted, and viewed as a pretext for the perpetuation of white supremacy. In East Africa, British hopes for a federation were dashed. In West Africa, Ghana's late President Nkrumah became a strong opponent of federalism in Africa generally; he advised the late President Lumumba of the Congo (Zaire) to resist federalism in that country, advice that had fateful consequences.

The Federation of Rhodesia and Nyasaland survived just one decade. Its dissolution, inevitable from the beginning, coincided with the ascent of Northern Rhodesia and Nyasaland to independence. The Zambezi dividing line had prevailed again.

The period following the end of World War II witnessed a growing international interest in the conditions prevailing in dependent territories. States possessing colonies were committed to report on the situation in their dependencies to the United Nations, whose independent commissions may investigate reports of abnormal circumstances.

Virtually all colonial powers submitted to this practice of voluntary cooperation. In Africa, the United Kingdom and France were in the process of decolonization and Belgium's timetable was hastened by developments in the Congo. But Portugal resisted the tide. When all of West Africa was independent, Portugal still retained its territory in Guinea. When Equatorial Africa became sovereign, Portugal managed to keep control of its tiny exclave of Cabinda. And when United Nations pressure for information about conditions in Mozambique and Angola grew stronger, Portugal once again found a way to avoid the issue. In 1951, the Portuguese government officially changed the status of its African dependencies to "provinces" of metropolitan Portugal. Now Portugal could maintain that it did not possess any colonies, and that it need not adhere to United Nations stipulations relating to nonself-governing territories.

Portugal had pervasive reasons for this course of action. Colonial practices in Portuguese Guinea, Angola, and Mozambique were repressive and exploitive, and reform was slow in coming. In Mozambique, for example, a system prevailed whereby male Africans between the ages of 18 and 55 were compelled to work for the state at minimal wages six months of each year, unless they could prove to be in some form of gainful employ or engaged in an approved activity (the military, for instance). By this *shibalo* system, the labor of thousands of Africans was obtained at the lowest possible cost; the laborers worked on road building projects, dam sites, railroads, ports, and farms. One alternative for the African adult male wishing to avoid such conscription was to volunteer to work in the South African mines, under a contractual arrangement whereby the Portuguese administration received a sum of money for each Mozambique laborer to cross the border legally for work in the Union. An ancillary provision benefiting the Portuguese territory stipulated that a certain number of laborers thus provided would also be rewarded by trade funneled through Lourenço Marques. The port of Lourenço Marques in this way became a major source of revenue, for the *shibalo* incentive led hundreds of thousands of Mozambique Africans to seek work in South Africa, and the quotas were always filled. Indeed, many Africans left Mozambique illegally, crossing the border to South Africa or Rhodesia, in order to seek employment and escape from Portuguese rule.

Where these means of exploitation could not succeed, the Portuguese administration instituted a system of compulsory cropping, whose intent was to force the African subsistence farmer into the cash economy. In northern Mozambique, for example, African villagers were instructed to grow a certain quantity of cotton in addition to their staple food crops. The seed was provided by the authorities and for their crop, the African farmers were paid returns that were far below those paid for cotton elsewhere in the world. The dislocation this system of forced cropping caused in the north was severe: local famines occurred and desperate peasants sabotaged the scheme by refusing to plant the seed, burning crops, and failing to harvest. Retribution was always severe, and the system gained notoriety even in Mozambique itself.

The Portuguese government did not want United Nations inspection of its colonial territories, and the change of status provided a convenient escape. But the conditions prevailing in Portuguese Africa nevertheless came to world attention, in part through the efforts of academicians whose research exposed some of them, through Africans who left Portuguese Africa to report on the situation, and through the writings of some Portuguese observers whose consciences were disturbed by what they knew. Still, at midcentury, all was quiet in Angola and Mozambique, and the image of Portuguese colonialism as perhaps severe but also color-blind with opportunities for "assimilation" still prevailed. While the convenience of isolation continued, the Portuguese did begin to modify certain of their policies and practices, with the confident expectation that such enlightened flexibility would forestall the sort of problems other colonial powers had experienced. But the "Wind of Change" would not miss Portuguese Africa, just as it did not fail to penetrate British southern Africa.

THE WIND OF CHANGE IN SOUTHERN AFRICA

In a speech before the South African Parliament during a visit in 1960, Harold Macmillan, then Prime Minister of the United Kingdom, termed Africa's drive toward self-determination and independence the "Wind of Change." It was a felicitous choice of words, for the process, in more ways than one, had freshness, force, and direction. The push for sovereignty had been strongest in West Africa, where Ghana led the way, becoming independent in 1957. Then, inexorably, the drive led from West Africa to Equatorial and East Africa, where independence came in the early 1960s (Zaire, 1960; Tanganyika, 1961: Uganda, 1962; Kenya, 1963). And eventually the Wind of Change penetrated southern Africa. The impression of a thrust toward South Africa is inescapable.

Nevertheless, more than half a generation after Ghana's rebirth, South Africa still is barely affected by the momentous changes that have marked the rest of the continent. In fact, most of the changes that have occurred in South Africa since 1957 have been designed to stop or slow African nationalist drive. Colonialism in its various forms has persisted and, we shall argue later, even intensified.

Six developments stand out significantly in southern Africa in the quarter century since 1950, all of them resulting from or responding to the pressure of the Wind of Change. These are: (1) the evolution and decay of a buffer zone between South Africa and black Africa; (2) the end of the Union in South Africa; (3) the failure of federation as Zambia and Malawi attained independence; (4) the rise and success of insurgent activities in Portuguese Africa; (5) the decision by white Rhodesians to declare an independent state in their colony; and (6) initial signs of moderation in South Africa's policies of separatism.

With the exception only of the quasi-independence of the former High Commission Territories, sovereignty in black Africa has come in a southward-moving wave that penetrated the region here defined as Southern Africa when Zambia and Malawi achieved it in 1964. This is reflected in Figure 31.1 which shows black Africa approaching southern Africa in stages from 1950 to 1972. Note that South Africa only as recently as 1975 shared boundaries with black independent Africa; the three High Commission Territories, though nominally sovereign, still remain very much in South Africa's sphere of influence.

The buffer zone had its maximum extent when the Central African Federation was still positioned between Angola and Mozambique, but the Federation broke up when Zambia and Malawi became independent. Subsequently, Angola and Mozambique attained independence. Rhodesia, however, still lies between South Africa and black Africa.

Both South Africa and black Africa are active in the belt of countries bordering the Republic. South Africa renders assistance of various kinds to Rhodesia. Indeed, South Africa has even sought to extend its arena of operations by establishing diplomatic and economic relations with Malawi, thereby weakening the black African front. And full-scale insurgency operations for more than a decade were carried on by African forces in Angola and for slightly less than a decade in Mozambique (Chapter 32). In addition, European-owned farms in the northern part of Rhodesia have been attacked by guerilla forces whose sanctuaries are in Zambia and Mozambique.

Symbolizing South Africa's increasing isolation, not only on the African continent but also in the Commonwealth and the world, was the termination in 1961 of the Union. Since 1948, South Africa has been governed by the Nationalist Party. The Nationalist Party represented the Afrikaner majority among the white population, the descendants of the Boer pioneers. During the period after 1948, South Africa's Nationalist government began to implement the program of racial-territorial segregation—*Apartheid*. In the process, the

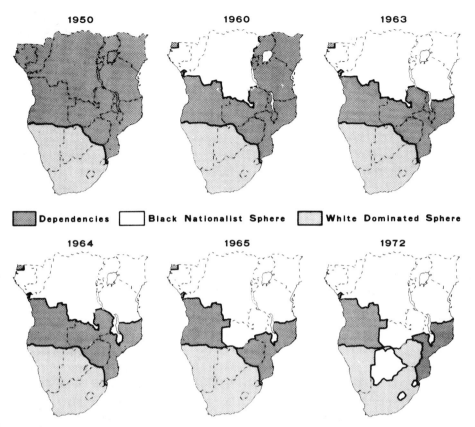

Figure 31.1 A Buffer Zone in Africa: Development and Decay.
Source: Provided by H.J. de Blij.

intercultural association among whites, envisaged a half century earlier by Campbell-Bannerman and championed by Smuts and others, was rejected. *Apartheid* is not simply the separation of black from white; it also involves the separation of blacks of different "nations" from each other, and the purification of white cultures as well. Parallel-medium schools, where subjects were taught alternately in English and Afrikaans, were phased out and replaced by schools using either Afrikaans or English. Nationalist fervor rekindled the flames doused by the Union, and things British took second place in the country's new list of priorities.

It was anomalous, therefore, that South Africa should still remain, however nominally, under the British Crown. World War II had revived old animosities as there was substantial Afrikaner opposition to Union participation in the conflict on the Allied side. The Nationalist government, it was felt, should terminate the Union and take South Africa out of the Commonwealth. These sentiments were strengthened by South Africa's increasing isolation in a world hostile to *Apartheid;* the United Kingdom was not supportive of the Union in this context. And as the number of decolonized Commonwealth member states increased, the South African position in that organization became untenable. The ouster occurred in the same year a Republic was re-established in South Africa—1961.

Thus, Africa's richest and most powerful state ceased to be a member of a multiracial organization in which several African states played prominent roles; it did not gain membership in the Organization of African Unity; and it faced continuous hostility in the United Nations. Still South Africa made no concessions to African or world opinion. The end of Union also symbolized the Afrikaners' determination to carry out the program of domestic colonialism that evolved from the original *Apartheid* principle—the program now referred to as *Separate Development.*

From the outset, African opposition to the Federation concept in the Rhodesias and Nyasaland was intense. That the government of Northern Rhodesia and Nyasaland should sit in Salisbury was unacceptable, nor was it palatable that the administration of the two protectorates was in the hands of a white clique dominated by Southern Rhodesians. Having first yielded to white settler pressures in the establishment of the Federation, the British government in the early 1960s reversed its direction and acknowledged that independence should come to Northern Rhodesia and Nyasaland. With this decision, the Federation was doomed, for the black sovereign states would not continue to participate in a political entity with Southern Rhodesia, where minority rule continued.

The independence of Zambia and Malawi constituted the first incursions of contiguous black Africa into southern Africa. It was also the first defeat for the region's white minority, whose framework to hold back the Wind of Change at the borders of Zaire and Tanzania had failed. Zambia's independence brought black Africa to the banks of the Zambezi River and Malawi's proximity to Mozambique contributed to insecurity along Mozambique's northwestern flank.

The federal experiment had both positive and negative consequences, the latter probably outweighing the former. Bitterness at having been forced into the Federation in the first place resulted in a militancy, especially in Zambia, that might not have developed under other circumstances. The brief lesson in multiracial government (the Salisbury-based federal assembly did have several African representatives in its ranks) failed, however, to generate a substantial segment of moderates among the Rhodesian white electorate and the prospect of a course of events similar to that of other British colonies and protectorates led to an unprecedented reaction (in the Africa of the postwar era): the colony's white minority declared independence from Britain in 1965. This had the effect of removing the restraints that British involvement might have had, and Rhodesia moved closer to South Africa ideologically. Thus a schism divided the former federal territories after the Federation broke up—a schism that was exacerbated by the federal misadventure. UDI—Rhodesia's unilateral declaration of independence—was sustained despite British pressure, an imperfect trade boycott, and the virtually complete severance of the territory's northern transport connections and functions.

Zambia and Malawi achieved independence by negotiation and consent; such political transformation could not be accommodated by the Portuguese state in its African dependencies. Angola and Mozambique could not escape the consequences of inflexibility, and rebellions against Portuguese authority broke out in the 1960s in both territories. Significantly, these insurgencies began shortly after neighboring countries became independent. Zaire (the former Belgian Congo) acquired independence in 1960 and sustained opposition to Portuguese rule began in Angola in 1961. Tanzania became a sovereign state in 1964 (after Tanganyika had attained independence in 1961) and serious revolutionary activities erupted in Mozambique shortly thereafter. The existence of a sanctuary in adjacent black Africa had a vital effect in making these hostilities possible.

This is not to suggest that the neighboring black African states provided their sanctuaries unconditionally, nor that cooperation was always given. Various Congolese governments acted at times to impede the liberation effort in Angola and Tanzania's government had sought to keep some check on the Mozambique insurgents. A major reason for such actions had been the division within the liberation movements themselves—in both Angola and Mozambique there was costly competition between insurgent groups which, at times, appeared to threaten the national security in the sanctuary states. Nevertheless, the rebels wrested sections of northern Angola and northern Mozambique from the Portuguese, and in both territories insurgent states arose before the colonial power yielded.

Also during the early 1970s, the hitherto isolated and rather sporadic incidents of guerilla activity in Rhodesia reached a new level of intensity. Rebel groups no longer carried out sorties across the Zambezi, then to retreat into Zambia: now those forces remained on Rhodesian soil, moving and eluding the Rhodesian army and air force. In 1973 the casualty toll on both sides was rising, white-owned farms had been attacked and European families killed, and South African military assistance was involved in the conflict.

PERSISTENT COLONIALISM IN SOUTHERN AFRICA

While Africa decolonizes, southern Africa's colonial condition remains—indeed, it intensifies. The effect of Rhodesia's UDI has been to concentrate even greater power in the white minority than it held when Rhodesia was still a colony. South Africa's program of Separate Development involves the creation of a set of "homelands" for African peoples in the Republic, a scheme that has been described as a case of "domestic colonialism" (Carter, Karis and Stultz, 1967). The practice of territorial separation of the races has been extended to South West Africa, in effect a dependency of South Africa. And even the independent black states in southern Africa have not escaped the colonial imprint. The former High Commission Territories are to a large extent controlled by South Africa, their economies (as those of colonies) tied to the Republic's economic machine. South Africa has reached beyond the buffer zone to involve itself in the affairs of Malawi, whose leadership proved receptive to the Republic's offers of economic assistance and diplomatic interaction. Malawi is no colony of South Africa, but its willingness to cooperate with South Africa has broken the unity of contiguous black Africa, a break the South Africans assiduously sought.

The pressure of the Wind of Change has produced major politico-territorial changes in southern Africa. It has virtually eliminated the interchanges that occurred across the Zambezi River (Zambia still uses Kariba power); problems created by the confrontation will be reduced by the completed Tanzania-Zambia rail line. South Africa's determination not to yield South West Africa relates to growing pressure to change the territory's status. And undoubtedly, the continued implementation of the Separate Development program in South Africa itself is based in part on external politico-geographical potentials.

When *Apartheid* became state policy in South Africa at midcentury, the fundamental reasons for its adoption were solely internal. Afrikaners had long objected to the slow but perceptible trend towards racial integration in the country (non-whites were attending "white" universities and riding on buses reserved for whites, for example). The establishment of firm practices of segregation was a Nationalist priority. There was no reason to look beyond South Africa's borders for any justification for *Apartheid*; Ghana's independence was years away and the precipitous course of events of the

1950s and 1960s could not be foreseen. The South African government implemented its *Apartheid* program in two ways. First, the Tomlinson Commission was created with a charge to develop a practicable blueprint for a South African "commonwealth of cultures," a racially and territorially segregated South Africa. Second, the government enacted a number of measures to initiate *ad hoc Apartheid*, measures to get non-whites out of the "white" universities, off the park benches, out of the elevators, even out of certain suburban areas known as "black spots." These measures were in anticipation of the broader national framework the Tomlinson Commission would recommend. The Commission reported to the country more than a half decade after its appointment, but when it did, it recommended a total transformation of South African living space.

Although a number of the Tomlinson Commission's specific recommendations were not accepted by the South African government, the program's essential element, the creation of a set of discrete "homelands" or *Bantustans* in which the black South African population would be concentrated, was adopted as policy. Since a substantial number of Bantu reserve areas already existed, the Commission proposed that 16 of these be recognized as "homelands," later to be consolidated into 7 Bantustans (Figure 31.2). The vanguard of the program was the Transkei, on the southeast coast. The Transkei became semi-autonomous in 1963, and acquired greater autonomy in stages subsequently. Its population of some four million, dominantly Xhosa, is represented in the capital, Umtata, by an all-black parliament. The next Bantu territory to achieve self-government was Kwazulu in Natal.

There are limits to the autonomy of the Bantu states in South Africa, and these are still established by the white regime that rules the Republic. The South African government involves itself heavily in the politics of the Transkei, and the country's leader, Kaiser Matanzima, is obliged to cooperate with South Africa's Separate Development planners. But the limits to sovereignty are not imposed by politicians alone. The Transkei, though better off than several of the other projected Bantustans, suffers from aridity, poor soils, excessive erosion, and other natural and man-induced environmental problems. Yet the Transkei has almost exclusively an agricultural economy; consequently a large number of residents must seek means of survival as transient workers in the South African mines, in factories, and on farms. It is officially estimated that over one million persons who are nominally Transkeians are employed elsewhere. This means that the Transkei must depend on white South Africa for job opportunities, and South Africa is in a position to throttle the coun-

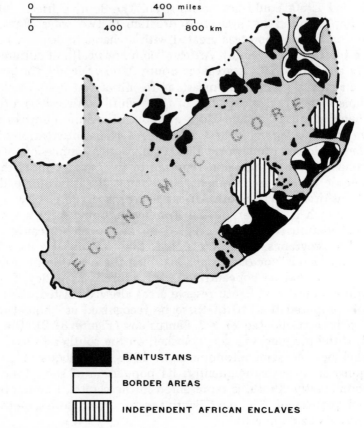

BANTUSTANS

BORDER AREAS

INDEPENDENT AFRICAN ENCLAVES

Figure 31.2 Shield of Proposed Bantustans.
Source: Provided by H.J. de Blij.

try at any time, simply by denying Transkeians entry rights into
white South Africa. The potential situation in several of the other
projected Bantustans is even less promising, so that these countries'
political quasi-independence is tied to a one-way economic dependence upon the powerful Republic.

When the Bantustan program is completed, the several autonomous African homelands will lie mainly along the land boundaries of
South Africa and South West Africa (Figure 31.3). In this position,
they will find themselves between sources of stress in the region—
between the core area of South Africa, with its power and strength,
and the forces of black African nationalism which, conceivably,
might achieve success in the external buffer zone at about the time
the Bantustan project nears completion. This leads to the conclusion

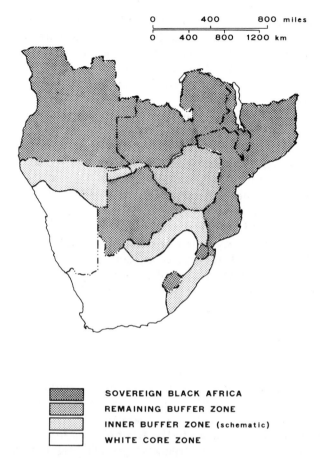

SOVEREIGN BLACK AFRICA
REMAINING BUFFER ZONE
INNER BUFFER ZONE (schematic)
WHITE CORE ZONE

Figure 31.3 Buffer Zones in Southern Africa.
Source: Provided by H.J. de Blij.

that if conflict were to spread into South Africa and South West
Africa as it did in Angola and Mozambique, and now Rhodesia,
these Bantu states (and not the white-held area) would be the first to
sustain the impact of guerilla incursions and insurgency. The white
areas of South Africa would lie somewhat protected, and thus the
Bantustan framework, intentionally or not, is in the process of creating an internal buffer zone for South Africa and South West Africa.

If indeed the South African Bantu states are to some degree
politically sovereign when such conflict arises, they will face a truly
murderous dilemma. Should there be cooperation with the insurgents? South African retribution undoubtedly would be severe. On
the other hand, resistance against the African nationalist forces (and

implied collaboration with South African authorities) also would have disastrous long-term effects. This choice has confronted smaller African communities in Angola and Mozambique, but not such substantial, clearly defined entities as the projected Bantustans. Caught between ideological adversaries, the Bantustans' role as buffer areas is just emerging.

The fruits of separate development in South Africa and South West Africa, then, are political as well as economic. Separate development is a variant of neocolonialism (perhaps not a unique one: there are other internal, domestic colonies in the world), and the Bantu homelands are colonies in the same sense that Ivory Coast and Kenya were colonies. It is not difficult to see the former High Commission Territories in the same category. Landlocked, economically unviable at present, and tied to South Africa, they perform for the white power structure the very functions the homelands are designed to fulfill. Only Swaziland appears at present to have the potential to escape this cycle, but the future of its outlet at Lourenço Marques is still uncertain. In South West Africa, South Africa has applied the doctrines of racial-territorial separation along lines similar to those in the Republic.

There are signs that South Africa is prepared to make minor modifications and adjustments in response to the momentous changes occurring across its borders. While assisting Rhodesia, the Republic played a moderating role in the Rhodesian crisis, and it did not interfere in Portugal's transfer of power in Angola and Mozambique. Some moves were made toward the extension of military service to Asians and Africans in the Republic, *ad hoc Apartheid* rules in the cities were slightly relaxed (hotels might under certain circumstances accept black registrants), Africans were once again permitted to own property in their suburbs near the country's major cities. But these changes still leave the essential system of separate development intact. In the larger sense, the direction of change in southern Africa still is not one of decolonization but, rather, greater degrees of colonization. Several varieties of the principle prevail: the domestic colonialism affecting the Bantustans, the implicit colonialism involving the former High Commission Territories, and the continuing system of rule in Rhodesia, where independence has served only to strengthen the subjugation already prevailing when the country was officially still a colony. The principles and practices of colonial rule continue to persist in Africa's southern tier.

32

Liberation Movements:
Guiné-Bissau and Mozambique

ROBERT W. MC COLL

Liberation movements can be viewed as an era in African history, one between a pre-European past and a nation-state future. It is precisely this transitional nature that makes a study of their patterns important.

Among the better known movements are those carried out by the PAIGC (African Party for Independence of Guiné and Cabo Verde) in the former Portuguese Guinea (Guiné-Bissau) and FRELIMO (Liberation Front of Mozambique) in Mozambique. Both have successfully ended over 500 years of foreign domination and have ushered in new areas of self-determination. Both also face the related problems of building modern nation-states.

The traditional approach to the study of liberation movements has been to focus upon their history and characteristics *en loco parentis*. To counter this rather parochial view, the present chapter focuses upon two widely separate movements, each in a unique physical and ethnic environment, with a different political history but with a common colonial government, the Portuguese. The methodological emphasis is on the political geographic elements necessary for the success of any liberation movement, which have been termed the four pillars of power—population, territory, organization, and force (McColl, 1975).

Population is a key element for the growth and survival of any revolutionary movement. Mao Tse-tung has termed population the "sea" in which the guerilla "swims," and thus one of the first tasks of a guerrilla is the recognition and preparation of the basic elements of such a "sea." These include the various social, economic, age, ethnic, and religious groups that could possibly contribute to the struggle for national power.

Two segments of the population that have long been recognized by insurgents as critical to their success are intellectuals and youths. They have always provided the leadership and backbone of revolutions. Today, the proportion of African populations below the age of 20 is exceedingly large (see Chapter 5). As more young people attend school, they come into contact with a wide range of political and social ideas and often become fanatic followers and supporters of a national revolution.

Territory is another key to guerrilla survival and success. This is especially important once the movement has been outlawed. A territorial base is an imperative if the movement hopes to continue. The insurgent army requires some territorial haven for training, stocking supplies, and for rest and recuperation from battle.

Obviously, not all territory has equal political or military value. Cities and major population clusters are the ultimate targets of the insurgent. However, action in rural areas provides sustenance for the revolution and room for battle. In addition, rural areas often contain the dissident population groups essential for popular support. Two classic uses of territory are the establishment of a military guerrilla base and the creation of "liberated areas"—extensive territories under insurgent control. A friendly neighboring country may provide an ideal haven or territorial base, but this further restricts the areas selected for activity.

Organization is the third pillar of success or failure. A supportive population and territorial base alone cannot bring success without effective political organization and an imaginative, often charismatic leader-organizer, such as a Mao, a Cabral, or a Mondlane. With good leadership it is possible to organize widely diverse populations into a national movement, all fighting for different specific "causes" but also all fighting simultaneously for a single national goal. Ultimately, the political struggle is between government and insurgent leaders; the winner will be the individual or the group who best organizes the various elements of power.

Force is the last of the four pillars. Once there is an organized following and some kind of territorial base for its expression, the insurgent needs a force capable of resisting and eventually overcoming the government. Military units or armies are not the only kinds of force available. Today we are very much aware of the uses of terror or threat of violence or kidnapping. In addition, outside support, especially by a neighboring country, often provides advisors and safe territory. There is also the underrated power of moral persuasion or psychological force. In some instances, the marshalling of public opinion has been sufficient to win what could not be won by force of arms alone. Certainly the psychological war waged by insurgents in Guiné-Bissau and Mozambique was as effective as its military efforts in forcing the Portuguese to abort their colonial wars. One can only speculate on how long the struggle would have continued without the Lisbon coup generated by the anticolonial General Antonio de Spinola. In addition, the control of a substantial portion of the state area (territory) is often used to substantiate the claim to "legitimate" political power. Especially important has been the creation of an "insurgent state" (McColl, 1969). Often it is through the creation of an insurgent state that the movement proceeds toward a final military or power confrontation.

GUINÉ-BISSAU

Guiné-Bissau provided a classic example of "commercial colonialism." It was never extensively colonized or settled by Europeans but merely provided raw materials and wealth for Portugal.

When the Portuguese arrived in the fifteenth century, they established coastal forts and only penetrated up the rivers as far as their ships could sail safely (Figure 31.1). It was a time when wealth was measured in terms of gold, ivory, and slaves and there was little interest in establishing any kind of colony except for the fortified settlements that protected the supplies of wealth.

In the interior uplands (the Fouta Jallon), the socially and politically organized Fulani had established their own colonies and were in the process of consolidating their position at about the same time that the Portuguese arrived at the coast. Because the well-organized Fulani controlled the trade in ivory and gold, the Portuguese reached economic and socio-political accommodation with them. Meanwhile, the coastal peoples were exploited by both groups.

The result of this history was a human geography that was a mixture of African and European spheres of influence. Portuguese settlements concentrated at the mouth of the Geba River (Bissau) and along its banks far into the interior (Pitche). The rest of the

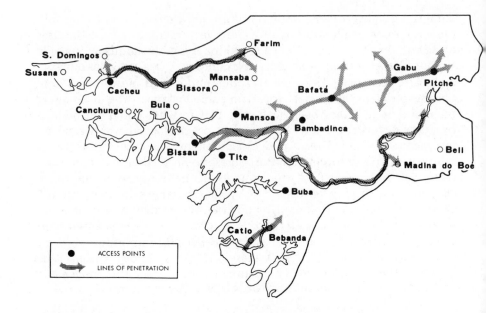

Figure 32.1   Portuguese Penetration of Guiné-Bissau.

country was divided among various African peoples, the most important of which were the Fulani and the Balante.

Recognizing this milieu and its antecedents, Amilcar Cabral (1969) did a "class analysis" of the population in Marxist terms. Cabral viewed class in terms of traditional ethnic groups and the urban classes created by the Portuguese. Of the two major rural groups, the Fulani and Balante, the Muslim Fulani were viewed as semi-feudal. They were better organized than other Africans and had chiefs, nobles, and religious leaders who ruled over a peasantry. According to Cabral, neither peasants nor women had any rights in this society. Their artisans were viewed as the embryo of industry (a point stretched for the convenience of Marxism) while the Dyulas (traders) could be persuaded to carry messages and provide intelligence for the insurgents but could not be trusted because they worked only for money.

Cabral saw the coastal Balante as having no well-defined socio-political organization. There was no social stratification parallel to that of the Fulani, only a council of elders in each village or for each group of villages. All property and land belonged to the village, and women were socially equal to men. Because these peoples had the longest and most bitter history of association with the Portuguese and exploitation by the Fulani, they actively participated in and supported the revolution. They accepted new leadership, whereas the Fulani leadership viewed the insurgents as a threat to their own positions. Naturally, the Fulani were least committed to the revolution and will pose a major problem for internal stability now that Guiné-Bissau is independent.

Cabral's analysis also noted an additional class or "pseudo-proletariat" associated with the urban-rural fringe. This consisted of what Cabral called the "intermediate classes or social groups," African peasant farmers who were numerically small but politically active. Finally, there were the urban "classes." These were composed of both Africans and Europeans, but the most important were the Africans who were petty officials and wage earners such as dockworkers, domestic servants, porters, and factory laborers. Especially significant were the youth who had only recently arrived from the rural areas and remained in contact with both the urban and rural populations. They generally had much energy and time to devote to the revolution.

This population analysis identified a specific political geography: the more conservative Fulani in the Fouta Jallon plateau; the Balante and other loosely organized groups along the coastal littoral, and the most active revolutionary groups in and around the cities and towns.

The insurgents also evaluated the more concrete or natural elements of geography such as suitable terrain and proximity to friendly neighbors. It was the access to Senegal and the Republic of Guinea that figured most prominently in the actual initiation of the "guerrilla war" or violent stage of the revolution. Initially, support by Senegal was largely passive; active support would bring reprisals from the powerful Portuguese air force and army. However, Sekou Touré and the Republic of Guinea gave active support and encouragement to the insurgents. With Senegalese and Guinean aid, the rebels were able to infiltrate supplies and men along the swampy coastlines and the contiguous land borders.

As with all insurgent groups, the PAIGC and its predecessors first attempted within-the-system changes and only gradually escalated their tactics to guerrilla war. Such moderate beginnings were clearly motivated by a desire to accomplish change peacefully but also through a fear of Portuguese reprisals.

As late as 1953 and 1954, there were still attempts at nonviolent political organization of the African population through the use of "recreational clubs." These were a necessary cover because the government refused to permit social or political organizations that might provide impetus to African political demands. In

September 1956 the PAIGC was created. Cabral's *class analysis* aimed the early efforts at organization toward the urban centers, not all of which were inside Guiné. Some of the earliest leaders met for the first time in Lisbon and Conakry. In addition, the leaders were often of the *assimilado* class of blacks and were hardly representative of any rural *vox populi* within Guiné.[1]

Between 1958 and 1962 political organization and political action rapidly escalated in both Guiné-Bissau and the neighboring Cabo Verde Islands. A famine in the Cabo Verde Islands and the Bissau dockworkers' strike resulted in a secret PAIGC conference held in Bissau in September, 1959. National issues now replaced purely local or ethnic issues and gave a new meaning to revolution.

Meanwhile, all African liberation movements were being gathered and coordinated at a Conference of Nationalist Organizations of Portuguese Territories (CONCP) held in Casablanca in 1961. It was at this time that Cabral first learned of the works of Mao. Along with other African leaders, Guineans began their training and preparation for a violent or guerrilla war stage in their political struggle.

Following the CONCP, active guerrilla war replaced persuasion. By 1962, acts of sabotage were planned and carried out and a number of rural autonomous guerrilla bases had been established. 1963 marked the start of open conflict ("armed struggle") especially in the north. By the end of the year, PAIGC forces claimed large contiguous areas in the south and center, and the Portuguese were evacuating Europeans from the outlying areas into fortified towns. In 1964, the PAIGC formed its first "regular" army. Action now shifted from local battles to a more coordinated national effort with attacks in widely separated parts of the country so coordinated that the government would be forced to keep its forces spread.

By 1966 the PAIGC had established large "liberated areas" and its own insurgent state government. The insurgents had also acquired heavy arms including several antiaircraft batteries.

Many PAIGC tactics and organizational forms were borrowed from other revolutionaries around the world, but their ability, willingness, and skill in organizing the territory and population they controlled was a major feature of the PAIGC struggle. In February 1964, leaders reorganized and democratized the PAIGC at a meeting in the southern forests of Guiné-Bissau. There was a decision to

[1] An *assimilado* is a Portuguese African who
1. can read, write, and speak fluent Portuguese;
2. has sufficient means to support his family;
3. is of good conduct; and
4. has the necessary education and individual and community habits to understand and observe the public and private law of Portugal.

create a Chinese Yenan-style insurgent state in their liberated areas. For purposes of military and political command, they divided the country into regions and zones. In 1966-1967 these were again reorganized and villages were given more voice in the affairs of their local areas. Each liberated village held an election for a Party committee which was composed of three men and two women. This committee was charged with the tasks of stepping up food production to support the area and the army, to control and oversee the fulfillment of Party-assigned tasks, and to care for the local militia, since the militia lived within the local area. The regular army moved from village to village and area to area. Clearly the PAIGC was gaining administrative experience for its later victory.

From 1966 to 1974, the struggle was see-saw, with the PAIGC controlling the rural areas, especially along the frontiers with Senegal and the Republic of Guinea and the Portuguese controlling the major towns and cities and the coastal littoral, especially along the Geba River. With each passing year, the PAIGC grew increasingly legitimate as a government for about two-thirds of Guiné-Bissau. In 1973, Guiné-Bissau officially declared the independence of controlled and contested territory, and in September 1974 this was formally granted by the new liberal government in Lisbon. Guiné-Bissau was admitted to the United Nations the same month. Unfortunately, Amilcar Cabral had been assassinated in 1973 in Senegal. His brother Luis was proclaimed the first president.

MOZAMBIQUE

Unlike Guiné-Bissau, Mozambique had a long history of political and commercial organization before the Portuguese arrival. Thus there evolved an entirely different social geography.

Eastern Africa was already well-developed along its coastal littoral and even in the interior before the arrival of the Portuguese. The Portuguese had to fight for a foothold on the coast and for any penetration to the interior (Figure 32.2). Eventually the Portuguese occupied Mozambique and settlers began to arrive.

Mozambique offered lands that could eventually be settled and farmed by Europeans, a practice that became most important in the twentieth century and that gave Mozambique strong alliance with European Rhodesia and South Africa as well as with Lisbon. It was a pattern distinct from the client-patron relationship of Portuguese Guiné.

A population analysis of Mozambique shows many significant

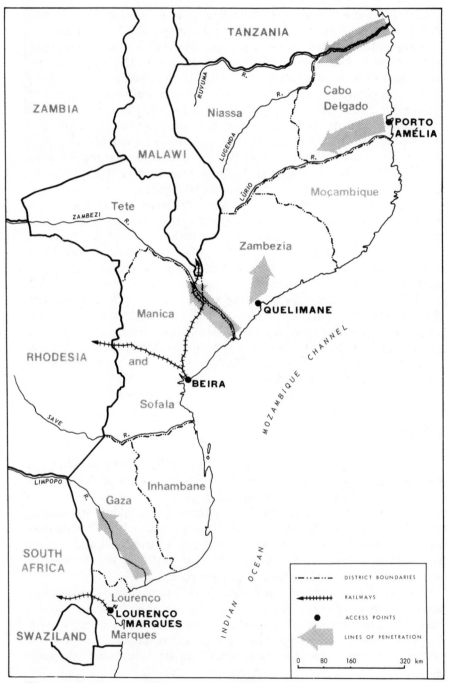

Figure 32.2 Portuguese Penetration of Mozambique.

ethnic groups, all of which are Bantu, and all of which have definable territories.

This multiplicity of peoples creates an ethnic pattern entirely different from that of Guiné Bissau.

However, just as in Guiné-Bissau, the urban environments provided an inter-ethnic environment that linked the various groups. As in all countries, the cities attract people from scattered regions and provide central locations for the exchange of ideas which are then carried back to the villages. In addition, it is to the cities that the potential elite migrate. Cities are the centers for the *assimilado* and, just as with Portuguese Guiné, the *assimilados* were the backbone of the movement. Nothing illustrates this quite as well as the history of FRELIMO.

In 1920, the *Liga Africana* was established in Lisbon. It was composed of African *assimilados* from all of Portugal's African colonies. Following a series of political and organizational ups and downs associated with internal European and Portuguese politics, the *Liga Africana* broke into various national groups. By 1949 the *Nucleo dos Estudantes Africanos Secundarios de Mocambique* (NESAM) was formed to organize and politicize secondary students in Mozambique. The insurgents continued to find limited legal expression for their views. Meanwhile, political events in Africa created a number of newly independent states and a willingness, in fact, a certain proclivity, for achieving such independence through the use of violence.

In 1960 at least 500 Makonde people were killed by the Portuguese at Mueda. Similar to the Bissau dockworkers' strike in Guiné-Bissau, this was the incident that generated a truly *national* concern over Portuguese treatment of Africans. In short, the Mueda incident provided an issue that focused and generated support for the movement. By 1963 strikes had been organized and carried out in other cities such as Lourenço Marques, Beira, and Nacola. It was clear that a *national* movement was now under way.

Meanwhile Tanzania (Tanganyika) had gained its independence in 1961, and Dar es Salaam became headquarters for liberation movements throughout southern Africa. At this time, there were three distinct movements for the liberation of Mozambique, all headquartered in Dar es Salaam. This profusion of liberation movements resulted in the CONCP Conference that met in Casablanca and called for fewer parties and more united fronts. Especially vocal in this regard were Ghana's Nkrumah and Tanzania's Nyerere, both of whom had strong impact upon Guiné-Bissau and Mozambique.

In 1962 FRELIMO was formed by Eduardo Mondlane. Throughout 1963 it established its political presence and intentions by organizing students and secondary school teachers and leading workers' strikes. In addition, it requested and was granted military training in Algeria. Meanwhile, Tanzania agreed to provide territorial sanctuary for FRELIMO troops and a base area was established inside Tanzania. FRELIMO's efforts now shifted from politics to armed conflict and from work in the major cities to the areas along the Tanzanian and Zambian borders. In the south, neighboring Rhodesia and South Africa clearly would provide no sanctuary for an African Liberation movement.

Arms and ammunition were stockpiled inside Mozambique from May to September 1964, prior to the infiltration of the newly trained FRELIMO troops. Only 250 men formed the initial nucleus of the FRELIMO "army," but from 1966 to 1968 FRELIMO attacks forced the Portuguese to commit troops and air power to hold a few fortified posts in the north. FRELIMO forces were able to establish their control or presence throughout the northern third of the country, with the exception of the fortified enclaves.

Because of its proximity to Tanzania and Zambia, only the Makonde plateau provided a haven for the insurgents. The long north-south shape of the country, combined with Portuguese control of the coast and South African and Rhodesian interests along the western borders created major difficulties in linking the forces and movements of the north (Cabo Delgado, Niassa, and Tete) with the peoples of the south. In short, the most important fact of political geography for the insurgents in Mozambique was the presence and willingness of Tanzania and Zambia to provide recruiting and training bases for the insurgents.

As with so many guerrilla movements, the creation of an "insurgent state" was a major FRELIMO theme and motivation. Eduardo Mondlane, president of FRELIMO until he was assassinated in 1969, opposed the idea of a "government in exile" as meaningless and contradictory (Mondlane, 1969:214):

> In the liberated areas of Mozambique, FRELIMO is in fact the government, a government operating within its national territory and not a government in exile.

Control of government territory and creation of an "insurgent state" became of sufficient importance that in 1967 a United Nations Special Committee made a number of recommendations designed to let various U.N. bodies give aid to liberation movements where they governed. A Liberated Area thus became a clear symbol of national as well as international legitimacy. FRELIMO's "insurgent state" was also designed to eliminate traditional ethnic divisions where they conflicted with FRELIMO's programs and efforts at "nation building." At a meeting in 1962, the Party Congress passed resolutions that made the basis of political structure in the liberated areas the same as the Party. In short, the political pattern was to be a "one party democracy." The army was a key element, in part because of "power from the gun" and in part because of the rationalization that since "everyone in the army lives and works with people from all over Mozambique in a complete new structure, the army can spread ideas and set an example" (Mondlane, 1969:165).

This "national" or Party organization had little meaning to on-the-spot groups and until the second Congress in 1968, there was not much local administrative organization or actual state-building. However, the second Congress, held in the liberated areas of Niassa province, made fundamental administrative changes. Most important were the recognition and formal integration of local leaders, especially "provincial secretaries." The questions of regional government were discussed and systematized. The liberated areas even formed their own schools and economic organizations (Mondlane, 1969). In the liberated zones FRELIMO made efforts to abolish various systems of exploitation, to eliminate or reduce heavy taxes, to establish more schools and health services, and to form local militias to protect the population from forays by the government or local bandits. In short, the first efforts at creating a unified African government for Mozambique were begun prior to liberation. Mozambique became independent in June 1975, the thirteenth anniversary of FRELIMO, but like Guiné-Bissau without its founder and facing a number of problems associated both with its ethnic diversity and with its neighbors.

CONCLUSIONS

Looking toward the future, it seems evident that the political geographic background of each movement will have a pronounced effect upon its future politics, including national viability. It seems evident, for example, that the purely exploitive history of Guiné-Bissau will leave few Portuguese residues. However, PAIGC reliance upon outside territory and the fact that ethnic groups such as the Fulani are distributed across national borders, along with the historic role of Sekou Touré in the internal politics of PAIGC, all may combine with the small size and economic vulnerability of the new country to create severe questions as to its long-term viability.

In contrast, the efforts of FRELIMO in Mozambique will now have to be devoted to a unification of a much more complex ethnic diversity. Each of the peoples in Mozambique had a long history prior to the arrival of the Portuguese and is also associated with a specific territorial realm. In addition, there are the wealthy and antiliberation countries of South Africa and Rhodesia and the large number of white colonists concentrated in the south. Whereas South Africa seems reconciled to the new African government in Mozambique, the Rhodesians have less sympathy because of their fear of its possible support for liberation movements within Rhodesia. Of particular note will be a solution to the north-south dichotomy that exists not only ethnically, but in terms of participation in the struggle. The fight was in the rural north but the seat of economic power remains in the south. In fact, in September, 1974, hundreds of rioting whites were joined by anti-FRELIMO blacks of the National Coalition Party to call for a renegotiation of the agreement signed with Samora Machel, leader of FRELIMO since Mondlane's assassination. Thus one can forecast a period of difficult regional problems.

The process of liberation, of politically organizing a diverse population, of creating territorial bases and the use of force to gain political ends often legitimizes violence and crystalizes regional differences and a sense of "in group" and "out group." Thus most successful revolutions require a period in which the four pillars (population, territory, organization and force) are reinterpreted to create political stability, not violence.

Bibliography

Abler, R., Adams, J. S., and Gould, P. 1971. *Spatial Organization: The Geographer's View of the World.* Englewood Cliffs, N.J.: Prentice-Hall.

Abrams, C. 1957. *Housing in Ghana.* New York: United Nations.

Achebe, C. 1960. *No Longer At Ease.* London: William Heinemann.

Achebe, C. 1961. *Things Fall Apart.* New York: I. Obolensky.

Ackerman, E. A. and Löf., G. O. G. 1959. *Technology in American Water Development.* Baltimore: Johns Hopkins.

Addo, N. O. 1972. "Differential Rural Migration in Ghana: Spatial, Demographic and Economic Dimensions." Unpublished manuscript.

Adegboye, R. O., Basu, A. C., and Olatungosun, D. 1969. "Impact of Western Nigerian Farm Settlements on Surrounding Farmers," *Nigerian Journal of Economic and Social Studies* 11:229-40.

Adejuwon, J. O. 1968. "Savanna Patches in the Forest Areas of Western Nigeria." Unpublished Ph.D. dissertation, University of London.

Adejuwon, J. O. 1971. "Savanna Patches Within Forest Areas in Western Nigeria: A Study of the Dynamics of the Forest Savanna Boundary." *Bulletin de l'Ifan,* Series A, 33: 327-43.

Adejuwon, J. O. and Ojo, G. J. A., eds. *Environmental Resource Management in Nigeria,* forthcoming conference proceedings.

Adelman, I. and Morris, C. T. 1967. *Society, Politics and Economic Development: A Quantitative Approach.* Baltimore: Johns Hopkins.

Africa Annual Review. 1972. London: Africa Journal Ltd.

Allan, W. 1965. *The African Husbandman.* Edinburgh: Oliver and Boyd.

Alonso, W. 1968. "Urban and Regional Imbalances in Economic Development." *Economic Development and Cultural Change* 17: 1-14.

Amoah, F. 1964. "Accra: A Study of the Development of a West African City." Unpublished M.A. thesis, Institute of African Studies, University of Ghana.

Ardener, E. and Ardener, S. 1960. *Plantation and Village in the Cameroons.* London: Oxford University Press.

Bailey, N. A. 1969. "Native and Labour Policy." In *Portuguese Africa.* D. M. Abshire and M. A. Samuels, eds. New York: Praeger.

Baker, P. R. 1971. "Stages in the Development of a Dairy Industry in Bunyoro, Western Uganda." *Transactions,* Institute of British Geographers, 53: 43-54.

Baldwin, J. 1957. *The Niger Agricultural Project.* Cambridge, Mass.: Harvard University Press.

Bank of Nova Scotia. 1972. "The Expanding Tourist Industry." *Monthly Review* (July).

Barber, W. J. 1961. *The Economy of British Central Africa.* Stanford, Calif.: Stanford University Press.

Barzun, J. 1965. *Race: A Study in Superstition.* 2nd edition. New York: Harper & Row.

Bates, M. 1952. *Where Winter Never Comes: A Study of Man and Nature in the Tropics.* New York: Scribner's.

Bauer, P. T. 1968. "Some Aspects and Problems of Trade in Africa." In *Markets and Marketing in Developing Economies.* R. Moyer and S. Hollander, eds. Homewood, Illinois: Richard D. Irwin, 48-69.

Baum, E. 1968. "Land use in the Kilombero Valley." In *Smallholder Farming and Smallholder Development in Tanzania.* H. Ruthenberg, ed. Munich: Weltforum Verlag.

Beals, R. E., Levy, M. B., and Moses, L. N. 1967. "Rationality and Migration in Ghana." *Review of Economics and Statistics* 49: 480-86.

Bell, R. H. V. 1971. "A Grazing Ecosystem in the Serengeti." *Scientific American* 225,1: 86-93.

Benedict, B., ed. 1967. *Problems of Smaller Territories.* London: Athlone Press.

Benneh, G. 1972. "Systems of Agriculture in Tropical Africa." *Economic Geography* 48: 244-57.

Bennett, C. F. 1964. "Savanna and Man in Middle America." *The Geographical Review* 54: 580-82.

Berg, E. J. 1960. "The Economic Basis of Political Economy in French West Africa." *The American Political Science Review* 54: 391-405.

Berg, E. J. 1965. "The Economics of the Migrant Labour System." In *Urbanization and Migration in West Africa.* H. Kuper, ed. Berkeley: University of California Press.

Bernstein, H. 1971. "Modernization Theory and the Sociological Study of Development." *The Journal of Development Studies* 7: 141-60.

Berry, B. J. L. 1969. "Relationships between Regional Economic Development and the Urban System, the Case of Chile." *Tijdschrift voor Economische en Sociale Geografie* 60: 283-307.

Berry, L., ed. 1970. *Tanzania in Maps.* London: University of London Press.

Berry, L. et al. 1971. *Pilot Studies of Human Adjustment to Agricultural Drought in Tanzania.* Natural Hazard Research Paper, no. 19, Toronto.

Bianca, W. 1961. "Heat Tolerance in Cattle—Its Concept, Measurement and Dependence on Modifying Factors." *International Journal of Biometerology* 5: 5-31.

Birmingham, W., Neustadt, I. and Omaboe, E. 1966. *A Study of Contemporary Ghana,* vol. 1. London: George Allen and Unwin.

Blum, H. F. 1954. "Effects of Sunlight on Man." *Meteorological Monographs* 8: 43-49.

Board, C., Davies, R. J., and Fair, T. J. D. 1970. "The Structure of the South African Space Economy: An Integrated Approach." *Regional Studies* 4: 367-92.

Bohannan, P. and Curtin, P. 1971. *Africa and Africans.* Garden City, N.Y.: Natural History Press.

Bohannan, P. and Dalton G., eds. 1962. *Markets in Africa.* Evanston, Ill.: Northwestern University Press.

Boserup, E. 1965. *The Conditions of Agricultural Growth.* Chicago: Aldine.

Boudeville, J. R. 1968. *L'Espace et les Pôles de Croissance.* Paris: Presse Universitaire de France.

Bourgeois-Pichat, J. 1965. "Problems of Population Size, Growth and Distribution in Africa," In *Man and Africa.* G. Wolstenholme and M. O'Connor, eds. London: Churchill.

Boyd, J. P. 1889. *Stanley in Africa.* New York: Union Publishing House.

Brand, R. 1971. "A Geographical Interpretation of the European Influence on Accra, Ghana, Since 1877." Unpublished Ed.D., Columbia University.

Brand, R. 1972a. "The Spatial Organization of Residential Areas in Accra, Ghana, with Particular Reference to 'Aspects' of Modernization." *Economic Geography* 48: 284-98.

Brand, R. 1972b. "The Role of Cocoa in the Early Economic Growth of Accra, Ghana." *African Studies Review* 15: 271-82.

Braun, O. 1971. "The External Economic Strategy: Outward- or Inward-looking?" In *Development in a Divided World.* D. Seers and L. Joy, eds. Hammondsworth, U.K.: Penguin Books.

Brokensha, D. and Scudder T. 1968. "Resettlement." In *Dams in Africa.* W. M. Warren and N. Rubin, eds. London: Frank Cass.

Brooke, C. 1967. "The Heritage of Famine in Central Tanzania." *Tanzania Notes and Records* 67: 15-22.

Brookfield, H. C. and Hart, D. 1971. *Melanesia: A Geographical Interpretation of an Island World.* London: Methuen.

Brown, L. R. 1970. *Seeds of Change—The Green Revolution and Development in the 1970's.* London: Praeger.

Bryden, J. and Faber, M. 1971. "Multiplying the Tourist Multiplier." *Social and Economic Studies* 20: 61-82.

Buck, W. K. and Elver R. B. 1971. "An Approach to Mineral Policy Formulation." *Natural Resources Forum.* 1: 16-21.

Cabral, A. 1969. *Revolution in Guinea: Selected Texts.* New York: Monthly Review Press.

Caldwell, J. C. 1963. *Population Growth and Family Change in Africa.* Canberra: Australian National Universities Press.

Caldwell, J. C. 1968. "Population Policy: A Survey of Commonwealth Africa. In *The Population of Tropical Africa.* J. C. Caldwell and C. Okonjo, eds. New York: Columbia University Press.

Caldwell, J. C. 1969. *African Rural-Urban Migration.* New York: Columbia University Press.

Canadian Imperial Bank of Commerce. 1970. "Leisure Time in Perspective." *Commercial Letter,* no. 2.

Carter, G. M., Karis, T. and Stultz, N. M. 1967. *South Africa's Transkei: The Politics of Domestic Colonialism.* Evanston, Ill.: Northwestern University Press.

Chambers, R. 1969. *Settlement Schemes in Tropical Africa.* New York: Praeger.

Chang, J. H. 1968. "The Agricultural Potential of the Humid Tropics." *Geographical Review* 58: 333-61.

Charsley, S. 1968. "The Group Farm Scheme in Uganda," In *Land Settlement and Rural Development.* R. Apthorpe, ed. Kampala: Nganga Editions.

Charter, J. R. and Keay, R. W. J. 1960. "Assessment of Olokemeji Fire Control Experiment (Investigation 254) 28 Years After Institution." *Nigeria Forestry Information Bulletin,* no. 3.

Chisholm, M. 1967. *Rural Settlement and Land Use.* New York: John Wiley.

Christaller, W. 1964. "Some Considerations of Tourism in Europe: The Peripheral Regions—Underdeveloped Countries—Recreation Areas." *Papers,* Regional Science Association 12: 95-105.

Christaller, W. 1966. *Central Places in Southern Germany.* Englewood Cliffs, N.J.: Prentice-Hall.

Claeson, C. F. and Egero, B. 1972. "Migration and the Urban Population: a Demographic Analysis of Population Data for Tanzania." *Geografiska Annaler* 54(B): 1-18.

Clarke, G. 1936. *The Balance Sheets of Imperialism.* New York: Columbia University Press.

Cliffe, L. 1971. "The Policy of Ujamaa Vijijini and the Class Struggle in Tanzania." *Rural Africana* 13: 5-27.

Cohen, A. 1969. *Custom and Politics in Urban Africa: A Study of Hausa Migrants in Yoruba towns.* London: Routledge and Kegan Paul.

Collinson, M. P. 1963. *Farm Management Survey No. 2.* Ukiriguru, Tanzania. Unpublished manuscript.

Collinson, M. P. 1964. *Farm Management Survey No. 3.* Ukiriguru, Tanzania. Unpublished manuscript.

Conant, F. P. 1965. "Korok: A Variable Unit of Physical and Social Space Among the Pokot of East Africa." *American Anthropologist* 67: 429-34.

Cornelisse, P. A. 1972. "An Economic View of Migration in West Africa: A Two Country Study." Unpublished manuscript.

Curtin, P. D. 1969. *"The Atlantic Slave Trade.* Madison: University of Wisconsin Press.

Curtin, P. D. 1973. "The Lure of Bambuk Gold," *Journal of African History* 14: 623-31.

Dagg, M. Woodhead, T., and Rijks, D. A. 1970. "Evaporation in East Africa." *Bulletin of the International Association of Scientific Hydrology* 15: 61-67.

Dalton, G. 1970. "Traditional Economic Systems." In *The African Experience.* J. N. Paden and E. W. Soja, eds. Evanston, Ill.: Northwestern University Press.

Darko, S. A. 1963. "The Effects of Modern Mining on Settlements in the Mining Areas of Ghana." *Bulletin of the Ghana Geographical Association* 8: 21-31.

Darkoh, M. B. K. 1971. "The Distribution of Manufacturing in Ghana: A Case Study of Industrial Location in a Developing Country." *Scottish Geographical Magazine* 87: 38-57.

Darwent, D. F. 1969. "Growth Poles and Growth Centers in Regional Planning—A Review," *Environment and Planning* 1:5-31.

Davidson, B. 1959. *The Lost Cities of Africa.* Boston: Little, Brown.

Davidson, B. and Buah, F. K. 1967. *The Growth of African Civilization: A History of West Africa 1000-1800.* London: Longmans.

Davies, D. H., ed. 1971. *Zambia in Maps.* London: University of London Press.

Davis, H. R. J. 1964. "The West African in the Economic Geography of the Sudan." *Geography* 49: 222-35.

Davis, K. and Blake J. 1956. "Social Structure and Fertility: An Analytic Framework," *Economic Development and Cultural Change* 4: 211-35.

Davis, K. 1969. *World Urbanization 1950-1970, Vol. 1: Basic Data for Cities, Countries, and Regions.* Population Monograph Series, no. 4. Berkeley: University of California Press.

deLattre, A. 1969. "Financial, Monetary and Trade Arrangements Between France and the African and Malagasy States." Unpublished research memorandum. Lagos: The Ford Foundation.

Demas, W. G. 1965. *The Economics of Development in Small Countries.* Montreal: McGill University Press.

Denis, J. 1958. *Le Phénomène Urbain en Afrique Centrale.* Brussels: Academie Royale des Sciences d'Outre-Mêr.

deSouza, A. R. and Porter, P. W. 1974. *The Underdevelopment and Modernization of the Third World.* Washington, D.C.: Association of American Geographers, Commission on College Geography. Resource Paper no. 28.

deVos, A. 1969. "Ecological Conditions Affecting the Production of Wild Herbivorous Mammals on Grasslands." *Advances in Ecological Research* 6: 137-84.

deWilde, J. C. et al. 1967. *Experiences with Agricultural Development in Tropical Africa.* Baltimore: Johns Hopkins.

Dieterich, B. and Henderson, J. M. 1963. *Urban Water Supply Conditions and Needs in Seventy-Five Developing Countries.* Public Health Papers 23. Geneva: World Health Organization.

Dowker, D. M. 1971. "A Note on the Reduction in Yield of Taboran Maize by Late Planting." *East African Agricultural and Forestry Journal* 30: 33-34.

Duckham, A. N. and Masefield, G. B. 1970. *Farming Systems of the World.* London: Chatto and Windus.

Dumanowski, B. 1968. "The Influence of Geographical Environments on Distribution and Density of Population in Africa." *Africa Bulletin 9:* 9-13.

Dumont, R. 1966. *False Start in Africa.* Translated by P. N. Ott. Paris: André Deutsch.

Dunyoh, F. 1968. "Transportation in Accra and Its Problems." Unpublished B.A. honors thesis, Department of Geography, University of Ghana.

Durand, J. D. 1967. "The Modern Expansion of World Population." *Proceedings,* American Philosophical Society 111:136-59.

Economic Commission for Africa. 1968. *Survey of Economic Conditions in Africa, 1967.* New York: United Nations.

Economic Commission for Africa. 1969. *Survey of Economic Conditions in Africa, 1968.* New York: United Nations.

Economic Commission for Africa. 1972. *Survey of Economic Conditions in Africa, 1971.* New York: United Nations.

Ehrlich, C. 1965. "The Uganda Economy, 1903-1945." *History of East Africa.* V. Harlow, E. M. Chilver and A. Smith, eds. Vol. 2. Oxford: Clarendon Press.

Eicher, C. K. and Witt, L. W., eds. 1964. *Agriculture in Economic Development.* New York: McGraw-Hill.

Eighmy, T. H. 1972. "Rural Periodic Markets and the Extension of an Urban System: A Western Nigeria Example." *Economic Geography* 48: 299-315.

Ekwensi, C. 1963. *Jagua Nana.* London: Hutchinson.

Ekwensi, C. 1965. *People of the City.* London: Heinemann.

Elkan, W. 1960. *Migrants and Proletarians: Urban Labour in the Economic Development of Uganda.* London: Oxford University Press.

Elliott, C., ed. 1971. *Constraints on the Economic Development of Zambia.* Nairobi: Oxford University Press.

Essex, B. 1972. "The Social and Economic Aspects of Schistosomiasis with Reference to Health Planning in Developing Countries." Unpublished M.Sc. thesis, London School of Economics and Political Science.

Ewing, A. F. 1968. *Industry in Africa.* New York: Oxford University Press.

Fagerfund, V. G. and Smith, R. H. T. 1970. "A Preliminary Map of Market Periodicities in Ghana." *Journal of Developing Areas* 4: 333-48.

Fair, T. J. D., Murdoch, G. and Jones, H. M. 1969. *Development in Swaziland,* Johannesburg: Witwatersrand University Press.

Fanon, F. 1965. *The Wretched of the Earth.* London: Mac Gibbon and Kee.

F.A.O. 1970. *Production Yearbook* Rome: United Nations.

Farvar, M. T. and Milton, J. P., eds. 1972. *The Careless Technology.* New York: Natural History Press.

Field, M. J. 1943. "The Agricultural System of the Manya-Krobo of the Gold Coast." *Africa* 14: 54-65.

Fitzgerald, W. 1955. *Africa.* 8th edition. London: Methuen.

Floyd, B. and Adinde, M. 1967. "Farm Settlements in Eastern Nigeria: A Geographical Appraisal." *Economic Geography* 43: 189-230.

Fogg, C. D. 1965. "Economic and Social Factors Affecting the Development of Small Holder Agriculture in Eastern Nigeria." *Economic Development and Cultural Change* 13: 280-86.

Forde, J. 1971. *The Role of the Trypanosomiases in African Ecology.* Oxford: Clarendon Press.

Foster, T. P. 1970. "Education for Self-Reliance: A Critical Review." In *Research and Action; Education in Africa.* R. Jolly, ed. Nairobi: East African Publishing House.

Frank, M. 1968. *Cooperative Land Settlements in Israel and their Relevance to African Countries.* Tubingen, Germany: Kylos-Verlag.

FRELIMO. n.d. "Aspects of the Mozambiean Struggle." Reprinted by Liberation Support Movement Information Centre, Richmond, British Columbia, Canada.

FRELIMO. 1973a. "The Struggle to Build a Healthy Mozambique." *Mozambique Revolution* 55: 17-18.

FRELIMO. 1973b. *Annual Report.* Dar es Salaam: Mozambique Institute.

Friedmann, J. R. 1966. *Regional Development Policy—A Case Study of Venezuela.* Cambridge, Mass.: M.I.T. Press.

Friedmann, J. R. 1968. "The future of urbanization in Latin America: some observations on the role of the periphery." Paper presented to the Congress of the Inter-American Planning Society. Lima, October 1968.

Gates, D. M. 1971. "The Flow of Energy in the Biosphere." *Scientific American* 224: 88-100.

Geertz, C. 1963. *Agricultural Involution: The Processes of Ecological Change in Indonesia.* Berkeley and Los Angeles: University of California Press.

Gillet, J. W., ed. 1970. *The Biological Impact of Pesticides in the Environment.* Corvallis: Oregon State University Press.

Good, C. M. 1970. *Rural Markets and Trade in East Africa.* University of Chicago. Department of Geography Research Paper no. 128.

Good, C. M. 1972. "Periodic Markets: A Problem in Locational Analysis." *The Professional Geographer* 24: 210-16.

Good, C. M. 1975. "Periodic Markets and Traveling Traders in Uganda." *Geographical Review* 65: 49-72.

Goodspeed, S. S. 1967. *The Nature and Function of International Organization.* New York: Oxford University Press.

Gould, P. R. 1960. *The Development of Transportation Patterns in Ghana.* Evanston: Northwestern University Studies in Geography no. 5.

Gould, P. R. 1970. "Tanzania 1920-63: The Spatial Impress of the Modernization Process," *World Politics* 22: 149-70.

Gould, P. R. 1972. "A Mental Map of Ghana." *African Urban Notes* 6: iv-v.

Gould, P. R. and Ola, D. 1970. "The Perception of Residential Desirability in the Western Region of Nigeria." *Environment and Planning* 2: 73-87.

Gould, W. T. S. and Prothero, R. M. 1975. "Space and Time in African Population Mobility." In *People on the Move.* L. A. Kosinski and R. M. Prothero, eds. London: Methuen.

Gourou, P. 1953. *The Tropical World.* London: Longmans, Green, and Co.

Gourou, P. 1961. *The Tropical World.* 3rd edition. London: Longmans, Green, and Co.

Graham, A. 1969. "Man-water Relations in the East-Central Sudan." In *Environment and Land Use in Africa.* M. F. Thomas and G. W. Whittington, eds. London: Methuen.

Great Britain, Colonial Reports 1886 and 1887. *Gold Coast Sanitary and Medical Reports.* Colonial Report no. 12.

Green, L. P. and Fair, T. J. D. 1962. *Development in Africa.* Johannesburg: Witwatersrand University Press.

Green, L. P. and Milone, V. 1973. *Urbanization in Nigeria: A Planning Commentary.* New York: Ford Foundation International Urbanization Survey.

Green, R. H. and Seidman, A. 1968. *Unity or Poverty: The Economics of Pan-Africanism.* Baltimore: Penguin Books.

Greenberg, J. H. 1966. *The Languages of Africa.* Bloomington: Indiana University.

Grove, A. T. 1970. *Africa South of the Sahara.* London: Oxford University Press.

Guggisberg, C. A. W. 1970. *Man and Wildlife.* New York: Arco.

Gugler, J. 1969. "On the Theory of Rural-Urban Migration: the Case of Sub-Saharan Africa." In *Migration, Sociological Studies.* J. A. Jackson, ed. Cambridge: Cambridge University Press.

Gulliver, P. H. 1962. "The Evolution of Arusha Trade." In *Markets in Africa.* P. Bohannan and G. Dalton, eds. Evanston, Ill.: Northwestern University Press.

Gutkind, P. C. W. 1963. *The Royal Capital of Buganda.* The Hague: Mouton and Co.

Hagen, E. E. 1962. *On the Theory of Social Change: How Economic Growth Begins.* Homewood, Ill.: Dorsey Press.

Hagerstrand, T. 1952. *The Propagation of Innovative Wares.* Lund, Sweden: Lund Studies in Geography.

Haggett, P. 1966. *Locational Analysis in Human Geography.* New York: St. Martins Press.

Haldane, D. 1971. "Nairobi." In *Urban Africa.* Nairobi: National Christian Council of Kenya.

Hall, E. T. 1969. *The Hidden Dimension.* Garden City, N.Y.: Doubleday.

Hall, R. 1965. *Zambia.* New York: Praeger.

Hall, S. A. and Langlands, B. W., eds. 1968. *Uganda Atlas of Disease Distribution.* Department of Preventive Medicine and Department of Geography. Occasional Paper no. 12. Makerere University College, Kampala.

Hance, W. A. 1967. *African Economic Development.* New York: Praeger.

Hance, W. A. 1970. *Population, Migration, and Urbanization in Africa.* New York: Columbia University Press.

Hance, W. A. 1975. *The Geography of Modern Africa.* 2nd ed. New York: Columbia University Press.

Hance, W. A., Kotschar, V. and Peterec, R. J. 1961. "Source Areas of Export Production in Tropical Africa." *The Geographical Review* 51: 487-99.

Harper, R. A. 1966. "The Geography of World Energy Consumption," *Journal of Geography* 65: 302-15.

Harris, M. 1959. "Labour Emigration among the Mozambique Thonga: Cultural and Political Factors." *Africa* 29: 50-65.

Harrison-Church, R. J. 1949. "The Evolution of Railways in French and British West Africa." Lisbon: *Congrès International de Géographie* 16, 4: 95-114.

Harrison-Church, R. J., et al. 1971. *Africa and the Islands.* New York: John Wiley.

Harvey, M. 1968. "Implications of Migration to Freetown: a Geographical Study of the Relationships Between Tribes, Housing and Occupation." *Civilisations* 10: 247-57.

Harvey, M. and Brand, R. 1974. "The Spatial Allocation of Migrants in Accra, Ghana." *The Geographical Review* 64: 1-30.

Harvey, M. and Greenberg, P. E. 1972. "Development Dichotomies, Growth Poles, and Diffusion Processes in Sierra Leone." *Rural Africana* 6: 117-36.

Hatchell, C. W. 1949. "An Early Sleeping Sickness Settlement in Southwest Tanganyika." *Tanganyika Notes and Records* 27: 60-64.

Hay, A. M. 1971. "Notes on the Economic Basis for Periodic Marketing in Developing Countries." *Geographical Analysis* 3: 393-401.

Hayter, T. 1966. *French Aid.* London: Overseas Development Institute, Inc.

Heijnen, J. 1972. *National Policy and Economic Development.* Unpublished manuscript.

Heisler, H. 1974. *Urbanization and the Government of Migration: the Inter-relation of Urban and Rural Life in Zambia.* London: Hurst.

Henty, G. 1874. *The March to Coomasie.* London: Tinsley Bros.

Herskovits, M. J. 1930. "The Culture Areas of Africa." *Africa* 3: 59-77.

Herskovits, M. J. 1962a. *The Human Factor in Changing Africa.* New York: Knopf.

Herskovits, M. J. 1962b. "Preface." In *Markets in Africa.* P. Bohannan and G. Dalton, eds. Evanston, Ill.: Northwestern University Press.

Hill, P. 1963. *Migrant Cocoa Farmers of Southern Ghana.* Cambridge: Cambridge University Press.

Hill, P. 1966. "Notes on Traditional Market Authority and Market Periodicity in West Africa." *Journal of African History* 7: 295-311.

Hirschman, A. O. 1958. *The Strategy of Economic Development.* New Haven: Yale University Press.

Hodder, B. W. 1959. "Tin Mining on the Jos Plateau." *Economic Geography* 35: 109-22.

Hodder, B. W. 1965a. "Some Comments on the Origins of Traditional Markets in Africa South of the Sahara." *Transactions,* Institute of British Geographers 36: 97-105.

Hodder, B. W. 1965b. "Distribution of Markets in Yorubaland." *Scottish Geographical Magazine* 81: 48-58.

Hodder, B. W. 1967. "The Markets of Ibadan." In *The City of Ibadan.* P. C. Lloyd, A. L. Mabogunje and B. Awe, eds. Cambridge: Cambridge University Press.

Hodder, B. W. 1968. *Economic Development in the Tropics.* London: Methuen.

Hodder, B. W. and Harris, D. R. 1967. *Africa in Transition.* London: Methuen.

Hodder, B. W. and Ukwu, U. I. 1969. *West African Markets.* Ibadan: Ibadan University Press.

Hopkins, B. 1966. *Forest and Savanna.* Ibadan: Heinemann.

Horowitz, R. 1967. *The Political Economy of South Africa.* New York: Praeger.

Hoselitz, B. F., ed. 1968. *The Role of Small Industry in the Process of Economic Growth.* The Hague: Mouton & Co.

Hughes, C. C. and Hunter, J. M. 1970. "Disease and Development in Africa," *Social Science and Medicine* 3:443-93.

Hunter, J. M. 1961. "Akotuadrom: A Devastated Cocoa Village in Ghana," *Transactions*, Institute of British Geographers 24: 161-86.

Hunter, J. M. 1965. "Regional Patterns of Population Growth in Ghana 1948-1960." In *Essays in Geography for Austin Miller.* J. B. Whittow and P. D. Wood, eds. Reading: University of Reading.

Hunter, J. M. 1966. "River Blindness in Nangodi, Northern Ghana: A Hypothesis of Cyclical Advance and Retreat." *The Geographical Review* 56: 398-416.

Hunter, J. M. 1967a. "Seasonal Hunger in a Part of the West African Savanna." *Transactions*, Institute of British Geographers 41: 167-85.

Hunter, J. M. 1967b. "Population Pressure in a Part of the West African Savanna: A Study of Nangodi, Northeast Ghana." *Annals*, Association of American Geographers 57: 101-14.

Hutton, J., ed. 1971. *Urban Challenge in East Africa.* Nairobi: East African Publishing House.

Huzlar, L. 1970. "Resettlement Planning." In *The Volta Resettlement Experience.* R. Chambers, ed. New York: Praeger.

Imperato, P. J. 1969. "The Use of Markets as Vaccination Sites in the Mali Republic." *Journal of Tropical Medicine and Hygiene* 72: 8-13.

International Bank for Reconstruction and Development. 1960. *The Economic Development of Tanganyika.* Baltimore: Johns Hopkins.

International Labour Office. 1970. *Towards Full Employment.* Geneva: International Labour Organization.

International Monetary Fund. 1971. *International Financial News Survey* 23: 422.

International Monetary Fund. 1973. *IMF Survey*, 18-20.

International Tourism Quarterly 1. 1971. London: The Economist Intelligence Unit.

Jackson, R. T. 1971. "Periodic Markets in Southern Ethiopia." *Transactions*, Institute of British Geographers 53: 31-42.

James, P. E. 1967. "On the Origin and Persistence of Error in Geography." *Annals*, Association of American Geographers 57:1-24.

Jarrett, H. R. 1949. "The Strange Farmers of the Gambia." *The Geographical Review* 39: 649-57.

Jennings, J. H. 1959. "Enugu—A Geographical Outline." *Nigerian Geographical Journal* 3: 28-38.

Johnson, H. B. 1967. "The Location of Christian Missions in Africa." *The Geographical Review* 57: 168-202.

Jones, E. W. 1963a. "The Forest Outliers in the Guinea Zone of Northern Nigeria." *Journal of Ecology* 51: 415-34.

Jones, E. W. 1963b. "The Cece Forest Reserve, Northern Nigeria." *Journal of Ecology.* 51: 461-66.

Jurgen, H. W., Tracey, K. A., and Mitchell, P. K. 1966. "Internal Migration in Liberia." *Bulletin*, Sierra Leone Geographical Association, no. 10.

Kalitsi, E. A. K. 1965. "The Organization and Economics of Resettlement." In *Volta Resettlement Symposium Papers.* Accra: Volta River Authority.

Kamarack, A. 1967. *The Economics of African Development.* New York: Praeger.

Kasfir, N. 1972. "Cultural Sub-Nationalism in Uganda." In *The Politics of Cultural Sub-Nationalism in Africa.* A. Olorunsola, ed. Garden City: Doubleday.

Kates, R. W., McKay, J., and Berry, L. 1968-69. "Twelve New Settlements in Tanzania: A Comparative Study of Success." *Conference Papers,* Makerere Institute of Social Research, 63-100.

Kay, G., 1965. "Resettlement and Land Use Planning: The Chipangali Scheme." *Scottish Geographical Magazine* 81: 163-75.

Kay, G., 1967. *A Social Geography of Zambia.* London: University of London Press.

Kay, G. 1970. *Rhodesia: A Human Geography.* New York: Africana Publishing Corp.

Keay, R. W. J. 1949. "An Example of Sudan Zone Vegetation in Nigeria." *Journal of Ecology* 37: 335-54.

Keay, R. W. J. 1959a. *An Outline of Nigerian Vegetation.* Lagos: Government Printer.

Keay, R. W. J. 1959b. *Vegetation Map of Africa South of the Sahara.* London: Oxford University Press.

Keay, R. W. J. 1959c. "Derived Savanna: Derived From What?" *Bulletin de l'Ifan* 21: 427-38.

Keay, R. W. J. 1960. "An Example of Northern Guinea Zone Vegetation in Nigeria." *Nigeria Forestry Information Bulletin,* no. 4. Lagos: Government Printer.

Keeble, D. E. 1967. "Models of Economic Development," In *Models in Geography.* R. J. Chorley and P. Haggett, eds. London: Methuen.

Kilby, P. 1962. *The Development of Small Industry in Eastern Nigeria.* Lagos: U.S. Agency for International Development.

Kilby, P. 1969. *Industrialization in an Open Economy: Nigeria.* Cambridge: Cambridge University Press.

Kimble, G. H. T. 1960. *Tropical Africa.* Baltimore: Johns Hopkins.

Kingsley, M. 1897. *Travels in West Africa.* London: Macmillan and Co.

Kirkman, J. 1966. "The History of the Coast of East Africa up to 1700," In *Prelude to East African History.* M. Posnansky, ed. London: Oxford University Press.

Kluckhohn, R. 1962. "The Konso Economy of Southern Ethiopia." In *Markets in Africa.* P. Bohannan and G. Dalton, eds. Evanston, Ill.: Northwestern University Press.

Knight, C. G. 1971. "The Ecology of African Sleeping Sickness." *Annals,* Association of American Geographers 61: 23-44.

Knight, C. G. 1974. *Ecology and Change: Rural Modernization in an African Community.* New York: Academic Press.

Kokot, D. F. 1967. "Is Water the Limiting Factor in the Development of South Africa?" *Optima* 17: 12-17.

Kuznets, S. 1966. *Modern Economic Growth: Rate, Structure and Spread.* New Haven: Yale University Press.

Laddel, W. S. S. 1949. "Physiological Classification of Climates." *Proceedings.* International West African Conference.

Laddel, W. S. S. 1957. "Influence of Environment in Arid Regions on the Biology." *Reviews of Research*, Arid Zone Research (UNESCO) 8: 43-99.

Landell-Mills, P. A. 1971. "The 1969 Southern African Customs Union Agreement." *The Journal of Modern African Studies* 9: 263-81.

Latham, M. 1965. *Human Nutrition in Tropical Africa.* Rome: Food and Agricultural Organization.

Lawson, R. M. 1972. *The Changing Economy of the Lower Volta 1954-1967.* London: Oxford University Press.

Le Moniteur africain. 1971. Special edition.

Lea, J. P. 1972. "The Differentiation of the Rural Periphery in Swaziland: A Multivariate Analysis." *South African Geographical Journal* 54: 105-23.

Lebon, J. H. G. 1965. *Land Use in Sudan.* Bude, U. K.: World Land Use Survey Monograph 4.

Leistner, G. M. E. and Smit, P. 1969. *Swaziland: Resources and Development.* Pretoria: Africa Institute of South Africa.

Lepawsky. A. 1963. "International Development of River Resources." *International Affairs* 39: 533-50.

Lerner, D. 1958. *The Passing of Traditional Society: Modernizing the Middle East.* Glencoe, Ill.: The Free Press.

Lerner, D. 1967. "Comparative Analysis of Processes of Modernization." In *The City in Modern Africa.* H. Miner, ed. New York: Praeger.

Levine, R. 1962. "Wealth and Power in Gusiiland." In *Markets in Africa.* P. Bohannan and G. Dalton, eds. Evanston, Ill.: Northwestern University Press.

Levine, R. and Campbell, D. 1972. *Ethnocentrism: Theories of Conflict, Ethnic Attitudes and Group Behavior.* New York: John Wiley.

Logan, M. I. 1970. "The Process of Regional Development and Its Implications for Planning," *Nigerian Geographical Journal* 13: 109-20.

Logan, M. I. 1972. "The Spatial System and Planning Strategies in Developing Countries." *The Geographical Review* 62: 229-44.

Lovering, T. S. 1969. "Mineral Resources from the Land." In *Resources and Man*, NAS-NRC. San Francisco: W. H. Freeman and Co.

Ludwig, H. D. 1968. "Permanent Farming on Ukara." In *Smallholder Farming and Smallholder Development in Tanzania.* H. Ruthenberg, ed. Munich: Weltforum-Verlag.

Mabogunje, A. L. 1962. "The Growth of Residential Districts in Ibadan." *The Geographical Review* 52: 56-77.

Mabogunje, A. L. 1968. *Urbanization in Nigeria.* New York: Africana Publishing Corp.

Mabogunje, A. L. 1970a. "Urbanization and Change." In *The African Experience.* J. N. Paden and E. W. Soja, eds. Evanston, Ill.: Northwestern University Press.

Mabogunje, A. L. 1970b. "A Systems Approach to a Theory of Rural-Urban Migration." *Geographical Analysis* 2: 1-18.

Mabogunje, A. L. 1970c. "A Typology of Population Pressure on Resources in West Africa." In *Geography and a Crowding World.* W. Zelinsky, L. Kosinski and M. Prothero, eds. New York: Oxford University Press.

Mabogunje, A. L. 1972. *Regional Mobility and Resource Development in Africa.* Montreal and London: McGill-Queen's University Press.

Mabogunje, A. L. 1973. "Manufacturing and the Geography of Development in Tropical Africa." *Economic Geography* 49: 1-20.

Mabogunje, A. L. 1974. "Urbanization Problems in Africa." In *Urbanization, National Development and Regional Planning in Africa.* S. El-Shakhs and R. Obudho, eds. New York: Praeger.

McCall, D. F. 1955. "Dynamics of Urbanization in Africa." *The Annals of the American Academy of Political and Social Sciences* 298: 151-60.

McClelland, D. C. 1961. *The Achieving Society.* Princeton, N.J.: Van Nostrand.

McColl, R. 1969. "The Insurgent State: Territorial Bases of Revolution." *Annals,* Association of American Geographers 59: 613-31.

McColl, R. 1975. "Geopolitical Themes in Contemporary Asian Revolutions." *Geographical Review* 65: 301-10.

McDermott, J. E. 1972. "Significance of the National Community Water Supply Study." In *Water Quality in a Stressed Environment: Readings in Environmental Hydrology.* W. A. Pettyjohn, ed. Minneapolis: Burgess Publishing Co.

McGlashan, N. D. 1966. The Distribution of Certain Diseases in Central Africa. Unpublished Ph.D. dissertation, University of London.

McKay, J. 1971. "Methodology of Road Feasibility Studies in Tanzania." Bureau of Resource Assessment and Land Use Planning *Research Report 11.* University of Dar es Salaam.

McKay, J. 1972. "Road Transport in Tanzania." Bureau of Resource Assessment and Land Use Planning *Research Notes,* no. 5. University of Dar es Salaam.

McMaster, C. 1968. "Towards a Settlement Geography of Uganda." *East African Geographical Review* 6: 23-36.

Makings, S. M. 1967. *Agricultural Problems of Developing Countries in Africa.* Lusaka: Oxford University Press.

Malcolm, D. W. 1953. *Sukumaland: An African People and its Country.* London: International African Institute.

Mangalam, J. 1968. *Human Migration.* Lexington: University of Kentucky Press.

Mansergh, N. 1962. *South Africa 1906-1961: the Price of Magnanimity.* New York: Praeger.

Marris, P. and Somerset, A. 1971. *African Businessmen: A Study of Entrepreneurship and Development in Kenya.* London: Routledge & Kegan Paul.

Marris, P. and Somerset, A. 1972. *The African Entrepreneur.* New York: African Publishing Co.

Mascarenhas, A. 1967a. "The Impact of Nationhood on Dar es Salaam." *East African Geographical Review* 5:39-46.

Mascarenhas, A. 1967b. *Some Aspects of Food Shortage in Tanganyika 1923-1945.* Kampala: East African Institute of Social Research.

Mascarenhas, A. 1971. "Agricultural Vermin in Tanzania." In *Studies in East African Geography and Development.* S. H. Ominde, ed. London: Heinemann.

Mascarenhas, A. and Claeson, C. 1972. "Factors Influencing Tanzania's Urban Policy." *African Notes* 6: 24-42.

Mason, M. 1969. "Population Density and 'Slave Raiding'—the Case of the Middle Belt of Nigeria." *Journal of African History* 10: 551-64.

May, J., ed. 1955. *World Atlas of Disease.* New York: American Geographical Society.

May, J. M. ed. 1958. *The Ecology of Human Disease.* New York: MD Publications.

May, J. M. ed. 1961. *Studies in Disease Ecology.* New York: Hafner.

May, J. 1965. *The Ecology of Malnutrition in Middle Africa.* Studies in Medical Geography, vol. 5. New York: Hafner.

May, J. 1968. *The Ecology of Malnutrition in the French Speaking Countries of West Africa and Madagascar.* Studies in Medical Geography, vol. 8. New York: Hafner.

May, J. 1970. *The Ecology of Malnutrition in Eastern Africa and Four Countries in Western Africa.* Studies in Medical Geography, vol. 9. New York: Hafner.

Mbilinyi, S. and Mascarenhas, A. C. 1969. "The Marketing of Cooking Bananas." Economic Research Bureau *Paper* 69/15. University of Dar es Salaam.

Mbithi, P. M. and Wisner, B. 1972. "Drought and Famine in Kenya: Magnitude and Attempted Solutions." *Discussion Paper* no. 144. Kenya: Institute for Development Studies, University of Nairobi.

Mechanic, D. 1968. *Medical Sociology.* New York: The Free Press.

Meillassoux, C. 1968. *Urbanization of an African Community, Voluntary Associations in Bamako.* Seattle: University of Washington Press.

Meillassoux, C., ed. 1971. *The Development of Indigenous Trade and Markets in West Africa.* London: Oxford University Press.

Michelin Tyre Company. *Africa* (Maps 153, 154, 155). London and Paris: Michelin Tyre Company (Pneu Michelin).

Miller, A. E. 1972. "The Expanding Definition of Disease and Health in Community Medicine." *Social Science and Medicine* 6: 573-81.

Mills, A. R. 1967. "A Comparison of Urban and Rural Populations in the Lunsar Area." *Sierra Leone Studies* 20: 173-90.

Ministère du Plan, République de Côte d'Ivoire. 1971. *Investir en Côte d'Ivoire.* Abidjan: République de Côte d'Ivoire.

Mitchell, J. C. 1959. "Labour Migration in Africa South of the Sahara: the Causes of Labour Migration." *Bulletin of the Inter-Africa Labour Institute* 6: 12-46.

Mondlane, E. 1969. *The Struggle for Mozambique.* London: Penguin.

Monteith, J. L. 1965. "Light Distribution and Photosynthesis in Field Crops." *Annals of Botany* 28: 17-37.

Morgan, W. T. W., ed. 1972. *East Africa: Its People and Resources.* Nairobi: Oxford University Press.

Morgan, W. B. 1969a. "Peasant Agriculture in Tropical Africa." In *Environment and Land Use in Africa.* M. F. Thomas and G. W. Whittington, eds. London: Methuen.

Morgan, W. B. 1969b. "The Zoning of Land Use Around Rural Settlements in Tropical Africa." In *Environment and Land Use in Africa.* M. F. Thomas and G. W. Whittington, eds. London: Methuen.

Morgan, W. B. and Pugh, J. C. 1969. *West Africa.* London: Methuen.

Morris, J. 1967. "The Evaluation of Settlement Scheme Performance." *Proceedings,* East African Institute of Social Research, no. 430.

Mortimore, M. J. and Wilson J. 1965. "Land and People in the Kano Close Settled Zone." Ahmadu Bello University, Department of Geography, *Occasional Paper* no. 1.

Mountjoy, A. B. and Embleton, C. 1967. *Africa: A New Geographical Survey.* New York: Praeger.

MPLA. 1970. "Medical Assistance Services." Richmond, B.C.: Liberation Support Movement.

MPLA. 1971. "Angola in Arms." *Information Organ of the People's Movement for the Liberation of Angola* 2: 4-5.

Murdock, G. P. 1959. *Africa: Its Peoples and Their Culture History.* New York: McGraw-Hill.

Murdock, G. P. 1960. "Staple Subsistence Crops of Africa." *The Geographical Review* 50: 523-40.

Mutharika, B. W. T. 1972. *Toward Multinational Economic Cooperation in Africa.* New York: Praeger.

Myers, N. 1972. "National Parks in Savanna Africa." *Science* 178: 1255-63.

Myrdal, G. 1957. *Economic Theory and Underdeveloped Regions.* London: Methuen.

Mywangavo, A. Y. 1969. "Population Pressure on Land in Kisanjuni Village." *Journal of Tanzania Geographical Association.*

National Liberation Council. 1968. *Budget Statement for 1968-1969.* Accra: Ministry of Finance.

Newman, J. L. 1970. *The Ecological Basis for Subsistence Change Among the Sandawe of Tanzania.* Washington, D.C.: National Academy of Sciences.

Newman, J. L. 1971. "The Culture Area Concept in Anthropology." *The Journal of Geography* 70: 8-15.

Newman, J. L., ed. 1975. *Drought, Famine and Population Movements in Africa.* Foreign and Comparative Studies/Eastern African Series 17, Syracuse University.

Nichols, V. 1969. "Growth Poles: an Evaluation of Their Propulsive Effect." *Environment and Planning* 1: 193-208.

Nortman, D. 1973. "Population and Family Planning Programs: A Factbook." *Reports on Population/Family Planning,* no. 2.

Nye, P. H. and Greenland, D. J. 1960. *The Soil Under Shifting Cultivation.* Farnham Royal, U.K.: Commonwealth Agricultural Bureaux.

Nyerere, J. 1967. *The Arusha Declaration.* Dar es Salaam: Government Printer.

O'Brien, D. C. 1972. "Modernization, Order and The Erosion of a Democratic Ideal: American Political Science, 1960-1970." *The Journal of Development Studies* 8: 351-78.

O'Connor, A. M. 1966. *An Economic Geography of East Africa.* New York: Praeger.

O'Connor, A. M. 1971. *The Geography of Tropical African Development.* Oxford: Pergamon Press.

Ojo, G. J. A. 1966. *Yoruba Culture.* London: University of London Press.

Ojo, G. J. A. 1968. "Some Cultural Factors in the Critical Density of Population in Tropical Africa." In *The Population of Tropical Africa.* J. C. Caldwell and C. Okonjo, eds. New York: Columbia University Press.

Okonjo, C. 1968. "A Preliminary Medium Estimate of the 1962 Mid-year

Population of Nigeria," In *The Population of Tropical Africa.* J. C. Caldwell and C. Okonjò, eds. New York: Columbia University Press.

Olayide S. O. and Idachaba, F. S. 1973. "The Supply, Demand and Management of Wildlife Resources in Nigeria." Presented to the Conference on Environmental Resource Management in Nigeria, University of Ife, Nigeria.

Oliver, R. and Fage, J. D. 1966. *A Short History of Africa.* London: Penguin Africa Library.

Ominde, S. H. 1968. *Land and Population Movements in Kenya.* London: Heinemann.

Oxford Regional Economic Atlas of Africa. 1967. Oxford, Clarendon Press.

Oyenuga, V. A. B. 1971. "Biological Productivity in West Africa." *Journal of the West Africa Science Association* 16: 93-115.

Paddock, W. and Paddock, P. 1967. *Famine 1975!* Boston: Little, Brown.

Page, H. J. and Coale, A. J. 1972. "Fertility and Child Mortality South of the Sahara," In *Population Growth and Economic Development in Africa.* S. H. Ominde and C. N. Ejiogn, eds. London: Heinemann.

PAIGC. 1974. "Bilan des dix Annees de La Lutte." Department de la Sante.

Pearson, D. S. 1969. *Industrial Development in East Africa.* New York: Oxford University Press.

Peel, C. 1952. "The Ventilation of Cinemas in Sierra Leone." *Journal of the Institute of Heating and Ventilating Engineers* 20: 295-312.

Peel, C. 1954. "Thermal Conditions in Sierra Leone," *Journal of the Institute of Heating and Ventilating Engineers* 22: 125-43.

Peel, C. 1961. "Thermal Comfort Zones in Northern Nigeria: An Investigation into the Physiological Reactions of Nursing Students to their Environment." *Tropical Medicine and Hygiene* 64: 113-21.

Peil, M. 1972. *The Ghanaian Factory Worker: Industrial Man in Africa.* Cambridge: University Press.

Pelletier, R. A. 1964. *Mineral Resources of South-Central Africa.* Cape Town: Oxford University Press.

Penman, H. L. 1948. "Natural Evaporation from Open Water, Bare Soil and Grass." *Proceedings of the Royal Society of London* (A) 193: 120-45.

Penman, H. L. 1963. *Vegetation and Hydrology.* Harpenden, U.K.: Commonwealth Bureau of Soils.

Perroux, F. 1950. "Economic Space, Theory and Application." *Quarterly Journal of Economics* 64: 89-104.

Petersen, W. 1968. "Migration: Social Aspects." In *International Encyclopaedia of Social Sciences* 10: 286-300.

Petterson, D. R. 1951. "The Witwatersrand." *Economic Geography* 27: 209-21.

Phipps, B. A. 1970. "Evaluating Settlement Schemes: Problems and Implications—A Malawi Case Study." *Provisional Council for the Social Sciences in East Africa* 5: 488-509.

Piault, M. 1971. "Cycles de Marches et 'Escapes' Socio-Politiques." In *The Development of Indigenous Trade and Markets in West Africa.* C. Meillassoux, ed. London: Oxford University Press.

Pool, D. I. 1971. "Urbanization and Fertility in Africa." *African Urban Notes* 6: 25-32.

Porter, P. W. 1965. "Environmental Potentials and Economic Opportunities: A Background for Cultural Adaptation." *American Anthropologist* 67: 409-20.

Potts, A. S. 1972. "Application of Harmonic Analysis to the Study of East African Rainfall Data." *Journal of Tropical Geography* 33: 31-42.

Powesland, P. G. 1954. "History of the Migration in Uganda." In *Economic Development and Tribal Change.* A. I. Richards, ed. Cambridge: W. Heffer & Sons, Ltd.

Prothero, R. M. 1953. "Land Use at Soba, Zaria Province." *Research Notes,* Department of Geography, University of Ibadan 2: 3-10.

Prothero, R. M. 1957. "Migratory Labour from Northwestern Nigeria." *Africa* 27: 251-61.

Prothero, R. M. 1958. "Migrant Labour from Sokoto Province, Northern Nigeria." Kaduna, Northern Nigeria: Government Printer.

Prothero, R. M. 1962. "Migrant Labour in West Africa." *Journal of Local Administration Overseas* 1: 149-55.

Prothero, R. M. 1965. *Migrants and Malaria.* London: Longmans, Green.

Prothero, R. M. 1968. "Migration in Tropical Africa." In *The Population of Tropical Africa.* J. C. Caldwell and C. K. Okonjo, eds. New York: Columbia University Press.

Prothero, R. M. 1972. "Problems of Public Health Among Pastoralists: A Case Study from Africa." In *Medical Geography: Techniques and Field Studies.* N. D. McGlashan, ed. London: Methuen.

Ramsay, D. M. 1963. "The Vegetation of the Climatic Middle Belt in Northern Nigeria." Mimeographed. Ministry of Agriculture and Natural Resources, Ibadan.

Rapp, A. et al. 1973. "Soil Erosion and Sedimentation in Four Catchments near Dodma Tanzania." *Geografiska Annaler* 54[A]: 255-318.

Rather, L. J., trans. 1958. *Disease, Life, and Man: Selected Essays by Rudolf Virchow.* Stanford Studies in the Medical Sciences, vol. 9. Stanford: Stanford University Press.

Rattray, J. M. 1960. *The Grass Cover of Africa.* Rome: FAO.

Reining, C. C. 1966. *The Zande Scheme.* Evanston, Ill.: Northwestern University Press.

Rempel, H. 1971. "The Rural-to-Urban Migrant in Kenya." *African Urban Notes* 6: 53-72.

Richards, A. I. ed. 1954. *Economic Development and Tribal Change.* Cambridge: Cambridge University Press.

Richards, P. W. 1952. *The Tropical Rainforest.* Cambridge: Cambridge University Press.

Riddell, J. B. 1970. *The Spatial Dynamics of Modernization in Sierra Leone.* Evanston: Ill.: Northwestern University Press.

Riddell, J. B. and Harvey, M. E. 1972. "The Urban System in the Migration Process: An Evaluation of Stepwise Migration in Sierra Leone," *Economic Geography,* 48: 270-83.

Riehl, H. 1954. *Tropical Meteorology.* New York: McGraw Hill.

Rigby, P. 1969. *Cattle and Kinship Among the Gogo.* London: Cornell University Press.

Riney, T. 1967. *Conservation and Management of African Wildlife.* Rome: FAO.

Rivkin, A. 1970. "Economic Systems Development," In *The African Experience.* J. N. Paden and E. W. Soja, eds. Evanston, Ill.: Northwestern University Press.

Robinson, E. A. G. ed. 1963. *Economic Consequences of the Size of Nations.* London: Macmillan.

Robinson, R. 1971. *Developing the Third World.* Cambridge: Cambridge University Press.

Robson, J. R. K. 1972. *Malnutrition, Its Causation and Control.* New York: Gordon and Breach.

Rodney, W. 1972. *How Europe Underdeveloped Africa.* Dar es Salaam: Tanzania Publishing House.

Rogers, E. M. 1962. *Diffusion of Innovations.* New York: Free Press.

Rogers, E. M. 1969. *Modernization Among Peasants, The Impact of Communication.* New York: Holt, Rinehart and Winston.

Roider, W. 1971. *Farm Settlements for Socio-Economic Development.* Munich: Weltforum Verlag.

Rosenzweig, M. L. 1968. "Net Primary Productivity of Terrestial Communities: Prediction from Climatological Data." *The American Naturalist* 102: 67-74.

Ross, R. 1954. "Ecological Studies on the Rain Forest of Southern Nigeria: III. Secondary Succession in the Shasha Forest Reserve." *Journal of Ecology* 42: 259-82

Rosser, C. 1973. *Urbanization in Tropical Africa.* New York: Ford Foundation International Urbanization Survey.

Roussel, L., Turlot, F. and Vaurs, R. 1968. "La Mobilité de la Population Urbaine en Afrique Noire: Deux Essais de Mésure, Abidjan et Yaoundé." *Population* 23:333-52.

Russell, C. S. and Landsberg, H. H. 1971. "International Environmental Problems—A Taxonomy." *Science* 172: 1307-14.

Ruthenberg, H. 1971. *Farming Systems in the Tropics.* Oxford: Clarendon Press.

Safier, M. 1970. "Urban Growth and Urban Planning in Subsaharan Africa." In *Urban Growth in Subsaharan Africa.* J. Gugler, ed. Kampala: Makerere Institute for Social Research.

Salcedo, R. N. 1971. "What Leads to Modernization?" *The Journal of Modern African Studies* 9: 626-33.

Schaller, K. F. 1969. *Ethiopia: A Geomedical Monograph.* Berlin: Springer-Verlag.

Schapera, I. 1956. "Migrant Labour and Tribal Life in Bechuanaland." In *Social Implications of Industrialization and Urbanization in Africa South of the Sahara.* D. Forde, ed. Rome: UNESCO.

Schneider, H. K. 1974. "Economic Development and Economic Change: The Case of East African Cattle." *Current Anthropology* 15: 259-76.

Schultz, T. W. 1964. *Transforming Traditional Agriculture.* New Haven: Yale University Press.

Schumpeter, J. A. 1934. *The Theory of Economic Development.* Cambridge, Mass.: Department of Economics, Harvard University.

Scott, Earl P. 1972. "The Spatial Structure of Rural Northern Nigeria: Farmers,

Periodic Markets, and Villages." *Economic Geography* 48: 316-32.

Scrimshaw, N. S. 1967. "Malnutrition, Learning and Behavior." *American Journal of Clinical Nutrition* 20: 493-507.

Scrimshaw, N. S., Taylor, C. E., and Gordon, J. E. 1968. *Interactions of Nutrition and Infection.* Geneva: World Health Organization.

Seers, D. 1972. "What Are We Trying to Measure?" *The Journal of Development Studies* 8: 21-36.

Segal, R. 1966. *The Race War.* London: Penguin.

Selwyn, P. 1972. "The Dual Economy Transcending National Frontiers: The Case of Industrial Development in Lesotho." *Institute of Development Studies Communications.* Brighton: University of East Anglia.

Shaw, D. J. 1964. "Labour Problems in the Sudan Gezira Scheme," *Agricultural Economics Bulletin for Africa* 5:1-41.

Shennan, D. H. 1968. *Tuberculosis Control in Developing Countries.* Edinburgh: E. & S. Livingstone.

Silberfein, M. 1971. "The Regional Impact of Tanzanian Settlement Schemes." Unpublished Ph.D. dissertation, Syracuse University.

Simmance, A. J. F. 1973. *Urbanization in Zambia.* New York: Ford Foundation International Urbanization Survey.

Simons, H. J. 1968. "Harnessing the Orange River." In *Dams in Africa.* W. M. Warren and N. Rubin, eds. London: Frank Cass and Co., Ltd.

Siradiou, D. 1970. "La Zone Franc et les États Africains après Dix Ans D'Indépendance." *Présence Africaine*, special edition.

Sjoberg, G. 1960. *The Preindustrial City: Past and Present.* Glencoe, Ill.: The Free Press.

Skinner, E. P. 1965. "Labour Migration among the Mossi of the Upper Volta." In *Urbanization and Migration in West Africa.* H. Kuper, ed. Berkeley: University of California Press.

Smith, R. H. T. 1971. "West African Marketing Places: Temporal Periodicity and Locational Spacing." In *The Development of Indigenous Trade and Markets in West Africa.* C. Meillassoux, ed. London: Oxford University Press.

Soja, E. W. 1968. *The Geography of Modernization in Kenya.* Syracuse: Syracuse University Press.

Soja, E. W. 1971. *The Political Organization of Space.* Washington, D.C.: Association of American Geographers, Commission on College Geography, Resource Paper no. 8.

Sommer, J. W. 1974. "Spatial Aspects of Urbanization and Political Integration in the Sudan." In *Urbanization, National Development and Regional Planning in Africa.* S. El-Shakhs and R. Obudho, eds. New York: Praeger.

Southall, A. W. 1954. "Alur Migrants." In *Economic Development and Tribal Change.* A. I. Richards, ed. Cambridge: Cambridge University Press.

Stamp, L. D. and Morgan, W. T. W. 1972. *Africa: A Study in Tropical Development.* 3rd ed. New York: Wiley.

Stanley, H. 1874. *Coomasie and Magdala.* New York: Harper and Bros.

Staples, R. R. 1938. "Report on Run-off and Soil Erosion Tests at Mpwapwa in Semi-Arid Tanganyika." *Annual Report*, Tanganyika Department of Veterinary Science.

Stine, J. H. 1962. "Temporal Aspects of Tertiary Production Elements in Korea." In *Urban Systems and Economic Development.* F. Pitts, ed. Eugene, Oregon: University of Oregon School of Business Administration.

Stolper, W. F. 1966. *Planning Without Facts.* Cambridge, Mass.: Harvard University Press.

Stren, R. 1972. "Urban Policy in Africa: A Political Analysis." *African Studies Review* 15: 489-516.

Stryker, R. E. 1971. "A Local Perspective on Development Strategy in the Ivory Coast." In *The State of the Nations: Constraints on Development in Independent Africa.* M. F. Lofchie, ed. Berkeley: University of California Press.

Sullivan, A. L. and Shaffer, M. L. 1975. "Biogeography of the Megazoo." *Science* 189: 13-17.

Swantz, M-L. 1970. "Traditional Concepts of Illness and Practices of Healing in Tanzania in Relation to Planning for Health Services." Mimeographed. University of Dar es Salaam.

Swift, J. 1972. "What Future for African National Parks?" *New Scientist* 55: 192-94.

Swynnerton, R. J. M. 1954. *A Plan to Intensify the Development of African Agriculture in Kenya.* Nairobi: Government Printer.

Taaffe, E. J., Morrill, R. L., and Gould, P. R. 1963. "Transport Expansion in Underdeveloped Countries: A Comparative Analysis." *The Geographical Review* 53: 503-29.

Talbot, L. M. 1963. "Comparison of the Efficiency of Wild Animals and Domestic Livestock in Utilization of East African Rangelands." *Publications of the International Union for the Conservation of Nature and Natural Resources* N.S. 1: 328-35.

Talbot, L. M., et al. 1965. *The Meat Production Potential of Wild Animals in Africa.* Farnham Royal, U.K.: Commonwealth Agricultural Bureaux.

Taylor, B. W., et al. 1962. "Report on the Land-Use Survey of the Oyo-Shaki Area, Western Nigeria." Ibadan: Ministry of Agriculture and Natural Resources.

Taylor, C. R. 1969. "The Eland and the Oryx," *Scientific American* 220, 1:89-95.

Taylor, D. R. F. 1969. "Agricultural Change in Kikuyuland." In *Environment and Land Use in Africa.* M. F. Thomas and G. W. Whittington, eds. London: Methuen.

Taylor, D. R. F. 1972. "The Role of the Smaller Urban Place in Development: A Case Study from Kenya." *African Urban Notes* 6: 7-23.

Terjung, W. H. 1966. "Physiologic Climates of the Conterminous United States: A Bioclimatic Classification Based on Man." *Annals,* Association of American Geographers, 56: 141-79.

Terjung, W. H. 1967. "The Geographical Application of Some Selected Physio-Climatic Indices to Africa." *International Journal of Biometeorology* 11: 5-19.

Terjung, W. H. 1968. "Bi-Monthly Physiological Climates and Annual Stresses and Regimes of Africa." *Geografiska Annaler* 50(A): 173-92.

Thomas, I. D. 1972. "Infant Mortality in Tanzania." *East African Geographical Review* 10: 5-26.

Thomas, M. F. and Whittington, G. W. 1969. *Environment and Land Use in Africa.* London: Methuen.

Thompson, V. and Adloff, R. 1958. *French West Africa.* London: Allen & Unwin.

Thornthwaite, C. W. 1962. "Average Climatic Water Balance Data for the Continents, Part I, Africa." *Publications in Climatology* 15: 115-287.

Tinkler, K. 1970. "Perception and Prejudice: Student Preferences for Employment and Residence in Uganda." *Occasional Paper* no. 15, Department of Geography, Makerere University, Kampala, Uganda.

Todaro, M. 1971a. "Education and Rural-Urban Migration: Theoretical Constructs and Empirical Evidence from Kenya." Unpublished paper delivered at the Conference on Urban Unemployment in Africa, Institute for Development Studies, University of Sussex.

Todaro, M. 1971b. "Income Expectations, Rural-Urban Migration and Employment in Africa." *International Labour Review* 104: 387-413.

Tomsett, J. E. 1969. "Average Monthly and Annual Rainfall Maps of East Africa." East African Meteorological Department, Technical Memorandum no. 14, Nairobi.

Turner, J. 1968. "Housing Priorities, Settlement Patterns, and Urban Development in Modernizing Countries." *Journal of American Institute of Planners* 34: 354-60.

Turner, T. 1972. "Congo-Kinshasa." In *The Politics of Cultural Sub-Nationalism in Africa.* Victor A. Olorunsola, ed. Garden City: Doubleday.

Udo, R. K. 1964. "The Migrant Tenant Farmer of Eastern Nigeria." *Africa* 34: 326-39.

Udo, R. K. 1970a. *Geographical Regions of Nigeria.* Berkeley: University of California Press.

Udo, R. K. 1970b. "Migrations in Nigeria." *Nigeria Magazine* 103: 616-24.

United Nations. 1960. *Statistical Yearbook 1959.* New York: United Nations.

United Nations. 1961. *Statistical Yearbook 1960.* New York: United Nations.

United Nations. 1962. *Statistical Yearbook 1961.* New York: United Nations.

United Nations. 1964. *Population Growth and Manpower in the Sudan.* New York: United Nations.

United Nations. 1965. *Housing in Africa.* New York: United Nations.

United Nations. 1968. *Demographic Handbook for Africa.* Addis Ababa: United Nations Economic Commission for Africa.

United Nations. 1969a. *Integrated River Basin Management,* revised. New York: United Nations.

United Nations. 1969b. *Growth of the World's Urban and Rural Population, 1920-2000.* New York: United Nations.

United Nations. 1969c. *Yearbook of National Accounts Statistics.* New York: United Nations.

United Nations. 1970. *Statistical Yearbook, 1969.* New York: United Nations.

United Nations. 1971a. *Demographic Yearbook 1970.* New York: United Nations.

United Nations. 1971b. *Final Draft Recommendations.* African Regional Seminar on the Human Environment. Document Number M71-2122. Addis Ababa: Economic Commission for Africa.

United Nations. Department of Economic and Social Affairs. 1971c. *Improvement of Slums and Uncontrolled Settlements: Report of the Interregional Seminar on the Improvement of Slums and Uncontrolled Settlements, Medellin, Columbia, 1970.* New York: United Nations.

United Nations. 1971d. "Housing, Building and Planning Problems and Priorities in Human Settlements, Report of the Secretary General." New York.

United Nations. 1971e. *Statistical Yearbook 1970.* New York: United Nations.

United Nations, Centre for Building, Housing and Planning. 1972a. *Human Settlements.* vol. 2: 1-28.

United Nations, Centre for Housing, Building and Planning. 1972b. *Sites and Services: the Experience and Potential.* Copenhagen: Paper presented at the ECAFE Seminar on Financing of Housing and Urban Development.

United Nations Children and Educational Fund. 1971. *Children and Adolescents in Slums and Shanty-towns in Developing Countries.* New York: United Nations.

U.S. AID. 1975. *U.S. Overseas Loans and Grants, July 1, 1945-June 30, 1974.* Washington, D.C.: Office of Financial Management, A.I.D.

U.S.D.A. 1973. *The Agricultural Situation in Africa and West Asia.* Washington, D.C.: U.S. Department of Agriculture.

Uzoigwe, G. N. 1970. "Pre-Colonial Markets in Bunyoro-Kitara." *Proceedings of the University of East Africa Social Sciences Conference.* Dar es Salaam.

Vail, D. 1975. *Technology for Socialist Development in Rural Tanzania.* Foreign and Comparative Studies/East African Series, 18, Syracuse University.

van der Lee, J. J. 1963. "Community Economic Relations with Associated African States and Other Countries." *The Annals of the American Academy of Political and Social Science* 348: 15-24.

Van de Walle, E. 1967. "Future Growth of Population and Changes in Population Composition: Tropical Africa." *Proceedings of the World Population Conference, 1965.* vol. 2. New York: United Nations.

Van de Walle, E. 1968. "Characteristics of African Demographic Data." In *The Demography of Tropical Africa.* W. Brass, et. al., eds. Princeton, N.J.: Princeton University Press.

Van Velsen, J. 1960. "Labour Migration as a Positive Factor in the Continuity of Tonga Tribal Society." *Economic Development and Cultural Change* 8: 265-78.

Van Velsen, J. 1963. "Some Methodological Problems in the Study of Labour Migration." In *Urbanization in Africa.* Edinburgh: Centre of African Studies.

Vernon, R. 1968. *Manager in the International Economy.* Englewood Cliffs, N.J.: Prentice-Hall.

Vogel, L. C., et al. 1974. *Health and Disease in Kenya.* Nairobi: East African Literature Bureau.

von Haugwitz, H. W. 1972. *Some Experiences with Smallholder Settlement in Kenya 1963/64-1966/67.* Munich: Weltforum Verlag.

von Rotenham, D. 1968. "Cotton Farming in Sukumuland." In *Smallholder Farming and Smallholder Development in Tanzania.* H. Ruthenberg, ed. Munich: Weltforum Verlag.

Wangati, F. J. 1969. "Methods of Estimating Photosynthesis in the Field and their Application in Land Use Planning." *Proceedings, 4th Specialist*

Meeting on Applied Meteorology. East African Agriculture and Forestry Research Organization.

Ward, B. and Dubos, R. 1972. *Only One Earth: The Care and Maintenance of a Small Planet.* New York: Norton.

Warren, W. M. and Rubin, N., eds. 1968. *Dams in Africa.* London: Frank Cass and Co., Ltd.

Watson, W. 1958. *Tribal Cohesion in a Money Economy.* Manchester, Manchester U.P.

Watts, S. 1966. "The South Busoga Settlement Scheme." *Occasional Papers.* Syracuse: Syracuse University Program of Eastern African Studies, no. 17.

Weinand, H. C. 1972. "A Spatio-temporal Model of Economic Development." *Australian Geographical Studies* 10: 95-100.

Weiner, M., ed. 1966. *Modernization: The Dynamics of Growth.* New York: Basic Books.

White, G. F. 1957. "A Perspective of River Basin Development." *Law and Contemporary Problems: River Basin Development.* Duke University School of Law, 23: 157-87.

White, G. F., Bradley, D. J., and White, A. U. 1972. *Drawers of Water: Domestic Water Use in East Africa.* Chicago: The University of Chicago Press.

White, H. P. and Gleave, M. B. 1971. *An Economic Geography of West Africa.* London: G. Bell and Sons.

Whittington, G. 1970. "Towards Urban Development in Swaziland." *Erdkunde* 24: 26-39

Whittlesey, D. 1954. "The Regional Concept and the Regional Method." In *American Geography, Inventory and Prospect.* P. James and C. Jones, eds. Syracuse: Syracuse University Press.

W.H.O. 1958. *The First Ten Years of the World Health Organization.* Geneva: W.H.O.

W.H.O. 1968. *The Second Ten Years of the World Health Organization.* Geneva: W.H.O.

Whyte, R. O. 1962. "The Myth of Tropical Grasslands." *Tropical Agriculture* 39: 1-11.

Wilcox, W. F. 1940. *Studies in American Demography.* Ithaca, N.Y.: Cornell University Press.

Williams, A. V. and Zelinsky, W. 1970. "On Some Patterns in International Tourist Flows." *Economic Geography* 46:549-67.

Williams, C. D. and Jelliffe, D. B. 1972. *Mother and Child Health.* (London: Oxford University Press.

Wisner, B. 1973. "Additional Report on the Medical Faculty—CDTF Water Survey: Analysis and Recommendations." Mimeographed. University of Dar es Salaam, Faculty of Medicine, Department of Community Health.

Wisner, B. 1975. "Famine Relief and People's War," *Review of African Political Economy* 3: 77-83.

Witthuhn, B. O. 1968. "The Spatial Integration of Uganda as a Process of Modernization." Unpublished Ph.D. dissertation, Pennsylvania State University.

Wood, A. 1950. *The Groundnut Affair.* London: The Bodley Head.

Wood, C. W. 1972. "Availability of Health Manpower." In *Health Care for*

Remote Areas. J. P. Hughes, ed. Oakland, California: Kaiser Foundation International. Quotation by permission.

Wraith, R. E. 1967. *Guggisberg.* London.

Wrigley, C. C. 1960. "Speculations on the Economic Pre-History of Africa." *Journal of African History* 1: 189-200.

Yudelman, M. 1964. *Africans on the Land.* Cambridge, Mass.: Harvard University Press.

Zambia, Ministry of Local Government and Housing. 1972. *Suggested Housing Policy in the Second National Development Plan.* Lusaka: Government Printer.

Zelinsky, W., Kosinski, L. A. and Prothero, R. M., eds. 1970. *Geography and a Crowding World: A Symposium on Physical and Social Pressures on Resources in the Developing Lands.* New York: Oxford University Press.

Zimmerman, E. 1951. *World Resources and Industries.* New York: Harper & Row.

Zolberg, A. R. 1964. *One-Party Government in the Ivory Coast.* (Princeton, N.J.: Princeton University Press.

Author Index

Subject Index

Dr. Newman, who received his degrees from the University of Minnesota, has held research grants for field work in Tanzania and Kenya. He is on the editorial board, *African Studies Review*, and was editor of *Eastern African Studies Series* at Syracuse University. His many publications include articles in the *Journal of Geography*, the *East African Geographical Review*, and *Annals*, Association of American Geographers.

DATE DUE